D0926466

WHAT DID THEY THINK OF THE JEWS?

WHAT DID THEY THINK OF THE JEWS?

collected and edited

by

Allan Gould

STEWART HOUSE

Permission to reprint various excerpts in this book will be found in
Acknowledgments on page 591.

Library of Congress Cataloging-in-Publication Data

What did they think of the Jews? / collected and edited by Allan Gould
    p. cm.
  Includes index.
  ISBN 0-87668-751-6
    1. Jews–Public opinion–History–Sources.   2. Antisemitism–
  History–Sources.   I. Gould, Allan, 1944-   .
  DS102.95.W43 1991
  305.8'924–dc20   90-43139

Manufactured in the United States of America. Jason Aronson Inc. offers books and cassettes.
For information and catalog write to Jason Aronson Inc., 230 Livingston Street, Northvale, New
Jersey 07647.

ISBN 1-895246-24-5
Published in Canada 1991 by
Stewart House
481 University Avenue
Toronto, Ontario
M5G 2E9

DS
102.95
.W43
1991

To my beloved wife Merle
and our brilliant, gifted children Judah and Elisheva—
who, like me, care very much about
what "they" thought about the Jews.

Contents

6. The Enlightenment   79

7. From the U.S. Industrial Revolution to the Civil War   *109*

8. The Romantic and Victorian Periods in England   *135*

11. The Communist Revolution and Regime   231

12. U.S. Writers and Leaders from Reconstruction to the Present   257

13. The Nazi Era in Europe   373

15. Afro-American Reflections on the Jews   553

Introduction

Growing up in postwar Detroit, I did not particularly care much about what "they" thought of the Jews. With the exception of a single "Dirty Jew!" shouted at me in second grade by a non-Jewish peer, anti-Semitism was simply not part of my experience. Much like Philip Roth's description of his own childhood in Newark, New Jersey, in the 1940s (in his recent "writer's autobiography," *The Facts*), being Jewish in a predominantly Jewish area was as normal and as accepted as breathing. It was to be *non*-Jewish that was out of the ordinary—at least in Roth's Newark of the 1940s and my own 1950s Detroit.

We knew of the destruction of European Jewry, of course, but it was almost too recent to confront. Hilberg's monumental work—with its brilliant "chart" showing how nearly every Nazi law had its precedent in papal bulls issued throughout the Middle Ages—was not to be published until 1961; the writings of Elie Wiesel and Primo Levi had not yet been translated into English; and the Eichmann trial in Jerusalem, which surely was the single greatest consciousness-raiser of the Holocaust—the legal equivalent of what Betty Friedan's *The Feminine Mystique* was to Feminism—would also not take place until 1961.

Still, as a fairly aware teenager in the midwestern United States, I knew that there had been a number of authors, politicians, businessmen, rulers, and clergymen who carried negative feelings toward my people. My own father would regale me with stories of Growing Up Jewish in Toronto, Canada, before the First World War, where zealous missionaries would accost young Jewish children on the street and outside their makeshift Hebrew schools, alternately taunting them and urging them to accept the True Faith. "I wasn't allowed to join the Lithographer's Union, because my name was Gold!" my father would tell me bitterly—a full half-century after the hurt—and remind me that our family name was now Gould for a *very* specific reason. My mother, too, would describe how every job application form in Toronto in the 1920s—and, I have been told, right into the 1950s—not only asked for one's age, sex, and marital status, but—how quaintly biased today!—religion and race. She never landed the job when she wrote down the truth, but (miraculously?) *always* got the position when she wrote down "Protestant." And, just as surely, she always lost that job when she asked for a day off for Rosh Hashanah or Yom Kippur.

Which is why my parents chose to make the simple, 250-mile trek to the southwest and the Promised Land of the United States—in their case, Detroit, Michigan—where Ford's astonishing offer of five dollars a day was irresistible to a young couple who had encountered far too much pain and offense in the also-white, but far more Anglo-Saxon, and exceedingly Protestant, Canada. (It was a much less difficult trip than their respective parents had experienced just a quarter-century before, escaping the pogroms of Latvia and Minsk, as well as the marauding Cossacks of Odessa. But then, we all *knew* what "antise-mitten" those Eastern Europeans were.)

Careful readers may have caught a rather disarming irony in the previous paragraph: My father left Canada to work for Henry Ford, of all people? Indeed—since Ford *didn't* mind hiring a hard-working white man with an Irish-sounding name like Earl Gould (who had wisely left Isaac Gold back in the unwelcoming town of Toronto). Of course, Ford was not hiring blacks in the 1920s, which was why, my father later explained to me, *he* always hired blacks when he started up his own little auto-parts distributing firm. "Ford was a bastard," Father would tell me, "but I could hide my Jewishness. The colored guys couldn't do that, and they ended up in the cold. Hiring them now is the least I can do, after what we both went through, at the hands of anti-Semites."

I begin with these little stories—especially the latter description of my father's mini reverse-discrimination program—to partially ex-plain my own journey toward an interest in What Did They Think of the Jews. And, perhaps not surprisingly, this came about through my involvement with the Civil Rights Movement of the 1960s. In 1964, I went down to Mississippi during the so-called Freedom Summer, where I taught English, world religion, French, and history in a Freedom School. (I was fond of my fellow Jews, but I was barely out of my teens and hadn't saved the world yet. The American version of apartheid then in vogue offended my sensibilities far more than the recent slaughter of two-fifths of my people in Europe; besides, I couldn't undo the latter, but I *could* teach my black brothers and sisters and help them register to vote.)

As a traditional Jew, I struggled to keep the dietary laws while working in the tiny Negro community of Harmony (just outside the larger all-white town of Carthage, a name that amused the visitors greatly). I ate the black-eyed peas, praying that they had not been cooked in pork—but too afraid to ask (and possibly offend)—and nibbled at the corn and squash. My mother would mail giant kosher salamis to our Mississippi village, to the eventual amusement of my hosts.

The big moment went like this: I was sitting under a tree with about a dozen black teenagers, discussing an American short story, when a young lad came running up to our informal school, shouting, "Hey, Allan! There's a funny-shaped package for you at the Post Office—and it *stinks!!*"

"Oh," I recalled. "That must be the meat!"

The mother of one of the teens, who often sat in on my classes, leaped up at that moment and could not contain her excitement. "Meat??" she boomed. "Your mama sends you MEAT?"

"Yes," I stammered.

"You *klosh??*" she asked, displaying a rather impressive awareness of the Jewish dietary laws for an illiterate black woman, until one recalls the number of times each day that references to things being "kosher" can be heard over TV sets.

"Yes, I am," I replied, not sure of what she was getting at.

"Allan!! Is *you* a Jew???"

My heart leaped into my mouth, as I feared—for only a moment—that this kindly woman of whom I had grown so fond, was a closet Henry Ford. "Yes, I'm a Jew," I murmured, thinking of the heavy irony of my risking my life down in Mississippi—the bodies of Goodman, Schwerner, and Chaney, two Jews and a black, were still missing, only a few miles away from where we were sitting, but we all assumed that they were dead—for a possible anti-Semite.

"Well, well, *well*," she declared, breaking into a wide-toothed grin. "No *wonder* you down here!"

Now I was totally confused. "Why is that?" I asked her.

"Because you is the *second* most hated group in the world!!!"

I was charmed. In other words, we despised folk had better stick together, since "they" hate us both. (See the words of Malcolm X, quoted in this volume, who eventually questioned the sincerity of Jews involved in the civil rights movement, and of Gore Vidal, who argues, like my black friend in Mississippi, that in a world where Jews with yellow stars and homosexuals with pink triangles both get gassed, they had better learn to stick up for each other.)

I wish I could end this anecdote there, but there is a comic, yet somehow touching, coda to the story. Back North, later that year, I was frequently invited to speak at black churches, white churches, and, of course, synagogues, about My Summer In Mississippi. Once, when I told the above story about the "klosh" meat and the woman's charming statement about Jews being "the second most hated group" after the blacks, an elderly Jewish woman leaped to her feet and screamed, "No!! *We* are!!" In other words, I assumed, in the great Hierarchy of Suffering, the Jews have had it far worse than the Negro (at least in the twentieth century, I have to add), and therefore, how *dare* that black woman accuse the Jews of coming in "only second" in the Great Hatred Olympics?

* * *

I share this story with you to help explain how I approached this anthology: I arrived late at an awareness of my Jewishness, and, by extension, of Jew-hatred. I was saddened by the ugly anti-Jewish references in T. S. Eliot and Hemingway, when I studied them, but I was willing to forgive, if not forget; after all (I would think to myself), if I refused to read the writings of everyone who had negative feelings toward Jews (or blacks, or gays, Catholics, and others), I would have a library so thin, I'd have to turn its few remaining books sideways to fill out the shelves. The do-gooder in me—the lover in me—longed to believe that one *had* to be a good person in order to create great Art, but I soon knew better; sexists have written great books; racists have painted great pictures; anti-Semites have built wonderful buildings, even impressive civilizations. *C'est la vie.*

Furthermore, I quickly discovered that you cannot always judge people's feelings about a religion or race by what they write; scholars call this the intentional fallacy, as I recall, and it means that it's fallacious to assume an author's intentions. Shakespeare created Shylock, of course, but since the Jews had been expelled from England some three centuries earlier (in 1290), he more than likely had never met one to hate (or love), and had to work within the conventions of his time—even if he did manage to create a far more sympathetic portrait of a Jew (and a far harsher depiction of Christians) than had most other artists of his age, in any medium.

Still, to quote from the fictional writings of men and women—which, with a handful of exceptions, I almost never do in this book—is to fall into possible error concerning the author's real intent. Louis Harap, in his most impressive *The Image of the Jew in American Literature*, explains this problem very well:

> There are those who challenge the view that a writer who introduces the Jewish literary stereotype is thereby manifesting anti-Semitism, whether conscious or unconscious. Is the stereotype, then, a literary convention that has esthetic but not necessarily social import? Rosenberg cites Louis Kronenberger's observation on this point. Within the literary tradition, writes Kronenberger, "Barabas and Fagin involve not how anti-Semitic but *only* how antirealistic a Marlowe and a Dickens are." Obviously, the stereotype is by definition anti- or nonrealistic, for it reduces the individual character to a mold that is outside any concrete time and place—a convention, in short. But is the stereotype *only* antirealistic? Does not its use by the writer and acceptance by the reader also presuppose anti-Semitic attitudes? Lest the charge of parochialism or paranoia be hurled at this position, it is clear that "anti-Semitism" is not a sharply defined quantity of anti-Jewish prejudice, but occurs within a continuous range of intensity, from passive acceptance of the convention to articulate, intense belief in it.
>
>   In any given instance of the use of the stereotype, the degree of intensity of anti-Semitism needs to be judged within

the entire context of the social milieu, personal history of the writer, and context of the work in which it appears.

Precisely. Which is why, for example, I have essentially refrained from quoting Hemingway or Fitzgerald in their often unpleasant depiction of fictional Jewish characters, except when a biographer chose to do so to illustrate various writers' anti-Semitic (or philo-Semitic) attitudes in their personal life.

Whenever possible, I have struggled to obtain the actual words uttered by these (usually) famous men and women about the Jews, preferably from their own correspondence, or from lectures, essays, or off-hand comments. In so doing I avoided, to the best of my ability, any "puff" speeches, such as an American president's address before a synagogue audience (hardly a place where anyone's true, inner feelings would be exposed) or interviews with specifically Jewish newspapers or magazines. For example, in a Yiddish periodical, the singer Paul Robeson discussed at length the influence of Jewish music on Negro spirituals; he had strong, pro-Jewish feelings, but declarations made in that context can hardly give much insight into his true attitudes toward the Jewish people.

Even autobiographies can be suspect, of course. Historical examples of men and women who hid their racism, homophobia, homosexuality, or anti-Semitism are legion. The best single example in this book is the selection on the famed muckraking author Upton Sinclair (*The Jungle*), who spoke affectionately about Jews in his self-portrait, but who displayed quite different attitudes in his words and actions. (Here, as in many other places in this book, an insightful biography transcended the "truth" of any autobiography.)

Since the Jews have been in the consciousness of the gentile world for over three millennia, I had to somehow limit this book in as many ways as I could. One easy way was to avoid quoting what Jews had to say about themselves. My only "exceptions"—if they are exceptions at all—are the Jewish-Christians in the Christian portion of the Bible; Karl Marx (his father was a convert to Protestantism), whose viciously anti-Semitic opinions placed him beyond the Jewish pale, at least in the eyes of his own people; the art historian Bernard Berenson, who was a convert to Christianity (even if described as a "kike" by Hemingway); and, inevitably, the Jewish historian Josephus, the only source to refute the ancient pagan historian Apion. For

Josephus, the fact that Apion apparently accused the Jews of killing and eating their enemies, a canard echoed throughout the Middle Ages and even during the Nazi era, was simply too shocking to omit.

Many problems arose in putting together an anthology such as this one. For one thing, there are few men and women with completely positive attitudes toward the Jews. (Completely negative ones, alas, are strikingly common.) But I could have easily—and unfairly— quoted the slurs against Jews in the letters of Polish-born novelist Joseph Conrad, without mentioning his deep love for his Jewish patron and agent. I could have quoted the scathing Jew-hatred of Martin Luther in his later years (after that stiff-necked people refused to join him in his quest to break away from the Roman Catholic Church), but omitted the powerful philo-Semitic speeches of his early years, giving the reader an incomplete portrait. Similarly, had I noted only the use of the offensive slang *zhid* ("kike") in the letters of the great Russian playwright and short-story writer Anton Chekhov, I would have unfairly painted him with an anti-Semitic brush; in fact, his outrage over the Dreyfus case and his warm friendship with the great Yiddish novelist Sholem Aleichem suggest a person who loved the Jews, but simply could not shake off the anti-Jewish language of his youth. And only God could explain the way H. L. Mencken and Dos Passos surrounded themselves with Jews and Jewish writers, yet wrote with such poison pens about their religion and nationality.

Some haters of the Jews are utterly irredeemable: Belloc, Céline, Pound, Ford, Dostoyevsky, Jack London, Katherine Anne Porter, and, of course, Hitler and his murderous cohorts, are all rather agonizing examples. (Still, in the writings of each, the pathology of racial and religious hatred often becomes more translucent than in any psychiatric study—or in Sartre's *Anti-Semite and Jew*, for that matter, which is also excerpted here.)

Yet even among those whose feelings toward the Jews are often decidedly negative, there are some gleams of insight: James Russell Lowell, Friedrich Nietzsche, and Theodore Dreiser admired, and simultaneously feared, Jewish "superiority"; John Buchan and Rider Haggard felt distaste for many Jews, but both also supported the concept of Zionism; and—my favorite—the Roman historian Tacitus, who *mocked* the Jews because they refused to put their own children to death as would any good citizen of Rome! (Criticism of this kind was always welcomed by the Jews.)

The Jew-*lovers*—George Eliot, Mark Twain, E. M. Forster, Robert Graves, C. P. Snow, Winston Churchill, Leo Tolstoy, Thornton Wilder, Dmitri Shostakovich, are not without their criticisms, but their affection appears sincere and often profoundly thoughtful and intelligent.

This book becomes haunting, I believe, when we read of the wonderful life-saving work of the future John Paul XXIII, yet recoil at his unwillingness to send some of the doomed European Jews to Palestine, since this flew in the face of his religious belief; and of the heartbreaking pacifism of the philo-Semite Gandhi, as he urged the German Jews (in 1938!) to refuse to leave Germany, to lie down in front of German tanks, and learn to love their enemy. (Had the Jews of World War II Europe faced a British enemy, as did Gandhi, instead of genocidal Nazis, the Indian leader may have had a good argument; but Nazi tanks were never as polite as British tanks. Surely the Nazis were an enemy before whom even Jesus could not have turned his other cheek; he would have been shot first.)

I have tried to make this anthology into a kind of history book as well, and an important reference guide. For instance, most people know that there are vaguely (and often savagely) anti-Jewish declarations in the New Testament and the Koran; I included many selections from each, as well as quotations from the ancient Greeks and Romans, various papal bulls, the words of numerous kings and princes, an Edict of Faith (from the Spanish Inquisition), excerpts from the Book of Mormon, the Covenant of the Palestine Liberation Organization, numerous laws and promulgations from the Nazi era, and much more. There are some stunning patterns here, some running through two thousand years of rage, envy, fear, and hate—and, yes, even of tolerance.

Still, the eternal question is never fully answered: What accounts for such differences in attitude among people living during the same era? Why did Dostoyevsky write an essay fit for *Der Stürmer* (Hitler's most offensive anti-Semitic periodical), while Tolstoy studied Hebrew and even donated the proceeds of several of his short stories to the survivors of the 1903 Kishinev pogrom? Why did Freud's biographer and fellow-psychiatrist Ernest Jones care for his Jewish co-workers so deeply, while Carl Jung flirted with "Aryan science" and Nazism? And how on earth can one explain why Upton Sinclair condescended to his Jewish friends, while fellow American novelist Sinclair Lewis refused to stay in any hotel that banned Jews? (The proto-Nazi ravings of Richard Wagner and the passionate philo-Semitism of Dmitri Shostakovich I will leave to Freud, Jones, and Jung to psychoanalyze.)

If anything is certain from this anthology, it is that the Jews, for whatever reasons (their brains, their lack of brains; their nationalism, their internationalism; their wealth, their poverty; their talent, their lack of talent; their religiosity, their secularism; their assimilation, their refusal to assimilate) tend to elicit strong reactions in their non-Jewish neighbors. What follows are the words of over two hundred important men and women over the past few thousand years, who expressed their views. Here can be found good Christians who despised the Jews *because* of their Christianity and haters of Christianity who despised the Jews because they gave birth to Christianity. But you will also discover good Christians who loved the Jews because of their own, deeply felt Christianity, and atheists and agnostics who loved the Jews because of what they have given the world.

Whether or not the Jews have been the "second most hated people" or the most hated, means little to me. They were also, surely, "God's First Love," to quote the German theologian Friedrich Heer, and they have shaped the civilized world through their acceptance of monotheism, their mothering both of Christianity and Islam, and in other ways that cannot be overestimated. As for myself, I love the Jewish people. But I have my own, vested interest in the Jewish Question. Here, in historical order, are some Gentile (but not always gentle) views of my sometimes difficult, often extraordinary, and always interesting fellow Jews. I trust that you'll find these views equally difficult, extraordinary, and interesting.

Allan Gould
Toronto, Canada
Fall 1990

1

Ancient Greece and Rome

CICERO   (106–43 B.C.E.)

Roman historian and orator

The attitude towards the Jews of Cicero, the greatest orator of Rome and a writer whose influence subsequently dominated European humanism, is, of course, of the greatest interest. From the outset one should stress the fact that the Jews and their religion are conspicuously absent from the whole range of Cicero's philosophical works, though one might have expected some reference to Judaism, if Cicero had taken even the slightest interest in it, in a treatise like *De Natura Deorum*. . . .

Jews appear only in the speeches . . . delivered in 59 B.C.E. and 56 B.C.E., respectively. In both cases it was the nature of the situation that imposed the speaker's disparaging remarks about Jews. . . . The Jews were instrumental in the prosecution of Flaccus, who was defended by Cicero. . . .

. . . First, he defines the religion of the Jews as "barbara superstitio." Then, he points to the "raging" of the Roman Jews. . . . Cicero finishes his outburst against the Jews by showing the contrast between the Jewish religion and Roman ancestral institutions, and by emphasizing the recent war waged by the Jews against Rome.

In assessing the contents of this passage we must bear in mind its judicial context and Cicero's common practice, wherever such a procedure suited the nature of the case, of denigrating opposing witnesses by incriminating their national character. Thus, little is left of Cicero's supposed anti-Semitism.

(Stern, *Greek and Latin Authors on Jews and Judaism*,
vol. I, pp. 193–194)

* * *

There follows the odium that is attached to Jewish gold. . . . Each state . . . has its own religious scruples, we have ours. Even while Jerusalem was standing and the Jews were at peace with us, the

3

practice of their sacred rites was at variance with the glory of our empire, the dignity of our name, the customs of our ancestors. But now it is even more so, when that nation by its armed resistance has shown what it thinks of our rule; how dear it was to the immortal gods is shown by the fact that it has been conquered, let out for taxes, made a slave.

(Cicero, *Pro Flacco*, 59 B.C.E.)

HORACE   *(65–8 B.C.E.)*

Latin lyric poet and satirist under the Emperor Augustus

There are four certain references to Jews in the poetry of Horace. This in itself well attests to the impact made by the Jews on the Roman society of the Augustan age, and is paralleled by some passages in the poetry of . . . Ovid.

Once Horace alludes to the missionary zeal of the Jews; a second time he laughs at their credulousness, which became proverbial. He also shows knowledge of Jewish circumcision and of the Sabbath. . . .

(Stern, *Greek and Latin Authors on Jews and Judaism*, vol. I, p. 321)

* * *

. . . "we, like the Jews, will compel you to make one of our throng."

. . . "Apella, the Jew may believe it, not I. . . ."

. . . "I mind it well, but I'll tell you at a better time. To day is the thirtieth day, a Sabbath. Would you affront the circumcised Jews?"

"I have no scruples," say I. . . .

(Horace, *Sermones* 127–129, in Stern, *Greek and Latin Authors*, p. 321)

SENECA   *(ca. 4 B.C.E.–65 C.E.)*

Roman philosopher, statesman, tragedian

Seneca was the first Latin writer to give vent to deliberate animadversions on the Jewish religion and its impact on Roman society. Cicero's outbursts against the Jews . . . are well explained by the special necessities of the case, though the personal antipathy of the speaker may have had something to do with it, while Horace's references to Jewish credulity and proselytizing zeal lack acrimony and have a touch of humour. . . .

Seneca's references to Jews derive from works that he composed in the sixties of the first century C.E., that is, at the height of the Jewish proselytizing movement and the diffusion of Jewish customs throughout the Mediterranean world. . . . Not only does he include the Jewish rites among the superstitions . . . but, in his criticism of ceremonial worship . . . he takes the Jewish custom of lighting lamps on Sabbath as his first example. The emphasis on Jewish customs in such contexts might be explained as an attempt to counter the claims of the Jews, who dwelt much on the excellence of Jewish abstract monotheism, and as a reply to those circles of Roman society that were impressed by this aspect of the Jewish religion.

We have no proof that Seneca preferred Christianity to Judaism. . . .

It should be remembered that the Roman government distinguished Christians from Jews only at the very end of Seneca's life; it is even reasonable to suppose that the spread of the new and dangerous sect could only serve in the eyes of Seneca as an additional argument to incriminate Judaism.

(Stern, *Greek and Latin Authors on Jews and Judaism,*
vol. I, pp. 429–430)

* * *

Along with other superstitions of the civil theology Seneca also censures the sacred institutions of the Jews, especially the Sabbath. He declares that their practice is inexpedient, because by introducing one day of rest in every seven they lose in idleness almost a seventh of their life, and by failing to act in times of urgency they often suffer loss. . . . But when speaking of the Jews he says: "Meanwhile the customs of this accursed race have gained such influence that they are now received throughout all the world. The vanquished have given laws to their victors." He shows his surprise as he says this, not knowing what was being wrought by the providence of God. But he adds a statement that shows what he thought of their system of sacred institutions: "The

Jews, however, are aware of the origin and meaning of their rites. The greater part of the people go through a ritual not knowing why they do so."

(Seneca, *De Superstitione*, in Stern, *Greek and Latin Authors*, p. 431)

* * *

Precepts are commonly given as to how the gods should be worshipped. But let us forbid lamps to be lighted on the Sabbath, since the gods do not need light, neither do men take pleasure in soot. Let us forbid men to offer morning salutation and to throng the doors of temples; mortal ambitions are attracted by such ceremonies, but God is worshipped by those who truly know him. Let us forbid bringing towels and flesh-scrapers to Jupiter, and proffering mirrors to Juno; for God seeks no servants. Of course not; he himself does service to mankind everywhere, and to all he is at hand to help.

(Seneca, *Epistulae Morales*, in *Greek and Latin Authors*, p. 433)

LIVY   *(59 B.C.E.–17 C.E.)*

Roman historian

Livy mentions the Jews at least twice in his History. The first time he does so in his account of Pompey's conquest of Syria, and the second time, when he relates the capture of Jerusalem by Antony's commanders (37 B.C.E.). In connection with the first event he seems to give a description of the Jewish religion that stresses the anonymity of the Jewish God and the absence in the Temple at Jerusalem of any statue to represent the Deity. . . .

(Stern, *Greek and Latin Authors on Jews and Judaism*, vol. I, p. 328)

* * *

And Judaea given over to the worship of an unknown God. Livy on Jews: "They do not state to which deity pertains the temple at Jerusalem, nor is any image found there, since they do not think the God partakes of any figure."

(102nd book of Livy's *History*, in Stern, *Greek and Latin Authors*, p. 330)

QUINTILIAN   (ca. 35–ca. 96 C.E.)

Latin teacher and writer

Quintilian, no less than the other great Spaniards in Latin literature of the first century C.E. – e.g. Seneca and Martial – had pronounced anti-Semitic views. This is evidenced by his reference to Moses as the father of Jewish superstition and as the man who was responsible for founding a nation pernicious to other people. In his hostility to Jews, Quintilian may have drawn inspiration from Domitian. . . .

   (Stern, *Greek and Latin Authors on Jews and Judaism*, vol. I, p. 512)

* * *

   The vices of the children bring hatred on their parents; founders of cities are detested for concentrating a race which is a curse to others, as for example the founder of the Jewish superstition; the laws of the Gracchi are hated, and we abhor any loathsome example of vice that has been handed down to posterity, such as the criminal form of lust which a Persian is said to have been the first to practise on a woman of Samos.

   (*Institutio Oratoria*, III, in Stern, *Greek and Latin Authors*, p. 513)

JOSEPHUS   (ca. 38–ca. 100 C.E.)

Jewish historian; author of Against Apion

After a six days' march, [Apion says] they developed tumours in the groin, and that was why, after safely reaching the country now called Judea, they rested on the seventh day, and called that day *sabbaton*, preserving the Egyptian terminology; for disease of the groin in Egypt is called *sabbo*.

   One knows not whether to laugh at the nonsense [writes Josephus], or rather to be indignant at the impudence, of such language. Clearly all these 110,000 persons were attacked by tumours. But if they were blind and lame and suffering from all kinds of disease, as represented by Apion, they could not have accomplished a single day's march. . . .

Within this sanctuary Apion has the effrontery to assert that the Jews kept an ass's head, worshipping that animal and deeming it worthy of the deepest reverence. . . . How did it escape him that the facts convict him of telling an incredible lie? Throughout our history we have kept the same laws, to which we are eternally faithful. . . .

. . . Finally, on consulting the attendants who waited upon him, he heard of the unutterable law of the Jews, for the sake of which he was being fed. The practice was repeated annually at a fixed season. They would kidnap a Greek foreigner, fatten him up for a year, and then convey him to a wood, where they slew him, sacrificed his body with their customary ritual, partook of his flesh, and while immolating the Greek, swore an oath of hostility to the Greeks. The remains of their victim were then thrown into a pit. The man [Apion continues] stated that he had now but a few days left to live, and implored the king, out of respect for the gods of Greece, to defeat this Jewish plot upon his life-blood and to deliver him from his miserable predicament.

A tale of this kind [writes Josephus] is not merely packed with all the horrors of a tragedy; it is also replete with the cruelty of impudence. . . .

(Josephus, *Against Apion*, trans. H. St. J. Thackeray, vol. I, pp. 233–248, 292–305, 325–337)

DAMOCRITUS   (*First century* C.E.?)

Ancient historian

Damocritus was a historian and the writer of a book on tactics. He is known to us only from Suda, according to which he was the author of a book about the Jews. We have no knowledge of Damocritus' time; we do not even know whether to date him before or after Apion. Like the latter, he knows the fable about the [Jewish] worship of the golden asinine head . . . and apart from Apion, he is the only Greek writer, as far as we know, to have maintained that the Jews practised ritual slaughter of foreigners. . . .

(Stern, *Greek and Latin Authors on Jews and Judaism*, p. 530)

Damocritus, an historian. — He wrote a work about tactics in two volumes, and a work *On Jews.* In the latter he states that they used to worship an asinine golden head and that every seventh year they caught a foreigner and sacrificed him. They used to kill him by carding his flesh into small pieces.

(*Greek and Latin Authors*, p. 531)

MARTIAL   *(ca. 41–ca. 103 C.E.)*

Early Roman writer

Martial, like the Senecas, Lucan, and Quintilian, is one of the great Spaniards who rose to fame in Latin letters. At least two of them — Seneca the Younger and Quintilian — were conspicuous for their anti-Semitic feelings. In the view of the nature of Martial's epigrams, we should not expect to find in them general statements of his opinion concerning the Jews. He does not even refer to what constituted, in the eyes of the Roman society, the chief danger of Judaism, namely the proselytizing zeal of the Jews and their success among the different classes of Roman society — a problem that bulked so large in the mind of Seneca, Tacitus and Juvenal. . . .

It is the Jewish rite of circumcision that serves as the main target for the epigrammatist's wit. . . . The only other Jewish rite mentioned by Martial is the observance of the Sabbath, which he mistakenly views as a fast — a mistake long-established in pagan literary tradition.

(Stern, *Greek and Latin Authors on Jews and Judaism*, p. 521)

* * *

. . . and for you from his Egyptian city comes sailing the gallant of Mephis, and the black Indian from the Red Sea; nor do you shun the lecheries of circumcised Jews. . . .

. . . and Bellona's raving throng does not rest, nor the canting ship-wrecked seaman with his swathed body, nor the Jew taught by his mother to beg, nor the blear-eyed huckster of sulpher-wares.

(Martial, *Epigrammata*, in Stern, *Greek and Latin Authors*, pp. 525, 529)

PLUTARCH   *(ca. 46–119* C.E.*)*

Greek biographer and author

Plutarch, scion of an old Boeotian family, was a priest of Delphi. He is the only resident of Greece proper among the Greek and Latin authors of the Roman imperial period who expressed views on the Jews and their religion. . . . [He] raises the problem of whether the Jews abstain from pork because they honour the pig or because they abhor it. . . .

(Stern, *Greek and Latin Authors on Jews and Judaism*, vol. I, p. 545)

* * *

"Greeks from barbarians finding evil ways!" [Euripides, *The Trojan Women*], because of superstition, such as smearing with mud, wallowing in filth, keeping of the Sabbath, casting oneself down with face to the ground, disgraceful besieging of the gods, and uncouth prostrations. . . .

But the Jews, because it was the Sabbath day, sat in their places immovable, while the enemy were planting ladders against the walls and capturing the defences, and they did not get up, but remained there, fast bound in the toils of superstition as in one great net.

(Plutarch, *De Superstitione*, in Stern, *Greek and Latin Authors*, p. 549)

* * *

. . . My grandfather used to say on every occasion, in derision of the Jews, that what they abstained from was precisely the most legitimate meat. But we shall say that of all delicacies the most legitimate kind is that from the sea. . . .

. . . do they abstain from eating pork by reason of some special respect for hogs or from abhorrence of the creature? Their own accounts sound like pure myth, but perhaps they have some serious reasons which they do not publish. . . .

My impression . . . is that the beast enjoys a certain respect among that folk; granted that he is ugly and dirty, still he is no more

absurd in appearance or crude in disposition than dung-beetle, croc-
odile, or cat, each of which is treated as sacred by a different group of
Egyptian priests. They say, however, that the pig is honoured for a
good reason: according to the story, it was the first to cut the soil with
its projecting snout, thus producing a furrow and teaching man the
function of a ploughshare. . . .

> (Plutarch, *Quaestiones Convivales*, IV, in Stern, *Greek and Latin
> Authors*, pp. 554–555)

EPICTETUS   *(ca. 50–130* C.E.*)*

Greek philosopher

While the other great Stoic, Seneca, was markedly hostile in his
references to Jews, Epictetus's references to them are of a neutral
character. The first mention appears in his discussion on the need for
a criterion of good and evil. Here Epictetus points out the differences
in the opinions of the Jews, the Syrians, the Egyptians and the
Romans on the subject of food, all of which were diametrically
opposed. These four nations are again listed as professing conflicting
views not over the principle of whether holiness should be pursued,
but on whether the particular act of eating the flesh of the swine is a
holy one or not. Both these examples are, thus, connected with Jewish
dietary laws. The third reference implies that Epictetus knew of the
significance of the rite of baptism in the conversion to Judaism—a rite
which was no less essential for converts to the Jewish religion than for
converts to Christianity. There is, therefore, no basis for the supposition that Epictetus confused Jews with Christians.

(Stern, *Greek and Latin Authors on Jews and Judaism*, vol. I, p. 541)

* * *

Do you not see in what sense men are severally called Jew,
Syrian, or Egyptian? For example, whenever we see a man halting
between two faiths, we are in the habit of saying, "He is not a Jew, he
is only acting the part." But when he adopts the attitude of mind of the

man who has been baptized and has made his choice, then he is both
a Jew in fact and is also called one. . . .

(Epictetus, *Dissertationes*, II in Stern, *Greek and Latin Authors*,
p. 543)

TACITUS   *(ca. 56–120 C.E.)*

Roman historian

Tacitus refers to Jews and Judaea in several places in the *Histories* and
Annals. . . . This is the most detailed account of the history and
religion of the Jewish people extant in classical Latin literature. . . .
Tacitus's account, written in the first decade of the second century C.E.,
reflects the feelings of influential circles of Roman society in the age
following the destruction of the Temple, when Judaism nevertheless
still constituted an important and militant factor in the Mediterranean world. . . .

Tacitus offers six explanations for the origin of the Jews. . . . A
third explanation mentioned by Tacitus indeed adds to the lustre of
the Jewish people by associating them with the Solymi celebrated in
the Homeric poems. The sixth and last version of the genesis of the
Jewish nation connects them with Egypt and presents the ancestors of
the Jews as people who had been disfigured by a plague, and were in
consequence expelled from Egypt. Their misfortune is said to account
for many of the religious practices introduced by their leader Moses.
This consistently hostile explanation of Jewish ancestry reflects the old
Graeco-Egyptian version which found its way into Latin literature at
least as early as the age of Augustus. . . .

However, Tacitus does not conceal his true opinion of Judaism,
the customs of which he declares to be sinister and abominable. Hate
and enmity towards other people are the counterpart to the strong
solidarity which the Jews display towards one another. Their prose-
lytes follow the same course and are imbued with contempt for the
gods and indifference to their country and families. Tacitus refers to
Jewish monotheism and to Jewish objections to material representa-
tions of God, but he does not state here his own views. He disapproves

of the comparison sometimes made between Jewish customs and the Dionysiac cult in strong terms. . . .

(Stern, Greek and Latin Authors on Jews and Judaism,
vol. II, pp. 1–2)

* * *

. . . Most authors agree that once during a plague in Egypt, which caused bodily disfigurement, King Bocchoris approached the oracle of Ammon and asked for a remedy whereupon he was told to purge his kingdom and to transport this race into other lands, since it was hateful to the gods. So the crowd was searched out and gathered together, then, being abandoned in the desert, while all others lay idle and weeping, one only of the exiles, Moses by name, warned them not to hope for help from gods or men; for they were deserted by both; but to trust to themselves. . . .

To establish his influence over this people for all time, Moses introduced new religious practices, quite opposed to those of all other religions. The Jews regard as profane all that we hold sacred; on the other hand, they permit all that we abhor. . . . They abstain from pork, in recollection of a plague, for the scab to which this animal is subject once afflicted them. By frequent fasts even now they bear witness to the long hunger with which they were once distressed, and the unleavened Jewish bread is still employed in memory of the haste with which they seized the grain. They say that they first chose to rest on the seventh day because that day ended their toils; but after a time they were led by the charms of indolence to give over the seventh year as well to inactivity. . . .

Whatever their origin, these rites are maintained by their antiquity: the other customs of the Jews are base and abominable, and owe their persistence to their depravity; for the worst rascals among other peoples, renouncing their ancestral religions, always kept sending tribute and contributing to Jerusalem, thereby increasing the wealth of the Jews; again, the Jews are extremely loyal toward one another, and always ready to show compassion, but toward every other people they feel only hate and enmity. They sit apart at meals and they sleep apart, and although as a race, they are prone to lust, they abstain from intercourse with foreign women; yet among themselves nothing is lawful. They adopted circumcision to distinguish themselves from other peoples by this difference. Those who are converted to their ways follow the same practice, and the earliest lesson they receive is to despise the gods, to disown their country, and to regard their parents, children, and brothers as of little account.

However, they take thought to increase their numbers; for they regard it as a crime to kill any late-born child. . . .

(Tacitus, *Historiae*, in Stern, *Greek and Latin Authors* II, pp. 24–27)

JUVENAL   (ca. 60–127? C.E.)

Roman satirist

Criticism of the intrusion of foreign elements into the capital of imperial Rome is frequently expressed by its greatest satirist; for Juvenal, Rome was fast deteriorating into a Greek city, and, even worse, an oriental Greek city. . . .

It was only to be expected that such a writer would include the Jews among the targets of his satire. Two main aspects of the contemporary position of Jews and Judaism emerge from Juvenal's allusions to the Jews of Rome. One was the spread of Judaism there, which gradually won over whole families. From among the specifically Jewish customs Juvenal singles out observance of the Sabbath, which was the first to gain ground among non-Jews. He also refers to the abstention of Jews from pork, and finally to their practice of circumcision. Juvenal saw conversion to Judaism mainly as the flouting of the laws of Rome aimed at the complete subjugation of its followers to the Jewish law, as handed down in the secret volume of Moses. Like Tacitus, Juvenal emphasizes Jewish misanthropy.

The second feature relating to the Jews that Juvenal brings into prominence is his picture of them as indigents. They are to be seen begging near the Porta Capena, and he relates that a Jew will interpret dreams for the minutest of coins. . . .

(Stern, *Greek and Latin Authors*, II, pp. 94–95)

* * *

. . . It was given as a present long ago by the barbarian Agrippa to his incestuous sister, in that country where kings celebrate festal sabbaths with bare feet, and where a long-established clemency suffers pigs to attain old age. . . .

No sooner has that fellow departed than a palsied Jewess, leaving her basket and her truss of hay, comes begging to her secret ear; she is an interpreter of the laws of Jerusalem, a high priestess of the tree, a trusty go-between of highest heaven. She, too, fills her palm, but more sparingly, for a Jew will tell you dreams of any kind you please for the minutest of coins. . . .

Some who have had a father who reveres the Sabbath, worship nothing but the clouds, and the divinity of the heavens, and see no difference between eating swine's flesh, from which their father abstained, and that of man; and in time they take to circumcision. Having been wont to flout the laws of Rome, they learn and practice and revere the Jewish law, and all that Moses handed down in his secret tome, forbidding to point out the way to any not worshipping the same rites, and conducting none but the circumcised to the desired fountain. For all which the father was to blame, who gave up every seventh day to idleness, keeping it apart from all the concerns of life.

(Juvenal, *Saturne*, in Stern, *Greek and Latin Authors* II, pp. 100, 101–103)

2

The Founding Fathers
of the Church
and the Rise of Islam

THE NEW TESTAMENT

Then Pilate entered into the judgment hall again, and called Jesus, and said unto him, Art thou the King of the Jews?

Jesus answered him, Sayest thou this thing of thyself, or did others tell it thee of me?

Pilate answered, Am I a Jew? Thine own nation and the chief priests have delivered thee unto me: what hast thou done? . . .

Pilate saith unto him, What is truth? And when he had said this, he went out again unto the Jews, and saith unto them, I find in him no fault at all.

But ye have a custom, that I should release unto you one at the passover: will ye therefore that I release unto you the King of the Jews?

Then cried they all again, saying, Not this man, but Barabbas. Now Barabbas was a robber.

Then Pilate therefore took Jesus, and scourged him. . . .

(John 18:33-35, 38-40; 19:1)

* * *

Tribulation and anguish, upon every soul of man that doeth evil, of the Jew first, and also of the Gentile;

But glory, honour, and peace, to every man that worketh good, to the Jew first, and also to the Gentile:

For there is no respect of persons with God.

For as many as have sinned without law shall also perish without law; and as many as have sinned in the law shall be judged by the law;

For not the hearers of the law are just before God, but the doers of the law shall be justified. . . .

(The Epistle of Paul to the Romans, 2:9-13)

* * *

Behold, thou art called a Jew, and restest in the law, and makest thy boast of God,

19

And knowest his will, and approvest the things that are more excellent, being instructed out of the law;

And art confident that thou thyself art a guide of the blind, a light of them which are in darkness,

And instructor of the foolish, a teacher of babes, which hast the form of knowledge and of the truth in the law.

Thou therefore which teachest another, teachest thou not thyself? thou that preachest a man should not steal, dost thou steal?

Thou that sayest a man should not commit adultery, dost thou commit adultery? thou that abhorrest idols, dost thou commit sacrilege?

Thou that makest thy boast of the law, through breaking the law dishonourest thou God?

For the name of God is blasphemed among the Gentiles through you, as it is written.

For circumcision verily profiteth, if thou keep the law: but if thou be a breaker of the law, thy circumcision is made uncircumcision. . . .

(Romans 2:17-25)

* * *

What advantage then hath the Jew? or what profit is there of circumcision?

Much every way: chiefly, because that unto them were committed the oracles of God.

But what if some did not believe? shall their unbelief make the faith of God without effect?

God forbid: yea, let God be true, but every man a liar. . . .

. . . as we be slanderously reported, and as some affirm that we say, Let us do evil, that good may come? whose damnation is just.

What then? are we better than they? No, in no wise; for we have before proved both Jews and Gentiles, that they are all under sin; As it is written, There is none righteous, no, not one.

(Romans 3:1-4, 8-10)

* * *

For there is no difference between the Jew and the Greek: for the same Lord over all is rich unto all that call upon him. . . .

(Romans 10:12)

Afterward Jesus findeth him in the temple, and said unto him, Behold, thou art made whole: sin no more, lest a worse thing come unto thee.

The man departed, and told the Jews that it was Jesus, which had made him whole.

And therefore did the Jews persecute Jesus, and sought to slay him, because he had done these things on the sabbath day.

But Jesus answered them, My Father worketh hitherto, and I work.

Therefore the Jews sought the more to kill him, because he not only had broken the sabbath, but said also that God was his Father, making himself equal with God. . . .

(John 5:14–18)

* * *

But the Jews did not believe concerning him, that he had been blind, and received his sight, until they called the parents of him that had received his sight. . . .

These words spake his parents, because they feared the Jews: for the Jews had agreed already, that if any man did confess that he was Christ, he should be put out of the synagogue. . . .

(John 9:18, 22)

* * *

His disciples say unto him, Master, the Jews of late sought to stone thee; and goest thou thither again?

(John 11:8)

* * *

And there abode three months. And when the Jews laid wait for him [Paul], as he was about to sail into Syria, he purposed to return through Macedonia. . . .

(Acts 20:3)

* * *

And when he was come unto us, he took Paul's girdle, and bound his own hands and feet, and said, Thus saith the Holy Ghost,

So shall the Jews at Jerusalem bind the man that owneth this girdle, and shall deliver him into the hands of the Gentiles.

(Acts 21:11)

* * *

And when it was day, certain of the Jews banded together, and bound themselves under a curse, saying that they would neither eat nor drink till they had killed Paul.

And they were more than forty which had made this conspiracy.

And they came to the chief priests and elders, and said, We have bound ourselves under a great curse, that we will eat nothing until we have slain Paul. . . .

(Acts 23:12–14)

* * *

Claudius Lysias unto the most excellent governor Felix sendeth greeting.

This man [Paul] was taken of the Jews, and should have been killed of them: then came I with an army, and rescued him, having understood that he was a Roman. . . .

And when it was told me how that the Jews laid wait for the man, I sent straightway to thee, and gave commandment to his accusers also to say before thee what they had against him. Farewell.

(Acts 23:27, 30)

* * *

And when he was come, the Jews which came down from Jerusalem stood round about, and laid many and grievous complaints against Paul, which they could not prove.

While he answered for himself, Neither against the law of the Jews, neither against the temple, nor yet against Caesar, have I offended any thing at all . . .

Then said Paul, I stand at Caesar's judgment seat, where I ought to be judged: to the Jews have I done no wrong, as thou very well knowest. . . .

(Acts 25:7, 8, 10)

Of the Jews five times received I [Paul] forty stripes save one.
Thrice was I beaten with rods, once was I stoned. . . .

(2 Corinthians 11:24–25)

* * *

I know thy works, and tribulation, and poverty, but thou art rich
and I know the blasphemy of them which say they are Jews, and are
not, but are the synagogue of Satan.

(The Revelation to John 2:9)

* * *

Behold, I will make them of the synagogue of Satan, which say
they are Jews, and are not, but do lie; behold, I will make them to come
and worship before thy feet, and to know that I have loved thee.

(Revelation 3:9)

* * *

And Pilate answered and said again unto them, What will ye
then that I shall do unto him whom ye call the King of the Jews?

And they cried out again, Crucify him.

Then Pilate said unto them, Why, what evil hath he done? And
they cried out the more exceedingly, Crucify him.

And so Pilate, willing to content the people, released Barabbas
unto them, and delivered Jesus, when he had scourged him, to be
crucified.

(Mark 15:12–15)

CONSTANTINE THE GREAT (ca. 280–337 C.E.)

*Roman emperor and convert to Christianity, who declared
Christianity the lawful religion of the Roman Empire*

Laws, 18 October 315:

We wish to make it known to the Jews and their elders and their
patriarchs that if, after the enactment of this law, any one of them

dares to attack with stones or some other manifestation of anger, another who has fled their dangerous sect and attached himself to the worship of God [Christianity], he must speedily be given to the flames and burnt together with all his accomplices.

Moreover, if any one of the population should join their abominable sect and attend their meetings, he will bear with them the deserved penalties.

(J. R. Marcus, *The Jew in the Medieval World*, p. 4)

SAINT GREGORY OF NYSSA   *(ca. 335–394 C.E.)*

Eastern Church Father

Slayers of the Lord, murderers of the prophets, adversaries of God, haters of God, men who show contempt for the law, foes of grace, enemies of their father's faith, advocates of the devil, brood of vipers, slanderers, scoffers, men whose minds are in darkness, leaven of the Pharisees, assembly of demons, sinners, wicked men, stoners, and haters of righteousness.

(Homilies on the Resurrection, 5)

SAINT JOHN CHRYSOSTOM   *(ca. 344–407 C.E.)*

Early Catholic theologian

[Of what to accuse the Jews?] Of their rapine, their cupidity, their deception of the poor, of thieveries, and huckstering? Indeed a whole day would not suffice to tell all.

(Homilies Against the Jews, pp. 843–942)

* * *

[How can Christians dare] have the slightest converse [with Jews], most miserable of all men [Homily 4:1] . . . [who are] lustful, rapacious, greedy, perfidious bandits.

. . . inveterate murderers, destroyers, men possessed by the devil [whom] debauchery and drunkenness have given them the manners of the pig and the lusty goat. They know only one thing, to satisfy their gullets, get drunk, to kill and maim one another. . . . They are impure and impious. . . .(1:4).

. . . they have surpassed the ferocity of wild beasts, for they murder their offspring and immolate them to the devil (1:6).

[The synagogue is a place of] shame and ridicule (1:3) . . . the domicile of the devil, as is also the soul of the Jews (1:4, 6); [their house of worship] an assembly of criminals . . . a den of thieves . . . a cavern of devils, an abyss of perdition (1:2, 6:6). . . . [their rites are] criminal and impure; [their religion] a disease (3:1).

[The Jews are corrupt because of their] odious assassination of Christ (6:4). . . . no expiation possible, no indulgence, no pardon (6:2).

[Their dispersion] was done by the wrath of God and His absolute abandon of you (6:4). . . .

[Why Christians must hate the Jews:] He who can never love Christ enough will never have done fighting against those [Jews] who hate Him (7:1).

Flee, then, their assemblies, flee their houses, and far from venerating the synagogue because of the books it contains, hold it in hatred and aversion for the same reason (1:5).

I hate the synagogue precisely because it has the law and prophets. . . . I hate the Jews also because they outrage the law. . . . (6:6).

SAINT AUGUSTINE   (354–430 c.e.)

Bishop of Hippo

. . . [Jesus] did many miracles that He might commend God in Himself, some of which, even as many as seemed sufficient to proclaim Him, are contained in the evangelic Scripture. The first of these is, that He was so wonderfully born, and the last, that with His body raised up again from the dead He ascended into heaven. But the Jews who slew Him, and would not believe in Him, because it behoved Him to die and rise again, were yet more miserably wasted by the Romans, and utterly rooted out from their kingdom, where aliens had already ruled over them, and were dispersed through lands (so that indeed there is no place where they are not), and are thus by their own Scriptures a testimony to us that we have not forged the prophecies

about Christ. And very many of them, considering this, even before
His passion, but chiefly after His resurrection, believed on Him, of
whom it was predicted, "Though the number of the children of Israel
be as the sand of the sea, the remnant shall be saved." But the rest are
blinded, of whom it was predicted, "Let their table be made before
them a trap, and a retribution, and a stumbling block. Let their eyes
be darkened lest they see, and bow down their back alway." Therefore,
when they do not believe our Scriptures, their own, which they
blindly read, are fulfilled in them, lest perchance any one should say
that the Christians have forged these prophecies about Christ which
are quoted under the sane of the sibyl, or of others, if such there be,
who do not belong to the Jewish people. For us, indeed, those suffice
which are quoted from the books of our enemies, to whom we make
our acknowledgment, on account of this testimony, which, in spite of
themselves, they contribute by their possession of these books, while
they themselves are dispersed among all nations, wherever the
Church of Christ is spread abroad. For a prophecy about this thing
was sent before in the Psalms, which they also read, where it is written,
"My God, His mercy shall prevent me. My God hath shown me
concerning my enemies, that Thou shalt not slay them, lest they
should at last forget Thy law: disperse them in Thy might." Therefore
God has shown the Church in her enemies the Jews the grace of His
compassion, since, as saith the apostle, "their offence is the salvation of
the Gentiles." And therefore He has not slain them, that is, He has not
let the knowledge that they are Jews be lost in them, although they
have been conquered by the Romans, lest they should forget the law
of God, and their testimony should be of no avail in this matter of
which we treat. But it was not enough that he should say, "Slay them
not, lest they should at last forget Thy law," unless he had also added,
"Disperse them"; because if they had only been in their own land with
that testimony of the Scriptures, and not everywhere, certainly the
Church which is everywhere could not have had them as witnesses
among all nations to the prophecies which were sent before concerning Christ. . . .

(Augustine, *The City of God*, trans. Marcus Dods, pp. 656–658)

* * *

"For the Lord will not cast off His people" — Psalms 94:14. Praise
be unto Him, and shouts of joy unto Him! What people shall He not

cast off? We have no right to make our own explanation here: for the Apostle hath prescribed this unto us, he has explained whereof it is said. For this was the Jewish people, the people where were the prophets, the people where were the patriarchs, the people begotten according to the flesh from the seed of Abraham.

(*Expositions on the Book of Psalms*, in *Select Library of the Nicene and Post-Nicene Fathers*, vol. VIII, p. 468)

* * *

The Jews held him [Jesus]; the Jews insulted him, the Jews bound him, they crowned him with thorns, dishonored him by spitting upon him, they scourged him, they heaped abuses upon him, they hung him upon a tree, they pierced him with a lance.

(*The Creed*, 3:10, p. 301)

* * *

. . . Let us preach to the Jews, whenever we can, with a spirit of love. . . . It is not for us to boast over them as branches broken off. . . . We shall be able to say to them without exulting over them—though we exult in God—"Come, let us walk in the light of the Lord."

(*Treatise Against the Jews*, p. 15)

* * *

Neither in the confusion of paganism, nor in the defilement of heresy, nor yet in the blindness of Judaism, is religion to be sought, but among those alone who are called Catholic Christians.

(*On the Christian Conflict*)

SAINT JEROME   (374–419 C.E.)

Early Church Father

The Jews . . . seek nothing but to have children, possess riches, and be healthy. They seek all earthly things, but think nothing of heavenly things; for this reason are they mercenaries.

(*Les Juifs dans L'Empire Romain*, p. 312)

CHRISTIAN LAW   *(ca. 412 C.E.)*

Let no one who has done no harm be molested on the ground that he is a Jew, nor let any aspect of his religion result in his exposure to contumely; in no place are their synagogues or dwellings to be set afire, or wantonly damaged, for, even if the case be otherwise and some one of them is implicated in criminal activities, obviously it is for precisely this that the vigor of the judiciary and the protection of public law have been instituted among us: That no one should have the right to permit himself private vengeance. But, just as it is Our will that this be the provision for those persons who are Jews, so too do We judge it opportune to warn the Jews that, elated, it may be, by their security, they must not become insolent and admit anything which is opposed to the reverence due to Christian worship.

(Codex Iustinianus, 1, 9, 14, 62)

SAINT FULGENTIUS OF RUSPE   *(ca. 467–533 C.E.)*

African bishop

Hold most firmly and doubt not that not all the pagans, but also all Jews, heretics, and schismatics who depart from their present life outside the Catholic Church, are about to go into eternal fire prepared for the devil and his angels.

(Writings, ca. 510 C.E.)

POPE GREGORY THE GREAT   *(ca. 540–604 C.E.)*

Architect of the medieval papacy

Hence, let us recognize in the "sheep" the faithful and innocent people of Judaea, long nourished by the Law; let us recognize in the "camels" those simple men, coming to the faith from paganism. These latter were formerly under a sacrilegious ceremonial; owing to a kind of deformity of their members, that is, by the foulness of their vices, they were extremely ugly in appearance. . . . Again, Israelites can be taken as represented by the "oxen," broken to the yoke of the Law, whereas by "asses," as has been said, the pagan peoples are designated, for these were accustomed to prostrate themselves for the worship of stones, with never a disclaimer from their intelligence, stupidly bending their backs; with, as it were, sense fit for brutes, they kept doing service to idols of every sort!

(Synan, *The Popes and the Jews in the Middle Ages*, p. 38)

THE KORAN   *(570–632* C.E.*)*

Ascribed to the Islamic prophet Mohammed

Verily, they who believe [Muslims], and they who follow the Jewish religion, and the Christians, and the Sabeites—whoever of these believeth in God and the last day, and doeth that which is right, shall have their reward with their Lord: fear shall not come upon them, neither shall they be grieved.

(Chapter XCI, Sura II, line 59)

* * *

A party among the people of the Book would fain mislead you: but they only mislead themselves, and perceive it not. O people of the Book! why disbelieve the signs of God, of which yourselves have been witnesses? O people of the Book! why clothe ye the truth with falsehood? Why wittingly hide the truth?

(Chapter XCVI, Sura XLVII, lines 62–64)

* * *

The Jews say "Ezra is a son of God"; and the Christians say, "The Messiah is a son of God." Such the sayings in their mouths! They resemble the saying of the Infidels of old! God do battle with them! How are they misguided!

(Chapter CXII, Sura IX, line 30)

* * *

Hast thou not remarked those who make friends of that people with whom God is angered? They are neither of your party nor of

theirs; and they swear to a lie, knowing it to be such. God hath got
ready for them a severe torment; for, evil is that they do. They make
a cloak of their faith, and turn others aside from the way of God:
wherefore a shameful torment awaiteth them. Not at all shall their
wealth or their children avail them aught against God. Companions
shall they be of the fire: they shall abide therein for ever. On the day
when God shall raise them all, they will swear to Him as they now
swear to you, deeming that it will avail them. Are they not – yes they –
the liars?

(Chapter CVI, Sura LVIII, lines 15-19)

* * *

"The hand of God," say the Jews, "is chained up." Their own
hands shall be chained up – and for that which they have said shall
they be cursed. Nay! outstretched are both His hands! At His own
pleasure does He bestow gifts. That which hath been sent down to
thee from the Lord will surely increase the rebellion and unbelief of
many of them; and we have put enmity and hatred between them that
shall last till the day of the Resurrection. Oft as they kindle a beacon
fire for war shall God quench it! and their aim will be to abet disorder
on the earth: but God loveth not the abettors of disorder.

But if the people of the Book believe and have the fear of God, we
will surely put away their sins from them, and will bring them into the
gardens of delight: and if that they observe the law and the Evangel,
and what hath been sent down to them from their Lord, they shall
surely have their fill of good things from above them and from beneath
their feet. Some there are among them who act aright; but many of
them – how evil are their doings!

(Chapter CXIV, Sura V, lines 69-70)

* * *

Ye shall assuredly be tried in your possessions and in yourselves.
And many hurtful things shall ye assuredly hear from those to whom
the Scriptures were given before you, and from those who join other
gods with God. But if ye be steadfast, and fear God – this verily is
needed in the affairs of life. Moreover, when God entered into a
covenant with those to whom the Scriptures had been given, and said,

"Ye shall surely make it known to mankind and not hide it," they cast it behind their backs, and sold it for a sorry price! But vile is that for which they have sold it.

(Chapter XCVII, Sura III, lines 184–185)

* * *

Hast thou not remarked those [the Jews and their rabbis] to whom a part of the Scriptures hath been given? Vendors are they of error, and are desirous that ye go astray from the way. But God knoweth your enemies; and God is a sufficient patron, and God is a sufficient helper! Among the Jews are those who displace the words of their Scriptures, and say, "We have heard, and we have not obeyed. Hear thou, but as one that heareth not; and look at us"; perplexing with their tongues, and wounding the Faith by their revilings. But if they would say, "We have heard, and we obey; hear thou, and regard us"; it were better for them, and more right. But God hath cursed them for their unbelief. Few only of them are believers!

(Chapter C, Sura IV, lines 48–49)

* * *

Of all men thou wilt certainly find the Jews, and those who join other gods with God, to be the most intense in hatred of those who believe; and thou shalt certainly find those to be nearest in affection to them who say, "We are Christians." This, because some of them are priests and monks, and because they are free from pride.

(Chapter CXIV, Sura V, 1.85)

* * *

So, for that they have broken their covenant, and have rejected the signs of God, and have put the prophets to death unjustly, saying the while, "Our hearts are uncircumcised,"—Nay, but God hath sealed them up for their unbelief, so that but few believe. And for their unbelief,—and for their having spoken against Mary a grievous calumny,—

And for their saying, "Verily we have slain the Messiah, Jesus, the son of Mary, an Apostle of God." Yet they slew him not, and they crucified him not, but they had only his likeness. And they who differed about him were in doubt concerning him: No sure knowledge had they about him, but followed only an opinion, and they did not really slay him, but God took him up to Himself. And God is Mighty, Wise!

There shall not be one of the people of the Book but shall believe in Him before his death, and in the day of resurrection, He will be a witness against them. For the wickedness of certain Jews, and because they turn away from the way of God, we have forbidden them goodly viands which had been before allowed them. And because they have taken usury, though they were forbidden it, and have devoured men's substance in frivolity, we have got ready for the infidels among them a grievous torment. . . .

(Chapter C, Sura IV, lines 155–159)

3

The Medieval Era

THE EASTER SEQUENCE

Composed by Wipo (d. 1050), chaplain to the Holy Roman Emperor

Credendum est magis
Mariae veraci soli quam Iudaeorum turbae fallaci

The truthful Mary alone
Is more to be believed than the deceitful crowd of Jews.

PETER ABÉLARD   *(1079–1142)*

French scholastic

From "The Divine Tragedy," in which Abélard has a Jew challenge Christian society:

No people is known ever to have suffered so much for God as we have suffered unremittingly; and there can be no sin so firmly established as not to have been consumed by the fire of our afflictions, as everyone must concede. Are we not among all the scattered nations alone without king or princes, harassed by such distressing expulsions that we pay almost each single day an intolerable ransom for our miserable lives? Is not the contempt and hatred of us so deep that any wrong done to us is accounted as a just retribution and an offering most acceptable to God?
 . . . Even the princes who rule over us, and whose shelter we purchase at so heavy a price, desire our death in order to seize our belongings. We are denied possession of the soil, of vineyards, of landed property, and there is none to shield us against open or

concealed malevolence. How, then, can we earn enough to sustain this miserable life but through the lending of money on interest to strangers, a circumstance which naturally makes us reprehensible to those who most feel themselves oppressed thereby! Our situation expresses far more clearly than language the horrible wretchedness of our existence and the dangers which we confront constantly.

(Abélard, *Dialogus inter Philosophum, Judaeum et Christianum*)

POPE INNOCENT III   *(1160/61–1216)*

Until today, in truth, the Jews are scandalized when they hear that God was scourged, was crucified, and that He died, holding it unworthy so much as to hear that God endured things unworthy . . . .

The Jew who denies that Messiah has come, and that he is God, lies.

Herod is the devil, the Jews demons; that one is King of the Jews, this one the King of demons . . . .

(Synan, *The Popes and the Jews in the Middle Ages*, p. 89)

PHILIP AUGUSTUS   *(1165–1223)*

King of France, 1179–1223

Recorded by the Monk Rigord:

[T]he Jews who dwelt in Paris were wont every year on Easter day, or during the sacred week of our Lord's Passion, to go down secretly into underground vaults and kill a Christian as a sort of sacrifice in contempt of the Christian religion. For a long time they had persisted in this wickedness, inspired by the devil, and in Philip's father's time, many of them had been seized and burned with fire. St. Richard, whose body rests in the church of the Holy Innocents-in-the-Fields in Paris, was thus put to death and crucified by the Jews, and through martyrdom went in blessedness to God. Wherefore many miracles have been wrought by the hand of God through the prayers and intercessions of St. Richard, to the glory of God, as we have heard.

And because the most Christian King Philip inquired diligently, and came to know full well these and many other iniquities of the Jews in his forefathers' days, therefore he burned with zeal, and in the same year in which he was invested at Rheims with the holy governance of the kingdom of the French, upon a Sabbath, the sixteenth of February, by his command, the Jews throughout all France were seized in their synagogues and then despoiled of their gold and silver and garments, as the Jews themselves had spoiled the Egyptians at their exodus from Egypt. This was a harbinger of their expulsion, which by God's hand soon followed. . . .

At this time a great multitude of Jews had been dwelling in France for a long time past, for they had flocked thither from divers parts of the world, because peace abode among the French, and liberality; for the Jews had heard how the kings of the French were prompt to act against their enemies, and were very merciful toward their subjects. And therefore their elders and men wise in the law of Moses . . . made resolve to come to Paris.

When they had made a long sojourn there, they grew so rich that they claimed as their own almost half of the whole city, and had Christians in their houses as menservants and maidservants, who were open backsliders from the faith of Jesus Christ, and judaized with the Jews. . . .

The most Christian King Philip heard of these things, and compassion was stirred within him. He took counsel with a certain hermit, Bernard by name, a holy and religious man, who at that time dwelt in the forest of Vincennes, and asked him what he should do. By his advice the King released all Christians of his kingdom from their debts to the Jews, and kept a fifth part of the whole amount for himself.

Finally came the culmination of their wickedness. Certain ecclesiastical vessels consecrated to God — the chalices and crosses of gold and silver bearing the image of our Lord Jesus Christ crucified — had been pledged to the Jews by way of security when the need of the churches was pressing. These they used so vilely, in their impiety and scorn of the Christian religion, that from the cups in which the body and blood of our Lord Jesus Christ was consecrated they gave their children cakes soaked in wine. . . .

In the year of our Lord's Incarnation 1182, in the month of April, which is called by the Jews Nisan, an edict went forth from the most serene king, Philip Augustus, that all the Jews of his kingdom should be prepared to go forth by the coming feast of St. John the Baptist. And then the King gave them leave to sell each his movable goods before the time fixed, that is, the feast of St. John the Baptist. But their real estate, that is, houses, fields, vineyards, barns, wine-presses, and such like, he reserved for himself and his successors, the kings of the French.

When the faithless Jews heard this edict some of them were born again of water and the Holy Spirit and converted to the Lord, remaining steadfast in the faith of our Lord Jesus Christ. To them the King, out of regard for the Christian religion, restored all their possessions in their entirety, and gave them perpetual liberty.

Others were blinded by their ancient error and persisted in their perfidy; and they sought to win with gifts and golden promises the great of the land—counts, barons, archbishops, bishops—that through their influence and advice, and through the promise of infinite wealth, they might turn the King's mind from his firm intention. But the merciful and compassionate God, who does not forsake those who put their hope in Him and who doth humble those who glory in their strength . . . so fortified the illustrious King that he could not be moved by prayers nor promises of temporal things. . . .

The infidel Jews, perceiving that the great of the land, through whom they had been accustomed easily to bend the King's predecessors to their will, had suffered repulse, and astonished and stupefied by the strength of mind of Philip the King and his constancy in the Lord, exclaimed with a certain admiration "Shema Israel!" and prepared to sell all their household goods. The time was now at hand when the King had ordered them to leave France altogether, and it could not be in any way prolonged. Then did the Jews sell all their movable possessions in great haste, while their landed property reverted to the crown. Thus the Jews, having sold their goods and taken the price for the expenses of their journey, departed with their

wives and children and all their households in the aforesaid year of
the Lord 1182.

(Marcus, The Jew in the Medieval World, pp. 24–27)

THIRD LATERAN COUNCIL OF THE CATHOLIC CHURCH   *(1179* c.e.*)*

In the second year of the pontificate of
Pope Innocent III:

Although in many ways the disbelief of the Jews must be reproved,
since nevertheless through them our own faith is truly proved, they
must not be oppressed grievously by the faithful, as the prophet says:
"Do not slay them, lest these be forgetful of Thy Law," [Psalms 58:12]
as if he were saying more openly: "Do not wipe out the Jews completely, lest perhaps Christians might be able to forget Thy Law,
which the former, although not understanding it, present in their
books to those who do understand it."

Just as, therefore there ought not to be license for the Jews to
presume to go beyond what is permitted them by law in their
synagogues, so in those which have been conceded to them, they
ought to suffer no prejudice. These men, therefore, since they wish
rather to go on in their own hardness than to know the revelations of
the prophets and the mysteries of the Law, and to come to a knowledge of the Christian faith, still, since they beseech the help of Our
defense, We, out of the meekness proper to Christian piety, and
keeping in the footprints of Our predecessors of happy memory
. . . admit their petition, and We grant them the buckler of Our
protection.

For We make the law that no Christian compel them, unwilling
or refusing, by violence to come to baptism. But, if any one of them
should spontaneously, and for the sake of the faith, fly to the
Christians, once his choice has become evident, let him be made a
Christian without any calumny. Indeed, he is not recognized to have
come to Christian baptism, not spontaneously, but unwillingly.

Too, no Christian ought presume, apart from the juridical

sentence of the territorial power, wickedly to injure their persons, or
with violence to take away their property, or to change the good
customs which they have had until now in whatever region they
inhabit.

Besides, in the celebration of their own festivities, no one ought
disturb them in any way, with clubs or stones, nor ought any one try
to require from them or to extort from them services they not owe,
except for those they have been accustomed from times past to
perform.

In addition to these, We decree, blocking the wickedness and
avarice of evil men, that no one ought to dare mutilate or diminish a
Jewish cemetery, nor, in order to get money, to exhume bodies once
they have been buried.

If anyone, however, shall attempt, the tenor of this decree once
known, to go against it—may this be far from happening!—let him be
punished by the vengeance of excommunication, unless he correct his
presumption by making equivalent satisfaction.

We desire, however, that only those be fortified by the guard of
this protection who shall have presumed no plotting for the subver-
sion of the Christian faith.

(Canon 25, given at Lateran, 17 October 1199)

* * *

The more the Christians are restrained from the practice of
usury, the more are they oppressed in this matter by the treachery of
the Jews, so that in a short time they exhaust the resources of the
Christians. Wishing, therefore, in this matter to protect the Christians against cruel oppression by the Jews, we ordain in this decree
that if in the future under any pretext Jews extort from Christians
oppressive and immoderate interest, the partnership of the Christians
shall be denied them till they have made suitable satisfaction for their
excesses. The Christians also, every appeal being set aside, shall, if
necessary, be compelled by ecclesiastical censure to abstain from all
commercial intercourse with them. We command the princes not to
be hostile to the Christians on this account, but rather to strive to
hinder the Jews from practicing such excesses. Lastly, we decree that
the Jews be compelled by the same punishment to make satisfaction
for the tithes and offerings due to the churches, which the Christians

were accustomed to supply from their houses and other possessions before these properties, under whatever title, fell into the hands of the Jews, that thus the churches may be safeguarded against loss.

(Canon 67)

* * *

In some provinces a difference of dress distinguishes the Jews and Saracens from the Christians, but in others confusion has developed to such a degree that no difference is discernible. Whence it happens sometimes through error that Christians mingle with the women of Jews and Saracens, and, on the other hand, Jews and Saracens mingle with those of the Christians. Therefore, that such ruinous commingling through error of this kind may not serve as a refuge for further excuse for excesses, we decree that such people of both sexes in every Christian province and at all times be distinguished in public from other people by a difference of dress, since this was also enjoined on them by Moses. On the days of the Lamentations and on Passion Sunday they may not appear in public, because some of them, as we understand, on those days are not ashamed to show themselves more ornately attired and do not fear to amuse themselves at the expense of the Christians, who in memory of the sacred passion go about attired in robes of mourning. That we most strictly forbid, lest they should presume in some measure to burst forth suddenly in contempt of the Redeemer. And, since we ought not to be ashamed to Him who blotted out our offenses, we command that the secular princes restrain presumptuous persons of this kind by condign punishment, lest they presume to blaspheme in some degree the One crucified for us.

(Canon 68)

FREDERICK II (THE BELLIGERENT)   *(1211–1246)*

Duke of Austria, 13th century C.E.

The "Charter of the Jews of the Duchy of Austria," 1 July 1244:

    I. We decree, therefore, first, that in cases involving money, or immovable property, or a criminal complaint touching the person or property of a Jew, no Christian shall be admitted as a witness against a Jew unless there is a Jewish witness together with a Christian . . . .

IX. Likewise, if a Christian should inflict any sort of wound upon a Jew, the accused shall pay to the Duke twelve marks of gold which are to be turned in to the treasury. He must also pay, to the person who has been injured, twelve marks of silver and the expenses incurred for the medicine needed in his cure.

X. Likewise, if a Christian should kill a Jew he shall be punished with the proper sentence, death, and all his movable and immovable property shall pass into the power of the Duke.

XI. Likewise, if a Christian strikes a Jew, without, however, having spilt his blood, he shall pay to the Duke four marks of gold, and to the man he struck four marks of silver. If he has no money, he shall offer satisfaction for the crime committed by the loss of his hand.

XII. Likewise, wherever a Jew shall pass through our territory no one shall offer any hindrance to him or molest or trouble him. If, however, he should be carrying any goods or other things for which he must pay duty at all custom offices, he shall pay only the prescribed duty which a citizen of that town, in which the Jew is then dwelling, pays.

XIII. Likewise, if the Jews, as is their custom, should transport any of their dead either from city to city, or from province to province, or from one Austrian land to another, we do not wish anything to be demanded of them by our customs officers. If however, a customs officer should extort anything, then he is to be punished for *praedatio mortui*, which means, in common language, robbery of the dead.

XIV. Likewise, if a Christian, moved by insolence, shall break into or devastate the cemetery of the Jews, he shall die, as the court determines, and all his property, whatever it may be, shall be forfeited to the treasury of the Duke.

XV. Likewise, if any one wickedly throw something at the synagogues of the Jews we order that he pay two talents to the judge of the Jews . . . .

XX. Likewise, if a Jew was secretly murdered, and if through the testimony it cannot be determined by his friends who murdered him, yet if after an investigation has been made the Jews begin to suspect some one, we are willing to supply the Jews with a champion against this suspect.

XXI. Likewise, if a Christian raises his hand in violence against a Jewess, we order that the hand of that person be cut off . . . .

(Marcus, *The Jew in the Medieval World*, pp. 28–32)

POPE GREGORY IX   *(ca. 1145–1241* C.E.*)*

In a letter sent to France to protest the "unwonted excess of cruelty" by Crusaders against the Jews:

Although the disbelief of the Jews must be reproved, it is, nevertheless, useful and necessary for Christians to have dealings with these same men, for they possess the image of our Saviour, they have been created by the Creator of all, and they must not be destroyed by His own creatures, namely, by those who believe in Christ: It is the Lord who forbids it! Now, to whatever point their median group may be perverse, their fathers were rendered friends of God, and their remnants will be saved.

(Synan, *The Popes and the Jews in the Middle Ages*, p. 110)

POPE GREGORY X   *(ca. 1210–1276)*

From "A Bull of Pope Gregory X," 7 October 1272:

. . . Even as it is not allowed to the Jews in their assemblies presumptuously to undertake for themselves more than that which is permitted by law, even so they ought not to suffer any disadvantage in those which have been granted them. Although they prefer to persist in their stubbornness rather than to recognize the words of their prophets and the mysteries of the Scriptures, and thus to arrive at a knowledge of Christian faith and salvation; nevertheless, inasmuch as they have made an appeal for our protection and help, we therefore admit their petition and offer them the shield of our protection through the clemency of Christian piety. . . .

We decree moreover that no Christian shall compel them or any one of their group to come to baptism unwillingly. But if any one of them shall take refuge of his own accord with Christians, because of conviction, then, after his intention will have been manifest, he shall be made a Christian without any intrigue. For, indeed, that person who is known to have come to Christian baptism not freely, but unwillingly, is not believed to possess the Christian faith.

Moreover no Christian shall presume to seize, imprison, wound, torture, mutilate, kill, or inflict violence on them. . . .

In addition, no one shall disturb them in any way during the celebration of their festivals, whether by day or by night, with clubs or stones or anything else. . . .

Since it happens occasionally that some Christians lose their Christian children, the Jews are accused by their enemies of secretly carrying off and killing these same Christian children and of making sacrifices of the heart and blood of these very children. It happens, too, that the parents of these children or some other Christian enemies of these Jews, secretly hide these very children in order that they may be able to injure these Jews, and in order that they may be able to extort from them a certain amount of money by redeeming them from their straits.

And most falsely do these Christians claim that the Jews have secretly and furtively carried away these children and killed them, and that the Jews offer sacrifice from the heart and the blood of these children, since their law in this matter precisely and expressly forbids Jews to sacrifice, eat, or drink the blood, or to eat the flesh of animals having claws. This has been demonstrated many times at our court by Jews converted to the Christian faith: nevertheless very many Jews are often seized and detained unjustly because of this.

We decree, therefore, that Christians need not be obeyed against Jews in a case or situation of this type, and we order that Jews seized under such a silly pretext be freed from imprisonment, and that they shall not be arrested henceforth on such a miserable pretext, unless — which we do not believe — they be caught in the commission of the crime . . . .

(Marcus, *The Jew in the Medieval World*, pp. 152–154)

GEOFFREY CHAUCER   (c. 1342/43–1400)

English writer; author of Canterbury Tales

The Prioress would speak of cursed Jews as naturally as cursed Turks. Anyone not a Christian was automatically damned, and the Jews were particularly damned because they had murdered the Lord Himself.

Even Chaucer would think of Jews as a diabolical abstraction, for it is doubtful if he ever saw a real one in his life. The Jews had been banished from England a century earlier, and Chaucer had no more reason for questioning the justice of their exile than he had for regretting that his home in Aldgate had been rebuilt in part with material from the ruined homes of the martyred "Hebrayk people."

(Marchette Chute, *Geoffrey Chaucer of England,* p. 296)

4

The Renaissance

JOHN REUCHLIN *(1455–1522)*

German humanist and Christian Hebraist; defender of the Talmud against the Dominicans

Christ himself ordained that the Talmud be preserved. This is the plain meaning of his words: "Search the scriptures; for in them ye think ye have eternal life: and they testify for me" (John 5:39).

The homilies and hymnodies of the Jews are not to be interfered with, in accordance with the edicts and decrees of Emperors and Popes—that the Jews be not disturbed in their synagogues, their religious worship and customs.

None of these books, as is claimed, contain statements hostile to Christians. For the Jews have their writings for the purpose of their own inspiration and the preservation of their faith in time of persecution by pagan, Christian or Mohammedan, but not to inflict harm on or cause shame to anybody. . . . It is obvious that they do not recognize Christ as God. That is their faith, but they do not intend to cast aspersion on anybody. . . .

The Jew belongs to God just as much as I do. If he holds his ground, he does so before his Lord. Every one of us will have to give an account of himself. Why, then, presume to judge the soul of another? Only God can do that, and He is mighty enough to set each soul right.

In matters of faith, Jews are responsible to themselves, not subject to any other judge, and no Christian should sit in judgment over them. They are not heretics, for those who were never of the Christian religion cannot be renegades from it. They are justified in complaining that the Christian Church annually on Good Friday calls them "perfidious Jews," i.e., such as are bereft of faith and fidelity.

In addition, the secular law, too, prohibits interference with the Jews, since they are members of the Roman Empire and fellow subjects of the Emperor . . . .

(L. Geiger, ed., *Johann Reuchlin, sein Leben und seine Werke*, Leipzig, 1871, pp. 227–240)

DESIDERIUS ERASMUS   *(1466–1536)*

Dutch humanist, translator, author, editor of Church writings

For my own part, provided the New Testament remain intact, I had rather that the Old should be altogether abolished, than that the peace of Christendom should be broken for the sake of the books of the Jews.

(Graetz, *Geschichte der Juden*, p. 435)

MARTIN LUTHER   *(1483–1546)*

Leader of the Protestant Reformation

I will therefore show by means of the Bible the causes which induce me to believe that Christ was a Jew born of a virgin. Perhaps I will attract some of the Jews to the Christian faith. For our fools—the popes, bishops, sophists, and monks—the coarse blockheads! have until this time so treated the Jews that to be a good Christian one would have to become a Jew. And if I had been a Jew and had seen such idiots and blockheads ruling and teaching the Christian religion, I would rather have been a sow than a Christian.

For they have dealt with the Jews as if they were dogs and not human beings. They have done nothing for them but curse them and seize their wealth. Whenever they converted them, they did not teach them either Christian law or life but only subjected them to papistry and monkery. When these Jews saw that Judaism had such strong scriptural basis and that Christianity [Catholicism] was pure nonsense without Biblical support, how could they quiet their hearts and become real, good Christians? I have myself heard from pious converted Jews that if they had not heard the gospel in our time [from us Lutherans] they would always have remained Jews at heart in spite of their conversion. For they admit that they have never heard anything about Christ from the rulers who have converted them.

I hope that, if the Jews are treated friendly and are instructed kindly enough through the Bible, many of them will become real Christians and come back to the ancestral faith of the prophets and patriarchs . . . .

I would advise and beg everybody to deal kindly with the Jews and to instruct them in the Scriptures; in such a case we could expect them to come over to us. If, however, we use brute force and slander them, saying that they need the blood of Christians to get rid of their stench and I know not what other nonsense of that kind, and treat them like dogs, what good can we expect of them? Finally, how can we expect them to improve if we forbid them to work among us and to have social intercourse with us, and so force them into usury?

If we wish to make them better, we must deal with them not according to the law of the pope, but according to the law of Christian charity. We must receive them kindly and allow them to compete with us in earning a livelihood, so that they may have a good reason to be with us and among us and an opportunity to witness Christian life and doctrine; and if some remain obstinate, what of it? Not every one of us is a good Christian.

I shall stop here now until I see what the results will be. May God be gracious to us all. Amen.

("That Jesus Christ was born a Jew," in Marcus,
The Jew in the Medieval World, pp. 166–167)

* * *

What then shall we Christians do with this damned, rejected race of Jews? Since they live among us and we know about their lying and blasphemy and cursing, we can not tolerate them if we do not wish to share in their lies, curses, and blasphemy.[1] In this way we cannot quench the inextinguishable fire of divine rage (as the prophets say) nor convert the Jews. We must prayerfully and reverentially practice a merciful severity. Perhaps we may save a few from the fire and the flames. We must not seek vengeance. They are surely being punished a thousand times more than we might wish them. Let me give you my honest advice.

First, their synagogues or churches should be set on fire, and whatever does not burn up should be covered or spread over with dirt so that no one may ever be able to see a cinder or stone of it. And this ought to be done for the honor of God and of Christianity in order that God may see that we are Christians, and that we have not wittingly tolerated or approved of such public lying, cursing, and blaspheming of His Son and His Christians. . . .

Secondly, their homes should likewise be broken down and

---

[1] Luther, and others, believed that the Jews curse the Christians in their daily prayers.

destroyed. For they perpetuate the same things there that they do in their synagogues. For this reason they ought to be put under one roof or in a stable, like gypsies, in order that they may realize that they are not masters in our land, as they boast, but miserable captives, as they complain of us incessantly before God with bitter wailing.

Thirdly, they should be deprived of their prayer-books and Talmuds in which such idolatry, lies, cursing, and blasphemy are taught.

Fourthly, their rabbis must be forbidden under threat of death to teach any more . . . .

Fifthly, passport and traveling privileges should be absolutely forbidden to the Jews. For they have no business in the rural districts since they are not nobles, nor officials, nor merchants, nor the like. Let them stay at home . . . .

Sixthly, they ought to be stopped from usury. All their cash and valuables of silver and gold ought to be taken from them and put aside for safe keeping. For this reason, as said before, everything that they possess they stole and robbed from us through their usury, for they have no other means of support. This money should be used in the case (and in no other) where a Jew has honestly become a Christian, so that he may get for the time being one or two or three hundred florins, as the person may require. This, in order that he may start a business to support his poor wife and children and the old and feeble. Such evilly acquired money is cursed, unless, with God's blessing, it is put to some good and necessary use . . . .

Seventhly, let the young and strong Jews and Jewesses be given the flail, the ax, the hoe, the spade, the distaff, and spindle, and let them earn their bread by the sweat of their noses as is enjoined upon Adam's children. For it is not proper that they should want us cursed *Goyyim* to work in the sweat of our brow and that they, pious crew, idle away their days at the fireside in laziness, feasting, and display. And in addition to this, they boast impiously that they have become masters of the Christians at our expense. We ought to drive the rascally lazy bones out of our system.

If, however, we are afraid that they might harm us personally, or our wives, children, servants, cattle, etc. when they serve us or work for us—since it is surely to be presumed that such noble lords of the world and poisonous bitter worms are not accustomed to any work and would very unwillingly humble themselves to such a degree among the cursed *Goyyim*—then let us apply the same cleverness as the other nations, such as France, Spain, Bohemia, etc., and settle with them for that which they have extorted usuriously from us, and after having divided it up fairly let us drive them out of the country for all time. For, as has been said, God's rage is so great against them that they only become worse and worse through mild mercy, and not much better through severe mercy. Therefore away with them . . . .

To sum up, dear princes and nobles who have Jews in your domains, if this advice of mine does not suit you, then find a better one so that you and we may be free of this insufferable devilish burden—the Jews.

("Concerning the Jews and Their Lies," 1543, in *The Jew in the Medieval World*, pp. 167–169)

* * *

For where God built a church there the Devil would also build a chapel. They imitated the Jews in this, namely, that as the Most Holiest was dark, and had no light, even so and after the same manner did they make their shrines dark where the Devil made answer. Thus is the Devil ever God's ape.

(*The Table Talk of Martin Luther*)

* * *

Jews and papists are ungodly wretches; they are two stockings made of one piece of cloth.

(*The Table Talk of Martin Luther*)

THE PASSION PLAY (OBERAMMERGAU) (ca. 1662)

But blind and deaf remains poor Jerusalem,
Thrusting away the hand lovingly held out to her.
Therefore the Highest from her His face hath turned.
So He leaveth her to sink down to destruction.

Queen Vashti once disdaining to attend the royal feast
Enraged thereby the king, who swore to banish her
From his presence and to choose
A gentler soul for his consort.

Thus too will the synagogue be thrust away,
From her will the kingdom of God be taken and
    entrusted
To another people who shall bring forth
The fruits of righteousness.

                                               (Anonymous)

POPE PIUS IV *(1499–1565)*

We order that each and every Jew of both sexes in our temporal dominions, and in all the cities, lands, places and baronies subject to them, shall depart completely out of the confines thereof within the space of three months and after these letters shall have been made public.

EDICT OF FAITH

A declaration from the Spanish Inquisition, 1519

We, Doctor Andres de Palacio, Inquisitor against the heresy and apostolic perversity in the city and kingdom of Valencia, etc.

To all faithful Christians, both men and women, chaplains, friars and priests of every condition, quality and degree; whose attention to this will result in salvation in our Lord Jesus Christ, the true salvation; who are aware that, by means of other edicts and sentences of the Reverend inquisitors, our predecessors, they were warned to appear before them, within a given period, and declare and manifest the things which they had seen, known, and heard tell of any person or persons, either alive or dead, who had said or done anything against the Holy Catholic Faith . . .

. . . cultivated and observed the law of Moses or the Mohammedan sect, or the rites and ceremonies of the same; or perpetrated diverse crimes of heresy; observing Friday evenings and Saturdays; changing into clean personal linen on Saturdays and wearing better clothes than on other days; preparing on Fridays the food for Saturdays, in stewing pans on a small fire; who do not work on Friday evenings and Saturdays as on other days; who kindle lights in clean lamps with new wicks, on Friday evenings; place clean linen on the beds and clean napkins on the table; celebrate the festival of unleavened bread, eat unleavened bread and celery and bitter herbs; observe the fast of pardon (Day of Atonement) when they do not eat all day until the evening after star-rise, when they pardon one another and break their fast; and in the same manner observe the fasts of Queen Esther, of *tissabav*,[2] and *rosessena*;[3]

who say prayers according to the law of Moses, standing up before the wall, swaying back and forth, and taking a few steps backwards; who give money for oil for the Jewish temple or other secret place of worship; who slaughter poultry according to the Judaic law, and refrain from eating sheep or any other animal which is *trefa*;[4] who do not wish to eat salt pork, hares, rabbits, snails, or fish that have not scales; who bathe the bodies of their dead and bury them in virgin soil according to the Jewish custom; who, in the house of mourning do not eat meat but fish and hard-boiled eggs, seated at low tables; who separate a morsel of dough when baking and throw it on the fire; who become, or know of others who become circumcised; who invoke demons, and give to them the honour that is due to God;

who say that the law of Moses is good and can bring about their salvation; who perform many other rites and ceremonies of the same; who say that our Lord Jesus Christ was not the true Messiah promised in Scripture, not the true God nor son of God; who deny that he died to save the human race; deny the resurrection and his ascension to heaven; and say that our Lady the Virgin Mary was not the mother of God or a virgin before the nativity and after; who say and affirm many other heretical errors; who state that what they had confessed before the inquisitors was not the truth. . . .

if any know of those who keep Jewish customs, and name their children on the seventh night after their birth and with silver and gold upon a table, pleasurably observe the Jewish ceremony; and if any know that when somebody dies, they place a cup of water and a lighted candle and some napkins where the deceased died, and for some days, do not enter there; if any know of the effort of a Jew or

---

[2]Tisha Bav, the ninth of Av, a fast day commemorating the destruction of the Jerusalem Temple.

[3]Rosh Hashanah, the Jewish New Year.

[4]Not slaughtered according to Jewish law.

convert, secretly to preach the law of Moses and convert others to this creed, teaching the ceremonies belonging to the same, giving information as to the dates of festivals and fasts, teaching Jewish prayers;

if any know of anyone who attempts to become a Jew, or being Christian walks abroad in the costume of a Jew; if any know of anyone, converted or otherwise, who orders that his dress shall be made of canvas and not of linen, as the good Jews do; if any know of those who, when their children kiss their hands, place their hands on their children's heads without making the Sign (of the Cross); or who, after dinner or supper, bless the wine and pass it on to everyone at the table . . . .

All these things, having been seen, heard or known, you, the above-mentioned faithful Christians, have, with obstinate hearts, refused to declare and manifest, greatly to the burden and prejudice of your souls; thinking that you were absolved by the bulls and indulgences issued by our holy father, and by promises and donations which you had made, for which you have incurred the sentence of excommunication and other grave penalties under statutory law; and thus you may be proceeded against as those who have suffered excommunication and as abettors of heretics, in various ways; but, wishing to act with benevolence, and in order that your souls may not be lost, since our Lord does not wish the death of the sinner but his reformation and life; by these presents, we remove and suspend the censure promulgated by the said former inquisitors against you, so long as you observe and comply with the terms of this edict, by which we require, exhort and order you, in virtue of the holy obedience, and under penalty of complete excommunication, within nine days from the time that the present edict shall have been read to you, or made known to you in whatsoever manner, to state all that you know, have seen, heard, or heard tell in any manner whatsoever, of the things and ceremonies above-mentioned, and to appear before us personally to declare and manifest what you have seen, heard, or heard tell secretly, without having spoken previously with any other person, or borne false witness against anyone.

Otherwise, the period having passed, the canonical admonitions having been repeated in accordance with the law, steps will be taken to give out and promulgate sentence of excommunication against you, in and by these documents; and through such excommunication, we order that you be publicly denounced . . . .

And we order the vicars, rectors, chaplains, and sacristans and any other religious or ecclesiastical persons to regard and treat the above-mentioned as excommunicated and accursed for having incurred the wrath and indignation of Almighty God, and of the glorious Virgin Mary, His Mother, and of the beatified apostles Saint Peter and Saint Paul, and all the saints of the celestial Court; and upon such rebels and disobedient ones who would hide the truth regarding the above-mentioned things, be all the plagues and maledictions which befell and descended upon King Pharaoh and his host for not having obeyed the divine commandments . . . .

. . . Accursed be they in living and dying, and may they ever be hardened to their sins, and the devil be at their right hand always; may their vocation be sinful, and their days be few and evil; may their substance be enjoyed by others, and their children be orphans, and their wives widows. May their children ever be in need, and may none help them; may they be turned out of their homes. . . .

. . . And if any persons incurring the said excommunications and maledictions, should persist therein for the space of a year, they should be regarded as heretics themselves, and shall be prosecuted by the same process as against heretics or suspects of the crime of heresy . . . .

(Cited in Roth, *The Spanish Inquisition*, pp. 76–83)

MIGUEL DE CERVANTES   *(1547–1616)*

Spanish author of Don Quixote

Forgetting a basic fact—that no other writer's work in Inquisitorial Spain is so saturated in ironic ambiguity as Cervantes', so elaborately encoded in the intellectual cryptography of the time—has led some Jews to accuse him of anti-Semitism. "O effeminate folk, infamous and of little worth," a Christian calls them in Cervantes' play *The Dungeons of Algiers*. But their persecution nevertheless "moves me to compassion," the Christian goes on. Cervantes' Jews obey the imperatives of

Inquisitorial orthodoxy; they are taunted and bullied and made fools of. But they are never deprived of their humanity, never caricatured as the bestial, unrelievedly evil monstrosities we see in so much Spanish and Flemish painting of the fifteenth and sixteenth centuries. The cruelty of their predicament is never lost from sight.

The plight of the Jews Cervantes saw in Algiers, perhaps the only avowed Jews he ever saw, was pitiable. Although the wealth they had brought with them into exile from Spain had largely contributed to North African prosperity, and although (perhaps partly because) they covertly controlled the Turkish provinces' trade, they were hated by the Moslems with whom they had sought refuge. Moslem religious tolerance toward them was barely that—tolerance. Jews were obliged to dress in distinct black; anyone, even a slave, could beat them publicly with impunity. Cervantes obliges his audience by making the Jews in his plays derisory; they cringe and fawn on their tormentors. But Cervantes' pity for them (and, by extension, for their kinsmen in Europe) is concealed by the flimsiest of veils . . . .

(Byron, *Cervantes, A Biography*, p. 27)

ROBERT BURTON   (1557–1640)

English scholar, writer, and clergyman

[The Jews have] goggle eyes [and] are most severe in their examination of time . . . . [they are] very industrious, while amongst Englishmen the badge of gentry is idleness, to be of no calling, not to labour . . . to be a mere spectator, a drone . . . .

As a company of vagabonds, they are scattered over all parts of the globe . . . . [The Jews are] so ignorant and self-willed withal, that amongst their most understanding Rabbis, you will find naught but gross dotage, horrible hardness of heart, and *stupend* obstinacy in all their actions, opinions, conversations, and yet so zealous withal, that no man living can be more, and vindicate themselves for the elect people of God.

(*Anatomy of Melancholy*, 1621)

OLIVER CROMWELL   *(1599–1658)*

Lord Protector of England

From his address at the Whitehall Conference on 18 December 1655, favoring the readmission of Jews into England:

You [English merchants] say that they are the meanest and most despised of all people. But in that case what becomes of your fears? Can you really be afraid that this contemptible and despised people should be able to prevail in trade and credit over the merchants of England, the noblest and most esteemed merchants of the whole world?

Great is my sympathy with this poor people whom God chose, and to whom He gave the law.

(Wolf, *Manasseh ben Israel's Mission to Oliver Cromwell*, p. iii)

* * *

The Jews had better success with Oliver Cromwell, when they desired leave to have a synagogue in London. They offered him, when Protector, sixty thousand pounds for that privilege. Cromwell appointed them a day, for his giving them an answer. He then sent to some of the most powerful among the clergy, and some of the chief merchants in the city, to be present among the clergy, and some of the chief merchants in the city, to be present at their meeting. It was in the long gallery at Whitehall. Sir Paul Rycaut, who was then a young man, pressed in among the crowd, and said he never heard a man speak so well in his life, as Cromwell did on this occasion. When they were all met, he ordered the Jews to speak for themselves. After that he turned to the clergy, who inveighed much against the Jews, as a cruel and cursed people.

Cromwell in his answer to the clergy called them "Men of God"; and desired to be informed by them whether it was not their opinion, that the Jews were one day to be called into the church? He then desired to know, whether it was not every Christian man's duty to forward that good end all he could? Then he flourished a good deal on the religion prevailing in this nation, the only place in the world where religion was taught in its full purity: was it not then our duty, in particular, to encourage them to settle here, where alone they could be taught the truth; and not to exclude them from the sight, and leave them among idolaters? This silenced the clergy.

He then turned to the merchants, who spoke much of [the Jews'] falseness and meanness, and that they would get their trade from them. " 'Tis true," says Cromwell, "they are the meanest and most despised of all people."—He then fell into abusing the Jews most heartily, and after he had said every thing that was contemptible and low of them: "Can you really be afraid," said he, "that this mean despised people, should be able to prevail in trade and credit over the merchants of England, the noblest and most esteemed merchants of the whole world!"—Thus he went on, till he had silenced them too; and so was at liberty to grant what he desired to the Jews [which was their readmission to England in 1656, for the first time since their expulsion in 1290 by Edward the First.]

(Singer, *Rev. Joseph Spence,*[5] *Anecdotes, Observations, and Characters of Books and Men [1728–1744],* pp. 77–79)

JOHN DONNE   *(1572–1631)*

English poet

Another passage in a sermon indicates that Donne had attended worship in a Jewish synagogue; he is speaking of the practice of offering up prayers for the dead:

> That is true that I have read, that after Christs time, the Rabbins laid hold upon it, and brought it into custome; And that is true which I have seene, that the Jewes at this day continue it in practice; For when one dies, for some certaine time after, appointed by them, his sonne or some other neere in blood or alliance, comes to the Altar, and there saith and doth some thing in the behalfe of his dead father, or grandfather respectively.

---

[5]Spence, a critic and friend of Alexander Pope, wrote this nearly a century after the event.

> . . . Donne . . . perhaps . . . attended Jewish worship as a lay-
> man . . . and may have done so in Holland.
>
> (Bald, *John Donne—A Life*, p. 262)

PHILIP III *(1578–1621)*

King of Spain

An edict to prevent the emigration of Marranos to the New
World, issued at the start of 17th century:

We command and decree that no one recently converted to our holy
faith, be he Jew or Moor, or the offspring of these, should settle in our
Indies without our distinct permission. Furthermore we forbid most
emphatically the immigration into New Spain of any one [who is at
the expiration of some prescribed penance] newly reconciled with the
Church; of the child or grandchild of any person who has ever worn
the 'san benito' [special costume] publicly; of the child or grandchild of
any person who was either burnt as a heretic or otherwise punished for
the crime of heresy, through either male or female descent. Should
any one [falling under this category] presume to violate this law, his
goods will be confiscated for the benefit of the royal treasury, and
upon him the full measure of our grace or disgrace shall fall, so that
under any circumstances and for all time he shall be banished from
our Indies. Whosoever does not possess personal effects, however,
should atone for his transgression by the public infliction of one
hundred lashes.

HUGO GROTIUS *(1583–1645)*

Dutch scholar and statesman

"An Address to the Jews"

Wherefore I desire the Jews that they would not look upon us as
adversaries. We know very well that they are the offspring of holy men

whom God often visited by His prophets and His angels; that the Messiah was born of their nation, as were the first teachers of Christianity. They were the stock into which we were grafted; to them were committed the oracles of God, which we respect as much as they.

(Grotius, *The Truth of the Christian Religion*, p. 208)

THOMAS HOBBES   *(1588–1679)*

British philosopher; author of Leviathan

To go on now, following the guidance of the Holy Scripture: the same covenant was renewed with Isaac (Genesis 26:3 f.), and with Jacob (28.13 f.), where God styles himself not simply God, whom nature doth dictate him to be, but distinctly the *God of Abraham and Isaac.* Afterward being about to renew the same covenant by Moses with the whole people of Israel (Exodus 3:6): "I am" saith he, "the God of thy father, the God of Abraham, the God of Isaac, and the God of Jacob." Afterward, when that people, not only the freest, but also the greatest enemy to human subjection, by reason of the fresh memory of their Egyptian bondage, abode in the wilderness near Mount Sinai, that ancient covenant was propounded to them all to be renewed in this manner (Exodus 19:5 f.): "Therefore if ye will obey my voice indeed, and keep my covenant," (to wit, that covenant which was made with Abraham, Isaac, and Jacob), "then shall ye be a peculiar treasure unto me, above all people; for all the earth is mine, and ye shall be to me a kingdom of priests, and a holy nation. And all the people answered together, and said, 'All that the Lord hath spoken, we will do.'"

(Hobbes, *The Questions Concerning Liberty, Necessity, and Chance,* 1656)

5

Colonial and Postrevolutionary America

ROGER WILLIAMS   (1603?–1683)

English clergyman; founder of Rhode Island colony

It hath fallen out sometimes that both papists and protestants, Jews and Turks, may be embarked upon one ship; upon which supposal I affirm, that all the liberty of conscience, that I ever pleaded for, turns upon these two hinges—that none of the papists, Jews, or Turks, be forced to come to the ship's prayers or worship, nor be compelled from their own particular prayers or worship.

(Morris, *American Jewish Archives*, vol. III, pp. 24–27)

PETER STUYVESANT   (1610–1672)

Dutch colonial governor in America

Extract from a letter from director Peter Stuyvesant to the West India Company, 22 September 1654:

The Jews who have arrived would nearly all like to remain here, but learning that they (with their customary usury and deceitful trading with the Christians) were very repugnant to the inferior magistrates, as also to the people having the most affection for you; the Deaconry [which takes care of the poor] also fearing that owning to their present indigence they might become a charge in the coming winter, we have, for the benefit of this weak and newly developing place and the land in general, deemed it useful to require them in a friendly way to depart; praying also most seriously in this connection, for ourselves as also for the general community of your worships, that the deceitful race—such hateful enemies and blasphemers of the name of Christ—be not allowed further to infect and trouble this new colony, to the detraction of your worships and the dissatisfaction of your worships' most affectionate subjects.

(Marcus, *The Jew in the Medieval World*, pp. 69–70)

West India Company to Stuyvesant, 26 April 1655:

We would have liked to effectuate and fulfill your wishes and request that the new territories should no more be allowed to be infected by people of the Jewish nation, for we foresee therefrom the same difficulties which you fear. But after having further weighed and considered the matter, we observe that this would be somewhat unreasonable and unfair, especially because of the considerable loss sustained by this nation, with others, in the taking of Brazil, as also because of the large amount of capital which they still have invested in the shares of this company. Therefore after many deliberations we have finally decided and resolved . . . that these people may travel and trade to and in New Netherland and live and remain there, providing the poor among them shall not become a burden to the company or to the community, but be supported by their own nation. You will now govern yourself accordingly. . . .

(*The Jew in the Medieval World*, p. 72)

SAMUEL PEPYS   (1633–1703)

English diarist and naval administrator

Diary entry of 14 October 1663 (the Festival of Sukkot):

". . . my wife and I . . . to the Jewish Synagogue: where the men and boys in their vayles, and the women behind a lattice out of sight; and some things stand up, which I believe is their Law, in a press to which all coming in do bow; and at the putting on their vayles do say something, to which others that hear him do cry Amen, and the party do kiss his vayle. Their service all in a singing way, and in Hebrew . . .

    . . . in the end they had a prayer for the King, which they pronounced his name in Portugall; but the prayer, like the rest, in Hebrew. But, Lord! to see the disorder, laughing, sporting, and no attention, but confusion in all their service, more like brutes than people knowing the true God, would make a man forswear ever seeing them more: and indeed I never did see so much, or could have imagined there had been any religion in the whole world, so absurdly performed as this. Away thence with my mind strongly disturbed with them, by coach and set down my wife in Westminster Hall. . . ."

(Wheatly, Diary of Samuel Pepy, vol. III, p. 303)

WILLIAM PENN   *(1644–1718)*

English Quaker; founder of Pennsylvania

Though the Jews, above all people, had the most to say for inspiration and restraint within their own dominions, having their religion instituted by so many signal proofs of divine original, it being delivered to them by the hand of God himself, yet such was their indulgence to dissenters, that if they held the common received Noahchical principles tending to the acknowledgement of One God and a just life, they had the free exercise of their distinct modes or ways of worship, which were numerous. Of this their own rabbis are witnesses. . . .

For we find that the ancient Jews did never punish the Sadducees, though they denied the doctrine of the resurrection. . . . I pass lightly over the Jews, by reason they had the knowledge of the true God, and were obliged not to engage in the superstitions of the heathens; yet were they not so rigid as to exclude the Gentiles from among them, but had their *Atrium Gentium* for their reception, although unconverted; nor did they refuse the sacrifices and oblations of the kings of Egypt, nor those of Augustus and Tiberius; all which they thought no breach of their laws to offer up in their holy temples.

(Penn, "The Great Case of Liberty of Conscience," 1670)

COTTON MATHER   *(1663–1728)*

American colonial clergyman

Mather's diary, 18 July 1696:

This day, from the dust, where I lay prostrate, before the Lord, I lifted my cries: For the conversion of the Jewish Nation, and for my own having the happiness, at some time or other, to baptize a Jew, that should by my ministry, be brought home unto the Lord.

(Friedman, "Cotton Mather and the Jews," in *American Jewish Historical Society Publications*, XXVI, p. 202)

* * *

Mather's diary, 9 April 1699:

This week, I attempted a further service to the name of the Lord. . . . I prefaced the Catechism with an address to the Jewish Nation, telling them in some lively terms, that if they would but return to the faith of the Old Testament, and believe with their own Ancient and blessed Patriarchs, this was all that we desired of them or for them. I gave this book to the Printer and it was immediately published. Its title is *The Faith of the Fathers*.

(p. 203)

* * *

Mather's diary, 21 May 1699:

I have advice from Heaven—Yea, more than this; That I shall shortly see some Harvest of my Prayers and Pains, and the Jewish Nation also.

(p. 205)

* * *

To the Jewish Nation:

One thing that satisfies us Christians, in the Truth of Christianity, is your obstinate aversion to that Holy Religion, our Blessed Jesus, the Author of our Faith, foretold your continuance under the circumstances now come upon you until the Ties of the Gentiles in the four monarchies, just now expiring, are expired. . . . Here is now put into your Hands an irresistible and inefragable demonstration that tho' you say, you are Jews you are not so. . . . Be amazed, O ye Rebellious and rejected People of our Great Lord Messiah. . . . Return O backsliding Israel!

(From the Dedication of *The Faith of the Fathers*)

Of all the states of Europe there is none where the Jews live more quietly than in Holland. Here they enrich the [country?] by trade and without fear profess their persuasions. There are two sorts of Jews in Holland, some are Germans, others come from Spain and Portugal. They are divided about some ceremonies and hate one another as if the essentials of religion were concerned. . . . [The Jews of America] are not of Ye Ten Tribes. They are only Jewish merchants drawn hither by their merchandise. . . .

(Friedman, *Pilgrims in a New Land*, p. 19)

BENJAMIN FRANKLIN   *(1706–1790)*

U.S. author, wit, and politician

. . . the most single-minded politicians could never long forget that there was a philosopher among them, incomparably able, when he chose, to speak with large wisdom, the pleasantest humour, and a happy grace. When he had more than a few words to say in the midst of debate he wrote out his speech in advance and, because standing was painful, had it read for him. His important speeches have been more accurately preserved than those of any other delegate. (Of course he did not make the speech against the Jews which, in 1934, was impudently forged and maliciously ascribed to him.)

(Van Doren, *Benjamin Franklin*, p. 745)

* * *

Franklin's respect for and tolerance of all religious groups was an important characteristic of the man, and the records bear out his statement of financial aid to all sects that asked him for it. The charge, made in 1934 by American Fascist sympathizers, renewed in the New York political campaign of 1938, and still occasionally repeated, that he was anti-Semitic and had delivered a speech against the Jews in the Federal Constitutional Convention of 1787, is based on a forgery and is utterly without historical foundation. On the other hand, the archives of Congregation Mikveh Israel in Philadelphia contain a subscription paper dated April 30, 1788, in which Franklin, together with forty-four other citizens of all faiths, contributed toward relieving the Congregation's debt incurred in building a synagogue. Franklin's donation and those of two others are the largest on the list.

(Larabee, ed., *The Autobiography of Benjamin Franklin*, pp. 146–147)

EDMUND BURKE   *(1729–1797)*

Irish political philosopher

During a debate regarding a British expedition against the island of Saint Eustasius in the Dutch West Indies, where the Jews were brutally mistreated:

The persecution was begun with the people whom of all others it ought to be the care and the wish of human nations to protect, the Jews. Having no fixed settlement in any part of the world, no kingdom nor country in which they have a government, a community and a system of laws, they are thrown upon the benevolence of nations and claim protection and civility from their weakness as well as from their utility. They were a people who, by shunning the profession of any, could give no well-founded jealousy to any state. If they have contracted some vices, they are such as naturally arise from their dispersed, wandering and proscribed state. It was an observation as old as Homer, and confirmed by the experience of all ages, that in a state of servitude the human mind loses half its value. From the east to the west, from one end of the world to the other, they are scattered and connected; the links of communication, in the mercantile chain; or, to borrow a phrase from electricity, the conductors by which credit was transmitted through the world. Their abandoned state and their defenceless situation calls most forcibly for the protection of civilized nations. If Dutchmen are injured and attacked, the Dutch have a nation, a government and armies to redress or revenge their cause. If Britons are injured, Britons have armies and laws, the laws of nations (or at least they once had the laws of nations), to fly to for protection and justice. But the Jews have no such power and no such friend to depend on. Humanity then must become their protector and ally. Did they find it in the British conquerors of St. Eustasius? No. On the contrary, a resolution was taken to banish this unhappy people from the island.

(From his address against Sir George Rodney
on 14 May 1781, in *The Parliamentary History of England
from the Earliest Period to the Year 1803*)

GEORGE WASHINGTON (1732–1799)

1st president of the United States, 1789–1797

A reply to Moses Seixas, sexton of the Hebrew Congregation of Newport, who had sent the president a letter of welcome on his visit to the town, 17 August 1790:

The citizens of the United States of America have a right to applaud themselves for having given to Mankind examples of an enlarged and liberal policy worthy of imitation. All possess alike liberty of conscience and immunities of citizenship. It is now no more that toleration is spoken of, as if it was by the indulgence of one class of people that another enjoyed the exercise of their inherent natural rights. For happily the Government of the United States, which gives bigotry no sanction, to persecution no assistance, requires only that they who live under its protection should demean themselves as good citizens, in giving it on all occasions their effectual support.

It would be inconsistent with the frankness of my character not to avow that I am pleased with your favorable opinion of my administration, and fervent wishes for my felicity. May the Children of the Stock of Abraham, who dwell in this land, continue to merit and enjoy the good will of the other Inhabitants, while every one shall sit in safety under his own vine and fig-tree, and there shall be none to make him afraid. May the father of all mercies scatter light and not darkness in our paths, and make us all in our several vocations useful here, and in his own due time and way everlastingly happy.

JOHN ADAMS (1735–1826)

2nd president of the United States, 1797–1801;
helped draft the Declaration of Independence

. . . in spite of Bolingbroke and Voltaire, I will insist that the Hebrews have done more to civilize men than any other nation. If I were an atheist, and believed in blind eternal fate, I should still believe that fate had ordained the Jews to be the most essential instrument for civilizing the nations. If I were an atheist of any other sect, who believe or pretend to believe that all is ordered by chance, I should believe that chance had ordered the Jews to preserve and propagate to all mankind the doctrine of a supreme, intelligent, wise, almighty sovereign of the universe, which I believe to be the great essential principle of all morality, and consequently all civilization. I cannot say that I love the Jews very much neither, nor the French, nor the English, nor the Romans, nor the Greeks. We must love all nations as well as we can, but it is very hard to love most of them.

(John Adams to F.A. Van Der Kemp, 16 February 1809)

* * *

. . . The Hebrew unity of Jehovah, the prohibition of all similitudes, appears to me the greatest wonder of antiquity. How could that nation preserve its creed among the monstrous theologies of all the other nations of the earth? Revelation, you will say, and especial Providence; and I will not contradict you. . . .

Christianity, you will say, was a fresh revelation. I will not deny this. As I understand the Christian religion, it was, and is, a revelation. But how has it happened that millions of fables, tales, legends, have been blended with both Jewish and Christian revelation that have made them the most bloody religion ever existed? How has it happened that all the fine arts, architecture, painting, sculpture, statuary, music, poetry, and oratory, have been prostituted, from the creation of the world, to the sordid and detestable purposes of superstition and fraud?

(Adams to F. A. Van Der Kemp, 27 December 1816)

* * *

. . . I have had occasion to be acquainted with several gentlemen of your nation, and to transact business with some of them, whom I found to be men of as liberal minds, as much honor, probity, generosity and good breeding, as any I have known in any sect of religion or philosophy.

I wish your nation may be admitted to all privileges of citizens in every country of the world. This country has done much. I wish it may do more; and annul every narrow idea in religion, government, and commerce. Let the wits joke; the philosophers sneer! What then? It has pleased the Providence of the 'first cause,' the universal cause, that Abraham should give religion, not only to Hebrews, but to Christians and Mahometans, the greatest part of the modern civilized world.

(Adams to Mordecai M. Noah, 31 July 1818)

THOMAS PAINE   (1737–1809)

English-American writer and political pamphleteer

I believe in one God, and no more; and I hope for happiness beyond this life.

I believe in the equality of man; and I believe that religious duties consist in doing justice, loving mercy, and endeavoring to make our fellow-creatures happy.

But, lest it should be supposed that I believe many other things in addition to these, I shall, in the progress of this work, declare the things I do not believe, and my reasons for not believing them.

I do not believe in the creed professed by the Jewish Church, by the Roman Church, by the Greek Church, by the Turkish Church, by the Protestant Church, nor by any church that I know of. My own mind is my own church.

All national institutions of churches, whether Jewish, Christian, or Turkish, appear to me no other than human inventions, set up to terrify and enslave mankind, and monopolize power and profit.

I do not mean by this declaration to condemn those who believe otherwise; they have the same right to their belief as I have to mine. But it is necessary to the happiness of man that he be mentally faithful to himself. Infidelity does not consist in believing, or in disbelieving; it consists in professing to believe what he does not believe. . . .

Soon after I had published the pamphlet "Common Sense," in America, I saw the exceeding probability that a revolution in the system of government would be followed by a revolution in the system of religion. The adulterous connection of church and state, wherever it has taken place, whether Jewish, Christian or Turkish, had so effectually prohibited by pains and penalties every discussion upon established creeds, and upon first principles of religion, that until the system of government should be changed, those subjects could not be brought fairly and openly before the world; but that whenever this should be done, a revolution in the system of religion would follow. Human inventions and priestcraft would be detected; and man would return to the pure, unmixed and unadulterated belief of one God, and no more. . . .

(*The Age of Reason*, 1794–1796)

* * *

Thomas Paine was an ardent deist who, in *The Age of Reason* and elsewhere, rivals Voltaire in the intensity of his denigration of the Bible and the ancient Hebrews. The Bible, he thought, far from being the "word of God," was an immense fraud, a thesis that he tried to prove by the methods of higher criticism taking shape in his time. The Bible narrative, he held, was a collection of Arabian stories that was not even entertaining. He disputed the Hebrew authorship of the Bible, asserting that it must be taken as anonymous except where Egyptian authorship was indicated. He polemicized against a leading contemporary Jewish Bible scholar, David Levi, whose defense of the Bible he considered full of "ignorance." The Hebrews, Paine asserts, were a "restless, bloody-minded people."

Viewing them from a distorted anthropological and historical perspective, Paine thought the ancient Hebrews guilty of the worst atrocities ever committed by any people. Further, in line with his Enlightenment predecessors he repeated that nowhere is it written that the Jews "were the inventors or the improvers of any one art or science." He thought Moses a drastically overrated figure. "The character of Moses as stated in the Bible," he writes, "is the most horrid that can be imagined. If those accounts be true, he was the wretch that first began and carried on wars on the score or on the pretence of religion; and under the mask, or that infatuation, committed the most unexampled atrocities that are to be found in the history of any nation."

There is no evidence, however, that Paine shared Voltaire's personal hatred of contemporary Jews. He made no exception of the Jews in his advocacy of the rights of man. Harry Hayden Clark has observed that "needless to say, Paine, the champion of tolerance, was not anti-Semitic toward contemporaries."

(Harap, *The Image of the Jew in American Literature*, p. 24)

THOMAS JEFFERSON   *(1743–1826)*

3rd president of the United States, 1801–1809

On looking over the summary of the contents of your book, it does not seem likely to bring into collision of those sectarian differences which you suppose may exist between us. In that branch of religion which regards the moralities of life, and the duties of a social being, which teaches us to love our neighbors as ourselves, and do good to all men, I am sure that you and I do not differ. We probably differ on the dogmas of theology, the foundation of all sectarianism, and on which no two sects dream alike; for if they did they would then be of the same. You say you are a Calvinist. I am not. I am of a sect by myself, as far as I know. I am not a Jew, and therefore do not adopt their theology, which supposes the God of infinite justice to punish the sins of the fathers upon their children, unto the third and fourth generations; and the benevolent and sublime reformer of that religion has told us only that God is good and perfect, but has not defined him. . . .

(Jefferson to Ezra Stiles, president of Yale University, 25 June 1819)

* * *

. . . [Jesus'] object was the reformation of some articles in the religion of the Jews, as taught by Moses. That sect had presented for the object of their worship, a being of terrific character, cruel, vindictive, capricious, and unjust. Jesus, taking for his type the best qualities of the human head and heart, wisdom, justice, goodness, and adding to them power, ascribed all of these, but in infinite perfection, to the Supreme Being, and formed him really worthy of their adoration. Moses had either not believed in a future state of existence, or had not thought it essential to be explicitly taught to his people. Jesus inculcated that doctrine with emphasis and precision. Moses had bound the Jews to many idle ceremonies, mummeries, and observances of no effect towards producing the social utilities which constitute the essence of virtue; Jesus exposed their futility and insignificance. The one instilled into his people the most anti-social spirit toward other nations; the other preached philanthropy and universal charity and benevolence. The office of reformer of the superstitions of a nation, is ever dangerous. Jesus had to walk on the perilous confines of reason and religion; and a step to right or left might place him within the grasp of the priests of the superstition, a blood-thirsty race, as cruel and remorseless as the being whom they represented as the family God of Abraham, of Isaac and of Jacob, and the local God of Israel. They were constantly laying snares, too, to entangle him in the web of the law. He was justifiable, therefore, in avoiding these by evasions, by sophisms, by misconstructions and misapplications of scraps of the prophets, and in defending himself with these their own weapons. . . .

(Jefferson to William Short, 4 August 1820)

* * *

. . . Jews. Their system was Deism; that is, the belief in one only God. But their ideas of him and his attributes were degrading and injurious. . . .

Their Ethics were not only imperfect, but often irreconcilable with the sound dictates of reason and morality, as they respect intercourse with those around us; and repulsive and anti-social, as respecting other nations. They needed reformation, therefore, in an eminent degree. . . .

(Jefferson to Dr. Benjamin Rush, 21 April 1803)

* * *

Jefferson to Joseph Marx, 1820:

[I have] ever felt regret at seeing a sect, the parent and basis of all those of Christendom, singled out by all of them for a persecution and oppression which proved they have profited nothing from the benevolent doctrines of him whom they profess to make the model of their principle and practice.

I have thought it a cruel addition to the wrongs which that injured sect [the Jews] have suffered, that their youth should be excluded from the instructions in science afforded to all others in our public seminaries, by imposing upon them a course of Theological Reading which their consciences do not permit them to pursue; and in the University lately established here, we have set the example of ceasing to violate the rights of conscience by any injunction on the different sects respecting their religion.

(S. K. Padover, *Democracy by Thomas Jefferson*, p. 179)

Sir:—I thank you for the discourse on the consecration of the Syna-gogue in your city, with which you have been pleased to favor me. I have read it with pleasure and instruction, having learnt from it some valuable facts in Jewish history which I did not know before. Your sect by its sufferings has furnished a remarkable proof of the universal spirit of religious intolerance inherent in every sect, disclaimed by all while feeble, and practiced by all when in power. Our laws have applied the only antidote to this vice, protecting our religious, as they do our civil rights, by putting all on an equal footing. But more remains to be done, for although we are free by the law, we are not so in practice; public opinion erects itself into an Inquisition, and exercises its office with as much fanaticism as fans the flames of an *Auto-da-fé*.

The prejudice still scowling on your section of our religion, although the elder one, cannot be unfelt by yourselves; it is to be hoped that individual dispositions will at length mould themselves to the model of the law, and consider the moral basis, on which all our religions rest, as the rallying point which unites them in a common interest; while the peculiar dogmas branching from it are the exclusive concern of the respective sects embracing them, and no rightful subject of notice to any other; public opinion needs reformation on that point. . . . Nothing, I think, would be so likely to effect this, as to your sect particularly, as the more careful attention to education, which you recommend, and which, placing its members on the equal and commanding benches of science, will exhibit them as equal objects of respect and favor. I salute you with great respect and esteem.

(Jefferson to M. M. Noah, 28 May 1818)

DANIEL WEBSTER *(1782–1852)*

U.S. politician and lawyer; Secretary of State

In a letter of 9 November 1849:

I feel, and have ever felt respect and sympathy for all that remains of that extraordinary people who preserved through the darkness and idolatry of so many centuries, the knowledge of one supreme spiritual

Being. . . . The Hebrew Scriptures I regard as the fountain from which we draw all we know of the world around us, and of our own character and destiny as intelligent, moral, and responsible beings.

(*Private Correspondence*, vol. II, p. 347)

6

The Enlightenment

SIR THOMAS BROWNE *(1605–1682)*

British scientific and religious writer

. . . I dare without usurpation assume the honourable Stile of a Christian. . . . I find my self obliged by the Principles of Grace, and the Law of mine own Reason, to embrace no other Name but this. Neither doth herein my zeal so far make me forget the general Charity I owe unto Humanity, as rather to hate than pity Turks, Infidels, and (what is worse,) Jews; rather contenting my self to enjoy that happy Stile, than maligning those who refuse so glorious a Title.

(Religio Medici, Part I, Section I, 1635)

* * *

I cannot but wonder with what exception the Samaritans could confine their belief to the Pentateuch, or five Books of Moses. I am ashamed at the Rabbinical Interpretation of the Jews upon the Old Testament, as much as their defection from the New: and truly it is beyond wonder, how that contemptible and degenerate issue of Jacob, once so devoted to Ethnick Superstition, and so easily seduced to the Idolatry of their Neighbours, should now in such an obstinate and peremptory belief adhere unto their own Doctrine, expect impossibilities, and, in the face and eye of the Church, persist without the least hope of Conversion. This is a vice in *them*, that were a vertue in *us*; for obstinacy in a bad Cause is but constancy in a good. . . .

. . . There are, I confess . . . men but of negative Impieties, and such as deny CHRIST, but because they never heard of Him. But the Religion of the Jew is expressly against the Christian, and the Mahometan against both. For the Turk, in the bulk he now stands, he is beyond all hope of conversion; if he fall asunder, there may be conceived hopes, but not without strong improbabilities. The Jew is obstinate in all fortunes; the persecution of fifteen hundred years hath but confirmed them in their Errour: they have already endured whatsoever may be inflicted, and have suffered in a bad cause, even to the condemnation of their enemies. Persecution is a bad and indirect way to plant Religion: it hath been the unhappy method of angry Devotions, not only to confirm honest Religion, but wicked Heresies, and extravagant Opinions. . . .

(*Religio Medici*, Part I, Section XXV)

* * *

. . . The Jews, that can believe the supernatural Solstice of the Sun in the days of Joshua, have yet the impudence to deny the Eclipse, which every Pagan confessed, at His Death: but for this, it is evident beyond all contradiction, the Devil himself confessed it. . . .

(*Religio Medici*, Part I, Section XXIX)

BLAISE PASCAL   *(1623–1662)*

French theologian and mathematician

I first see that they [the Jews] are a people wholly composed of brethren, and whereas all others are formed by the assemblage of an infinity of families, this, though so wonderfully fruitful, has all sprung from one man alone, and, being thus all one flesh, and members one of another, they constitute a powerful state of one family. This is unique.

This family, or people, is the most ancient within human knowledge, a fact which seems to me to inspire a peculiar veneration for it, especially in view of our present inquiry; since if God has from all time revealed Himself to men, it is to these we must turn for knowledge of the tradition.

This people is not eminent solely by their antiquity, but is also singular by their duration. . . . For whereas the nations of Greece and of Italy, and others who came long after, have long since perished, these ever remain, and in spite of the endeavors of many powerful kings who have a hundred times tried to destroy them, . . . and extending from the earliest times to the latest, their history comprehends in its duration all our histories. . . .

The law by which this people is governed is at once the most ancient law in the world, the most perfect, and the only one which has been always observed without a break in a state.

(Pascal, "Advantages of the Jewish People" in *Thoughts*, 1669)

JOHN LOCKE   *(1632–1704)*

British philosopher

No private person has any right, in any manner, to prejudice another person in his civil enjoyments because he is of another church or religion. . . . If any man err from the right way, it is his own misfortune, no injury to thee: nor therefore art thou to punish him in the things of this life because thou supposest he will be miserable in that which is to come. . . .

The magistrate ought not to forbid the preaching or professing of any speculative opinions in any church; because they have no manner of relation to the civil rights of the subjects. If a Roman Catholic believe that to be really the body of Christ which another man calls bread, he does no injury thereby to his neighbor. If a Jew do not believe the New Testament to be the Word of God, he does not thereby alter any thing in men's civil rights. If a Heathen doubt of both Testaments, he is not therefore to be punished as a pernicious citizen. The power of the magistrate, and the estates of the people may be equally secure, whether any man believe these things or no. . . .

. . . neither pagan, nor Mahumetan, nor Jew ought to be excluded from the civil rights of the commonwealth because of his religion. The Gospel commands no such thing. The Church, *which judges not those that are without*, wants it not. And the commonwealth, which embraces indifferently all men that are honest, peaceable and industrious, requires it not. Shall we suffer a pagan to deal and trade with us, and shall we not suffer him to pray unto, and worship God? If we allow the Jews to have private houses and dwellings amongst us, why should we not allow them to have synagogues? Is their doctrine more false, their worship more abominable, or is the civil peace more endangered, by their meeting in public than in their private houses? But if these things may be granted to Jews and pagans, surely the

condition of any Christian ought not to be worse than theirs in a
Christian commonwealth. . . .

(Locke, *A Letter Concerning Toleration*, 1689)

GOTTFRIED WILHELM VON LEIBNITZ   (1646–1716)

German philosopher and mathematician

Among all the ancient peoples the Hebrews are the only ones known
to have had public principles regarding their religion. Abraham and
Moses established the belief in the one God, the Source of all good,
the Author of all things. The Hebrews speak of it in a manner worthy
of the Supreme Being, and it is astonishing to see the inhabitants of an
insignificant territory more enlightened than the rest of the human
race. The sages of other nations have perhaps said as much occasionally, but they did not have the good fortune of being followed and of
having their teachings assume the force of law.
(From the Preface to *Essais de Théodicée sur la bonté de Dieu, la liberté
de l'homme et l'origine du mal*, 1710)

GIOVANNI BATTISTA VICO   (1668–1744)

Italian jurist, philosopher, and Catholic historian

The religion preached by Moses taught the concept of a true God, not
of the sky as the pagans thought, not of a world structure as the
philosophers envisaged, but of a God who was above the heavens and
the world. Beyond Israel such a concept was reached only by the
divine Plato, when the Greeks had attained the highest rung of their
culture. . . .

In his code, Moses proscribed not only unjust acts but also unjust
intentions. He assumed a standpoint which the heathens reached
much later, with the more advanced culture in Greek philosophy. . . .

The descendants of Abraham represent humanity in its purest
form, without brutish giants, just as their religion is pure of superstitious rites. All the religious institutions of the Hebrew people were

designed to maintain and promote the knowledge of God and to shield man against sinking into pagan vulgarity. While the pagan priests concealed carefully their religious mysteries, the prescriptions of the Jewish religion were put down in writing, and made accessible to all who could read. The Hebrews had no arcana. . . .

The pagan religions prescribed certain purification ceremonies and ritual ablutions, but these pertained only to the body. The purity of the soul, the contrition of the heart crushed by the consciousness of its moral impurity, was demanded only by the religion of the Hebrews. . . .

JOSEPH ADDISON   (1672–1719)

English essayist

As I am one, who, by my profession, am obliged to look into all kinds of men, there are none whom I consider with so much pleasure, as those who have anything new or extraordinary in their characters, or ways of living. For this reason I have often amused myself with speculations on the race of people called Jews, many of whom I have met with in most of the considerable towns which I have passed through in the course of my travels. They are, indeed, so disseminated through all the trading parts of the world, that they are become the instruments by which the most distant nations converse with one another, and by which mankind are knit together in a general correspondence: they are like the pegs and nails in a great building, which, though they are but little valued in themselves, are absolutely necessary to keep the whole frame together.

. . . The Jews are looked upon by many to be as numerous at present, as they were formerly in the land of Canaan. This is wonderful, considering the dreadful slaughter made of them under some of the Roman emperors, which historians describe by the death of many hundred thousands in a war; and the innumerable massacres and persecutions they have undergone in Turkey, as well as in all Christian nations of the world. The Rabbis, to express the great havoc which has sometimes been made of them, tell us, after their usual manner of hyperbole, that there were such torrents of holy blood shed as carried rocks of an hundred yards in circumference above three miles into the sea.

Their dispersion is the second remarkable particular in this people. They swarm over all the East, and are settled in the remotest parts of China; they are spread through most of the nations of Europe and Africa, and many families of them are established in Europe and Africa, and many families of them are established in the West Indies. . . .

Their firm adherence to their religion is no less remarkable than their numbers and dispersion, especially considering it as persecuted or contemned over the face of the whole earth. This is likewise the more remarkable, if we consider the frequent apostasies of this people when they lived under their kings, in the land of Promise, and within sight of their temple.

If in the next place we examine, what may be the natural reasons for these three particulars which we find in the Jews, and which are not to be found in any other religion or people, I can, in the first place, attribute their numbers to nothing but their constant employment, their abstinence, their exemption from wars, and above all, their frequent marriages; for they look on celibacy as an accursed state, and generally are married before twenty, as hoping the Messiah may descend from them.

The dispersion of the Jews into all the nations of the earth is the second remarkable particular of that people, though not so hard to be accounted for. They were always in rebellions and tumults while they had the temple and holy city in view, for which reason they have often been driven out of their old habitations in the land of Promise. They have as often been banished out of most other places where they have settled, which must very much disperse and scatter a people, and oblige them to seek a livelihood where they can find it. Besides, the whole people is now a race of such merchants as are wanderers by profession, and at the same time are in most, if not all, places incapable of either lands or offices, that might engage them to make any part of the world their home.

This dispersion would probably have lost their religion, had it not been secured by the strength of its constitution: for they are to live all in a body, and generally within the same enclosure; to marry among themselves, and to eat no meats that are not killed or prepared their own way. This shuts them out from all table conversation, and the most agreeable intercourses of life; and, by consequence, excludes them from the most probable means of conversion.

If, in the last place, we consider what providential reason may be assigned for these three particulars, we shall find that their numbers, dispersion, and adherence to their religion, have furnished every age and every nation of the world with the strongest arguments for the Christian faith, not only as these very particulars are foretold of them, but as they themselves are the depositaries of these and all the other prophecies, which tend to their own confusion. Their number furnishes us with a sufficient cloud of witnesses that attest the truth of the old Bible. Their dispersion spreads these witnesses through all parts of the world. The adherence to their religion makes their testimony unquestionable. Had the whole body of the Jews been converted to Christianity, we should certainly have thought all the prophecies of the Old Testament, that relate to the coming and history of our blessed Saviour, forged by Christians, and have looked upon them, with the prophecies of the Sibyls, as made many years after the events they pretended to foretell.

(Addison, "The Jews," in *The Spectator*, 27 September 1712, quoted in Thomas Arnold, ed., *Addison: Selections from Addison's Papers Contributed to "The Spectator"*)

FREDERICK WILLIAM   (1620–1688)

Elector of Brandenburg

On "The Readmission of Jews into Brandenburg"
21 May 1671:

. . . for special reasons and upon the most humble request of Hirshel Lazarus, Benedict Veit, and Abraham Ries, Jews, and moved particularly by the desire to further business in general, we have been influenced to take and receive graciously into our land of Electoral and March Brandenburg, under our special protection, a few Jewish families, namely, fifty of them, that have left other places. We do this on the following conditions, by virtue of the power vested in us.

1. We admit into our above mentioned land . . . the above mentioned fifty families. . . .

2. . . . We allow them explicitly to have public shops and booths, to sell and to retail cloth and similar wares by the piece or by the yard, and to keep large and small weights which must not deviate in the least from the town-scales or the large scales used by the city authorities. The Jews must not practice any deception with their weights in buying or selling. We permit them to trade in new and old clothes, to slaughter meat in their own homes, and to sell that part of the slaughtered animal which they do not require for their own use or which their laws do not allow them to eat. And finally they are allowed to seek their livelihood everywhere—in places where they live, and in other spots too. They are specifically permitted to earn their livelihood by dealing in wool and groceries, just like the other inhabitants of these territories, and they are also allowed to sell their goods at the fairs and markets. . . .

6. Although they are not permitted to have a synagogue they are allowed to arrange an assembly in their houses where they may offer their prayers and perform their ceremonies, without, however, offering any offense to the Christians. They must particularly refrain from all abuse and blasphemy, under the threat of heavy penalties. They are also herewith allowed to have a ritual slaughterer as well as a schoolteacher for the instruction of their children. . . .

7. Moreover they should everywhere evidence and show themselves to be decent, peaceful, and considerate, and must take particular care that they do not carry any good coins out of the country and bring worthless ones back in. . . .

9. If the now oft-mentioned Jewry will act in accordance with that above which has been laid upon them and has been promised by them, that we most graciously promise them our most benign protection and defense in these our territories from this time forth for twenty years, and, after this termination, the continuation thereof by us and our heirs, as we see fit. Failing this, we reserve for ourselves the right, after proper consideration, to recall our protection even before the twenty years have passed.

10. Should the tumult of war—God forbid—rise in our land during these twenty years, the oft-mentioned Jewry, like our other subjects, shall not be forbidden to take refuge in our fortresses with their families, but shall be admitted and tolerated there.

Accordingly we command all our subjects and followers without regard to station and dignity, that from this day forth, for the whole twenty years, they allow the oft-mentioned Jewry to pass about freely and safely everywhere in our entire Electorate and the lands mentioned with it. . . . No one shall lay violent hands upon them. Furthermore, every magistrate and official of the courts shall aid them, at their request, in that to which they are entitled; shall accord them, like others, the right of civic hospitality; and shall not treat them in any other way, if they would avoid our high disfavor – to say nothing of a penalty of fifty golden gulden and even more, according to circumstances.

(Marcus, *The Jew in the Medieval World*, pp. 75–79)

PHILIP DORMER STANHOPE   (1694–1773)

4th Earl of Chesterfield; British statesman, diplomat, and wit

Stanhope to his son, 26 November 1753:

The Ministers here, intimidated on the absurd and groundless clamors of the mob, have, very weakly in my mind, repealed, this session, the bill which they had passed in the last for rendering Jews capable of being naturalized by subsequent acts of Parliament. The clamorers triumph and will doubtless make further demands; which, if not granted, this piece of complaisance will soon be forgotten. . . .

Wise and honest governors will never, if they can help it, give the people just cause to complain; but then, on the other hand, they will firmly withstand groundless clamor. Besides that this noise against the Jew Bill proceeds from that narrow mob-spirit of *intoleration* in religious, and inhospitality in civil matters; both which all wise governments should oppose.

(*Letters of the Earl of Chesterfield*, vol. II, p. 591)

VOLTAIRE   (1694–1778)

French philosopher and writer

Let the fanatics, the superstitious, the persecutors, become men. . . . What was the Jews' crime? None other than that of being born.

(Voltaire, *Sermon du Rabbin Akib*, quoted in Hertzberg, *The French Enlightenment and the Jews*, p. 280)

[Let Christians] stop persecuting and exterminating the Jews, who as men are their brothers and who as Jews are their fathers. Let each man serve God in the religion in which he is born. . . . Let each man serve his kind and his country, without ever using obedience to God as the excuse for disobeying the law.

(Voltaire, *Sermon du Rabbin Akib*, in *The French Enlightenment and the Jews*, p. 281)

* * *

Letter in English to Nicolas Thieriot, 26 October 1726, telling about his unfortunate dealing with a Jewish banker:

At my coming to London I found the damned Jew was broke. I was without a penny, sick to death of a violent ague, a stranger, alone, helpless, in the midst of a city wherein I was known to nobody.

(*Correspondence*, II, p. 36)

* * *

To Jean Baptiste Nicolas de Lisle de Sales:

I know that there are some Jews in the English colonies. These marranos go wherever there is money to be made. . . . But that these circumcized Jews who sell old clothes to the savages claim that they are of the tribe of Naphtali or Issachar is not of the slightest importance. They are, nonetheless, the greatest scoundrels who have ever sullied the face of the globe.

(*Correspondence*, LXXXVI, p. 166)

* * *

They are, all of them, born with raging fanaticism in their hearts, just as the Bretons and the Germans are born with blond hair. I would not be in the least bit surprised if these people would not some day become deadly to the human race.

(*Lettres de Memmius à Ciceron*, 1771, in *The French Enlightenment*, p. 300)

(Hertzberg adds: "Voltaire had thus, being an ex-Christian, abandoned entirely the religious attack on the Jews as Christ-killers or Christ-rejectors. He proposed a new principle on which to base his hatred of them, their innate character.")

* * *

[To the Jews]: You seem to me to be the maddest of the lot. The Kaffirs, the Hottentots, and the Negroes of Guinea are much more reasonable and more honest people than your ancestors, the Jews. You have surpassed all nations in impertinent fables, in bad conduct, and in barbarism. You deserve to be punished, for this is your destiny.
(*Il faut prendre une partie*, 1772, in *The French Enlightenment*, p. 301)

* * *

. . . one must state that this people had no idea of that which we call taste, delicacy, or proportion.
(Hertzberg, *Oeuvres Completes*)

* * *

If we must talk of Jewry, we must state that they were a wretched Arabic tribe without art or science, hidden in a small hilly, and ignorant land. . . .
(*Un Chrétien contre sit Juifs*, in *The French Enlightenment*, pp. 303–304)

* * *

If it were permitted to reason consistently in religious matters, it is clear that we all ought to become Jews, because Jesus Christ our Saviour was born a Jew, lived a Jew, died a Jew, and He said expressly that He was fulfilling the Jewish religion.
(*Philosophical Dictionary*, 1764)

* * *

. . . when Voltaire went on to make the first of his pathetic efforts to become a diplomat, we can only shake our heads sadly; and even more sadly when we find that the form taken by his effort was a report on an obscure affair of espionage centering round one Solomon

Levy, a report containing such phrases: "He passed over to the enemy with the facility the Jews have of being received and dismissed everywhere." This was the first manifestation of Voltaire's anti-se-mitism (if so anachronistic a term may be used), or rather of his willingness to use any tool that came to hand, for in fact he recognised intellectually the vulgar error of anti-semitic prejudices. Voltaire's language was the language of his time, and we must not expect even the greatest of men always to rise above their environment. Indeed, his language became stronger and stronger as his campaign against the *Bible* and Christianity itself became more violent. And the Jews, as the chosen people of the former and the progenitors of the latter, were an all too tempting target. However, when a Jew wrote courteously to complain of a particularly severe passage, Voltaire replied: "The lines of which you complain are violent and unjust. Your letter alone convinces me that there are highly cultivated and very respectable men among you. I shall take care to insert a cancel in the new edition. When one has done a wrong one should put it right, and I was wrong to attribute to a whole nation the vices of some individuals."

Voltaire's fundamental attitude is expressed in an anecdote recorded in his *Notebooks*. When an abbé tried to convert a Jewish lady, she asked, "Was your god born a Jew?" – "Yes." – "Did he live a Jew?" – "Yes." – "Did he die a Jew?" – "Yes." – "Well then, be a Jew."

(Besterman, *Voltaire*, p. 86)

THOMAS NEWTON   *(1704–1782)*

British clergyman; Bishop of Bristol

The preservation of the Jews is really one of the most signal and illustrious acts of Divine Providence. . . .

The Jews can go up higher than any other nation, they can even deduce their pedigree from the beginning of the world. They may not know from what particular tribe or family they are descended, but they know certainly that they all sprung from the stock of Abraham. And yet the contempt with which they have been treated and the hardships which they have undergone in almost all countries, should, one would think, have made them desirous to forget or renounce that original; but they profess it, they glory in it: and after so many wars, massacres, and persecutions, they still subsist, they still are very numerous: and what but a supernatural power could have preserved them in such a manner as none other nation upon earth hath been preserved?

Nor is the providence of God less remarkable in the destruction of their enemies, than in their preservation. . . . We see that the great empires, which in their turns subdued and oppressed the people of God, are all come to ruin; because though they executed the purposes of God, yet that was more than they understood; all that they intended was to satiate their own pride and ambition, their own cruelty and revenge. And if such hath been the fatal end of the enemies and oppressors of the Jews, let it serve as a warning to all those, who at any time or upon any occasion are for raising a clamor and persecution against them.

(Newton, *Dissertations on the Prophecies*, vol. I, pp. 216ff., 241f)

* * *

All over the world, the Jews are in all respects treated as if they were of a different species.

DAVID HUME   *(1711-1776)*

Scottish historian and philosopher

In 1250, Henry renewed his oppressions, and the same Aaron was condemned to pay him thirty thousand marks upon an accusation of forgery. The high penalty imposed upon him and which, it seems, he was thought able to pay, is rather a presumption of his innocence than of his guilt. In 1255, the king demanded eight thousand marks from the Jews and threatened to hang them if they refused compliance. . . . He then delivered over the Jews to the Earl of Cornwall, that those whom the one brother had flayed, the other might disembowel. . . .

To give a better pretence for extortions, the improbable and absurd accusation, which has been at different times advanced against that nation, was revived in England that they had crucified a child in derision of the sufferings of Christ. Eighteen of them were hanged at once for this crime—though it is nowise credible that even the antipathy borne them by the Christians, and the oppressions under which they labored, would ever have pushed them to be guilty of that dangerous enormity. . . .

Though these acts of violence against the Jews proceeded much from bigotry, they were still more derived from avidity and rapine. So far from desiring in that age to convert them, it was enacted by law in France that if any Jew embraced Christianity, he forfeited all his goods, without exception, to the king or his superior lord. These plunderers were careful lest the profits accruing from their dominion over that unhappy race should be diminished by their conversion.

(*History of England*, 1761, vol. 1, ch. 12)

FREDERICK THE GREAT   *(1712–1786)*

Frederick II, King of Prussia, 1740–1786

The *Charter* for Prussian Jews:[1]

. . . We have noticed in our kingdom of Prussia . . . and particularly also in this capital various faults and abuses among the licensed and tolerated Jews, and have particularly observed that the rampant increase of these abuses has caused enormous damage and hardship, not only to the public, particularly to the Christian inhabitants and merchants, but also to Jewry itself. For this reason and because of the surreptitious entry of unlicensed Jews: foreigners and those who are all but without any country, many complaints and difficulties have arisen. . . .

For this reason we have found it necessary to make such provision that this, our most gracious purpose, may be attained, so that a proportion may be maintained between Christian and Jewish business opportunities and trades, and especially that neither be injured through a prohibited expansion of Jewish business activity. For this purpose we have again made an exact investigation of the condition, in our kingdom and in the other above mentioned imperial lands, of

---

[1]This *Charter* for Prussian Jews was drafted in 1750 and promulgated six years later.

all Jewry, of their families, their means of subsistence, and their business activity. We have considered certain feasible proposals which have as their basis justice, fairness, and common safety, and have also deemed them useful for the attainment of our ultimate object and the attendant welfare of all inhabitants of the country who live by means of business activity. As a result of these proposals we wish to prepare and to put into effect a special regulation and constitution for all Jewry. There we establish, regulate, and order, herewith and by virtue of this, that. . . .

II. No Other Jews Are to Be Tolerated except Those Named in the Lists That Are Attached to the End of These Regulations. . . .

V. . . . Foreign Jews are not allowed to settle in our lands at all. However, if one should really have a fortune of ten thousand Reichsthalers and bring the same into the country and furnish authentic evidence of the fact, then we are to be asked about this and concerning the fees he is to pay. . . .

XI. The Jews Must Not Pursue Any Manual Trade. . . .

XII. Jews Are Forbidden the Smelting of Gold and Silver. . . .

XIII. The Slaughter of Meat for Their Own Consumption Is Permitted the Jews If They Kill the Animals in Christian Slaughterhouses. . . .

XIV. The Jews in Berlin Are Not Allowed to Have Dealings in Raw Wool Or Woolen Yarns Or to Manufacture Woolen Goods. . . .

XV. Jews Are Further Allowed to Sell One Another Beer and Spirits. . . . With the Exception of Kosher Wines They Are Not Allowed to Do Any Business in Wines. . . .

XVII. Under Special Conditions They May Sell Choice Groceries and Spices to Other Jews. . . . The Jews Are Forbidden to Trade in Raw Tobacco, to Manufacture Tobacco, And to Carry a Line of [Staple] Groceries. . . .

XIX. The Jews . . . May Not Peddle in Cities except at the Time of the Fairs. . . .

XX. No Foreign Jews and Jewish Boys Shall Do Business in Berlin. Outside of Exceptional Cases Herein Specified, Those Who Remain over Twenty-Four Hours in Berlin Must Pay One Specie-Ducat to the Potsdam Orphan Home. . . .

XXII. What Is to Be Done with Jewish Beggars

It has already been decreed many times that Jewish beggars are nowhere to be allowed to cross our borders. We not only repeat this, but order that in the event any such Jewish beggars nevertheless reach our capital surreptitiously, they shall be brought at once to the Poor-Jews Home at the Prenzlau Gate. There they are to be given alms and on the following day evicted through the gate without being allowed to enter the city. . . .

XXVIII. In the Future the Jews Shall Not Buy Houses of Their Own. The Forty Houses Owned by Jews in Berlin Shall Not Be Increased in Number. . . . In Other Cities Where There Are Five Jewish Families Only One of Them May Buy a House. . . .

XXX. The Jews Are to Be Protected in Their Religion, Ceremonies, and Synagogue, and That Which Is Related to It.

We have everywhere most graciously and firmly protected all these Jewish families in their religion and in their Jewish customs and ceremonies which they have practiced till now. We also herewith confirm anew the [right to possess the] synagogues which they have built in Berlin, Konigsberg, Halberstadt, Halle, and Frankfort on the Oder, as well as the schools in the other provinces, the cemeteries, and the small houses belonging to the synagogues and the cemeteries. This, however, on the condition that they must always refrain, under penalty of death and complete expulsion of the entire Jewry from Berlin and our other cities, from such abuses as the Jewish prayer which begins *Alenu* etc., as has already been emphatically decreed in detail in the edicts of 1703 and 1716. They must refrain likewise from other prayers of the same type, and also from all improper excesses in their festivals, particularly during the so-called Haman or Purim festival. . . .

(Marcus, *The Jew in the Medieval World*, pp. 85–97)

JEAN-JACQUES ROUSSEAU   *(1712–1788)*

French philosopher, social reformer, and author

Do you know many Christians who have taken the trouble to inquire what the Jews allege against them? If any one knows anything at all about it, it is from the writings of Christians. What a way of ascertaining the arguments of our adversaries! But what is to be done? If any one dared to publish in our day books which were openly in favor of the Jewish religion, we should punish the author, publisher and bookseller. This regulation is a sure and certain plan for always being in the right. It is easy to refute those who dare not venture to speak.

Those among us who have the opportunity of talking with Jews are little better off. These unhappy people feel that they are in our power; the tyranny they have suffered makes them timid; they know that Christian charity thinks nothing of injustice and cruelty; will they dare to run the risk of an outcry against blasphemy? Our greed inspires us with zeal, and they are so rich that they must be in the wrong. The more learned, the more enlightened they are, the more cautious. You may convert some poor wretch whom you have paid to slander his religion; you get some wretched old-clothes man to speak, and he says what you want; you may triumph over their ignorance and cowardice, while all the time their men of learning are laughing at your stupidity.

But do you think you would get off so easily in any place where they knew they were safe? At the Sorbonne it is plain that the Messianic prophecies refer to Jesus Christ. Among the rabbis of Amsterdam it is just as clear that they have nothing to do with him. I do not think I have ever heard the arguments of the Jews as to why they should not have a free state, schools and universities, where they can speak and argue without danger. Then alone can we know what they have to say.

At Constantinople the Turks state their arguments, but we dare not give ours; then it is our turn to cringe. Can we blame the Turks if they require us to show the same respect for Mahomet, in whom we do not believe, as we demand from the Jews with regard to Jesus Christ in whom they do not believe? Are we right? On what grounds of justice can we answer this question?

(Rousseau, *Emile*, 1762)

DENIS DIDEROT   *(1713–1784)*

French philosopher, writer, and encyclopedist

A third horde, consisting of more than 200,000 people, half of whom were women and the rest priests, peasants, and school children, followed in the footsteps of Peter and Dodescal; but the fury of this last horde fell particularly on the Jews. They massacred them whenever they could find them: these brutish impious people believed that they could properly avenge the death of Jesus by slitting the throats of the little children of those who had crucified him.[2]

(*Encyclopedie*, vol. xiv, s.v. "Crusades")

* * *

[Among the Jews one will not find] any rightness of thought, any exactness in reasoning or precision of style, in a word, any of that which ought to characterize a healthy philosophy. One finds among them, on the contrary, only a confused mélange of the principles of reason and revelation, a pretentious and often impenetrable obscurity, principles that lead to fanaticism, blind respect for the authority of the rabbis and for antiquity, in a word, all the faults that mark an ignorant and superstitious people.

(*Oeuvres Complets*, XV, p. 378)

* * *

This people should be kept separate from others.

(*Oeuvres Complets*, II, p. 97)

GOTTHOLD EPHRAIM LESSING   *(1720–1781)*

German critic, dramatist, and leader of the Enlightenment

In response to an attack on Judaism by Jerome Cardan, a physician from Italy (1501–1576), who had claimed that God permitted the religion to perish:

Has the Jewish religion really perished? Is not its present circumstance rather a prolonged Babylonian captivity? The arm which delivered His people then is still unimpaired. Perhaps the God of Abraham heaped such difficulty on the return path of the posterity of Abraham to their inheritance, and rendered it so insurmountable, in

---

[2]In the *French Revolution and the Jews*, A. Hertzberg wrote: "He managed to attack the Inquisition and the church all his life without mentioning the persecution of the Jews at its hands. There was only one such passage in defense of the Jews, and not a very warm one, in all his writings," on the Crusades.

order to manifest His might and wisdom in all the more glorious splendor to the dismay of their oppressors.

"Do not be mistaken, Cardan," a pious Jew could undoubtedly retort. "Our God has so far from forsaken us that He has rather remained our protector even amidst His judgments. If He had not watched over us, would we not long since have been swallowed up by our enemies, would they not long since have exterminated us from the face of the earth and wiped our name off from the book of the living? Scattered to all corners of the globe, oppressed, maligned and persecuted everywhere, we are nevertheless the same today as we were a thousand and more years ago. Recognize His hand, or else name us another people that have met sorrow with such invincible powers, and amidst all their afflictions have worshipped God, from whom their afflictions have come, have worshipped even after the manner of their forebears upon whom He showered His blessings.

"As God said to Satan, when He was about to test Job, 'Behold, he is in thy hand; only spare his life,' so He spoke to our enemies, 'My people is in your hand, only spare his life.' Here are the boundaries of your fury, here is the shore on which the waves of your pride shall break! Thus far and no farther! Proceed to afflict us, oppress us without end; you shall not achieve the goal which you seek. He spoke the word 'Spare!' and His word is true. In vain will Bildads and Zophars arise out of our own race to doubt our good cause. In vain will our own commiserating wives call out to us: 'Do you still hold fast your integrity? Blaspheme God and die!' We shall not blaspheme Him, for He will most assuredly descend at last in a whirlwind, and turn our captivity, and give us double of what we had."

I shall not let my Jew continue. Let this suffice as a proof of how easy it is to refute the fallacies of Cardan.

(Lessing, *Rettung des Hieronimus Cardanus*, 1754)

IMMANUEL KANT   *(1724–1804)*

German philosopher

Kant to Moses Mendelssohn, 16 August 1783:

You have succeeded [in his book, *Jerusalem*] in combining your religion with such a degree of freedom of conscience as was never imagined possible and of which no other faith can boast. You have, at the same time, so thoroughly and clearly demonstrated the necessity of unlimited liberty of conscience of every religion, that ultimately our Church will also be led to reflect how to remove from its midst everything that disturbs and oppresses conscience which will finally unite all men in their view of the essential points of religion.

(F. Ohmann, *Kants Briefe*, p. 112)

JOSEPH PRIESTLEY   *(1733–1804)*

British theologian, philosopher, and chemist

No heathen ever conceived an idea of so great an object as that of the institutions of Moses, which appears to be nothing less than the instruction of all mankind in the great doctrine of the unity and universal government of God as the Maker of the world and the common parent of all the human race, in opposition to the polytheism and idolatry which then prevailed, which, besides being grossly absurd in its principles and leading to endless superstitions, threatened the world with a deluge of vice and misery.

For this purpose the Hebrew nation was placed in the most conspicuous situation among all the civilized nations of the world, which were universally addicted to idolatry of the grossest kind. . . . As all mankind imagined that their outward prosperity depended upon the observance of their respective religions, that of the Hebrew nation was made to do so in the most conspicuous manner, as a visible lesson to all the world. They were to prosper beyond all other nations while they adhered to their religion; and to suffer in a manner equally exemplary and conspicuous in consequence of their departure from it. Of this all mankind might easily judge. These great ideas occur in the sacred books of the Hebrews and nowhere else. They are all distinctly advanced by Moses and more fully unfolded in the writings of the later prophets. But certainly nothing so great and sublime could have been suggested to Moses from anything that he saw in Egypt, or could have heard of in other countries.

(Priestley, *A Comparison of the Institutions of Moses With Those of the Hindoos and Other Ancient Nations*, 1799)

JOHANN WOLFGANG VON GOETHE   *(1749–1832)*

German dramatist, novelist, and poet

Energy is the basis of everything. Every Jew, no matter how insignificant, is engaged in some decisive and immediate pursuit of a goal. . . .

(*Maximen und Reflexionen*)

* * *

It is the most perpetual people of the earth; it was, it is, it will be to glorify the name of Jehovah through all the times.

(*Wilhelm Meister's Travels*, ch. 10)

* * *

I was opposed to the new law regarding Jews, which permitted intermarriage between members of both faiths. I believe that the superintendent ought to resign his office rather than tolerate the marriage ceremony of a Jewess in the name of the Holy Trinity. Any expression of contempt for the religious sentiment in a people leads to disaster. But I do not hate the Jews. The aversion which I felt against them in my early youth was more of a timidity before the mysterious, the ungraceful. The scorn which used to stir within me was more a reflection of the Christian men and women around me. Only later, when I became acquainted with many talented and refined men of this race, respect was added to the admiration which I entertained for this people that created the Bible, and for the poet who sang the Song of Songs.

It is despicable to pillory a nation which possesses such remarkable talents in art and science. . . .

(*Gespräche*, 1909)

JOSEPH MARIE COMTE DE MAISTRE   *(1753–1821)*

French writer and statesman

These Jews, represented as a fierce and intolerant people, were none the less, in certain respects, the most tolerant of all, so much so that it is sometimes difficult to understand how the exclusive professors of the truth could appear so obliging to foreign relations. The wholly liberal manner in which Elisha settled the case of conscience proposed by a captain of the Syrian guard is well known. If the prophet had been a Jesuit, Pascal would no doubt have placed him, though wrongly, in .his *Provincial Letters*, for his decision. Philo, if I am not mistaken, observes somewhere that the High Priest of the Jews, alone in the whole world, prayed for foreign nations and powers. Indeed, I believe that there is not another example of it in antiquity. The Temple of Jerusalem had a portico designed for strangers who came to pray there freely. A multitude of these Gentiles had faith in this God (whoever He might be) worshipped on Mt. Zion. Nobody disturbed them or asked them for an account of their national beliefs. We see them again in the Gospel, coming on the festival of Passover to worship in Jerusalem, without the least mark of disapproval or surprise on the part of the sacred historian.

(*Les Soirées de Saint-Petersbourg, ou, Entretiens sur le Gouvernement Temporal de la Providence*, 1806)

CHARLES LAMB   *(1755–1834)*

British essayist

I should not care to be in habits of familiar intercourse with any of that [Jewish] nation. . . . Old prejudices cling about me. I cannot shake off the story of Hugh of Lincoln. . . . A Hebrew is nowhere congenial to me. He is least distasteful on the 'Change,[3] — for the mercantile spirit levels all distinctions, for all are beauties in the dark. . . .

("Jews, Quakers, Scotchmen and other Imperfect Sympathies," in *London Magazine*, IV, p. 152)

FRIEDRICH VON SCHILLER   *(1759–1805)*

German poet and dramatist

The establishment of the Jewish state by Moses is one of the most memorable events recorded in history. It is important as a manifesta-

---

[3]"Change" refers to the Stock Exchange.

tion of the intelligence with which it was consummated, and even more so because of its abiding effect on the world. The two religions which control the larger portion of the inhabited globe, Christianity and Islam, are both based on the religion of the Jews.

Yes, in a certain sense it is indisputable that we are indebted to the religion of Moses for a large share of the culture which we now enjoy. Through it, a precious truth became popularly known, the doctrine of one God, which, if left to the intellect alone, would have been discovered only after a slow process of evolution.

The Hebrew system enjoyed this extraordinary advantage, that the religion of its sages and the religion of its folk were not in direct mutual contradiction, as was the case among the enlightened pagans. From this standpoint, the Jewish nation must appear to us historically as of universal significance. All the evil which has been imputed to them, all the efforts of literary men to disparage them, will not prevent us from doing them justice.

("Die Sendung Moses," in *Thalia*, 1790)

NAPOLEON BONAPARTE   *(1769–1821)*

French general and emperor

My policy is to govern men as the great majority of them wish to be governed. That, I believe, is the way to recognize the sovereignty of the people. It was as a Catholic that I won the war in the Vendee, as a Moslem that I established myself in Egypt, and as an Ultramontane that I won the confidence of the Italians. If I were governing Jews, I should rebuild the temple of Solomon. . . .

[I plan] to revive among the Jews . . . the sentiments of civic morality that unfortunately have been moribund among too large a number of them by a state of abasement in which they have long languished.

(Told to the Council of State in August 1801)

* * *

Napoleon to Portalis, 25 December 1807:

It is against the divine law to prevent the Jew from working on Sundays in order to gain his bread; the Jew has his necessities on

Sunday as well as on the week days. The government could pass such a law only if it were to give bread to those who have none; police and Government have, therefore, no business to interfere. . . .

Mr. Portalis had better, therefore, be careful, because these concessions once made, the Government undertaking to interfere in matters that are outside of its sphere, it will not be long before we will be taken back to the unfortunate period of the issue of letters patent of absolution, or the miserable epoch when the priest imagined the right to order the burning alive of the Jew, or to maltreat the citizen who refused to attend mass. The power of the clergy must be confined to the sermon; it is time that the sorely persecuted Jews were left in peace. As long as I live, however, police and dungeon shall never be resorted to in France to tyrannize the citizen of another faith. There are many erring sheep in the Christian fold; let the priest lead these back to the practices of religion.

(Quoted in *Selected Addresses and Papers of Simon Wolf*)

SIR WALTER SCOTT   *(1771–1832)*

Scottish novelist, poet, and historian

. . . it is hard that the vagabond stock-jobbing Jews should, for their own purposes, make such a stroke of credit as now exists in London, and menace the credit of men trading on sure funds like Hurst and Robinson. It is just like a set of pickpockets, who raise a mob, in which honest folks are knocked down and plundered, that they may pillage safely in the midst of the confusion they have excited.

(Lockhart, *Memoirs of Sir Walter Scott*, vol. IV, p. 364)

* * *

One does not naturally and easily combine with [the Jews'] habits and pursuits any liberality of principle, although certainly it may, and I believe, does, exist in many individual instances. They are money-lenders and money-brokers by profession, and it is a trade which narrows the mind.

(Douglas, *Familiar Letters of Sir Walter Scott*, vol. I, p. 435)

FRIEDRICH SCHLEGEL (1772–1829)

German philosopher and critic

The superiority of the Hebrews over all the other Asiatic peoples consists solely and simply in this—that they alone preserved that original truth and higher knowledge, which was intrusted to them pure and unfalsified, with the strongest faith . . . while among all other nations these things were either altogether forgotten or abandoned, or mixed up with the wildest fictions and the most odious errors and abominations. . . . In these writings whatever is meant to be a practical law to the nation is expressed with the greatest accuracy and precision. . . .

Whatever, on the other side, can serve only as an amusement of our curiosity, is wrapped by Moses in obscurity and mystery. What he tells us with hieroglyphical brevity concerning the ten first fathers of the primitive world, has been spun out by the Persians, the Indians, and the Chinese, into whole volumes of mythology and been invested with a crowd of half poetical, half metaphysical traditions. The praise of a more ardent and poetical fancy and of more inventive metaphysics, as well as of a deeper acquaintance with nature and her powers, we may easily grant to the Persians. . . .

But if we are perplexed with any of these dark questions which make man tremble to look into futurity, where among any other nation shall find such answers as the Hebrews can point to us in their narrative of the sorrows of Job? . . .

That peculiar faith and confidence in God which were the inheritance of the Jews, are expressed with less of the Mosaic mystery as we advance in the sacred volume and appear in their full light in the Psalms of David, the allegories of Solomon and the Prophecies of Isaiah. These works indeed set them forth with a splendor and a sublimity which, considered merely as poetry, excite our wonder and disdain all comparison with any other compositions; they form a fountain of fiery and Godlike inspiration, of which the greatest of modern poets have never been weary of drinking, which has suggested to them their noblest images and animated them for their most magnificent flights.

(*Lectures on the History of Literature,
Ancient and Modern*, vol. 1, p. 188)

ROBERT SOUTHEY   *(1774–1843)*

English poet

All Oriental poetry that I have seen is bad, and the superiority of the Hebrews is truly marvelous; it almost requires a belief in inspiration to account for it.

> (In a letter 16 October 1808)

* * *

. . . the corruptions of Judaism have found a most curious parallel with those of Popery, and in both, tradition has been set up above the written word. . . . [The Jews] are found everywhere, [but] as long as they are Jews, they will continue to be, however corrupted, a peculiar people, all whose observances are intended to keep them so. . . . The society for converting the Jews has wasted more money than any other society in this country, which is saying a great deal.

DANIEL O'CONNELL   *(1775–1847)*

19th-century Irish patriot and member of Parliament

I have the happiness of being acquainted with some Jewish families in London, and among them more accomplished ladies, more humane, cordial, high-minded or better educated gentlemen, I have never met. It will not be supposed that when I speak of Disraeli as the descendant of a Jew that I mean to tarnish him on that account. They were once the chosen people of God. . . .

There were miscreants among them, however, and it certainly must have been from one of them that Disraeli descended. [Roars of laughter.] He possesses just the qualities of the Impenitent Thief who died upon the cross, whose name, I verily believe, must have been Disraeli. [Roars of laughter.] For aught I know, the present Disraeli is descended from him, and, with the impression that he is, I now forgive

the heir-in-law of the blasphemous thief who died upon the cross.
[Loud cheers and roars of laughter.]

(from House of Commons debate, ca. 1850)

7

From the U.S. Industrial Revolution to the Civil War

WILLIAM CULLEN BRYANT   (1794–1878)

U.S. poet and editor of The New York Evening Post

In terming Shylock "the Jew whom Shakespeare drew," there is a perfect logic, for Shylock is, of all Shakespeare's characters, the only one untrue to nature. He is not a Jew, but a fiend presented in the form of one; and whereas he is made a ruling type, he is but an exception, if even that, and the exception is not to be met with either in the Ghettos of Venice or Rome. . . .

Revenge is not a characteristic of the Jew. He is subject to sudden fits of passion, but that intellect which always stands sentinel over the Hebrew soon subdues the gust. However strong in Shylock's time might have been the hatred of the Jew toward the Christian, the lust of lucre was even more strong, and Shakespeare might have ransacked every Ghetto in Christendom without finding a Jew, or a Christian either, who would have preferred a pound of flesh to a pound of sterling, and Jews also shrink from physical contests. Their disposition is to triumph by intellect rather than violence. . . .

The contempt of a daughter for her parent is equally uncharacteristic of the Jew. The Jews are universally admired for the affections which adorn their domestic life. . . . No one can ever have visited the houses of the Jews without having been struck by the glowing affection with which the daughter greets the father as he returns from the day's campaign and the slights and sneers his gaberdine and yellow cap provoke, and without observing how those small, restless eyes that sparkle and gleam, shine out in a softened, loving luster as they fall upon the face of Rebecca or Jessica, or Sarah, and how he stands no longer with crooked back, but erect and commanding, as he blesses his household goods with exultations vehement as the prejudices which during the day have galled and fretted his nature.

To do justice to the grandeurs of the Jewish race, and to brand with infamy its infirmities, it is not enough to produce a repulsive delineation of the latter. It would be only just to give an expression to

111

the former, and to exhibit that superiority of intellect which has survived all persecution and which, soaring above prejudices of the hour, has filled us with reluctant admiration on finding how many of the great events which mark the progress of the age or minister to its improvements, or elevate its tastes, may be traced to the wonderful workings of the soul of the Hebrew, and the supremacy of that spiritual nature which gave mankind its noblest religion, its noblest laws and some of its noblest poesy and music.

(New York Post, January 1867)

RALPH WALDO EMERSON   (1803–1882)

U.S. poet, lecturer, and essayist

The Hebrew nation compensated for the insignificance of its members and territory by its religious genius, its tenacious belief; its poems and histories cling to the soil of this globe like the primitive rocks. . . . In Puritanism, how the whole Jewish history became flesh and blood in those men, let Bunyan show.

(from the address "The Man of Letters," 1863)

* * *

. . . In his writing, allusions to modern Jews are few and rely on the conventional stereotype. In 1828 he wrote complainingly from Cambridge to his brother William, who was running a newspaper, that he does not write to him much; he suspects that "you are sunk into the vulgarest man of business who has no correspondence for any but the Jews with whom you have dealings." A few years later (1831) he again wrote William: "Do you not die of the Jews to whom you pay usance?" Pejorative allusions recur in the following years. In a journal entry for July 3, 1839, he writes of a visit to an exhibit of Washington Allston's paintings. Referring to several paintings of Polish Jews, he comments: "In the Allston Gallery the Polish Jews are an offense to me; they degrade and animalize. As soon as a beard becomes any thing but an accident, we have not a man but a Turk, a Jew, a satyr, a dandy, a goat. So we paint angels." Later, in the essay "Fate," he echoes the conventional view of Jewish power. "A man must think of his defects," he writes, "and stand in some terror of his talents—a transcendent talent draws so largely on his forces as to lame him; a defect pays him revenues on the other side. The sufferance which is the badge of the Jew, has made him, in these days, the ruler of rulers of the earth"—the popular stereotype of Jewish bankers who control the thrones of Europe by their financial power.

. . . his thinking about this people was largely limited to their religious significance in Western history and reflected the usual Christian viewpoint. But his views were riddled with inconsistencies. On one hand, he writes that "the Jewish Law answered its temporary purpose. It set aside. Christianity is completing its purpose as an aid to educate man." The Jews adhered to an obsolete system of ethics and were superseded. "If ethics were an immovable science," he writes, "the primeval altar of the Jews might serve as a model of our holy place." But modern man, he adds, "are standing on a higher stage. . . . We leave the ritual, the offering and the altar of Moses, we cast off the superstitions that were the swaddling clothes of Christianity."

Many years later, however, he was far from complacent concerning the superiority of Christianity as it was interpreted by the clergy. In a speech given in 1869, he decried the disparagement of wisdom in other faiths:

> I find something stingy in the unwilling and disparaging admissions of these foreign opinions—opinions from all parts of the world—by our churchmen, as if only to enhance by their dimness the superior light of Christianity. . . . You cannot bring me too good a word, too dazzling a hope, too penetrating an insight from the Jews. I hail every one with delight, as showing the riches of my brother, my fellow soul, who could thus think and thus greatly feel.

Yet in another lecture in 1853, as Philip L. Nicoloff points out, Emerson asserted that, in Nicoloff's words, "the Jews had flowered in Jesus and ended as a nation." Considering the very lively and often tragic history of the Jewish people since Jesus' time, Emerson was here misled by his own rhetoric. Indeed, in his essay "Fate" he writes, as was obvious enough and more realistic, "we see how much has been expended to extinguish the Jew, in vain." And in his *Journal* during 1867 Emerson calls attention to white Christian responsibility for what he calls the "base" condition of both Negroes and Jews. "You complain," he writes, "that the Negroes are a base class. What makes and keeps the Jew or the Negro base, who but you, who exclude them from the rights which others enjoy?" Note Emerson's concession to popular opinion by his designation "base."

(Harap, The Image of the Jew in American Literature,
pp. 102–104)

NATHANIEL HAWTHORNE   *(1804–1864)*

U.S. novelist; author of Twice-Told Tales, The Scarlet Letter

Although Jews figured very little in Hawthorne's experience, they did engage his imagination and in important ways entered into his explorations of the moral dilemmas of man. The legend of the Wandering Jew particularly attracted him as literary material, and this theme of moral death in physical deathlessness runs through his fiction in direct and indirect ways. How the ideas he associated in his fiction with this legendary character are related to his personal feelings toward the Jews is a subtle question. . . .

More frequent allusions to Jews occurred in the European notebooks, and, significantly, nearly all are infused with repugnance, which even seems justified in some instances. In the Italian notebooks he describes a visit to a Jewish synagogue in Leghorn. "It looked very like a Christian church," he writes, but the likeness stopped with the form, for he adds, perhaps accurately, that "it was dirty, and had an odor not of sanctity." And at the Barberini Palace in Rome his attention was drawn to Dürer's "Christ Disputing with the Doctors." He describes the repulsive figure at Christ's left as "the ugliest, most evil-minded, stubborn, practical, and contentious old Jew that ever lived under the law of Moses. . . ."

One misses any note of compassion in these expressions of disgust and revulsion. Inferences about his feelings concerning Jews do not have to be drawn from these passages alone, for others equally betray a hostile attitude. . . .

The fact is that Hawthorne simply did not like Jews. He said as much quite plainly and unequivocally in a revealing passage in his *English Notebooks*. In 1856 he was a guest at a formal dinner given by the lord mayor of London, David Salomons, who was the first Jew to be elected to that post. Sitting opposite Hawthorne were the lord mayor's brother and sister-in-law; his charged description of these two supplies the key to Hawthorne's opinions of the Jews. Underlying his words are the assumptions of the Rebecca and Shylock-Iscariot stereotypes. . . . First, the Jewish woman:

> My eyes were mostly drawn to a young lady who sat nearly opposite me. . . . Her hair was a wonderful deep, raven black, black as night, black as death; *not* raven black, for that has a shiny gloss, and hers had not; but it was hair never to be painted, nor described—wonderful hair, Jewish hair. Her nose had a beautiful outline, though I could see that it was Jewish too. . . . looking at her, I saw what were the wives of the old patriarchs, in their maiden or early married days—what Rachel was, when Jacob wooed her seven years, and seven more—what Judith was; for, womanly as she looked, I doubt not she could have slain a man, in a good cause—what Batsheva was; only she seemed to have no sin in her—perhaps what Eve was, though one could hardly think her weak enough to eat the apple. I should never thought of touching her, nor desired to touch for; for, whether owing to distinctness of race, my sense that she was a Jewess, or whatever else, I felt a sort of repugnance, simultaneously with my perception that she was an admirable creature.

Note the elements of the female Jewish stereotype: she is beautiful, idealized, yet essentially untouchable because of the barrier of "race." Hawthorne's feeling is love-hate, the sexual attraction–repulsion of a self-regarded superior for a female of an outcast people. . . .

Then her husband is described:

> But, at the right hand of this miraculous Jewess, there sat the very Jew of Jews; the distilled essence of all the Jews that have

been born since Jacob's time; he was Judas Iscariot; he was the Wandering Jew; he was the worst, and at the same time, the truest type of his race, and contained within himself, I have no doubt, every old prophet and every old clothesman, that ever the tribes produced; and he must have been circumcised as much as ten times over. I never beheld anything so ugly and disagreeable, and preposterous, and laughable, as the outline of his profile; it was so hideously Jewish, and so cruel, and so keen; and he had such an immense beard that you could see no trace of a mouth, until he opened it to speak, or to eat his dinner,— and then, indeed, you were aware of a cave, in this density of beard. And yet his manners and aspect, in spite of all, were those of a man of the world, and a gentleman. Well; it is as hard to give an idea of this ugly Jew, as of the beautiful Jewess. . . . I rejoiced exceedingly in this Shylock, this Iscariot; for the sight of him justified me in the repugnance I have always felt towards his race.

It is hard to credit the intensity of prejudice so explicitly brought to expression. As far as I can ascertain, this passage has been ignored in studies about Hawthorne. Even if the Jewish man *was* repulsive, Hawthorne was not satisfied to stop with the individual, but seized the occasion to attribute to the entire Jewish people the physical and moral ugliness he imputed to the individual. (Jewish women seem to be chivalrously exempt from these characterizations.) He is for Hawthorne the essential Jew, the "Jew of Jews." The "worst" type of Jew is "the truest type of his race." Hawthorne finally "rejoiced" that "this Shylock, this Iscariot . . . justified me in the repugnance I have always felt towards his race."

Hawthorne used no restraint in this shocking characterization of the Jews because these notes were not meant for publication. When he came to fashion the notes of his English sojourn into articles for publication, which he later gathered in *Our Old Home*, he rewrote these passages under the tutelage of his censor. All references to Jews and Jewishness are omitted. The beautiful woman in his rewritten version has for him an unexplained "strange repulsion and unattainableness in the very spell that made her beautiful." The invidious characteristics of her husband are muted, but he is called a "Blue-beard."

(Harap, *The Image of the Jew in American Literature*, pp. 107–110)

THE BOOK OF MORMON   *1827–1830*

The Revelation received by Joseph Smith (1805–1844)

And it came to pass that the Jews did mock him ["Lehi"] because of the things which he testified of them; for he truly testified of their wickedness and their abominations; and he testified that the things which he saw and heard, and also the things which he read in the book, manifested plainly of the coming of a Messiah, and also the redemption of the world.

And when the Jews heard these things they were angry with him; yea, even as with the prophets of old, whom they had cast out, and stoned, and slain; and they also sought his life, that they might take it away. . . .

(1 Nephi, Ch. 1, v. 19–20)

* * *

And it came to pass after my father had spoken these words he spake unto my brethren concerning the gospel which should be preached among the Jews, and also concerning the dwindling of the Jews in unbelief. And after they had slain the Messiah, who should come, and after he had been slain he should rise from the dead, and should make himself manifest, by the Holy Ghost, unto the Gentiles.

(1 Nephi, Ch. 10, v. 11)

* * *

And as for those who are at Jerusalem, saith the prophet, they shall be scourged by all people, because they crucify the God of Israel, and turn their hearts aside, rejecting signs and wonders, and the power and glory of the God of Israel.

(1 Nephi, Ch. 19, v. 13)

And now, my beloved brethren, I have read these things that ye might know concerning the covenants of the Lord that he has covenanted with all the house of Israel—

That he has spoken unto the Jews, by the mouth of his holy prophets, even from the beginning down, from generation to generation, until the time comes that they shall be restored to the true church and fold of God; when they shall be gathered home to the lands of their inheritance, and shall be established in all their lands of promise.

(2 Nephi, Ch. 9, v. 1, 2)

* * *

Yea, and my soul delighteth in the words of Isaiah, for I came out from Jerusalem, and mine eyes hath beheld the things of the Jews, and I know that the Jews do understand the things of the prophets, and there is none other people that understand the things which were spoken unto the Jews like unto them, save it be that they are taught after the manner of the things of the Jews.

But behold I, Nephi, have not taught my children after the manner of the Jews; but behold, I, of myself, have dwelt at Jerusalem, wherefore I know concerning the regions round about; and I have made mention unto my children concerning the judgments of God, which hath come to pass among the Jews, unto my children, according to all that which Isaiah hath spoken. . . .

And as one generation hath been destroyed among the Jews because of iniquity, even so have they been destroyed from generation to generation according to their iniquities; and never hath any of them been destroyed save it were foretold them by the prophets of the Lord.

. . . for woe unto them that fight against God and the people of his church.

Wherefore, the Jews shall be scattered among all the nations; yea, and also Babylon shall be destroyed; wherefore, the Jews shall be scattered by other nations.

And after they have been scattered, and the Lord God hath scourged them by other nations for the space of many generations, yea, even down from generation to generation until they shall be persuaded to believe in Christ, the Son of God. . . .

(2 Nephi, Ch. 25, v. 5–6, 9, 14–16)

* * *

But, behold, in the last days, or in the days of the Gentiles – yea, behold all the nations of the Gentiles and also the Jews, both those who shall come upon this land and those who shall be upon other lands, yea, even upon all the lands of the earth, behold, they will be drunken with iniquity and all manner of abominations. . . .

(2 Nephi, Ch. 27, v. 1)

* * *

And because my words shall hiss forth – many of the Gentiles shall say: A Bible! A Bible! We have got a Bible, and there cannot be any more Bible.

But thus saith the Lord God: O fools, they shall have a Bible; and it shall proceed forth from the Jews, mine ancient covenant people. And what think they the Jews for the Bible which they receive from them? Yea, what do the Gentiles mean? Do the labors, and the pains of the Jews, and their diligence unto me, in bringing forth salvation unto the Gentiles?

O ye Gentiles, have ye remembered the Jews, mine ancient covenant people? Nay; but ye have cursed them, and have hated them, and have not sought to recover them. But behold, I will return all these things upon your own heads; for I the Lord have not forgotten my people.

(2 Nephi, Ch. 29, v. 3–4)

* * *

For behold, I say unto you that as many of the Gentiles as will repent are the covenant people of the Lord; and as many of the Jews as will not repent shall be cast off; for the Lord covenanteth with none save it be with them that repent and believe in his Son, who is the Holy One of Israel. . . .

And it shall come to pass that the Jews which are scattered also shall begin to believe in Christ; and they shall begin to gather in upon the face of the land; and as many as shall believe in Christ shall also become a delightsome people.

(2 Nephi, Ch. 30, v. 2, 7)

ANDREW JOHNSON   (1808–1875)

17th president of the United States, 1865–1869

On the evening of February 28, 1861, Charles Francis Adams, of the distinguished Boston family, was chatting with Senator Andrew Johnson, later to become the seventeenth President of the United States. Johnson discoursed on many subjects, and finally came around to two of his Senatorial colleagues:

[Andrew Johnson] was amusingly severe over the secession of Florida. "There's that Yulee," he said, "miserable little cuss! I remember him in the House—the contemptible little Jew—standing there and begging us—yes! begging us to let Florida in as a State. Well! we let her in, and took care of her, and fought her Indians; and now that despicable little beggar stands up in the Senate and talks about *her* rights." Toward Jews, he evidently felt a strong aversion; for, after finishing with Yulee he began on Benjamin, exclaiming: "There's another Jew—that miserable Benjamin! He looks on a country and a government as he would on a suit of old clothes. He sold out the old one; and he would sell out the new if he could in so doing make two or three millions!"

Thirteen years later ex-President Johnson was an honored guest at the dedication of the new synagogue in Nashville, Tenn. He rode in a carriage with Rabbi Kalisch of the Nashville congregation, and Rabbi Isaac M. Wise, and was accompanied by them to the pulpit. After the two dedicatory addresses, the chairman introduced him to the assemblage. He said he would not take much of their time, according to the report in the *Nashville Republican Banner*, because they had already heard two very stimulating speeches. "No one felt a deeper interest in the success and prosperity of them and their temple than he did. He hoped that it would ever remain a monument to the industry, prosperity, and welfare of the Jewish citizens of Nashville. He thanked them for the attention and retired amidst applause."

(Korn, *American Jewry and the Civil War*, p. 169)

OLIVER WENDELL HOLMES   *(1809–1894)*

U.S. poet and essayist

The golden rule should govern us in dealing with those whom we call unbelievers, with heathen, and with all who do not accept our religious views. The Jews are with us as a perpetual lesson to teach us modesty and civility. The religion we profess is not self-evident. It did not convince the people to whom it was sent. We have no claim to take it for granted that we are all right, and they are all wrong. And, therefore, in the midst of all triumphs of Christianity, it is well that the stately synagogue should lift its walls by the side of the aspiring cathedral, a perpetual reminder that there are many mansions in the Father's earthly house as well as in the heavenly one; that civilized humanity, longer in time and broader in space than any historical form of belief, is mightier than any one institution or organization it includes.

(*Over the Teacups*, 1891, p. 197)

* * *

. . . the story of sweating gold was only one of the many fables got up to make the Jews odious and afford a pretext for plundering them.

(*The Autocrat of the Breakfast-Table*, 1860)

* * *

One set of questions, however, he treated seriously. They were addressed to him and to others and were printed in the *American Hebrew* for April 4, 1890. The questions asked individuals to account for their racial prejudice and to suggest ways to dispel it. Holmes's answers are worth reading. Free of cant and self-righteousness, always honest and personal, he replied from his own experience. "I shared more or less the prevailing prejudices against the persecuted race." He traced that prejudice to Christian teaching and, in his own case, to puritan exclusiveness.

"It was against the most adverse influences of legislation, of religious feeling, of social repugnance, that the great names of Jewish origin made themselves illustrious; that the philosophers, the musicians, the financiers, the statesmen, of the last centuries forced the world to recognize and accept them. . . . Christians, as they called themselves, have insulted, calumniated, oppressed, abased and outraged "the chosen race" during the succession of centuries since the Jewish contemporaries of the Founder of Christianity made up their minds that he did not meet the conditions of their Scriptures. . . .

It seems as if there should be certain laws of etiquette regulating the relation of different religions to each other. Still more, there should be something like politeness in the bearing of Christian sects toward each other, and of believers in the new dispensation toward those who still adhere to the old. . . . I doubt if a convert to the religion of Mahomet was ever made by calling a man a Christian dog. I doubt if a Hebrew ever became a good Christian if the baptismal rite was performed by spitting on his Jewish gabardine. . . ."

(Tilton, *Amiable Autocrat — the Biography of Dr. Oliver Wendell Holmes*, pp. 380–381)

ABRAHAM LINCOLN   (1809–1865)

16th president of the United States, 1861–1865

"Brethren, the lamented Abraham Lincoln believed himself to be bone from our bone and flesh from our flesh. He supposed himself to be a descendant of Hebrew parentage. He said so in my presence." These words were spoken by Rabbi Isaac M. Wise during the eulogy which he delivered five days after the assassination of the President. There is no shred of evidence to substantiate Wise's assertion, and Lincoln is not known to have said anything resembling this to any of his other Jewish acquaintances. He could not, however, have been any friendlier to individual Jews, or more sympathetic to Jewish causes, if he had stemmed from Jewish ancestry. . . .

In March, 1863, Lincoln conferred with a strange and visionary man, Henry Wentworth Monk, the Canadian-born Judaeophile and early Zionist, who had come to Washington to urge upon the President a plan for the abandonment of the war. Lincoln was not seriously disposed to listen to his proposals, so Monk went on to discuss one of his pet projects: the restoration of European Jewry to Palestine. The President agreed that the vision which Monk had of a Jewish state in Palestine was worthy of consideration, but protested that the United States was in no position to take a leading role in international affairs until it had set its own house in order and reunited the two warring sections. This is what he said of the Jews: ". . . I myself have a regard for the Jews. My chiropodist is a Jew, and he has so many times 'put me upon my feet' that I would have no objection to giving his countrymen 'a leg up'. . . .

This passing reference to [Dr. Isachar] Zacharie was the only known opinion Lincoln ever registered in regard to the Jews, beyond . . . the Grant Order[1] and . . . the chaplaincy clause. In those two cases he had expressed an interest in seeing justice done to the Jews, and was willing to take upon himself the responsibility for the necessary action. He understood the quality of democratic equality well enough to know that no group could be deprived of its rights without endangering the whole structure of democracy.

(Korn, *American Jewry and the Civil War*, pp. 189, 202, 203)

HORACE GREELEY   *(1811–1872)*

U.S. newspaper editor and crusader against slavery

We choose our own company at all times, and that of our own race, but cherish little of that spirit which for eighteen centuries has held the kindred of M. M. Noah[2] accursed of God and man, outlawed and outcast, and unfit to be the associates of Christians and Musselmen,

---

[1]See the entries under Ulysses S. Grant.

[2]Mordecai M. Noah, a 19th-century playwright.

or even self-respecting Pagans. Where there are thousands who would not eat with a Negro, there are (or lately were) tens of thousands who would not eat with a Jew. We leave to such renegades as the Judge of Israel the stirring up of prejudices and the prating of "usages of society," which over half the world make him an abhorrence, as they not long since would have done here. . . .

(Goldberg, Major Noah, pp. 241–242)

HARRIET BEECHER STOWE   (1811–1896)

U.S. novelist and abolitionist

The strongest impulse in the character of Moses appears to have been that of protective justice, more particularly with regard to the helpless and down-trodden classes. The laws of Moses, if carefully examined, are a perfect phenomenon; an exception to the laws of either ancient or modern nations in the care they exercised over women, widows, orphans, paupers, foreigners, servants and dumb animals. No so-called Christian nation but could advantageously take a lesson in legislation from the laws of Moses. There is a plaintive, pathetic spirit of compassion in the very language in which the laws in favor of the helpless and suffering are expressed, that it seems must have been learned only of superhuman tenderness. Not the gentlest words of Jesus are more compassionate in their spirit than many of these laws of Moses. Delivered in the name of Jehovah, they certainly are so unlike the wisdom of that barbarous age as to justify of them to Him who is Love.

(Stowe, "Moses and his Laws," in the Christian Union)

* * *

Harriet's interest in Negroes being what it was, it may be interesting to glance at her attitude toward certain other minority groups. What she says about Jews is all favorable. Their moral superiority she attributes to the wise, humane provisions of the Law of Moses. But I do not find that she had any real interest in Judaism except as it prepared the way for Christianity. In 1854 she wrote to [prominent rabbi] Isaac Meyer Wise, who had sent her his *History of the Israelitish Nation*, of "that singular and sacred nation to whom I, in common with all the world, am indebted for the preservation and transmission of the oracles of God." She added that she never meets a Jew or enters a synagogue without thinking of these things.

(Wagenknecht, *Harriet Beecher Stowe, The Known and the Unknown*, p. 178)

HENRY WARD BEECHER   *(1813–1887)*

U.S. clergyman, abolitionist, and brother of Harriet B. Stowe

Are [Jews] in our poorhouses? In which? Are they in our jails? Where? Are they in our reformatories? Point them out. Do their women defile our streets? You cannot find another people in America among whom the social virtues are more rigorously taught and observed than among the Israelites. . . . They are a temperate people, and we are a drunken people. They are a virtuous people, and we largely tend to be a lascivious people. They are a people excessively careful of their children, and there is a great laxity among us in the education of the household. We may well take lessons of them. They were the school-masters of our fathers, and we may well go to school to the same masters.

(In his sermon "Jew and Gentile," in *Menorah*, 1887, p. 203)

ELIZABETH CADY STANTON   *(1815–1902)*

U.S. reformer and suffragette

I found nothing grand in the history of the Jews nor in the morals inculcated in the Pentateuch. I know of no other books that so fully teach the subjection and degradation of women.

(*Eighty Years and More*, p. 395)

HENRY DAVID THOREAU   *(1817–1862)*

U.S. author and naturalist

The fact is that contemporary Jews figured peripherally, if at all. . . . This is not surprising in the case of Thoreau, considering that he spent most of his life in Concord. No allusion to contemporary Jews can be found in any of his works and journals. One reference to the traditional Hebrew does occur in his journals. Of his quiet search for "The Ineffable" he records on September 7, 1851, that it must be pursued without sadness. "These Jews," he writes, "were too sad: to another people a still deeper revelation may suggest only joy. . . . In the Hebrew gladness, I hear but too distinctly still the sound of sadness retreating. Give me a gladness which has never given place to sadness."

(Harap, The Image of the Jew in American Literature, p. 101)

JAMES RUSSELL LOWELL   *(1819–1891)*

U.S. poet and critic; editor of Atlantic Monthly

In "Democracy," an address given on 6 October 1884
in Birmingham, England

One of the most curious of these frenzies of exclusion was that against the emancipation of the Jews. All share in the government of the world was denied for centuries to perhaps the ablest, certainly the most tenacious, race that had ever lived in it—the race to whom we owed our religion and the purest spiritual stimulus and consolation to be found in all literature—a race in which ability seems as natural and hereditary as the curve of their noses, and whose blood, furtively mingling with the bluest blood in Europe, has quickened them with its own indomitable impulse.

(Literary and Political Addresses, in Writings, p. 18f)

* * *

[Lowell] detected a Jew in every hiding-place and under every disguise, even when the fugitive had no suspicion of himself. To begin with nomenclature: all persons named for countries or towns are Jews; all with fantastic, compound names, such as Lilienthal, Morgenroth; all with names derived from colors, trades, animals, vegetables, minerals; all with Biblical names, except Puritan first names; all patronymics ending in *son*, *sohn*, *sen*, or any other version; all Russells, originally so called from red-haired Israelites; all Walters, by long descended derivation from wolves and foxes in some ancient tongue; the Caecilii, therefore Cecilia Metella, no doubt St. Cecilia too, consequently the Cecils, including Lord Burleigh and Lord Salisbury; he cited some old chronicle in which he had cornered one Robert de Caecilia and exposed him as an English Jew.

(Scudder, *James Russell Lowell*, vol. II, p. 303)

* * *

Mr. Lowell said more, much more, to illustrate the ubiquity, the universal ability of the Hebrew, and gave examples and statistics for every statement, however astonishing, drawn from his inexhaustible information. He was conscious of the sort of infatuation which possessed him, and his dissertation alternated between earnestness and drollery; but whenever a burst of laughter greeted some new development of his theme, although he joined in it, he immediately returned to the charge with abundant proof of his paradoxes. Finally he came to a stop, but not to a conclusion, and as no one else spoke, I said, 'And when the Jews have got absolute control of finance, the army and navy, the press, diplomacy, society, titles, the government, and the earth's surface, what do you suppose they will do with them and with us?' "That," he answered turning toward me, and in a whisper audible to the whole table, "that is the question which will eventually drive me mad."

(*James Russell Lowell*, II, p. 305)

* * *

On a map of the world you may cover Judea with your thumb, Athens with a finger tip; but they still lord it in the thought and action of every civilized man.

(*Harvard Anniversary Literary and Political Addresses*, vol. VI, p. 174)

* * *

Lowell was most likely to bore or insult a dinner partner if he got off on what had become a favorite topic with him—the Jews. He had come to delight in the bizarre pastime of discovering that everyone of talent was in some way descended from Jewish ancestors, and he would play the game of "detection" with a relish that approached monomania. He based his discoveries less on physiognomy than names; every name which could not be instantly derived from Latin or Anglo-Saxon became "Jewish," resulting, needless to say, in the ascription of Hebrew origins to the majority of people he met. Among others whom he believed descended from Jews were Gladstone, Lord Granville (the telltale family name was *Leveson*-Gower) and, he rather contentedly admitted, himself (that middle name, Russell). Sometimes Lowell relied on still less tangible factors in "proving" the Jewish origins of some noted man. Thus Browning, though he tried to conceal the fact, *obviously* had Jewish blood. Why? Because he *looked* Jewish, because he had once used a Hebrew line in a poem and then canceled it in a later edition, and because whenever you dined with a Jew in London, Browning was sure to be there.

Conscious of his own obsession, Lowell would discuss The Jewish Origins of Practically Everyone with at least occasional drollery. Still, it was difficult for one to know whether he meant his "discoveries" to be taken as compliments or accusations. In fact he was uncertain himself, his admiration for the Jews alternating with stereotypic fears about them. Thus he could describe them as "a people remarkable above almost all others for the possession of the highest and clearest intellect" and yet in an official despatch could ascribe some of the passion of Spanish politics to the large infusion of Jewish blood in the upper and middle classes: "the most intense, restless, aspiring and unscrupulous blood of all." He could speak of the prejudice against Disraeli as "medieval, of a piece with the enlightened public opinion which dictated the legend of Hugh of Lincoln," and yet he could demonstrate some medievalisms of his own by rhetorically asking, "Where would a Jew be among a society of primitive men without pockets, and therefore *a fortiori* without a hole in them?"

Lowell's ambivalent fascination with the Jews reflected the contradictory strains of his divided New England inheritance. On the one side was the Puritan tradition, with its respect for the chosen people of the Old Testament and its direct identification with those upright, austere, sternly moral Israelites who had searched for a Promised Land. But the Puritan view of the Jews conflicted with an image which had become manifest in the late nineteenth century: the degraded immigrant Jew, the vendor, the money changer, the despised outcast. Lowell, even while deploring the conditions under which Jews currently suffered, exhibited some of the mythic fears which helped to justify and perpetuate those conditions—especially the fear (mixed, in his case, with a little hopeful anticipation) of Jewish "domination." Richard Henry Dana, Jr.,[3] in a public speech in 1868 before the Massachusetts legislature, denounced the state's usury law as one benefiting only "the Jews emerging from their alleys." And Norton,[4] in a private letter to Lowell, expressed concern that Jewish students beginning to "inundate" Harvard might "keep the Christian youths away."

Yet Lowell, and most of his friends, were incapable of the harsher anti-Semitism which seized upon such New England aristocrats of the next generation as Brooks and Henry Adams and such patricians of New England ancestry as John Jay Chapman. By then Jewish immigration had waxed while the Puritan tradition had still further waned. The pessimism, moreover, with which this later generation of aristocrats regarded the country's heightened devotion to materialism found a convenient scapegoat in the Jew. . . . Thus Henry Adams, as early as the 1870s, could write while traveling in Spain, "I have now seen enough of Jews and Moors to entertain more liberal views in regard to the Inquisition, and to feel that, though the ignorant may murmur, the Spaniards saw and pursued a noble aim." And John Jay Chapman, approaching the point of phobia by the 1920s, could laud the Ku Klux Klan for being on "the right track" in recognizing the peril in the Catholic and Jewish Questions.

With Lowell, on the other hand, uneasiness about Jewish "aggression" was offset by respect for Jewish history and for the Jewish commitment to learning and achievement. If he felt some distaste for what he believed the nineteenth-century Jew had become, he also felt some responsibility for that decline. In a public address in 1884, he spoke disapprovingly of the "frenzies of exclusion" which for centuries had denied

---

[3]An American novelist and reformer, 1815–1882.

[4]Charles Eliot Norton (1827–1908), professor of the history of art at Harvard and co-founder of *The Nation.*

all share in the government of the world . . . to perhaps the
ablest, certainly the most tenacious, race that had ever lived in it
. . . We drove them in to a corner, but they had their revenge, as
the wronged are always sure to have it sooner or later. They
made their corner the counter and banking-house of the world,
and thence they rule it and us with the ignobler sceptre of
finance.

Much of Lowell's fear was fantasy, but not fantasy impervious to
compassion; he refused to condone any measures of discrimination
and repression. And he and his friends at least felt some guilt for such
anti-Jewish feeling as they harbored. They could say apologetically
with Norton (as representatives of the next generation, like Henry
Adams, never could): "My pet prejudices are two, one against Jews, the
other against Germans. I hope to outlive them. . . ."

(Duberman, *James Russell Lowell, Poet, Critic,
Editor*, pp. 307–310)

WILLIAM TECUMSEH SHERMAN
(1820–1891)

Union Army general during the U.S. Civil War

Letter written in September 1858:

. . . Individuals may prosper in a failing community such as San
Francisco, but they must be Jews, without pity, soul, heart or bowels
of compassion; but in a rising, growing, industrious community like
St. Louis, all patient, prudent, honest men can thrive . . .

Letter to Colonel John A. Rawlins, from Fifth Division
Headquarters, 30 July 1862:

I have been very busy in answering the innumerable questions of
civilians and hope they are now about through. I found so many Jews
and speculators here trading in cotton, and secessionists had become
so open in refusing anything but gold, that I have felt myself bound to

stop it. . . . Of course, I have respected all permits by yourself or the Secretary of the Treasury, but in these new cases (swarms of Jews) I have stopped it. . . .

* * *

Letter to Hon. S.P. Chase, Secretary of the Treasury, 11 August 1862:

The flock of Jews had disappeared, but will again overrun us.

* * *

Letter to the Adjutant-General of the Union Army, 11 August 1862:

The country will swarm with dishonest Jews who will smuggle powder, pistols, percussion-caps, etc., in spite of all the guards and precautions we can give.

(Korn, *American Jewry and the Civil War*, pp. 147–148)

ULYSSES S. GRANT *(1822–1885)*

Union Army general during the U.S. Civil War; 18th president of the United States, 1869–1877

It was in the midst of this nightmare of profiteering that the most sweeping anti-Jewish regulation in all American history was issued. It was wired from General Grant's headquarters in Holly Springs, Mississippi on December 17, 1862, and provided for the expulsion "within twenty-four hours" of "the Jews, as a class," without trial or hearing, from the Department of the Tennessee. . . .

(Korn, *American Jewry and the Civil War*, p. 122)

[Jewish leaders met with President Lincoln, and on January 4, 1863, a letter went out from the War Department to Grant: "A paper purporting to be General Orders, No. 11, issued by you December 17, has been presented here. By its terms, it expels all Jews from your department. If such an order has been issued, it will be immediately revoked."]

". . . the specie regulations of the Treasury Department have been violated, and that mostly by Jews and other unprincipled traders. So well satisfied have I been of this that I instructed the commanding officer at Columbus to refuse all permits to Jews to come South, and I have frequently had them expelled from the department, but they come in with their carpet-sacks in spite of all that can be done to prevent it. The Jews seem to be a privileged class that can travel everywhere. . . ."

(Letter of U. S. Grant to the Assistant Secretary of War in Washington written the same day as Order #11)

* * *

I have no prejudice against sect or race, but want each individual to be judged by his own merit. Order No. 11 does not sustain this statement, I admit, but then I do not sustain that order. It never would have been issued if it had not been telegraphed the moment it was penned, and without reflection.

(Grant, during the presidential campaign of 1868, to Congressman I.N. Morris of Illinois)

* * *

He had a whole month in which to reflect upon these orders, and they were never withdrawn; one is entitled to conclude that Grant himself was the author of General Order No. 11 and that it never would have been withdrawn if Cesar Kaskel had not organized the pressure campaign against it.

(Korn, *American Jewry and the Civil War*, p. 144)

* * *

Perhaps . . . Grant was not consciously anti-Jewish at all. At any rate, however, he came to bury the prejudice which expressed itself in The Order – Grant never again revealed any antipathy towards Jews. During his presidential terms, he appointed many Jews to minor and major public offices. . . . Grant offered . . . the position of Secretary of the Treasury . . . to Joseph Seligman [who] declined the post, but

served the nation in good stead in many financial crises. . . . It is a fact
that the State Department took an unusual interest in antisemitic
persecutions in Roumania and Russia during the Grant Administration. In 1870, when pogroms broke out in Roumania with renewed
violence, Grant performed a major service for the Jews of the world.
He appointed the Grand Master of B'nai B'rith, Benjamin Franklin
Peixotto, to serve as Consul at Bucharest, without remuneration, in
an effort to bring pressure on the Roumanian government for the
cessation of attacks on the Jews. The President added to Peixotto's
official credentials a note in his own handwriting:

". . . Mr. Peixotto has undertaken the duties of his present office
more as a missionary work for the benefit of the people he represents
than for any benefit to accrue to himself—a work in which all citizens
wish him the greatest success. The United States, knowing no distinction of her citizens on account of religion or nativity, naturally
believes in a civilization the world over which will secure the same
universal view."

He had come to recognize the inner meaning of the words he
used, and the true contours of the concept of democratic equality.

(Korn, *American Jewry and the Civil War*, pp. 145–146)

EMILY DICKINSON   *(1830–1886)*

U.S. poet

Far more sequestered than even Thoreau, there is no evidence of
contact with any Jew whatsoever in her life. But she does mention the
Jew in four poems, probably written during 1861 and 1862. In all cases
the Jew begs for a smile—from one of those men whom she is said to
have loved—in terms of a commercial transaction at a "counter." She
would "buy a smile" in exchange for diamonds or rubies, "like a star!"
The exchange would be a " 'Bargain' for a *Jew!*" In another poem she
longs to see the face of a beloved, and bargains with his wife,
presumably, for "*One hour*—of her Sovereign's face!" The poet offers
stocks, bonds, money for the privilege.

> Now—have I bought it—
> "Shylock?" Say!
> Sign me the Bond!

In another poem Dickinson says of an orchard at the coming of day that it "sparkled like a Jew." And in a fourth poem she writes that she knows only "the names, of Gems," but if her lover's smiles could only be hers, she would "but be a Jew." It is altogether likely that this exquisite mind had no immediate knowledge of the modern Jew, but was introducing the literary stereotype as she might any other established metaphor.

(Harap, *The Image of the Jew in American Literature*, pp. 101–102)

8

The Romantic and Victorian Periods in England

WILLIAM BLAKE   *(1757–1827)*

British poet and painter

If humility is Christianity, you, O Jews! are the true Christians.
(Selections from Jerusalem, 1804–1820)

SAMUEL TAYLOR COLERIDGE   *(1772–1834)*

British poet

I have had a good deal to do with Jews in the course of my life, although I never borrowed any money from them. Once I sat in a coach opposite a Jew—a symbol of old clothes' bag—an Isaiah of Holywell Street. He would close the window; I opened it. He closed it again; upon which, in a very solemn tone, I said to him: 'Son of Abraham! thou smellest; son of Isaac! thou art offensive; son of Jacob! thou stinkest foully. See the man in the moon! He is holding his nose at thee in the distance; dost thou think that I, sitting here, can endure it any longer?' My Jew was astounded, opened the window forthwith himself, and said he was sorry he did not know before I was so great a gentleman.

(The Complete Works of Samuel Taylor Coleridge, 1884; VI, p. 474)

* * *

The other day I was *floored* by a Jew. He passed me several times, crying for old clothes, in the most nasal and extraordinary tone I ever heard. At last, I was so provoked that I said to him, 'Pray, why can't you say "old clothes" in a plain way, as I do now?' The Jew stopped, and looking very gravely at me, said in a clear and even fine accent, 'Sir, I can say "old clothes" as well as you can; but if you had to say it ten times a minute, for an hour together, you would say *ogh clo* as I do

137

now'; and so he marched off. I was so confounded with the justice of his retort, that I followed and gave him a shilling, the only one I had.
(*The Complete Works of Samuel Taylor Coleridge*, 1884, VII, p. 474)

WILLIAM HAZLITT   (1778–1830)

British critic

The Jews are shut up here in a quarter by themselves. I see no reason for it. . . . There was a talk (it being *Anno Santo*) of shutting them up for the whole of the present year. . . . Owing to the politeness of the age, they no longer burn them as of yore, and that is something. Religious zeal, like all other things, grows old and feeble.
(From *Notes of a Journey Through France and Italy*, 1826, on the ghetto of Rome)

* * *

The Emancipation of the Jews is but a natural step in the progress of civilization. . . . it is said, "The Jews at present have few grievances to complain of; they are well off, and should be thankful for the indulgence they receive." It is true, we no longer burn them at a stake, or plunder them of their goods: why then continue to insult and fix an idle stigma on them? At Rome, a few years ago, they made the Jews run races (naked) in the Corso on Good Friday. At present, they only oblige them to provide asses to run races on the same day for the amusement of the populace, and to keep up the spirit of the good old custom, though by altering it they confess that the custom was wrong, and that they are ashamed of it. They also shut up the Jews in a particular quarter of the city (called Il Ghetto Judaico) and at the same time will not suffer the English as heretics to be buried within the walls of Rome. An Englishman smiles or is scandalized at both these instances of bigotry; but if he is asked, "Why then do you not yourselves emancipate the Catholics and the Jews?" he may answer, "We *have* emancipated the one." And why not the other? "Because we are intolerant." This, and this alone, is the reason.

We throw in the teeth of the Jews, that they are prone to certain sordid vices. If they are vicious, it is we who have made them so. Shut out any class of people from the path to fair fame, and you reduce them to grovel in the pursuit of riches and the means to live. A man has long been in dread of insult for no just cause, and you complain that he grows reserved and suspicious. You treat him with obloquy and contempt, and wonder that he does not walk by you with an erect and open brow.

We also object to their trades and modes of life; that is, we shut people up in close confinement, and complain that they do not live in the open air. The Jews barter and sell commodities, instead of raising or manufacturing them. But this is the necessary traditional consequence of their former persecution and pillage by all nations. They could not set up a trade when they were hunted every moment from place to place, and while they could count nothing their own but what they could carry with them. They could not devote themselves to the pursuit of agriculture, when they were not allowed to possess a foot of land. You tear people up by the roots, and trample on them like noxious weeds, and then make an outcry that they do not take root in the soil like wholesome plants. You drive them like a pest from city to city, from kingdom to kingdom, and then call them vagabonds and aliens. . . .

The proposal to admit Jews to a seat in Parliament in this country is treated as an irony or a burlesque on the Catholic question. . . . as everything in this country is done by money alone, the Stock Exchange would soon buy up the House of Commons; and if a single Jew were admitted, the whole would shortly be a perfect Sanhedrin. This is a pleasant account of English patriotism, and the texture of the House of Commons. All the wealth of the Jews cannot buy them a single seat there; but if a certain formal restriction were taken off, Jewish gold would buy up the fee simple of the consciences, prejudices and interests of the country, and turn the kingdom *topsy-turvey*. Thus the bedrid imagination of prejudice sees some dreadful catastrophe in every improvement, and no longer feeling the ground of custom under its feet, fancies itself on an abyss of ruin and lawless change. . . .

. . . Hatred is the food and growth of ignorance. While we know nothing but ourselves and our own notions, we can conceive of nothing else as possible; and every deviation from our practice or opinions gives a shock to our faith that nothing can expiate but blows. Those who differ from us in the smallest particular are considered as of a different species, and we treat them accordingly. But this barrier of prejudice, which is founded on ignorance, is thrown down by the diffusion of light and knowledge; nor can any thing build it up again. In the good old times, a Jew was regarded by the vulgar and their betters as a sort of monster . . . whose existence they could not account for, and would not tolerate. The only way to get rid of the obnoxious opinion was to destroy the *man*. . . . While it was supposed that "the Jews eat little children," it was proper to take precautions against them. But why keep up ill names and the ill odour of a prejudice, when the prejudice has ceased to exist? It has long ceased amongst the reflecting part of the community; and, although the oldest prejudices are, it is to be lamented, preserved longest in the highest places, and governments to have been slow to learn good manners, we cannot but be conscious that these days are passing away. We begin to see, if we do not fully see, that we have no superiority to boast of but reason and philosophy, and that it is well to get rid of vulgar prejudices and nominal distinctions as fast as possible.

(Hazlitt, "On Jewish Emancipation," in *The Tatler*, 28 March 1831)

THOMAS DE QUINCEY   *(1785–1859)*

British critic and author of Confessions of an English Opium Eater

Greece was, in fact, *too* ebullient with intellectual activity—an activity too palestric and purely human—so that the opposite pole of the mind, which points to the mysterious and the spiritual, was, in the agile Greek, too intensely a child of the earth, starved and palsied; whilst in the Hebrew, dully and inert intellectually, but in his spiritual organs awake and sublime, the case was precisely reversed. Yet, after all, the result was immeasurably in favor of the Hebrew.

Speaking in the deep sincerities of the solitary and musing heart which refuses to be duped by the whistling of names, we must say of the Greek—*laudatur et alget*: he has won the admiration of the human race, he is numbered amongst the chief brilliancies of earth, but on the deeper and more abiding nature of man he has no hold. He will perish when any deluge of calamity overtakes the libraries of our planet, or if any great revolution of thought remoulds them, and will be remembered only as a generation of flowers is remembered; with the same tenderness of feeling and with the same pathetic sense of a natural predestination to evanescence. Whereas the Hebrew, by introducing himself to the secret places of the human heart and sitting there as incubator over the awful germs of the spiritualities that connect man with the unseen worlds, has perpetuated himself as a power in the human system: he is co-enduring with man's race, and careless of all revolutions in literature or in the composition of society.

("Language," in *Works*, vol. IX, p. 81)

GEORGE GORDON BYRON   *(1788–1824)*

British poet

Needing literary occupation, Byron turned to writing some notes for *Childe Harold* in which he attempted to formulate his ideas on the Greeks as a people and a nation. . . .

He wrote with feeling and conviction: ". . . it seems to me rather hard to declare so positively and pertinaciously, as almost everybody has declared, that the Greeks, because they are very bad, will never be better. . . . At present, like the Catholics of Ireland and the Jews throughout the world . . . they suffer all the moral and physical ills that can afflict humanity. . . .

(L. A. Marchand, *Byron—A Portrait*, p. 94)

SIR ROBERT PEEL   *(1788–1850)*

British prime minister and founder of Conservative Party

"For the Jews I see no place of justice whatever; they are voluntary strangers here, and have no claim to become citizens but by conforming to our moral law, which is the Gospel."

(In the House of Commons, 17 April 1833, quoting the words of Dr. Thomas Arnold, headmaster of Rugby)

PERCY BYSSHE SHELLEY   *(1792–1822)*

British poet

All that miserable tale of the Devil and Eve, and an Intercessor with the childish mummeries of the God of the Jews, is irreconcilable with the knowledge of the stars.

(A Philosophical View of Reform, 1819)

THOMAS BABINGTON MACAULAY   *(1800–1859)*

British historian and essayist

. . . If no man has a right to political power, than neither Jew nor Christian has such a right. The whole foundation of government is taken away. . . . It is because men are not in the habit of considering what the end of government is, that Catholic disabilities and Jewish disabilities have been suffered to exist so long. We hear of essentially Protestant governments and essentially Christian governments— words which mean just as much as essentially Protestant cookery, or essentially Christian horsemanship. . . . why a man should be less fit to exercise that power because he wears a beard, because he does not eat ham, because he goes to the synagogue on Saturdays instead of going to the church on Sundays, we cannot conceive.

The points of difference between Christianity and Judaism have very much to do with a man's fitness to be a bishop or rabbi. But they have no more to do with his fitness to be a magistrate, a legislator, or a minister of finance, than with his fitness to be a cobbler. Nobody has ever thought of compelling cobblers to make any declaration on the true faith of a Christian. . . . We have surely had two signal proofs within the last twenty years, that a very good Christian may be a very bad Chancellor of the Exchequer.

But it would be monstrous, say the persecutors, that a Jew should legislate for a Christian community. This is a palpable misrepresenta-tion. What is proposed is not that Jews should legislate for a Christian community, but that a legislature composed of Christians and Jews, should legislate for a community composed of Christians and Jews.

On nine hundred and ninety-nine questions out of a thousand, — on all questions of police, of finance, of civil and criminal law, of foreign policy, the Jew, as a Jew, has no interest hostile to that of the Christian, or even of the Churchman. . . .

If it is our duty as Christians to exclude the Jews from political power, it must be our duty to treat them as our ancestors treated them — to murder them, and banish them, and rob them. For in that way, and in that way alone, can we really deprive them of political power. If we do not adopt this course, we may take away the shadow, but we must leave them the substance.

. . . It has always been the trick of bigots to make their subjects miserable at home, and then complain that they look for relief abroad; — to divide society, and to wonder that it is not united; — to govern as if a section of the state were the whole, and to censure the other sections of the state for their want of patriotic spirit. If the Jews have not felt toward England like children, it is because she has treated them like a step-mother. There is no feeling which more certainly develops itself in the minds of men living under tolerably good government, than the feeling of patriotism. Since the beginning of the world, there never was any nation, or any large portion of any nation, not cruelly oppressed, which was wholly destitute of that feeling. To make it therefore ground of accusation against a class of men, that they are not patriotic, is the most vulgar legerdemain of sophistry. It is the logic which the wolf employs against the lamb. It is to accuse the mouth of the stream of poisoning the source. It is to put the effect before the cause. It is to vindicate oppression, by pointing at the depravation which oppression has produced.

If the English Jews really felt a deadly hatred to England — if the weekly prayer of their synagogues were that all the curses denounced by Ezekiel on Tyre and Egypt might fall on London; — if in their solemn feasts, they called down blessings on those who should dash our children to pieces on the stones, still, we say, their hatred to their countrymen would not be more intense than that which sects of Christians have often borne to each other. But, in fact, the feeling of the Jews is not such. It is precisely what, in the situation in which they are placed, we should expect it to be. . . .

. . . it passes for an argument to say that a Jew will take no interest in the prosperity of the country in which he lives, that he will not care how bad its laws and police may be . . . because God has pronounced that by some unknown means, and at some undetermined time, perhaps a thousand years hence, the Jews shall migrate to Palestine. Is not this the most profound ignorance of human nature? Do we not know that what is remote and indefinite affects men far less than what is near and certain? Besides, the argument applies to Christians as strongly as to Jews. The Christian believes, as well as the Jew, that at some future period the present order of things will come to an end. Nay, many Christians believe that the Messiah will shortly establish a kingdom on earth, and reign visibly over all its inhabitants. . . .

Now, wherein does this doctrine differ, as far as its political tendency is concerned, from the doctrine of the Jews? If a Jew is unfit to legislate for us, because he believes that he or his remote descendants will be removed to Palestine, can we safely open the House of Commons to a fifth-monarchy-man, who expects that, before this generation shall pass away, all the kingdoms of the earth will be swallowed up in one divine empire? . . .

("Civil Disabilities of the Jews," in
The Edinburgh Review, January 1831)

JOHN STUART MILL   *(1806–1873)*

British philosopher and political economist

In contrast with these nations [Egypt and China], let us consider the example of an opposite character afforded by another and a comparatively insignificant Oriental people—the Jews. They, too, had an absolute monarchy and a hierarchy, and their organized institutions were as obviously of sacerdotal origin as those of the Hindoos. These did for them what was done for other Oriental races by their institutions—subdued them to industry and order, and gave them a national life. But neither their kings nor their priests ever obtained, as in those other countries, the exclusive moulding of their character.

Their religion, which enabled persons of genius and a high religious tone to be regarded and to regard themselves as inspired from heaven, gave existence to an inestimably precious unorganized institution—the Order (if it may be so termed) of Prophets. Under the protection, generally though not always effectual, of their sacred character, the Prophets were a power in the nation, often more than a match for kings and priests, and kept up, in that little corner of the earth, the antagonism of influences which is the only real security for continued progress. Religion consequently was not there, what it has been in so many other places—a consecration of all that was once established, and a barrier against further improvement.

The remark of a distinguished Hebrew, M. Salvador, that the Prophets were, in Church and State, the equivalent of the modern liberty of the press, gives a just but not an adequate conception of the part fulfilled in national and universal history by this great element of Jewish life; by means of which, the canon of inspiration never being complete, the persons most eminent in genius and moral feeling could not only denounce and reprobate, with the direct authority of the Almighty, whatever appeared to them deserving of such treatment, but could give forth better and higher interpretations of the national religion, which thenceforth became part of the religion. . . .

Conditions more favorable to Progress could not easily exist: accordingly, the Jews, instead of being stationary like other Asiatics, were, next to the Greeks, the most progressive people of antiquity, and, jointly with them, have been the starting-point and main propelling agency of modern cultivation.

(*Considerations on Representative Government*, p. 51)

WILLIAM EWART GLADSTONE   (1809–1898)

British Liberal prime minister

But indeed there is no need, in order to [give] a due appreciation of our debt to the ancient Greeks, that we should either forget or disparage the function which was assigned by the Almighty Father to His most favored people. . . .

No poetry, no philosophy, no art of Greece ever embraced, in its most soaring and widest conceptions, that simple law of love towards God and towards our neighbor, on which "two commandments hang all the law and the prophets," and which supplied the moral basis of the new dispensation.

There is one history, and that the most touching and most profound of all, for which we should search in vain through all the pages of the classics—I mean the history of the human soul in its relations with its Maker; the history of its sin, and grief, and death, and of the way of its recovery to hope and life and to enduring joy. For the exercises of strength and skill, for the achievements and for the enchantments of wit, of eloquence, of art, of genius, for the imperial games of politics and war—let us seek them on the shores of Greece.

But if the first among the problems of life be how to establish the peace, and restore the balance, of our inward being; if the highest of all conditions in the existence of the creature be his aspect towards the God to whom he owes his being and in whose great hand he stands; then let us make our search elsewhere. All the wonders of the Greek civilization heaped together are less wonderful, than is the single Book of Psalms.

(From his address "Place of Ancient Greece in the Providential Order," 1865)

CHARLES DICKENS   (1812–1870)

British novelist and reformer

[At the coronation of Edward I], there was such eating and drinking, such music and capering, such a ringing of bells and tossing of caps, such a shouting, and singing, and revelling, as the narrow overhanging streets of old London City had not witnessed for many a long day. All the people were merry—except the poor Jews, who, trembling within their houses, and scarcely daring to peep out, began to foresee that they would have to find the money for this joviality sooner or later.

To dismiss this sad subject of the Jews for the present, I am sorry to add that in this reign they were mostly unmercifully pillaged. They were hanged in great numbers, on accusations of having clipped the King's coin—which all kinds of people had done. They were heavily taxed; they were disgracefully badged; they were, on one day, thirteen years after the coronation, taken up with their wives and children and thrown into beastly prisons, until they purchased their release by paying to the King twelve thousand pounds. Finally, every kind of property belonging to them was seized by the King, except so little as would defray the charge of their taking themselves away into foreign countries. Many years elapsed before the hope of gain induced any of their race to return to England, where they had been treated so heartlessly and suffered so much.

(*Child's History of England*, ch. 16)

* * *

With the close of the summer [1864] Dickens's thoughts were turning more and more purposefully to his new serial, *Our Mutual Friend.* . . . Only a short time earlier there had come to him a communication that curiously influenced the design of his story. Mrs. Eliza Davis, the wife of the gentleman who had bought Tavistock House, wrote him a letter telling him that Jews regarded his portrayal of Fagin in *Oliver Twist* as "a great wrong" to their people. Only once before had this reproach come to his eyes, in 1854, when the *Jewish Chronicle* had asked "why Jews alone should be excluded from the sympathizing heart" of this great author and powerful friend of the oppressed. At that time, responding to an invitation to an anniversary dinner of the Westminster Jewish Free School, he had replied: "I know of no reason the Jews can have for regarding me as 'inimical' to them. On the contrary, I believe I do my part toward the assertion of their civil and religious liberty, and in my *Child's History of England* I have expressed a strong abhorrence of their persecution in old time." Now he felt impelled to defend himself in more detail.

If Jews thought him unjust to them, he replied, they were "a far less sensible, a far less just, and a far less good-tempered people than I have always supposed them to be." Fagin, he pointed out, was the only Jew in the story (he had forgotten the insignificant character of Barney) and "all the rest of the wicked *dramatis personae* are Christians." Fagin had been described as a Jew, he explained, "because it unfortunately was true of the time to which that story refers, that that class of criminal almost invariably was a Jew." (Which was not to say, of course, that all, or even many, Jews were receivers of stolen goods.) And finally, Dickens continued, in calling Fagin a Jew no imputation had been suggested against the Jewish religion; the name had been intended in the same way in which one might call a Frenchman or

Spaniard or Chinese by those names. "I have no feeling towards the Jews but a friendly one," Dickens concluded his letter. "I always speak well of them, whether in public or private, and bear my testimony (as I ought to do) to their perfect good faith in such transactions as I have ever had with them. . . ."

Nevertheless, although Dickens felt it absurd to regard Fagin as typifying his feelings about Jews, he was troubled at being so seriously misinterpreted. In *Our Mutual Friend* he therefore included a group of Jewish characters, of whom the most important is Mr. Riah, a gentle and upright old Jew caught in the toils of a *Christian* moneylender. Lizzie Hexam, one of the two heroines, takes refuge in affliction among a community of Jews, who treat her with the most generous tenderness. To a clergyman worried about her remaining with them, she defends her Jewish employers: "The gentleman certainly is a Jew," she says, "and the lady, his wife, is a Jewess, and I was brought to their notice by a Jew. But I think there cannot be kinder people in the world."

Near the end of the book there is a passage showing that Dickens had reflected upon Mrs. Davis's reproach and understood how it came to be made, even though it imputed to him an injustice he had never intended. "For it is not in Christian countries with the Jews as with other peoples," Mr. Riah reflects. "Men say, 'This is a bad Greek, but there are good Greeks. This is a bad Turk, but there are good Turks.' Not so with the Jews. Men find the bad among us easily enough— among what peoples are the bad not easily found?—but they take the worst of us as samples of the best; they take the lowest of us as presentations of the highest; and they say 'All Jews are alike.'"

Mrs. Davis saw the meaning of this group of Jewish characters. During the course of the novel's serial publication she wrote to Dickens in terms that can be inferred from his reply: "I have received your letter with great pleasure, and hope to be (as I have always been in my heart) the best of friends with the Jewish people." Some years later she gave him a copy of Benisch's *Hebrew and English Bible*, inscribed: "Presented to Charles Dickens, in grateful and admiring recognition of his having exercised the noblest quality men can possess—that of atoning for an injury as soon as conscious of having inflicted it." These words, Dickens told her, were more gratifying than he could possibly express, "for they assure me that there is nothing but good will left between you and me and a people for whom I have a real regard, and to whom I would not willfully have given an offense or done an injustice for any worldly consideration."

(Johnson, Charles Dickens—His Tragedy and Triumph,
vol. II, pp. 1010–1012)

ROBERT BROWNING *(1812 1889)*

British poet

In accounting for the Jewish element in Browning's poems, it may be well to examine the ground for rumors to the effect that the author was himself a Jew. Many persons will remember that at the time of the poet's death such statements were common. Some time since, I wrote to Mr. Oswald John Simon, a distinguished member of the Hebrew race in London, asking if he could give me definite information on this head. In response he says,—

"I am not aware that there is any truth in the reports regarding the connection of Robert Browning with the Jewish race. My opinion is that such reports have arisen in consequence of the fact that members of his family have held positions in the eminent house of Rothschild both in Paris and in London. I do not know that there is any evidence of the poet having descended from the Jewish race. He certainly was not personally of it. He was, however, as everybody knows, a most valued champion and defender of our people, and entertained the highest admiration for Jewish history."

To my mind this assurance from one in a position to know whereof he speaks is conclusive, and I feel satisfied that the broad and liberal basis upon which our poet has created such gems as "Rabbi Ben Ezra," "Jochanan," and "Holy Cross Day" is one not to be apologized for on the grounds of racial sympathy, but admired, gloried in as proof of true Christian feeling, of the "charity which thinketh no evil," of a nobility of soul which found good in everything. . . .

. . . Jewish clergymen make comparatively no use of the philosophical and practical lessons to be derived from a study of ["Rabbi Ben Ezra"]. . . . And yet Browning has in it seized the essence of Jewish faith and hope, holding it aloft in the crystal of language. There is no doubt that the writer had drunk deeply at the well of Hebraic thought;

not otherwise could he have composed verses which in their majestic music and their noble meaning seem to echo something of the solemn earnestness and inspiration of Isaiah or Job. . . . If the Jewish people do not appreciate what Browning has done for them in "Rabbi Ben Ezra," then I think it is high time to alter the Hebrews of this land. The value of the Hebrew element in Browning's poems is that it does much to remove prejudice, and to place the philosophy of the Jew in its true place among the world's "Credos." A Ben Ezra and a Jochanan may supplant a Shylock and a Fagin in public estimation. This is an effect much to be desired. When in looking through a graphic and beautiful picture of the life of Montefiore by Samuel W. Cooper, I am reminded of the condition of the Jewish people in England a hundred years ago, it may be held a blessing that one of England's greatest poets has shown such intelligent comprehension of the claims of the "little drop in the ocean." The most satisfying assurance is that he who is capable of this generous spirit will entertain it for all peoples, not for one alone. . . .

I find the poet astonishingly correct, as a rule, in his grasp of the Hebraic nature. In but one poem does he seem to me to introduce a feature with which I can justly find fault; I mean the anachronism and unfitness of attaching the Trinitarian idea to such a distinctly Jewish poem as "Saul." It is natural that the writer, from his own point of view and his personal belief, should wish to connect the old and the new, the monotheistic faith of the Hebrew prophet and king with the later dictum of the Founder of Christianity; but of course to the Jewish student, the introduction of this incompatible feature mars the otherwise unified beauty of a glorious production. . . .

(M. M. Cohen, "Browning's Hebraic Sympathies," in
Poet-Lore, vol. III, 1891, pp. 250–254)

ANTHONY TROLLOPE   (1815–1882)

British novelist

Trollope's attitude toward Jews is not so clearly marked. In the novels he makes less use of the Jew than of the Roman Catholic, principally, one judges, because his contacts with the former were not broad. Of course, he introduces the Jew conventionally as a usurer; and since so many of his plots turn upon or at least involve a "bit of paper," the usurer is a familiar type in the novels. In the bitter days of his junior clerkship Trollope had become wearisomely acquainted with the discounter of bills, and it was no doubt difficult for him to think of the Jew in any other connection. Nevertheless, it is instructive of his broadness in matters of race and religion to examine *Nina Balatka*, a novel given an unfamiliar setting among the Jewish colony of Prague. The Victorian pattern of fiction provided, in general, for two Jewish characterizations—both stereotypes: the ogre, such as Fagin of *Oliver Twist*; and the demigod, such as Riah of *Our Mutual Friend*. Whatever function these characters might have in a morality play, they are unsuccessful in a realistic novel, for each represents an extreme of aberrant human conduct. The use of these types, unless obviously for allegorical purposes, argues on the part of the novelist either a willful perversion of human nature or a fundamental failure to understand it. In *Nina Balatka* Trollope does not entirely avoid the stereotype, for Rebecca Loth is something of a demigoddess; but the Trendellsohns are carefully individualized and very human. Stephen, the father, is an idealist, but he has not conquered all his prejudices. Anton, the son, a remarkably acute study in racial history, rises above the ghetto environment of his youth. In a more ambitious and infinitely more difficult psychological portrait than he usually attempted, Trollope develops in Anton the disabling experiences of ghetto segregation and persecution. Anton has a number of regrettable character traits: he is stubborn, haughty, suspicious; but he is honest, sincere, and honorable. In him Trollope traces the disintegration of European ghetto society and the emergence of a more self-reliant Jewish individualist who can escape environmental neuroses. Where Fagin and Riah are copybook studies in black and white and appeal to the critically naive, Anton is delicately drawn in subtle gray shadings more likely to appeal to the critically mature. Whether or not Trollope's handling of Jewish scenes and characters indicates any affection for the group, it is pretty clear that he could use Jews objectively for artistic purposes, seeing in them the same mixed qualities of mind and heart that animated the Anglicans of Barchester.

Trollope shows no such tolerance toward the Evangelical faiths. . . .

(Booth, *Anthony Trollope: Aspects of His Life and Art*,
pp. 30–31)

. . . He is showing irritation against religious bigotry and against narrow sectarianism, as he always did. *Some* Protestant groups, he felt, were guilty of perverting Christian ideals. The Jews and the Catholics are portrayed in a softer, kindlier light than are the Protestants, but Trollope is merely preaching religious tolerance, not arguing the blessings of any religion. In England Catholics and Jews were minority religious groups, and perhaps scorned by some of the thoughtless. In Prague and Nuremberg Protestants were the minority group. To bring Protestantism to the bar and arraign it for bigotry under such circumstances of reversed situation is to teach the lesson of tolerance very effectively. Trollope never had anything but affection for his own church, but the excesses of a withering sectarianism he fought bitterly.

(Booth, *Anthony Trollope: Aspects of His Life and Art*, p. 68)

GEORGE ELIOT (MARY ANNE EVANS)   *(1819–1880)*

British novelist; author of Silas Marner, Middlemarch

. . . even at this stage of European culture one's attention is continually drawn to the prevalence of that grosser mental sloth which makes people dull to the most ordinary prompting of comparison—the bringing things together because of their likeness. . . .

To take only the subject of the Jews: it would be difficult to find a form of bad reasoning about them which has not been heard in conversation or been admitted to the dignity of print; but the neglect of resemblances is a common property of dullness which unites all the various points of view—the prejudiced, the puerile, the spiteful, and the abysmally ignorant. . . .

. . . The European world has long been used to consider the Jews as altogether exceptional, and it has followed naturally enough that they have been excepted from the rules of justice and mercy, which are based on human likeness. But to consider a people whose ideas have determined the religion of half the world, and that the more cultivated half, and who made the most eminent struggle against the power of Rome, as a purely exceptional race, is a demoralizing offence against rational knowledge, a stultifying inconsistency in historical interpretation. Every nation of forcible character—*i.e.*, of strongly marked characteristics, is so far exceptional. The distinctive note of each bird-species is in this sense exceptional, but the necessary ground of such distinction is a deeper likeness. The superlative peculiarity in the Jews admitted, our affinity with them is only the more apparent when the elements of their peculiarity are discerned.

From whatever point of view the writings of the Old Testament may be regarded, the picture they present of a national development is of high interest and speciality, nor can their historic momentousness be much affected by any varieties of theory as to the relation they bear to the New Testament or to the rise and constitution of Christianity. Whether we accept the canonical Hebrew books as a revelation or simply as part of an ancient literature, makes no difference to the fact that we find there the strongly characterized portraiture of a people educated from an earlier or later period to a sense of separateness unique in its intensity, a people taught by many concurrent influences to identify faithfulness to its national traditions with the highest social and religious blessings. Our too scanty sources of Jewish history, from the return under Ezra to the beginning of the desperate re-sistance against Rome, show us the heroic and triumphant struggle of the Maccabees, which rescued the religion and independence of the nation from the corrupting sway of the Syrian Greeks, adding to the glorious sum of its memorials, and stimulating continuous efforts of a more peaceful sort to maintain and develop that national life which the heroes had fought and died for, by internal measures of legal administration and public teaching. Thenceforth the virtuous elements of the Jewish life were engaged, as they had been with varying aspects during the long and changeful prophetic period and the restoration under Ezra, on the side of preserving the specific national character against a demoralizing fusion with that of foreigners whose religion and ritual were idolatrous and often obscene. . . .

. . . I share the spirit of the Zealots. I take the spectacle of the Jewish people defying the Roman edict, and preferring death by starvation or the sword to the introduction of Caligula's deified statue into the temple, as a sublime type of steadfastness. But all that need be noticed here is the continuity of that national education (by outward and inward circumstance) which created in the Jews a feeling of race, a sense of corporate existence, unique in its intensity. . . .

We must rather refer the passionate use of the Hebrew writings to affinities of disposition between our own race and the Jewish. Is it true that the arrogance of a Jew was so immeasurably beyond that of a Calvinist? And the just sympathy and admiration which we give to the ancestors who resisted the oppressive acts of our native kings, and by resisting rescued or won for us the best part of our civil and religious liberties—is it justly to be withheld from those brave and steadfast men of Jewish race who fought and died, or strove by wise administration to resist, the oppression and corrupting influences of foreign tyrants, and by resisting, rescued the nationality which was the very hearth of our own religion? At any rate, seeing that the Jews were more specifically than any other nation educated into a sense of their supreme moral value, the chief matter of surprise is that any other nation is found to rival them in this form of self-confidence.

More exceptional—less like the course of our own history—has been their dispersion and their subsistence as a separate people through ages in which for the most part they were regarded and treated very much as beasts hunted for the sake of their skins, or of a valuable secretion peculiar to their species. The Jews showed a talent for accumulating what was an object of more immediate desire to Christians than animal oils or well-furred skins, and their cupidity and avarice were found at once particularly hateful and particularly useful: hateful when seen as a reason for punishing them by mulcting or robbery, useful when this retributive process could be successfully carried forward. Kings and emperors naturally were more alive to the usefulness of subjects who could gather and yield money; but edicts issued to protect "the King's Jews" equally with the King's game from being harassed and hunted by the commonalty were only slight mitigations to the deplorable lot of a race held to be under the divine curse, and had little force after the Crusades began. As the slave-holders in the United States counted the curse on Ham a justification of negro slavery, so the curse on the Jews was counted a justification for hindering them from pursuing agriculture and handicrafts; for marking them out as execrable figures by a peculiar dress; for torturing them to make them part with their gains, or for more gratuitously spitting at them and pelting them; for taking it as certain that they killed and ate babies, poisoned the wells, and took pains to spread the plague; for putting it to them whether they would be baptized or burned, and not failing to burn and massacre them when they were obstinate; but also for suspecting them of disliking the baptism when they had got it, and then burning them in punishment of their insincerity; finally, for hounding them by tens on tens of thousands from the homes where they had found shelter for centuries, and inflicting on them the horrors of a new exile and a new dispersion. All this to avenge the Saviour of mankind, or else to compel these stiff-necked people to acknowledge a Master whose servants showed such beneficent effects of His teaching.

With a people so treated one of two issues was possible: either from being a feebler nature than their persecutors, and caring more for ease than for the sentiments and ideas which constituted their distinctive character, they would everywhere give way to pressure and get rapidly merged in the populations around them; or, being endowed with uncommon tenacity, physical and mental, feeling peculiarly the ties of inheritance both in blood and faith, remembering national glories, trusting in their recovery, abhorring apostasy, able to bear all things and hope all things with the consciousness of being steadfast to spiritual obligations, the kernel of their number would harden into an inflexibility more and more insured by motive and habit. They would cherish all differences that marked them with a sense of virtual though unrecognized superiority; and the separateness which was made their badge of ignominy would be their inward pride, their source of fortifying defiance. Doubtless such a people would get confirmed in vices. An oppressive government and a persecuting religion, while breeding vices in those who hold power, are well known to breed answering vices in those who are powerless and suffering. What more direct plan than the course presented by European history could have been pursued in order to give the Jews a spirit of bitter isolation, of scorn for the wolfish hypocrisy that made victims of them, of triumph in prospering at the expense of the blunderers who stoned them away from the open paths of industry? – or, on the other hand, to encourage in the less defiant a lying conformity, a pretence of conversion for the sake of the social advantages attached to baptism, an outward renunciation of their hereditary ties with the lack of real love towards the society and creed which exacted this galling tribute? – or again, in the most unhappy specimens of the race, to rear transcendent examples of odious vice, reckless instruments of rich men with bad propensities, unscrupulous grinders of the alien people who wanted to grind *them*?

No wonder the Jews have their vices: no wonder if it were proved (which it has not hitherto appeared to be) that some of them have a bad pre-eminence in evil, an unrivalled superfluity of naughtiness. It would be more plausible to make a wonder of the virtues which have prospered among them under the shadow of oppression. But instead of dwelling on these, or treating as admitted what any hardy or ignorant person may deny, let us found simply on the loud assertions of the hostile. The Jews, it is said, resisted the expansion of their own religion into Christianity; they were in the habit of spitting on the cross; they have held the name of Christ to be *Anathema*. Who taught them that? The men who made Christianity a curse to them: the men who made the name of Christ a symbol for the spirit of vengeance, and, what was worse, made the execution of the vengeance a pretext for satisfying their own savageness, greed, and envy: the men who sanctioned with the name of Christ a barbaric and blundering copy of pagan fatalism in taking the words "His blood be upon us and on our children" as a divinely appointed verbal warrant for wreaking cruelty from generation to generation on the people from whose sacred writings Christ drew his teaching. Strange retrogression in the professors of an expanded religion, boasting an illumination beyond the spiritual doctrine of Hebrew prophets! . . .

. . . It is more reverent to Christ to believe that He must have approved the Jewish martyrs who deliberately chose to be burned or massacred rather than be guilty of a blaspheming lie, more than He approved the rabble of crusaders who robbed and murdered them in His name. . . .

. . . mediaeval types of thinking—insisting that the Jews are made viciously cosmopolitan by holding the world's money-bag, that for them all national interests are resolved into the algebra of loans, that they have suffered an inward degradation stamping them as morally inferior, and—"serve them right," since they rejected Christianity. All which is mirrored in an analogy, namely, that of the Irish, also a servile race, who have rejected Protestantism though it has been repeatedly urged on them by fire and sword and penal laws, and whose place in the moral scale may be judged by our advertisements, where the clause, "No Irish need apply," parallels the sentence which for many polite persons sums up the question of Judaism—"I never *did* like the Jews." . . .

. . . a varied, impartial observation of the Jews in different countries tends to the impression that they have a predominant kindliness which must have been deeply ingrained in the constitution of their race to have outlasted the ages of persecution and oppression.

The concentration of their joys in domestic life has kept up in them the capacity of tenderness: the pity for the fatherless and the widow, the care for the women and the little ones, blent intimately with their religion, is a well of mercy that cannot long or widely be pent up by exclusiveness. And the kindliness of the Jew overflows the line of division between him and the Gentile. On the whole, one of the most remarkable phenomena in the history of this scattered people, made for ages "a scorn and a hissing," is, that after being subjected to this process, which might have been expected to be in every sense deteriorating and vitiating, they have come out of it (in any estimate which allows for numerical proportion) rivalling the nations of all European countries in healthiness and beauty of *physique*, in practical ability, in scientific and artistic aptitude, and in some forms of ethical value. A significant indication of their natural rank is seen in the fact that at this moment [1879] the leader of the Liberal party in Germany is a Jew, the leader of the Republican party in France is a Jew, and the head of the Conservative ministry in England is a Jew.

And here it is that we find the ground for the obvious jealousy which is now stimulating the revived expression of old antipathies. "The Jews," it is felt, "have a dangerous tendency to get the uppermost places not only in commerce but in political life. Their monetary hold on governments is tending to perpetuate in leading Jews a spirit of universal alienism (euphemistically called cosmopolitanism), even where the West has given them a full share in civil and political rights. A people with oriental sunlight in their blood, yet capable of being everywhere acclimatized, they have a force and toughness which enables them to carry off best prizes; and their wealth is likely to put half the seats in Parliament at their disposal."

There is truth in these views of Jewish social and political relations. But it is rather too late for liberal pleaders to urge them in a merely vituperative sense. Do they propose as a remedy for the impending danger of our healthier national influences getting over-ridden by Jewish predominance, that we should repeal our emancipatory laws? . . .

. . . Are we to adopt the exclusiveness for which we have punished the Chinese? Are we to tear the glorious flag of hospitality which has made our freedom the world-wide blessing of the oppressed? It is not agreeable to find foreign accents and stumbling locutions passing from the piquant exception to the general rule of discourse.

But to urge on that account that we should spike away the peaceful foreigner, would be a view of international relations not in the long-run favorable to the interests of our fellow-countrymen; for we are at least equal to the races we call obstrusive in the disposition to settle wherever money is to be made and cheaply idle living to be found. . . .

. . . Apart from theological purposes, it seems to be held surprising that anybody should take an interest in the history of a people whose literature has furnished all our devotional language; and if any reference is made to their past or future destinies some hearer is sure to state as a relevant fact which may assist our judgment, that she, for her part, is not fond of them, having known a Mr. Jacobson who was very unpleasant, or that he, for his part, thinks meanly of them as a race, though on inquiry you find that he is so little acquainted with their characteristics that he is astonished to learn how many persons whom he has blindly admired and applauded are Jews to the backbone. Again, men who consider themselves in the very van of modern advancement, knowing history and the latest philosophies of history, indicate their contemptuous surprise that any one should entertain the destiny of the Jews as a worthy subject, by referring to Moloch and their own agreement with the theory that the religion of Jehovah was merely a transformed Moloch-worship, while in the same breath they are glorifying "civilization" as a transformed tribal existence of which some lineaments are traceable in grim marriage customs of the native Australians. . . .

For less theoretic men, ambitious to be regarded as practical politicians, the value of the Hebrew race has been measured by their unfavorable opinion of a prime minister who is a Jew by lineage. But it is possible to form a very ugly opinion as to the scrupulousness of Walpole, or of Chatham; and in any case I think Englishmen would refuse to accept the character and doings of those eighteenth-century statesmen as the standard of value for the English people and the part they have to play in the fortunes of mankind.

If we are to consider the future of the Jews at all, it seems reasonable to take as a preliminary question: Are they destined to complete fusion with the peoples among whom they are dispersed, losing every remnant of a distinctive consciousness as Jews; or, are there in the breadth and intensity with which the feeling of separateness, or what we may call the organized memory of a national consciousness, actually exists in the world-wide Jewish communities — the seven millions scattered from east to west — and again, are there in the political relations of the world, the conditions present or approaching for the restoration of a Jewish state planted on the old ground as a centre of national feeling, a source of dignifying protection, a special channel for special energies which may contribute some added form of national genius, and an added voice in the councils of the world?

They are among us everywhere: it is useless to say we are not fond of them. Perhaps we are not fond of proletaries and their tendency to form Unions, but the world is not therefore to be rid of them. If we wish to free ourselves from the inconveniences that we have to complain of, whether in proletaries or in Jews, our best course is to encourage all means of improving these neighbors who elbow us in a thickening crowd, and of sending their incommodious energies into beneficent channels. Why are we so eager for the dignity of certain populations of whom perhaps we have never seen a single specimen, and of whose history, legend, or literature we have been contentedly ignorant for ages, while we sneer at the notion of a renovated national dignity for the Jews, whose ways of thinking and whose very verbal forms are on our lips in every prayer which we end with an Amen? Some of us consider this question dismissed when they have said that the wealthiest Jews have no desire to forsake their European palaces, and go to live in Jerusalem. But in a return from exile, in the restoration of a people, the question is not whether certain rich men will choose to remain behind, but whether there will be found worthy men who will choose to lead the return. Plenty of prosperous Jews remained in Babylon when Ezra marshalled his band of forty thousand and began a new glorious epoch in the history of his race, making the preparation for that epoch in the history of the world which has been held glorious enough to be dated from forevermore. The hinge of possibility is simply the existence of an adequate community of feeling as well as widespread need in the Jewish race, and the hope that among its finer specimens there may arise some men of instruction and ardent public spirit, some new Ezras, some modern Maccabees, who will know how to use all favoring outward conditions, how to triumph by heroic exemplar over the indifference of their fellows and the scorn of their foes, and will steadfastly set their faces towards making their people once more one among the nations.

Formerly, evangelical orthodoxy was prone to dwell on the fulfilment of prophecy in the "restoration of the Jews." Such interpretation of the prophets is less in vogue now. The dominant mode is to insist on a Christianity that disowns its origin, that is not a substantial growth having a genealogy, but is a vaporous reflex of modern notion. . . . Modern apostles, extolling Christianity, are found using a different tone: they prefer the medieval cry translated into modern phrase. But the mediaeval cry too was in substance very ancient — more ancient than the days of Augustus. Pagans in successive ages said, "These people are unlike us, and refuse to be made like us: let us punish them." The Jews were steadfast in their separateness, and through that separateness Christianity was born. A modern book on Liberty has maintained that from the freedom of individual men to persist in idiosyncrasies the world may be enriched. Why should we not apply this argument to the idiosyncrasy of a nation, and pause in our haste to hoot it down? There is still a great function for the steadfastness of the Jew: not that he should shut out the utmost illumination which knowledge can throw on his national history, but that he should cherish the store of inheritance which that history has left him. Every Jew should be conscious that he is one of a multitude possessing common objects of piety in the immortal achievements and immortal sorrows of ancestors who have transmitted to them a physical and mental type strong enough, eminent enough in faculties, pregnant enough with peculiar promise, to constitute a new beneficent individuality among the nations, and, by confuting the traditions of scorn, nobly avenge the wrongs done to their Fathers.

There is a sense in which the worthy child of a nation that has brought forth illustrious prophets, high and unique among the poets of the world, is bound by their visions.

Is bound?

Yes, for the effective bound of human action is feeling, and the worthy child of a people owning the triple name of Hebrew, Israelite, and Jew, feels his kinship with the glories and the sorrows, the degradation and the possible renovation of his national family.

Will any one teach the nullification of this feeling and call his doctrine a philosophy? He will teach a blinding superstition — the superstition that a theory of human well-being can be constructed in disregard of the influences which have made us human.

("The Modern Hep! Hep! Hep!" in Impressions of
Theophrastus Such, 1879)

JOHN RUSKIN   *(1819–1900)*

British art critic, poet, and author

In religion, which with me pervaded all the hours of life, I had been moved by the Jewish ideal, and as the perfect color and sound gradually asserted their power on me, they seemed finally to agree in the old article of Jewish faith that things done delightfully and rightfully were always done by the help and spirit of God. . . .

("Morals and Religion," *The True and the Beautiful*, VII)

SIR RICHARD BURTON   *(1821–1890)*

British scholar, explorer, and Orientalist

Physically and mentally, the Jewish man and woman are equal in all respects to their Gentile neighbors; and in some respects are superior to them. . . . We visit [the Jew], we dine with him, and we see him at all times and places, except perhaps at the Sunday service. We should enjoy his society but for a certain coarseness of manner, especially an offensive familiarity, which seems almost peculiar to him. We marvel at his talents, and we are struck by the adaptability and the universality of his genius. We admire his patience, his steadfastness and his courage, his military prowess and his successful career in every post and profession—statesman and senior wrangler, poet and literato, jurist, surgeon and physician, capitalist, financier and merchant, philosopher and engineer; in fact, everything that man can be. When we compare the Semite Premier with his Anglo-Saxon rival, it is much to the advantage of the former; while jesting about the Asian mystery, we cannot but feel there is something in the Asiatic which we do not expect, which eludes our ken, which goes beyond us. . . .

Of the middle and lower classes of Jews, the Englishman only hears that they are industrious, abstinent, and comparatively cleanly in person; decent, hospitable and as strict in keeping the Sabbath as the strictest Sabbatarians could desire. He is told that they are wondrous charitable in their dealings with those of the same faith, always provided that some mite of religious difference does not grow to a mountain size. . . .

To my mind, there are few things so admirable and wonderful as the "getting on" of the Hebrew race. Most Jews seem to rise. . . . The average Englishman smiles at their intense love of public amusements and their excessive fondness for display. . . .

(The Jew, the Gypsy, and El Islam, 1869–1871)

* * *

[Burton] himself was an adherent of no religion. He appears to have believed in some sort of providence—which he usually referred to as "Provy"—but not the deity of any existing religion. "The more I study religions," he wrote, "the more I am convinced that man never worshipped anything but himself." But he makes it quite clear that he preferred Islam to Christianity.

"There is no more immoral work than the Old Testament," he said. "Its deity is an ancient Hebrew of the worst type, who condones, permits or commands every sin in the Decalogue to a Jewish patriarch, *qua* patriarch." He cites passages in the Bible of "obscenity and impurity"; he lists other passages containing "horrors forbidden to the Jews, who, therefore have practiced them"; and still another series of Biblical passages are cited of which he says, "For mere filth what can be fouler." This part of the essay is an outright attack on Christianity. While he does not accept wholeheartedly the teachings of Mohammed, he uses Islam to make comparisons with Christianity that are never to the credit of the latter. . . .

(Farwell, Burton, pp. 380–381)

MATTHEW ARNOLD   *(1822–1888)*

British poet and critic

No people ever felt so strongly as the people of the Old Testament, the Hebrew people, that conduct is three-fourths of our life and its largest concern. No people ever felt so strongly that succeeding, going right, hitting the mark in this great concern, was *the way of peace*, the highest possible satisfaction. . . .

Then there is the practical force of their example; and this is even more important. Everyone is aware how those who want to cultivate any sense of endowment in themselves must be habitually conversant with the works of people who have been eminent for that sense, must study them, catch inspiration from them. Only in this way, indeed, can progress be made. And as long as the world lasts, all who want to make progress in righteousness will come to Israel for inspiration, as to the people who have had the sense for righteousness most glowing and strongest; and in hearing and reading the words Israel has uttered for us, carers for conduct will find a glow and a force they could find nowhere else.

(*Literature and Dogma*, pp. 26, 57)

THOMAS HENRY HUXLEY   (1825–1895)

British biologist and botanist

It seems to me that the moral and intellectual life of the civilized nations of Europe is the product of that interaction, sometimes in the way of antagonism, sometimes in that of profitable interchange, of the Semitic and the Aryan races, which commenced with the dawn of history, when Greek and Phoenician came in contact, and has been continued by Carthaginian and Roman, by Jew and Gentile, down to the present day. Our art (except, perhaps, music) and our science are the contributions of the Aryan; but the essence of our religion is derived from the Semite. In the eighth century B.C., in the herd of a world of idolatrous polytheists, the Hebrew prophets put forth a conception of religion which appears to me to be as wonderful an inspiration of genius as the art of Pheidias or the science of Aristotle.

"And what doth the Lord require of thee, but to do justly, to love mercy, and to walk humbly with thy God?"

If any so-called religion takes away from this great saying of Micah, I think it wantonly mutilates, while, if it adds thereto, I think it obscures, the perfect ideal of religion.

. . . The captivity made the fortune of the ideas which it was the privilege of these men [the prophets] to launch upon an endless career. With the abolition of the Temple-services for more than half a century, the priest must have lost and the scribe gained influence. The puritanism of a vigorous minority among the Babylonian Jews rooted out polytheism from all its hiding-places in the theology which they had inherited; they created the first consistent, remorseless, naked monotheism . . . ; and they inseparably united therewith an ethical code, which, for its purity and for its efficiency as a bond of social life, was and is unsurpassed. . . .

The world being what it was, it is to be doubted whether Israel would have preserved intact the pure ore of religion, which the prophets had extracted for the use of mankind as well as for their nation, had not the leaders of the nation been zealous, even to death, for the dross of the law in which it was embedded. The struggle of the Jews, under the Maccabean house, against the Seleucidae was as important for mankind as that of the Greeks against the Persians. And, of all the strange ironies of history, perhaps the strangest is that "Pharisee" is current as a term of reproach among the theological descendants of that sect of Nazarenes who, without the martyr spirit of those primitive Puritans, would never have come into existence. They, like their historical successors, our own Puritans, have shared the general fate of the poor wise men who save cities.

(Huxley, "The Interpreters of Genesis and the Interpreters of Nature" in *Science and Hebrew Tradition*, p. 161. 1885)

ROBERT LOUIS STEVENSON   *(1850–1894)*

Scottish novelist and poet

Stevenson to Miss Adelaide Boodle, May 1891:

What a strange idea, to think me a Jew-hater! Isaiah and David and Heine are good enough for me; and I leave more unsaid. Were I of Jew blood, I do not think I could ever forgive the Christians; the ghettos would get in my nostrils like mustard or lit gunpowder. . . . were he of mine, I should not be struck at all by Mr. Moss of Bevis Marks; I should still see behind him Moses of the Mount and the Tables and the shining face. We are all nobly born; fortunate those who know it; blessed those who remember.

(Colvin, *The Letters of Robert Louis Stevenson*, vol. II, p. 273)

RIDER HAGGARD   *(1856–1925)*

British author

The conflict within him between the fanciful and the practical made his character complex and inconsistent. There is ample evidence that in his everyday life he was charitable toward his fellow-man, and yet he also had his prejudices. We know that for a long time he hated the Boers but that he was later able to develop some understanding of them. . . . He believed the conventional stereotypes of the Jews (see *Benita*), although he clearly admired ancient Hebrew civilization and learning and wrote a number of tales favourable to the Hebrews; furthermore, in a letter to *The Times*, Haggard asked that Palestine be made a home for Jews under British rule. He could hardly be called a xenophobe, but he did believe in the superiority of the Anglo-Saxons as a race. During World War I, he expressed his hope that the Empire would "cease to be so fond of admitting Germans and other foreigners within its gates and . . . stick to Anglo-Saxons." . . .

(M. Cohen, *Rider Haggard, His Life and Work*, pp. 150–151)

RUDYARD KIPLING   *(1865–1936)*

British novelist and poet

But of all the planks on which the platform of the Imperialist Radicals of the Right, of whom Kipling was the Laureate, was built, the weakest was their home social policy. In origin, this should not have been so. Radical Imperialism descended from notable social reformers—Sir Charles Dilke and Ruskin back in the seventies. Their dream of the Anglo-Saxon Empire as the basis of civilisation had been closely bound with social change and the reinvigoration of England itself. Incidentally, it is this that ties the radical Charles Dickens, the advocate of emigration to the colonies as a panacea, the co-supporter with Ruskin and Tennyson of violent suppression of the black rebellion in Jamaica, to Kipling. This link, which united their common fears of social disorder, has always intrigued me as an admirer of the art of two such different men. . . .

The whole concept of racialist Anglo-Saxon superiority which these clever men truly believed seems now as absurd as it is repugnant. But its practical weakness lay surely in the demands of experience it asked for, experience and knowledge of real life and not of theory in its supporters. When it came to important social aspects of English life they seem curiously deficient. And Kipling, their literary spokesman, was no exception. . . .

The discussion of Kipling's positive political ideas in those years has been a great deal befogged by an unwillingness to associate a man of high ideals, a generous benevolent man, and a considerable artist, with corporate social ideas at all, because, in their later European forms, they accrued enormities so detestable to our generations. There can be no doubt whatsoever of how much Kipling would have abhorred the form right-wing corporativism took under Hitler in Germany. Apart from his continuing apprehension, as expressed in poems and speeches of his last years, of the resurgence of the German absolutism he had spent most of his life in fighting, again and again in his work he expresses his respect for the Jewish contribution to Western civilisation. It is notable that in his most direct statement about his ideal of a reformed English society finding its corporate expression in national military service, "The Army of a Dream," he goes out of his way to make the Jewish school contingents the victors in the day's military exercises. That this respect for the Jews is often mixed up with a sort of slang, common to the whole Victorian and Edwardian age, that we have come to associate with anti-semitism — "To your tents, O Israel. The Hebrew schools stop the mounted troops . . . Pig, were you scuppered by Jew-boys?" — should not for a moment allow us to confuse Kipling with the world of Belloc. If I seem to labour this it is because even excellent and enlightened critics like Lord Annan refer loosely to "Kipling's anti-semitism."

By contrast, we must, I fear, convict Shaw, the Fabian, of an acceptance of the brutalities carried out in the Stalinist name of collectivist efficiency. But then, as has often been pointed out, there is nothing in Shaw's work, even at its best, to lead us to expect him to have any proper realisation of the meaning of individual suffering. Kipling is an artist at almost the opposite extreme from Shaw in this, a man hyper-sensitive to human feelings. He often wilfully accepted cruelty as a means of punishing or suppressing evil, and he did so sometimes with an attractive relish. But he is quite incapable of confusing it with the ordering of human happiness or of reducing men to figures as Shaw could. His artistic heart is not in his collectivist dreams.

(A. Wilson, *The Strange Ride of Rudyard Kipling*, pp. 240–242)

* * *

Many of Kipling's most cherished themes are embodied in these stories—the desolate obligation of obedience in the Roman Wall stories—the only ones where didacticism overcomes the evocation; the political wisdom of mercy in "Old Men at Pevensey"; the special civilising contribution of the Jews to society in "The Treasure and The Law." . . .

(*The Strange Ride of Rudyard Kipling*, p. 294)

ERNEST JONES   *(1879–1958)*

British psychoanalyst; author of The Life and Work of Sigmund Freud

The situation was still further complicated to some extent by the curious circumstance that, with the exception of the small Swiss group—who nearly all parted company after four or five years—and myself, all the early workers in psycho-analysis were Jews. I imagine the reasons for this were mainly local ones in Austria and Germany, since, except to some slight extent in the United States, it is a feature that has not been repeated in any other country; in England, for example, only two analysts have been Jews (apart from refugee immigrants). In Vienna it was obviously easier for Jewish doctors to share Freud's ostracism, which was only an exacerbation of the life they were accustomed to, and the same was true of Berlin and Budapest, where anti-Semitism was almost equally pronounced. The aptness of Jews for psychological intuition, and their ability to withstand public obloquy, may also have contributed to this state of affairs. It was one that had some influence on the form taken, especially at first, by the psycho-analytical "movement." It also had personal results for myself, since I found, to my surprise, that henceforth my life was to be lived mainly in Jewish company and that my best friends would for the greater part be Jews. This could not but be a matter of interest to me, and it makes it inevitable that I should say something about my attitude to this vexed and delicate topic.

Until this time I had had no friends among Jews, and had met very few of them. In childhood I remember my grandmother telling me that Jews were people who kept pawnshops, a fact with hardly any meaning to me, and that they were obstinate people who kept apart from the rest, even going to the length of having non-Christian synagogues of their own. So I suppose I started life with the usual vague prejudice against them. There were none in any school I went to, and only one or two in college or hospital; there was nothing, therefore, to arouse my interest in them. I doubt if I connected them much with the ancient Jews of the Old Testament, about whom I was of course fully informed. These lived far away and long ago, and had presumably disappeared, for the remarkable and incredible stories one read of their doings were hard to connect with any real everyday world.

The Jews I was now to get to know were of course all foreigners, from whom one must expect standards of all sorts and attitudes of mind different from English ones, so it was some time before I came to discriminate between them and other foreigners and to remark on their own distinguishing characteristics. As time went on, however, my position as the only Gentile sharing deeply their main preoccupation with, I think I may say, my own unusual capacity for adaptation and sympathetic understanding, led to my being admitted to their intimacy on practically equal terms. They would almost forget my Gentile extraction, and would freely share with me their characteristic jokes, anecdotes, points of view, and outlook on life. After a quarter of a century's such experience I came to feel that I knew their characteristics with an intimacy that must have fallen to the lot of few Gentiles, and I have reflected much on them and the social problems that surround their lives. I am going to prove this to any Jewish readers of this book by an anecdote which I shall not attempt to translate to others. When the Nazis took possession of Vienna one of the urgent problems that arose was how to help the patients of the Psycho-Analytical Clinic there. The Nazis said we might for the moment continue to treat them, but that the Directorship of the Clinic must be in "Aryan" hands. On inquiring about Dr. Sterba, one of our colleagues who happened to be a Gentile, I was told he had left for Switzerland, whereupon, to the general amusement, I exclaimed, "*O weh, unser einziger Shabbes-Goy ist fort.*" [Woe unto us, our only Sabbath-Gentile is gone!]

In one important respect, however, my knowledge on this topic is singularly deficient. It has never been my fortune to know a Jew possessing any religious belief, let alone an orthodox one. It may well be said that this quite disqualifies me from holding any opinion worth anything on any Jewish question, for to empty it of its religious kernel is surely to make it into a *Hamlet* without the Danish Prince. I should not myself agree, however. I fully admit that the greater part of what is called the Jewish problem emanates from their remarkable religious history, but I am sufficiently familiar with that history both from my first-hand experience in childhood and from extensive subsequent reading.

Well, after this preamble, all I am going to say here on a topic that might well fill an interesting book amounts to two personal expressions of opinion. The first is that the greater part of this bulky Jewish problem is related to a central characteristic of Jews that may very reasonably be derived from their peculiar belief of being God's Chosen People: namely, their intense, and practically universal, determination not merely to regard themselves as different from other people but also fundamentally to remain so despite any superficial compromise they may appear to make. Although every distinct community possesses something of this quality, no other seems to possess it in anything like the same degree, and no other maintains it when living as a minority amidst other communities.

My second observation is that, whatever other qualities Jews may possess, likeable or the reverse, no one who knows them well can deny that they are personally interesting. By that I mean, specially alive, alert, quick at comprehending people or events and at making pungent or witty comments on them. My Celtic mind, a little impatient of Anglo-Saxon placidity, complacency, and slowness of imagination, responded gratefully to these qualities, and it was perhaps the chief reason why I enjoyed Jewish society. One might at times find the rather hothouse family atmosphere, with its intensities and frictions, somewhat trying, but one could be sure of never being bored. These are the qualities, together with the resulting swift facility in apprehension of knowledge, that go to support the Jewish belief, which they

ELIZAVETA PETROVNA *(1709-1762)*

Empress of Russia, 1741-1762

Upon being asked to admit Jews into the country for economic reasons:

I do not wish to obtain any benefits from the enemies of Christ.

(Hay, The Foot of Pride, pp. 18–19)

GAVRILA DERZHAVIN *(1743-1816)*

Catherine the Great's court poet; later Minister of Justice under Alexander I of Russia

Upon surveying the situation of the Jews in the western provinces for Czar Paul in 1799:

Since Providence, for the realization of some unknown purpose, has left this dangerous people on the face of the world and has not destroyed it, the government under whose rule it lives ought to tolerate it. It is also their duty to take care of them in such a manner that the Jews be useful to themselves and to society at large in whose midst they live.

VICTOR HUGO *(1802-1885)*

French novelist, poet, and dramatist

At a protest of Czar Alexander's anti-Jewish policies, 19 June 1882:

The hour for decision is at hand. Dying religions clutch at their last resources. What appears before us at this moment is no longer crime. It is monstrosity. A people turning monster, a frightful phenomenon.

It seems as though a curtain were rent asunder, and a voice were heard saying: Humanity, behold and see!

Two solutions loom before our eyes:

On the one side we see man advancing slowly but surely toward an ever brightening horizon. . . .

On the other side we see man stepping backwards. The horizon grows darker. The masses plod and grope in the shadow. . . . The falsehoods devour each other. Christianity tortures Judaism. Thirty towns (twenty-seven, according to others) are at this very moment a prey to plunder and destruction. Events in Russia are terrifying. An immense crime is being committed, or, to put it more correctly, an action is taking place, for this ravaging populace has no longer any consciousness of crime. They are no longer even at that state. In their bestiality they banished their cults. They are possessed of the terrible innocence of tigers. The old centuries of the Albigenses, of the Inquisition, of the Holy Office . . . hurl themselves on the nineteenth century in an attempt to smother it. The mutilation of men, the violation of women, the burning of children, that is the suppression of the future. The past does not wish to end. It holds humanity in its clutch. The thread of life is between its ghostly fingers.

On the one side the people, on the other side the mob. On the one side light, on the other side darkness. Choose!

(*Stars and Sand*, 1882, p. 230)

FYODOR MIKHAYLOVICH DOSTOYEVSKY
(1821–1881)

Russian novelist; author of The Brothers Karamazov,
Crime and Punishment

Oh, please don't think that I mean to raise "the Jewish question"! I wrote the title jestingly. To raise a question of such magnitude as the status of the Jew in Russia, and the status of Russia which among her sons has three million Jews—is beyond my power. The question exceeds my limits. Still, I can have a certain opinion of my own, and it now appears that some Jews begin to take interest in it. For some time I have been receiving letters from them in which they seriously and with bitterness have reproached me for the fact that I am attacking them, that "I hate the Yiddisher," that I hate him not for his vices, "not as an exploiter," but specifically as a race. . . .

. . . when and how did I declare hate against the Jews as a people? — Since there never has been such a hatred in my heart, and those Jews who are acquainted with me and have dealt with me know it, from the very outset, and before I say a word, I withdraw from myself this accusation, once and forever, so as not to make special mention of it later.

Am I not accused of hatred because sometimes I called the Jew "Yiddisher"? But, in the first place, I did not think that this is so abusive, and secondly, as far as I can remember, I have always used the word "Yiddisher" in order to denote a certain idea: "Yiddisher, Yiddishism, Yiddish reign," etc. This denotes a certain conception, orientation, characteristic of the age. One may argue about this idea, and disagree with it, but one shouldn't feel offended by a word. . . .

True, it is very difficult to learn the forty-century-long history of a people such as the Jews; but, to start with, this much I know, that in the whole world there is certainly no other people who would be complaining as much about their lot, incessantly, after each step and word of theirs, — about their humiliation, their suffering, their martyrdom. One might think that it is not they who are reigning in Europe, who are directing there at least the stock exchanges, and therefore politics, domestic affairs, the morality of the states. . . .

I am ready to believe that Lord Beaconsfield[1] has, perhaps, forgotten about his descent — some time in the past — from Spanish Yiddishers (for sure, however, he hasn't forgotten); but that during the last year he did "direct English conservative policy" *partly* from the standpoint of a Yid is, in my opinion, impossible to doubt. "Partly" — cannot but be admitted.

But let all this be merely verbalism on my part, — light tone and light words. I concede. Nevertheless, I am unable fully to believe the screams of the Jews that they are so downtrodden, oppressed and humiliated. In my opinion, the Russian peasant, and generally, the Russian commoner, virtually bears heavier burdens than the Jew. . . .

. . . the Jews vociferated about rights which the Russian people themselves did not have; they shouted and complained that they were downtrodden and martyrs, and that when they should have been

---

[1] Benjamin Disraeli.

granted more rights, "then demand from us that we comply with the duties toward the state and native population."[2]

But then came the Liberator and liberated the native people. And who was the first to fall upon them as on a victim? Who preeminently took advantage of their vices? Who tied them with that sempiternal gold pursuit of theirs? By whom—whenever possible—were the abolished landowners promptly replaced, with the difference that the latter, even though they did strongly exploit men, nevertheless endeavored—perhaps in their own interest—not to ruin the peasants in order to prevent the exhaustion of labor, whereas the Jew is not concerned about the exhaustion of Russian labor: he grabs what's his, and off he goes.

I know that upon reading this, the Jews will forthwith start screaming that this is a lie; that this is a calumny; that I am lying; that I believe all this nonsense because I "do not know the forty-century-old history of these chaste angels who are incomparably purer morally not only than the other nationalities but also than the Russian people deified by me." (according to the words of my correspondent.) . . .

Let it be conceded that I am not firm in my knowledge of the Jewish modes of living, but one thing I do know for sure, and I am ready to argue about it with anyone, namely, that among our common people there is no preconceived, *a priori*, blunt religious hatred of the Jew, something along the lines: "Judas sold out Christ." Even if one hears it from little children or drunken persons, nevertheless our people as a whole look upon the Jew, I repeat, without a preconceived hatred. I have been observing this for fifty years. I even happened to live among the people, in their very midst, in one and the same barracks, sleeping with them on the same cots. There there were several Jews, and no one *despised* them, no one shunned them or persecuted them. When they said their prayers (and Jews pray with screams, donning a special garment) nobody found this strange, no one hindered them or scoffed at them,—a fact which precisely was to be expected from such a coarse people—in your estimation—as the Russians. On the contrary, when beholding them, they used to say: "such is their religion, and thus do they pray"; and would pass by calmly, almost approvingly.

And yet these same Jews in many respects shunned the Russians,

---

[2]The writer is quoting from a letter to him by a Jew.

they refused to take meals with them, looked upon them with haughtiness (and where?—in a prison!) and generally expressed squeamishness and aversion towards the Russian, towards the "native" people. The same is true in the case of soldiers' armories, and everywhere—all over Russia: make inquiries, ask if a Jew, as a Jew, as a Yiddisher, is being abused in armories because of his faith, his customs. Nowhere is he being abused, and that is also true of the people at large.[3] On the contrary, I assure you that in armories, as elsewhere, the Russian commoner perceives and understands only too well (besides, the Jews themselves do not conceal it) that the Jew does not want to take meals with him, that he has an aversion toward him, seeking as much as possible to avoid him and segregate himself from him. And yet, instead of feeling hurt, the Russian commoner calmly and clearly says: "such is his religion; it is because of his faith that he does not take meals with me and shuns me" (i.e., not because he is spiteful). And having comprehended this supreme cause, he wholeheartedly forgives the Jew.

However, at times, I was fancying: now, how would it be if in Russia there were not three million Jews, but three million Russians, and there were eighty million Jews,—well into what would they convert the Russians and how would they treat them? Would they permit them to acquire equal rights? Would they permit them to worship freely in their midst? Wouldn't they convert them into slaves? Worst than that: wouldn't they skin them altogether? Wouldn't they slaughter them to the last man, to the point of complete extermination, as they used to do with alien peoples in ancient times, during their ancient history?

Nay, I assure you that in the Russian people there is no preconceived hatred of the Jew, but perhaps there is a dislike of him, and especially in certain localities, maybe—a strong dislike. Oh, this cannot be avoided; this exists; but it arises not at all from the fact that he is a Jew, not because of some racial or religious hate, but it comes from other causes of which not the native people but the Jew himself is guilty.

. . . Even in my childhood I have read and heard a legend about Jews to the effect that they are supposed to be undeviatingly awaiting

---

[3]For much of the 19th century, Jewish boys were forcibly drafted for up to 25 years as part of the "recrutzia."

the Messiah, all of them, both the lowest Yiddisher and the highest
and most learned one—the philosopher and the cabalist–rabbi; that
they all believe that the Messiah will again unite them in Jerusalem
and will bring by his sword all nations to their feet; that this is the
reason why the overwhelming majority of the Jews have a predilection
but for one profession—the trade in gold, and at the utmost—for
gold-smithery; and all this, so it is alleged, in order that, when Messiah
comes, they should not need to have a new fatherland and to be tied
to the land of aliens in their, the Jews' possession, but to have
everything converted into gold and jewels, so that it will be easier to
carry them away when

> The ray of dawn begins to shine:
> Our flute, our tabor and the cymbal,
> Our riches and our holy symbol
> We will bring back to our old shrine,
> To our old home—to Palestine.

All this—I repeat—I heard as a legend, but I believe that the
substance of the matter unfailingly is there, in the form of an instinctively irresistible tendency. . . .

. . . instead of raising, by its influence, the level of education,
instead of increasing knowledge, generating economic fitness in the
native population,—instead of this, the Jew, wherever he has settled,
has still more humiliated and debauched the people; there humane-
ness was still more based and the educational level fell still lower; there
inescapable, inhuman misery, and with it despair, spread still more
disgustingly. Ask the native people in our border regions: What is
propelling the Jew—has been propelling him for centuries? You will
receive a unanimous answer: *mercilessness*. . . .

Thus, it is not for nothing that over there the Jews are reigning
everywhere over stock-exchanges; it is not for nothing that they
control capital, that they are the masters of credit, and it is not for
nothing—I repeat—that they are also the masters of international
politics, and what is going to happen in the future is known to the Jews
themselves: their reign, their complete reign is approaching! We are
approaching the complete triumph of ideas before which sentiments of
humanity, thirst for truth, Christian and national feelings, and even
those of national dignity, must bow. On the contrary, we are ap-

proaching materialism, a blind, personal accumulation of money by any means – this is all that has been proclaimed as the supreme aim, as the reasonable thing, as liberty, in lieu of the Christian idea of salvation only through the closest moral and brotherly fellowship of men. . . .

. . . despite all considerations already set forth by me, I am decidedly favoring full extension of Jewish rights in formal legislation, and, if possible, fullest equality with the native population (N.B., although, perhaps, in certain cases, even now they have more rights, or – to put it better – *more possibilities of exercising them* than the native population itself).

Of course, the following fantasy, for instance, comes to my mind: "Now, what if somehow, for some reason, our rural commune should disintegrate, that commune which is protecting our poor native peasant against so many ills; what if, straightway, the Jew, and his whole *kehillah* should fall upon that liberated peasant, – so inexperienced, so incapable of resisting temptation, and who up to this time has been guarded precisely by the commune? – Why, of course: instantly, this would be his end; his entire property, his whole strength, the very next day, would come under the power of the Jew, and there would ensue such an era as could be compared not only with the era of serfdom but even with that of the Tartar yoke."

Despite all the "fantasies" and everything I have written above, however, I feel full and complete equalization of rights because such is Christ's law, such is the Christian principle. . . .

(*The Diary of a Writer*, pp. 637–653)

KONSTANTIN PETROVICH POBEDONOSTSEV
(1827–1907)

Head of Holy Synod of Russia; tutor to Alexander III and Nicholas II

In a letter to Dostoyevsky, 14 August 1879:

What you write about the Yids [Zhidi] is extremely just. The Jews have engrossed everything, they have undermined everything, but the spirit of the century supports them. They are at the root of the

revolutionary socialist movement and of regicide, they own the periodical press, they have in their hands the financial markets, the people
as a whole fall into financial slavery to them; they even control the
principles of contemporary science and strive to place it outside
Christianity.

(Byrnes, *Pobedonostsev*, p. 205)

LEO TOLSTOY   *(1828–1910)*

Russian author of War and Peace, Anna Karenina

From a letter found in the archives of the Bulgarian
statesman F. Gabai:

What is a Jew? This question is not at all so odd as it seems. Let us see
what kind of peculiar creature the Jew is, which all the rulers and all
the nations have together and separately abused and molested, oppressed and persecuted, trampled and butchered, burned and
hanged—and in spite of all this is yet alive? What is a Jew, who has
never allowed himself to be led astray by all the earthly possessions
which his oppressors and persecutors constantly offered him in order
that he should change his faith and forsake his own Jewish religion?

The Jew is that sacred being who has brought down from heaven
the everlasting fire and has illuminated with it the entire world. He is
the religious source, spring and fountain out of which all the rest of the
peoples have drawn their beliefs and their religions.

The Jew is the pioneer of liberty. Even in those olden days, when
the people were divided into but two distinct classes, slaves and
masters—even so long ago had the law of Moses prohibited the
practice of keeping a person in bondage for more than six years.

The Jew is the pioneer of civilization. Ignorance was condemned
in olden Palestine more even than it is today in civilized Europe.
Moreover, in those wild and barbarous days, when neither the life nor
the death of any one counted for anything at all, Rabbi Akiba did not
refrain from expressing himself openly against capital punishment, a
practice which is recognized today as a highly civilized way of punishment.

The Jew is the emblem of civil and religious toleration. "Love the
stranger and the sojourner," Moses commands, "because you have
been strangers in the land of Egypt." And this was said in those remote

and savage times when the principal ambition of the races and nations consisted in crushing and enslaving one another. As concerns religious toleration, the Jewish faith is not only far from the missionary spirit of converting people of other denominations, but on the contrary the Talmud commands the rabbis to inform and explain to every one who willingly comes to accept the Jewish religion, all the difficulties involved in its acceptance, as to point out to the would-be proselyte that the righteous of all nations have a share in immortality. Of such a lofty and ideal religious toleration not even the moralists of our present day can boast.

The Jew is the emblem of eternity. He whom neither slaughter nor torture of thousands of years could destroy, he whom neither fire nor sword nor inquisition was able to wipe off the face of the earth, he who was the first to produce the oracles of God, he who has been for so long the guardian of prophecy, and who transmitted it to the rest of the world—such a nation cannot be destroyed. The Jew is everlasting as is eternity itself.

(In *Der Israelit* of Frankfurt am Main)

* * *

In a letter of Countess Tolstoy, Fall 1882:

"Levochka was at first very merry and animated, now he is learning Hebrew and has become more gloomy."

* * *

Tolstoy to V. I. Alexeev, 1882:

". . . All this time I am very assiduously engaged on Hebrew and have almost mastered that language. I already read and understand it. The Moscow Rabbi, Minor, teaches me. He is a very good and wise man. I have learnt a great deal, thanks to this occupation, and above all I am kept very busy. . . ."

* * *

From one of Tolstoy's letters of April 1903, protesting the Jew-baiting and pogroms in Kishinev and Gomel:

". . . the real culprit in the whole matter, namely our Government, with its priesthood which stupefies the people and makes fanatics of them, and its robber-band of officials. The Kishinev crime is a direct consequence of the propaganda of lies and violence carried on with such intensity and insistence by the Russian Government."

"[Tolstoy] contributed *Esarhaddon* and two other short stories for the relief of the sufferers in these riots."

(Maude, The Life of Tolstoy, vol. II, p. 438)

ALEXANDER III   *(1845–1894)*

Czar of Russia

Written in 1890 by the czar, in the margin of a draft of an official report suggesting that the oppression of the Jews of his empire might be relaxed:

But we must not forget that the Jews crucified Christ.

S. Y. WITTE   *(1849–1915)*

Russian Finance Minister

From the diaries of Theodor Herzl, who had interviewed several government ministers in St. Petersburg in 1903 to try and drum up support for his Zionist movement. The "liberal" finance minister declared to him:

One has to admit that the Jews provide enough reasons for hostility. There is a characteristic arrogance about them. Most Jews however are poor, and because they are poor they are filthy and make a repulsive impression. They also engage in all sorts of ugly pursuits, like pimping and usury. So you see it is hard for friends of the Jews to come to their defence. And yet I am a friend of the Jews. [Herzl noted here, "If so, we certainly do not need enemies." Then, when asked by Herzl why Witte complained of the large number of Jews in the revolutionary movement, Witte replied]:

"I believe it is the fault of our government. The Jews are too oppressed. I used to say to the late Tsar, Alexander III, "Majesty, if it were possible to drown the six or seven million Jews in the Black Sea, I would be absolutely in favour of that. But if it is not possible, one must let them live." What, then, do you want from the Russian government? [Herzl: "Certain encouragements." Witte: "But the Jews are given encouragements—to emigrate. Kicks in the behind, for example."

(from O'Brien's *The Siege*, 1986)

ANTON CHEKHOV   *(1860–1904)*

Russian dramatist and short-story writer

In the complete eight-volume edition of Chekhov's letters, [some sentences end] with three dots in brackets, designating a suppressed word or words. In the two-volume *Selected Letters*, the omission is restored. It is *zhidovka*, the feminine form of *zhid*, which, with its derivatives—not unlike the English "Yid" and its synonyms—has a derogatory connotation. Oddly, along with *yevrey*, the neutral word for Jews, and its forms, Chekhov used the offensive words in letters to his family and friends, his scrupulous humanity and devotion to justice notwithstanding. That devotion is clearly exemplified in an incident of his schooldays, recalled by a classmate. An upperclassman, on being called a "Yid," slapped the offender and was himself expelled. Chekhov rallied the classmates of the expelled boy to sign a declaration to the effect that they would boycott classes unless the Jewish boy were reinstated, which he was.

(Yarmolinsky, *Letters of Anton Chekhov*, p. 61)

* * *

Letter from Tomsk, 16 May 1890:

On the road I examined a Jew with cancer of the liver. He was emaciated and scarcely breathing, but this did not prevent the nurse from placing twelve cupping glasses on him. By the way, a word about the Jews. Here they till the soil, work as coachmen, run ferryboats, trade, and are called peasants, because they are peasants *de jure* and *de facto*. They are universally respected and, according to the police officer, are not rarely elected village elders. I saw a tall, lean Jew

scowling with distaste and spitting when the policeman was telling
risqué stories, an undefiled soul; his wife cooked a delicious fish soup.
The wife of the Jew with cancer regaled me with pike roe and excellent
white bread. Exploitation by Jews is unheard of. . . .

(*Letters of Anton Chekhov*, p. 144)

* * *

Letter of Chekhov's wife, Olga Knipper, 29 August 1902:

. . . My good darling, find out if Colonel Stakhovich could give you a
letter (his own or someone else's) to Senger, Minister of Education,
urging the admittance of a Jew to the Yalta high school. For the last
four years this Jew has passed his examinations with the highest
marks, yet they don't admit him, though he's the son of a Yalta
house-owner. They admit little Yids from other towns, though. Do
find out, darling, and write me without delay.

(*Letters of Anton Chekhov*, pp. 425–426)

* * *

Chekhov to Olga Knipper, 23 February 1903:

To young ladies going abroad to study here's what should be said: (1)
first complete your studies in Russia and then go abroad to improve
upon them, if you are preparing yourself for work in the sciences; our
institutions of higher learning for women, medical schools, for instance, are excellent; (2) do you know foreign languages? (3) Jews go
abroad to study from necessity, for they are hampered, but why do
you go?

(*Letters of Anton Chekhov*, p. 445)

* * *

Chekhov to Yiddish author Sholom Aleichem,
19 June 1903:

Much esteemed Solomon Naumovich!
       Generally speaking, I do not write nowadays, or write very little,
so I can only give a conditional promise. I shall write a story with

pleasure, if illness does not interfere. As for my published stories, they
are wholly at your disposal, and their translation into Yiddish and
their publication in a collection for the benefit of the Jews victimized
in Kishinev would give me nothing but heartfelt pleasure.

(Letters of Anton Chekhov, pp. 452–453)

* * *

Chekhov to A. S. Suvorin, 6 February 1898:

You write that you are vexed by Zola, but here the general feeling is as
if a new, better Zola has been born. In this trial of his he has been
cleansed of superficial grease spots as by turpentine, and shines forth
before the French in his true splendor. It is a purity, a moral loftiness
that no one suspected. Trace the entire affair from the very start. The
degradation of Dreyfus, whether just or not, made a painful, dismal
impression on everyone (including you, too, as I remember). It was
noticed that when he was being sentenced Dreyfus conducted himself
as an honorable, well-disciplined officer, while the onlookers, journalists, for instance, shouted at him, "Keep still, you Judas!"—that is,
behaved badly, indecently. Everyone came away from the scene
disgruntled, with a troubled conscience. Dreyfus's lawyer, Demange,
was especially dissatisfied—an honest man who even during the
preliminaries had felt that something shady was going on behind the
scenes; then the experts, to convince themselves that they were not
mistaken, spoke only of Dreyfus, of his being guilty, meanwhile
roaming through Paris, just roaming. . . . One of the experts turned
out to be demented, the author of a monstrously absurd scheme, two
others were eccentrics. Willy-nilly attention turned to the intelligence
department of the Ministry of War, a military consistory occupied
with hunting spies and reading other people's letters. . . . Furthermore, a whole series of gross violations of court procedure came to
light. Little by little the belief came to prevail that Dreyfus had in
reality been condemned on the evidence of a secret document that
had been shown neither to him nor to his attorney—and people who
had due process at heart saw this as a basic abrogation of law: had the
letter been written by Kaiser Wilhelm or by the sun itself, it should
have been shown to Demange. All kinds of guesses as to the contents

of the letter became current, cock-and-bull stories were repeated. Dreyfus was a Jew, and so the Jews pricked up their ears. . . . Militarism, the Yids, became topics of conversation. Such utterly contemptible figures as Drumont raised their heads, gradually trouble was stirred up on the ground of anti-Semitism, a ground that reeks of the slaughterhouse. When something does not go well with us, we seek causes outside of ourselves and find them soon enough: "It's the French playing scurvy tricks, the Yids, the Kaiser. Capital, masons, the Syndicate, the Jesuits, bugaboos, are ghosts, how will they relieve our unease? They are, of course, a bad sign. If the French start talking about the Yids, the Syndicate, it is a sign that they feel all is not well with them, that a worm is gnawing at them, that they need these ghosts to appease their disturbed consciences. . . .

. . . The best people, the leaders of the nation had to be the first to sound the alarm—that is just what happened. The first to raise his voice was Scherer-Koestner, whom his French intimates call . . . "the dagger's blade"—so irreproachable and stainless he is. The second was Zola. And now he is being tried.

I know the case from the stenographic report, which is totally different from what is in the newspapers, and I see Zola plainly. Above all, he is sincere: he builds his judgments solely on what he sees, and not on ghosts, as others do. True, sincere people can make mistakes, but such mistakes cause less harm than reasoned insincerity, prejudices, or political considerations. Even if Dreyfus is guilty, Zola nevertheless is right, because the business of writers is not to accuse, not to persecute, but to side even with the guilty, once they are condemned and suffer punishment. People will say: but politics? but the interests of the State? Well, great writers and artists should engage in politics only to the extent needed to defend themselves against politics. Even without them there are plenty of accusers, prosecutors, and gendarmes, and in any event the role of Paul suits them better than that of Saul. And no matter what the verdict will be, Zola will nevertheless rejoice, his old age will be a good age and he will die with a conscience at peace or at least at ease. . . .

(*Letters of Anton Chekhov*, pp. 303–305)

10

European Nationalism, the Dreyfus Affair, and the Rise of Fascism

ADAM MICKIEWICZ   (1798–1855)

Polish poet; author of Pan Tadeusz

Lecture of 26 December 1843:

There is another very important task before Polish philosophy. Messianism is also to solve the oldest and most difficult of all questions, that of the people of Israel. It is not in vain that this people chose Poland as its fatherland. The most spiritual among all peoples on earth, it is capable of understanding what is most sublime in humanity; but delayed hitherto on the road to progress, and unable to see anywhere the attainment of the promises made to them by Providence, the Jews have dissipated their mental powers in earthly pursuits, and deteriorated. However, they have never ceased to await their Messiah, and this faith of theirs has certainly not been without influence on the character of Polish Messianism. . . .

A futile endeavor has thus far been made to link the case of this people with that of Poland by promising them landed property and a better material existence. Could this people forget the centuries of suffering they experienced, and sell their glorious past for a piece of land? Would it not have been a misfortune for the world if this last remnant of an ancient tribe, the only one that has never doubted God, would have fallen into apostasy?

(*Kurs Literaturny Slowianskiej*, vol. III, p. 322)

HONORÉ DE BALZAC   (1799–1850)

French novelist

When we look around us, and calmly contemplate the present condition of the Hebrew race in those countries, where, as in the United States of America, and to a considerable extent in England and in

189

France, the benign influences of modern civilization have been allowed full sway, and compare that ameliorated and daily improving condition with the state of social degradation which these persecuted people have had to endure for centuries, in consequence of the barbarous enactments of wicked and oppressive rulers, we feel, indeed, as if the fulfillment of the prophecy was not very far distant.

("The Influence of the Jews on the Progress of the World," 1888 in S. Wolf, *Selected Addresses*)

LOUIS KOSSUTH   *(1802–1894)*

Hungarian patriot

Kossuth to Ignacz Helfy, 15 October 1882, concerning the Independence Party Convention:

I have never discriminated between men on account of race, language or religion, and I shall never resort to such discrimination. As for the anti-Semitic agitation, I feel ashamed of it as a son of the nineteenth century, injured by it as a Hungarian, and I condemn it as a patriot. I condemn it because, with respect to the prevailing social and economic evils, it misrepresents symptoms for causes, and, as if it had entered some sinister foreign service to hinder the welfare of our country, it diverts the attention from the investigation of real motives.

I condemn it because it serves no useful practical purpose at all. I cannot conceive that any thoughtful Hungarian would be stupid enough to agree with the agitators that the "nullification of the emancipation," and even the expulsion from the country of six, seven hundred thousand men would be possible in Europe in the nineteenth century, even if the idea were not a monstrosity from the moral standpoint. I condemn it because the agitators, through their provocations, can only help to achieve that of which they complain, the segregation of the Jews and their work to the harm of others, for persecution must inevitably drive the victims to solidarity.

GIUSEPPE MAZZINI (1805–1872)

Italian patriot and champion of the Risorgimento[1]

If our fathers were to teach their children that the true definition of life is not a search after happiness, but a preparation, through the fulfilment of our earthly duties, for a higher stage of earthly existence—if our mothers, who think themselves Christians, would meditate upon and teach their sons some of the words of Christ and the whole of that book of Maccabeus which appears as if written for the Italians—they would better fulfil the duties of love, and our Italy would not be doomed to weep over the flower of her sons, lost to her one by one in solitary death on the scaffold, or by the soul's slow atrophy in exile. . . .

(Stubbs, *God and the People*, p. 195)

HANS CHRISTIAN ANDERSEN (1805–1875)

Danish author of fairy tales

The evening came. I was present at the concert [in Amsterdam in 1866] when was given one of Gade's symphonies, and this was especially applauded, and people looked at me as much as to say— "Carry our enthusiasm to your gifted countryman."

There was an elegantly dressed audience; but it was unpleasant to me not to see a face of the people, whose men in our time are those who have given us the most remarkable musical works, the people who gave us Mendelssohn, Halevy, and Meyerbeer. I did not see a single Jew and mentioned my surprise, and it was still greater when I heard—would I had misunderstood my ears!—that they were not admitted here. On several occasions I received the impression that there is a strong division here between men in social, religious and artistic relations.

. . . In Denmark, God be praised, we do not know such distinctions.

(*The Story of My Life*, p. 519)

---

[1]Nineteenth-century movement for Italian political unity.

SØREN KIERKEGAARD   (1813–1855)

Danish philosopher

O venerable father Abraham! When you returned home from Mount Moriah, you needed no praise to console you for your loss: for, indeed, did you not win everything and keep Isaac? . . .

O venerable father Abraham! Thousands of years have passed since those days, but you have no need of a tardy lover to snatch your memory from the power of oblivion: for every language reminds men of you—and yet you reward your lover more gloriously than anyone, since in Heaven you grant him blessedness in your bosom and on earth captivate his heart and his eyes with the miracle of your action. O venerable father Abraham! Second father of our race! You who were the first to know and the first to bear witness to that vast passion which disdains the fury of the elements and the powers of creation in order to battle with God, you who were the first to know that supreme passion, that humble, holy, and pure expression of the divine madness which was the admiration of the heathen—forgive him who would speak in your praise, if he has spoken idly. He has spoken humbly, according to the desire of his heart: he has spoken briefly, because brevity is seemly; but he will never forget that you required a hundred years to obtain the son of your old age against all hope and that you had to draw your knife before you could keep Isaac; nor will he ever forget that in a hundred and thirty years you never went beyond faith.

(*Fear and Trembling*, 1843, p. 24)

RICHARD WAGNER   (1813–1883)

German composer of operas Lohengrin, Die Meistersinger

It is in particular the purely sensuous manifestation of the Jewish speech that revolts us. Culture was unsuccessful in eradicating the peculiar stubbornness of the Jewish nature with respect of the characteristics of the Semitic manner of expression despite two thousand years of inter-course with European nations. Our ear perceives especially the hissing, shrill-sounding, buzzing and grunting tonal expression of the Jewish way of speech as thoroughly foreign and unpleasant. In addition, the arbitrary twisting of words and phrase constructions, which is totally uncharacteristic of our national language, gives this tonal expression

the character of a completely insufferable confused babbling in listening to which our attention involuntarily dwells on this revolting *how*
of the Jewish speech than on the *what* contained in it.

(*Das Judenthum in der Musik*, 1869, p. 15)

* * *

. . . [Wagner] was loved by his adoptive father and took his name
until some years after Geyer's death, but he suffered from a lifelong,
tormenting suspicion (in fact groundless) that Geyer was of Jewish
birth. The fear of belonging to a race considered almost universally at
the time as inferior (though redeemable through assimilation) was
aggravated by the awkward facts that he was born in Bruhl, the Jewish
quarter of Leipzig, and that he had the prominent nose and high
forehead generally associated with the Jewish physiognomy. It was the
perceived necessity of proving to the world that he was without taint
that underlay the virulence of his later anti-Semitism.

(S. Spencer and B. Millington, *Selected Letters of
Richard Wagner*, p. 3)

* * *

Another essay from the *Opera and Drama* period, *Das Judenthum
in der Musik* (Judaism in Music), caused concern within the circle of his
friends and considerable anger beyond. It should be seen as Wagner's
contribution to a debate on a theme increasingly exercising the minds
of his contemporaries: the extent to which Jews affected the artistic
climate of the country in which they lived. Wagner's argument—that
the rootlessness of Jews in Germany and their historical role as usurers
and entrepreneurs condemned them to cultural sterility—was overlaid
with uncompromisingly anti-Semitic observations. A letter to Liszt
makes clear too how far personal animus was responsible for the
tirade: Meyerbeer, he tells Liszt, reminds him of the "darkest" period of
his life, one in which the necessity for recognition led inevitably to
insincere, dishonest relationships. Above all, the frequently voiced
opinion that he was in some ways indebted also musically to Meyerbeer goaded Wagner beyond endurance: with *Das Judenthum in der
Musik* he intended to make clear once and for all how Meyerbeer and
everything he stood for were the very antithesis of his own ideals.

(*Selected Letters of Richard Wagner*, p. 159)

Wagner to Franz Liszt, 18 April 1851:

. . . You ask me about "Judaism." You know of course that the article is by me: so why do you ask? It was not out of fear, but to prevent the question from being dragged down by the Jews to a purely personal level that I appeared in print pseudonymously. I harboured a long suppressed resentment against this Jewish business, and this resentment is as necessary to my nature as gall is to the blood. The immediate cause of my intense annoyance was their damned scribblings, so that I finally let fly: I seem to have struck home with terrible force, which suits my purpose admirably, since that is precisely the sort of shock that I wanted to give them. For they will always remain our masters—that much is as certain as the fact that it is not our princes who are now our masters but bankers and philistines. . . .
                    (*Selected Letters of Richard Wagner*, pp. 221–222)

* * *

Wagner to Liszt, 7 June 1855:

. . . We may allow that Christianity is such a contradictory phenomenon because we know it only through its contamination by narrow-minded Judaism and through its resultant distortion, whereas modern research has succeeded in proving that pure, uncontaminated Christianity is no more and no less than a branch of that venerable Buddhist religion which, following Alexander's Indian campaign, found its way, among other places, to the shores of the Mediterranean. . . .
                    (*Selected Letters of Richard Wagner*, pp. 346–347)

* * *

Wagner to Liszt, 11 January 1858:

. . . Send me the money, even if it is from the most Jewish of Jews. . . .
                    (*Selected Letters of Richard Wagner*, p. 374)

* * *

Wagner to Hans Von Wolzogen, 17 January 1880:

. . . what we are happy to abandon to the most pitiless destruction is all that impairs and distorts this saviour of ours: that is why we ask for sensitivity and care in the way we express ourselves, lest we end up working with the Jews and for the Jews.

(*Selected Letters of Richard Wagner*, p. 899)

* * *

Wagner to King Ludwig II of Bavaria, 30 December 1880:

. . . I shall continue and speak of another man who is, however, merely something of a curiosity. He is the opera director of the Leipzig Municipal Theatre, Angelo Neumann, a man of Jewish extraction, and strangely energetic and extremely devoted to me, in a way which — oddly enough! — I find even today is true of the Jews whom I know. He was the first person to put on a complete performance of the "Ring of the Nibelung" in Leipzig, which he did with lasting success; proud of his achievements, he now intends to win the highest renown for himself. . . .

(*Selected Letters of Richard Wagner*, p. 905)

* * *

Wagner to Angelo Neumann, 23 February 1881:

Dear friend and benefactor,

I have absolutely no connection with the present "anti-Semitic" movement: an article of mine which is shortly to appear in the *Bayreuther Blätter* will prove this so conclusively that it will be impossible for anyone of *intelligence* to associate me with that movement. —

. . . Our Nibelungs were not made to be hounded by courtiers and Jews — and that because of some totally absurd misunderstandings!

(*Selected Letters of Richard Wagner*, p. 906)

* * *

Wagner to King Ludwig of Bavaria, 22 November 1881:

. . . The man in question is the curious figure of Joseph Rubinstein, who first approached me ten years ago while I was at Triebschen, begging me to save him from the Jewishness of which he was a part. I allowed him to have personal dealings with me — he is, in any case, an outstanding musician — although it must be said that he — no less than the good Levi—has caused me a good deal of trouble. What both these unhappy men lack is the basis of a Christian education which instinctively enables the rest of us to appear similar in kind—however different we may in fact be—and the result, for them, is the most painful mental anguish. Faced with these circumstances—and very often having to combat their tendency towards suicide—I have had to exercise the most extreme patience, and if it is a question of being humane towards the Jews, I for one can confidently lay claim to praise. But I simply cannot get rid of them: the director Angelo Neumann sees it as his calling in life to ensure that I am recognized throughout the world. There is no longer anything I can say to all this, but simply have to put up with energetic Jewish patronage, however curious I feel in doing so. . . . If I have friendly and sympathetic dealings with many of these people, it is only because I consider the Jewish race the born enemy of pure humanity and all that is noble in man: there is no doubt but that we Germans especially will be destroyed by them, and I may well be the last remaining German who, as an artist, has known how to hold his ground in the face of a Judaism which is now all-powerful.

(Selected Letters of Richard Wagner, p. 918)

OTTO VON BISMARCK   *(1815–1898)*

Chancellor of German Empire, 1871–1890

In a speech at the Prussian States General in 1847, where Bismarck was a delegate:

I am no enemy of the Jews; if they become my enemies I will forgive them. Under certain circumstances I love them; I am ready to grant them all rights but that of holding the magisterial office in a Christian state. This they now claim; they demand to become *Landrat*, general, minister, yes even, under circumstances, minister of religion and education. I allow that I am full of prejudices, which, as I have said, I have sucked in with my mother's milk; I cannot argue them away; for if I think of a Jew face to face with me as a representative of the king's sacred Majesty, and I have to obey him, I must confess that I should feel myself deeply broken and depressed; the sincere self-respect with

which I now attempt to fulfill my duties towards the state would leave
me. I share these feelings with the mass of the lower strata of the
people, and I am not ashamed of their society. . . .
(J. W. Headlam, *Bismarck and the Foundations of the German Empire*,
pp. 41–42)

* * *

As a matter of fact they [the Jews] have no real home. So to
speak, they are European in a general sort of way; cosmopolitans – in
a word, nomads. Their fatherland is Zion; Jerusalem. Outside that,
they belong, as it were, to the whole world, and hang together all over
the earth. The petty Jew alone experiences anything like a feeling of
local patriotism. Among Hebrews of that class may be found some
decent, honest people. . . .
Even Jews, however, have their good qualities; they are renowned for respect to their parents, conjugal fidelity and benevolence.
(In a conversation with the author Moritz Busch,
25 September 1870)

* * *

Indeed, I am of the opinion that Jews must be improved by
crossing their breed [intermarrying with Christians]. The results are
really not so bad. . . . On the whole it is better the other way – I mean,
by the conjunction of a Christian stallion of German breed with a
Jewish mare. The Jews' money is thus brought into circulation again;
and the result of the cross is a very fair breed. I really do not know
what I shall advise my sons to do, one of these days. . . .
(In a conversation with Moritz Busch, 10 January 1871)

* * *

He [Bismarck] did not see any way by which the aims of the
anti-Semites might be realized. . . . Nor could the Jews be expelled
without grave injury to the national welfare. Any measures by which
the Jews would be excluded from judicial and other positions in the
state would only increase the evil which the anti-Semites thought they
had to do away with. For then the same Jewish intelligence, to which
public careers would be closed, would embrace those fields in which

the overweight of the Jews is already said by the anti-Semites to be intolerable, *i.e.,* those of commerce.

The prince then stated his opinion that the Jewish movement sprang less from religious and social instincts than from economic reasons. He mentioned as a fact that the Jews are greatly superior to the other elements of the population in making money. Their superiority rests on qualities which, whether they are pleasing or not, cannot be removed by measures of state. The Jews, by reason of their natural dispositions, were generally more clever and skillful than Christians. They were also, at any rate so long as they had not made their fortunes, if perhaps not more industrious at least more frugal and saving than their Christian competitors. To this must be added the fact that the Jew would risk something more readily once in a way in order to gain a commercial advantage, and in applying his methods to gain his object, would also act more kindheartedly than his Christian competitor. All this gives him an advantage in commerce which could not legally be taken away. Even the anti-Semites had up till then been unable to suggest anything which might paralyze this advantage and its effect on the economic life of the nation. Their proposals had hitherto been impracticable, and no government would be found able to carry them out. It was also inadvisable for the state to put obstacles in the way of the pursuit of gain and fortune, for the other elements of the population would thereby suffer equally, and the national wealth would decrease.

It is not necessary on that account to allow the Jews to dominate, or to make one's self dependent on them financially, as is the case in some states. In his own dealings, as a minister, with the *haute finance,* he had always placed them under an obligation to him.

He considered the Jews to be useful members of the state of today, and thought it unwise to molest them. The rich Jew especially was generally a regular taxpayer and a good subject.

Finally the prince spoke about his personal relations with Jews, and remarked *inter alia* that he had really reaped ingratitude at their hands. No statesman had done more for their emancipation than he had; yet, in spite of this, it was just the progressive and radical papers, in the hands of the Jews, which attacked him most violently. But he did not take that too much to heart; the reason was, probably, that the owners of the papers considered it due to their liberal or radical spirit not to allow the memory of that, for which they as Jews had to thank him, to influence the attitude of their papers with regard to him and his policy.

(H. von Poschinger, *Conversations with Bismarck*, pp. 164–166)

* * *

In reply to a question in 1880 as to whether he agreed with anti-Semitism:

Nothing can be more incorrect. I absolutely disapprove of this campaign against Jews, whether it be waged on grounds of religious or of racial differences. By similar reasoning, one might some day wish to attack Germans of Polish or of French descent, claiming that they are not Germans. That Jews prefer to engage in trade is, of course, a matter of personal predilection; and it may well be explained by their former exclusion from other vocations. But surely this does not justify us in making inciting remarks about their wealth, which remarks I find altogether objectionable because they lead to envy and jealousy.

I shall never agree to have the constitutionally accorded rights of the Jews curtailed in any wise. The spiritual organization of the Jews makes them generally inclined to be critical, hence they appear usually allied with the Opposition; but I do not differentiate between Christian and Jewish political opponents.

(O. Johlinger, *Bismarck und die Juden*, p. 79)

CHARLES BAUDELAIRE   *(1821–1867)*

French poet

The Jews who are [our] librarians and bear witness to the Redemption.

(*Intimate Journals*)

HENRIK IBSEN   *(1828–1906)*

Norwegian dramatist; author of The Doll's House, Hedda Gabler, An Enemy of the People

Ibsen to Georg Brandes, Dresden, 17 February 1871:

Yes, to be sure, it is a benefit to possess the franchise, the right of self-taxation, etc., but for whom is it a benefit? For the citizen, not for the individual. Now there is absolutely no reasonable necessity for the individual to be a citizen. On the contrary—the State is the curse of the individual. With what is the strength of Prussia bought? With the merging of the individual in the political and geographic concept. The waiter makes the best soldier.

Now, turn to the Jewish nation, the nobility of the human race. How has it preserved itself—isolated, poetical—despite all the barbarity from without? Because it had no State to burden it. Had the Jewish nation remained in Palestine, it would long since have been ruined in the process of construction, like all the other nations. The State must be abolished! In that revolution I will take part. Undermine the idea of the State; make willingness and spiritual kinship the only essentials in the case of a union—and you have the beginning of a liberty that is of some value. The changing of forms of government is mere toying with degrees—a little more or a little less—folly, the whole of it.

(Letters of Henrik Ibsen, p. 208)

ÉMILE ZOLA   (1840–1902)

French novelist; author of Nana, Germinal

"I ACCUSE . . . !"

Letter to M. Félix Faure, president of the French Republic, 1895–1899

Monsieur Le Président:

Will you permit me, in my gratitude for the kindly welcome that you once extended to me, to have a care for the glory that belongs to you, and to say to you that your star, so lucky hitherto, is threatened with the most shameful, the most ineffaceable, of stains?

You have emerged from base calumnies safe and sound; you have conquered hearts. . . . But what a mud stain on your name—I was going to say on your reign—is this abominable Dreyfus affair! . . . France has this stain upon her cheek; it will be written in history that under your presidency it was possible for this social crime to be committed.

Since they have dared, I too will dare. I will tell the truth, for I have promised to tell it, if the courts, once regularly appealed to, did not bring it out fully and entirely. It is my duty to speak; I will not be an accomplice. My nights would be haunted by the specter of the innocent man who is atoning, in a far-away country, by the most frightful of tortures, for a crime that he did not commit.

And to you, *Monsieur le Président*, will I cry this truth, with all the force of an honest man's revolt. Because of your honor I am convinced that you are ignorant of it. And to whom then shall I denounce the malevolent gang of the really guilty, if not to you, the first magistrate of the country?

First, the truth as to the trial and conviction of Dreyfus. . . .

Ah! the emptiness of this indictment! That a man could have been condemned on this document is a prodigy of iniquity. I defy honest people to read it without feeling their hearts leap with indignation and crying out their revolt at the thought of the unlimited atonement yonder, on Devil's Island [where Dreyfus was presently imprisoned]. Dreyfus knows several languages—a crime; no compromising document was found on his premises—a crime; he sometimes visits the neighborhood of his birth—a crime; he is industrious, he is desirous of knowing everything—a crime; he does not get confused—a crime; he gets confused—a crime. And the simplicities of this document, the formal assertions in the void! We were told of fourteen counts, but we find, after all, only one,—that of the *bordereau*. And even as to this we learn that the experts were not in agreement; that one of them, M. Gobert, was hustled out in military fashion, because he permitted himself to arrive at another than the desired opinion. We were told also of twenty-three officers who came to overwhelm Dreyfus with their testimony. We are still in ignorance of their examination, but it is certain that all of them did not attack him, and it is to be remarked, furthermore, that all of them belonged to the war offices. It is a family trial; there they are all at home; and it must be remembered that the staff wanted the trial, sat in judgment at it, and has just passed judgment a second time. . . .

These, then, *Monsieur le Président*, are the facts which explain how it was possible to commit a judicial error; and the moral proofs, the position of Dreyfus as a man of wealth, the absence of motive, this continual cry of innocence, complete the demonstration that he is a victim of the extraordinary fancies of Major du Paty de Calm, of his clerical surroundings, of that hunting down of the "dirty Jews" which disgraces our epoch. . . .

. . . And the beautiful result of this prodigious situation is that the one honest man in the case, Lieutenant-Colonel Picquart, who alone has done his duty, is to be the victim, the man to be derided and punished. O justice, what frightful despair grips the heart! They go so far as to say that he is a forger; that he manufactured the telegram, to ruin Esterhazy. But, in heaven's name, why? For what purpose? Show a motive. Is he, too, paid by the Jews? The pretty part of the story is that he himself was an anti-Semite. Yes, we are witnesses of this infamous spectacle, — the proclamation of the innocence of men ruined with debts and crimes, while honor itself, a man of stainless life, is stricken down. When a society reaches that point, it is beginning to rot. . . .

. . . the war offices, by all imaginable means, by press campaigns, by communications, by influences, have covered Esterhazy only to ruin Dreyfus a second time. Ah! with what a sweep the Republican Government should clear away this band of Jesuits, as General Billot himself calls them! Where is the truly strong and wisely patriotic minister who will dare to reshape and renew all? How many of the people I know are trembling with anguish in view of a possible war, knowing in what hands lies the national defense! And what a nest of base intrigues, gossip, and dilapidation has this sacred asylum, entrusted with the fate of the country, become! We are frightened by the terrible light thrown upon it by the Dreyfus case, this human sacrifice of an unfortunate, of a "dirty Jew." Ah! what a mixture of madness and folly, of crazy fancies, of low police practices, of inquisitorial and tyrannical customs, the good pleasure of a few persons in gold lace, with their boots on the neck of the nation, cramming back into its throat its cry of truth and justice, under the lying and sacrilegious pretext of the *raison d'État!*

And another of their crimes is that they have accepted the support of the unclean press, have suffered themselves to be championed by all the knavery of Paris, so that now we witness knavery's insolent triumph in the downfall of right and of simple probity. It is a crime to have accused of troubling France those who wish to see her generous, at the head of the free and just nations, when they themselves are hatching the impudent conspiracy to impose error, in the face of the entire world. It is a crime to mislead opinion, to utilize for a task of death this opinion that they have perverted to the point of delirium. It is a crime to poison the minds of the little and the humble, to exasperate the passions of reaction and intolerance, while seeking shelter behind odious anti-Semitism, of which the great liberal France of the rights of man will die, if she is not cured. It is a crime to exploit patriotism for works of hatred, and, finally, it is a crime to make the sword the modern god, when all human science is at work on the coming temple of truth and justice. . . .

As for the people whom I accuse, I do not know them, I have never seen them, I entertain against them no feeling of revenge or hatred. They are to me simple entities, spirits of social ill-doing. And the act that I perform here is nothing but a revolutionary measure to hasten the explosion of truth and justice.

I have but one passion, the passion for the light, in the name of humanity which has suffered so much, and which is entitled to happiness. My fiery protest is simply the cry of my soul. Let them dare, then, to bring me into the Assize Court, and let the investigation take place in the open day.

I await it.[2]

Accept, *Monsieur le Président*, the assurance of my profound respect.

("*J'Accuse!*" in *L'Aurore*, 13 January 1898)

AUGUSTE RENOIR   (1841–1919)

French Impressionist painter

In politics, Renoir's friends probably had certain leanings, though differing among themselves, but they were all too busy with their painting to take much interest in them. Manet was the perfect type of middle-class Liberal. Pissarro was for the Commune. Dégas would have been a Royalist if he had had the time for it. Renoir liked human beings too much not to approve of all parties whatever their colour.

---

[2] Anatole France described the publication of "*J'Accuse!*" as "a moment in the conscience of mankind." Within five days, the charge of defamation was indeed made against Zola, and he was summoned before the Court of Assizes on 7 February 1898.

He liked the Commune because of Courbet's association with it; and the Catholic Church because of Pope Julius II and Raphael.

While on the subject of politics, I should like to say a word about the Dreyfus Affair. Almost everyone knows, of course, how once more all France was divided when the Jewish artillery captain was unjustly convicted on a charge of espionage. "Always the same camps," said Renoir, "but with different names for each century. Protestants against Catholics, Republicans against Royalists, Communards against the Versailles faction. The old quarrel has been revived again. People are either pro- or anti-Dreyfus. I would like to try to be simply a Frenchman. And that is the reason I am for Watteau and against Monsieur Bourguereau. . . ."

Renoir knew how grave the question was, but he also realized that when the hour for settling it struck the answer would not be long in coming. He feared the answer might take the form of anti-Semitism among the lower middle class. He could envisage armies of grocers and similar tradesmen, wearing hoods and treating the Jews the way the Ku-Klux-Klan treated the Negroes. His advice was to stay quiet and wait for the ferment to pass. "That fool of a Deroulède did a great deal of harm." Pissarro [the fellow Impressionist and a Jew] was all for taking some sort of action; Dégas wanted action too, but of an opposite kind. Renoir admired both men enormously, but he had real affection for Pissarro. He did his best to avoid embroiling himself with either, though in the case of Dégas, he "just missed it by a hair's breadth" when Dégas asked him in astonishment, "How can you stand associating with that Jew?"

(J. Renoir, *Renoir, My Father*, pp. 229–230)

GEORGES CLEMENCEAU   (1841–1929)

French physician, journalist, and premier of France

We deceive ourselves with fulsome praise of our civilization: at the first savage cry resounding in our midst, the barbarian within us comes back to the surface. [On anti-Semitic riots in Algiers]

We need only to cross the great inland sea, the highway of the oldest civilization, in order to bring to the attention of the Africans the rude barbarism of our police. One call was sufficient: "Death to the Jews!" And the people threw themselves furiously into an orgy of sacking, ravaging and massacring, expecting the end of their misery through this outburst of savagery.

"Death to the Jews!" today; "Death to whom?" tomorrow? If murder were all that were necessary to liberate humanity from its shackles and to secure for it the fruit of social bliss, the human race would long ago have been surfeited with happiness.

When Moses came down from Sinai, after the Lord had spoken to him amidst thunder and lightning, he found no other means of defending the pure faith than to slaughter the idolatrous Israelites. The Christians took delight in the rack and the stake, and it was necessary to rob them of worldly weapons in order to compel them to respect human life. And secular authority showed itself no milder when it came into power.

When shall we at last be satiated with slaughter? When shall we all, whether we call ourselves Catholics or Atheists, who are enjoined to love one another, agree at last not to hate each other, and if that be too much to expect, at least to refrain from giving full vent, like savages, to our paroxysms of hate?

We believe that we are still far removed from that time and that it is far easier to invent the steamboat, the telegraph and the Roentgen rays than to alter an iota of the atavism of our hearts. We have come to the point when the masses are roused by the cry of "Long live France! Long live the Army!" to plunder, arson and murder, and when the mere demand for justice exposes one to the charge of being a traitor or of being in the pay of the enemy. The latter is perhaps the less pardonable, for it has not even the excuse of mob frenzy and ignorance. . . .

"What does it matter to you whether Dreyfus is innocent or guilty?" a general asked of Col. Picquart. "You are not on Devil's Island!" And in daily conversation we hear many people exclaim, apparently in order to acquit themselves of some doubt which may attach to them: "Why should it concern us whether Dreyfus was judged aright or not! After all, he is only a Jew!"

These words will remain in the memory of men, for they characterize an age!

(From an editorial in *L'Aurore*, 1897)

FRIEDRICH NIETZSCHE   *(1844–1900)*

German philosopher

[What does Europe owe to the Jews?]

Many things, good and bad, and above all one thing of the nature both of the best and the worst: the grand style in morality, the fearfulness and majesty of infinite demands, of infinite significations, the whole Romanticism and sublimity of moral questionableness — and consequently just the most attractive, ensnaring, and exquisite element in those iridescences and allurements to life, in the aftersheen of which the sky of our European culture, its evening sky, now glows — perhaps glows out. For this, we artists among the spectators and philosophers are grateful to the Jews.

(*Beyond Good and Evil*, Aphorism 250)

* * *

I want all anti-Semites shot.

(Quoted in R. M. Lonsbach, *Nietzsche und die Juden*, p. 55)

* * *

I have never yet met a German who was favorably inclined to the Jews; and however decided the repudiation of actual anti-Semitism may be on the part of all prudent and political men, this prudence and policy is not perhaps directed against the nature of the sentiment itself, but only against its dangerous excess, and especially against the distasteful and infamous expression of this excess of sentiment; — on this point we must not deceive ourselves. That Germany has amply sufficient Jews, that the German stomach, the German blood, has difficulty (and will long have difficulty) in disposing only of this quantity of *Jew* — as the Italian, the Frenchman, and the Englishman have done by means of a stronger digestion: — that is the unmistakable declaration and language of a general instinct, to which one must listen and according to which one must act. "Let no more Jews come in! And shut the doors, especially towards the East (also towards Austria)!" — thus commands the instinct of a people whose nature is still feeble and uncertain, so that it could be easily wiped out, easily extinguished by a stronger race. The Jews, however, are beyond all doubt the strongest, toughest, and purest race at present living in Europe; they know how to succeed even under the worst conditions (in fact better than under favorable ones) by means of virtues of some sort, which one would like nowadays to label as vices—owing above all to a resolute faith which does not need to be ashamed before "modern ideas." . . .

It is certain that the Jews, if they desired—or if they were driven to it, as the anti-Semites seem to wish—could now have the ascendancy, nay, literally the supremacy, over Europe; that they are not working and planning for that end is equally certain. Meanwhile, they rather wish and desire, even somewhat importunely, to be inscribed and absorbed by Europe; they long to be finally settled, authorized, and respected somewhere, and wish to put an end to the nomadic life, to the "wandering Jew"—and one should take account of this impulse and tendency and make advances to it (it possibly betokens a mitigation of the Jewish instincts): for which purpose it would perhaps be useful and fair to banish the anti-Semitic bawlers out of the country. One should make advances with all prudency and with selection: pretty much as the English nobility do. It stands to reason that the more powerful and strongly marked types of new Germanism could enter into relation with the Jews with the least hesitation, for instance, the nobleman officer from the Prussian border: it would be interesting in many ways to see whether the genius for money and patience (and especially some intellect and intellectuality—sadly lacking in the place referred to) could not in addition be annexed and trained to the hereditary art of commanding and obeying—for both of which the country in question has now a classic reputation.

(*Beyond Good and Evil*, Aphorism 251)

* * *

One of the spectacles which the next century will invite us to witness is the decision regarding the fate of the European Jews. It is quite obvious now that they have cast their die and crossed their Rubicon: the only thing that remains for them is either to become masters of Europe or to lose Europe, as they once centuries ago lost Egypt where they were confronted with similar alternatives. In Europe, however, they have gone through a schooling of eighteen centuries such as no other nation has ever undergone, and the experiences of this dreadful time of probation have benefited not only the Jewish community but, even to a greater extent, the individual. As a consequence of this, the resourcefulness of the modern Jews, both in mind and soul, is extraordinary. Amongst all the inhabitants of Europe it is the Jews least of all who try to escape from any deep distress by recourse to drink or to suicide, as other, less gifted, people are prone to do. Every Jew can find in the history of his own family and his ancestors a long record of instances of the greatest coolness and perseverance amid difficulties and dreadful situations, an artful cunning in fighting with misfortune and hazard.

And above all it is their bravery under the cloak of wretched submission . . . that surpasses the virtues of all the saints. People wished to make them contemptible by treating them contemptibly for nearly twenty centuries, and refusing them access to all honorable positions and dignities, and by pushing them further down into the meaner trades—and under this process indeed they have not become any cleaner. But contemptible? They have never ceased for a moment from believing themselves qualified for the very highest functions, nor have the virtues of the suffering ever ceased to adorn them. Their manner of honoring their parents and children, the rationality of their marriages and marriage customs, distinguishes them amongst all Europeans. Besides this, they have been able to create for themselves a sense of power and eternal vengeance from the very trades that were left to them (or to which they were abandoned). Even in palliation of their usury we cannot help saying that, without this occasional pleasant and useful torture inflicted on their scorners, they would have experienced difficulty in preserving their self-respect for so long. For our self-respect depends upon our ability to make reprisals in both good and evil things. Nevertheless, their revenge never urges them on too far, for they all have that liberty of mind, and even of soul, produced in men by frequent changes of place, climate, and customs of neighbors and oppressors; they possess by far the greatest experience in all human intercourse, and even in their passions they exercise the caution which this experience has developed in them. They are so certain of their intellectual versatility and shrewdness that they never, even when reduced to the direst straits, have to earn their bread by manual labor as common workmen, porters, or farm hands. In their manners we can still see that they have never been inspired by chivalric and noble feelings, or that their bodies have ever been girt with fine weapons: a certain obtrusiveness alternates with a submissiveness which is often tender and almost always painful.

Now, however, that they unavoidably intermarry more and more year after year with the noblest blood of Europe, they will soon have a considerable heritage of good intellectual and physical manners, so that in another hundred years they will have a sufficiently noble aspect not to render themselves, as masters, ridiculous to those whom they will have subdued. And this is important! and therefore a settlement of the question is still premature. They themselves know very well that the conquest of Europe or any act of violence is not to be thought of; but they also know that some day or other Europe may, like a ripe fruit, fall into their hands, if they do not clutch at it too eagerly. In the meantime, it is necessary for them to distinguish themselves in all departments of European distinction and to stand in the front rank: until they shall have advanced so far as to determine themselves what distinction shall mean. Then they will be called the pioneers and guides of the Europeans whose modesty they will no longer offend.

And then where shall an outlet be found for this abundant wealth of great impressions accumulated during such an extended period and representing Jewish history for every Jewish family, this wealth of passions, virtues, resolutions, resignations, struggles, and conquests of all kinds—where can it find an outlet but in great intellectual men and works! On the day when the Jews will be able to exhibit to us as their own work such jewels and golden vessels as no European nation, with its shorter and less profound experience, can or could produce, when Israel shall have changed its eternal vengeance into an eternal benediction for Europe, then that seventh day will once more appear when old Jehovah may rejoice in Himself, in His creation, in His chosen people—and all, all of us, will rejoice with him!

(*The Dawn of Day*, pp. 210–214)

* * *

On the Gospels:

One is among Jews—the first consideration to keep from losing the thread completely—Paul and Christ were little superlative Jews. . . . One would no more associate with the first Christians than one would with Polish Jews—they both do not smell good. . . . Pontius Pilate is the only figure in the New Testament who commands respect. To take a Jewish affair seriously — he does not persuade himself to do that. One Jew more or less — what does it matter?

. . . The Jews have made mankind so thoroughly false that even today the Christian can feel anti-Jewish without realizing that he is himself the *ultimate Jewish consequence*.

(From *The Antichrist*, quoted in O'Brien, *The Siege: the Saga of Israel and Zionism*, p. 58)

ANATOLE FRANCE   *(1844–1924)*

French novelist and critic

What is called the triumph of Christianity is more accurately the triumph of Judaism, and to Israel fell the singular privilege of giving a god to the world.

(*Epigrams, Oeuvres complet*)

PAUL VON HINDENBURG   *(1847–1934)*

German military and political leader; 2nd president of the Weimar Republic, 1925–1934

The Imperial military rules and regulations which were discriminatory to the Jews of our country were not drawn up by me. As a subordinate to the high military command, I had to abide by these laws, of course. But let me assure you, that I was never in favor of any discriminatory laws against any element of our citizenship. . . .

The Jewish people have given to humanity some of its greatest men. Germany is proud to have among its citizens a scholar of the caliber of Prof. Einstein. I do not need to tell you that in Germany your race has a significant share in the development of German culture. . . . Informed as I am of the multiple activities of the Jewish race, familiar with their history and coming in contact with the outstanding representatives of your race, I fully appreciate the part

Jews play in Germany and all over the world in the advancement of humanity toward a better world. . . .

No, there is no room for intolerance and prejudice, if permanent world peace is to be established. That is why I granted you this interview, despite my aversion to talking for the press, in order to make it clear once and for all that democratic Germany will not tolerate any prejudice towards any race or creed.

(From an interview granted to Miriam Sterner, in *American Jewish World*, 29 June 1928)

ARTHUR JAMES   *(1848–1930)*

Earl of Balfour; Prime Minister of England, 1902–1905

During a Parliamentary debate on the second reading of the Aliens Bill of 1904, which was to control immigration into Britain more strictly:

The treatment of the [Jewish] race has been a disgrace to Christendom, a disgrace which tarnishes the fair fame of Christianity even at this moment, and which in the Middle Ages gave rise to horrors which whoever makes himself acquainted with them even in the most superficial manner, reads of with shuddering and feelings of terror lest any trace of the blood-guiltiness then incurred should have fallen on the descendants of those who committed the deeds.

(*Hansard*, vol. 145, col. 795, 2 May 1905)

SIR WILLIAM OSLER   *(1849–1919)*

Canadian physician and educator

From an open letter written in Berlin and published in the *Canada Medical and Surgical Journal*, July 1884:

The modern "hep, hep, hep" shrieked in Berlin for some years has by no means died out, and to judge from the tone of several of the papers devoted to the Jewish question there are not wanting some who would gladly revert to the plan adopted on the Nile some thousands of years ago for solving the Malthusian problem of Semitic increase. Doubtless there were then, as now, noisy agitators . . . who clamored for the hard laws which ultimately prevailed, and for the taskmasters, whose example so many Gentile generations have willingly followed, of demanding, where they safely could, bricks without straw of their Israelitish brethren. Should another Moses arise and preach a Semitic exodus from Germany, and should he prevail, they would leave the land impoverished far more than was ancient Egypt by the loss of the "jewels of gold and jewels of silver" of which the people were "spoiled."

To say nothing of the material wealth—enough to buy Palestine over and over again from the Turk—there is not a profession which would not suffer the serious loss of many of its most brilliant ornaments and in none more so than our own. I hope to be able to get the data with reference to the exact number of professors and docents of Hebrew extraction in the German Medical Facilities. The number is very great, and of those I know their positions have been won by hard and honorable work; but I fear that, as I hear has already been the case, the present agitation will help to make the attainment of university professorships additionally difficult. One cannot but notice here, in any assembly of doctors, the strong Semitic element; at the local societies and at the German congress of Physicians it was particularly noticeable, and the same holds good in any collection of students. All honor to them!

(Cushman, *The Life of Sir William Osler*, vol. I, p. 214)

THOMÁŠ G. MASARYK   (1850–1937)

Czech scholar and patriot; chief founder and first president of Czechoslovakia, 1918–1935

In the fifties of the last century every Slovak child in the vicinity of Goding was nurtured in an atmosphere of anti-Semitism,—in school, church and society at large. Mother would forbid us to go near the Lechners because, as she said, Jews were using the blood of Christian children. I would therefore make a wide turn to avoid passing their house; and so did all my schoolmates. . . .

The superstition of Christian blood used for Passover cakes had become so much part and parcel of my existence that whenever I chanced to come near a Jew—I wouldn't do it on purpose—I would look at his fingers to see if no blood were there. For a long time I continued this practice. . . .

At the high school of Auspitz I had a single Jewish fellow student. I used to pass him by and look at his fingers. We would torture him in un-Christian manner, even though he was a most good-natured fellow. He was not very clever, was one of the poorer students and opposed our attitude. This Jewish fellow-student converted me away from anti-Semitic ideas.

We once took an excursion into the Poku Mountains. On the way back we rested in an inn at Danujowitz, where we took our repast. We drank wine and beer, we smoked, our teachers enjoyed all with us, and the target of our jokes became "Leopold" (I can recall his face, but I have forgotten his name.) The sun was about to set when Leopold disappeared from the table, and we went to look for him. Boys found him behind a gate, as though praying. Others also went out to observe him and tease him at his prayer. I also went to look at him. I shall never forget how Leopold startled me. He stood behind the gate in an unclean spot, apparently so as not to be observed. He kept on bowing and praying.

All at once I forgot to tease him and to poke fun at him. While we were enjoying ourselves Leopold did not forget his praying. From that moment on my anti-Semitism suffered a shock, even though it was not fully overcome as yet.

My parents again moved to Goding, and I had occasion to study the ghetto of that time and a number of Jews living there. My acquaintance with the Jews brought about a feeling of friendship—a friendship both faithful and full of beauty. In Brunn and Vienna the circle of my Jewish friends became larger and larger, so that prejudice vanished into the thin air, even though my childhood days would claim their toll from time to time. Past experience is mighty and dreadful.

By becoming acquainted with each other, by living together, by economic mutual relations, blood will be forgotten. A new generation brought up in a public school cannot conceive of anti-Semitism in the form in which we had conceived it, when they had their Jewish ghetto and we Christians had ours. . . . Would that I may unmake all that anti-Semitism caused me to do in my childhood days.

(Capek, *President Masaryk Tells His Story*, p. 28)

JOSEPH CONRAD   *(1857–1924)*

Polish-British novelist

. . . Conrad's biography begins here, with the marginality thrust upon him even by birth. His names were a career in themselves, part of that dare to achieve or fail. As Jozef Teodor Konrad Korzeniowski, he would, like Proteus, always be in a state of defining and redefining himself. . . .

For the Korzeniowskis and other members of their class, money-making was shunned; was, indeed, considered a dirty enterprise better left to vulgarians and Jews. Apollo, then, was born into a traditional society, with certain class, caste, and family pretensions, and his attitude toward money and money-making was clearly transmitted to the young Conrad. Later, when Conrad wrote to his friend Cunninghame Graham about "making money," he referred to it in mock-Yiddish terms as the "shent-per-shent" business, clearly attributing the money business to Jewish elements. And to Garnett, Conrad mentioned that his maternal grandfather, also a member of the land-owning gentry, never wrote anything but letters "and a large number of promissory notes dedicated to various Jews."

(Karl, *Joseph Conrad: The Three Lives*, pp. 22–23)

* * *

To Cunninghame Graham, as noted above, Conrad speaks of the "shent-per-shent" business: "I am making preparations to receive [Graham's essay] which [sic] all the honours due to his distinguished position. I always thought a lot of that man. He was no philistine anyhow—and no Jew, since he had no eye for the shent-per-shent business the other fellow spotted at once" (January 7, 1898). Conrad's early letters are dotted with contemptuous references to Unwin, Conrad's first publisher and Edward Garnett's employer, as an "Israelite" intent only on profit.

(Joseph Conrad, p. 82)

* * *

. . . This parallelism of dislike of Jews and yet reliance of their merchant abilities runs, as we shall see, straight through Conrad's entire career, as he found himself in the hands of one Jew after another and depended heavily on their good will, from Fisher Unwin to Heinemann to James Brand Pinker, his agent and devoted patron.

(Joseph Conrad, p. 84)

* * *

. . . Conrad was heartened by Fisher Unwin's agreement to collect the stories into a volume, although by this time he was disillusioned by the latter's niggardly terms. The two men, author and publisher, could not have been more different and lacking in understanding of the other. Unwin found it almost impossible to handle individuals, and he tended to drive a hard bargain with his authors. On the other hand, Conrad did not sell, and Unwin could not expect much in the way of return except prestige for a well-received author. Conrad, for his part, mocked Unwin's Jewishness, making fun of him to Garnett and Graham, portraying him as the stereotypical Hebrew tight with money and deceptive in business affairs. . . .

(Joseph Conrad, p. 379)

* * *

The *Outlook* also printed Conrad's piece on Alphonse Daudet, in the April 9 issue. It was a publication Conrad could only scorn: ". . . its price three pence sterling, its attitude—literary; its policy— Imperialism, tempered by expediency; its mission—to make money for a Jew. . . ."

(Joseph Conrad, p. 422)

Even more sorrowfully, he heard of the death of [his agent] Pinker, in New York, on February 8, something totally unexpected and a loss of tremendous proportions to Conrad. Not only had Pinker nurtured him in his apprentice years, they had become inseparable friends, true survivors of the publishing wars. Pinker was Conrad's junior by six years, and his death was the first of any close friend. . . .

In another sense, Conrad's attitude toward Jews was altered by his association with Pinker. The anti-Semitic assumptions which underlay some of his earlier comments disappeared almost entirely, except for an occasional remark such as Berenson's being a "noxious old Jew." Conrad's anti-Semitism, as noted earlier, was never of the virulent kind, but rather a not very deeply held feeling that came with his birth and class. He took the alleged coarseness and vulgarity of Jews for granted, and he also, to some extent, saw them as part of that radical or revolutionary world he detested. In his nurturing years, he had not observed them as individuals but as men involved in money matters—lending, selling, serving as middlemen—or on the European scene in politically extreme activities. Once he saw them as individuals, Rothenstein, Pinker, Winawer, Knopf, among others, his reactions were directed at the man, not the race. In no way did he enter into the fashionable and often virulent anti-Semitism of many of his contemporaries—Eliot, Lawrence, Pound, Wyndham Lewis, Woolf, Hemingway, or the French writers around Charles Maurras.

(*Joseph Conrad*, pp. 867–868.)

BEATRICE WEBB   (1858–1943)

British socialist; co-founder of the London School of Economics and Political Science

Why is it that everyone who has dealing with Jewry ends up being prejudiced against the Jews?

(N. Mackenzie, *Letters of Sidney and Beatrice Webb*, p. 334)

Beatrice Webb, in a reference to the 1929 massacres in Palestine:

I can't understand why the Jews make such a fuss over a few dozen of their people being killed in Palestine. As many are killed every week in London in traffic accidents, and no one pays any attention.

(Quoted by Chaim Weizmann, in *Trial and Error*, p. 331)

ALFRED NORTH WHITEHEAD   *(1861–1947)*

British mathematician and philosopher; co-author with Bertrand Russell of Principia Mathematica

Our modern progressive civilization owes its origin mainly to the Greeks and the Jews. The progressiveness is the point to be emphasized . . . the Greeks and the Jews, in the few centuries before and after the beginning of the Christian era, intensified an element of progressive activity which was diffused throughout the many peoples in the broad belt from Mesopotamia to Spain. . . . So far as the Greeks and Jews were active, progress was not in a rut degenerating into conservatism. . . . The Greeks have vanished, the Jews remain. . . .

("An Appeal to Sanity," in *Atlantic Monthly*, vol. 163, p. 315, 1939)

RICHARD STRAUSS   *(1864–1949)*

German composer

Rehearsing Hans Sommer's *Loreley* was a depressing business because "the thing is so badly scored." (To his father, 28 May 1892) After the premiere he wrote to his sister on 14 June:

> It was a gigantic slog, but it went capitally and was well received. Sommer was called to take a bow after the love duet. . . . Sommer, I'm afraid, will never grasp that nowadays one can't just haul Loreleis out of the romantic attic; he is very pleased; and I'm glad that we have once again done a little honour to a German composer who isn't a Jew.

Once again we are reminded of how susceptible Strauss still was at that date to the anti-semitism of his father and Alexander Ritter, and of his fervent nationalism. . . .

(Schuh, *Richard Strauss*, p. 197)

. . . On Corfu he visited "the beautiful, poetic villa of Empress Elisabeth [of Austria], whose unhappy notion, born of misguided, feminine, emotional silliness, to erect a monument to Heine introduces an ugly discord into the whole." Once again the anti-semitism fired by Ritter reveals itself.

(Schuh, *Richard Strauss*, p. 298)

ERICH LUDENDORFF   *(1865–1937)*

German army general in World War I

I decline Christianity because it is Jewish, because it is international, and because, in cowardly fashion, it preaches Peace on Earth.

(Belief in a German God)

BERNARD BERENSON   *(1865–1959)*

Lithuanian-born art historian and Jewish convert to Christianity

The Jew still has a mission. . . . In the future he should cultivate the qualities that anti-Dreyfusards and other anti-Semites have reproached him with. He should not identify himself with the rest of the nation in its chauvinism, in its overweening self-satisfaction, self-adulation, and self-worship. He should be in every land the element that keeps up standards of human value and cultivates a feeling for proportion and relations. He should be supernational as the Roman Church claims to be. . . .

From Ezra down, this Jewish exclusiveness was due less and less to a feeling of superiority, certainly not in the ways of this world, but rather to a fear of contamination. Rabbinical Judaism is first and foremost an organization for keeping a small minority, scattered among the nations, from dissolving and disappearing. It was thus based on fear. . . .

(*Rumor and Reflection*, Simon & Schuster, New York 1952)

... In assimilating the high culture of his greatly admired Boston, Bernard assimilated as well the current anti-Semitism and anti-foreignism of the business and fashionable world. He learned to shudder at the crudity of immigrant manners and the strident vulgarity of many of the fugitives from the ghetto. He convinced himself that he had successfully escaped from his blighting heritage and had achieved a new identity. The truce—for it proved only that—which he made with his buried feelings would last for decades; suppress them utterly he could not; nor could he deny himself at times a lurking sense of pride in the Jewish roots of much of Christian culture or in the fact that his Hebraic puritanism had ancestral sources more ancient than the New England puritanism which he had adopted. He learned that life would be a prolonged accommodation to the prejudices of the great world and its upper crust. He would never quite lose the traces of Jewish self-hatred which at the turn of the century his sharp-eyed friend Henry Adams was quick to spot in his emancipated Jewish friends. He had much more to learn of the subtle ramifications of anti-Semitism against which the garment of Christianity which he put on would not protect him. The path to a personal identity would prove strewn with unexpected hazards and ambiguous guideposts.

(Samuels, *Bernard Berenson: The Making of a Connoisseur*, 1979, pp. 39–40)

JÓZEF PILSUDSKI *(1867–1935)*

Polish patriot; leader of pre-World War II Poland

September, 1894:

Looking now at the most recent period, we find one paramount factor commanding the Jews to go hand in hand with us—namely, the solidarity of the Polish and Jewish proletariats who, living together and suffering together from the same oppression and exploitation, should combine their forces. This they will undoubtedly do some day. The solidarity of their interests is at the same time a guarantee that when independence will be consummated, even though under a capitalist regime, the Jewish proletarian in the Polish Republic will have a sure and strong ally in the person of the conscious Polish worker who, until the day of victory, will not desist from the life and death struggle against every kind of injustice, national, economic, or political.

(In *Przedswit*, the Polish émigré paper in London, No. 9)

JOHN BUCHAN   (1875–1940)

1st Baron of Tweedsmuir; Scottish-Canadian novelist;
Governor-General of Canada, 1935–1940

To my mind the Jew is the natural bridge between the East and the West. . . . The prosperity of the old inhabitants, the Arabs, depends upon the prosperity of Palestine as a whole, and to this the newcomers have most nobly contributed. . . .

Zionism has never been more important than at this moment. . . . In these days, when most countries are jealously restricting their immigration, Palestine is the one city of refuge left to the persecuted. Of course it cannot meet the whole problem. The number of Jews who can be admitted must depend rigidly upon Palestine's economic capacity to absorb them. But that there should be such a city of refuge, even though its capacity for reception is limited, gives beyond doubt a certain hope and comfort to the Jews in the darkest hour that they have known since Titus captured Jerusalem. The success of Zionism is no less important to Britain. Palestine holds the key to the strategical position on the great route between West and East. . . .

These are utilitarian arguments which I have given you, but there is another which must appeal to any man of imagination and humanity. The Jews have never forgotten Jerusalem, but till a few years ago their Holy Land has been only an inspiration and a dream. Now it is being made a reality. Perhaps this appeals specially to a Scotsman, for we Scots, like the Jews, have always been a far-wandering race, scattered over every part of the globe. But in our wanderings we have always had Scotland behind us, our mother country, the shrine of our sentiments and memories. Is it not right and

fitting that the Jew, after long wanderings, should again find his homeland?
(From his address at a Zionist dinner in Montreal on 20 April 1936)

* * *

John Buchan has quite often been accused of anti-Semitism. Such accusations have referred to certain slighting remarks about Jews which are to be found in his novels, and to one brief passage in particular. "A little, white-faced Jew with an eye like a rattlesnake," working as prime mover of a vile, international conspiracy has been taken by one or two by no means futile or unintelligent critics to imply a rooted racial dislike on my father's part. That there are only about half a dozen disobliging references to Jews in all of JB's many works of fiction goes for nothing against that sharp-edged and fatally memorable phrase. And here, I think, JB has been the victim of his own style, and of a radical change in attitude to racial difference which he was never to live to know. He was guilty, for once, of thoughtlessness, of using a commonplace of his time without considering its implications. For the man who gives, in *The Dancing Floor* a most attractive portrait of a benevolent Jewish financier and who, in *The Prince of the Captivity* gives another Jew an impressive history of courage and integrity, the line quoted above might charitably be thought of as no more than a lapse in taste, as true feeling sacrificed to a brilliant phrase. *Qui s'excuse s'accuse:* I shall not labour this point, beyond remarking that a strong distaste for the Rand financiers – who, as all Milner's young men saw it, hampered their purpose and muddied their good intentions after the South African war – remained with JB for a long time. It is, I would submit, the basis for those disobliging references to which I have referred. That those financiers happened to be Jewish, of a not very exalted variety, was inevitable at the time; and they were as cordially disliked by the more thoughtful and sensitive elements of their own people as by any Anglo-Saxon theorist of Europe. John Buchan was a man of sensibility. One hint from any of his Jewish friends that he was doing them a disservice would have been quite enough to change his mind. Yet no such hint ever came. What is puzzling to me is that John Buchan should have been so persistently tarred with this particular brush, when so many other well-known writers from Henry James to T. S. Eliot could equally well have been indicted. As I have tried to show, my father's character was far from negative. He was never immovably "anti" anything or anyone, except the forces of evil. Proof that he had no prejudice against Jews, perhaps, was his friendship with Chaim Weizmann, and the work he did inside and outside Parliament to further the Zionist cause. It was scarcely an anti-Semite whose name was inscribed in Israel's Golden Book for his work for the Jewish National Fund. Finally, even John Buchan's prophetic imagination, continually engaged as it was with the dangers threatening civilization, the permanent presence of evil, simply could not have stretched to encompass the horrors of Auschwitz and Ravensbruck. On a lighter note JB, as a connoisseur of human ambivalences, would have been amused to see a well-known Jewish Canadian writer, Mordecai Richler, one of his most savage accusers, happily accepting the Governor-General's prize for literature, which he himself had instituted.

(William Buchan, *John Buchan: A Memoir*, pp. 250–251)

LA CIVILITÀ CATTOLICA

A semi-official journal of the Vatican

From a series of unsigned articles written by Giuseppe Oreglia de San Stefano:

The practice of killing children for the Paschal Feast is now very rare in the more cultivated parts of Europe, more frequent in Eastern Europe, and common, all too common, in the East. . . . [In the West, the Jews] have now other things to think of than to make their unleavened bread with Christian blood, occupied as they are in ruling almost like kings in finance and journalism.

(20 August 1881, p. 478)

* * *

It remains therefore generally proved . . . that the sanguinary Paschal rite . . . is a general law binding on the consciences of all Hebrews to make use of the blood of a Christian child, primarily for the sanctification of their souls, and also, although secondarily, to bring shame and disgrace to Christ and to Christianity.

(3 December 1881, p. 606)

* * *

Every year the Hebrews crucify a child. . . . In order that the blood be effective, the child must die in torments.

(21 January 1882, p. 214)

EDUARD BENEŠ (1884–1948)

Czech statesman, and president of the League of Nations

Statement issued in London by Beneš as president of the Czechoslovakian Government-in-Exile, 5 October 1941:

The Jewish problem, along with many other problems relating to the reconstruction of the life of our State after the conclusion of the war, has greatly occupied my mind. It represents an important factor in our efforts to secure civil liberty and social justice in Czechoslovakia within the framework of a genuine and improved new order which, as a sequel to the chaos let loose upon the world by the insane Nazi experiment, is certainly destined to come into existence. In a restored Czechoslovakia all sections of the population, as far as they have shown themselves, and will show themselves in the future, as capable of aiding in the work of the State, must receive due justice.

The Nazis incite people to intolerance and to racial, religious and ideological fanaticism. They expel those who are not so cowardly as to accept their regime, or those who in their eyes sinned only by the fact that they were not born of "Aryan" parents, while at the same time they drive their own youth to their grave on battlefields. But all this is only transitional, like everything which is in contradiction with the laws of humanity. Hold on, therefore, to the end and be sure that the renewed Czechoslovakian republic will have no other program than the program of religious tolerance maintained by the First Republic of President Masaryk.

(Beneš, *Democracy Today and Tomorrow*, 1939, pp. 161 f.)

KEMAL ATATURK   *(1882–1938)*

Turkish patriot, soldier, and statesman; founder and first president of the Turkish Republic

Statement at Izmir, 2 February 1923:

We have in our midst faithful elements, who have linked their destiny with that of the dominant element, the Turkish people. Above all, the Jews, having proved their loyalty to this nation and fatherland, have led hitherto a comfortable existence and will continue in the future to live prosperously and happily.

(Galante, *Turcs et Juifs*, p. 84)

D. H. LAWRENCE   *(1885–1930)*

British novelist

Lawrence to Mark Gertler, 9 October 1916:

My dear Gertler: Your terrible and dreadful picture has just come. This is the first picture you have ever painted: it is the best *modern* picture I have seen. . . . It would take a Jew to paint this picture. It would need your national history to get you here, without disintegrating you first. You are of an older race than I, and in these ultimate processes, you are beyond me, older than I am. But I think I am sufficiently the same, to be able to understand.

. . . At last your race is at an end—these pictures are its death-cry. And it will be left for the Jews to utter the final and great death-cry of this epoch: the Christians are not reduced sufficiently. I must say, I have, for you, in your work, reverence, the reverence for the great articulate extremity of art.

. . . You are twenty-five, and have painted this picture—I tell you, it takes three thousand years to get where this picture is—and we Christians haven't got two thousand years behind us yet. . . .

(Moore, *The Collected Letters of D. H. Lawrence*,
vol. I, pp. 477–478)

Lawrence to S. S. Koteliansky, 3 July 1917:
... Why humanity has hated Jews, I have come to the conclusion, is
that the Jews have always taken religion—since the great days, that
is—and used it for their own personal and private gratification, as if it
were a thing administered to their own importance and well-being and
conceit. This is the slave trick of the Jews—they use the great religious
consciousness as a trick of personal conceit. This is abominable. With
them, the conscious ego is the absolute, and God is a name they flatter
themselves with.—When they have learned again pure reverence to
the Holy Spirit, then they will be free, and not slaves before men.
Now, a Jew cringes before men, and takes God as a Christian takes
whiskey, for his own self-indulgence.

(*The Collected Letters of D. H. Lawrence*, p. 517)

* * *

Lawrence to Waldo Frank, 17 July 1917:
... I hear Huebsch is a Jew. Are you a Jew also? The best of Jews is,
that they *know* truth from untruth. The worst of them is, that they are
rather slave-like, and that almost inevitably, in action, they betray the
truth they know, and fawn to the powers that be. But they *know* the
truth. Only they must cringe their legs and betray it. The material
world dominates them with a base kind of fetish domination. Yet they
know the truth all the while. Yet they cringe their buttocks to the
fetish of Mammon, peeping over their shoulders to see if the truth is
watching them, observing their betrayal.—I have got Jewish friends,
whom I am on the point of forswearing for ever. ...

(*The Collected Letters of D. H. Lawrence*, p. 520)

* * *

Lawrence to Waldo Frank, 15 September 1917:
... So Judas was a Super-Christian! And Jews are Super-Christian
lovers of mankind! No doubt it is true. It makes me dislike Judas and
Jews very much.—To learn plainly to hate mankind, to detest the
spawning human-being, that is the only cleanliness now.

We shall disagree too much.—I believe in Paradise and Paradisal
beings: but humanity, mankind—*crotte!* We shall disagree too much,
from the root. ... God, I *don't want* to be sane, as men are counted
sane. It all stinks.

(*The Collected Letters of D. H. Lawrence*, p. 525)

Lawrence to Edith Eder, 21 May 1918 [?]:

. . . I feel queer and desolate in my soul—like Ovid in Thrace. And the world is such a useless place. But I set potatoes and mow the grass and write my never-to-be-finished *Studies in Classic American Literature*. I am reading Gibbon. He says the Jews are the great *haters* of the human race—and the great *anti-social* principle.—Strikes me that is true—for the last 2500 years, at least.—I feel such a profound hatred myself, of the human race, I almost know what it is to be a Jew. . . .

(The Collected Letters of D. H. Lawrence, p. 553)

* * *

Lawrence to B. W. Huebsch, 30 September 1919:

. . . I swear people are no longer people, over there with you—sort of stalking emotional demons. You no doubt are a Jew—capable of the eternal detachment of judgment—connoisseurs of the universe, the Jews—even connoisseurs of human life—dealers in fine arts and treasures—dealers—you might just tell me what you *really* think of the United States.

(The Collected Letters of D. H. Lawrence, p. 595)

* * *

Lawrence to Mabel Luhan, 23 September 1926:

. . . We leave here on Tuesday, and stay a few days in Paris, on our way to Florence. . . . I have seen a few of the old people: and yesterday the Louis Untermeyers: extraordinary, the *ewige Jude*, by virtue of not having a real core to him, he is eternal. *Plus ça change, plus c'est la même chose*: that is the whole history of the Jew, from Moses to Untermeyer: and all by virtue of having a little pebble at the middle of him, instead of an alive core.

(The Collected Letters of D. H. Lawrence, vol. II, p. 938)

* * *

Lawrence to Dr. Trigant Burrow, 6 June 1925:

Dear Dr. Burrow: I found your letter and the two reprints when I got back here. I am in entire sympathy with your idea of social images. In fact, I feel myself that the Jewish consciousness is now composed entirely of social images: there is no new-starting "reality" left. Nothing springs alive and new from the blood. All is a chemical reaction, analysis and decomposition and reprecipitation of social images. It is what happens to all old races. They lose the faculty for real experience, and go on decomposing their test-tubes full of social images. One fights and fights for that living something that stirs way down in the blood, and *creates* consciousness. But the world won't have it. To the present human mind, everything is ready-made, and since the sun cannot be new, there can be nothing new under the sun. But to me, the sun, like the rest of the cosmos, is alive, and therefore not ready-made at all. . . .

(*The Collected Letters of D. H. Lawrence*, II, pp. 842–843)

ISAK DINESEN (KAREN BLIXEN)   *(1885–1962)*

Danish-born author of Out of Africa

Letter to Ingeborg Dinesen, 4 November 1928:

I am reading a book: *Disraeli*, by a French author, André Maurois. If you can get a hold of it you should read it, it is very enjoyable. I think I would have been completely happy if I had been married to Disraeli, but so of course was his wife; you know I have always been mad about Jews, and he was an exceptionally brilliant and charming Jew. . . .

(*Letters from Africa, 1914–1931*, p. 385)

RUPERT BROOKE   *(1887–1915)*

British poet

In fact the thought of London appalled him [Brooke] leading him to use language unsuited to the ears of an infant of six months, saying its ways were thronged with "lean and vicious people, dirty hermaphrodites and eunuchs, moral vagabonds, pitiable scum." Troubled with a brief recurrence of the old bitterness, he even vented the spleen of his anti-Semitism—which at times could be virulent (a disagreeable result

of his admiration for Belloc) . . . —so grim was the prospect of a return
to the modern world.

(C. Hassall, *Rupert Brooke, A Biography*, p. 438)

T. E. LAWRENCE   *(1888–1935)*

British soldier and scholar, a.k.a. "Lawrence of Arabia"

Lawrence hoped that the Zionist movement would have the result of
bringing the Jews into a position of technological leadership in the
Arab regions of Asia and North Africa and that they would help to
raise the material level of their Arab neighbors. "The Jewish experiment," he wrote in 1920, "is a conscious effort, on the part of the least
European people in Europe, to make head against the drift of the ages,
and return once more to the Orient from which they came. The colonists will take back with them to the land which they occupied for
some centuries before the Christian era samples of all the knowledge
and technique of Europe. They propose to settle down amongst the
existing Arabic-speaking population of the country, a people of kindred origin, but far different social condition. They hope to adjust their
mode of life to the climate of Palestine, and by the exercise of their skill
and capital to make it as highly organised as a European state. The
success of their scheme will involve inevitably the raising of the present
Arab population to their own material level, only a little after themselves in point of time, and the consequences might be of the highest
importance for the future of the Arab world. It might well prove a
source of technical supply rendering them independent of industrial
Europe, and in that case the new confederation might become a for-
midable element of world power. However, such a contingency will not
be for the first or even for the second generation, but it must be borne
in mind in any laying out of foundations of empire in Western Asia.
These to a very large extent must stand or fall by the course of the
Zionist effort, and by the course of events in Russia."

There is no evidence that Lawrence anticipated the intransigence and hostility that would develop between Arabs and Jews. . . .

(Mack, *A Prince of Our Disorder; The Life of
T. E. Lawrence*, pp. 252–253)

EVELYN WAUGH   (1902–1966)

British novelist

The "scrapes" he discovered [in Kenya] were those concerning the friction between the Europeans, Indians and African Nationalists. Adopting the tone of a mild-mannered, quizzical outsider, he devotes nearly twelve pages to the defence of the white settlement. While strenuously condemning all proven injustice he nevertheless concludes: "It is just worth considering the possibility that there may be something valuable behind the indefensible and inexplicable assumption of superiority by the Anglo-Saxon race." There is little doubt that Waugh shared this assumption.

(Stannard, *Evelyn Waugh, The Early Years, 1903–39*, p. 263)

* * *

Waugh to _____ , 6 March 1947:

. . . I was not the least anti-Semitic before I came here [to Hollywood, California]. I am now. It is intolerable to see them enjoying themselves. . . .

(Amory, *The Letters of Evelyn Waugh*, p. 248)

11

The Communist Revolution
and Regime

KARL MARX   (1818–1883)

Prussian social philosopher; author of Das Kapital,
The Communist Manifesto

Let us consider the real Jew: not the Sabbath Jew . . . but the everyday Jew.

Let us not seek the secret of the Jew in his religion, but let us seek the secret of his religion in the real Jew.

What is the profane basis of Judaism? Practical need, self-interest. What is the worldly cult of the Jew? Huckstering. What is his worldly god? Money.

Very well; then in emancipating itself from huckstering and money, and thus from real and practical Judaism, our age would emancipate itself.

An organization of society which would abolish the preconditions and thus the very possibility of huckstering, would make the Jew impossible. His religious consciousness would evaporate. . . . On the other hand, when the Jew recognizes his practical nature as invalid and endeavors to abolish it, he begins to deviate from his former path of development, works for general human emancipation and turns against the supreme practical expression of human self-estrangement.

We discern in Judaism, therefore, a communal antisocial element of the present time, whose historical development, zealously aided in its harmful aspects by the Jews, has now attained its culminating point, a point at which it must necessarily begin to disintegrate.

In the final analysis, the emancipation of the Jews is the emancipation of mankind from Judaism.

Judaism has maintained itself alongside Christianity, not only because it constituted the religious criticism of Christianity . . . but equally because the practical Jewish spirit — Judaism or commerce — has perpetuated itself in Christian society and has even attained its highest development. . . . It is from its own entrails that civil society ceaselessly engenders the Jew.

What was, in itself, the basis of the Jewish religion? Practical need, egoism. . . . Money is the zealous god of Israel. . . . The god of the Jews has been secularized and become the god of this world.

In its perfected practice the spiritual egoism of Christianity becomes the material egoism of the Jew. . . . The social emancipation of the Jew is the emancipation of society from Judaism.

(*Early Writings*, trans. T. B. Bottomore, pp. 34ff)

PETER ALEXEIVICH KROPOTKIN
(1842–1921)

Russian revolutionary and anarchist

Another teacher conquered our rather uproarious form in a quite different manner. It was the teacher of writing, the last one of the teaching staff. If the "heathen"—that is, the German and the French teachers—were regarded with little respect, the teacher of writing, Ebert, who was a German Jew, was a real martyr. To be insolent with him was a sort of *chic* amongst the pages. His poverty alone must have been the reason why he kept to his lesson in our corps. The old hands, who had stayed for two or three years in the fifth form without moving higher up, treated him very badly; but by some means or other he had made an agreement with them: "One frolic during each lesson, but no more,"—an agreement which, I am afraid, was not honestly kept on our side.

One day, one of the residents of the remote peninsula soaked the blackboard sponge with ink and chalk and flung it at the calligraphy martyr. "Get it, Ebert!" he shouted, with a stupid smile. The sponge touched Ebert's shoulder, the grimy ink spurted into his face and down on to his white shirt.

We were sure that this time Ebert would leave the room and report the fact to the inspector. But he only exclaimed, as he took out his cotton handkerchief and wiped his face, "Gentlemen, one frolic,—no more today!" "The shirt is spoiled," he added, in a subdued voice, and continued to correct some one's book.

We looked stupefied and ashamed. Why, instead of reporting, he had thought at once of the agreement! The feeling of the class turned in his favor. "What you have done is stupid," we reproached our comrade. "He is a poor man, and you have spoiled his shirt! Shame!" somebody cried.

The culprit went at once to make excuses. "One must learn, learn, sir," was all that Ebert said in reply, with sadness in his voice.

All became silent after that, and at the next lesson, as if we had settled it beforehand, most of us wrote in our best possible handwriting, and took our books to Ebert, asking him to correct them. He was radiant; he felt happy that day.

This fact impressed me, and was never wiped out from my memory. To this day I feel grateful to that remarkable man for his lesson.

(*Memoirs of a Revolutionist*, pp. 89–90)

* * *

During my journey I had bought a number of books and collections of socialist newspapers. In Russia, such books were "unconditionally prohibited" by censorship; and some of the collections of newspapers and reports of international congresses could not be bought for any amount of money, even in Belgium. "Shall I part with them, while my brother and my friends would be so glad to have them at St. Petersburg?" I asked myself; and I decided that by all means I must get them into Russia.

I returned to St. Petersburg via Vienna and Warsaw. Thousands of Jews live by smuggling on the Polish frontier, and I thought that if I could succeed in discovering only one of them, my books would be carried in safety across the border. However, to alight at a small railway station near the frontier, while every other passenger went on, and to hunt there for smugglers, would hardly have been reasonable; so I took a side branch of the railway and went to Cracow. "The capital of old Poland is near to the frontier," I thought, "and I shall find there some Jew who will lead me to the men I seek."

I reached the once renowned and brilliant city in the evening, and early the next morning went out from the hotel on my search. To my bewilderment I saw, however, at every street corner and wherever I turned my eyes in the otherwise deserted market-place, a Jew, wearing the traditional long dress and locks of his forefathers, and watching there for some Polish nobleman or tradesman who might send him on an errand and pay him a few coppers for the service. I wanted to find *one* Jew; and now there were too many of them. Whom should I approach? I made the round of the town, and then, in my despair, I decided to accost the Jew who stood at the entrance gate of my hotel,—an immense old palace, of which, in former days, every hall was filled with elegant crowds of gayly dressed dancers, but which now fulfilled the more prosaic function of giving food and shelter to a few occasional travelers. I explained to the man my desire of smuggling into Russia a rather heavy bundle of books and newspapers.

"Very easily done, sir," he replied. "I will just bring to you the representative of the Universal Company for the International Exchange of (let me say) Rags and Bones. They carry on the largest smuggling business in the world, and he is sure to oblige you." Half an hour later he really returned with the representative of the company,—a most elegant young man, who spoke in perfection Russian, German, and Polish.

He looked at my bundle, weighed it with his hands, and asked what sort of books were in it.

"All severely prohibited by Russian censorship: that is why they must be smuggled in."

"Books," he said, "are not exactly in our line of trade; our business lies in costly silks. If I were going to pay my men by weight, according to our silk tariff, I should have to ask you a quite extravagant price. And then, to tell the truth, I don't much like meddling with books. The slightest mishap, and 'they' would make of it a political affair, and then it would cost the Universal Rags and Bones Company a tremendous sum of money to get clear of it."

I probably looked very sad, for the elegant young man who represented the Universal Rags and Bones Company immediately added: "Don't be troubled. He [the hotel commissionnaire] will arrange it for you in some other way."

"Oh, yes. There are scores of ways to arrange such a trifle, to oblige the gentleman," jovially remarked the commissionnaire, as he left me.

In an hour's time he came back with another young man. This one took the bundle, put it by the side of the door, and said, "It's all right. If you leave to-morrow, you shall have your books at such a station in Russia," and he explained to me how it would be managed.

"How much will it cost?" I asked.

"How much are you disposed to pay?" was the reply.

I emptied my purse on the table, and said: "That much for my journey. The remainder is yours. I will travel third class!"

"Wai, wai, wai!" exclaimed both men at once. "What are you saying, sir? Such a gentleman travel third class! Never! No, no, no, that won't do. . . . Five dollars will do for us, and then one dollar or so for the commissionaire, if you are agreeable to it, — just as much as you like. We are not highway robbers, but honest tradesmen." And they bluntly refused to take more money.

I had often heard of the honesty of the Jewish smugglers on the frontier; but I had never expected to have such a proof of it. Later on, when our circle imported many books from abroad, or still later, when so many revolutionists and refugees crossed the frontier in entering or leaving Russia, there was not a case in which smugglers betrayed any one, or took advantage of circumstances to exact an exorbitant price for their services.

Next day I left Cracow; and at the designated Russian station a porter approached my compartment, and, speaking loudly, so as to be heard by the gendarme who was walking along the platform, said to me, "Here is the bag your highness left the other day," and handed me my precious parcel.

I was so pleased to have it that I did not even stop at Warsaw, but continued my journey directly to St. Petersburg, to show my trophies to my brother.

(Memoirs of a Revolutionist, pp. 293–295)

SAKI (HECTOR HUGH MUNRO)   (1870–1916)

Scottish short-story writer

Hector flirted with endangering his reputation by these gestures to a coterie, but in his treatment of another minority he was unimpeachably on the side of the prevailing prejudice. Twice Reginald mentions Jews in his conversations, and although each time he is careful to say something placating about their virtues, Hector's own disdain shows through. In one instance, Reginald describes the Anglo-Saxon Empire as becoming a suburb of Jerusalem. "A very pleasant suburb, I admit, and quite a charming Jerusalem. But still a suburb." At another point, he remarks, "Personally, I think the Jews have estimable qualities; they're so kind to their poor — and our rich."

One man who knew Hector suggested that his remarks betrayed no anti-Jewish feelings — even though Ethel [his sister], who lived to see the results of Hitler's final solution, harbored them through an unshakable lifetime. Rather, he said, they represented the response of a social satirist to the pavan of changing mores. The same man pointed out that Hector never scorned Jews as Jews, only as people with pretensions, figures fit for ridicule whether Jewish or Gentile. But Hector's response to Jews, as he would show in his newspaper dispatches, was more complex than that. He was a product of his age, and his rebelliousness was spent on Christianity and conventional sexuality. Otherwise, he accepted with the air he breathed the monarchy, the Empire and a wariness toward Jews.

(A. J. Langguth, *Saki: A Life of H. H. Munro*, p. 83)

* * *

With its huge ghetto population, Warsaw exposed Hector to more Jews than he had ever known, and his reflections on the subject of anti-Semitism showed that he had not resolved his ambiguity. Everything in his experience with Jews seems to have been positive, yet he could never overcome the ingrained suspicions of his time, country and social class. "To the Jew in Warsaw is meted out a wealth of disfavour and contempt that is hardly pleasant to witness. The British stranger, however, who normally lives far from any personal contact with these huge Jewish populations, is not altogether in a position to pass judgment on this deeply-seated Anti-Semitic rancour. It pervades all classes of Polish society, and finds expression in a variety of ways. The youth who obligingly performs my minor marketing for me, in return for a tolerant attitude on my part on the subject of small change, was interested in the fate of an egg which I had pronounced to have passed the age limit of culinary usefulness.

" 'Don't throw it away,' he begged; 'give it to me.'

" 'What do you want it for?'

" 'Oh, it will do to throw at a Jew.'

"Personally I have found the Jew in several Slav-inhabited countries easier to deal with than some of his Christian neighbours. He understands that it takes two to make a bargain, and if he haggles it is always with the view of doing business; with the Slav haggling seems often to be carried out on the principle of art for art's sake. For that reason the Russians will never rid themselves of the economic pressure of the Jews, and if they absorb any considerable mass of Chinese subjects these, too, will soon have a tenacious grip on the trade affairs of the Empire."

(*Saki*, pp. 123–124)

* * *

By May [1905], the Russian government was trying to win support with religious concessions that would eliminate discrimination against Roman Catholics, Mohammedans, every sect but the Jews. "Any relaxation of anti-Jew restrictions would be extremely unpopular in the country districts," Hector wrote. But there was a subdued trace of gratification two weeks later when he reported that the Jews of Little Russia were organizing armed resistance to threats of attacks by Christians: "A militantly defensive Jewish organization will involve considerable additional embarrassment to the Government, which has hitherto been able to rely on the Jews not hitting back." Hector's attitude toward the Jews was undergoing an evolution. As recently as Warsaw, he had been inclined to think the Poles were justified in resenting the sure business instincts of the Jewish minority. Now, in St. Petersburg, he was wondering whether the real problem was not more basic. Perhaps Jews were simply smarter than their neighbors, and if so, what could be done about that?

The Russian moves in a narrow world, he noted, its horizon bounded by the most minute interests. "Incessantly sipping syrup-sweetened tea, munching sunflower seeds, smoking cigarettes, chatting and chaffing endlessly with his neighbors. . . ."

This laggard, this dullard, could hardly claim that his intellect or his future was straitened: ". . . nothing could be in more marked contrast than the alert and keenly-trained brainpower which makes the Jew such an awesome competitor in the Russian world. With the same, or perhaps fewer, possibilities and with many disadvantages added to those under which the youthful Russian labours, the Jewish working-class lad begets himself an education which seems to leave very little out of its purview."

(*Saki*, pp. 138–139)

VLADIMIR ILYICH ULYANOV (LENIN) *(1870–1924)*

Founder of Bolshevik Communism

From a speech before the Council of Peoples Commissars,
9 August 1918:

The Jewish bourgeoisie are our enemies, not as Jews but as bourgeoisie.
The Jewish worker is our brother.

* * *

"Until Lenin moved to Austrian Poland in 1912, his polemics on nationalism had been almost exclusively with the Jewish Bund. Despite Jewish dispersion and lack of a distinct territory, the Bund insisted on considering the Jews as a nationality, and on speaking for all Jews anywhere in Russia. For their scattered peoples, they did not dream of demanding the "right of secession" to form an independent state. Instead of "territorial autonomy" and the "right of secession," they limited self-determination to the more modest demand for "cultural autonomy" or "national-cultural autonomy." By this they meant that the Jewish communities should control their own schools, theaters, press and religious life, free from interference or handicap on the part of the state, should elect their own school and community administrators, and speak for and defend the "national-cultural" interests of people anywhere in Russia who chose to regard themselves as Jews. Still worse, in Lenin's opinion, they wanted the same autonomy to prevail in the Party, for themselves and for other national groups. Lenin was willing to concede nationality to Ukrainians, White Russians, Poles, etc., because they had a distinct territory and language and a strong will to secede from the Russian Empire, and therefore constituted a movement which would weaken tsarism. But Jews, he maintained, were not a nationality but a caste; they spoke not one language but various, lived not in a definite territory but scattered throughout the Empire, and, insofar as they were not "bourgeois-minded" were internationalists. The only "progressive solution" of the Jewish question was emancipation and assimilation. Above all in the Social Democratic Party there was no room for nationalism. The "best and most class-conscious" Jews had set an example by rejecting the Jewish Bund in favor of membership in the local mixed units of the

Russian Social Democratic Party. If the Bund were to have its way, it would lead to the recognition of national divisions in the labor movement, and to a federated party in which Jews, Ukrainians, Georgians, Armenians, Great-Russians, White-Russians, Poles, etc., would each be organized separately. Then the Party and the Party Central Committee, instead of being centralized would be a mere federated body. And the new Russia to issue out of the revolution would be a federated, not a centralized, republic."

(B. D. Wolfe, *Three Who Made a Revolution*, p. 579)

* * *

He who would serve the proletariat must unite the workers of all nations and struggle unwaveringly against bourgeois nationalism, both his "own" and foreign. . . .

The same applies to the most oppressed and downtrodden nation, the Jews. Jewish national culture is the slogan of the rabbis and the bourgeoisie—the slogan of our enemies. But there are other elements in Jewish culture and in the whole history of Jewry. Out of some ten and a half million Jews in the world, a little more than half live in Galicia and Russia, backward and semi-barbarian countries which keep the Jews *by force* in the position of an outlawed caste. The other half live in the civilized world, where there is no caste segregation of the Jews. There the great and universally progressive features of Jewish culture have made themselves clearly felt: its internationalism, its responsiveness to the advanced movements of our times (the percentage of Jews in democratic and proletarian movements is everywhere higher than the percentage of Jews in the general population).

. . . Those Jewish Marxists who join up in the international Marxist organizations with the Russian, Lithuanian, Ukrainian and other workers, adding their might (both in Russian and in Jewish) to the creation of an international culture of the working class movement, are continuing the best traditions of Jewry and struggling against the slogan of "national culture."

(From an article in *Northern Pravda*, October-December 1913, quoted in *Lenin on the Jewish Question*, p. 10)

* * *

. . . Lenin himself did not deal with the Jewish question systematically but in numerous, scattered references. His first detailed state ment appeared . . . in the October 22, 1903 issue of *Iskra,* the party paper which Lenin edited. In an article entitled "The Bund's Position Within the Party," Lenin called the Bundist idea of Jewish national autonomy a

> Zionist idea . . . false and reactionary in its essence. . . . The idea of a separate Jewish people, which is utterly untenable scientifically is reactionary in its political implications. . . . Everywhere in Europe the downfall of medievalism and the development of political freedom went hand in hand with the political emancipation of the Jews . . . and their . . . progressive assimilation by the surrounding population . . . The Jewish question is this exactly: assimilation or separateness? And the idea of a Jewish "nationality" is manifestly reactionary . . . [It] is in conflict with the interests of the Jewish proletariat, for, directly or indirectly, it engenders in its ranks a mood hostile to assimilation, a "ghetto" mood.

This thesis approximated the Bolshevik position, and when discussing Jewish issues, the Bolshevik press frequently quoted from Lenin's views. . . .

After the conference [of the party's central committee, in 1913], Lenin started work on "Critical Remarks on the National Question." . . . Those who wish to serve the proletariat must unite the workers of all nations and fight bourgeois nationalism, both domestic and foreign. The same struggle applies to the

> most oppressed and persecuted nation, the Jews. Jewish national culture is the slogan of rabbis and bourgeoisie, the slogan of our enemies. But there are other elements in Jewish culture and . . . history as a whole. Out of ten and a half million Jews throughout the world, somewhat over a half live in Galicia and Russia, backward and semi-barbarous countries, where the Jews are *forcibly* kept in the status of a caste. The other lives in the civilised world, and there the Jews do not live as a segregated caste. There the great world-progressive features of Jewish culture stand clearly revealed . . . Whoever, directly or indirectly puts forward the slogan of Jewish "national culture" is (whatever his good intentions may be) an enemy of the proletariat, a supporter of all that is *outmoded* and connected with *caste* among

the Jewish people; he is an accomplice of the rabbis and the bourgeoisie . . . In advocating the slogan of national culture and building upon it an entire plan . . . of what they call "cultural-national autonomy," the Bundists are *in effect* instruments of bourgeois nationalism among the workers.

Thus, argued Lenin, who knew little of Jewish history, literature, or religious tradition, Jewish reactionaries and Bundists who oppose assimilation are "turning back the wheel of history." Bourgeois nationalism and proletarian internationalism are "irreconcilably hostile," and those, like the Bund, who advance the idea of national culture are guilty of "the most refined, most absolute and most extreme nationalism."

However,

. . . those Jewish Marxists who merge with the Russian, Lithuanian, Ukrainian, and other workers in international Marxist organizations, contributing their share (in both Russian and Yiddish) to the creation of an international culture of the labor movement—those Jews carry on (in defiance of the separatism of the Bund) the best Jewish tradition when they combat the slogan of "national culture."

In the Bund struggle against Lenin, no one quoted from Marx's essay "Zur Judenfrage," very possibly because of its shocking and vulgar anti-Semitism, but Marxists generally, including Lenin and Stalin, accepted the Marxist dogma that the Jews would ultimately disappear as a definable group, and that, as individual and class exploitation ends, national differences and antagonisms would disappear as well.

(N. Levin, *The Jews in the Soviet Union since 1917*, vol. I, pp. 17–19)

JOSEPH STALIN (DZHUGASHVILI) *(1879–1953)*

Secretary-General of the Communist party; premier of the USSR

Stalin's "Report on the London Congress" of 1907:

"Not less interesting . . . is the composition of the Congress from the standpoint of nationalities. Statistics showed that the majority of the

Menshevik faction consists of Jews—and this of course without counting the Bundists—after which come Georgians and then Russians. On the other hand, the overwhelming majority of the Bolshevik faction consists of Russians, after which come Jews—not counting of course the Poles and Letts—and then Georgians, etc. For this reason, one of the Bolsheviks observed in jest (it seems, Comrade Alexinsky) that the Mensheviks are a Jewish faction, the Bolsheviks a genuine Russian faction, whence it wouldn't be a bad idea for us Bolsheviks to arrange a pogrom in the party."

(B. D. Wolfe, *Three Who Made a Revolution*, p. 468)

* * *

We leave it to the reader to judge the factional purpose of this coarse-grained jest and its possible effect in a Russian that had just gone through three years of pogroms. In passing we might note that this same Alexinsky whom Stalin was citing against the Mensheviks would one day point to Zinoviev, Kamenev, and Trotsky as evidence of the number of Jews in the leadership of the Bolshevik Party!

(*Three Who Made a Revolution*, pp. 468–469)

* * *

He was a raging anti-Semite, and liked to introduce lengthy attacks against Jews into his speeches. What Stalin seemed to like most about the Bolshevik party was that it included fewer Jews than the Menshevik party. "It exasperates Lenin that God sent him such comrades as the Mensheviks!" Stalin used to say, according to Arsenidze. "Martov, Dan, Alexandrov—they are nothing but uncircumcised Jews! So is that old *baba* Vera Zasulich! Go and work with them! You will find that they won't fight and there is no rejoicing at their banquets! They are cowards and shopkeepers! The workers of Georgia ought to know that the Jewish nation produces only cowards and people who are no use at fighting!"

It is not surprising that Stalin should have been anti-Semitic in his early years, for he was to show an abundance of anti-Semitic feeling when he came to power. In 1909 he wrote that he preferred the Bolsheviks because they were more Russian than the Mensheviks; his anti-Semitism would seem to have been accompanied by a growing sense of nationalism. Yet his bitterness against the Jews is not easily explained, for traditionally the Georgians were far less anti-Semitic than the Russians. There were no pales or ghettos in Georgia.

(R. Payne, *The Rise and Fall of Stalin*, pp. 110–111)

* * *

Stalin and Hitler, according to Ribbentrop, were almost brothers in arms. Stalin was imitating Hitler even to the extent of mounting an anti-Jewish campaign; all Jews had been removed from positions of power in the Soviet Union with the exception of Kaganovich, "who looks more like a Georgian than a Jew."

(*The Rise and Fall of Stalin*, p. 609)

* * *

Visiting Communist leaders found him as unyielding and demanding as ever. Milovan Djilas, invited to Moscow to discuss a Yugoslav quarrel with Albania, found that nothing had changed. . . . "In our Central Committee there are no Jews," Stalin laughed, and went on to taunt Djilas for being pro-Jewish.

(*The Rise and Fall of Stalin*, pp. 705–706)

* * *

In Stalin's eyes the Jews presented a mortal danger to his regime, and had not Voroshilov married a woman of Jewish extraction? And not only Voroshilov—there were others among his immediate associates who were tainted with Semitic blood. Kaganovich was a Jew, Molotov had married a Jewess, Beria's mother was half-Jewish, and Khrushchev had permitted his daughter to marry a young Jewish journalist. There was no end to the ramifications of the Jews in the Soviet Union, and now at last he had decided to put an end to this source of corruption. A plan, which had been long maturing in his diseased brain, now seemed ripe for fulfillment. In addition to the giant *chistka* ["purge" or "massacre"] which would cleanse the entire body of the nation, there would be another, relatively milder *chistka* reserved for the Jews, who were to be transported to some region far in the north, where they could die quietly of cold and starvation.

He summoned a meeting at the Kremlin and outlined his plans. When Mikoyan and Voroshilov protested vigorously, pointing out that they had fought a war against Hitler and nothing was to be gained by imitating him, Stalin worked himself into a fury. Kaganovich wept and pleaded, but to no avail. He even offered to surrender his party card. The Communist leaders left the meeting with the knowledge that Stalin was mentally deranged, but perfectly capable of carrying out his threats. From that moment they knew—they could not help knowing—that their lives were in danger.

. . . Suddenly, on January 13, 1953, both *Pravda* and *Izvestiya* printed long announcements which showed that the terror was beginning its work. The ten-paragraph announcement proclaimed that a sinister plot by the Kremlin doctors had been uncovered. The doctors, who were named, were accused of "using improper techniques to murder their patients. . . ." Six of the doctors were Jews. . . .

. . . Stalin's threat to send all Russian Jews and everyone who was in any way related to the Jews to the frozen north involved half the members of the Presidium.

(*The Rise and Fall of Stalin*, pp. 740–743)

* * *

From a reply given on 12 January 1931 to an enquiry
made by the Jewish Telegraphic Agency of America:

National and race chauvinism is a survival of the man-eating ethics characteristic of the period of cannibalism. Anti-Semitism, as an extreme form of race chauvinism, is the most dangerous survival of cannibalism. Anti-Semitism benefits the exploiters, for it serves as a lightning conductor to divert from capitalism the blow of the toilers. Anti-Semitism is dangerous for the toilers, for it is a false track which diverts them from the proper road and leads them into the jungle. Hence Communists, as consistent internationalists, cannot but be irreconcilable and bitter enemies of anti-Semitism. In the U.S.S.R., anti-Semitism is strictly prosecuted as a phenomenon hostile to the Soviet system. According to the laws of the U.S.S.R. active anti-Semites are punished with death.

(*Stars and Sand,* p. 316)

* * *

To help him prepare materials for his critical essays on the national question (1913–14), Lenin sent Stalin to Vienna. The result was Stalin's "Marxism and the National and Colonial Question," published in a party journal in the spring of 1913, an essay which repeated Lenin's attacks on cultural autonomy and which remains the basic statement in Communist party literature on the Jewish national question, but subject to revision. Stalin defines the nation as a "historically evolved stable community of language, territory, economic life and psychological make-up manifested in a community of culture." Only when all these characteristics are present do we have a nation. By definition, Jews were thus excluded. The Austrian definitions of a nation as a "cultural community no longer tied to the soil," or "an aggregate of people bound into a community of character by a community of fate" (Bauer), were sharply criticized for blocking the right of self-determination by maintaining the multinational state, substituting equality of cultural rights for sovereign political rights, and for perpetuating national prejudices.

When Stalin deals specifically with Jews, he does not analyze the linguistically homogeneous population in the Pale [of Settlement, the area where Russian Jews were forced to live] that the Bund was concerned with, but with disparate Jewries:

> What ... national cohesion can there be ... between the Georgian, Daghestanian, Russian and American Jew? ... If there is anything common left to them it is their religion, their common origin and certain relics of national character. How can it be seriously maintained that petrified religious rites and fading psychological relics affect the "fate" of these Jews more powerfully than the living ... environment that surrounds them?

Moreover, Stalin added, few Jews live on the soil; nor do Jews constitute a majority in any province in Russia. Interspersed as national minorities in areas inhabited by other nationalities, they serve "foreign" nations as manufacturers and traders and professionals, adapting themselves to the "foreign nations." All this, taken together with the increasing reshuffling of nationalities in developed forms of capitalism, will inevitably lead to the assimilation of Jews. The abolition of the Pale of Settlement will hasten this process. ...

Stalin acknowledged that Jews rejected inevitable assimilation by demanding an autonomous status and protection of minority rights. But, he argued, autonomy for Jews would mean guarding the "harmful" as well as the "useful" traits; it would also foster "national narrow-mindedness and the spread of prejudice" and would disorganize and demoralize the labor movement.

Stalin, in fact, was echoing Lenin's views, and it seems likely that Lenin edited Stalin's essay. . . .

(N. Levin, *The Jews in the Soviet Union since 1917*, vol. I, pp. 16–17)

* * *

The popular Jewish reactions to Mrs. Meyerson [Golda Meir, visiting the Soviet Union from the new State of Israel] in the fall of 1948 were unprecedented and apparently took Stalin and other Soviet authorities by surprise. The depth and passion of Jewish feeling was startling—and disquieting. After thirty years of Communist rule, "sovietization" of Soviet Jews, and rapid assimilation, these fires had not been quenched. Stalin also apparently began to fear and suspect Soviet Jewry's contacts with the West . . . and the brief flowering of Yiddish culture. All of that would have to end and the standard bearers of that revival be reviled, exposed as dangerous, isolated, and removed from Soviet life. How much of this alleged threat Stalin himself believed and how much he exploited craftily for internal purposes is difficult to assess. Many observers have reported his growing paranoia and obsession with personal as well as national security, which reached a bizarre pitch of suspicion in the so-called doctors' plot of 1953. . . . He was also becoming obsessed with the alleged dangers of Soviet contamination by the West, with Jewish contacts in the West that took their minds out of rigid Soviet control. Moreover, he was giving more noticeable rein to a long-harbored dislike of Jews.

His daughter Svetlana has said that Stalin's feelings over the years changed "from political hatred to racial aversion for all Jews," and that his vehement anti-Semitism caused her divorce from her first husband Grigory Morozov, who was a Jew, and his deportation. Stalin accused him of shirking military service. After their divorce, Stalin told her that "that first husband of yours was thrown your way by the Zionists," and that "the entire older generation is contaminated with Zionism and now they are teaching the young people too." Svetlana as well as Khrushchev agreed that Stalin eventually regarded all Jews as "treacherous and dishonest." . . . Charles Bohlen, a former American ambassador to the Soviet Union, quoted Stalin as saying that "he did not know what to do" with the Jews: "I can't swallow them, I can't spit them out; they are the only group that is completely unassimilable." Stalin had a number of Jews around him both officially and within his family but apparently never really liked them. The wife of his oldest son was Jewish, a situation that displeased him, and when his son was taken prisoner by the Nazis, Stalin's suspicions were aroused and he implicated his daughter-in-law. The mixture of hope, anxiety, and then joyful relief among many Soviet Jews when the Jewish state was established unleashed these partially dissembled feelings and infuriated him. . . .

(*The Jews in the Soviet Union since 1917*, pp. 483–484)

* * *

Khrushchev, too, has described Stalin's uncanny ability to disguise his own anti-Semitism, and officially rejecting it as shameful. He is described as often imitating "with an exaggerated accent the way Jews talk," possibly "a means of establishing some rapport with his Russian anti-Semitic subordinates." On the other hand, Khrushchev says that he, Stalin, "would have strangled anyone whose actions would have discredited his name, especially with something as indefensible and shameful as anti-Semitism. . . ."

(*The Jews in the Soviet Union since 1917*, p. 507)

ALEKSANDR KERENSKY   *(1881–1970)*

Russian revolutionary leader; head of the Provisional Government in 1917

From a statement in the *Jewish Chronicle* of London, November, 1918

When in the first days of the Revolution I was Minister of Justice, I decreed the full emancipation of the Jews, thus granting to them the same rights as to all other citizens. Ninety-nine per cent of the Russian Jews are against the Bolshevists, and during the whole of the Revolution, the Jewish intellectuals and the Jewish masses, were, of all non-Russian races, the most faithful supporters of the Revolution with which they were closely linked as well as with the general interests of the country. . . .

During the Revolution the Jews everywhere worked together with the parties who had coalesced to organize and support the Provisional Government. The Jewish bankers, firms, workers' unions—they were all for national defense and for cooperation with the moderate "bourgeois" elements in the upbuilding of the new State.

(quoted in S. M. McCall, *Patriotism of the American Jew,* 1924, p. 162)

DMITRI SHOSTAKOVICH   *(1906–1975)*

Russian composer

And there is also the Jewish theme from the Piano Trio in this quartet. I think, if we speak of musical impressions, that Jewish folk music has made a most powerful impression on me. I never tire of delighting in it, it's multifaceted, it can appear to be happy while it is tragic. It's almost always laughter through tears.

This quality of Jewish folk music is close to my ideas of what music should be. There should always be two layers in music. Jews were tormented for so long that they learned to hide their despair. They express despair in dance music.

All folk music is lovely, but I can say that Jewish folk music is unique. Many composers listened to it, including Russian composers, Mussorgsky, for instance. He carefully set down Jewish folk songs. Many of my works reflect my impressions of Jewish music.

This is not a purely musical issue, it is also a moral issue. I often test a person by his attitude toward Jews. In our day and age, any person with pretensions of decency cannot be anti-Semitic. This seems so obvious that it doesn't need saying, but I've had to argue the point for at least thirty years. Once after the war I was passing a bookstore and saw a volume with Jewish songs. I was always interested in Jewish folklore, and I thought the book would give the melodies, but it contained only the texts. It seemed to me that if I picked out several texts and set them to music, I would be able to tell about the fate of the

Jewish people. It seemed an important thing to do, because I could see anti-Semitism growing all around me. But I couldn't have the cycle performed then, it was played for the first time much later, and later still I did an orchestral version of the work.

My parents considered anti-Semitism a shameful superstition, and in that sense I was given a singular upbringing. In my youth I came across anti-Semitism among my peers, who thought that Jews were getting preferential treatment. They didn't remember the pogroms, the ghettos, or the quotas. In those years it was almost a mark of *sangfroid* to speak of Jews with a mocking laugh. It was a kind of opposition to the authorities.

I never condoned an anti-Semitic tone, even then, and I didn't repeat anti-Semitic jokes that were popular then. But I was much gentler about this unworthy trait than I am now. Later I broke with even good friends if I saw that they had any anti-Semitic tendencies.

But even before the war, the attitude toward Jews had changed drastically. It turned out that we had far to go to achieve brotherhood. The Jews became the most persecuted and defenseless people of Europe. It was a return to the Middle Ages. Jews became a symbol for me. All of man's defenselessness was concentrated in them. After the war, I tried to convey that feeling in my music. It was a bad time for Jews then. In fact, it's always a bad time for them.

Despite all the Jews who perished in the camps, all I heard people saying was, "The kikes went to Tashkent to fight." And if they saw a Jew with military decorations, they called after him, "Kike, where did you buy the medals?" That's when I wrote the Violin Concerto, the Jewish Cycle, and the Fourth Quartet.

Not one of these works could be performed then. They were heard only after Stalin's death. I still can't get used to it. The Fourth Symphony was played twenty-five years after I wrote it. There are compositions that have yet to be performed, and no one knows when they will be heard.

I'm very heartened by the reaction among young people to my feelings on the Jewish question. And I see that the Russian intelligentsia remains intractably opposed to anti-Semitism, and that the many years of trying to enforce anti-Semitism from above have not had any visible results. . . .

. . . It would be good if Jews could live peacefully and happily in Russia, where they were born. But we must never forget about the dangers of anti-Semitism and keep reminding others of it, because the infection is alive and who knows if it will ever disappear.

That's why I was overjoyed when I read Yevtushenko's "Babi Yar"; the poem astounded me. It astounded thousands of people. Many had heard about Babi Yar, but it took Yevtushenko's poem to make them aware of it. They tried to destroy the memory of Babi Yar, first the Germans and then the Ukrainian government. But after Yevtushenko's poem, it became clear that it would never be forgotten. That's the power of art.

People knew about Babi Yar before Yevtushenko's poem, but they were silent. And when they read the poem, the silence was broken. Art destroys silence. . . .

(Volkov, *Testimony, The Memoirs of Dmitri Shostakovich,*
pp. 156–159)

* * *

Shostakovich came out openly against anti-Semitism in his Thirteenth Symphony. It was 1962 then and Khrushchev was in power, not Stalin, but the official attitude toward Jews was, as always, hostile. The moralizing Thirteenth (which incorporated Yevgeny Yevtushenko's famous poem "Babi Yar") was the cause of the last sharp and well-known conflict between Soviet power and the composer.

(*Testimony,* p. xxxvii)

MILOVAN DJILAS   *(1911–   )*

Yugoslavian writer and dissident

. . . The problems are very simple.

In January of 1948 I was dining with Stalin. Other Soviet leaders were present. The atmosphere was unlike any before; there was reserve on both sides, many thoughts remained unuttered, and we had a few flare-ups. Stalin asked me: "With the exception of Pijade, why don't you have more Jews in your Central Committee?" I explained to him how our movement had developed. He started to laugh heartily and sarcastically. With sympathy he called me and the other

Yugoslav Communists anti-Semites. I heard a lot, talked a lot about this anti-Semitic theme in the USSR. One man from the apparatus of the Central Committee of the Soviet party bragged how Zhdanov had weeded out all the Jews from the apparatus of the Central Committee. The deputy of the Chief of Staff of the Soviet Army, Antonov, had by chance been discovered to be a Jew. This had ended his brilliant career.

The struggle against "cosmopolitans" in the USSR is really a covert struggle against Jewish intellectuals in the USSR. During the war anti-Semitism was more or less openly expressed in the army. In Moscow in 1948 there was a lot of discussion about the Hungarian Central Committee, which, as is well known, is made up mostly of Jews. And in the Moscow trials Jews always played a major role. There are no longer any Jews in the public life of the USSR. They are citizens of the lowest rank of public life in the USSR. The same thing is now taking place in Eastern Europe. And all that over a handful of people — sufferers who survived the fascist extermination. And all this happens, and continues to happen, regardless of whether some of the Jews are bourgeois or socialist.

The Prague trial revealed the conscious, organized anti-Semitic line without any doubt. It showed, as is common in the case of Stalin, that reality is often disguised. Anti-Semitism is hiding behind the struggle against Zionism and Americanism and even behind the struggle against anti-Semitism — which is quite in the style of Stalinist absurdities. . . .

Anti-Semitism has already become the rule in Eastern Europe. It attains monstrous forms, which would be grotesque if they were not so bloody. The Hungarian leadership is the most anti-Semitic in its propaganda just because it is made up primarily of Jews. They want to prove that way that they have freed themselves from the "Jewish cosmopolitan mentality" and that they are totally faithful to Stalin and his "Great Russian" imperialism. They are not only crawling, but they are also attempting to guess the secret wishes of the master. This is not strange. The Hungarian leadership finds itself doubly despised by the Hungarian people: because it is the servant of Moscow and, traditionally, because it is Jewish. The past bane of capitalism, which was presented to the Hungarian peasants and craftsmen in the image of the Jew-miser, today becomes the "socialist" bane, again in the image of the Jew, but this time a bureaucrat. This is convenient for all kinds of combinations of the Soviet government. Stalin only smiles like a devil while Rakosi and Gero and others of the Jewish bunch, with their anti-Semitic propaganda, braid the rope that will hang around their necks. . . .

From history we know that each order became reactionary the moment it began to turn anti-Semitic; the pogroms against the Jews were the surest sign of the blackest social reaction. History does not repeat itself, but it is very seldom wrong. Great Russian bureaucratic state capitalism had to become not only nationalistic but also racist. This is inevitable, for how else can one justify the struggle for world hegemony and the oppression of other peoples except through one's own "special" merits? Thus it must inevitably become, indeed, it already is, anti-Semitic. Because of their history, Jews became the carriers of trade and of the city way of life, creating channels through which flowed the separate regions into the first common life. Some of them some of the time tried to be feudal lords and good Christians, but they didn't succeed. Their usury and trade, regardless of how callous and inhumane, undermined feudal relationships and spread ties among regions and peoples. They were the yeast of the new civilization. Those who condemn them are thus undermining their own world. But it has been a long time since the Jews were such an "evil" yeast. They are not the only channels or the only merchants. Christian usurers and merchants are greater "Jews" than the Jews themselves. The cosmopolitan spirit remained and still remains, but only there where they are scattered. It is also mainly because they are scattered that they are persecuted. In Palestine they are as nationalistic and as socialistic as the people in any other state. . . .

It is not easy to understand how during the last war the Jews, helplessly, stupefied, paralyzed, waited without struggle patiently for Hitler's slaughterhouses and "obediently" walked into them. But is it not also true that other reactionary regimes excluded them from the life of the nation? Had not the USSR already begun to exclude them from its life? Did anyone in the world really protect them? Isn't it true that everything was done to exclude them, to cast them out of the history of each people and out of history in general? What can such a neglected people do? This was a people without a stable class, without a territory, without stable fighting organizations, a people saturated with the traditional spirit of adaptability and obedience. Yes, that resignation in the face of extermination was "unexplainable," especially in our country where revolutionary struggles were going on all around us. This is exactly the most tragic historical event of this quiet and meek people—which through prior development was so handicapped that it could not struggle to save itself even there where the struggle could have been successful. They died peacefully or ran aimlessly. Imbued with a spirit of the past, as in the past, as in the Middle Ages, they gave themselves up to a fate they could not explain and thus could not resist.

At the execution ground many Jews tried without success to convince the Nazis that they were anti-Bolsheviks. Today in vain they are doing the same thing—trying to convince Stalin that they are not against the USSR, that they are for socialism. They are supposed to stop being that which they are—a people of specific characteristics formed through historical development, a people imbued with an international spirit (regardless of which one, because it is not the same for all Jews). And they are imbued with that spirit mainly because they are a people scattered throughout the world. The spirit is strongest there where they are persecuted. They cannot kill the spirit within themselves, and thus they have to be persecuted wherever there is a regime enclosed within its own fortresses.

But because of that, the fully human and humanistic duty today is not only to uncover anti-Semitism as the basic element in Stalin's bloody game, but also to struggle for the defense of this small, unfortunate but beautiful people, to whom all despots in history have denied the right to breathe the air and to enjoy the sun, of whom one can say that, although persecuted, resettled and scattered, burned, tortured, and exterminated through thousands of years, of whom one can say—if such comparisons were not senseless—that it gave humanity nothing less than any other "chosen" people, and further, they did not give [their] part, part of the progressive, democratic forces, in isolation, but always within the framework of, and together with, the people with whom it lived. It is not a question of defending capitalism or socialism, or, least of all, Palestine, which is a state the same as any other, with its own way of life and its ties and which will defend itself as best it can. It is a question of defending a people who are still subject to the most terrible and longest-enduring crimes known to history.

And not in medieval times or even in Hitler's times, but in "socialist," "revolutionary" countries. Precisely socialism and democracy must come to their defense if they do not wish to undermine themselves, to lull the democratic and peace-loving consciousness and the revolutionary spirit of their own people into some kind of Stalinist socialism. For Stalinism is nothing but common imperialism, chauvinism and racism, new only in that it emerges in a state-capitalist form, decorated with "socialist" feathers and hostile to private capital, but in reality it is even more deeply hostile to real socialism and real democracy. That struggle must be carried on for the sake of that small and unfortunate people and also because of the spirit for which that people is persecuted. And also for the sake of socialism, which preaches the idea of the brotherhood and equality of all peoples.

Anti-Semitism soils and extinguishes everything human and democratic in man. The imprint of its shame cannot be erased from history. The intensity of anti-Semitism is the measure of how much a reactionary order has succeeded in enslaving its own people. History also proves that those who use it, even if their power is still growing, are at the beginning of their own end.

(From *Borba*, 14 December 1952, in Djilas, *Party of a Lifetime*, pp. 358–362)

ANDREY DONATOVICH SINYAVSKY   *(1925–   )*

Russian novelist and dissident; author of The Trial Begins, A Voice from the Chorus

In an interview with *Time Magazine*, 25 December 1989, when asked why he used the name of a Jewish hero in a ballad about Russian thieves:

I chose the name [Abram Tertz, the pseudonym] because a Jew in the Soviet Union is considered a foreigner, one who is chased and persecuted.

(R. Z. Sheppard, "Notes from the Underground," *Time*, 25 December 1989)

12

U.S. Writers and Leaders from Reconstruction to the Present

HERMAN MELVILLE *(1819–1891)*

U.S. novelist; author of Moby Dick, Billy Budd

The most striking evidence of the negative side of Melville's thought, however, is the unfriendly allusions embedded in passages exalting freedom from national prejudice. In *Redburn* [an autobiographical adventure] Melville pays eloquent tribute to the United States as an international amalgram of immigrants. "There is something in the contemplation of the mode in which America has been settled," he writes, "that, in the noble breast, should forever extinguish the prejudices of national dislikes. . . . You can not spill a drop of American blood without spilling the blood of the whole world." Then to reinforce his point he adds: "We are not a narrow tribe of men, with a bigoted Hebrew nationality—whose blood had been debased in the attempt to ennoble it, by maintaining an exclusive succession among ourselves." Melville here shows no awareness that separation and exclusiveness were forced upon the Jew by ghettoization, or that the Christian world was no less separatistic in relation to the Jews than the reverse. Nor does the passage betray any sensitivity to the fact that, in the land where Jews were freer than anywhere else in the world at the time, they were less separatistic and participated more fully in the national life than elsewhere. Melville's reference to the "bigoted Hebrew nationality" reveals that he accepts here without thought the deep-seated, prejudiced conception of the Jew. . . .

It would be a mistake to conclude from Melville's invidious references to Jews that he was a true anti-Semite. What is indicated is rather that his attitude was conventionally anti-Semitic. . . .

(Harap, *The Image of the Jew in American Literature*, pp. 120–121)

* * *

Toward Judaism itself Melville felt repugnance. In this respect he followed the Enlightenment tradition of scorning Old Testament religion. . . . His feelings toward Judaism are explicitly expressed by his meditations on the pyramids in the *Journal*. They "oppressed" him

259

with their awful, mysterious, inhuman magnitude. They were to him "something vast, undefiled, incomprehensible, and awful." And he speculates that Moses "conceived his idea of Jehovah" from the pyramids. Just as the "wise men" of Egypt could create out of the crude, unformed masses of earth a "transcendent," overpowering work of art in the pyramids, so Moses was inspired to organize "insignificant thoughts that are in all men" into "the transcendent conception of a God." The terror and giddiness he experienced at the top of the pyramids reminded him of Judaism. He felt a similar revulsion against the "extraordinary physical aspect" of Jerusalem. And the "diabolical landscapes [in a] great part of Judea must have suggested to the Jewish prophets their ghastly theology." He clearly felt an antipathy for the "ghastly theology," to which his observations in Palestine gave imaginative support.

(*The Image of the Jew*, p. 124)

ROBERT G. INGERSOLL   *(1833–1899)*

U.S. statesman, lecturer, lawyer, known as "the great agnostic"

The "Sabbath" was born of asceticism, hatred of human joy, fanaticism, ignorance, egotism of priests and the cowardice of people. . . .

To hate man and worship God seems to be the sum of all creeds. . . .

A false friend, an unjust judge, a braggart, hypocrite, and tyrant, sincere in hatred, jealous, vain and revengeful, false in promise, honest in curse, suspicious, ignorant, infamous and hideous – such is the God of the Pentateuch.

(Ingersoll, *Some Mistakes of Moses*, 1879)

BENJAMIN HARRISON   *(1833–1901)*

23rd president of the United States, (1889–1893)

Message to Congress, 9 December 1891:

This Government has found occasion to express, in a friendly spirit, but with much earnestness, to the Government of the Czar, its serious concern because of the harsh measures now being enforced against the Hebrews in Russia. By the revival of antisemitic laws, long in abeyance, great numbers of those unfortunate people have been constrained to abandon their homes and leave the empire by reason of the impossibility of finding subsistence within the pale to which it is sought to confine them. The immigration of these people to the United States—many other countries being closed to them—is largely increasing and is likely to assume proportions which may make it difficult to find homes and employment for them here and to seriously affect the labor market.

It is estimated that over one million will be forced from Russia within a few years. The Hebrew is never a beggar; he has always kept the law—life by toil—often under severe and oppressive civil restrictions. . . .

(*Foreign Relations*, 1892, pp. xii–xiii)

MARK TWAIN   *(1835–1910)*

U.S. novelist; author of The Adventures of Huckleberry Finn, Tom Sawyer

Some months ago I published a magazine article descriptive of a remarkable scene in the Imperial Parliament in Vienna. Since then I have received from Jews in America several letters of inquiry. They were difficult letters to answer, for they were not very definite. But at last I have received a definite one. It is from a lawyer, and he really asks the questions which the other writers probably believed they were asking. By help of this text I will do the best I can to publicly answer this correspondent, and also the others—at the same time apologizing for having failed to reply privately. The lawyer's letter reads as follows:

I have read "Stirring Times in Austria." [*Harper's*, March, 1898] One point in particular is of vital import to not a few thousand people, including myself, being a point about which I have often wanted to address a question to some disinterested person. The show of military force in the Austrian Parliament, which precipitated the riots, was not introduced by any Jew. No Jew was a member of that body. No Jewish question was involved in the Ausgleich or in the language proposition. No Jew was insulting anybody. In short, no Jew was doing any mischief toward anybody whatsoever. In fact, the Jews were the only ones of the nineteen different races in Austria which did not have a party — they are absolutely non-participants. Yet in your article you say that in the rioting which followed, all classes of people were unanimous only on one thing, viz., in being against the Jews. Now will you kindly tell me why, in your judgment, the Jews have thus ever been, and are even now, in these days of supposed intelligence, the butt of baseless, vicious animosities? I dare say that for centuries there has been no more quiet, undisturbing, and well-behaving citizens, as a class, than that same Jew. It seems to me that ignorance and fanaticism cannot alone account for these horrible and unjust persecutions.

Tell me, therefore, from your vantage-point of cold view, what in your mind is the cause. Can American Jews do anything to correct it either in America or abroad? Will it ever come to an end? Will a Jew be permitted to live honestly, decently, and peaceably like the rest of mankind? What has become of the golden rule?

I will begin by saying that if I thought myself prejudiced against the Jew, I should hold it fairest to leave this subject to a person not crippled in that way. But I think I have no such prejudice. A few years ago a Jew observed to me that there was no uncourteous reference to his people in my books, and asked how it happened. It happened because the disposition was lacking. I am quite sure that (bar one) I have no race prejudices, and I think I have no color prejudices nor caste prejudices nor creed prejudices. Indeed, I know it. I can stand any society. All that I care to know is that a man is a human being — that is enough for me; he can't be any worse. I have no special regard for Satan; but I can at least claim that I have no prejudice against him. . . .

In the present paper I shall allow myself to use the word Jew as if it stood for both religion and race. It is handy; and besides, that is what the term means to the general world.

In the above letter one notes these points:

1. The Jew is a well-behaved citizen.
2. Can ignorance and fanaticism *alone* account for his unjust treatment?

3. Can Jews do anything to improve the situation?
4. The Jews have no party; they are non-participants.
5. Will the persecution ever come to an end?
6. What has become of the golden rule?

Point No. 1 — We must grant proposition No. 1, for several sufficient reasons. The Jew is not a disturber of the peace of any country. Even his enemies will concede that. He is not a loafer, he is not a sot, he is not noisy, he is not a brawler nor a rioter, he is not quarrelsome. In the statistics of crime his presence is conspicuously rare — in all countries. With murder and other crimes of violence he has but little to do: he is a stranger to the hangman. In the police court's daily long roll of "assaults" and "drunk and disorderlies" his name seldom appears. That the Jewish home is a home in the truest sense is a fact which no one will dispute. The family is knitted together by the strongest affections; its members show each other every due respect; and reverence for the elders is an inviolate law of the house. The Jew is not a burden on the charities of the state nor of the city; these could cease from their functions without affecting him. When he is well enough, he works; when he is incapacitated, his own people take care of him. And not in a poor and stingy way, but with a fine and large benevolence. His race is entitled to be called the most benevolent of all the races of men. A Jewish beggar is not impossible, perhaps; such a thing may exist, but there are few men that can say they have seen that spectacle. The Jew has been staged in many uncomplimentary forms, but, so far as I know, no dramatist has done him the injustice to stage him as a beggar. Whenever a Jew has real need to beg, his people save him from the necessity of doing it. The charitable institutions of the Jews are supported by Jewish money, and amply. The Jews make no noise about it; it is done quietly; they do not nag and pester and harass us for contributions; they give us peace and set us an example — an example which we have not found ourselves able to follow; for by nature we are not free givers, and have to be patiently and persistently hunted down in the interest of the unfortunate.

These facts are all on the credit side of the proposition that the Jew is a good and orderly citizen. Summed up, they certify that he is quiet, peaceable, industrious, unaddicted to high crimes and brutal dispositions; that his family life is commendable; that he is not a

burden upon public charities; that he is not a beggar; that in benevolence he is above the reach of competition. These are the very
quintessentials of good citizenship. If you can add that he is as honest
as the average of his neighbors—but I think that question is affirma-
tively answered by the fact that he is a successful businessman. The
basis of successful business is honesty; a business cannot thrive where
the parties to it cannot trust each other. In the matter of numbers the
Jew counts for little in the overwhelming population of New York; but
that his honesty counts for much is guaranteed by the fact that the
immense wholesale business of Broadway, from the Battery to Union
Square, is substantially in his hands. . . .

The Jew has his other side. He has some discreditable ways,
though he has not a monopoly of them, because he cannot get entirely
rid of vexatious Christian competition. We have seen that he seldom
transgresses the laws against crimes of violence. Indeed, his dealings
with the courts are almost restricted to matters connected with
commerce. He has a reputation for various small forms of cheating,
and for practising oppressive usury, and for burning himself out to get
the insurance, and for arranging cunning contracts which leave him
an exit but lock the other man in, and for smart evasions which find
him safe and comfortable just within the strict letter of the law, when
court and jury know very well that he has violated the spirit of it. He
is a frequent and faithful and capable officer in the civil service, but he
is charged with an unpatriotic disinclination to stand by the flag as a
soldier—like the Christian Quaker.

Now if you offset these discreditable features by the creditable
ones summarized in the preceding paragraph beginning with the
words "These fact are all on the credit side," and strike a balance, what
must the verdict be? This, I think: that, the merits and demerits being
fairly weighed and measured on both sides, the Christian can claim no
superiority over the Jew in the matter of good citizenship.

Yet in all countries, from the dawn of history, the Jew has been
persistently and implacably hated, and with frequency persecuted.

Point No. 2.—"Can fanaticism alone account for this?"

Years ago I used to think that it was responsible for nearly all of
it, but latterly I have come to think that this was an error. Indeed, it
is now my conviction that it is responsible for hardly any of it. . . .

I wish to . . . refer to a remark made by one of the Latin
historians. I read it in a translation many years ago, and it comes back

to me now with force. It was alluding to a time when people were still living who could have seen the Saviour in the flesh. Christianity was so new that the people of Rome had hardly heard of it, and had but confused notions of what it was. The substance of the remark was this: Some Christians were persecuted in Rome through error, they being *"mistaken for Jews."*

The meaning seems plain. These pagans had nothing against Christians, but they were quite ready to persecute Jews. For some reason or other they hated a Jew before they even knew what a Christian was. May I not assume, then, that the persecution of the Jews is a thing which *antedates* Christianity and was not born of Christianity? I think so. What was the origin of the feeling? . . .

The Jew is being legislated out of Russia. The reason is not concealed. The movement was instituted because the Christian peasant and villager stood no chance against his commercial ability. He was always ready to lend money on a crop, and sell vodka and other necessaries of life on credit while the crop was growing. When settlement day came he owned the crop; and next year or year after he owned the farm. . . .

In the dull and ignorant England of John's time everybody got into debt to the Jew. He gathered all lucrative enterprises into his hands; he was the king of commerce; he was ready to be helpful in all profitable ways; he even financed crusades for the rescue of the Sepulchre. To wipe out his account with the nation and restore business to its natural and incompetent channels he had to be banished from the realm.

For the like reasons Spain had to banish him four hundred years ago, and Austria about a couple of centuries later.

In all the ages Christian Europe has been obliged to curtail his activities. If he set up as a doctor, he was the best one, and he took the business. If he exploited agriculture, the other farmers had to get at something else. Since there was no way to successfully compete with him in any vocation, the law had to step in and save the Christian from the poorhouse. Trade after trade was taken away from the Jew by statute till practically none was left. He was forbidden to engage in agriculture; he was forbidden to practise law; he was forbidden to practise medicine, except among Jews; he was forbidden the handi-crafts. Even the seats of learning and the schools of science had to be closed against this tremendous antagonist. Still, almost bereft of employments, he found ways to make money, even ways to get rich. Also ways to invest his takings well, for usury was not denied him. In the hard conditions suggested, the Jew without brains could not survive, and the Jew with brains had to keep them in good training and well sharpened up, or starve. Ages of restriction to the one tool which the law was not able to take from him—his brain—have made that tool singularly competent; ages of compulsory disuse of his hands have atrophied them, and he never uses them now. This history has a very, very commercial look, a most sordid and practical commercial look, the business aspect of a Chinese cheap-labor crusade. Religious prejudices may account for one part of it, but not for the other nine.

Protestants have persecuted Catholics, but they did not take their livelihoods away from them. The Catholics have persecuted the Protestants with bloody and awful bitterness, but they never closed agriculture and the handicrafts against them. Why was that? That has the candid look of genuine religious persecution, not a trade-union boycott in a religious disguise.

The Jews are harried and obstructed in Austria and Germany, and lately in France; but England and America give them an open field and yet survive. . . .

I feel convinced that the Crucifixion has not much to do with the world's attitude toward the Jew; that the reasons for it are older than that event. . . . I am persuaded that in Russia, Austria, and Germany nine-tenths of the hostility to the Jew comes from the average Christian's inability to compete successfully with the average Jew in business—in either straight business or the questionable sort.

In Berlin, a few years ago, I read a speech which frankly urged the expulsion of the Jews from Germany; and the agitator's *reason* was as frank as his proposition. It was this: *that eighty-five per cent* of the successful lawyers of Berlin were Jews, and that about the same percentage of the great and lucrative businesses of all sorts in Germany were in the hands of the Jewish race! Isn't it an amazing confession? It was but another way of saying that in a population of 48,000,000, of whom only 500,000 were registered as Jews, eighty-five per cent of the brains and honesty of the whole was lodged in the Jews. I must insist upon the honesty—it is an essential of successful business, taken by and large. Of course it does not rule out rascals entirely, even among Christians, but it is a good working rule, nevertheless. The speaker's figures may have been inexact, but *the motive of persecution* stands out as clear as day. . . .

. . . the argument is that the Christian cannot *compete* with the Jew, and that hence his very bread is in peril. To human beings this is a much more hate-inspiring thing than is any detail connected with religion. With most people, of a necessity, bread and meat take first rank, religion second. I am convinced that the persecution of the Jew is not due in any large degree to religious prejudice.

No, the Jew is a money-getter; and in getting his money he is a very serious obstruction to less capable neighbors who are on the same quest. I think that that is the trouble. In estimating worldly values the Jew is not shallow, but deep. With precocious wisdom he found out in the morning of time that some men worship rank, some worship heroes, some worship power, some worship God, and that over these ideals they dispute and cannot unite—but that they all worship money; so he made it the end and aim of his life to get it. He was at it in Egypt thirty-six centuries ago; he was at it in Rome when that Christian got persecuted by mistake for him; he has been at it ever since. The cost to him has been heavy; his success has made the whole human race his enemy—but it has paid, for it has brought him envy, and that is the only thing which men will sell both soul and body to get. He long ago observed that a millionaire commands respect, a two-millionaire homage, a multi-millionaire the deepest deeps of adoration. We all know that feeling; we have seen it express itself. We have noticed that when the average man mentions the name of a multi-millionaire he does it with that mixture in his voice of awe and reverence and lust which burns in a Frenchman's eye when it falls on another man's centime.

Point No. 4.—"The Jews have no party; they are non-participants."

Perhaps you have let the secret out and given yourself away. It seems hardly a credit to the race that is able to say that; or to you, sir, that you can say it without remorse; more, that you should offer it as a plea against maltreatment, injustice, and oppression. Who gives the Jew the right, who gives any race the right, to sit still, in a free country, and let somebody else look after its safety? The oppressed Jew was entitled to all pity in the former times under brutal autocracies, for he was weak and friendless, and had no way to help his case. But he has ways now, and he has had them for a century, but I do not see that he has tried to make serious use of them. When the Revolution set him free in France it was an act of grace – the grace of other people; he does not appear in it as a helper. I do not know that he helped when England set him free. Among the Twelve Sane Men of France who have stepped forward with great Zola at their head to fight (and win, I hope and believe)[1] the battle for the most infamously misused Jew of modern times, do you find a great or rich or illustrious Jew helping? In the United States he was created free in the beginning – he did not need to help, of course. In Austria and Germany and France he has a vote, but of what considerable use is it to him? He doesn't seem to know how to apply it to the best effect. With all his splendid capacities and all his fat wealth he is to-day not politically important in any country. In America, as early as 1854, the ignorant Irish hod-carrier, who had a spirit of his own and a way of exposing it to all that he must be politically reckoned with; yet fifteen years before that we hardly knew what an Irishman looked like. As an intelligent force, and numerically, he has always been away down, but he has governed the country just the same. It was because he was *organized*. It made his vote valuable – in fact, essential.

You will say the Jew is everywhere numerically feeble. That is nothing to the point – with the Irishman's history for an object-lesson. But I am coming to your numerical feebleness presently. In all parliamentary countries you could no doubt elect Jews to the legislatures – and even *one* member in such a body is sometimes a force which counts. How deeply have you concerned yourselves about this in Austria, France, and Germany? Or even in America, for that matter? You remark that the Jews were not to blame for the riots in this Reichsrath here, and you add with satisfaction that there wasn't one in that body. That is not strictly correct; if it were, would it not be in order for you to explain it and apologize for it, not try to make a merit of it? But I think that the Jew was by no means in as large force there as he ought to have been, with his chances. Austria opens the suffrage to him on fairly liberal terms, and it must surely be his own fault that he is so much in the background politically.

As to your numerical weakness. I mentioned some figures awhile ago – 500,000 – as the Jewish population of Germany. I will add some

---

[1]The article was written in the summer of 1898, while Alfred Dreyfus was still in disgrace.

more—6,000,000 in Russia, 5,000,000 in Austria (Austro-Hungarian Empire), 250,000 in the United States. I take them from memory; I read them in the Cyclopaedia Britannica ten or twelve years ago. Still, I am entirely sure of them. If those statistics are correct, my argument is not as strong as it ought to be as concerns America, but it still has strength. It is plenty strong enough as concerns Austria, for ten years ago 5,000,000 was nine per cent of the empire's population. The Irish would govern the Kingdom of Heaven if they had a strength there like that. . . .

. . . Look at the city of New York; and look at Boston, and Philadelphia, and New Orleans, and Chicago, and Cincinnati, and San Francisco—how your race swarms in those places!—and everywhere else in America, down to the least little village. Read the signs on the marts of commerce and on the shops: Goldstein (gold stone), Edelstein (precious stone), Blumenthal (flower-vale), Rosenthal (rose-vale), Veilchenduft (violet odor), Singvogel (song bird), Rosenzweig (rose branch), and all the amazing list of beautiful and enviable names which Prussia and Austria glorified you with so long ago. It is another instance of Europe's coarse and cruel persecution of your race; not that it was coarse and cruel to outfit it with pretty and poetical names like those, but that it was coarse and cruel to make it *pay* for them or else take such hideous and often indecent names that to-day their owners never use them; or, if they do, only on official papers. And it was the many, not the few, who got the odious names, they being too poor to bribe the officials to grant them better ones.

Now why was the race renamed? I have been told that in Prussia it was given to using fictitious names, and often changing them, so as to beat the tax-gatherer, escape military service, and so on; and that finally the idea was hit upon of furnishing all the inmates of a house with *one and the same surname*, and then holding the house responsible right along for those inmates, and accountable for any disappearances that might occur; it made the Jews keep track of *each other*, for self-interest's sake, and saved the government the trouble.

If that explanation of how the Jews of Prussia came to be renamed is correct, if it is true that they fictitiously registered themselves to gain certain advantages, it may possibly be true that in America they refrain from registering themselves as Jews to fend off the damaging prejudices of the Christian customer. I have no way of knowing whether this notion is well founded or not. . . . I may, of course, be mistaken, but I am strongly of the opinion that we have an immense Jewish population in America.

Point No. 3. — "Can Jews do anything to improve the situation?"

I think so. If I may make a suggestion without seeming to be trying to teach my grandmother how to suck eggs, I will offer it. In our days we have learned the value of combination. . . . Whatever our strength may be, big or little, we *organize* it. We have found out that that is the only way to get the most out of it that is in it. We know the weakness of individual sticks, and the strength of the concentrated faggot. Suppose you try a scheme like this, for instance. In England and America put every Jew on the census-book *as* a Jew (in case you have not been doing that). Get up volunteer regiments composed of Jews solely, and, when the drum beats, fall in and go to the front, so as to remove the reproach that you have few Massenas among you, and that you feed on a country but don't like to fight for it. Next, in politics, organize your strength, band together, and deliver the casting vote where you can, and where you can't, compel as good terms as possible. You huddle to yourselves already in all countries, but you huddle to no sufficient purpose, politically speaking. You do not seem to be organized, except for your charities. There you are omnipotent; there you compel your due of recognition — you do not have to beg for it. It shows what you can do when you band together for a definite purpose.

And then from America and England you can encourage your race in Austria, France, and Germany, and materially help it. . . . You seem to think that the Jews take no hand in politics here, that they are "absolutely non-participants." I am assured by men competent to speak that this is a very large error, that the Jews are exceedingly active in politics all over the empire, but that they scatter their work and their votes among the numerous parties, and thus lose the advantages to be had by concentration. I think that in America they scatter too, but you know more about that than I do.

Speaking of concentration, Dr. Herzl has a clear insight into the value of that. Have you heard of his plan? He wishes to gather the Jews of the world together in Palestine, with a government of their own — under the suzerainty of the Sultan, I suppose. At the convention of Berne, last year, there were delegates from everywhere, and the proposal was received with decided favor. I am not the Sultan, and I am not objecting; but if that concentration of the cunningest brains in the world was going to be made in a free country . . . , I think it would be politic to stop it. It will not be well to let that race find out its strength. If the horses knew theirs, we should not ride any more.

Point No. 5. – "Will the persecution of the Jews ever come to an end?"

On the score of religion, I think it has already come to an end. On the score of race prejudice and trade, I have the idea that it will continue. That is, here and there in spots around the world, where a barbarous ignorance and a sort of mere animal civilization prevail; but I do not think that elsewhere the Jew need now stand in any fear of being robbed and raided. Among the high civilizations he seems to be very comfortably situated indeed, and to have more than his proportionate share of the prosperities going. It has that look in Vienna. I suppose the race prejudice cannot be removed; but he can stand that; it is no particular matter. By his make and ways he is substantially a foreigner wherever he may be, and even the angels dislike a foreigner. I am using this word foreigner in the German sense – *stranger*. Nearly all of us have an antipathy to a stranger, even of our own nationality. We pile gripsacks in a vacant seat to keep him from getting it; and a dog goes further, and does as a savage would – challenges him on the spot. The German dictionary seems to make no distinction between a stranger and a foreigner; in its view a stranger *is* a foreigner – a sound position, I think. You will always be by ways and habits and predilections substantially strangers – foreigners – wherever you are, and that will probably keep the race prejudice against you alive.

But you were the favorites of Heaven originally, and your manifold and unfair prosperities convince me that you have crowded back into that snug place again. Here is an incident that is significant. Last week in Vienna a hailstorm struck the prodigious Central Cemetery and made wasteful destruction there. In the Christian part of it, according to the official figures, 621 windowpanes were broken; more than 900 singing-birds were killed; five great trees and many small ones were torn to shreds and the shreds scattered far and wide by the wind; the ornamental plants and other decorations of the graves were ruined, and more than a hundred tomb-lanterns shattered; and it took the cemetery's whole force of 300 laborers more than three days to clear away the storm's wreckage. In the report occurs this remark – and in its italics you can hear it grit its Christian teeth: ". . . lediglich die *israelitische* Abtheilung des Friedhofes vom Hagelwetter *ganzlich verschont* worden war." Not a hailstone hit the Jewish reservation! Such nepotism makes me tired.

Point No. 6.—"What has become of the golden rule?"

It exists, it continues to sparkle, and is well taken care of. It is Exhibit A in the Church's assets, and we pull it out every Sunday and give it an airing. But you are not permitted to try to smuggle it into this discussion, where it is irrelevant and would not feel at home. It is strictly religious furniture, like an acolyte, or a contribution-plate, or any of those things. It has never been intruded into business; and Jewish persecution is not a religious passion, it is a business passion.

To conclude.—If the statistics are right, the Jews constitute but *one per cent* of the human race. It suggests a nebulous dim puff of star dust lost in the blaze of the Milky Way. Properly the Jew ought hardly to be heard of; but he is heard of, has always been heard of. He is as prominent on the planet as any other people, and his commercial importance is extravagantly out of proportion to the smallness of his bulk. His contributions to the world's list of great names in literature, science, art, music, finance, medicine, and abstruse learning are also away out of proportion to the weakness of his numbers. He has made a marvellous fight in this world, in all the ages; and has done it with his hands tied behind him. He could be vain of himself, and be excused for it. The Egyptian, the Babylonian, and the Persian rose, filled the planet with sound and splendor, then faded to dream-stuff and passed away; the Greek and the Roman followed, and made a vast noise, and they are gone; other peoples have sprung up and held their torch high for a time, but it burned out, and they sit in twilight now, or have vanished. The Jew saw them all, beat them all, and is now what he always was, exhibiting no decadence, no infirmities of age, no weakening of his parts, no slowing of his energies, no dulling of his alert and aggressive mind. All things are mortal but the Jew; all other forces pass, but he remains. What is the secret of his immortality?

(Twain, "Concerning the Jews," in *Harper's Magazine*, June 1899)

* * *

... it cannot be said, despite his patent goodwill, that Twain understood the situation of the Jews. He writes in his notebook (1899) that "the Jews are the only race who work wholly with their brains and never with their hands. There are no Jewish beggars, no Jew tramps, no Jew ditchers, hod-carriers, day laborers or followers of toilsome, mechanical trades." This is, of course, a conventional notion. But at that very time there were, in fact, many Jewish immigrants who were not only beggars but also cigar-makers and clothing workers, who must have attracted general notice in the 1870s by their participation in strikes. . . .

Twain's mixture of openhearted goodwill and incomplete apprehension reached its most extended expression in an essay, "Concerning the Jews," which Twain published in *Harper's* in June 1899. In March of the previous year an article of his had appeared in *Harper's*, describing the stormy debate he had witnessed in the Austrian parliament on the proposal that the official language of Bohemia be Czech, rather than German. The deputies, writes Twain, "are religious men. They are earnest, sincere, devoted, and they hate the Jews." In the rioting and turbulence that followed the vote, the Jews were the targets of both sides "in all cases the Jew had to roast, no matter what side he was on." Twain received a number of letters from Jews on this article, but one letter in particular stimulated him to write an article in reply. . . .

No one, Twain asserts, can complain that the Jews are not acceptable as citizens, for they are not a burden on the civic organization of society, since they are law-abiding in all respects. This was accurate enough, for it had statistical support. But Twain then goes on to set forth the Jews' "discreditable ways," and he apparently agrees with this "reputation" of the Jews for various forms of sharp practice in business, even though he adds that Jews do not have "a monopoly of them." Although there was some basis in reality for this stereotype, Twain was following the popular fallacy of identifying the whole with a part—so often the basis for prejudice. Twain adds the charge that the Jew has "an unpatriotic disinclination to stand by the flag as a soldier—like the Christian Quaker," an assertion that he was later to retract. . . .

. . . It is because "the Christian cannot *compete* with the Jew," rather than religious prejudice, that accounts for persecution of the Jew. The Jew's "success made the whole human race his enemy." Here Twain oversimplifies a very complex phenomenon, and underestimates the staying power that Jew-hatred because of the Jews' supposed role in the crucifixion has proved to have, even to our own day. Competition often does set off anti-Semitic feeling, but there are other factors as well. For instance, in the Austrian rioting that occasioned this article the Jew served as a scapegoat, a diversion from real problems.

Twain then criticizes the Jewish community for not organizing into political parties, so that it might defend itself, instead of letting "somebody else look after its safety." Here again, Twain underesti-mates the extent to which Jews have participated in government and national life where tolerance permitted. In the United States, for instance, Jews have held public office since colonial times. His assump-tion that Jews were passive everywhere and did not participate in revolutions that resulted in their liberation (e.g., the French Revolu-tion) only reveals that Twain was historically beyond his depth. His suggestion that the Jews organize politically in defense of their inter-ests did have the virtue of discerning the need to organize for defense, even if not in the forms proposed by Twain. Jews did organize in this century, following the pogroms and persecution in Eastern Europe and the rise of aggressive anti-Semitism.

Twain is unduly optimistic in his belief that religious persecution has "already come to an end." True, the day of the religious auto-da-fé was over (the gas chambers of secular anti-Semitism were still to come), but the momentum of religious anti-Semitism was still far from expended, nor is it to this day. He is quite right, however, in his assertion that "on the score of race prejudice and trade," persecution will continue. He even believes that this will never end. . . .

As could be anticipated, the article aroused comment and controversy in the Jewish press all over the world. While most acknowledged the goodwill behind the article, objection was made to Twain's historical allusions concerning Jewish passivity in the struggle for freedom of the countries in which they lived and for their own people, and to the imputed nonparticipation in the military. To Twain's complaint that important Jews had not fought back in the Dreyfus case, contrary evidence was given. Interestingly enough, Twain himself, in a letter from Sweden to the Jewish historiographer Simon Wolf on September 15, 1899, offered the view that "the Jews did wisely in keeping quiet during the Dreyfus agitation — the other course would have hurt Dreyfus's cause, and I see now that *nothing* could have helped it." Twain thus not only negates his own criticisms, but shows that he is unaware of the many protesting letters and petitions and resolutions by American Jews to President McKinley to intervene for

Dreyfus. In this letter Twain thanked Wolf for his *American Jew as Patriot, Soldier and Citizen* (1895), which refutes Twain's assertions of Jewish passivity and nonparticipation. . . .

But Twain's errors did not rise out of ill will; it was just that his talents did not run to history of social analysis. The greatness of *Huckleberry Finn* lies in his insight into character within a social context, not in social-scientific analysis of slavery and frontier life. Obviously, he did not know the Jew as well as he knew Huck and Jim; and his venture into the much-misunderstood territory of the Jewish question led to some unhappy results. When his errors were pointed out to him, he did try to make amends. He studied official figures of Jewish participation in American wars and in 1904 published his results in a widely publicized postscript to his article, under the title "The American Jew as Soldier." The "slur," he writes, "that the Jew is willing to feed on a country but not to fight for it," is false; and "ought to be pensioned off now, and retired from active service."

The genuineness of his feelings about the Jews is attested to by his attitude toward the great pianist Osip Gabrilowitsch, who met Twain's daughter, Clara, at the turn of the century and married her in 1909. When Clara first became friendly with the Jewish pianist, she writes, she

> thought of my father. Since childhood I had heard him rail at the crass stupidity and barbarity of race prejudice. Oftenest, of course, he ridiculed the persecution of Jews, a member of whose race the entire world worships. . . . Father used to find it particularly laughable that so-called Christians, filled with contempt for the Jew, were themselves often the most insignificant or reprehensible members of the human race!

Clara Clemens earlier remarks that her father's comments on the Jews were so often repeated that he was suspected of being a Jew himself. Indeed, beginning in 1910 attempts were made in Germany to prove that he was Jewish and that his name was *Salamon* Clemens. The Nazis publicized these efforts. . . .

. . . His feeling for the Jews as a persecuted people was one aspect of his total outlook. Wherever he saw it he condemned injustice, whether economic or racial, within the limits of his knowledge and understanding. Once he reached maturity he threw off racist attitudes toward Negroes, Jews, Chinese, and Indians. He supported trade unionism in its pioneer days in the 1880s, and was an anti-imperialist in relation to the Spanish-American War and the imperialist adventures of European powers (like Belgian King Leopold's appropriation of the Congo). Mark Twain was no social scientist and there were inconsistencies in his social attitudes, but the will for genuine equality was present in his as in few major American writers.

(L. Harap, *The Image of the Jew in American Literature*, pp. 352–357)

HENRY ADAMS   *(1838–1918)*

U.S. historian and novelist

Adams to—, 1896:

. . . We are in the hands of Jews; they can do what they please with our values.

* * *

Adams to Sir Robert Cunliffe, 1898:

You dear simple-minded Britisher, and bucolic, I love you, but I don't love your Lombard Street Jews who rule you. . . . What with your Jew crusade for gold, and your hopeless subservience to the speculative interests of the city of London, we were drifting very far apart.

* * *

Adams to Charles Gaskell, 19 February 1914:

The winter is nearly over, I am seventy-six years old, and nearly over too. . . . It is quite astonishing how the circle narrows. I think that in reality as many people pass by, and I hear as much as I ever did, but it is no longer a part of me. I am inclined to think it is not wholly my fault. The atmosphere has become a Jew atmosphere. . . . We are still in power, after a fashion. Our sway over what we call society is undisputed. We keep the Jews far away, and the anti-Jew feeling is quite rabid. We are anti-everything and we are wild up-lifters; yet we somehow seem to be more Jewish every day.

Adams to—, 23 December 1916:

I am dining tonight in a palace of gold plate and shall talk Jew-baiting with a very able American woman, wife of an English peer.

* * *

Adams to—, 29 December 1917:

Judea—Israel—the Lost Tribes—lost no more! Found—very much found, increased—multiplied—as the sands of the sea—upon the sands of the sea—in the city of the sea—Atlantic City—with cliff dwellings of 10,000 each,—and regurgitating with Hebrews—only Hebrews. Families of tens and dozens—grave old plodders, gay young friskers—angel Jews, siren Jewesses,—puppy Jews—mastiff Jews—bulging matrons—spectacled backfish—golden-haired Jewish Dianas, sable-eyed Jewish Pucks, Jewish Mirandas—Romeos and Juliets, Jew Caesars—only no Shylock. It is a heathen menagerie of Israel.

(Henry Adams, Letters (1892–1918), p. 111)

HENRY GEORGE (1839–1897)

U.S. journalist and economist; author of Progress and Poverty

From the free spirit of the Mosaic law sprang the intensity of family life that amid all dispersions and persecution has preserved the individuality of the Hebrew race; that love of independence that under the most adverse circumstances has characterized the Jew; that burning patriotism that flamed up in the Maccabees and bared the breasts of Jewish peasants to the serried steel of Grecian phalanx and the resistless onset of Roman legion; that stubborn courage that in exile and in torture held the Jew to his faith.

It kindled that fire that has made the strains of Hebrew seers and poets phrase for us the highest exaltations of thought; that intellectual vigor that has over and over again made the dry staff bud and blossom. And passing outward from one narrow race it has exerted its power wherever the influence of the Hebrew Scriptures has been felt. It has toppled thrones and cast down hierarchies. It strengthened the

Scottish Covenanter in the hour of trial, and the Puritan amid the
snows of a strange land. . . .

("Moses: A Lecture," in *The Writings of Henry George*,
vol. VIII, p. 21)

WILLIAM JAMES   *(1842–1910)*

U.S. philosopher and psychologist

Need and struggle are what excite and inspire me; our hour of triumph
is what brings the void. Not the Jews of the captivity, but those of the
days of Solomon's glory are those from whom the pessimistic utterances in our Bible come.

(*The Will to Believe*, 1897)

AMBROSE BIERCE   *(1842–1914)*

American journalist; author of Devil's Dictionary

Hebrew. A male Jew, as distinguished from a Shebrew, an altogether
superior creation.

(*Devil's Dictionary*, 1906)

HENRY JAMES   *(1843–1916)*

U.S. novelist; author of The Europeans, Daisy Miller

Alice James, sister of Henry and William, makes a tart comment in her
journal for May 7, 1891, that exposes the hypocrisy of some restric-
tionists. "What a spectacle," she writes; "the Anglo-Saxon races ad-
dressing remonstrances to the Czar against expelling Jews from Russia,
at the very moment when their governments are making laws to forbid
their immigration." One brother, the philosopher William James, who

was as free from prejudice as any man of his generation, summarily wished that "the Anglo-Saxon race would drop its sniveling cant."

For his part, their brother, Henry James, assumed the conventional social attitude to the Jews, as he amply manifests in his fiction. Leon Edel reports that Bernard Berenson once said that "he didn't get along very well with James because James didn't like Jews." Edel assigns this unfriendliness to James's lack of interest in art "expertise or connoisseurs." In any case, however, his anti-Semitism did not approach in intensity or irrationality the attitude of Henry Adams. The difference is clear from their respective attitudes toward the Dreyfus case. While Adams condemned the Dreyfusards and the Jews, whether or not Dreyfus was guilty, because they were an evil force, Henry James was profoundly disgusted by the false accusations against Dreyfus. When Zola was tried in February 1898 for publishing J'accuse, every day James felt himself "in Paris by the side of the big, brave Zola, whom I find really a hero." After Zola's conviction, James wrote him a letter of support that has never been found. . . .

. . . Discussing Jules Lemaitre as a critic, James regrets that his convictions were of the "ugliest" kind — "his voice was loud throughout the 'Affair' . . . in the anti-revisionist and anti-Semitic interest." While Henry James's unequivocal private feelings about the Dreyfus case are creditable, one wishes he had spoken out — as he admired Zola for doing — even if he was not French.

Leon Edel seems to conclude too much from this aspect of James's life. James, writes Edel, "had no hatred for any people. He might satirize national manners or national idiosyncrasies, or use national stereotypes, but there was no touch of bigotry or racism in his make-up." "Hatred" is surely too strong a word for James's attitude toward the Jews. But social condescension and an incapacity to see the Jew as an individual and not a type is evinced by his fiction. . . .

(Harap, *The Image of the Jew in American Literature*, pp. 368–369)

* * *

. . . Only the gross injustice of the Dreyfus case was unsubtle enough to affront James, to move him to opposition — if only privately.

Like most Americans, the Jews were alien to James; just how distant from them James felt is evinced in his comments on the condition of the Jewish ghetto in New York. During his last long visit to the United States in 1904–5, he was given a conducted tour of the East Side, which he recounts in *The American Scene* (1907). Of course, it was not only the Jew who was alien to the aging James. If the young James considered the cultural soil of the United States too sterile for his creativity, the older James, returning to America after two decades, found a country radically different from the one he had left and even more alien to his mentality than before. The "swarming" Jews of New York, "a Jewry that had burst all bounds," was only one aspect of the new America that repelled him. To be sure, the impression that the teeming population of the East Side made on an eye and mind unaccustomed to the sight must have been overpowering. James reports that "with the exception of some shy corner of Asia, no district in the world known to the statistician has so many inhabitants to the yard."

James's response to this unprecedented sight was not humane and compassionate and comprehending, but rather disgusted and dehumanized. To James, this concentration of the Jewish population intensified the Jewishness of the individuals, in that "the unsurpassed strength of the race permits the chopping into myriads of fine fragments without loss of race-quality." He was reminded of "small, strange animals, known to natural history, snakes or worms, I believe, who, when cut into pieces, wriggle away contentedly as in the whole. So the denizens of the New York Ghetto, heaped as thick as the splinters in the table of a glass-blower, had each, like the fine glass particle, his or her individual share of the whole hard glitter of Israel."

The unconscious process that went into creating this striking imagery tells much of James's human distance from the Jews. Jews are "snakes or worms" and Jewry as a whole has a "hard glitter." The unfeeling images continue: the Jews "were all there for race, and not, as it were, for reason"; the old ones conveyed an "excess of lurid meaning"; the "ethnic' apparition" sat "like a skeleton at the feast"; James can see "the spectre grin" as he is told facts and figures about "the extent of the Hebrew conquest of New York." Everywhere, it seems to him, the faces are "insistent, unhumorous, exotic."

Easier for us to understand, even if we do not concur, is James's shock at what is happening to the English language in the ghetto. The "East-Side cafés," James writes, are "torture-rooms of the living idioms" and he despairs of the future of the language.

The Jews, finally, are a mysterious, incomprehensible, and perhaps sinister people. "Who can ever tell, moreover, in any conditions and in presence of any apparent anomaly, what the genius of Israel may, or may not, really be 'up to'?"

It would not be fair to James, however, if we did not mention that when his view of the East Side leads him to think about "the poor" and the depersonalization of the individual under the operation of the "Trusts and . . . the new remorseless monopolies," he displays great social insight. He discerns that "the living unit's property in himself" comes under unconditional subjection to these "properties overwhelmingly greater." He concludes that "there is such a thing, in the United States, it is hence to be inferred, as freedom to grow up blighted, and it may be the only freedom in store for the smaller fry of future generations." Such social insight, however, emerges after his specific discussion of the ghetto. For the Jews his response is curiosity mixed with revulsion.

(The Image of the Jew, pp. 375–376)

THOMAS ALVA EDISON   (1847–1931)

U.S. inventor of the light bulb, mimeograph, and phonograph

Was Edison . . . anti-Semitic? There are some indications that he was. Edison told a *Detroit Journal* reporter in 1914 that the rise of commerce in Germany fostered the war, and that Jews were responsible for Germany's business success. He added that he believed the military government to be a pawn of the Jewish business sector. Within two weeks, however, Edison wrote to Herman Bernstein saying that he had been badly misquoted. What he actually had said was, "If one went down to the bottom of things in the great and most successful industries, one would dig up a Jew who furnished the ability to make them a success."

During the series of anti-Semitic articles appearing in the *Dearborn Independent*, Edison gave indications of support for that effort. In December 1920, for instance, Edison corresponded with Liebold on the anti-Semitic articles, saying that "they don't like publicity." On several other occasions he sent notes that implied at least tacit support, and in a note dated November 28, 1924, Edison sent Liebold a news clipping entitled "Jews are Ruling Soviet Russia," which stated that out of the forty-eight leaders of the Soviet government, only five were of pure Russian blood. Edison's attached note says only, "Liebold: This is interesting. Edison." Moreover, Ford sent Edison a complete set of volumes of the *International Jew*, in a special leather presentation binding. Edison graciously accepted with "thanks."

The evidence on Edison's anti-Semitism is far from conclusive. It is known that he employed Jews in his laboratory and, except for the few notes to Liebold in his late seventies, never made an anti-Semitic comment to anyone. Also, we have the testimony of Harry Bennett, who said that "more than once I heard Edison rebuke Mr. Ford for his prejudice. Mr. Ford always denied it to him."

Was he or wasn't he? The evidence seems to indicate that Edison shared the Populist notion that Wall Street was dominated by Jews, and it was the Jews in the financial professions whom Edison resented. Edison could have applauded the first articles pointing a finger at Jewish international bankers; but, as the articles continued, it is doubtful that he could have accepted the bizarre accusations [of Ford's newspaper].

There are some indications that Edison encouraged Ford to drop the anti-Semitic series. For one, Ford said that his reason for stopping the attack was to bring down the gold standard. The gold standard was Edison's obsession during these years. In his eulogy of Edison in 1931, Ford said: "Latterly he turned his mind to economic questions because he believed the present system hindered the best in men. . . . He was convinced that our money machinery was badly in need of attention." If Edison was anti-Semitic, as his notes to Ford indicate, then it appears to be the unique form of the disease . . . economic anti-Semitism.

(Lee, *Henry Ford and the Jews*, pp. 155–156)

WOODROW WILSON (1856–1924)

*28th president of the United States, 1913–1921; founder of the
League of Nations*

The invading hosts who came from across the Rhine in the fifth century of our era found Roman law and institutions everywhere in possession of the lands they conquered. Everywhere there were towns of the Roman pattern and populations more or less completely under the dominion of Roman legal conceptions and practices. Their dealings with their institutions, the action and reaction upon one another of Roman law and Teutonic habit, constitute in no small part the history of government in the Middle Ages.

It would be a mistake, however, to ascribe to Roman legal conceptions an undivided sway over the development of law and institutions during the Middle Ages. The Teuton came under the influence, not of Rome only, but also of Christianity; and through the Church there entered into Europe a potent leaven of Judaic thought. The laws of Moses as well as the laws of Rome contributed suggestion and impulse to the men and institutions which were to prepare the modern world; and if we could but have the eyes to see the subtle elements of thought which constitute the gross substance of our present habit, both as regards the sphere of private life and as regards the action of the state, we should easily discover how very much besides religion we owe to the Jew.

(Wilson, *The State*, p. 143)

* * *

In an address at Carnegie Hall in New York,
6 December 1911:

Here is a great body of our Jewish Citizens from whom have sprung men of genius in every walk of our varied life; men who have conceived of its ideals with singular clearness; and led its enterprises with spirit and sagacity. . . . They are not Jews in America; they are American citizens.

(*Public Papers of Woodrow Wilson*, vol. II, pp. 318–319)

THORSTEIN VEBLEN   *(1857–1929)*

U.S. political economist; author of The Theory of the Leisure Class

Among all the clamorous projects of national self-determination which surround the return of peace [1919], the proposal of the Zionists is notable for sobriety, good will, and a poise of self-assurance. More confidently and perspicuously than all the others, the Zionists propose a rehabilitation of their national integrity under a regime of live and let live, "with charity for all, with malice toward none." Yet it is always a project for withdrawal upon themselves, a scheme of national demarcation between Jew and gentile; indeed, it is a scheme of territorial demarcation and national frontiers of the conventional sort, within which Jews and Jewish traits, traditions, and aspirations are to find scope and breathing space for a home-bred culture and a free unfolding of all that is best and most characteristic of the endowment of the race. There runs through it all a dominant bias of isolation and inbreeding, and a confident persuasion that this isolation and inbreeding will bring great and good results for all concerned. The Zionists aspire to bring to full fruition all that massive endowment of spiritual and intellectual capacities of which their people have given evidence throughout their troubled history, and not least during these concluding centuries of their exile.

The whole project has an idyllic and engaging air. And any disinterested bystander will be greatly moved to wish them godspeed. Yet there comes in a regret that this experiment in isolation and inbreeding could not have been put to the test at an earlier date, before the new order of large-scale industry and universal intercourse had made any conclusive degree of such national isolation impracticable, before this same new order had so shaped the run of things that any nation or community drawn on this small scale would necessarily be dependent on and subsidiary to the run of things at large. It is now, unhappily, true that any "nation" of the size and geographical emplacement of the projected Zion will, for the present and the calculable future, necessarily be something of a national make-believe. The current state of the industrial arts will necessarily deny it a rounded and self-balanced national integrity in any substantial sense. The days of Solomon are long past. . . .

It is a fact which must strike any dispassionate observer that the Jewish people have contributed much more than an even share to the intellectual life of modern Europe. So also it is plain that the civilization of Christendom continues today to draw heavily on the Jews for men devoted to science and scholarly pursuits. It is not only that men of Jewish extraction continue to supply more than a proportionate quota to the rank and file engaged in scientific and scholarly work, but a disproportionate number of the men to whom modern science and scholarship look for guidance and leadership are of the same derivation. Particularly is this true of the modern sciences, and it applies perhaps especially in the field of scientific theory, even beyond the extent of its application in the domain of workday detail. So much is notorious. . . .

. . . the Chosen People have quite characteristically never been addicted to missionary enterprise; nor does the Jewish scheme of right and honest living comprise anything of the kind. This, too, is notorious fact; so much so that this allusion to it may well strike any Jew as foolish insistence on a commonplace matter of course. In their character of a Chosen People, it is not for them to take thought of their unblest neighbors and seek to dispel the darkness that overlies the soul of the gentiles.

The cultural heritage of the Jewish people is large and rich, and it is of ancient and honorable lineage. And from time immemorial this people has shown aptitude for such work as will tax the powers of thought and imagination. Their home-bred achievements of the ancient time, before the Diaspora, are among the secure cultural monuments of mankind. . . .

It appears to be only when the gifted Jew escapes from the cultural environment created and fed by the particular genius of his own people, only when he falls into the alien lines of gentile inquiry and becomes a naturalised, though hyphenate, citizen in the gentile republic of learning, that he comes into his own as a creative leader in the world's intellectual enterprise. It is by loss of allegiance, or at the best by force of a divided allegiance to the people of his origin, that he finds himself in the vanguard of modern inquiry. . . .

("The Intellectual Pre-eminence of Jews in Modern Europe," 1919, in *The Portable Veblen*, pp. 467–479)

THEODORE ROOSEVELT   *(1858–1919)*

26th president of the United States, 1901–1909

While I was Police Commissioner [1895] an anti-Semitic preacher from Berlin, Rector Ahlwardt, came over to New York to preach a crusade against the Jews. Many of the New York Jews were much excited and asked me to prevent him from speaking and not to give him police protection. This, I told them, was impossible; and if possible would have been undesirable because it would have made him a martyr. The proper thing to do was to make him ridiculous.

Accordingly I detailed for his protection a Jew sergeant and a score or two of Jew policemen. He made his harangue against the Jews under the active protection of some forty policemen, every one of them a Jew.

It was the most effective possible answer; and incidentally it was an object lesson to our people, whose greatest need is to learn that there must be no division by class hatred, whether this hatred be that of creed against creed, nationality against nationality, section against section, or men of one social or industrial condition against men of another social or industrial condition.

(*Theodore Roosevelt, an Autobiography*, p. 186)

HENRY FORD   (1863–1947)

Father of the automobile assembly line and the Model T

For some time past I have given consideration to the series of articles concerning Jews which since 1920 have appeared in the *Dearborn Independent*. Some of them have been reprinted in pamphlet form under the title *The International Jew*. Although public publications are my property, it goes without saying that in the multitude of my activities it has been impossible for me to devote personal attention to their management or to keep informed as to their contents. It has therefore inevitably followed that the conduct and policies of [my] publications had to be delegated to men whom I placed in charge of them and upon whom I relied implicitly.

To my great regret I have learned that Jews generally, and particularly those in this country, not only resent these publications as promoting anti-Semitism, but regard me as their enemy. Trusted friends with whom I have conferred recently have assured me in all sincerity that in their opinion the character of the charges and insinuations made against the Jews, both individually and collectively, contained in the many of the articles which have been circulated periodically in the *Dearborn Independent*, and have been reprinted in the pamphlets mentioned, justifies the righteous indignation entertained by Jews everywhere toward me because of the mental anguish occasioned by the unprovoked reflections made upon them.

This has led me to direct my personal attention to the subject, in order to ascertain the exact nature of these articles. As a result of this survey I confess I am deeply mortified that this journal, which is intended to be constructive and not destructive, has been made the medium for resurrecting exploded fictions, for giving currency to the so-called *Protocols of the Wise Men of Zion*, which have been demonstrated, as I learn, to be gross forgeries, and for contending that the Jews have been engaged in a conspiracy to control the capital and the industries of the world, besides laying at their door many offenses against decency, public order, and good morals.

Had I appreciated even the general nature, to say nothing of the details, of these utterances, I would have forbidden their circulation without a moment's hesitation. . . . I deem it my duty as an honorable man to make amends for the wrong done to the Jews as fellow-men and brothers, by asking their forgiveness for the harm that I have unintentionally committed, by retracting so far as lies within my power the offensive charges laid at their door by these publications, and by giving them the unqualified assurance that henceforth they may look to me for friendship and good will.

(Lee, Henry Ford[1] and the Jews, pp. 78–81)

* * *

Jews have always controlled the business. . . . The motion picture influence of the United States and Canada . . . is exclusively under the control, moral and financial, of the Jewish manipulators of the public mind.

(The Dearborn Independent, 12–19 February 1921)

---

[1]Retraction made by Henry Ford, appearing in every major newspaper in the United States and written by two prominent Jews of the time, Louis Marshall and Congressman Nathan Perlman. Ford refused to either sign or read the retraction; his signature was forged by his anti-Semitic assistant, Harry Bennett.

Two signs on the gates of employee parking lots at the Ford
Motor Company's Rouge plant in Dearborn, Michigan, in
1939:

"Jews are traitors to America and should not be trusted – Buy Gentile."

"Jews Teach Communism
Jews Teach Atheism
Jews Destroy Christianity
Jews Control the Press
Jews Produce Filthy Movies
Jews Control Money"
                    (Reprinted in *Henry Ford and the Jews*, pp. 100–101)

* * *

Later on it would be suggested by Ford apologists that anti-Semitism was a virus Ford brought back from Europe as part of his
disillusion with the Peace Ship. In fact it predated that doomed
voyage. Rosika Schwimmer recalled that during a luncheon when her
antiwar collaboration with Ford was beginning, he had suddenly
slapped a breast pocket containing one of his notebooks and blurted
out, "I know who started the war – the German Jewish bankers. I have
the evidence here. Facts. The German Jewish bankers caused the war.
I can't give out the facts now, because I haven't got them all yet. But I'll
have them soon."

Schwimmer thought the comment was "cheap and vulgar,"
although she didn't say so at the time for fear of alienating Ford.
(Ultimately he came to believe that his mission to Europe had failed in
large part because this "Jewess" led him astray.) But while the war
hadn't caused his anti-Semitism, it did reinforce it. When he returned
from Europe he told Liebold, whose Prussian background and character made him the perfect detail man for this new obsession, that he
was "going to go after the Jews who had started the war."

. . . There was a cultural factor in Ford's anti-Semitism: the
notion that the Jew, with his presumed cosmopolitanism and money-
lending, was the villain in the populists' soap opera of American
capitalism. His own personal prejudices extended to Catholics as

well. . . . He would explain Jews and Catholics who were his friends as exceptions to the general rule of racial and religious inferiority. Ford might say of a Jew he liked, "Oh, he's mixed, he's not *all* Jewish." Or of a Catholic, "Well, you know he's not a *good* Catholic." The difference between him and other respectable men who were also prejudiced was that he insisted on systematizing his bigotry, transforming it from a personal quirk to an architectonic truth he could demonstrate.

His proofs appeared in the Dearborn *Independent*, which he bought in 1919 when he became concerned about the quality of the press he was receiving. . . . Eventually most dealers capitulated and factored a subscription fee into the purchase of a car to satisfy their quota. Since over a million Model T's a year were being sold in 1919–21, this meant that the *Independent* went from a fortnightly filled with gossip about a sleepy suburb of Detroit to a mass-circulation weekly whose news was almost exclusively the Jews.

For ninety-one consecutive weeks it flogged "the Jewish question," excoriating the "International Jew" for grasping every lever of power and leaving nothing sacred, not even the Christian religion. Ford played an active role. He once wrote an editorial offering a reward of $1,000 to anyone able to give him an example of a Jewish farmer, part of his belief that Jews avoided "honest" manual labor in favor of "criminal" activities in the banking industry. But most of the material in the paper was far more serious and damaging in its implications than this piece of whimsy.

. . . Claiming that the Jews had connived in everything from the discovery of the New World (Queen Isabella was a "Jewish front") to the destruction of Europe as a result of World War I, "The Protocols" was a sort of encyclopedia of ethnic virulence. Its assertions were repeatedly repackaged and inserted into the *Independent*. . . .

Edsel and others in the company were disturbed by the way the Ford name was being systematically linked to anti-Semitism. But Henry believed that he was purveying "science," not prejudice, and that the "truths" appearing in the *Independent* could not hurt individuals. In fact, he was convinced that the "good" Jews appreciated his efforts. Employing his best Jewish accent, he liked to tell about a time he went to a pawnshop in Washington: "The elderly pawnbroker kept looking at me. He said, 'Hey, you're Henry Ford, aren't you?' I said, 'Yes.' He said, 'Well, I been reading that Dearborn *Independent* of yours. It's all right. It tells the truth about us.' " Ford was genuinely hurt when Rabbi Leo Franklin, his friend and former neighbor in Detroit, sent back a Model T he had given him. Ford called him on the phone and asked, "What's wrong, Dr. Franklin? Has anything come between us?" . . .

Longtime Ford defenders in the press were disgusted. Former presidents Taft and Wilson and other national leaders pleaded with him to stop. But he forged ahead. The Jews were a fixation that penetrated into the operations of the Ford Motor Company itself. A new employee was dumbfounded his first day on the job when he was told by an old-timer, "Don't ever let Mr. Ford see you using brass. It's a Jew metal." Foreman William Klamm later said, "There was a policy not to have Jewish boys working in the shop. Of course it wasn't outspoken, but you knew it when you were told to 'fire that Jewish fellow over there.' "

Ford formed the Dearborn Publishing Company to reprint a series of anti-Semitic pamphlets which were later called, when collected into a single volume, *The International Jew.* While the book had a modest circulation in the United States, it did better elsewhere in the world and fell on especially receptive ears in Germany, where it was a best-seller and where a New York *Times* reporter, during a visit in 1922, found it on the desk of the as yet largely unknown Adolf Hitler, along with a large photograph of Ford.

The anti-Semitism subsided only when Ford was threatened with another potentially embarrassing legal action. . . .

After the recantation, the "Journal of the Neglected Truth," as the Dearborn *Independent* had called itself, sank out of sight, leaving behind only an oil slick of bigotry.

Now that the anti-Semitic campaign had ended, a friend screwed up his courage to ask Ford why he had begun it in the first place. "The Jews have gone along during the ages making themselves disliked, right?" he answered. "They ignored their own splendid teachers and statesmen. Even they could not get their people to change some of their obnoxious habits."

"Well?" the friend prompted him.

"Well, I thought that by taking a club to them, I might be able to do it."

(P. Collier & D. Horowitz, *The Fords—An American Epic,*
pp. 101–106)

Although Franklin D. Roosevelt assiduously courted him, Ford hated the new president. Asked what Roosevelt had talked about at one private meeting at the White House, Ford snapped, "Well, he took up the first five minutes telling me about his ancestors. I don't know why, unless he wanted to prove he had no Jewish blood." The only good thing Ford had to say about the New Deal had to do with the appointment of Henry Morgenthau, Jr., as Secretary of the Treasury, a move he supported because he felt it made sense to have the nation's money under the control of a Jew. . . .

(*The Fords*, pp. 130–131)

WILLIAM RANDOLPH HEARST   *(1863–1951)*

U.S. newspaper publisher

Hearst's love affair with National Socialism has often been denounced by his critics as proof that he was really a kind of native fascist. . . . It was said, too, that he approved of Hitler's anti-Semitism. Those views were held not only by distinguished liberals, but by Stalin, who referred to him in *Pravda* as a "gangster journalist" and a friend of Hitler's.

Apparently Hitler, at least, knew better. Taking note of the fact that a good share of Hearst's ablest executives and writers were Jewish, the chancellor asserted in one speech: "A gigantic organization of press lies was built up, and again it was a Jewish concern, the Hearst press, which laid down the tone of the agitation against Germany."

Anyone who knew Hearst well knew that he was no anti-Semite. On the other hand, his myopic political views led him into the company of anti-Semites and American fascists. Hearst never thought it necessary to repudiate the nightshirt crowd which applauded him, though he considered it President Roosevelt's duty to disavow publicly the Communists who gave him unsought support.

The root of Hearst's affinity for National Socialism was easy to discover. It stemmed directly from his Anglophobia and Francophobia and from his blind isolationism. . . .

The appearance in the Hearst papers of syndicated articles by Hermann Goering, and of pseudo-news stories describing the "amazing economic recovery" brought about by the Hitler regime, and fervent praise of Germany's desire for peace and struggle against Communism could not have failed to put both Hearst and his papers under the same shadow of doubt that cloaked them in 1914 and thereafter.

Yet Hearst stubbornly refused to believe that anyone but a Communist could fail to agree with him, until the overwhelming evidence of persecution of Jews and Catholics and the rising protest against his pro-Hitler articles convinced him at last that he would have to give up the campaign. He still thought he was right. One editorial excused the excesses of the regime on the ground that Hitler's ministers had got out of hand and were acting without orders. But he denounced anti-Semitism specifically, and although he had no sympathy for a war on Germany, on the other hand he made no further flagrant attempts to defend Hitler's actions, since they were now clearly indefensible.

(Tebbel, *The Life and Good Times of William Randolph Hearst*,
pp. 235–237)

LINCOLN STEFFENS   *(1866–1936)*

U.S. journalist, lecturer, and political philosopher

A synagogue that burned down during a service introduced me to the service; I attended another synagogue, asked questions, and realized that it was a bit of the Old Testament repeated after thousands of years, unchanged. And so I described that service and other services [in the *New York Post* in 1896]. They fascinated me, these old practices, and the picturesque customs and laws of the old orthodox Jews from Russia and Poland. Max, an East Side Jew himself, told me about them; I read up and talked to funny old, fine rabbis about them, and about their conflicts with their Americanized children. The *Post* observed all the holy days of the Ghetto. There were advance notices of their coming, with descriptions of the preparations and explanations of their sacred, ancient, biblical meaning, and then an account of them as I saw these days and nights observed in the homes and the churches of the poor. A queer mixture of comedy, tragedy, orthodoxy, and revelation, they interested our Christian readers.

The uptown Jews complained now and then. Mr. Godkin himself required me once to call personally upon a socially prominent Jewish lady who had written to the editor asking why so much space was given to the ridiculous performances of the ignorant, foreign East Side Jews and none to the uptown Hebrews. I told her. I had the satisfaction of telling her about the comparative beauty, significance, and character of the uptown and downtown Jews. I must have talked well, for she threatened and tried to have me fired, as she put it. Fortunately, the editorial writers were under pressure also from prominent Jews to back up their side of a public controversy over the blackballing of a rich Jew by an uptown social club. "We" were fair to the Jews, editorially, but personally irritated. I was not "fired"; I was sent out to interview the proprietor of a hotel which excluded Jews, and he put his case in very few words.

"I won't have one," he said. "I have had my experience and so learned that if you let one in because he is exceptional and fine, he will bring in others who are not exceptional, etc. By and by they will occupy the whole house, when the Christians leave. And then, when the Christians don't come any more, the Jews quit you to go where the Christians have gone, and there you are with an empty or a second-class house."

It would have been absurd to discharge me since I at that time was almost a Jew. I had become as infatuated with the Ghetto as Eastern boys were with the Wild West, and nailed a *mazuza* on my office door; I went to the synagogue on all the great Jewish holy days; on Yom Kippur I spent the whole twenty-four hours fasting and going from one synagogue to another. The music moved me most, but I knew and could follow with the awful feelings of a Jew the beautiful old ceremonies of the ancient orthodox services. My friends laughed at me; especially the Jews among them scoffed. "You are more Jewish than us Jews," they said, and since I have traveled I realize the absurdity of the American who is more French than the French, more German than the Kaiser. But there were some respecters of my respect. When Israel Zangwill, the author of *Tales of the Ghetto*, came from London to visit New York, he heard about me from Jews and asked me to be his guide for a survey of the East Side; and he saw and he went home and wrote *The Melting Pot*.

The tales of the New York ghetto were heart-breaking comedies of the tragic conflict between the old and the new, the very old and the very new; in many matters, all at once: religion, class, clothes, manners, customs, language, culture. We all knew the difference between youth and age, but our experience is between two generations. Among the Russian and other eastern Jewish families in New York it was an abyss of many generations; it was between parents out of the Middle Ages, sometimes out of the Old Testament days hundreds of years B.C., and the children of the streets of New York today. We saw it everywhere all the time. Responding to a reported suicide, we would pass a synagogue where a score or more of boys were sitting hatless in their old clothes, smoking cigarettes on the steps outside, and their fathers, all dressed in black, with their high hats, uncut beards, and temple curls, were going into their synagogues, tearing their hair and rending their garments. The reporters stopped to laugh; and it was comic; the old men, in their thrift, tore the lapels of their coat very carefully, a very little, but they wept tears, real tears.

It was a revolution. Their sons were rebels against the law of Moses; they were lost souls, lost to God, the family, and to Israel of old. The police did not understand or sympathize. If there was a fight — and sometimes the fathers did lay hands on their sons, and the tough boys did biff their fathers in the eye; which brought out all the horrified elders of the whole neighborhood and all the sullen youth — when there was a "riot call," the police would rush in and club now the boys, now the parents, and now, in their Irish exasperation, both sides, bloodily and in vain. I used to feel that the blood did not hurt, but the tears did, the weeping and gnashing of teeth of the old Jews who were doomed and knew it. Two, three, thousand years of continuous devotion, courage, and suffering for a cause lost in a generation.

(*The Autobiography of Lincoln Steffens*, pp. 243–245)

FINLEY PETER DUNNE   *(1867–1936)*

American humorist; creator of Mr. Dooley

In the *Boston Globe*, 16 November 1902:

"'Tis ye'er idee that ivry Jew is a rich man. Maybe ye're right. Maybe all thim Jews that lives down in Canal sthreet, twinty in a room, is

Rothschilds. . . . Th' raison th' Jews is all in business is because they'se nawthin' else fr thim to do. . . . They cudden't be sojers or pollyticians or lawyers or judges. But they'se wan pursoot where prejudice has no hand. Whin a man wants to borrow money he niver inquires about th' charackter or religion iv th' fellow he touches. . . . an' not payin' back money to a Jew is a Christyan varchue. . . . In figures th' Jews is strong. Where thy're weak is not carin' about money. . . . A Jew makes down town an' spinds up town. It's aisy come aisy go with a Jew. . . . Whin all th' money in th' wurruld is gathered in th' hands iv anny wan class th' Jews won't have it. Most iv it'll be in New England with a few odd dollars in Scotland. . . . Why ain't th' Jew a sojer, says ye? . . . He knows he niver cud get to be a gin'ral. . . ."

(Bander, Mr. Dooley & Mr. Dunne, pp. 221–222)

JANE ADDAMS   (1869–1935)

U.S. social reformer and social worker

Upon observing "the charged atmosphere" in Chicago between philanthropists and new Russian immigrants in the 1880s:

It seems to me there is more ill feeling between Reform and Orthodox Jews than there is between Jew and Gentile.

THEODORE DREISER   (1871–1945)

U.S. novelist; author of An American Tragedy, Sister Carrie, The Titan

. . . a report that the Hitler government had banned [Dreiser's] works convinced him that the reason was the belief that he was Jewish. He was more interested in continuing a profitable German sale than in withdrawing his books on principle from a country where savagery toward the Jews had become notorious. "What procedure could I apply," he asked Mencken, "to disabuse the authorities over there of the notion that I am Jewish?" He sent a similar query to George Douglas the same day.

His attitude came out in the open when Hutchins Hapgood at last published his correspondence with Dreiser in *The Nation* under the title, "Is Dreiser Anti-Semitic?" He did so with the permission of Dreiser, who was quite willing to stand behind his opinions. His communist brethren had closed their eyes to his earlier *Spectator* statements, Dreiser being so useful to them, but this new and sharper blast could not be ignored. One can envision tense conferences at the communist Thirteenth Street headquarters under Alexander Trachtenberg, the powerful Yale-educated party member known as Moscow's "Cultural Commissar" to the United States. How to coax the temperamental novelist to retract without antagonizing him? Dreiser was invited to call at the *New Masses* office and clarify his position. . . .

. . . the *New Masses* later put it, "It was only with the greatest hesitation, with continual shifting of his position, with the use of analogies which have their roots in hoary fable and race-hatred, with repeated confusion of the interests of the Jewish masses with those of the Jewish masters, that Mr. Dreiser came around to see a few of the contradictions of his stand, and eventually acknowledged that, with fascist gangsters on every hand encouraging the same ideas, his words had a widespread and dangerous effect." The *Masses* ended forgivingly, "We decline to believe that it will be impossible for Theodore Dreiser to regain his traditional place as a fighter for human liberty."

Dreiser wrote a short statement appearing in the same issue that fell far short of the recantation expected. In fact, he retracted nothing, though he repudiated the use of his views by Nazi propagandists and wrote, "I have no hatred for the Jews and nothing to do with Hitler or fascism."

Mike Gold was so angry that, speaking for himself, he wrote a piece titled "The Gun is Loaded, Dreiser," accusing him of nationalistic, fascist leanings and writing, "It is now my belief he can undo this damage only by years of devoted battle against anti-Semitism and Fascism." But the party contented itself with slapping Dreiser's wrist, needing his voice even if his ideology was shaky.

(Swanberg, *Dreiser*, pp. 426–428)

... Though he was now more than three years late with the novel promised to Simon & Schuster, he saw himself as the victim of a Jewish plot to suppress all his works in retaliation for his writings about the Jews. He suspected that Arthur Pell, head of the Liveright firm, and Simon & Schuster were parties to the plot. He wrote Lengel:

"... This constant under-cover talk about my anti-Judaism ... has caused all sorts of people who are inimical to me ... to not only play this up but exaggerate it in every quarter, so that I feel that Simon & Schuster may themselves be joined in this issue to the end of taking me off the market entirely. It may be that they identify me with Germany and have decided to include me in their campaign against Teutonic Culture." ...

To another New York friend, Dayton Stoddart, he wrote, "Get me the names of a number of fairly recently organized non-Jewish publishers," adding, "Can you tell me whether W.W. Norton or anyone connected with his organization in a financial control sense is Jewish? All this is strictly private. ..."

... His defeat by the film censors 39 years after *Carrie* was published—long after it had become a classic—was maddening ... To Dayton Stoddart he amplified the description: "This is a selfish, self-concentrated, mean, loafing town. The business and political world is hard boiled & cruel. The movies are solidly Jewish [.] They've dug in, employ only Jews with American names and buy only what they cannot abstract and disguise. And the dollar sign is the guide— mentally & physically. That America should be led—the mass—by their direction is beyond all believing. In addition they are arrogant, insolent, and contemptuous."

(*Dreiser*, pp. 462–463)

* * *

Dreiser to H. L. Mencken, 20 September 1920:

New York to me is a scream—a Kyke's dream of a Ghetto. The lost tribe has taken the island.

(*Letters of Theodore Dreiser*, vol. II, p. 405)

* * *

Left to sheer liberalism ... they could possess America by sheer numbers, their cohesion, and their race tastes. ... The Jew insists that when he invades Italy or France or America or what you will, he becomes a native of that country—a full-blooded native of that country. You know yourself, if you know anything, that that is not true. He has been in Germany for all of a thousand years, if not longer, and he is still a Jew. He has been in America all of two hundred years, and he has not faded into a pure American by any means, and he will not. As I said before, he maintains his religious dogmas and his racial sympathies, race characteristics, and race cohesion as against all the types of nationalities surrounding him whatsoever.

(Dreiser in *The Nation*, 17 April 1935)

WILLA CATHER   *(1873–1947)*

U.S. novelist; author of My Antonia *and* Death Comes for the Archbishop

Those first brief but pungent character studies with which Willa started her newspaper career read like exercises for her future work and frequently, as in her stories, the observer is a man and the viewpoint male. . . . Clubwomen and drifters, all the small-town types that Willa knew so well, are there in embryo. Her prejudices are apparent also. In one unpleasant little sketch she describes a baby "with the unmistakable nose of an unmistakable race" grasping for a penny with which his mother tries to comfort him when he cries. "Not an orange or a bonbon," writes Willa, "but a penny. He . . . looks at it carefully on both sides as though seeing if it were genuine."

The greedy infant might be overlooked except that it is the first of many stereotyped portraits of Jews in Willa's fiction. She romanticized other nationalities and cultures, the Bohemians, the Swedes, the French, but where Jews were concerned, she seemed to have a blind spot. For the biblical Hebrews she had respect and admiration, and people she knew, like the Wieners, were certainly not included in her antipathy, but one wonders what they and other Jewish friends who came later made of the obnoxious Jews who populate her stories.

Her prejudice was not uncommon in the Midwest of her day but it was deep-seated. In 1923 she could sit in a New York theatre watching *Loyalties*, John Galsworthy's powerful play about anti-Semitism and, while admiring the performance, still comment to a friend about the fat Jewesses in the audience and suggest that Galsworthy might have changed the ending of his play if he had sat beside them. Ten years later, at the height of her career, Willa Cather surprised a magazine editor by asking him if he was "of the Jewish persuasion." When he said he was, she inquired whether he had experienced anti-Semitism and seemed skeptical when he told her he had not. She questioned him about his background, wanted to know what his mother was like, what she read, what she did for amusement. It interested her that his parents had been born in America and that he had grown up in a small town on the Hudson. Neither he nor his parents matched the Jewish stereotype of her imagination. It was as though, late in life, she was trying to understand a people who had escaped her sympathy for so long, and who fared so badly in her fiction.

(Robinson, *Willa — The Life of Willa Cather*)

* * *

"Scandal," however, besides being a poor story, contains a savage portrait of the Jewish millionaire Stein. He is an ogre, a caricature of the social-climbing, department-store-owning Jewish businessman. Stein is described as "one of the most hideous men in New York" with a "long nose, flattened as if it had been tied down; a scornful chin, long, white teeth; flat cheeks, yellow as a Mongolian's; tiny, black eyes, with puffy lids and no lashes; dingy, dead-looking hair — looks as if it were glued on." This description following hard after a similar one in "The Diamond Mine" of Cressida Garnet's accompanist, Miletus Poppas, comes as something of a shock to Cather readers. Poppas, who has been with Garnet for many years, is thoroughly disagreeable, has a "tin, lupine face," and yellowish green eyes, "always gleaming with something like defeated fury." "He was a vulture of the vulture race, and he had the beak of one," and at the end of the story "he look[s] as old as Jewry" as he waits to read the list of survivors of the *Titanic*.

Characters like Stein and Poppas have led some critics to charge that Cather was anti-Semitic. They cite also other unflattering Jewish figures in her work: the Jewish baby described in one of her earliest newspaper columns, the despicable art dealer in "The Marriage of

Phaedra," the villain in "The Affair at Grover Station," who looks
Jewish but turns out to be oriental. And in addition Louis Marcellus
in *The Professor's House* has been seen as a character created out of an
anti-Semitic bias. Marcellus, however, is for most readers a sympathetic figure, despite his brashness and aggressive behavior, and Jews
in Cather's fiction represent a minuscule fraction of the totality. There
are a good many villains in her works who are white, Anglo-Saxon
Protestants: Wick Cutter, Ivy Peters, Jerome Brown, and Buck Scales,
to name some; and others, who if not villains, are figures who reap the
author's scorn: Alexandra's brothers, Nat Wheeler and his son Bay-
liss, the bad priests in *Death Comes for the Archbishop*, and so forth.
Then there are the good Jews in her fiction such as the Rosens and the
Nathanmeyers, the former being modeled after Cather's old friends
and neighbors in Red Cloud, the Wieners; and later in her life there
was her much beloved Menuhin family—all of them, Yehudi, his
sisters, and the parents. She had what one might call a typical
Midwestern bias against Jews in the aggregate, the result of growing up
in a culture almost devoid of Jews; but to call her anti-Semitic is to
exaggerate considerably. She had many loves and many hates, and
among each were a few Jews. . . .

    (Woodress, *Willa Cather, A Literary Life*, pp. 283–284)

EDGAR RICE BURROUGHS (1875–1950)

American novelist; creator of Tarzan

"What to Do With Germany," 15 April 1945:

I would make Germany a Jewish republic. . . . Under this plan Jews
who thought they were getting the worst of it could move to Germany. . . . [Not all Jews would move, though, because] all Jews are not
fond of Jews. . . .

  The Jews are a clever race. That is one reason why they are
disliked by less clever people. They would build up a rich and powerful
nation that would need 'living room.' Then up pops a modern Joshua,
and—bingo!

  (Quoted in I. Porges, *Edgar Rice Burroughs—The Man Who Created
Tarzan*, vol. II, pp. 984–985)

JACK LONDON (1876–1916)

U.S. novelist and short story writer

Elsie Martinez . . . stated in "San Francisco Bay Area Writers and Artists" (manuscript) that Strunsky "was very much in love with [Jack London], yet claimed there was no affair, which we all believed. Bessie had told us of the evening when Anna and Jack were working. . . . She found her sitting in Jack's lap. That was enough for Bessie. . . . Jack once confided to Sterling that he wouldn't marry her because he was pure Anglo-Saxon and she was Semitic, although he loved her."

(*The Letters of Jack London*, vol. I, p. 384)

* * *

Letter to Hughes Massie, 20 November 1910:

. . . Mr. Heinemann I like very much; but he has in his employ a man whom he has delegated to treat with me, namely a Mr. Sydney Pawling, who seems to be 99 percent Jew and the rest of him Cad. It's on account of him that I feel very prone to finish my contract with Heinemann, and go off on my own again. . . .

(*The Letters of Jack London*, vol. II, p. 945)

* * *

Letter to Sydney S. Pawling, 22 January 1911:

Dear sir:

In reply to yours of January 5. I sometimes wonder if you think that in your dealings with me you feel that you are compelled to play a sharp and baffling game of business enterprise. As a business man and a horse trader, these things might go with me; but being neither a business man nor a horse trader, but just an ordinary common-sense sort of a man, they don't go. I have no patience with bafflement nor with cleverness. . . .

. . . A better thing would be to let me deal with Mr. Heinemann directly. You, Mr. Pawling, may be a very excellent Englishman; but you're not the right kind of Englishman to meet an American like me. I am quite confident that I can deal with Mr. Heinemann, but I cannot deal with you. There is a smack of the shop and of petty cleverness about you, and of small caddish ways, that turns my gorge. From the beginning of my correspondence with you, after I finished my correspondence with Mr. Heinemann, you have dealt with me in the spirit of a Jew pawnbroker trying to buy several moth-eaten undershirts from an impecunious sailor. Now, we won't go on this way. Personally, my feeling is that if ever I should meet you, I should pull your nose. . . .

Please take this letter as the expression of one who is temperamentally not akin to you. You [and] I live in different worlds and talk different languages. I care never again to howl on your door-step, and I wish never again to have you slink under my window when I'm trying to sleep. . . .

(*The Letters of Jack London*, II, pp. 974–975)

* * *

Letter to Hughes Massie, 18 May 1911:

. . . Thank you for the tip you gave me on Heinemann. [In a postscript to a letter of the earlier month, London wrote, "Confidentially – I am absolutely convinced that Mr. Sydney Pawling is all kinds of a Petticoat Lane Jew in his nature; but I am in doubt concerning Mr. Heinemann. So in the spirit of confidence, can you give me any line upon the nationality of Mr. Heinemann?" – ED.] I see that when I laid it into Pawling I was hitting Heinemann over Pawling's shoulders. In all my experience I never struck such Shylocking as that passed out to me by Heinemann. It was not merely the limit, it was grotesquely inconceivable. It seems that Pawling must have been the fall guy.

(*The Letters of Jack London*, II, p. 1003)

* * *

Letter to the Editor of the *American Hebrew and Jewish Messenger*, 27 August 1911:

I have made villains, scoundrels, weaklings, and degenerates, of Cockneys, Scotchmen, Englishmen, Americans, Frenchmen and Irish, and I don't know what other nationalities. I have no recollection of having made a Jew serve a mean fictional function. But I see no reason why I should not, if the need and the setting of my story demanded it.[2] I cannot reconcile myself to the attitude that in humor and fiction the Jew should be a favored race, and therefore be passed over, or used only for his exalted qualities.

I have myself, not as an American, but personally and with the name so little different from mine that it was not even a thin disguise, been exploited before Jewish audiences in the most despicable of characters. The only sensation I experienced was regret at not being able to be present to enjoy the fun.

Finally, I am a terrific admirer of the Jews; I have consorted more with Jews [than with any other nationality]; I have among the Jews some of my finest and noblest friends; and, being a Socialist, I subscribe to the Brotherhood of Man. In this connection, let me add that it is as unfair for a writer to make villains of all races except the Jews, as it is to make villains only of Jews. To ignore the Jew in the matter of villainy is so invidious an exception as to be unfair to the Jews.

(*The Letters of Jack London*, II, p. 1024)

* * *

Letter to Jack L. London, 11 March 1913:

. . . I wonder if we are related. Please find herewith a short biography of yours truly. Tell me about yourself; send me a photo of yourself. Let me know if you think we are related, and what the branch of the family is from which you have descended. The Londons, as you know, are a very large family.

In fact, there are two great London families. One is a Jewish family which came to England from Austria about 200 years ago, and changed its name to London. I am not a member of this family. I am a member of the English family of Londons, hundreds of whom now reside in the City of the London. . . .

(*The Letters of Jack London*, III, pp. 1142–1143)

* * *

Letter to Joseph Noel, 6 July 1914:

. . . you were warned of it in advance by me when I was in New York before I sailed around the Horn—that I had to hold my entire

---

[2]London had been asked to contribute to an article, "The Jew in English Fiction: A Symposium."

moving-picture rights, covered by my name, intact. And now you begin to tell me that the Jews you deal with tell you that you can go ahead and split a commission with an agent and sell out the present moving-picture rights in *The Sins of The Fathers, System, The Judge.* . . .

. . . The only way you can hurt me is to hurt me in the spirit – and you always hurt me in the spirit when you deal technically with me. You cannot do one thing with *The Judge* that I cannot kibosh. You just try, aided and abetted by your Jew friends, to put out the moving-pictures of *The Judge,* and see what will happen to your Jewish friends. I do not care a whoop to hell – I'll be willing to pay ten dollars for every dollar that I make them lose; and I'll make them sick in the end, because they are money-grubbers and I am not a money-grubber. . . .

(*The Letters of Jack London,* III, p. 1143)

UPTON SINCLAIR   *(1878–1968)*

U.S. novelist; author of The Jungle

Upton had inherited from his father and his early background an automatic and unconscious anti-Semitism and racism, which, along with anti-intellectualism, resentment of "the effete East," and Anglophobia, has formed the traditional American demonology. Upton's Progressive and Socialist beliefs were to a degree influenced by the lower-class expression of anti-Semitism repeatedly found in Populism. But he was especially heir to an upper-class anti-Semitism that often accompanies such strident claims to aristocracy as his mother's, as well as to the Christian parochialism and racism of the Episcopal hymnal.

In his autobiography, Upton insisted on more than one occasion and at some length that neither in his youth nor later was he ever in the slightest anti-Semitic. ". . . When I was sounded out for a 'frat' I actually didn't know what it was, and could make nothing of the high-sounding attempts at explanation. If the haughty upperclass man with the correct clothes and the Anglo-Saxon features had said to me in plain words, 'We want to keep ourselves apart from the kikes and wops who make up the greater part of our student-body,' I would have told him that some of the kikes and wops interested me, whereas he did not.

"About two thirds of the members of my class were Jews. I had never known any Jews before this, but here were so many that one took them as a matter of course. I am not sure if I realized they were Jews; I seldom realize it now about the people I meet. The Jews have lived in Central Europe for so long, and have been so mixed with the population, that the border-line is hard to draw. In my case, as a socialist writer, half my friends and half my readers have been Jews. I sum up my impression of them in the verses about the little girl who had a little curl right in the middle of her forehead, and when she was good she was very, very good, and when she was bad she was horrid."

Upton's claim that he seldom realized when people were Jewish is repeatedly proven untrue by his published work as well as his correspondence. When he was aware that anyone about whom he wrote or spoke was Jewish, Upton almost invariably pointed it out, even when it was obvious from the name and whether or not it was important in the context. For example, in the same autobiography, he had felt it was mandatory to point out that a classmate was "a Jewish boy" whose short story was accepted by a monthly magazine "published by a Hebrew orphan home," when neither was relevant to the fact that the episode inspired Upton's first commercial literary effort.

When the autobiography appeared, Upton expressed dismay when this former classmate wrote him: "In my autobiography will be this: In my class was a short-panted Christian lad named Upton Beall Sinclair. He was blatantly Christian; fearfully Jew and Catholic conscious; lasciviously chaste; he was a hot-biscuit addict and showed early signs of disturbed metabolism."

Upton was no more anti-Semitic than were most non-Jews in his America, and far less so than many. The most obvious statement of his anti-Semitism was in a brief article he wrote for a labor group in Vienna. He ascribed to Jews a superior commercial ability, the ability to create great religions such as Christianity and Socialism, and a powerful sex instinct which combined with their business ability enabled Jews to produce films that stimulated sensuality and thereby corrupted youth. "In olden times, Jewish traders sold Christian girls into concubinage and into prostitution, and even today they display the same activity in the same field in southern California, where I live."

When various Jews objected that Sinclair's premise was anti-Semitic or at least promoted anti-Semitism, his replies further revealed his prejudice and insensitivity. "I think that the Jewish race has a remedy at hand; . . . They can reprobate and ostracize these persons [such as the Schuberts and Laskys of Broadway and Hollywood] and they can make it plain that the decent Jewish people are as much in

revolt against commercialized sensuality as are the American people. . . . I think we need a Jewish prophet right now. . . . We Americans have a great many intelligent and noble-minded members of our
race, who have risen above our national vices of bragging and
bunkum, and I understand that likewise there are a great many
members of the Jewish race who do not make millions out of selling
depravity to our children."

The projection of one's own sexual fantasies (whether aberrant
or normal but deemed wicked because of one's own puritanism) onto
objects of one's prejudice (Jews, blacks, Latins, *et alia*) has long served
multiple purposes. Many delude themselves that their indulgence in
racial prejudice is acceptable by disguising it as condemnation of
sexual excess or irregularity, and conversely, some are enabled to
enjoy sexual fantasies they would otherwise consider unacceptable by
attaching these to some other group. . . .

. . . The fact that Sinclair's disavowals of anti-Semitism were so
regularly accompanied by at least an admonitory sentence or two
concerning the excessive sensuality and prurience of his good friends
and good customers, the Jews, derived from the prejudice learned from
the pathetic Southern aristocrats of his youth and expecially from his
failed drummer father. It may also evidence an otherwise usually
well-sublimated or suppressed prurience of his own.

Although most of the muckrakers ignored all aspects of racism in
America, a few understood and wrote about prejudice against blacks
or Jews. Steffens nailed a mezuzah to his office door and Hutchins
Hapgood's *The Spirit of the Ghetto* displayed an understanding no less
extraordinary for a gentile in 1902 than at any other time.

There were writers of the period other than Upton, of course,
who were anti-Semitic, Dreiser for example. But unlike Upton, who
was unable to recognize it, Dreiser once he saw it in himself fought
against it. Dreiser had also revealed his feelings in an essay in *The
American Spectator* where he stated that "the world's quarrel with the
Jew is not that he is inferior, but that he is superior," and he proposed
that the Jews establish their own nation. When Hutchins Hapgood
wrote him criticizing the essay, Dreiser's answer revealed his prejudice
against Jewish movie executives, not like Sinclair because of their
sensuality, but because: "If you listen to Jews discuss Jews, you will find
that they are money-minded, very pagan, very sharp in practice."

Upton, like the Russians for the last half century, was never able to take Lenin's position: "The Jewish bourgeoisie are our enemies, not as Jews but as bourgeoisie. The Jewish worker is our brother."

(Harris, *Upton Sinclair: American Rebel*, pp. 215–217)

WALLACE STEVENS   *(1879–1955)*

U.S. poet

A discussion of his poem, *Winter Bells:*

. . . I suppose I thought that the strength of the church stands for little more than propriety, and that, after all, in a world without religion, propriety and a capon and Florida were all one. Notwithstanding his exacting intelligence, the Jew is a good example of the man who drifts from fasting to feasting. I ought to say that it is a habit of mind with me to be thinking of some substitute for religion. I don't necessarily mean some substitute for the church, because no one believes in the church as an institution more than I do. My trouble, and the trouble of a great many people, is the loss of belief in the sort of God in Whom we were all brought up to believe. Humanism would be the natural substitute, but the more I see of humanism the less I like it. . . .

(H. Stevens, *Letters of Wallace Stevens*, p. 348)

H. L. MENCKEN   *(1880–1956)*

U.S. journalist and critic; editor of American Mercury

On the Continent, the day is saved by the fact that the plutocracy tends to be more and more Jewish. Here the intellectual cynicism of the Jew almost counterbalances his social unpleasantness. . . . The case against the Jews is long and damning; it would justify ten thousand times as many pogroms as now go on in the world. But whenever you find a *Davidsbundlerschaft* making practise against the Philistines, there you will find a Jew laying on. Maybe it was this fact that caused Nietzsche to speak up for the children of Israel quite as often as he spoke against them. He was not blind to their faults, but when he set them beside Christians he could not deny their general superiority. Perhaps in America and England, as on the Continent, the increasing Jewishness of the plutocracy, while cutting it off from all chance of ever developing into an aristocracy, will yet lift it to such a dignity that it will at least deserve a certain grudging respect.

But even so, it will remain in a sort of half-world, midway between the gutter and the stars. . . .

(From Mencken's introduction to Nietzsche's *The Antichrist*, pp. 29–31)

* * *

Mencken to Constance Black, 29 May 1919:

I think you once asked me about the Freud books. I have all of them — in fact, nearly the whole literature in English. If you ever want any of them I'll be glad to send it or them. They are very large books and very solemn. I lately read the latest Freud opus in German. I found it chiefly piffle. . . . Freud did excellent exploratory work, but has become self-hypnotized. There is good ground for hoping that, as a Jew, he will fall a victim to some obscure race war in Vienna. The Poles are doing nobly.

(Bode, *The New Mencken Letters*, p. 101)

* * *

Mencken to August Mencken, 10 August 1922:

I am writing, not because I have anything to say, but because I have nothing to do. This is the third day out and I have not spoken to a living soul save the stewards and a small boy who stopped me on deck and asked me to police his brother, who had a box of matches and was trying to set a lifeboat afire. The Jews aboard outnumber the Christians by at least 15 to 1. They all seem to be department store buyers, and it is bad enough to look at them, without speaking to them. . . .

(*The New Mencken Letters*, p. 156)

* * *

When in the early 1930s Nazism came to public notice many people suspected that Mencken, long a pro-German, would become an ardent sympathizer. He did not. However, he made the grave mistake of underestimating Hitler and when Hitler engaged in the persecution of the German Jews, he failed to feel all the outrage that most people felt.

(*The New Mencken Letters*, p. 288)

Mencken to James Rosenberg, 24 April 1934:

The Evening Sun has sold out the issues containing my two articles on Palestine, and so I am forced to send you my own copies. If you don't return them after you have read them and prayed over them I shall get out some kind of writ. As you will notice, they are rather superficial. I had planned to do several more pieces, one of them dealing with the probable prospect of Zionism as a practical concern, but the local Jewish weekly has already denounced me for the two within, and so I am not inclined to go on with the subject.

I only wish that you had really come to Palestine. The boys of the Jewish agency came to see me as soon as they heard I was in town and proposed an all day trip by motor through the happier parts of the country. As you know, Palestine is very small and all of it that is worth seeing is above Jerusalem. We were thus able to cover nearly everything of interest in one day, and I enjoyed that day immensely. . . . The thing that struck me most forcibly—I have barely hinted at it in my articles—is that there is little if any sign of orthodox Judaism in the colonies. All of the farmers looked to me to be skeptics of a somewhat extreme wing, and I suspect that if a rabbi with long whiskers came among them and tried to set up his stand they would chase him out. This seems to me to be a good joke on the pious Jews who are contributing their pennies to Zionism. To be sure, there are some orthodox colonies but they are so rare that on the official list the fact that they are orthodox is specifically mentioned. This seems to be a sort of warning to the unwary.

. . . The Untermeyers and other such wind machines have begun to make the American Jew look like the most extreme hyphenate ever heard and so the way is open for professional patriots to whoop up an anti-Semitic movement. All such imbecilities, of course, are inevitable in human affairs. I begin to believe that the whole world is mashuggah.

(*The New Mencken Letters*, pp. 309–310)

* * *

Mencken to Julia Harris, 24 March 1933:

. . . The German news is probably at least nine-tenths bogus. Certainly the Germans are not beating up Jews, as such. It simply happens that a good many Communists are Jews. As you know, I am in favor of letting Communists howl, but that scheme seems to be in ill-favor in all countries, including the United States as well as Germany. The agitations carried on by such quacks as Rabbi Stephen S. Wise would be comic if it were not so tragic. Wise is always eager to grab publicity, but during the late war he was one of the most active denouncers of German kultur. . . .

(The New Mencken Letters, p. 284)

* * *

Mencken to George Schuyler, 14 May 1935:

. . . The Dreiser uproar gave me some loud laughs. Dreiser's anti-Semitism is simply a reaction of disgust against Jewish Communists. They are such God-awful swine that he simply can't stomach them.

(The New Mencken Letters, p. 352)

* * *

Mencken to Ewald Netzer, 6 January 1936:

It goes without saying that that report is not true. Some time ago the *Sturmer* listed me as a Jew, thus adding one more note to its immemorial repertoire of false reports. I should add that I am entirely out of sympathy with the method used by Hitler to handle the Jewish question. It seems to be that the gross brutality to harmless individuals must needs revolt every decent man. I am well aware that reports from Germany have been exaggerated, but am also well aware that intolerable brutalities have been practised. I don't know a single man of any reputation in America who is in favor of the Nazi scheme. As it stands, Germany has completely lost the sympathy it had during the years following 1920.

(The New Mencken Letters, p. 370)

* * *

Mencken to Ezra Pound, 1 March 1937:

. . . Despite the obvious comforts of life in Italy, I wish you would come home, at least for a while. You'd find a United States that would really astonish you. New York [ha]s now become al[most] wholly Jewish. I am not sure that it is a change for the worse, but nevertheless it is somewhat startling. The principal holiday of the year in the town is Yom Kippur. Virtually all offices are closed, and the streets are almost deserted.

(The New Mencken Letters, pp. 404–405)

The Jews were a puzzle to Mencken. He loved them and feared them. He told me that for years his personal physician was a Jew. He once said to me: "I go only to a Jewish doctor. Medicine requires brains, and the Jews got it. *Goyim* make bum doctors. Whenever anyone asks me to recommend a doctor, well, if I like him, I send him to a Jewish doctor, and if I don't, I send him to a *goy* doctor. The Jewish doctor saves his patient, and the *goy* kills him." Mencken's closest editorial and publishing associates over the years were mainly Jews. Many years later we met, he said to me, "One of the things I first liked about you was that you were never baptised." In that same conversation, he added, "I can't understand how anybody can be an anti-Semite. I have never been to a Jewish home that didn't serve good grub, and I have never known a Jew who was a Prohibitionist."

Because of his close and long relationship with Jews, Mencken learned a great many Jewish words and posed as something of an authority on Jewish affairs. When I asked him why he permitted a Jewish book of reference to list him as a Jew, he said, among other things: "Well, in the first place, they didn't ask me. They assumed I was Jewish and cribbed the facts about my life from *Who's Who*. In the second place, they may be right. From long wear and tear, much of it with fine Jewish girls, I am practically circumcised. I believe in Yahweh as much, well, maybe a little more, than I believe in Jesus, Buddha, Ramzu, and all the other godly bastards. And I do believe in stuffed derma, gefilte fish, sacramental wines, tsimes, and matzoh-ball soup. That, my boy, makes me at least as good a Jew as you are. Oh, one more thing. I dislike Christians. So what more do you want?"

". . . I keep a kosher house anyway. I have given strict orders to my nigger cook never to put pork meat and cow meat on the same plate, and to keep cheese and milk at least six inches removed from the meat plate. Sure, I insist on that. Ask Goodman.[3] He doesn't observe these rules. I'm a better Jew than he is."

. . . But while Mencken had many pleasant and profitable relations with Jews, he sometimes wrote about them as though some of them at least had personally harmed or offended him. Whatever unfavorable views he had of Jews as a group, he nevertheless continued to see them and do business with them and be friends with them—and keep me as his assistant. This attitude puzzled me. It

---

[3]Philip Goodman was a publisher, producer of plays, and one of Mencken's closest friends.

puzzled Goodman. When the relations between the two became
strained, Goodman discussed the matter with me more and more
frequently. "Mencken is a case for Freud," he said. "He loves the Jews
and he hates them. He hates them because they have done so much for
him. I published a couple of his books. Knopf publishes his books now
and has taken plenty of chances on him. There's you. There's Nathan.
No wonder he hates us!"

In spite of Mencken's reservations about Jews, he often filled the
Mercury with Jewish authors and Jewish articles and stories. Even
more significant, Mencken did not comment upon the fact that now
and then the names in the contents of the magazine were preponder-
antly Jewish. . . .

. . . [Yet] he continued to make remarks that appeared to be
anti-Jewish. And there is his strange behavior during the Hitler
madness. He predicted that Hitler would not last very long, that the
Germans were too intelligent to be taken in by such a "hoodlum and
second-rate paperhanger." Still, he wrote nothing that I can recall
against the Nazis or against the Germans as a whole for voting him
into office. . . .

. . . Mencken certainly was not a violent anti-Semite, who
preached or practiced physical harm to the Jews, or who openly
espoused any form of discrimination against them. He was too shrewd
to do that. Even his belief in the morality of the *numerous clausus* with
regard to Jewish students in colleges he expressed only verbally.
Mencken's anti-Semitism – or perhaps one should say fear and distrust
of Jews – was of the rarer and more intellectual sort – one might even
say, more dangerous sort, since what the intellectual elite believe or
fail to denounce tends to seep down to the majority of the people and
to mold and color their thinking. . . .

Then how did Mencken's "anti-Semitism" reveal itself? It revealed itself indirectly. He prided himself upon being a champion of
the rights of minorities, especially what he liked to call "civilized
minorities," but he never raised his voice in defense of the Jewish
minorities who were being deprived of all civil rights by his beloved
Germans, and as I have already said, he covered up his indifference
with the claim that the Germans as a people would not long stand for
Hitler. When events proved Mencken wrong, he still did not lift his
voice in behalf of the Jews – nor did he find much to criticize in the
German people or, for that matter, in the Nazis. He kept on going to

the East Side for "the mammoth, *zaftig* meals," that he loved so much, but often, in the office, he would supplement his expressions of satisfaction with the remark: "But what a dirty, impolite people is down there in the bowels of Manhattan! . . ."

A few months before he died in 1940, I met Philip Goodman. . . . He said he was worried. I asked him about what.

"About the Jews," he said. "The Jews and how dumb they are. Even you and me. We get taken in by people we think are all right, free and civilized and in love with free speech and free press and decency. Mark my words. We're gonna learn that some of our best friends are anti-Semites . . . well, some of our most liberal preachers and educators are going to keep goddamn dumb as the Germans begin to kill more and more Jews. Even some of your Harvard professors. And Mencken. What do you think he did?"

"What?"

"I've refused to have anything more to do with him, since I learned he was a Hitler lover. But he still sends me all sorts of mail, embalmers' cards, stuff like that. But the other day he did something that made me squirm. The sonofabitch is really no good. He sent me a note on the letter-paper of the *Deutscher Weckruf*, a lousy Nazi sheet published in Yorkville. He asked me how my gallstones were, and he signed himself, Heil Hitler. Funny, eh? Now, what do you think of that?"

I gasped.

"We Jews never learn," said Goodman. Then he added: "The Dark Ages are upon us again."

(Angoff, *H. L. Mencken, A Portrait from Memory*, pp. 161–169)

FATHER CHARLES E. COUGHLIN   *(1881–1979)*

Famed "Radio Priest" of the 1930s in the U.S.

[We need a] Christian Front which will not fear being called anti-Semitic because it knows the term "anti-Semitic" is only another pet phrase of castigation in Communism's glossary of attacks.

(*Social Justice*, 25 July 1938)

. . . because Jews reject Christ, it is impossible for them to accept His doctrine of spiritual brotherhood in the light in which Christians accept it.

(*Social Justice*, 25 July 1938)

* * *

Editor's note: From 1926 to 1940, when he finally left the air, Father Coughlin had built up an audience as high as 3.5 million each week. His weekly magazine continued for several years after. In 1942, following several anti-Jewish attacks, the American Catholic bishops proclaimed in their annual statement: "We feel a deep sense of revulsion against the cruel indignities heaped upon the Jews in conquered countries and upon defenseless peoples not of our faith."

("Victory and Peace," in *Our Bishops Speak*, 1952, p. 113)

FRANKLIN DELANO ROOSEVELT   (1882–1945)

32nd president of the United States, 1933–1945

The State Department remained officially silent regarding Nazi mistreatment of the Jews [in 1933], taking the position that, as much as Americans might privately deplore such actions, the United States could not intervene in the internal affairs of another nation. When George H. Earle, the American minister to Austria, warned that Americans had little sympathy with the rising tide of anti-Semitism, his remarks were regarded as a blunder in some diplomatic circles. FDR said nothing publicly, but he wrote Earle: "Strictly between ourselves, I am glad that you committed what some have suggested was a diplomatic blunder. I can assure you that it did not embarrass me at all!" FDR to Earle, Dec. 22, 1933.

(N. Miller, *FDR—An Intimate History*, p. 322)

* * *

Following the annexation of Austria, the Nazis stepped up the persecution of the Jews. A trickle of German Jews had reached the United States since Hitler had come to power in 1933, but Congress had refused to broaden immigration quotas out of fear of adding to the unemployment and relief rolls. American consular officials interpreted the statutes so rigorously that almost three quarters of the German quota went unfilled. Three thousand Jews besieged the American consulate in Vienna, and Representative Emanuel Celler, of New York, thought the State Department's heart was "muffled in protocol." The President, who was sympathetic to the plight of the Jews but had done little to alleviate it, was under pressure to do something to assist the refugees. He invited thirty-two nations to an international conference at Evian, France, to establish a committee to facilitate the emigration of the victims of Nazism, but he cut the ground out from under it with the declaration that there would be no changes in American immigration laws.

On November 10, 1938, the Nazis burned 195 synagogues in Germany, savagely beat every Jew they could find, hauled 25,000 people to concentration camps, and shattered the windows of 800 Jewish-owned shops in a fit of rage and destruction that came to be known as *Kristallnacht*. "I myself could scarcely believe that such things could occur in a twentieth-century civilization," Roosevelt told the press. The American ambassador to Berlin was recalled, and about 15,000 German and Austrian refugees in the United States on visitors permits were allowed to remain. But there was no relaxation of immigration quotas. Public opinion remained a barrier to revision, but the feeling persists that had Roosevelt mounted an effort to permit the victims of Nazism to come to the United States in greater numbers, the nation's humane instincts might have been aroused. Thousands of people who later died in the Nazi gas chambers could have been saved had Roosevelt been more concerned about their fate.

(*FDR — An Intimate History*, pp. 428–429)

* * *

. . . the President had extolled the Bill of Rights on its one-hun-dred-fiftieth anniversary, but without protest he signed an order authorizing the internment of the West Coast Japanese. Frightened and bewildered, the Japanese were given a week to sell homes, farms, and businesses, usually at a fraction of true value, and were herded into relocation centers in remote desert areas that were little more than concentration camps. There they remained until almost the end of the war. Why did Roosevelt permit an action that bore, in Justice Frank Murphy's words, a "melancholy resemblance" to the Nazi treatment of the Jews? Never a strong civil libertarian, he gave in to public and congressional pressure with little thought of the consequences. . . .

Roosevelt was also blind to the destruction of six million European Jews by the Nazis. The situation of the Jews worsened with the coming of the war and the expansion of Hitler's domain, for the State Department actually tightened visa requirements for refugees. The President was curiously ambivalent about the problem. Although personally sympathetic to the plight of the Jews, he left the refugee question in the less-than-compassionate hands of assistant Secretary of State Breckenridge Long. An old Wilsonian and large contributor to the Democratic party, Long had jurisdiction over refugee problems. If not anti-Semitic, he was least sympathetic to the Jews and feared that letting down immigration barriers would flood the nation with Communist and Nazi spies disguised as refugees. Along with other officials, he thwarted numerous efforts to rescue Jews and suppressed information about Hitler's plans to exterminate them.

By early 1942 details of Hitler's plan for the Final Solution had reached the State Department, but many officials refused to believe the reports. . . . Following an Anglo-American conference in Bermuda in 1943 to discuss the refugee problem, Secretary Hull told Roosevelt, "The unknown cost of removing an undetermined number of persons from an undisclosed place to an unknown destination, a scheme advocated by certain pressure groups, is of course out of the question."

It may have been so for Hull but not for Henry Morgenthau. As a Jew he was anguished by the reports reaching Washington, and early in 1944 he instructed Randolph Paul, the Treasury Department's general counsel, to prepare a study of the State Department's handling of the refugee question. Paul produced a bluntly worded indictment, "Report to the Secretary on the Acquiescence of This Government in the Murder of the Jews," which pulled no punches. State Department officials, it charged, "have not only failed to use the Governmental machinery at their disposal to rescue Jews from Hitler, but have even gone so far as to use this Governmental machinery to prevent the rescue of these Jews." Morgenthau personally presented these findings to the President, who appeared surprised. Within a week, Roosevelt created a War Refugee Board outside of the State Department to take over the refugee problem. Representatives of the Board, including Raoul Wallenberg, a Swedish businessman who worked in Budapest, rescued thousands of Jews from the gas chambers. But had Roosevelt acted sooner, other hundreds of thousands of people might also have been saved. As in the case of the Japanese, his sin was not one of commission but omission—with even more tragic results.

(*FDR—An Intimate History*, pp. 489–490)

* * *

Roosevelt left Yalta on February 11, 1945, in an optimistic mood about the continued unity of the Big Three. . . . [He] flew to Egypt, where he rejoined the *Quincy*. As the cruiser lay at anchor in the Great Bitter Lake, he met with three kings on successive days: Farouk of Egypt, Haile Selassie of Ethiopia, and Ibn Saud of Saudi Arabia. The President, a self-proclaimed Zionist, tried to persuade Ibn Saud to allow more Jewish survivors of Hitler's death camps to enter Palestine, but the grizzled old desert warrior said the Arabs would fight to the death to prevent it. . . .

(*FDR—An Intimate History*, p. 505)

ELEANOR ROOSEVELT   *(1884–1962)*

Humanitarian, wife of president Franklin Delano Roosevelt

In view of what is confronting us, the Jew is almost powerless today. It depends almost entirely on the course of the Gentiles what the future holds. It can be cooperative: mutual assistance, gradual slow assimilation, with justice, fair-mindedness toward all the racial groups living together in different countries, or it can be injustice, hatred and death.

It looks to me as though the future of the Jews were tied up, as it has always been, with the future of all the races of the world. If they perish, we perish sooner or later. . . .

(In *Liberty Magazine*, 31 December 1938)

SINCLAIR LEWIS   *(1885–1951)*

U.S. novelist, social critic, and Nobel laureate; author of Elmer Gantry, Babbitt, Main Street

[His] lecture to the Sunday Afternoon Club of the First Presbyterian Church of Evanston . . . began with an attack on the anti-Semitism of

Henry Ford, deduced that Ford's phobia showed that he did not read, and concluded that if Henry Ford had read more in the history of the Jewish race, he would not have frightened people into believing that America was in danger of subjugation by New York Jewish millionaires. . . .

(Schorer, *Sinclair Lewis, An American Life*, p. 305)

* * *

Such reticence did not give Lewis pause as his impulse to scramble society [in Duluth, Minnesota, in 1945] grew to a kind of mania. Now he extended his guest lists to include ministers of various denominations, Jews, and gentiles white and black. We can credit him, if not with social imagination, with an honest indignation over any intolerance (years before, when his secretary Louis Florey took rooms for them in the best hotel in Bermuda, known to discriminate against Jews, Lewis said, "I won't stay there," and did not), and there is something touching about his fumbling attempts to correct it. He badgered his fashionable friends, not only Mrs. Banning, but those, like Mrs. Anneke, of whom he was genuinely fond: Why don't you have Jews at your parties? Have you ever had a Negro in your house? Why not?

(*Sinclair Lewis*, p. 730)

EZRA POUND   *(1885–1972)*

American poet

From broadcast 32, delivered during World War II from
Rome, 30 April 1942:

I naturally mistrust newspaper news from America. I grope in the mass of lies, knowing most of the sources are wholly UNtrustworthy.

It nevertheless seems to transpire, or expire that there is a difference of opinion between quite a fair sized number of Americans, and an equally large number of Jews, Jews-playfellows, and the bedfellows of Jews and of Jewesses, from Eve Curie to Lehman, and Lippmann. . . .

BUT clarity has not come and will not come till an accurate

census of the ORIGINAL bellifiyers is made and until every pro-war
Jew has his name listed. I think the NON-war Jews (at least those who
were non-war before the WAR started) will be found to be very, very
verrrreeee small.

In fact, apart from the thefts and extractions of the gang back of
the Treasury music hall, it becomes increasingly difficult to discuss
American affairs EXCEPT on a racial basis.

Whether America will wake to this now or in 20 years, will
depend on Yankee enterprise, I suppose. Whatever you read in
America, we read here that the Americans, U.S.A.'ers, are irritated at
finding 'emselves in war UNPREPARED. Disappointed in British
FLOP.

SOMETIME the Anglo Saxon may AWAKE to the fact that the
Jewish kahal and secret forces concentrated or brought to focus in the
unappetizin' carcass of Franklin D. Roosevelt do NOT shove Aryan or
non-yittisch nations into WARS in order that those said nations may
WIN wars. The non-Jew nations are shoved into wars in order to
destroy themselves, to break up their structure, to destroy their
populations. And no more flaming and flagrant case appears in
history than our own American Civil War, said to be an occidental
record for size of armies employed and only surpassed by the more
recent triumphs of Warburgs, the wars of 1914 and the present
one. . . .

No one in the United States will be more surprised at the talk of
hook up between Masonry, its central control, Jewry, Anglo-Israel,
and the British Intelligence Service [than will the rank and file of
American Masons.] . . .

Rothschild, the stink of hell gittin' hold of Austrian postal
service and censorship in time of Napoleon. Hundred years after
Austria is the dumbest, and LEAST mentally awake country in
Europe, and FLOPS. France was awake, Rothschilds git into bank or
stank of France in, I think, 1843. Inside a hundred years, France walks
down her pirate Reynaud, and flops into the discard.

You'll find out, brother, before or after the belly-flop. England is
on the teeter. The central stink betrayed the United States in 1863.
Keeping up the hostilities, keepin' the rebels at it, *divide et impera*. Now
the same bunch of Kikes is doing [it] in England. NOT for the benefit
of the American people.

Sassoons baboons, Rothschilds, etc. migrating to the United

States and stinking up the whole country, in the wake of Zukor and the other fine flowers of Semite culture.

Look at Litvinov's face. The SOUL shining in beauty. Greek philosophy jettisoned, Justinian, jettisoned, the sense of LAW that built up all Europe, puked into the discard.

Sense of ENGLISH law, that was built up out of the Roman, puked into the discard. You will find out, brother, later or soon, and I should prefer it sooner, so as I should be able to meet some survivors.

Interested ONLY in Bunk, says the sheeny lawyer, seein' what you can put over. Immoral geometry, Freud, Bergson, crawlin' in through all the crevices. HONESTY of [thought] in all and every department filched away, undermined, dry rotted, wet rotted. And simple hearted elegiac poets like Archie put out in front as top dressin'. No, brother, the American people will have to start askin' questions.

WHAT ARE THE MASONS? Where do they git their money? And WHO controls 'em? Who is the big SILENT noise at their center?

WHAT is the British Intelligence Service? Secret Service? Fighting for the British people? How did Willie Wiseman git there? Why don't the OPPOSITION papers, papers that say they opposed Frankie Finklestein Roosevelt, why don't they LOOK into these matters?

What is the KAHA[L]? Why don't you examine the Talmud? Talmud, said to have corrupted the Jews. Some Jews disparage it. What is really said in the Talmud about creatin' disorder? Why did the firm, publishing firm that printed the Protocols, go out of business?

Waaal, maybe they went out of business cause they hadn't enough sense to GO ON printin' me. But look into it. Don't git excited until you have got some real evidence. There is a buildin' outside of Washington, and so forth, go look at it.

Don't start a pogrom. That is, not an old style killing of small Jews. That system is no good whatsoever. Of course if some man had a stroke of genius and could start pogrom UP AT THE top, there might be something to say for it.

But on the whole legal measures are preferable. The sixty Kikes who started this war might be sent to St. Helena as a measure of world prophylaxis. And some hyper-kike, or non-Jewish kikes along with 'em. . . .

(Doob, "*Ezra Pound Speaking*," pp. 113–115)

RUTH BENEDICT   *(1887–1948)*

U.S. anthropologist and author

When I was growing up in the hinterland of America I did not know any Jews. In the public schools I went to, there were no Jews, and, later, it would not have occurred to me to see anything in common among the few Jews I came to know. There was the daughter of the rich clothing merchant, the threadbare student who kept me on my toes discussing European philosophy, and the itinerant peddler who kept the farmers supplied with store goods and who stayed on to swap words of wisdom with my grandfather. They all fell, in my mind and in their own, into the usual American pigeonholes which have to do first and foremost with money income. The clothing merchant's family in Buffalo consorted with the other rich merchants of the city; they made no common cause with itinerant peddler or with schoolboy living on crusts. There was no issue that drew these Jews together.

Anti-Semitism was no issue in my childhood and we thought it had been outmoded. It has been a cruel teacher, but it has laid the basis in the last decades for a Jewish fellowship which overspans all class and national schisms. Jews have learned the hard way, but they have learned, better than any other group, that outrages on Jews in Germany or on Yorkville tenement-dwellers are ultimately threats to all Jews. They have learned too that discriminations against any minority group, whether it is Irish or Negro, Italian or Japanese, are potentially threats to the Jewish minority. They have had to recognize from their own experience that they themselves can live decently only insofar as all human beings have opportunity to live without being the butt of outrages and discriminations.

It is an eternal truth for all men, but human beings have to learn it over and over again from their own experience. Democracy has taken this truth as its foundation stone, but the democracies have been halfhearted. It has to be brought home afresh. And in our great need for drastic reaffirmation of this truth in this war and in the peace to follow, Jews can speak clearly and work courageously. More than any other minority group—and all such groups have learned this lesson also in their own persons—Jews are represented among the rich and the poor, business, the professions, and the trades. They therefore span the usual schisms in American life. More than any other group they are international. They therefore span the great modern schisms among the nations. Jews are therefore in a doubly strategic position. It would be tragedy indeed if any timidities, any wisdom of this world, made them turn their eyes away when affronts are perpetrated. Let them not be silent. There are many Gentiles who have not yet learned the truth Jews know, and that truth must be made clear to them. No other issue in the world today is of greater importance. America desperately needs those who have learned from their own experience that altruism and self-interest coincide in every effort to secure for all human beings the right and the obligation of full and decent participation in our common life. Such efforts are the bond of fellowship which unite in one great crusade, not only Jews of every nation and of every income; it unites also the Jew and the intelligent Gentile.

("The Bond of Friendship," quoted in Margaret Mead, *An Anthropologist at Work: Writings of Ruth Benedict*, pp. 356–357)

T.S. ELIOT   *(1888–1965)*

American-born British poet and critic

Reasons of race and religion combine to make any large number of free-thinking Jews undesirable.

(*After Strange Gods*, p. 20)

* * *

When he returned to England in the middle of December, the winter again affected him. . . . He was well enough in February [1951], however, to attend a poetry reading at the Institute of Contemporary Arts; but it was not a pleasant occasion. Apparently without Eliot having been warned, the poet Emmanuel Litvinoff read a poem which attacked his attitude toward the Jews. At the end of the reading there was some consternation but Eliot, who was sitting at the back of the room, was heard to mutter, "It's a good poem, it's a very good poem." The incident was reported in the press, however, and his secretary was quoted in one newspaper as saying, "Many Jewish people have written to him accusing him of anti-semitism. It is not true."

Since it is the charge still most frequently levelled against him, it is perhaps worth examining the evidence for it. In his published writings there are two egregious instances: the line 'The Jew is underneath the lot,' in 'Burbank with a Baedeker: Bleistein with a Cigar' and the reference to the undesirability of a large number of 'free-thinking Jews' in *After Strange Gods*. In his unpublished correspondence there are four references. On two occasions he used the word 'Jew' as a perjorative adjective—once in a letter to John Quinn, dated 12 March 1923, and once in a letter to Ezra Pound, dated 31 October 1917. In a letter to Herbert Read, dated '16 February' (probably written in 1925) he described a racial prejudice from which he was not immune—although he did not specify that prejudice, its nature is clear from the context, in which he offered Disraeli as an example of what he meant. Finally in a letter to Bonamy Dobree—dated by Dobree 'about March 1929'—he made a number of supercilious remarks about the Jews. All the available evidence suggests, then, that on occasions he made what were then fashionably anti-semitic remarks to his close friends. Leonard Woolf, himself a Jew, has said, 'I think T.S. Eliot was slightly anti-semitic in the sort of vague way which is not uncommon. He would have denied it quite genuinely,' which suggests Eliot's ability to seem quite different to different people. But there is one further distinction which needs to be made. He was drawn to the traditions of Sephardism, he had once explained; that rigorous and secluded tradition appealed to his own sensibility, in the same way that 'free-thinking' Jews seemed to him to come too close to the rational Unitarianism which he despised. On a less theoretical level, it is also true that his expressions of anti-semitism occur in the Twenties or just before, when he was inclined to make misogynistic remarks also; it was a period when his own personality threatened to break apart, and it seems likely that his distrust of Jews and women was the sign of an uneasy and vulnerable temperament in which aggression and insecurity were compounded. This is an explanation, however, and not a justification.

(Ackroyd, *T. S. Eliot, A Life*, pp. 303–304)

JOSEPH P. KENNEDY *(1888–1969)*

U.S. businessman, ambassador to Great Britain, father of President John F. Kennedy

The sourness of these days roused Kennedy's concern about Jewish pressure to keep the war going. It was a concern he shared with Neville

Chamberlain. After the British guarantee to Poland, so Kennedy told Herbert Hoover in later years, Chamberlain had said to him that "he hoped the Americans and the Jews would now be satisfied but that he (Chamberlain) felt that he had signed the doom of civilization." Kennedy later wrote in a draft autobiography that "a number of Jewish publishers and writers" assailed him after the Trafalgar Day speech. They wanted war, he thought. "They should not be condemned for such an objective. After all, the lives and fortunes of their compatriots were being destroyed by Hitler. Compromise could hardly cure that situation; only the destruction of Nazism could do so. . . . [But] they did not hesitate to resort to slander and falsehood to achieve their aims. . . . I was hardly prepared . . . for the full viciousness of this onslaught."

On the other hand, he attacked religious persecution in the fascist states. He called the anti-Semitic outrages of November 1938 "the most terrible things I have ever heard of." He busied himself with schemes for the rescue of Jewish refugees to an extent that led the Arab National League of Boston to call him a "Zionist Charlie McCarthy." Nor was he at all anti-Jewish in individual relations. In Palm Beach he played golf at a predominantly Jewish country club. "One of his most constant riding companions and closest collaborators in the Embassy," noted D. W. Brogan, who knew more about America than any other Briton, "was a Jew whose career in the Department was not helped by this part of his record." Still, the ambassador's fear of war now moved him for a moment to speak of Jews collectively as a menacing influence.

By the autumn of 1940, Kennedy wanted to come home. . . .

(A. M. Schlesinger, Jr., *Robert Kennedy and His Times*, p. 34)

* * *

His disaffection grew. "Dissatisfaction is rife and lack of confidence in the leaders and in Congress is definitely high," he wrote to Beaverbrook in August 1942, "and there is a great undercurrent of dissatisfaction with the appointment of so many Jews in high places in Washington. . . . If you want everybody yelling for our team, Mr. Roosevelt is certainly not attaining that end."

(*Robert Kennedy and His Times*, p. 47)

DWIGHT DAVID EISENHOWER   *(1890–1969)*

Supreme Commander of the Allied Forces, World War II;
34th president of the United States, 1953–1961

Eisenhower and Patton immediately became and remained fast friends, despite their much different personalities and backgrounds. Patton came from a wealthy, aristocratic family. . . . Where Eisenhower tended to qualify all his observations and statements, Patton was dogmatic. Where Eisenhower had no particularly strong views on race or politics, Patton was viciously anti-Semitic and loudly right wing. Where Eisenhower was patient and let things happen to him, Patton was impatient and took charge of his own career. . . .

(Ambrose, Eisenhower, vol. I, p. 70)

* * *

That same year, 1938, Eisenhower had an unusual job offer. At social functions in Manila, the Spanish community (and some of the American businessmen) expressed their admiration for Hitler. Eisenhower thought this a "strange" attitude and said so. The resulting arguments were loud and long. Eisenhower had friends among the small Jewish community in Manila, and his anti-Nazi feelings were well known to them. They were also aware of his abilities. They formed a committee that asked Eisenhower to take on the job of finding a haven for Jewish refugees from Nazi Germany in China, Indochina, Indonesia, or anywhere else in Asia. The committee guaranteed him a salary of $60,000 a year plus expenses, and promised to place the first five years' salary in escrow to be paid to him in full if for any reason he had to leave the job. Tempting though it was, Eisenhower turned down the offer, saying he thought it best to stay in the Army.

He did so because he could see that war was coming and he felt that America would not be able to stay out of it. He also knew that within a year MacArthur would have to allow him to return to the States, as the law said that any officer who was on detached duty for more than four years either had to resign his commission or return to active duty, and even MacArthur could not force him to resign his commission.

(Eisenhower, pp. 113–114)

[In 1945] Eisenhower put Lucian Truscott in Patton's place. Before Truscott left for Bavaria, Eisenhower called him into his office and told him that the "most acute and important problems . . . were those involving denazification and the handling of those unfortunate persons who had been victims of Nazi persecution." Eisenhower told Truscott to be "stern" toward the Nazis and to give preferential treatment to Jewish displaced persons.

(Eisenhower, p. 424)

* * *

On September 2 [1952], Eisenhower began his campaign. . . . He created the organization and picked the team. Adams was his administrative assistant who carried out his wishes and followed his orders. For example, Eisenhower told Adams he wanted at least one Jew and one Catholic among his advisors; Adams found them.

(Eisenhower, p. 550)

KATHERINE ANNE PORTER   *(1890–1980)*

U.S. novelist and short-story writer; Pulitzer Prize, 1966

"Even in Berlin, when I met all those people . . . the one I talked to most was Goering. It was at this little party and we just sat by the fire and discussed Germany and he explained to me what they were going to do to the Jews and I said, 'Well, you know, I wonder how you dare to do it because it's never done any good and it doesn't suppress them. It does do great damage to the country. Look what happened to Spain. Nobody has ever prospered harassing the Jews. They are rooted and they are going to stay and I don't see what you have against them.' He said the time had come to clear out the degenerate forces in the country. 'We've got to restore that good clean German blood,' he said. I argued with him a little bit that they had pure blood by this time. I could say with confidence that I was a mixture of British, Scotch, Irish and Welsh. We're all the whole white race. . . ."

(Quoted by Mary Anne Dolan in the
Washington Star, 11 May 1975)

Porter, on the idiom in American writing:

"These others have fallen into a curious kind of argot more or less originating in New York, a deadly mixture of academic, guttersnipe, gangster, fake-Yiddish, and dull old worn-out dirty words—an appalling bankruptcy in language, as if they hate English and are trying to destroy it along with all other living things they touch."

(Hank Lopez, "A Country and Some People I Love,"
Harper's, September 1965)

* * *

"The charge [of anti-Semitism, based on her portrayal of the salesman Julius Lowenthal in *Ship of Fools*] was not unfounded, and comments in the margins of some of her books show that her virulent anti-Semitism was part of a general racism. On the jacket of *Portrait of a Jew*, by Albert Memmi . . . she wrote beside the author's photograph, 'This writer is completely typically Jewish, nose and mouth especially—But it is not a question of features. It is a *look*, an expression, a manner, that identifies them. And it is not a question of ugliness.' In the book itself she wrote, 'Everybody except the Jews knows the Jews are not chosen but are a lot of noisy, arrogant, stupid, pretentious people and then what?' This was more than a reaction to a personal attack, which she had recorded when [the Jewish critic Leslie] Fiedler criticized her. She also made a note in Memmi's book that in the United States Jews made up 4 percent of the population but about 60 percent of the criminals, Negroes about 10 percent of the population but about 25 percent of the criminals. She did not of course give any sources for her statistics. . . . At first glance it seems that in public she would express an opinion that she felt would be acceptable to the audience at hand and in private and among friends who shared her opinions she was frankly racist. On the other hand, *Ship of Fools* is perhaps the accurate expression of the ambivalence of her attitudes. She could not depict a likable Jewish character and yet the book consciously shows the irrational, mindless, dangerous nature of such prejudice, and, by implications, its devastating course toward the Holocaust."

(Givner, *Katherine Anne Porter, A Life*, pp. 450–453)

REINHOLD NIEBUHR   (1892–1971)

U.S. Protestant theologian and philosopher

I offer "a" solution rather than "the" solution to the problem of anti-Semitism precisely because a prerequisite for any solution for a basic social problem is the understanding that there is no perfect satisfactory formula. . . .

We must . . . preserve and if possible extend the democratic standards of tolerance and of cultural and racial pluralism which allow the Jews "Lebensraum" as a nation among nations. We must on the other hand support more generously than in the past the legitimate aspiration of Jews for a "homeland" in which they will not be simply tolerated but which they will possess. . . .

The Jews require a homeland, if for no other reason, because even the most generous immigration laws of the Western democracies will not permit all the dispossessed Jews of Europe to find a haven in which they may look forward to a tolerable future. . . .

A much mightier justification of Zionism is that every race finally has a right to a homeland where it will not be "different," where it will neither be patronized by "good" people nor subjected to calumny by bad people.

(*The Nation*, 28 February 1942)

* * *

The case of the Jews presents an equally difficult problem for modern democratic society. It must be admitted that bourgeois liberalism did emancipate Jewish life from the restraints of the medieval ghetto. By creating an impersonal society in which money and credit relations became more important than organic ties it laid the foundations for ethnic pluralism. But the hope that the liberties derived from this situation would be infinitely extensible has proven to be mistaken. While fascist mania and fury have aggravated anti-Semitism and while some of the noxious fruits of race prejudice which have recently been harvested in the democratic world must be attributed to seeds scattered by the Nazis, we should be blind to attribute this evil altogether to this one specific cause. The Nazis have accentuated but they did not create racial pride. The ideals of democracy do contradict this pride; but it is an illusion of idealistic children of light to imagine that we can destroy evil merely by avowing ideals. The ideal of racial brotherhood is the "law of God" in which we delight "after the inward man"; but racial arrogance is "the law in our members which wars against the law that is in our mind."

Racial bigots bring all kinds of charges against the Jewish minority; but these charges are rationalizations of a profounder prejudice. The real sin of the Jews is twofold. They are first of all a nation scattered among the nations; and therefore they cannot afford to become completely assimilated within the nations; for that would mean the sacrifice of their ethnic existence. Secondly, they are a group which affronts us by diverging doubly from the dominant type, both ethnically and culturally. It is idle to speculate on whether the primary source of anti-Semitism is racial or religious; for the power of the prejudice is derived from the double divergence. If the Jews were only a religious and not an ethnic group, as some of them claim to be, they would arouse some prejudice by their cultural uniqueness. If they were only a unique ethnic group with the same religion as the majority they would also arouse prejudice. But in either case the prejudice would be more moderate. They are actually an ethnic group with a universalistic religious faith which transcends the values of a single people but which they are forced to use as an instrument of survival in an alien world.

There is no simple solution for a problem of such complexity. No democratic society can afford to capitulate to the pride of dominant groups. The final end of such appeasement is the primitivistic homogeneity of Nazism. On the other hand it is foolish to regard race pride as a mere vestige of barbarism when it is in fact a perpetual source of conflict in human life. . . .

(*The Children of Light and the Children of Darkness*, pp. 141–145)

DOROTHY THOMPSON   (1893–1961)

U.S. journalist

"It's been an amazing experience," she wrote [in 1920]. "The ship is crowded with Zionists whose presence in the first cabin has led to our being extended all the privileges of the place except meals."

It was, of course, through Barbara De Porte [a Jewish close friend]
that Dorothy met this remarkable group who were en route to a World
Zionist Conference in London, the first such gathering since Britain in
1917 had, through the Balfour Declaration, announced its support for
"the establishment of a national home in Palestine for the Jewish
people."

"To an anti-Semite, the trip would be torture probably," Dorothy wrote to Beatrice [Sorchan], whose father was Jewish, "but to
me, to whom an alien temperament is always stimulating, it has been
altogether amusing. The delegation numbers several extraordinary
people, notably Max Radin of the University of California, Dr. David
de Sola Pool (without exception the handsomest man I *ever* laid eyes
on), a Portuguese Jew and a radical rabbi . . . With Max Radin and Dr.
Pool I have had a *delightful* time to the scandal of the ship's Jewry. It
has become known that he chose a particularly delightful moonlit spot
in which to recite to me in impassioned tones his own dramatic and
original translation of the 'Song of Songs which is Solomon's!' We
have flirted, in other words, quite and wholly outrageously, the whole
episode enhanced by his rabbinical character. Besides this we've had
seemingly endless discussions of Zionism . . . I think I shall perhaps
become the leading Gentile authority on Judaism. . . . I have, as you
know, a very real admiration for this extraordinary race, and an
appreciation of qualities in them . . ."

(Sanders, *Dorothy Thompson — A Legend in Her Time*,
pp. 37–38)

* * *

. . . Following the signing of the Hitler-Stalin pact in August
1939, German and Russian armies had dismembered Poland. Although Britain and France had responded by declaring war on
Germany, there was still a military lull. Postponing comment on the
European scene until she could report firsthand observations, Dorothy fashioned lively columns out of shipboard encounters with
young Americans. Some were planning to join the volunteer ambu-
lance corps in Britain; others were Jewish medical students en route to
Europe, where they were forced to seek their education because of the
quotas that were still enforced by American medical schools. "We also
have our modified versions of Hitler's racial laws," she observed, "only

they are not enforced by the state but in a silent and unpublicized manner by our so-called free universities."

(*Dorothy Thompson*, pp. 258–259)

* * *

Through firsthand observation and interviews she learned [in 1945] of the intransigence and brutality of the Soviet conquerors. In weekly broadcasts over the Mutual Network and in cabled columns she reported on her disillusionment with the Russian allies. After a harrowing visit to a newly liberated death camp she fashioned a moving article whose sophistication foreshadowed Hannah Arendt's reflections on "the banality of evil" during the Eichmann trial in 1961. "The Germans are in many ways *like us*," Dorothy wrote. "That is what is terrifying about the concentration camps, with their millions of victims murdered en masse by the most modern and hygienic methods. . . . They are in many ways *like us*—these people in whose country victims descended to cannibalism . . . While they did so the administrators of the camps lived in pleasant and civilized villas . . . Nothing to me, in visiting these camps, was so shattering as the sight of the homes of the SS administrators—of the men who, in a modern bureaucratic manner, according to card catalogues, dossiers and files, gave the orders which resulted in tortures, carefully calculated famine and corpses piled like cordwood when the crematories were too full. Their homes were *civilized*. I pulled out of the library of one of them the lyric poems of Goethe. . . . On the piano of one of them I found the lovely *lieder* of Schubert and Hugo Wolf. . . . The Nazi concentration camps themselves were testing places of mass reactions. Does the world realize that some of the worst crimes in these camps were committed by the inmates? . . ."

(*Dorothy Thompson*, pp. 318, 319)

* * *

[Thompson and her second husband] wound up their voyage in May in the Holy Land, where Dorothy was accorded an enthusiastic welcome by Jewish leaders, deeply grateful for her unflagging championship of Zionism. Of her many appeals in behalf of the cause, one of the best-remembered was a column published in the *Herald Tribune* in

1939 when a British White Paper proposed drastic limitation of Jewish immigration. "The 'Arab rebellion' in Palestine," she wrote, "is actually limited to . . . rebel gangs . . . more or less directed by the Mufti and the Higher Arab Committee. . . . The Jews in Palestine numbered 75,000 in 1919. They now number about 450,000 . . . They have developed beautiful agricultural settlements, built fine cities . . . And they have not ousted any Arabs. On the contrary whereas there were 600,000 Arabs in 1919, there are now 900,000. . . . Palestine has become a problem by reason of the incitation of the Arab population by Arabian nationalists operating with terrorist gangs and assisted by Italian and German propaganda, and Britain has decided that the safest thing for her to do is to come to terms with the Arab leaders. . . ."

Her position was equally forthright in 1943 when she contributed a glowing essay to a volume commemorating Dr. Chaim Weizmann's 70th birthday. Unequivocally endorsing the concept of a Jewish national home, she wrote: "The best place to send people, or allow them to go, is the place to which they want to go. The Jews of Europe want to go to Palestine. They want to go to the one place on earth where they will not be received out of charity or bad conscience but joyfully—where they will not only be admitted but welcomed. I know that the Arab situation creates a woeful problem. But I also know that the Arabian world is an empty and neglected world. It is an impoverished world, not because it is overcrowded, but because it is backward. From a long view the exclusion of the Jews will do nothing whatever for the welfare of the Arabs. They had far better emulate the agricultural and industrial example of modern Jewish Palestine. . . ."

. . . The gravity of the problem was apparent during Dorothy's stay [in 1945]. Initially the Jewish response to Arab attacks on their settlements had been purely defensive. But now organized groups of Jewish extremists had begun to counter terror with terror, and frightened Palestinian Arabs were fleeing their homeland in large numbers.

When she returned to the United States, Dorothy spoke at several Zionist meetings but her zeal for the cause had been undermined. Over the years, she offered a variety of explanations for her change of heart. According to Vincent Sheean, she claimed that while she was hospitalized in Jerusalem, Jesus of Nazareth appeared to her in a vision, holding out his arms to the dispossessed Palestinian Arabs. To [Marcel] Fodor, Dorothy said that her faith in the validity of

Zionism was shaken when she overheard a Jewish soldier in British uniform say, "Their war is over, ours begins."

Whatever the immediate trigger, Dorothy began, in her column, to voice concern for the Arab refugees and dismay at the tactics of the Jewish terrorists. Meyer Weisgal, her closest friend in the Zionist movement, was in Palestine at the time. Weisgal, who subsequently became chancellor of the Weizmann Institute of Science in Rehovoth, wrote in his memoir: "I got a cable from New York asking me to intervene with Dorothy and get her to desist from her attacks on the terrorists. I answered that I could not pass judgment before I received a telegraphic summary of what she had written. I got it, and cabled back that I could not in all honesty repudiate her; she was sincere in what she wrote, no matter how noble the motives ascribed to some of the terrorists. . . . Weizmann was deeply and irrevocably committed against the Jewish terrorists; his was the warning and moral voice; and his was the moral authority. Dorothy was not Jewish, she could not speak with that all-commanding directness. She was bound to be misunderstood; the result was that her utterances against Jewish terrorism were violently resented by the leadership of the Zionist Organization of America . . . [The *Post* dropped her column by 1947].

. . . For Dorothy, the bitterest blow was the discovery that Zionists equated criticism of their policies with anti-Semitism. "I refuse to become an anti-Semite by designation," she said, recalling not only her long record of benevolence to Jewish refugees, her steadfast battle against Hitler, and, perhaps, the fact that she had once been ridiculed for walking out of a dinner party where an anti-Semitic joke was told with the comment, "I will not remain in the same house with traitors to the United States." Indeed, in her personal and public life, Dorothy's stance had always been—and remained—the antithesis of even that casual anti-Semitism typified for example in the pages of *Time* magazine, which in the days before Hitler commonly wrote, "Fannie Hurst, Smart, Semite Novelist" or "Smart Jew David Lilienthal" and identified the premier of France as "Leon Blum, lean, spiderly, Socialist and Jew" or "Jew Blum." Nor did she share the feelings of her friend Harold Nicolson, whose attitude was typical of the British and American upper class when he wrote in his diary: "Although I loathe anti-semitism, I do dislike Jews."

"Dorothy was never anti-Semitic," said Anita Daniel, whose

differences with her on the issue of Zionism never impaired their friendship. "And to accuse her of having been bought — as some did — was shocking. I never knew anyone of more absolute integrity."

(*Dorothy Thompson*, pp. 321–323, 327)

* * *

Rejected and even ostracized by her once-devoted Jewish constituency, Dorothy was eagerly embraced by the opposing camp — the small circle of Americans concerned, for reasons variously compassionate, political, or economic, with the plight of the displaced Palestinian Arabs and bitterly critical of America's pro-Zionist policy, which culminated in the instant recognition of the state of Israel in May 1948. Encouraged by these new advisors, she reached the view that a religious state was inherently wrong and that the existence of Israel would lead to endless trouble in the Mideast. . . .

. . . She never fully recovered from the slightly paranoid state that frequently afflicts partisans in the Arab-Israeli controversy. Regarding herself as the persecuted victim of a Zionist conspiracy, she became increasingly suspicious and intolerant particularly of "fuzzy-minded liberals," whom she blamed for her exclusion from the *Post* and the leading papers of other cities. In dropping her column the *Post* had behaved no differently from the *Herald Tribune*, which had also parted with her for political reasons. But in 1940 she was at the peak of her career and could take the setback in stride. By the 1950s she was weary and out of sympathy with the society in which she lived, increasingly nostalgic for the world of simple Christian values in which she had grown up. "Politically, she was like a great ship left stranded on the beach after the tide had gone out," said one friend. . . .

According to Meyer Weisgal, one of the "errors in judgment" that she now admitted was her turnabout on the question of Israel, which they discussed far into the night . . . Weisgal urged her to use her influence to advance a peaceful resolution of the conflict. In his memoir, *Meyer Weisgal . . . So Far*, he wrote, "This was one of the rare occasions in our friendship when she was absolutely silent for a long, long time. When she spoke at last it was to say slowly, 'Meyer, what you have said has touched me very deeply. I want to think about it . . . What you have told me will not be forgotten . . .' " She did not live

long enough to take any action that might have mitigated the anger of
those who never forgave her defection from the Israeli cause. . . .

(*Dorothy Thompson*, pp. 334, 341, 359–360)

DASHIELL HAMMETT   (1894–1961)

U.S. novelist; author of The Maltese Falcon, The Thin Man

Hammett associated himself with two magazines. In April [1939]
appeared the first issue of *Equality*, a "monthly journal to defend
democratic rights and combat anti-Semitism and racism," with an
editorial council that included Hammett, [Bennett] Cerf, Moss Hart,
Lillian [Hellmann, his lover], Arthur Kober, Louis Kronenberger,
Dudley Nichols, Dorothy Parker and Donald Ogden Stewart. The
first issue contained, among other things, an open letter to the
Catholic hierarchy of America "to examine and stop the activities of
those Catholics" who were spreading hate and prejudice against the
American Jewish people and an article, "Anti-Semitism is Anti-Christian," by Harry Emerson Fosdick. Hammett was also on the editorial
board of *Jewish Survey*, along with Albert Maltz, Rockwell Kent, Max
Leiber and others.

(D. Johnson, *Dashiell Hammett, A Life*, p. 156)

e.e. cummings   (1894–1962)

American poet

Cummings to Steffi Kiesler, "Sunday [1950]":

Dear SK —
    please don't be stupid!
    I wasn't laughing for scorn, but from joy; because (if my telephone
didn't deceive me) you said you liked best the poem about "a nigger and
a little star" — & it so happens that this poem(24) is one of two poems(46
being the other) which a "friend" & "critic", who saw XAIPE in ms, did
his very worst to dissuade me from including . . . on the ground that

the word "nigger"(like the word "kike")would hurt a lot of sensitive human beings & create innumerable enemies for the book. Of course I said to hell with him but the incident depressed me; just how much,I never quite realized until your voice took the curse off those eight lines & put glory upon them

or so I seemed to hear. But even if I misheard you entirely,the point remains

(*Selected Letters of E. E. Cummings*, p. 187)

EDMUND WILSON   (1895–1972)

U.S. literary critic and author

New York, 53rd Street, 1932–1933:

A house with the only real colonial mezuzah he'd ever seen.— Mezuzah's the Ten Commandments in a gold scroll that you kissed as you went into orthodox Jewish houses.

Mrs. Perelman had eaten with the Mankowitzes—big fat Jews, swinish, what's really meant by the word "swinish"—pigs!—awful fat boy who sat there with his mouth open—her husband started talking Jewish (Yiddish) and everybody talked Jewish till somebody said something in English—then the daughter said, "We come from Riga!— they said his Jewish accent was terrible. Snobbery: Litvaks (good); Galicianos (low). A feud that was obsolete everywhere but there. Big Tudor house they lived in with colonial mezuzah as above. . . .

(L. Edel, *The Thirties, From Notebooks and Diaries of the Period*, p. 313)

* * *

Perelmans; Hollywood. Jewish girl, very nice and intelligent, not fancy, who had lost her husband out there after three years—her theory that Jewish men thought themselves ugly, so had to keep proving to themselves what they could do in the way of getting Gentile girls—she thought you had to have a permanent relation with some- body but they would go crazy when they got out to Hollywood—any little dumbbell from Indiana—the Jewish situation very important out there—Thalberg and Norma Shearer had nothing for each other—Thalberg just wanted to show what he could do.—Everybody scared—she'd seen prominent Jewish executives break chairs because their wives had used the wrong fork. . . .

(*The Thirties, From Notebooks and Diaries of the Period*, p. 329)

* * *

Meeting of League of Professional Groups afterwards—I never saw such groping—Rorty and Cowley were the only Gentiles there—they tend naturally perhaps to exclude non-Jews—love excluding people, asserting moral superiority (Communism, psychoanalysis). . . .

(*The Thirties, From Notebooks and Diaries of the Period*, p. 339)

* * *

Griffin Barry's anti-Semitism with Morrie Werner, whom he was meeting for the first time—first said of Nathanael West that he didn't like that kind of looking Jew—then, that when a Jew insulted you at the opera in Russia, you understood Hitler's anti-Semitism. (Hitler's persecutions, in some cases, instead of arousing indignation, brought out anti-Semitism.)—Morrie later said that you were always a Jew first—that at Columbia the Jews couldn't make the fraternities, so they went in for being students. . . .

(*The Thirties, From Notebooks and Diaries of the Period*, p. 354)

* * *

The Jew lends himself easily to Communism because it enables him to devote himself to a high cause, involving all of humanity, characteristics which are natural to him as a Jew—he is already secretive, half alien, a member of an opposition, a member of a minority, at cross purposes with the community he lives in. The [middle-class] radical must be all those things, he must perhaps lack abnormally (like Rousseau) the kind of sense of solidarity with one's social group which makes the ordinary person defend the interests of his group against humane considerations (toward people outside it) and reason–the radical lacks this kind of human relationship; he can only identify his interests with those of an outlawed minority– sometimes not in any immediate way (like Trotsky) even with these: his human solidarity lies only in his imagination of general human improvement–a motive force, however, the strength of which cannot be overestimated–what he loses in immediate human relationships is compensated by his ability to see beyond them and the persons with whom one has them: one's family and one's neighbors–he can see who and what they are in the larger scheme of life. He is always a foreigner like the Jew who has the foreigner's advantage of being able to see things objectively.

* * *

The Jews have the sense of the revolt of the industrial workers in the cities–they have no sense of the American revolutionary tradition created by our farmers–don't know how to talk to people along these lines.

(*The Thirties, From Notebooks and Diaries of the Period*, pp. 379–380)

* * *

To look into, to contemplate Judaism after living with Christianity is to feel at first a certain emptiness. But it is something of a relief, also, to get rid of the Christian mythology. The half-human figure of the Savior is likely to introduce a disquieting personal element. The Christian must refer himself to Jesus. What would Jesus have done? What does He want me to do? How should a Christian behave? Or– in the case of a more fervent person–he may go further and identify himself with Christ: struggle with temptations, endure ordeals, offer himself to martyrdoms. There is always an emotional relationship to another half-human being, and–since this being the Son of God– through him, to a Heavenly Father who is bound to be more or less anthropomorphic. But the God of the Jews is remote: one cannot speak or write his name. He has no go-between but the prophets, and these are human beings, whose words one uses in praying but to whom one does not pray. In the Calvinist church, to be sure, Jesus Christ played a minor role, could hardly, in some cases, be said to figure; yet, in contrast to this kind of "Christianity," too, the theology of Judaism affords a relief: no worry about being Elected, no preoccupation with Hell.

Thus if the outlook of Judaism seems somewhat bleak, if its observances—to a non-Jew—mean little, some contact with it is nonetheless bracing. We are living with God in an empty room—in a room without pictures: the synagogue, where the only things displayed on the walls are words. These words declare the power of the Spirit, the authority of the moral sense. The source of this power and authority gains dignity from not being seen, from not being given a name, from being communicated with—not through the bread and wine of Christ's flesh and blood—but only through thought and prayer. There is only the conviction of its eternal reality, and sometimes of its actual presence.

(Wilson, "The Jews," in *A Piece of My Mind: Reflections at Sixty*, pp. 106–107)

JOHN DOS PASSOS   *(1896–1970)*

U.S. *author of* The Forth-ninth Parallel

When it was published, *The Ground We Stand On* was favorably received for the vitality of the individual chapters . . . and for its appreciation of American democracy. . . .

One of his longtime friends, Gilbert Seldes, cautioned him about what Seldes was sure was an unintentional hint of bigotry. He wrote Dos Passos that he had almost set aside *The Ground We Stand On* because in the opening chapter Dos Passos had implied that "the selfgoverning tradition had been diluted by the diverse habits of the stream of newcomers from Europe." This was "the most poisonous kind of doctrine," Seldes warned. There was no evidence to support it, he added, and Dos Passos needed to recognize that "Americans are not Anglo-Saxons and that the 'bedrock habits' of Americans were not formed by Anglo-Saxons but by Jews and Portuguese, Bulgars and

Italians and Germans and twenty-one other races." The meaning of
the term *American*, Seldes continued, "is that it was formed by the
action upon one group of all the other groups and vice versa."

Dos Passos deserved Seldes's strictures because, while he scorned
bigotry, he was coming close to it with his blend of nationalism and
Anglo-Saxon pride. He did distrust the influence of outsiders; he had
said as much to Jack Lawson in the 1930s when he criticized "the
whole New York Jewish Theatre Guild, Damrosch, Otto Kahn, Mike
Gold culture" which he accused of being "an echo of the liberal
mitteleuropa culture . . . in Europe." As long as he remained skeptical
of the American system, he remained open-minded. After he had
embraced the United States, however, too often he sounded intolerant, although his harsh tone reflected less his complete conviction or
a bigot's complacency than the fervor of his concern about American
"selfgovernment." But hyperbole on the written page was nothing new
for the man who was in person shy and diffident.

(Ludington, *John Dos Passos, A Twentieth-Century*
Odyssey, pp. 406–407)

WILLIAM FAULKNER   *(1897–1962)*

U.S. novelist, Intruder in the Dust, the Sound and the Fury,
Pulitzer Prize, 1955, 1963

Instead of going on with *Liberator Story*, Faulkner found himself
shifted on November 23 [1942] to another picture, based on Eric
Ambler's espionage thriller *Uncommon Danger*. Renamed *Background*
to Danger, it starred George Raft, with Raoul Walsh as the director. . . . Faulkner was assigned to it with a young writer named Daniel
Fuchs. . . . Communication between Fuchs and Faulkner was [poor].
Later, without actually naming his collaborators, Fuchs described the
problem: "I was paralyzed with awe. It happened that I had a deep,
long-time admiration for this man and his achievement." But he could
scarcely talk to him. One day Faulkner told Fuchs he understood.

"You don't cozy to me because you think I'm anti-Semitic."

"Yes," Fuchs said. "How about that?"

"Well, it's troo-oo," Faulkner said. "I don't like Jews—but I don't
like Gentiles neither."

(Blotner, *Faulkner, A Biography*, vol. II, p. 1113)

. . . he wrote to Malcolm at Camp Robinson in Arkansas. [In July, 1942] He told him who Bob Haas[4] was, and added, "During the times when I would be broke, year after year sometimes, I had only to write him and he would send me money—no hope to get it back, unless I wrote another book. He's a Jew." Now his only son had been killed and his daughter was still flying planes from factories to bases in the Women's Ferry Squadron. They were that kind of family. "All Jews. I just hope I dont run into some hundred percent American Legionnaire until I feel better.

"There is a squadron of negro pilots. They finally got congress to allow them to learn how to risk their lives in the air. They are in Africa now, under their own negro lt. colonel, did well at Pantelleria, on the same day a mob of white men and white policemen killed 20 negroes in Detroit. Suppose you and me and a few others of us lived in the Congo, freed seventy-seven years ago by ukase; of course we cant live in the same apartment hut with the black folks, nor always ride in the same car nor eat in the same restaurant, but we are free because the Great Black Father says so. Then the Congo is engaged in War with the Cameroon. At last we persuade the Great Black Father to let us fight too. You and Jim say are flyers. You have just spent the day trying to live long enough to learn how to do your part in saving the Congo. Then you come back down and are told that 20 of your people have just been killed by a mixed mob of civilians and cops at Little Poo Poo. What would you think?

"A change will come out of this war. If it doesn't, if the politicians and the people who run this country are not forced to make good the shibboleth they glibly talk about freedom, liberty, human rights, then you young men who dont live through it will have died in vain.". . .

(*Faulkner, A Biography*, vol. II, pp. 1146–1147)

* * *

He made a quick trip to New York during the last week in February [1955]. At first it seemed to be an interesting and challenging undertaking. He began work immediately from the material provided by the network's research department and soon had a six-page syn-

---

[4]The father of Lieutenant Robert K. Haas, lost in action at Casablanca during World War II.

opsis with brief passages of dialogue. It was built around the conflict of Donald Hobson, a successful young businessman and reserve lieutenant commander, over whether or not he would make an affidavit attesting the loyalty of Abe Chasanow, suspended as a result of charges made against him by a committee. The conflict was resolved in a dream sequence in which Uncle Sam watched as Hobson's wife threatened to leave him if he did not help. Then Uncle Sam showed him the next day's paper, reporting Chasanow's suicide. Awaking, Hobson called Chasanow's lawyer about making his affidavit. Neither Faulkner's hatred of anti-Semitism nor his detestation of Senator McCarthy had been enough to infuse life into the script. . . .

(*Faulkner, A Biography*, vol. II, p. 1529)

* * *

He said there had been a gratifying degree of agreement in letters and phone calls, [in response to his letters about integration in 1955] mostly from young people. There had also been bitter denunciations, some of them anonymous, and a number of nuisance phone calls, some as late as two or three in the morning from as far away as Florida. Apparently these people preferred the impractical solution of ignoring the problem. "It's like living in Alaska and saying you don't like snow," Faulkner said; "you have to live with it, and you might as well make the best of it." He had explained his feelings on a deeper level in a letter to Else Jonsson the day before. "We have much tragic trouble in Mississippi now about Negroes," he had told her. "The Supreme Court has said that there shall be no segregation, difference in schools, voting, etc., between the two races, and there are many people in Mississippi who will go to any length, even violence, to prevent that, I am afraid. I am doing what I can. I can see the possible time when I shall have to leave my native state, something as the Jew had to flee from Germany during Hitler. I hope that wont happen of course. But at times I think that nothing but a disaster, a military defeat even perhaps, will wake America up and enable us to save ourselves, or what is left. This is a depressing letter, I know, but human beings are terrible. One must believe well in man to endure him, wait out his folly and savagery and inhumanity."

(*Faulkner, A Biography*, vol. II, pp. 1538–1539)

ERNEST HEMINGWAY   *(1898–1961)*

U.S. novelist; author of For Whom the Bell Tolls, The Old Man
and the Sea; *Pulitzer Prize 1953.*

A paradoxical aspect of Hemingway's friendships was the relation
between his occasional but distinct anti-Semitism (which appears
most notably in his animus against Robert Cohen in *The Sun Also
Rises*) and his large number of Jewish friends: girls, writers, agents,
publishers, painters, bullfighters, bibliographers, lawyers, fishermen,
photographers, doctors, soldiers, art historians, journalists and critics.
Hemingway's expression of sympathy for pogrom victims in his Kansas
City article, "Kerensky, the Fighting Flea" suggests that his anti-Semitism developed after he left Oak Park [Illinois] (for no Jews lived in
that town). The workmen in Kiev, he wrote, "made a cross of ice and
set it up on the frozen river. It fell over and they blamed the Jews.
Then the workmen rioted, breaking into stores and smashing windows." Hemingway's fashionably hostile feelings about Jews probably
began when he entered artistic circles in Paris and met wealthy Jews
who lived (as Hemingway himself did) on unearned income and
seemed to him to exploit, rather than contribute to, the world of art
and literature. His hostility, though sometimes vociferous, was actually quite mild, for he spent a good deal of time with Jewish friends,
established professional relationships with them and told Harvey Breit
that the only very rich people who were generous with money were
Jews.
    . . . From 1949 to 1957 he corresponded with (though never met)
Bernard Berenson. . . . In June 1928 he had condemned Berenson as
an empty asshole and kike patron of the arts. By August 1949, he had
shed his anti-Semitism and told Berenson: "you are one of the living
people that I respect most."
                          (Meyers, *Hemingway, A Biography*, pp. 72, 429)

* * *

    . . . In the same era in which Anthony Patch, the hero of Scott
Fitzgerald's *The Beautiful and Damned*, detected something sinister in
the faces of Semitic New Yorkers and T. S. Eliot defined the univer-
salist Jew in terms of "A saggy bending of the knees/And elbows, with

the palms turned out,/Chicago Semite Viennese," Hemingway found
it easy to revile Jewish acquaintances with anti-Semitic epithets,
especially those he hated, like Lincoln Steffens' new wife, Ella Winter.
"You heard of course of Steffens' marriage to a 19 year old Bloomsbury
kike intellectual," he wrote to Pound from Burguete, Spain, on July 19,
1924, having forgotten that two and a half months earlier he had
written him from Paris to say that "Abe Linc Steffens [has] gone off to
Italy with objectionable 22 year old Jewine who treats him like Gaugin
[sic] treated Van Gogh."

Of homosexuals he was even more intolerant. . . .

(Lynn, *Hemingway*, pp. 236–237)

* * *

A much more self-controlled bigot than his friend Ezra Pound
(and a good thing, too: Hemingway, did, after all, want to sell "Fifty
Grand" to a mainstream American magazine like *Collier's* or the
Saturday Evening Post), he further muted the signs of his prejudice by
being somewhat vague about the ethnic identity of the fighter who
finally squares off against Jack in Madison Square Garden. Hemingway certainly thought of him as Jewish, not only because he had
written "Fifty Grand" with the Jack Britton–Benny Leonard fight in
mind, but because he identified his hero's opponent with Horace
Liveright. . . .

Two other characters in the story are Jews—at least in Hemingway's mind. At the training camp one afternoon, a couple of poolroom
operators show up in the company of John Collins, Jack's manager.
Morgan and Steinfelt are their names and gambling on the outcome of
sports events could be called their game, except that—in Jack's
words—"they don't take any chances, those two." . . . Despite his
unawareness that he is being set up, Jack sarcastically says of these
sharks, they are a "fine bunch," and through their slimy presence
Hemingway covertly degraded two Jews whom he had gone after
before. In Steinfelt, he struck at Gertrude Stein for the second time in
less than a month. In Morgan—a name that was even more legendary
on Wall Street than Kuhn, Loeb—he made a contemptuous addition
to the assault on Harold Loeb that he was in the process of mounting
in *The Sun Also Rises*.

(*Hemingway*, pp. 308–309)

HENRY R. LUCE *(1898–1967)*

U.S. publisher of Time *and* Life *magazines*

. . . The great and first impression I got . . . is that National Socialism is a socialism which works mightily for the masses however distasteful it may be to them personally in many ways. . . . [I]t was there [Bayreuth] I first saw the paper edited by Streicher and entirely devoted to attacking Jews . . . there has been no exaggeration as to the important role which anti-Semitism has played in the Third Reich or as to the intensity of this brand of hatred. Our friend [the driver] . . . was anything but a "natural" Nazi, but even he accepted anti-Semitism as, at least, a necessary evil in the rebuilding of Germany under the Third Reich. . . . We read of Germany as if it were the private domain of Hitler with just enough people to serve him for an audience occasionally, and with an Army to parade around and amuse him. But the *visual* impression of Germany is of a People's land. I never saw Hitler. I saw many soldiers casually here and there but I saw no Army. I saw only The People and The People and The People. I do not know what they are but they do not seem to be slaves. Their chains are not visible.

(Swanberg, *Luce and His Empire,* p. 155)

* * *

"On the basis," [Luce] wrote, "of a two-day rather low-pressure visit to Baghdad [in 1950], I will not put myself forward as an expert on Iraq." Still he was a quick observer and his tendency toward instant expertise was strong. "The main points about Iraq are quickly stated," he wrote. "The first point is about Jews and the second is about Nationhood." He was astonished at the Arab feeling against the Jews and against America as being on the side of the Jews, and he was indignant at the plight of the Arab refugees. "The Jews of America are always making a great hubbub about humanitarianism—the really great thing for the Jews of America to do would be to raise a fund of $1,000,000,000 to take care of the refugee Arabs whom they banished out of their homeland. Time Inc. would undoubtedly suffer Jewish reprisals if we took up the subject vigorously, but there is evidently need of some courage in this matter. . . . And in any case America—

including American Jews—ought to be told at how great a price of American good-will Zion has been purchased."

This was one of those rare moments when he showed genuine sympathy for human beings. The warmth for humanity simply as humanity, quite separate from his usual concentration on power, was so unexpected and appealing as to underline its gradual disappearance from his consideration.

(*Luce and His Empire*, p. 295)

THOMAS WOLFE   (1900–1938)

U.S. writer; author of Look Homeward, Angel, You Can't Go Home Again

Like most Southerners of the time, the Wolfes were anti-Semitic. Tom was brought up to think of Jews as "beaknosed Shylocks from Yankeedom," and he and his playmates took joy in terrorizing the Jewish boys of their age and in spying on their parents. Though there were only sixteen Jewish families in all of Buncombe County in 1906, they were so readily identifiable by their exotic names and their Sabbath observances that it was easy for Wolfe, both as a boy and a man, to believe that their numbers in the town were rapidly increasing "by that strange advertisement of the race which brings stealthily the swarm where honey is found."

(Donald, *Look Homeward—A Life of Thomas Wolfe*, p. 21)

* * *

Wolfe found the students at Washington Square College[5] unlike any that he had known at the University of North Carolina or at Harvard. Most were second-generation immigrants; many were Jews. Years later, in *Of Time and the River*, he described Eugene Gant's sense of drowning in "the brawling and ugly corridors of the university," which were flooded with the "swarming, shrieking, shouting tides of dark amber Jewish flesh," only to be swept "into the comparative sanctuary of the class room with its smaller horde of thirty or forty Jews and Jewesses."

---

[5]At New York University in Greenwich Village.

Much of the time he found it exhilarating to be plunged into this unfamiliar ethnic world. "I am making a contact which shall prove itself to be of the greatest value to me," he explained to Frederic Day, one of the few Workshop members with whom he kept in touch. "I came without racial sentimentality—indeed with a strong racial prejudice concerning the Jew, which I still retain," he admitted. . . .

(*Look Homeward—A Life of Thomas Wolfe*, pp. 113–114)

* * *

Deeply hurt [by attacks on his novels as anti-Semitic], Wolfe replied that the charge of anti-Semitism was "absolutely groundless." He asked Calo [Harold, a member of Wolfe's first class at New York University] "to consider fairly whether you ever saw or heard me do anything that was unfair, intolerant, or unjust to any member of your faith," and he added the conventional cliche: "some of the best and most valued friends I have ever had here in New York have been Jews." Perkins also told Simon Pearl that Wolfe had "no anti-Semitic leanings" and that "he numbers Jews among his best friends." The editor pointed out that Wolfe was equally harsh in his descriptions of other American ethnic groups, particularly the Irish.

These were, at best, partial answers to an embarrassing question. Wolfe was, in fact, anti-Semitic. As a child he was brought up to deride and torment the few Jewish families in Asheville. At the same time he, like all the other members of his family, feared them. "In our small towns," he wrote, "we see our small tradesmen steadily driven to the wall, outwitted and outreached on every side by their Jewish competitor." In Cambridge and Boston he for the first time encountered a considerable number of Jews, and he disliked them. They were, he thought, materialistic, avaricious, money-grubbing—and, worst of all, successful. The chief tenet of the Jewish faith, he observed, was "keeping an eye on the main chance—a regulation the Jew observes with an iron pertinacity." A dramatic skit that he wrote at this time began: "Enter two Jews, arm in arm, gesticulating and exhorting each other loudly. Each bears a money bag in his free hand." They say to each other: "To de bank, to de bank, to de bank."

His move to New York reinforced his prejudices. He came to believe that Jews controlled the world of the theater, where Jewish producers catered to the demands of predominantly Jewish audiences for "the sensual, the thinly veiled, or the materialistic." Aline Bernstein was, of course, Jewish, and every quarrel with her reinforced his belief that Jews were treacherous, conniving, money-loving, and ostentatious.

But Wolfe usually tried to conceal his anti-Semitism. When he was growing up in the South he was taught that being a Jew was an unfortunate but ineradicable handicap and of course no gentleman would publicly refer to this deformity. What he said in his private letters or recorded in his pocket notebook was another matter—as were his virulently anti-Semitic outbursts when he was in his cups.

In his fiction, however, he intended to offer a portrait of America, and all his characters—except, perhaps, the immediate members of the Gant family—were not so much individuals as representative figures. Consequently he always took pains to identify the Jews in his stories by their ethnic, or as he thought of it, racial origins. In his own provincial way Wolfe thought that he was giving a balanced picture of Jewish life in America. Arrogance and aggressiveness, extravagance and sensuality were pairs of negative "racial" traits that he attributed to Jews in his fiction. But on the positive side he praised the "richness, color, and humor" of Jewish life, along with high intellectual achievement and love for rich foods, sumptuous clothing, and passionate sexual enjoyment, which made them "the most lavish and opulent race on earth." Since that balance was so much more flattering than his own personal assessment of Jews, he was both angered and baffled by critics who found his novels anti-Semitic.

(*Look Homeward—A Life of Thomas Wolfe*, pp. 356–357)

* * *

In February [1938] Aline Bernstein published her second book, *The Journey Down*, a novel about her love affair with Wolfe. The unnamed hero of her story was easily recognizable: he was gigantic physically, had grandiose ideas about himself as a writer, composed indescribably magnificent prose, and made love to the heroine by telling her that she came from the dung hill of the theater, that her breasts were like melons, and that she smelled like a Jew. Because of the danger of libel, reviewers did not openly identify him as Wolfe, but Bernard DeVoto, in the *Saturday Review of Literature*, gave hints that were obvious to readers who had followed his earlier attacks on Wolfe.

Wolfe was infuriated. Though he planned to publish his own fictional account of his affair with Aline, he was deeply upset by *The Journey Down*. Late one night, after brooding and drinking, he stormed up to the Bernsteins' apartment in the Gotham Hotel. He "started the most awful row about the Jews," Aline told a friend shortly afterward; "he denounced them at the top of his voice, said they should be wiped off the face of the earth." After attacking her Jewish friends by name, he called for three cheers for Adolf Hitler. At the end of her patience, Aline "launched out and punched him in the nose." Taken by surprise, he fell flat on his back on the floor, and she called for the porter to put him out. "It was the most sickening experience of my life," she wrote; "horrible, but it succeeded in finally freeing me from the spell. . . . I have always protected him so far as I could, and always allowed for his behavior because of a certain greatness I have felt about him; but this was too much."

(*Look Homeward — A Life of Thomas Wolfe*, pp. 443–444)

JOHN STEINBECK *(1902–1968)*

U.S. Nobel Prize-winning author of Of Mice and Men, The Grapes of Wrath; *Pulitzer Prize 1940*

. . . significantly, ["The Murder," published in the April 1934 issue of *North American Review* and winner of the O. Henry Award as the best short story of that year] marked the beginning of Steinbeck's career as a writer of "social protest." Although there was little in the way of social protest in "The Murder," there was a palpable social conscious-ness that presaged his most significant and successful works.

In retrospect, one is compelled to recall the words of Steinbeck's high school English teacher, Ora Cupp, who questioned the sincerity of his later devotion to social idealism in his work. "These people were good copy," she said. "Let the reader cry over them . . . I'm willing to wager there were times when . . . he stood off and grinned at his own indignation." One is also compelled to recall Steinbeck's own words, written late in his life in *Travels With Charley*, about the absence of any racial or ethnic prejudice in his life.

Why? Because despite its literary virtues, "The Murder" is suffused with an underlying feeling of ethnic superiority. Steinbeck had grown up in an Anglo-Saxon Protestant household and in an ethnically and racially divided town in which the Anglo-Saxons were the elite. Although humanists to a degree, the Steinbecks were not without a sense of their own intellectual and behavioral superiority. Their middle-class respectability had repelled John as a young man, but more lately, with his parents on the verge of death, he had rallied to their side with a belated sense of love and duty and probably guilt. . . .

. . . Steinbeck was the repository of a reflexive anti-Semitism as a young adult. Because anti-Semitism was powerfully endemic in Christian, Anglo-Saxon America, this was not surprising. But it gave lie to his later claims that he was without racial and ethnic prejudice. In its curious way, so too did "The Murder" and other works he was later to write. Despite their throbbing social consciousness and idealism, they were often to be infused by a narrative attitude that subtly looked down or patronized their subjects. His aim was compassion, but it was always to be mixed with a certain condescension—as it was in his cautionary tale about the Slavs in "The Murder."

> (Kiernan, *The Intricate Music, A Biography of John Steinbeck*, pp. 187–188)

* * *

. . . his refusal to stay in New York through the play's [*Of Mice and Men*] rehearsals and his unwillingness to appear at the opening deeply offended George Kaufman and several others who had worked on the production. Kaufman, already puzzled by John's personal remoteness and lack of amiability during their pre-production working sessions, credited Steinbeck's attitude to the fact that he, Kaufman, was a Jew. Kaufman had heard gossip, months before when he was trying to acquire the stage rights to *Of Mice and Men*, that Steinbeck had expressed misgivings about Kaufman's involvement in the play. "What would a wiseacre New York Jew know about people like George and Lenny?" Steinbeck was purported to have said to someone that no one else seemed willing to identify to Kaufman. Steinbeck's alternating unease and diffidence evidently confirmed Kaufman's suspicions that Steinbeck disliked Jews. And although John wrote him a warm letter of appreciation after the opening of the play, Kaufman would refuse to talk to him for years.

> (*The Intricate Music*, p. 222)

[President] Roosevelt saw Steinbeck and listened to him outline a plan that called for the movie and radio industries to be mobilized to subvert the Nazi propaganda machine and to develop a mass resistance to German intentions in Central and South America. Steinbeck offered to drop everything else he was doing and organize the mobilization himself. Roosevelt expressed gratitude for Steinbeck's concern but failed to act on his proposal. Nevertheless, Steinbeck's first venture into the halls of high power gave him a sense of political self-importance that he would cultivate with increasing gusto in the months and years to come. . . . Steinbeck did not realize that Roosevelt had been giving him his time only to humor his wife Eleanor, who had become an advocate of Steinbeck the author.

Although the vast majority of the population of the United States was complacent about the government's position on the hostilities in Europe late in 1940, war fever had broken out among the country's intelligentsia. Steinbeck had caught the fever, and when he returned to Mexico in October to work on the actual filming of [a] documentary, it intensified. Several of the people connected with the production were Jewish, and from them he heard tales and rumors of the anti-Jewish measures that were being implemented in Europe by the Nazis. From the film's director he received an education in the entire history of anti-Jewish pogroms in Europe—a history of which he had been unaware. He experienced deepening embarrassment about his own German heritage, and his views about Jews underwent a rapid, sympathetic change.

(*The Intricate Music*, pp. 250–251)

CHARLES LINDBERGH *(1902–1974)*

U.S. aviator

Lindbergh continued to speak. He did not submit his speeches to America First leaders for approval before he made them. Thus when he spoke in Des Moines, on September 11, 1941, at an America First rally, no one but Lindbergh knew what he was going to say. It, more than any other of his speeches (and his speeches were the most important ones made by any America Firster, invariably drawing overflow crowds), smeared his reputation and that of America First.

In this speech Lindbergh, who had been referring darkly for many months to "powerful elements" which were trying to lead the United States into war, identified specifically the interventionist groups. These groups, "responsible for changing our national policy from one of neutrality and independence to one of entanglement in European affairs . . . are the British, the Jewish and the Roosevelt administration," he said to the enthusiastic Iowans. "Behind these groups, but of lesser importance, are a number of capitalists, Anglophiles, and intellectuals who believe that their future, and the future of mankind, depends upon the domination of the British Empire. . . . [This] . . . minority . . . control . . . a tremendous influence."

Then he went on to speak his mind. . . . "It is not difficult to understand why Jewish people desire the overthrow of Nazi Germany. The persecution they suffered in Germany would be sufficient to make bitter enemies of any race. No person with a sense of dignity of mankind can condone the persecution the Jewish race suffered in Germany. But no person of honesty and vision can look on their pro-war policy here today without seeing the dangers involved in such a policy, both for us and for them.

"Instead of agitating for war the Jewish groups in this country should be opposing it in every possible way, for they will be among the first to feel its consequences. Tolerance is a virtue that depends upon peace and strength. A few farsighted Jewish people realize this and stand opposed to intervention. But the majority still do not. Their greatest danger to this country lies in their large ownership and influence in our motion pictures, our press, our radio, and our government."

Professor Wayne S. Cole, in his detailed book *America First, the Battle Against Intervention, 1940-1941,* says, "It would be difficult to exaggerate the magnitude of the explosion which was set off by this speech. . . . Undoubtedly much of this uproar was due to genuine disapproval of Lindbergh's key statement regarding the Jews. Many may have denounced the speech publicly to protect themselves from any possible charge of anti-Semitism. But there can be no doubt that interventionists exploited this incident."

. . . There were pamphlets, statements by such men as Willkie and Thomas E. Dewey, speeches by opposition groups—all aimed at Lindbergh. He was called everything from a Hitlerite to a fool; even many of America First's leading members disapproved publicly.

However, Norman Thomas said in his defense that Lindbergh was "not as anti-Semitic as some who seize the opportunity to criticize him." This was a tack taken by several people who disliked Lindbergh's statement but felt the attacks on him were extreme. . . .

Lindbergh himself did not attempt to explain or amplify his statement, and he never made another like it. However, a few days later in Fort Wayne, Indiana, he said that he had always spoken what he believed to be the truth, and that his statements had been distorted and his motives and meanings "falsely ascribed." He also said that he did not "speak out of hate for any individuals or any people."

This did not wash away the stain, a stain that is still implicit in the wrongheadedness of some of his Des Moines statements.

That speech destroyed Lindbergh's effectiveness for America First and greatly damaged the organization and its cause. Between September and December 7, 1941, America First was shrill but less and less effective. . . .

(Ross, *The Last Hero: Charles A. Lindbergh*, pp. 312–314)

* * *

Lindbergh's fight against intervention in what he considered "Europe's war" and for isolationism doubtless had its roots in his father's isolationism during World War I. . . .

Lindbergh had seen the same strain of barbarism in his own time. He had felt its force in his private life. He had seen what anti-Semitism could do in Germany. There was certainly reason to fear it in the United States. His warning to the Jews could be read, in this context, as the advice of a friend, not the threat of an enemy.

In a critical article published in *Life* magazine some months before the Des Moines speech, Roger Butterfield reported that Lindbergh "believes Jews will be blamed for American entry into the war and will suffer for it. If that happens, he has said, the anti-Jewish outbreaks that will occur here will surpass those in Nazi Germany, for Americans are 'more violent' than the Germans.

"Yet [the Butterfield article continued] Lindbergh is not anti-Semitic. In personal conversation he has expressed indignation over the German treatment of Jews in Europe." But Butterfield pointed out that Lindbergh had never condemned these persecutions publicly.

When friends and associates pleaded with him to do so, Lindbergh invariably refused, saying, "I must be neutral."

Much later, after the war, one of Lindbergh's daughters was dating a Jewish boy. The boy's parents made him stop seeing the Lindbergh girl because they said her father was an anti-Semite. The girl, naturally troubled by this, asked Lindbergh about it.

Lindbergh told her it was not true. He had never been anti-Semitic. It was just a convenient peg for his enemies to hang their attacks on, he said.

Lindbergh, in his Des Moines speech, had identified the Jews as a "race," though there is no scientific definition of race that would encompass all Jews. Further, he had assumed that Jews needed "tolerance" to exist. This could seem like a threat: behave or you won't be tolerated. Yet it could also be traced to Lindbergh's firsthand experience with the lack of tolerance in this country and the Nazi demonstration of what this could mean to the Jews. His assumption that Jews controlled the press, movies, and radio, and were using this control to push the country toward war to get even with the Nazis, was certainly erroneous. Jews did not exert nearly as much control of the press and radio as he had said, and they were certainly not united on interventionism. The Keep America Out of War Congress had at least four Jews on its governing committee.

Lindbergh had used some of the language of anti-Semites, but this does not make him an anti-Semite. His own private statements exculpate him of the charge; it would be out of character for him to lie on a subject as vital as this. His actions before and since do not add up to bigotry.

Nevertheless, he suffered because he got the reputation of an anti-Semite, and also because of his isolationism. Some of his closest friends, both Jewish (Harry Guggenheim) and Christian (Colonel Henry Breckinridge) stopped seeing him for a time. Mrs. Dwight Morrow took a strong public stand against her son-in-law and her daughter by supporting the Committee to Defend America by Aiding the Allies, and Anne Lindbergh's sister Constance Morgan opposed Anne and supported her own husband, who was head of British Information Services in New York. . . .

(*The Last Hero: Charles A. Lindbergh*,
pp. 316–318)

ANNE MORROW LINDBERGH   (1906–   )

U.S. writer, wife of aviator Charles Lindbergh

12 November 1938:

We are very depressed by accounts in the newspaper of German riots on Jews [Kristallnacht; Nov. 9, 1938]. Apparently there were terrible demonstrations, supposedly "spontaneous"—smashing shops, driving out Jews, harassing them all over Germany. . . .

You just get to feeling you **can** understand and work with these people when they do something stupid and brutal and undisciplined like that. I am shocked and very upset.

How *can* we go there to live?
(A. M. Lindbergh, *The Flower and the Nettle, Diaries and Letters, 1936–1939,* p. 450)

* * *

10 December 1938:

Mail from home, including another letter from Dr. Carrel, very much upset by the insidious "campaign" directed against C. [her husband Charles Lindbergh] in the United States, sending us an article in *The New Yorker* to illustrate this attitude. The story is that we are going to live in Germany in a house of an evicted Jew.[6]

The press have of course used this situation to the best (or worst, rather) advantage. I hate to have such unfair labeling going on and have a body of hatred building up against C. for something that is not true. He is not and never has been anti-Semitic. C. is marvelously untouched by all this. Their scorn does not touch him any more than their praise once did.

Only, I think, if he felt he had betrayed his own integrity would he mind.

Femininely, I mind the injustice of it.
(*The Flower and the Nettle,* pp. 469–470)

---

[6]In answer to Dr. Carrel's letter, C.A.L. replied that his decision to take an apartment in Paris was not based on the reaction of the press but he simply did "not want to make a move which would seem to support the German actions in regard to the Jews."

11 December 1938:

Mother darling,

    We have been one week in Paris today.

    Dr. Carrel and Mrs. S. have written us several times about the widespread "campaign" against C. in the United States. C. hissed in the movie theaters, name taken off the *Lindburgh Line*, and Jewish booksellers boycotting my book, etc.

    This does distress me as I feel it is unfair labeling due to a series of circumstances, inaccurately reported, with a large amount of malicious gossip on top. The press, I feel, is responsible (the stories that we could easily get a house in Berlin from some evicted Jew) plus, of course, the naturally oversensitive Jews. But it is too bad, all the way round. C. is not and never has been antisemitic. . . .

(The Flower and the Nettle, p. 471)

JOSEPH CAMPBELL   (1904–1987)

Popular scholar of mythology; author of The Power of Myth

    At least five persons have gone on the record regarding first-person encounters with Campbell's anti-Semitism. They are author Brendan Gill (who was a friend of Campbell); Carol Wallace Orr, director of the University of Tennessee Press (who worked on one of Campbell's books while she was at Princeton University Press); Carol Luther (who attended a lecture by Campbell); Sarah Lawrence faculty member Arnold Krupat (who was a colleague of Campbell); and Sarah Lawrence graduate Eve Sidorov Feldman (who studied with Campbell until he aimed an anti-Semitic tirade at her).

    In September, 1989, Brendan Gill set off a public controversy by writing in the *New York Review of Books* of Campbell's "bigotry" and "seemingly ineradicable anti-Semitism." Gill stated that "by the time I came to know him, he had learned to conceal its grosser manifestations, but there can be no doubt that it existed and that it tainted not only the man himself but the quality of his scholarship."

    Gill's article provoked angry responses from Campbell's defenders. However, Carol Wallace Orr, in a letter to the *New York Review of Books*, wrote of her years of working with Campbell in the early 1970s: "It was amazing to me that this man of cosmic vision could harbor such mean-spirited and seemingly unexamined biases against much of humankind. In addition to anti-Semitism, I remember in particular his vexation over blacks being admitted to Sarah Lawrence" (where Campbell had taught for 38 years).

In a reply to letters published in the *New York Review of Books*, Brendan Gill revealed that "when the astronauts landed on the moon, Joe made the repellant jest to a member of my family, who was a student of his at the time, that the moon would be a good place to put the Jews." Gill also made public the experience of a correspondent, Carol Luther, who had written to him of an exchange with Campbell during a lecture. When Campbell presented a favorite Indian fable of his about how we are all bloodthirsty tigers who do well to prey upon lower species of animals, Luther rose from her chair and shouted: "What about the six million who were gassed during World War II?" According to Luther, Campbell shrugged and said, "That's your problem."

Arnold Krupat, in a letter published in the *New York Times*, recalled a Sarah Lawrence faculty function at which Campbell told Krupat "something to the effect that he could always spot a Jew." According to Krupat, Campbell went on and on "in the most charming and amiable fashion" about how the New York Athletic Club "had ingeniously managed for years to keep Jews out." Krupat states that Campbell "obviously relished the notion of keeping Jews out of anywhere, anytime, forever."

When Eve Feldman told Campbell in 1968 that she was Jewish and wanted to do a serious study of the Old Testament, he told her that the God of the Hebrews was an evil God. Then, in Feldman's words, as quoted in Amy Taubin's 1989 article in the *Village Voice*: "He was sweating and pacing and running his fingers through his hair. He began to spew out this garbage, about how the college was going Jewish. . . . He went down his class roster identifying the students who were Jewish. He said that the Jews had ruined 20th century culture and went through a list of Jewish artists." Feldman told Taubin that "it was horrifying. It was like watching someone have a fit or having them vomit uncontrollably all over you."

Joseph Campbell's books and videos are everywhere. Sarah Lawrence College continues to maintain a Joseph Campbell Chair in the Humanities. If Bill Moyers [the producer and host of the popular PBS (Public Broadcasting System) series starring Campbell and presenting his theories of myth] and others wish to enshrine their guru, then let them at least be honest about Joseph Campbell's ugly views concerning Jews, African-Americans, and other minorities.

(From a study by Bob Lamm, New York free-lance writer, 1990)

WILLIAM SAROYAN   (1908–1981)

American novelist and short-story writer; author of The Human Comedy

Carol Matthau (his Jewish ex-wife, interviewed):

It started so insanely. I had been seeing Bill. He took me to a party, and I don't remember where it was, whose house it was, but there were a lot of Armenians there, and of course the war had started and they were talking about the war.

The Jews. The Jews started the war. The Jews were clever. New York Jews. All the phrases you've ever heard. And I winced.

And he turned around and said, "What's the matter with you, kid? I mean, *you're* not Jewish, are you?"

Suddenly there was a silence and I was looking at all these people who had said all these horrible things, and I was so embarrassed that I didn't know what to do.

I said, "Oh, ah – well, no. No, of course not."

I just didn't have the guts to say, "Well, of course I *am*."

After that he said, "I hate liars more than anything," and I realized that that night at the party I was so embarrassed, I didn't think it really mattered anyway. But because I didn't have that kind of background that it meant anything, I didn't know what it was all about, but I lived to regret that.

I think it came from his – he was brought right up with it. His whole family were like that.

I remember when I invited his mother and sister to New York before he went overseas. They went out one afternoon, and when they came back I said, "Did you have a nice time?"

They said, "Too much juice, too much juice."

I said, "Where did you go?" (I thought they had juice or something.) And then Bill told me what they meant.

But he did drive me on a very beautiful street in Fresno, and I said, "Oh, this is so pretty," and they had very pretty houses. And he said, "Armenians can't live here." I said, "Really? How horrible!" And he said, "No, the Jews have this all sewed up."

This was festering. I had to tell him, and I did.

In Carol's account of the breakup, reported in their son's biography, *William Saroyan*, Bill and Carol were lying in bed after making love when she told Saroyan that she was, in fact, Jewish. Saroyan moved immediately to the living-room sofa, but returned to the bedroom in the wee hours, turned on a light, tore off the covers and pointed at her. "Look at you, all white and pink and perfect. Do you mean to tell me that you're Jewish? How can that be possible? Come on, kid. You're not Jewish. How could someone as beautiful as you are be Jewish?"

"My God, what do you think a Jew *is?* What do you think I'm supposed to look like?"

In bitter hindsight, Saroyan wrote, "The little bride had confessed it—she had taken six years to do so, and she had chosen the moment that suited her best. She hoped I would continue the marriage anyway. Really she did, she said. Really."

Exactly *what* his wife had confessed, Saroyan left to the reader's imagination, with only his rage as a clue: "I understood instantly how a father might destroy his entire family and himself. I couldn't look at the woman."

(Lee and Gifford, *Saroyan, A Biography*, pp. 153–155)

Paul Gitlin (Saroyan's lawyer, interviewed):

* * *

I remember Bill being very upset about Carol. She was living near the Hampton House then. She was dating. He was suspicious because, after all, she was the mother of his children.

We had her followed. The whole purpose of that was to show she was an unfit mother. That was his idea, to get the kids back. He was capable of these temper tantrums that would last for years. He wasn't doing anything much except blowing his own legal situation. . . .

It was one of these erratic moments in his life.

She lied to him, the fact that she's Jewish. I said, "I'm Jewish, too."

"That's beside the point, she lied to me."

I even, out of sheer curiosity, said, "Why are you so mad about this?" And he started giving this whole story. But I resented the fact—I told him I personally resented the fact that it smelled of anti-Semitism.

"Oh, *no*: she just *lied*."

I said, "Would you have married her anyway?"

He said, "Sure."

(*Saroyan, A Biography*, pp. 243–244)

MARY McCARTHY   (1912–1989)

U.S. novelist, essayist, critic; author of The Group.

[Upon meeting a colonel on a train in March, 1953, who accuses Harvard of being Communist and mocks Jews]

. . . I had always scoffed at the notion of liberals "living in fear" of political demagoguery in America, but now I had to admit that if I was not fearful, I was at least uncomfortable in the supposition that anybody, anybody whatever, could think of me, precious me, as a Communist. A remoter possibility was, of course, that back there my departure was being ascribed to Jewishness, and this too annoyed me. I am in fact a quarter Jewish, and though I did not "hate" the idea of being taken for a Jew, I did not precisely like it, particularly under these circumstances. I wished it to be clear that I had left the club car for intellectual and principled reasons; I wanted those men to know that it was not I, but my principles, that had been offended. To let them conjecture that I had left because I was Jewish would imply that only a Jew could be affronted by an anti-Semitic outburst; a terrible idea. Aside from anything else, it voiced the whole concept of transcendence, which was very close to my heart, the concept that man imore than his circumstances, more even than himself. . . . For the colonel, anti-Semitism was simply an aspect of urbanity, like a knowledge of hotels or women. . . .

. . . He was waiting for me as I descended the car steps. "Aren'ts you coming to lunch with me?" he called out and moved up to take my elbow. I began to tremble with audacity. "No," I said firmly, picking up my suitcase. . . . I took a deep breath. "I have to tell you. I think you should be *ashamed* of yourself, Colonel, for what you said in the club car." The colonel stared: I mechanically waved for a redcap, who took my bag and coat and went off. The colonel and I stood facing each other on the emptying platform. "What do you mean?" he inquired in a low, almost clandestine tone. "Those anti-Semitic remarks," I muttered, resolutely. "You ought to be *ashamed*." The colonel gave a quick, relieved laugh. "Oh, come now," he protested. "I'm sorry," I said. "I can't have lunch with anybody who feels that way about the Jews." The colonel put down his attache case and scratched the back of his lean neck. "Oh, come now," he repeated, with a look of amusement. "You're not Jewish, are you?" "No," I said quickly. "Well then . . ." said the colonel, spreading his hands in a gesture of bafflement. I saw that he was truly surprised and slightly hurt by my criticism, and this made me feel wretchedly embarrassed and even apologetic, on my side, as though I had called attention to some physical defect in him, of which he himself was unconscious. "But I might have been," I stammered. "You had no way of knowing. You oughtn't to talk like that." I recognized, too late, that I was strangely reducing the whole matter to a question of etiquette: "Don't start anti-Semitic talk before making sure there are no Jews present." "Oh, hell," said the colonel easily. "I can tell a Jew." "No, you can't," I retorted, thinking of my Jewish grandmother, for by Nazi criteria I was Jewish. "Of course I can," he insisted. "So can you. . . ."

". . . Hell," he conceded. "You've got me wrong. I've nothing against the Jews. Back there in the club car, I was just stating a simple fact: you won't find an Irishman sounding off for the Commies. You can't deny that, can you?"

"There *have* been Irishmen associated with the Communist party," I said suddenly, when the drinks came. "I can think of two." "Oh, hell," said the colonel, "every race and nation has its traitors. What I mean is, you won't find them in numbers. You've got to admit the Communists in this country are ninety per cent Jewish." "But the Jews in this country aren't ninety per cent Communist," I retorted.

As he stirred his drink, I began to try to show him the reasons why the Communist movement in America had attracted such a large number, relatively, of Jews: how the Communists still capitalized on a

Jewish fear of fascism; how many Jews had become, after Buchenwald, traumatized by this fear. . . .

But the colonel was scarcely listening. An impatient frown rested on his jaunty features. "I don't get it," he said slowly. "Why should you be for them, with a name like yours?" "I'm *not* for the Communists," I cried. "I'm just trying to explain to you—" "For the Jews," the colonel interrupted, irritable now himself. "I've heard of such people but I never met one before." "I'm not 'for' them," I protested. "You don't understand. I'm not for *any* race or nation. I'm against those who are against them." This word, *them*, with a sort of slurring circle drawn round it, was beginning to sound ugly to me. Automatically, in arguing with him, I seemed to have slipped into the colonel's style of thought. It occurred to me that defense of the Jews could be a subtle and safe form of anti-Semitism, an exercise of patronage: as a rational Gentile, one could feel superior both to the Jews and the anti-Semites. There could be no doubt that the Jewish question evoked a curious stealthy lust or concupiscence. I could feel it now vibrating between us over the dark table. If I had been a good person, I should unquestionably have got up and left. . . .

But the colonel's hide was tough. "You've got me wrong," he reiterated, with an almost plaintive laugh. "I don't dislike the Jews. I've got a lot of Jewish friends. Among themselves, they think just as I do, mark my words. I tell you what it is," he added ruminatively, with a thoughtful prod of his muddler, "I draw a distinction between a kike and a Jew." I groaned. "Colonel, I've never heard an anti-Semite who didn't draw that distinction. You know what Otto Kahn said? 'A kike is a Jewish gentleman who has just left the room.' " The colonel did not laugh. "I don't hold it against some of them," he persisted, in a tone of pensive justice. "It's not their fault if they were born that way. That's what I tell them, and they respect me for my honesty. I've had a lot of discussions; in procurement, you have to do business with them, and the Jews are the first to admit that you'll find more chiselers among their race than among the rest of mankind." "It's not a race," I interjected wearily, but the colonel pressed on. . . .

"Look," I said, "you may be dealing with an industry where the Jewish manufacturers are the most recent comers and feel they have to cut corners to compete with the established firms. I've heard that said about Jewish cattle-dealers, who are supposed to be extra sharp. But what I think, really, is that you notice it when a Jewish firm fails to meet an agreement and don't notice it if it's a Yankee." "Hah," said the colonel. . . .

A dispirited silence followed. I was not one of those liberals who believed that the Jews, alone among peoples, possessed no character-istics whatever of a distinguishing nature—this would mean they had no history and no culture, a charge which should be leveled against them only by an anti-Semite. Certainly, types of Jews could be noted and patterns of Jewish thought and feeling: Jewish humor, Jewish rationality, and so on, not that every Jew reflected every attribute of Jewish life or history. But somehow, with the colonel, I dared not concede that there was such a thing as a Jew: I saw the sad meaning of the assertion that a Jew was a person whom other people thought was Jewish.

Hopeless, however, to convey this to the colonel. The desolate truth was that the colonel was extremely stupid, and it came to me, as we sat there, glumly ordering lunch, that for extremely stupid people anti-Semitism was a form of intellectuality, the sole form of intellec-tuality of which they were capable. It represented, in a rudimentary way, the ability to make categories, to generalize. Hence a thing I had noted before but never understood: the fact that anti-Semitic state-ments were generally delivered in an atmosphere of profundity. Fur-rowed brows attended these speculative distinctions between a kike and a Jew, these little empirical laws that you can't know one without knowing them all. To arrive, indeed, at the idea of a Jew was, for these groping minds, an exercise in Platonic thought, a discovery of essence, and to be able to add the great corollary, "Some of my best friends are Jews," was to find the philosopher's cleft between essence and existence. From this, it would seem, followed the querulous obstinacy with which the anti-Semite clung to his concept; to be deprived of this intellectual tool by missionaries of tolerance would be, for persons like the colonel, the equivalent of Western man's losing the syllogism: a lapse into an-imal darkness. In the club car, we had just witnessed an example: the colonel with his anti-Semitic observation had come to the mute young man like the paraclete, bearing the gift of tongues. . . .

. . . I leaned forward. "You know, Colonel," I said quickly, "anti-Semitism is contrary to the Church's teaching. God will make you do penance for hating the Jews. Ask your priest; he'll tell you I'm right. You'll have a long spell in Purgatory, if you don't rid yourself of this sin. It's a deliberate violation of Christ's commandment, 'Love thy neighbor.' The Church holds that the Jews have a sacred place in God's design. Mary was a Jew and Christ was a Jew. The Jews are under God's special protection. The Church teaches that the millenium can't come until the conversion of the Jews; therefore, the Jews must be preserved that the Divine Will may be accomplished. Woe to them that harm them, for they controvert God's Will!" In the course of speaking, I had swept myself away with the solemnity of the doctrine. The Great Reconciliation between God and His chosen people, as envisioned by the Evangelist, had for me at that moment a piercing, majestic beauty, like some awesome Tintoretto. I saw a noble spectacle of blue sky, thronged with grey clouds, and a vast white desert, across which God and Israel advanced to meet each other, while below in hell the demons of disunion shrieked and gnashed their teeth.

"Hell," said the colonel jovially, "I don't believe in all that. I lost my faith when I was a kid. I saw that all this God stuff was a lot of bushwa."

. . . We both glanced at our watches. "See you some time," he called. "What's your married name?" "Broadwater," I called back. The whistle blew again. "Brodwater?" shouted the colonel, with a dazed look of unbelief and growing enlightenment; he was not the first person to hear it as a Jewish name, on the model of Goldwater. "B-r-o-a-d," I began, automatically, but then I stopped. I disdained to spell it out for him; the victory was his. "One of the chosen, eh?" his brief grimace seemed to commiserate. . . .

(M. McCarthy, "Artists in Uniform," in *On the Contrary*, pp. 61–74)

WILLIAM S. BURROUGHS   *(1914–   )*

U.S. writer; author of Naked Lunch, The Soft Machine

By this time, Burroughs had finished the novel he had been working on since 1974, *Cities of the Red Night*, and had sent a typescript to Brion Gysin to look at. Brion urged him to delete a couple of phrases that he felt would be construed as anti-Semitic, to which Burroughs replied: "As regards the Jew jokes . . . there is no basis to assume that opinions expressed by a writer's characters are the opinions of the writer. You have a Nazi character, he is going to talk like a Nazi. . . . Look at my other books—*Naked Lunch*: 'All a Jew wants to do is diddle a Christian girl.' *Nova Express*: 'Take your ovens with you and pay

Hitler on the way out. Nearly got the place hot enough for you Jews, didn't he?' *Exterminator!*: 'And I want to say this to followers of the Jewish religion. We like nice Jews with Jew jokes so watch yourself Jewboy or we'll cut the rest of it off.' In *Cities*, Hitler Jugend boys sing 'And the dance that they do is enough to kill a Jew.' Well, what would one expect from Hitler Jugend boys?"

Burroughs told Brion that he had full confidence in his editor. . . . Anyway, he wasn't writing for the Book-of-the-Month ladies and would lose his present readers if he tried. He was not going to be a commercial writer, he was trying to be the best writer. He wasn't going to change a scene to sell books or get a review in *The New Yorker*. Concession was the thin edge of a very thick wedge. At the same time, he assured Brion, he wasn't an anti-Semite at all. "With Reagan and these born-again assholes putting in their two cents' worth," he wrote, "us minorities have to stick together." He recalled his embarrassment when someone had said about *The New Yorker*, "Smart bunch of kids run that mag. Went to school with 'em." It took him awhile to register that the person had said "yids," not kids. . . .

> (T. Morgan, *Literary Outlaw: The Life and Times of*
> *William S. Burroughs*, pp. 554–555)

ORSON WELLES   *(1915–1986)*

U.S. filmmaker and actor; starred in Citizen Kane,
The Magnificent Ambersons

In an editorial, "Race Hate Must Be Outlawed" (July 1944), he . . . pointed out that the war was being fought against the very causes of racial hatred and that the fight was against the denial of man's equal dignity. He made no direct mention of the Holocaust, which had already been revealed by *The New Republic*, yet the implication was clearly there.

> Race hate isn't human nature; race hate is the abandonment of human nature . . . the Indian is on our conscience, the Negro is on our conscience, the Chinese and the Mexican American are on our conscience. The Jew is on the conscience of Europe, but our neglect gives us communion in that guilt, so that their dance [sic] is even here the lunatic spectre of anti-Semitism. This is [to be] deplored; it must be fought, and the fight must be won.

These were brave if ill-written words indeed at a time when many people in America were still avoiding the Jewish issue and few were prepared to consider their own guilt, a time of moral righteousness in which the conquest of Germany and Japan was seen as the act of a clean and guiltless America. If Welles's intention was to ruffle feathers in both the Democratic and the Republican parties, he achieved his purpose.

(Higham, *Orson Welles*, p. 216)

CARSON McCULLERS　*(1917–1967)*

U.S. writer; author of The Heart Is a Lonely Hunter

More immediately unsettling to Carson than her father's health, however, was an anonymous letter which came in the mail the morning after her arrival home. There were several fan letters relative to *The Ballad of the Sad Cafe* and on the whole her readers seemed to like it. But among the batch was one letter, a single paragraph, unsigned except for the phrase "An American". . . . It read: "To the distinguished young writer whose story I started to read but at the bottom of the second page you poke fun at the Jew. . . . Why don't you leave race alone. . . . Will certainly pan Harper's Bazaar until you and your kind learn to be human like the Jews are."

The reference to which the letter writer took offense read as follows:

At last one of the twins said: "I'll be damned if he [the hunchback] ain't a regular Morris Finestein."

Everyone nodded and agreed, for that is an expression having a certain special meaning. But the hunchback cried louder because he could not know what they were talking about. Morris Finestein was a person who had lived in the town years before. He was only a quick, skipping little Jew who cried if you called him Christkiller, and ate light bread and canned salmon every day. A calamity had come over him and he had moved away to Society City. But since then if a man were prissy in any way, or if a man ever wept, he was known as a Morris Finestein.

Carson found the accusation incredible, and since it was not signed, she was frustrated because she could not respond to it directly.

Instead, her whole being was thrown out of kilter. She wrote many frantic letters seeking advice. First she wrote to Newton Arvin, reminding him that he had read the manuscript and had seen no cause for offense. She told him that Philip Rahv, a Russian-American Jew, had read it the preceding summer, too, and had found nothing objectionable. Carson wrote next to Alfred Kazin, also Jewish, to learn his response. Certainly no one hated prejudice and cruelty any more than she did, Carson insisted, but she wondered if one who did not know her and saw the reference to the Jew might rightfully find it offensive. It was agonizing for her to think that anyone could have misunderstood her story. She had ridiculed or made light of not only the Jew, but everyone else in the novel as well. She explained in each letter that the book was her fairy tale—all in the manner of satire and the style of that particular work. The whole story was laid against a background of neglect, narrowness, meanness, and barbarity, but the sadness and grief in the tale were due to her awareness of the cruelty inherent in everyone. Carson sent the anonymous letter to Kazin and asked him to read it and see what he thought, then to keep it so that she herself would not have to see it again. To Kazin, "it was a tempest in a teapot," and he wrote back reassuringly for her to ignore it.

In the meantime, Carson prepared in her defense an "Open Letter" which she planned to ask Carmel Snow and Mary Lou Aswell to run in the December issue of *Harper's Bazaar*. In it, she explained that when one is insensitive to irony or misunderstands it, it is difficult for the author to rationalize the point intended. *The Ballad of the Sad Cafe* was a light tale, told in a jesting manner, but beneath its simple narrowness were purposeful and bitter implications. The Jew, said Carson, was treated in the traditional and light way that she handled all of her characters. There was no intent to poke fun at the Jewish people. It was a tale of menacing tragedy indicting not the Jew, but the society which allowed such degradations to occur. For Carson to have to defend her work, when those who had read her writings knew of her loathing for the Fascist elements in her country and her hatred of discrimination against any minority group—especially the undemocratic principles which she felt extant in her southern region—all seemed to Carson a grotesque joke. Yet she could not rest so long as anyone misunderstood her.

Carson's "Open Letter" was a brilliant one, but it remained unpublished. Mary Lou Aswell, who had succeeded George Davis as literary editor of *Harper's Bazaar*, wanted to run it, but the Hearst office refused permission. . . . Carson was finally reconciled to believe that there was no reason to defend what had never occurred to anyone else, especially to anyone who understood her intent in the story; yet during her agonizing turmoil, she wrote five letters to Alfred Kazin, three to Diamond, four to Arvin, and other assorted missives relative to the matter to George Davis, Mary Lou Aswell, and to countless others, begging each one to please get in touch with someone else who might also be able to advise her, pleading for a telephone call or wire advising her as to how he felt. In the meantime, she mailed copies of her "Open Letter" to Kazin, to Diamond, and to the magazine. For a week Carson lived in an eerie world, unable to believe that this strange accusation had actually happened to her. It had challenged her whole sense of good and evil and was alien to her very soul. She told Kazin that it was as though one of her favorite stories by Chekhov, "Rothschild's Fiddle," had been interpreted as an anti-Semitic story, or that a reader of "A Modest Proposal" had accused Swift of actually cooking the babies. Soon she had telegrams from Kazin, *Harper's Bazaar*, and George Davis and phone calls from Diamond and Arvin. She had blown the whole affair out of proportion, they assured her, and she must forget it. It was almost the end of August before Carson could think about writing again, but finally, with rest and reassurance from her friends, she returned to her typewriter.

(Carr, *The Lonely Hunter*, pp. 236–238)

FRANKLIN H. LITTELL   (1917–   )

U.S. Protestant theologian and educator

It has become popular among some churchmen and general historians, to deal with Nazism as a "pagan" irruption—essentially atavistic, tribal, anti-Christian. There is much to be said for the argument. . . . The trouble with this line of argument [however] is that it relieves the Christians and their leaders of their guilt for what happened. . . . If dthe churches had used the means of spiritual government at their disposal to call the Nazi leaders to repentance, to return to minimal Christian standards, if the Nazi elite had been excommunicated for failure to respond, then today the churches could say truthfully, "They were pagans. They left our fellowship in the covenant. They were not of us." But the churches did not do this. Instead they retained in their membership and accorded signal honors to traitors to human liberty, mass murderers, apostate Christians. Adolf Hitler died a Roman Catholic, and an annual mass is celebrated in his memory in Madrid. Hermann Goering died a Lutheran. We Christians cannot come back today and claim no responsibility for what they did in the name of law and order and anti-Bolshevism, claiming to protect "religion."

(Littell, The Crucifixion of the Jews, pp. 47–48)

FLANNERY O'CONNOR *(1925–1964)*

U.S. short-story writer

. . . I'll be interested in the symposium on "The Jew in American Culture." The declaration on the Jews and on religious liberty seems to have got sidetracked at the [Vatican] council. I hope they manage to get it going again. . . .

(Fitzgerald, Letters of Flannery O'Connor – The Habit of Being, pp. 550–551)

THE AMERICAN SPECTATOR

A Literary Newspaper (September, 1933)

EDITORIAL CONFERENCE
(With Wine)

Theodore Dreiser
[American novelist, 1871–1945]
Well, to begin with, I offer that the world's quarrel with the Jew is not that he is inferior, but that he is superior. He is uniformly altogether too successful in the professions, as well as in science,

philosophy, education, trade, finance, religious theory, musician-
ship—also musical composition, painting, poetry, and the other arts.

George Jean Nathan
[American editor and critic, 1882–1958]
Poetry! Nonsense! In the entire history of literature since the
time of Christ, there has been but one first-rate Jewish poet, Heine.

Dreiser
You are forgetting that compendium not only of religious but of
pure poetry—the Old Testament—its Song of Songs, its Psalms,
Ecclesiastes, the Book of Job, the poetic flights of Isaiah and Jeremiah.
Weren't they written by Jews?

Eugene O'Neill
[American playwright, 1888–1953]
The Bible, as we know it, was written by a coterie of Church of
England literary gents under King James. But for them, its influence
would be nil.

Dreiser
. . . From the period that produced the Old Testament on, the
Jews were not only dispersed, but suppressed. Social, and hence to a
degree, artistic expression were denied them for nearly 2000 years.
Ended as a nation by Rome, they proceeded to wander. They were
dispersed, and worse, frustrated by Christianity. But now turn to the
Jew since the bans were lifted and he has been allowed to step into the
arena of social, political, and intellectual activity. As I see it, in this
period—which cannot be much over 200 years . . . how do you explain
the astounding development of a race that has, according to your
assertions, small claim to art, science, or what have you? In 200 years
we have had Jewish composers, musicians, painters, philosophers,
statesmen, and scientists: Schumann, Schlegel, Marx, Bloch, Satie,
Rodin, Epstein, Lewisohn, Loeb, Freud, Feuchtwanger, Disraeli, Ca-
han, Einstein, Schubert, etc., etc.

Nathan
Painters and composers? Name one really first-rate Jewish
painter! Composers? Meyerbeer and Mendelssohn, second-raters,—
who else, save third-raters like Schoenberg? . . .

Dreiser

The Jews claim many more, and perhaps justly.

Nathan

The reason for this emergence of the Jews that you speak of is due to what seems to me a very simple thing. For 2000 years the members of the other faiths have been dissipating their energies hating the Jews so violently and indignantly that they have exhausted themselves. In all this time, the Jews have sat back very quietly and humorously and have done their job.

Dreiser

My real quarrel with the Jew is not that he is inefficient or ignorant or even unaesthetic. It is that he is really too clever and too dynamic in his personal and racial attack on all other types of persons and races. Some races, like some individuals in athletics, and some horses in races, must justly carry handicaps. The Jew, to me, particularly in the realm of commerce and some practical professions, wherein shrewdness rather than any creative labor is the chief issue, might well be compelled to accept a handicap—limitation as to his numbers in given lines. Thus 100,000 Jewish lawyers might be reduced to ten and the remainder made to do farming. . . . He finds himself scattered in all countries, but still retaining all of his racial if not national characteristics, and desiring, first and foremost, as he should, to racially further the Jew. Now it may be the genius of the Jew to inspire, to advance, and even, if given time enough, to control the world, but that wouldn't be comfortable or pleasant for the rest of the races and nations. Who would want a whole world of English, of Irish, of Chinese, or of Negroes? Not even the Jews would want that for themselves. But we could and would admire and rejoice in a distinguished and powerful Jewish nation, leading the world if it pleased.

O'Neill

[A territory for the Jews could be] one place in Africa, just north of British South Africa—a semi-temperate nation as large as the United States and extending from the Atlantic to the Indian Ocean. Politically and territorially, as things stand today, I am sure it could be arranged.

Dreiser

. . . I would ask the Jew with all his ability and his wealth and admiration of power, with all the genius he shows when he enters an alien land and becomes a powerful factor in its welfare, or its domination, I would ask him, I say, personally to consider whether in just plain fairness to nations that want to be themselves, that don't care to be dominated by a church or race or theory of life, and are not, in short, as clever as he is, why he shouldn't step up before the peoples of the world and ask for just such a territory in which to develop a nation of his own and with which he could deal on the basis of his own genius in all lines. With the Jews nationally so placed, we could deal, just as they could deal with every other nation in the world. And by degrees all should benefit from their very great ability to organize and construct. What I cannot understand is their present objection to doing so. But this may be the result of their scattering in historic times, and it may, for all we know, be presently overcome by the Jew himself.

O'Neill

Such, at least, appears to be the opinion of Mr. Ludwig Lewisohn, who, if I read him aright, is anxious for just such a Jewish land and nation.

Dreiser

Whatever the outcome, it should not be an insupportable hardship for the Jews to nationalize themselves, and it should not, I hope, involve bloodshed or enormous cruelty. If I had any way to influence the Jews, it would be in the direction of their taking the matter in their own hands, and so solving their own problems, which certainly they have the genius to do.

Nathan

You visualize, Dreiser, one of the most extensive territories in the world inhabited and run by Jews. You believe that they would, by their genius, presently establish themselves as one of the most successful national enterprises in the present world. Within two years, I contend, the dominating element of that population would have joined the Episcopalian Church.

Dreiser

And, now, gentlemen, a cool drink.

(*The American Spectator*, September 1933)

13

The Nazi Era in Europe

ADOLF HITLER   *(1889–1945)*

Nazi leader of Germany, 1933–1945

... Not until my fourteenth or fifteenth year did I begin to come across the word "Jew," with any frequency, partly in connection with political discussions. This filled me with a mild distaste, and I could not rid myself of an unpleasant feeling that always came over me whenever religious quarrels occurred in my presence.

At that time I did not think anything else of the question.

There were few Jews in Linz. In the course of the centuries their outward appearance had become Europeanized and had taken on a human look; in fact, I even took them for Germans. The absurdity of this idea did not dawn on me because I saw no distinguishing feature but the strange religion. The fact that they had, as I believed, been persecuted on this account sometimes almost turned my distaste at unfavorable remarks about them into horror.

Thus far I did not so much as suspect the existence of an organized opposition to the Jews.

Then I came to Vienna.

Preoccupied by the abundance of my impressions in the architectural field, oppressed by the hardship of my own lot, I gained at first no insight into the inner stratification of the people in this gigantic city. Notwithstanding that Vienna in those days counted nearly two hundred thousand Jews among its two million inhabitants, I did not see them. In the first few weeks my eyes and my senses were not equal to the flood of values and ideas. Not until calm gradually returned and the agitated picture began to clear did I look around me more carefully in my new world, and then among other things I encountered the Jewish question.

I cannot maintain that the way in which I became acquainted with them struck me as particularly pleasant. For the Jew was still characterized for me by nothing but his religion, and therefore, on grounds of human tolerance, I maintained my rejection of religious attacks in this case as in others. Consequently, the tone, particularly that of the Viennese anti-Semitic press, seemed to me unworthy of the cultural tradition of a great nation. I was oppressed by the memory of certain occurrences in the Middle Ages, which I should not have liked to see repeated. . . .

I was not in agreement with the sharp anti-Semitic tone, but from time to time I read arguments which gave me some food for thought. . . .

My views with regard to anti-Semitism thus succumbed to the passage of time, and this was my greatest transformation of all.

It cost me the greatest inner soul struggles, and only after months of battle between my reason and my sentiments did my reason begin to emerge victorious. Two years later, my sentiment had followed my reason, and from then on became its most loyal guardian and sentinel. . . .

Once, as I was strolling through the Inner City, I suddenly encountered an apparition in a black caftan and black hair locks. Is this a Jew? was my first thought.

For, to be sure, they had not looked like that in Linz. I observed the man furtively and cautiously, but the longer I stared at this foreign face, scrutinizing feature for feature, the more my first question assumed a new form:

Is this a German?

. . . since I had begun to concern myself with this question and to take cognizance of the Jews, Vienna appeared to me in a different light than before. Wherever I went, I began to see Jews, and the more I saw, the more sharply they became distinguished in my eyes from the rest of humanity. Particularly the Inner City and the districts north of the Danube Canal swarmed with a people which even outwardly had lost all resemblance to Germans.

And whatever doubts I may still have nourished were finally dispelled by the attitude of a portion of the Jews themselves.

Among them there was a great movement, quite extensive in Vienna, which came out sharply in confirmation of the national character of the Jews: this was the *Zionists*.

. . . By their very exterior you could tell that these were no lovers of water, and, to your distress, you often knew it with your eyes closed. Later I often grew sick to my stomach from the smell of these caftan-wearers. Added to this, there was their unclean dress and their generally unheroic appearance.

All this could scarcely be called very attractive; but it became positively repulsive when, in addition to their physical uncleanliness, you discovered the moral stains on this "chosen people."

In a short time I was made more thoughtful than ever by my slowly rising insight into the type of activity carried on by the Jews in certain fields.

Was there any form of filth or profligacy, particularly in cultural life, without at least one Jew involved in it?

If you cut even cautiously into such an abscess, you found, like a maggot in a rotting body, often dazzled by the sudden light – a kike!

What had to be reckoned heavily against the Jews in my eyes was when I became acquainted with their activity in the press, art, literature, and the theater. All the unctuous reassurances helped little or nothing. It sufficed to look at a billboard, to study the names of the men behind the horrible trash they advertised, to make you hard for a long time to come. This was pestilence, spiritual pestilence, worse than the Black Death of olden times, and the people were being infected with it! It goes without saying that the lower the intellectual level of one of these art manufacturers, the more unlimited his fertility will be, and the scoundrel ends up like a garbage separator, splashing his filth in the face of humanity. And bear in mind that there is no limit to their number; bear in mind that for one Goethe Nature easily can foist on the world ten thousand of these scribblers who poison men's souls like germ-carriers of the worst sort, on their fellow men.

It was terrible, but not to be overlooked, that precisely the Jew, in tremendous numbers, seemed chosen by Nature for this shameful calling.

Is this why the Jews are called the "chosen people"? . . .

The fact that nine tenths of all literary filth, artistic trash, and theatrical idiocy can be set to the account of a people, constituting hardly one hundredth of all the country's inhabitants, could simply not be talked away; it was the plain truth.

And I now began to examine my beloved "world press" from this point of view.

And the deeper I probed, the more the object of my former admiration shriveled. The style became more and more unbearable; I could not help rejecting the content as inwardly shallow and banal; the objectivity of exposition now seemed to me more akin to lies than honest truth; and the writers were – Jews. . . .

But then a flame flared up within me. I no longer avoided discussion of the Jewish question; no, now I sought it. And when I learned to look for the Jew in all branches of cultural and artistic life in its various manifestations, I suddenly encountered him in a place where I would least have expected to find him.

When I recognized the Jew as the leader of the Social Democracy, the scales dropped from my eyes. A long soul struggle had reached its conclusion. . . .

. . . One thing had grown clear to me: the party with whose petty representatives I had been carrying on the most violent struggle for months was, as to leadership, almost exclusively in the hands of a foreign people for, to my deep and joyful satisfaction, I had at last come to the conclusion that the Jew was no German.

Only now did I become thoroughly acquainted with the seducer of our people. . . .

I didn't know what to be more amazed at: the agility of their tongues or their virtuosity at lying.

Gradually I began to hate them. . . .

For me this was the time of the greatest spiritual upheaval I have ever had to go through.

I had ceased to be a weak-kneed cosmopolitan and become an anti-Semite. . . .

If, with the help of his Marxist creed, the Jew is victorious over the other peoples of the world, his crown will be the funeral wreath of humanity and this planet will, as it did thousands of years ago, move through the ether devoid of men.

Eternal Nature inexorably avenges the infringement of her commands.

Hence today I believe that I am acting in accordance with the will of the Almighty Creator: *by defending myself against the Jew, I am fighting for the work of the Lord.*

(From *Mein Kampf*, trans. Ralph Manheim, pp. 51–65)

* * *

The only reference to Zionism in *Mein Kampf*:

. . . while Zionism tries to make the other part of the world believe that the national self-consciousness of the Jew finds satisfaction in the creation of a Palestinian State the Jews again most slyly dupe the stupid *goiim*. They have no thought of building up a Jewish State in Palestine, so that they can inhabit it, but they only want a central organization of their international world cheating, endowed with prerogatives, withdrawn from the seizure of others; a refuge for convicted rascals and a high school for future rogues.

("Nation and Race" in *Mein Kampf*, ch. II)

* * *

My prophecy shall be fulfilled that this war will not destroy Aryan humanity but it will exterminate the Jew. Whatever the battle may bring in its course or however long it may last, that will be its final course.

(*Keesings Archiv der Gegenwart*, 1940, p. 5409)

* * *

Spoken in mid-October 1941:

But the first thing, above all, is to get rid of the Jews. Without that, it will be useless to clean the Augean stables. . . . From the rostrum of the Reichstag, I prophesied to Jewry that, in the event of war's proving inevitable, the Jew would disappear from Europe. That race of criminals has on its conscience the two million dead of the First World War, and now already hundreds and thousands more. Let nobody tell me that all the same we can't park them in the marshy parts of Russia! Who's worrying about our troops? It's not a bad idea, by the way, that public rumor attributes to us a plan to exterminate the Jews. Terror is a salutary thing.

(*Hitler's Secret Conversations*, pp. 91, 108–109, 111)

* * *

In a speech at the Berlin Sports Palace, 30 September 1942

. . . if Jewry should plot another world war in order to exterminate the Aryan peoples of Europe, it would not be the Aryan peoples who would be exterminated, but Jewry. . . .

At one time the Jews of Germany laughed about my prophecies. I do not know whether they are still laughing or whether they have already lost all desire to laugh. But right now I can only repeat: they will stop laughing everywhere, and I shall be right also in that prophecy.

Hitler to Himmler, 19 June 1943:

For us, this has been an essential process of disinfection, which we have prosecuted to its ultimate limit and without which we should ourselves have been asphyxiated and destroyed. On the eve of the war, I gave them one final warning. I told them that, if they precipitated another war, they would not be spared and that I would exterminate the vermin throughout Europe, and this time once and for all. To this warning they retorted with a declaration of war and affirmed that wherever in the world there was a Jew, there, too, was an implacable enemy of National Socialist Germany. Well, we have lanced the Jewish abscess; and the world of the future will be eternally grateful to us.

(Krausnick, *Anatomy of the SS State*, p. 123)

* * *

In a speech on the 9th anniversary of National
Socialism's rise to power

I do not even want to speak of the Jews. They are simply our old enemies, their plans have suffered shipwreck through us, and they rightly hate us, just as we hate them. We realize that this era can only end either in the wiping out of the Germanic nations, or by the disappearance of Jewry from Europe. For the first time, it will not be the others who will bleed to death, but for the first time the genuine ancient Jewish law, 'an eye for an eye, a tooth for a tooth,' is being applied. The more this struggle spreads, the more anti-Semitism will spread — and world Jewry may rely on this. It will find nourishment in every prison camp, it will find nourishment in every family which is being enlightened as to why it is being called upon to make such sacrifices, and the hour will come when the worst enemy in the world will have finished his part for at least a thousand years to come.

(Toland, *Adolph Hitler*, pp. 705–706)

* * *

Hitler's last will:

Above all, I enjoin the leaders of the nation and those under them to uphold the racial laws to their full extent and to oppose mercilessly the universal poisoner of all peoples, International Jewry.

(*Adolph Hitler*, pp. 884–885)

CANONICAL LAW AND ANTI-JEWISH MEASURES

CANONICAL LAW	NAZI MEASURE
Prohibition of intermarriage and of sexual intercourse between Christians and Jews, Synod of Elvira, 306	Law for the Protection of German Blood and Honor, September 15, 1935 (RGB1 I, 1146.)
Jews and Christians not permitted to eat together, Synod of Elvira, 306	Jews barred from dining cars (Transport Minister to Interior Minister, December 30, 1939, Document NG-3995.)
Jews not allowed to hold public office, Synod of Clermont, 535	Law for the Re-establishment of the Professional Civil Service, April 7, 1933 (RGB1 I, 175.)
Jews not allowed to employ Christian servants or possess Christian slaves, 3d Synod of Orleans, 538	Law for the Protection of German Blood and Honor, September 15, 1935 (RGB1 I, 1146.)
Jews not permitted to show themselves in the streets during Passion Week, 3d Synod of Orleans, 538	Decree authorizing local authorities to bar Jews from the streets on certain days (i.e., Nazi holidays), December 3, 1938 (RGB1 I, 1676.)
Burning of the Talmud and other books, 12th Synod of Toledo, 681	Book burnings in Nazi Germany
Christians not permitted to patronize Jewish doctors, Trulanic Synod, 692	Decree of July 25, 1938 (RGB1 I, 969.)
Christians not permitted to live in Jewish homes, Synod of Narbonne, 1050	Directive by Göring providing for concentration of Jews in houses, December 28, 1938 (Borman to Rosenberg, January 17, 1939, PS-69.)[1]
Jews obliged to pay taxes for support of the Church to the same extent as Christians, Synod of Gerona, 1078	The "Sozialausgleichsabgabe" which provided that Jews pay a special income tax in lieu of donations for Party purposes imposed on Nazis, December 24, 1940 (RGB1 I, 1666.)
Prohibition of Sunday work, Synod of Szabolcs, 1092	
Jews not permitted to be plaintiffs, or witnesses against Christians in the Courts, 3d Lateran Council, 1179, Canon 26	Proposal by the Party Chancellery that Jews not be permitted to institute civil suits, September 9, 1942 (Bormann to Justice Ministry, September 9, 1942, NG-151.)

Table is from Raoul Hilberg, *The Destruction of the European Jews.*

[1]This refers to separate housing for Jews, or ghettoization.

CANONICAL LAW	NAZI MEASURE
Jews not permitted to withhold inheritance from descendants who had accepted Christianity, 3d Lateran Council, 1179, Canon 26	Decree empowering the Justice Ministry to void wills offending the "sound judgment of the people," July 31, 1938 (RGB1 I, 937.)
The marking of Jewish clothes with a badge, 4th Lateran Council, 1215, Canon 68 (Copied from the legislation by Caliph Omar II [634–44], who had decreed that Christians wear blue belts and Jews, yellow belts.)	Decree of September 1, 1941 (RGB1 I, 547.)
Construction of new synagogues prohibited, Council of Oxford, 1222	Destruction of synagogues in entire Reich, November 10, 1938 (Heydrich to Göring, November 11, 1938, PS-3058.)
Christians not permitted to attend Jewish ceremonies, Synod of Vienna, 1267	Friendly relations with Jews prohibited, October 24, 1941 (Gestapo directive, L-15.)
Jews not permitted to dispute with simple Christian people about the tenets of the Catholic religion, Synod of Vienna, 1267	
Compulsory ghettos, Synod of Breslau, 1267	Order by Heydrich, September 21, 1939 (PS-3363.)
Christians not permitted to sell or rent real estate to Jews, Synod of Ofen, 1279	Decree providing for compulsory sale of Jewish real estate, December 3, 1938 (RGB1 I, 1709.)
Adoption by a Christian of the Jewish religion or return by a baptized Jew to the Jewish religion defined as a heresy, Synod of Mainz, 1310	Adoption by a Christian of the Jewish religion places him in jeopardy of being treated as a Jew, Decision by Oberlandesgericht Königsberg, 4th Zivilsenat, June 26, 1942 (*Die Judenfrage* [*Vertrauliche Beilage*], November 1, 1942, pp. 82–83.)
Sale or transfer of Church articles to Jews prohibited, Synod of Lavour, 1368	
Jews not permitted to act as agents in the conclusion of contracts between Christians, especially marriage contracts, Council of Basel, 1434, Sessio XIX	Decree of July 6, 1938, providing for liquidation of Jewish real estate agencies, brokerage agencies, and marriage agencies catering to non-Jews (RGB1 I, 823.)
Jews not permitted to obtain academic degrees, Council of Basel, 1434, Sessio XIX	Law against overcrowding of German schools and universities, April 25, 1933 (RGB1 I, 225.)

NUREMBERG LAWS

Laws passed by the Nazis in the mid-1930s

Article II. A citizen of the Reich is only that subject who is of German or kindred blood and who through his conduct, shows that he is both desirous and fit to serve faithfully the German people and the Reich. . . .

(Reich Citizenship Law of 15 September 1935)

* * *

Article IV. A Jew cannot be a citizen of the Reich. He cannot exercise the right to vote; he cannot occupy public office.

Article V. A Jew is anyone who is descended from at least three grandparents who were racially full Jews. . . .

A Jew is also one who is descended from two full-Jewish grandparents if:

a. He belonged to the Jewish religious community at the time this law was issued or who joined the community later.

b. At the time the law was issued he was married to a person who was a Jew or was subsequently married to a Jew. . . .

(First Supplementary Decree of 14 November 1935)

* * *

Imbued with the knowledge that the purity of the German blood is the necessary condition for the continued existence of the German people, and animated by the inflexible will to ensure the existence of the German nation for all future times, the Reichstag has unanimously adopted the following law . . .

Article I. Marriage between Jews and subjects of the German or kindred blood are forbidden. Marriages concluded despite this law are invalid, even if they are concluded abroad in order to circumvent this law.

Article II. Extra-marital relations between Jews and subjects of German or kindred blood are forbidden.

Article III. Jews may not employ in domestic service female subjects of German or kindred blood who are under the age of 45 years.

Article IV. Jews are forbidden to display the Reich and national flag or to show the national colors. The display of the Jewish colors, however, is permitted for them. . . .

(The Law for the Protection of German Blood and Honor,
15 September 1935)

* * *

Jews are forbidden to attend German schools—They are permitted to attend Jewish schools only. . . . All Jewish boys and girls still attending German schools are to be dismissed immediately.

(Dismissal of Jewish Children from All German Schools,
15 November 1938)

* * *

Insofar as Jews have other given names than those which they are permitted to bear . . . they are obligated to acquire an additional given name beginning with January 1, 1939, namely, Jewish male persons must add the given name Israel and Jewish female persons must add the given name Sara.

(Laws on Jewish Given Names, August 1938)

* * *

Streets, squares, parks and buildings, from which the Jews are to be banned, are to be closed to Jewish subjects of the State and stateless Jews, both pedestrians and drivers.

The ban on Jews in Berlin comprises the following districts:

1. All theatres, cinema, cabarets, public concert and lecture halls, museums, amusement places, . . . all athletic fields including ice-skating rinks;

2. All public and private bathing places.

3. Wilhelmstrasse from Leipsizerstrasse up to Unter den Linden. . . .

(Ghetto Laws, 1938)

GEORGE BERNARD SHAW   *(1856–1950)*

Irish playwright; wrote Pygmalion, Man and Superman

. . . Hitler was able to go further than Mussolini because he had a defeated, plundered, humiliated nation to rescue and restore, whereas Mussolini had only an irritated but victorious one. He carried out a persecution of the Jews which went to the scandalous length of outlawing, plundering, and exiling Albert Einstein, a much greater man than any politician, but great in such a manner that he was quite above the heads of the masses and therefore so utterly powerless economically and militarily that he depended for his very existence on the culture and conscience of the rulers of the earth. Hitler's throwing Einstein to the Antisemite wolves was an appalling breach of cultural faith. It raised the question which is the root question of this preface: to wit, what safeguard have the weaponless great against the great who have myrmidons at their call? It is the most frightful betrayal of civilization for the rulers who monopolize physical force to withhold their protection from the pioneers in thought. Granted that they are sometimes forced to do it because intellectual advances may present themselves as quackery, sedition, obscenity, or blasphemy, and always present themselves as heresies. Had Einstein been formally prosecuted and sentenced by the German National Socialist State, as Galileo was prosecuted by the Church, for shaking the whole framework of established physical science by denying the infallibility of Newton, introducing fantastic factors into mathematics, destroying human faith in absolute measurement, and playing an incomprehensible trick with the sacred velocity of light, quite a strong case could have been made out by the public prosecutor. But to set the police on him because he was a Jew could be justified only on the ground that the Jews are the natural enemies of the rest of the human race, and that as a state of perpetual war necessarily exists between them any Gentile has the same reason for killing any Jew at sight as the Roman leader had for killing Archimedes.

Now no doubt Jews are most obnoxious creatures. Any competent historian or psycho-analyst can bring a mass of incontrovertible evidence to prove that it would have been better for the world if the Jews had never existed. But I, as an Irishman, can, with patriotic relish, demonstrate the same of the English. Also of the Irish. If Herr Hitler would only consult the French and British newspapers and magazines of the latter half of 1914, he would learn that the Germans are a race of savage idolaters, murderers, liars, and fiends whose assumption of the human form is thinner than that of the wolf in Little Red Riding Hood.

We all live in glass houses. Is it wise to throw stones at the Jews? Is it wise to throw stones at all?

Herr Hitler is not only an Antisemite, but a believer in the possibility and desirability of a pure-bred German race. I should like to ask him why. All Germans are not Mozarts, nor even Mendelssohns and Meyerbeers, both of whom, by the way, though exceptionally desirable Germans, were Jews. Surely the average German can be improved. I am told that children bred from Irish colleens and Chinese laundrymen are far superior to inbred Irish or Chinese. Herr Hitler is not a typical German. I should not be at all surprised if it were discovered that his very mixed blood (all our bloods today are hopelessly mixed) got fortified somewhere in the past by that of King David. He cannot get over the fact that the lost tribes of Israel expose us all to the suspicion (sometimes, as in Abyssinia, to the boast) that we are those lost tribes, or at least that we must have absorbed them.

One of my guesses in this matter is that Herr Hitler in his youth was fascinated by Houston Chamberlain's *Foundations of the XIX Century*, an interesting book which at the time of its appearance I recommended everybody to read. Its ethnology was not wholly imaginary. A smattering of Mendelism is all that one needs to know that the eternal fusion of races does not always blend them. The Jews will often throw up an apparently pure-bred Hittite or a pure-bred Philistine. The Germans throw up out-and-out blond beasts side by side with dark Saturnine types like the Fuhrer himself. I am a blond, much less an antique Roman than a Dane. . . .

. . . the notion that they can be segregated as races or species is bosh. We have nations with national characteristics (rapidly fading, by the way), national languages, and national customs. But they deteriorate without cross fertilization; and if Herr Hitler could put a stop to cross fertilization in Germany and produce a population of brainless Bismarcks Germany would be subjugated by crossfertilized aliens, possibly by cosmopolitan Jews. There is more difference between a Catholic Bavarian and a Lutheran Prussian, between a tall fair Saxon and a stocky Baltic Celt, than there is between a Frankfort

Jew and a Frankfort Gentile. . . . The intelligent Jew is a Fusionist as between Jew and Gentile stock, even when he is also a bit of a Zionist. Only the stupidest or craziest ultra-Nationalists believe that people corralled within the same political frontier are all exactly alike, and that they improve by continuous inbreeding.

Now Herr Hitler is not a stupid German. I therefore urge upon him that his Antisemitism and national exclusiveness must be pathological: a craze, a complex, a bee in his bonnet, a hole in his armor, a hitch in his statesmanship, one of those lesions which sometimes prove fatal. As it has no logical connection with Fascism or National Socialism, and has no effect on them except to bring them into disrepute, I doubt whether it can survive its momentary usefulness as an excuse for plundering raids and coups d'état against inconvenient Liberals or Marxists. A persecution is always a man hunt; and man hunting is not only a very horrible sport but socially a dangerous one, as it revives a primitive instinct incompatible with civilization: indeed civilization rests fundamentally on the compact that it shall be dropped. . . .

(Preface to *The Millionairess*, pp. 23–27)

* * *

From an interview in the *London Daily Express*, 26 March 1938:

Hitler hasn't solved the Jewish problem. He's created it. It has damaged his intellectual credit to an extraordinary extent. Europe could hardly be more disagreeably surprised if he had revived witch burning.

The exiling of Einstein and the confiscation of his property was Hitler's stupidest single act. Einstein may yet be the winner.

. . . We will have no more anti-Semitism when Jews cease to be Jews and Christians cease to be Christians.

(Quoted in *The Churchman*, 15 November 1938)

POPE PIUS XI   *(1857–1939)*

A message to a delegation of Belgian Catholic leaders, 5 December 1938:

Sacrifice of Abel, sacrifice of Abraham, sacrifice of Melchisedek. In three acts, in three links, in three stages, behold the whole religious history of humanity. Sacrifice of Abel: era of Adam. Sacrifice of

Abraham: era of religion and the wonderful history of Israel. Sacrifice of Melchisedek: announcement of the Christian era and religion.

Sacrifice of Abraham our Patriarch. Note well how Abraham is called our patriarch, our ancestor. Anti-Semitism is not compatible with the thought and sublime realities which are expressed in this text. It is a movement in which we, as Christians, cannot have any part whatsoever.

Concerning the promise made to Abraham and his descendants, the text "saith not," St. Paul remarks (Galatians 3:16), "And to seeds, as of many; but as of one, And to thy seed, which is Christ." Through Christ, then, we are the spiritual descendants of Abraham. No, it is not possible for Christians to participate in anti-Semitism. We acknowledge the right of everyone to defend himself, to take legitimate measures to protect himself against all that menaces his legitimate interests. But anti-Semitism is inadmissible. Spiritually, we are Semites.

(Catholic Worker Press Service, in *Stars and Sand*, p. 327)

HAVELOCK ELLIS   (1859–1939)

British physician, scientist, editor, and social reformer

For me indeed there has never been any Jewish question. The background from which I come had no Jewish element, save indeed the Bible, which for me is Jewish throughout and has an importance I would never belittle.

Even in later life when I have gained many friends who are Jews, and experienced in large measure those qualities of generosity and receptivity which often mark the Jew, I have been conscious of no Jewish problem. Myself English in the narrowest sense, the Jew is not more alien to me than the Cornishman or the Irishman, or even many so-called Englishmen, often less so. . . .

Misoneism, the hatred of novelty, was the name old Lombroso (who happened to be a Jew) gave to a characteristic of mankind in all lands and ages. What is new and superior—for if it is not superior it is not worth hating—always arouses suspicion and dislike. Not even the best-endowed nations are free from this tendency. Even the Greeks persecuted, imprisoned, exiled, or slew the creators of their own "modern culture," whom now that they are no longer new we all revere. Even the Jews themselves exhibited the same spirit; the ancient story of Jesus is still remembered, and the more recent story of Spinoza.

We see how the matter stands in Germany. "Modern culture" there—it is a familiar fact in the records of science and medicine and literature and music—is represented by Jews in a proportion altogether in excess to their numbers in the general population. This is shown by all the tests that can be applied. Meyerson and Goldberg [*The German Jew: His Share in Modern Culture*] may not be counted impartial witnesses, but they present the situation fairly. They might choose as their text the words of Renan: "The enemies of Jewry are for the most part the enemies of the modern spirit."

All sorts of reasons are assigned for hostility to the Jews. They are not always baseless, and Jews themselves are often prepared to find Jews objectionable. But those reasons remain side-issues beside the central fact.

The result, of course, is that those who seek to injure the Jews in the end only injure themselves and benefit the world. We may think of Louis XIV, by the Revocation of the Edict of Nantes impoverishing France of much of her best blood, to enrich neighboring countries with Huguenots who in the end had no cause to regret their exile. So I expect to see the Jews still carrying on successfully, much as they have any time during the past three thousand years. . . .

Looking broadly at the matter, even with but a small knowledge of human nature, it is easy to account for anti-Semitism. The four thinkers to whom, above all others, we owe the development of the modern spirit have been Jews: Marx, Bergson, Freud, and Einstein.

(Ellis, "The Jewish Question" in *Questions of Our Day*, pp. 37–40)

DAVID LLOYD GEORGE   *(1863–1945)*

British Prime Minister, 1916–1922

Of all the bigotries that savage the human temper there is none so stupid as the anti-Semitic.

It has no basis in reason, it is not rooted in faith, it aspires to no ideal—it is just one of those dank and unwholesome weeds that grow in the morass of racial hatred.

How utterly devoid of reason it is may be gathered from the fact that it is almost confined to nations that worship the Jewish prophets and apostles and revere the national literature of the Hebrews as the only inspired message delivered by the Deity to mankind, and whose only hope of salvation rests on the precepts and promises of the great teachers of Judaism.

Still, in the sight of these fanatics Jews of today can do nothing right. If they are rich, they are birds of prey. If they are poor, they are vermin. If they are in favor of war, that is because they want to exploit the bloody feuds of Gentiles to their own profit. If they are anxious for peace, they are either instinctive cowards or traitors. If they give generously—and there are no more liberal givers than the Jews—they are doing it for some selfish purpose of their own. If they don't give—then what would you expect of a Jew?

If labor is oppressed by great capital, the greed of the Jew is held responsible. If labor revolts against capital as it did in Russia—the Jew is blamed for that also. If he lives in a strange land, he must be persecuted and pogrommed out of it. If he wants to go back to his own, he must be prevented. . . .

The latest exhibition of this wretched indulgence is the agitation against settling poor Jews in the land their fathers made famous.

> (George, "What Has the Jew Done?" in *Zionism and Anti-Semitism: The Absurd Folly of Jew-Baiting*, p. 27)

H. G. WELLS   *(1866–1946)*

British novelist, historian, and social commentator; author of
The Time Machine, The War of the Worlds

And now we can tell of the Hebrews, a Semitic people, not so important in their own time as in their influence upon the later history of the world. . . .

Their importance in the world is due to the fact that they produced a written literature, a world history, a collection of laws, chronicles, psalms, books of wisdom, poetry and fiction and political utterances which became at last what Christians know as the Old Testament, the Hebrew Bible. . . .

Before [the Babylonian Exile] the Jews do not seem to have been a very civilized or united people. Probably only a very few of them could read or write. In their own history one never hears of the early books of the Bible being read; the first mention of a book is in the time of Josiah. The Babylonian captivity civilized them and consolidated them. They returned aware of their own literature, an acutely self-conscious and political people. . . .

But it is well to keep the proportion of things in mind. At the climax of his glories Solomon was only a little subordinate king in a little city. . . . The account of Solomon's magnificence given in the books of Kings and Chronicles is questioned by many critics. They say that it was added to and exaggerated by the patriotic pride of later writers. But the Bible account read carefully is not so overwhelming as it appears at the first reading. Solomon's temple, if one works out the measurements, would go inside a small suburban church, and his fourteen hundred chariots cease to impress us when we learn from an Assyrian monument that his successor Ahab sent a contingent of two thousand to the Assyrian army. It is also plainly manifest from the Bible narrative that Solomon spent himself in display and overtaxed and overworked his people. . . .

The prosperity of the Hebrew people was short-lived. . . .

It was in Babylon that the Hebrew people got their history together and evolved their tradition. The people who came back to Jerusalem at the command of Cyrus were a very different people in spirit and knowledge from those who had gone into captivity. They had learnt civilization. In the development of their peculiar character a very great part was played by certain men, a new sort of men, the Prophets, to whom we must now direct our attention. These Prophets mark the appearance of new and remarkable forces in the steady development of human society.

(Wells, *A Short History of the World*, pp. 115–121)

* * *

. . . Foremost of these Jewish ideas was this, that their God was invisible and remote, an invisible God in a temple not made with hands, a Lord of Righteousness throughout the earth. All other peoples had national gods embodied in images that lived in temples. If the image was smashed and the temple razed, presently that god died out. But this was a new idea, this God of the Jews, in the heavens, high above priests and sacrifices. And this God of Abraham, the Jews believed, had chosen them to be his peculiar people, to restore Jerusalem and make it the capital of Righteousness in the World. They were a people exalted by their sense of a common destiny. This belief saturated them all when they returned to Jerusalem after the captivity in Babylon.

Is it any miracle that in their days of overthrow and subjugation many Babylonians and Syrians and so forth and later on many Phoenicians, speaking practically the same language and having endless customs, habits, tastes and traditions in common, should be attracted by this inspiring cult and should seek to share in its fellowship and its promise? After the fall of Tyre, Sidon, Carthage and the Spanish Phoenician cities, the Phoenicians suddenly vanish from history; and as suddenly we find, not simply in Jerusalem but in Spain, Africa, Egypt, Arabia, the East, wherever the Phoenicians had set their feet, communities of Jews. And they were all held together by the Bible and by the reading of the Bible. Jerusalem was from the first only their nominal capital; their real city was this book of books. This is a new sort of thing in history. It is something of which the seeds were sown long before, when the Sumerians and Egyptians began to turn their hieroglyphics into writing. The Jews were a new thing, a people without a king and presently without a temple (for as we shall tell Jerusalem itself was broken up in 70 A.D.), held together and consolidated out of heterogeneous elements by nothing but the power of the written word.

And this mental welding of the Jews was neither planned nor foreseen nor done by either priests or statesmen. Not only a new kind of community but a new kind of man comes into history with the development of the Jews. In the days of Solomon the Hebrews looked like becoming a little people just like any other little people of that time clustering around court and temple, ruled by the wisdom of the priest and led by the ambition of the king. But already, the reader may learn from the Bible, this new sort of man of which we speak, the Prophet, was in evidence. . . .

These fulminations were written down and preserved and studied. They went wherever the Jews went, and wherever they went they spread a new religious spirit. They carried the common man past priest and temple, past court and king and brought him face to face with the Rule of Righteousness. That is their supreme importance in the history of mankind. In the great utterances of Isaiah the prophetic voice rises to a pitch of splendid anticipation and foreshadows the whole earth united and at peace under one God. Therein the Jewish prophecies culminate.

All the Prophets did not speak in this fashion, and the intelligent reader of the prophetic books will find much hate in them, much prejudice, and much that will remind him of the propaganda pamphlets of the present time. Nevertheless it is the Hebrew Prophets of the period round and about the Babylonian captivity who mark the appearance of a new power in the world, the power of individual moral appeal, of an appeal to the free conscience of mankind against the fetish sacrifices and slavish loyalties that had hitherto bridled and harnessed our race.

(*A Short History of the World*, pp. 123–126)

* * *

The Jews were persuaded that God, the one God of the whole world, was a righteous god, but they also thought of him as a trading god who had made a bargain with their Father Abraham about them, a very good bargain indeed for them, to bring them at last to predominance in the earth. With dismay and anger they heard Jesus sweeping away their dear securities. God, he taught, was no bargainer; there were no chosen people and no favourites in the Kingdom of Heaven. God was the loving father of all life, as incapable of showing favour as the universal sun. . . . In the parable of the labourers he thrust aside the obstinate claim of the Jews to have a special claim upon God. . . . There are no privileges, no rebates and no excuses in the Kingdom of Heaven.

But it is not only the intense tribal patriotism of the Jews that Jesus outraged. They were a people of intense family loyalty, and he would have swept away all the narrow and restrictive family affections in the great flood of the love of God. . . .

And not only did Jesus strike at patriotism and the bonds of family loyalty in the name of God's universal fatherhood and brotherhood of all mankind, but it is clear that his teaching condemned all the gradations of the economic system, all private wealth, and personal advantages. . . .

. . . In the white blaze of this kingdom of his there was to be no property, no privilege, no pride and precedence; no motive indeed and no reward but love. Is it any wonder that men were dazzled and blinded and cried out against him? Even his disciples cried out when he would not spare them the light. Is it any wonder that the priests realized that between this man and themselves there was no choice but that he or priestcraft should perish? Is it any wonder that the Roman soldiers, confronted and amazed by something soaring over their comprehension and threatening all their disciplines, should take refuge in wild laughter, and crown him with thorns and robe him in purple and make a mock Caesar of him? For to take him seriously was to enter upon a strange and alarming life, to abandon habits, to control instincts and impulses, to essay an incredible happiness. . . .

(A Short History of the World, pp. 215–221)

* * *

. . . We have seen how the Arabs were the means of restoring Aristotle to Europe, and how such a prince as Frederick II acted as a channel through which Arabic philosophy and science played upon the renascent European mind. Still more influential in the stirring up of men's ideas were the Jews. Their very existence was a note of interrogation to the claims of the church. . . .

(A Short History of the World, p. 294)

* * *

Wells had travelled widely in Europe before the war [1914]. . . . He was as aware as anyone else of the strains of nationalism, and when the war broke out, some of his initial newspaper articles offered his views on what was needed to stabilize Europe.

After ten days of fighting, he said, "We begin a new period in history. . . . That means that we have to redraw the map so that there shall be, for just as far as we can see ahead, as little cause for warfare among us Western nations as possible. That means that we have to redraw justly. And very extensively. . . ."

A few days later he urged the United States to enter the war, at least symbolically, so that she could be part of the peace-making effort. . . . He also called for restoration of Palestine to the Jews, creating a real Judaea. . . .

(D. C. Smith, *H. G. Wells, Desperately Mortal*, p. 236)

* * *

. . . it becomes apparent [in *The Anatomy of Frustration*, 1936] that education is for all life, not just the young. In this discussion Wells uses the concept of Jewishness as something which had had great value in sustaining the member group, but must now be set aside to the greater good of all. Others, such as Catholics, Moslems, Communists, Nazis, all would have to give over their creeds as well, which were essentially selfish ways of maintaining life in the face of the growing need for change. Without doing this, frustration, already present in the world, would become unbearable.

(H.G. *Wells, Desperately Mortal*, p. 314)

* * *

. . . he felt the Jewish question was 'a particularly bad instance of the distortions of human life by the poison called history', which was useless as the basis for an ideology of peace. The most astounding story, he said, 'masked and hidden under the misrepresentation of the old history', was the imposition of 'Judaeo-Christian mythology', first upon the Mediterranean world, and then, 'less effectively', upon the rest of Europe and America. 'I can imagine no more dreadful position in the world today than to be an intelligent Jew, with a clear sense of reality.'

(H.G. *Wells, Desperately Mortal*, p. 348)

* * *

. . . Among others to whom Wells addressed for his special pleas for help [with his "Declaration" in 1943] were Chaim Weizmann, to whom he apologized for his general tactlessness on the matter of Jewish desire for a homeland, saying, 'In these urgent days there is a need for a fundamental solidarity in creative work that should rule out these minor resentments'. . . .

(H.G. *Wells, Desperately Mortal*, p. 445)

MAHATMA M. K. GANDHI   (1869–1948)

Indian leader and pacifist

In late November 1938, just after Kristallnacht:

Several letters have been received by me asking to declare my views about the Arab-Jew question in Palestine and the persecution of the Jews in Germany. It is not without hesitation that I venture to offer my views on this very difficult question.

My sympathies are all with the Jews. I have known them intimately in South Africa. Some of them became lifelong companions. Through these friends I came to learn much of their age-long persecution. They have been the untouchables of Christianity. The parallel between their treatment by Christians and the treatment of untouchables by Hindus is very close. Religious sanction has been invoked in both cases for the justification of the inhuman treatment meted out to them. . . .

But my sympathy does not blind me to the requirements of justice. The cry for a national home for the Jews does not make much appeal to me. . . . Why should they not, like other peoples of the earth, make that country their home where they are born and where they earn their livelihood?

The nobler course would be to insist on a just treatment of the Jews wherever they are born and bred. The Jews born in France are French in precisely the same sense that Christians born in France are French. If the Jews have no home but Palestine, will they relish the idea of being forced to leave the other parts of the world in which they are settled? . . .

But the German persecution of the Jews seems to have no parallel in history. . . .

Germany is showing to the world how efficiently violence can be worked when it is not hampered by any hypocrisy or weakness masquerading as humanitarianism. It is also showing how hideous, terrible and terrifying it looks in its nakedness.

Can the Jews resist this organized and shameless persecution? Is there a way to preserve their self-respect, and not to feel helpless, neglected and forlorn? I submit there is. . . . If I were a Jew and were born in Germany and earned my livelihood there, I would claim Germany as my home even as the tallest gentile German might, and challenge him to shoot me or cast me in the dungeon; I would refuse to be expelled or to submit to discriminating treatment. And for doing this I should not wait for the fellow-Jews to join me in civil resistance, but would have confidence that in the end the rest were bound to follow my example. If one Jew or all the Jews were to accept the prescription here offered, he or they cannot be worse off than now. And suffering voluntarily undergone will bring them an inner strength and joy which no number of resolutions of sympathy passed in the world outside Germany can. . . .

I am convinced that, if someone with courage and vision can arise among them to lead them in non-violent action, the winter of their despair can in the twinkling of an eye be turned into the summer of hope. And what has today become a degrading manhunt can be turned into a calm and determined stand offered by unarmed men and women possessing the strength of suffering given to them by Jehovah. It will be then a truly religious resistance offered against the Godless fury of dehumanized man. The German Jews will score a lasting victory over the German gentiles in the sense that they will have converted the latter to an appreciation of human dignity. They will have rendered service to fellow-Germans and proved their title to be the real Germans as against those who are today dragging, however unknowingly, the German name into the mire.

And now a word to the Jews in Palestine. I have no doubt that they are going about things in the wrong way. The Palestine of theBiblical conception is not a geographical tract. It is in their hearts. But if they must look to the Palestine of geography as their national home, it is wrong to enter it under the shadow of the British gun. A religious act cannot be performed with the aid of the bayonet or the bomb. They can settle in Palestine only by the goodwill of the Arabs. They should seek to convert the Arab heart. They can offer Satyagraha[2] in front of the Arabs and offer themselves to be shot or thrown into the Dead Sea without raising a finger against them. They will find the world opinion in their favor in their religious aspiration. There are hundreds of ways of reasoning with the Arabs, if they will only discard the help of the British bayonet. As it is, they are co-sharers with the British in despoiling a people who have done no wrong to them.

---

[2]"Hold unto truth," used by Gandhi in the sense of penance or fasting.

. . . Every country is their home, including Palestine, not by aggression but by loving service. . . .

(From *Harijan*, 26 November 1938, in *The Essential Gandhi, An Anthology*, pp. 328–330)

* * *

. . . I happen to have a Jewish friend (Herman Kallenbach, who purchased the farm for Gandhi's first ashram in South Africa) living with me. He has an intellectual belief in non-violence. But he says he cannot pray for Hitler. He is so full of anger over the German atrocities that he cannot speak of them with restraint. I do not quarrel with him over his anger. He wants to be non-violent, but the sufferings of his fellow-Jews are too much for him to bear. What is true of him is true of thousands of Jews who have no thought even of "loving the enemy." With them, as with millions, "revenge is sweet, to forgive is divine."

(From *Harijan*, 18 February 1939)

* * *

. . . If [the Jewish people] were to adopt the matchless weapon of non-violence, whose use their best prophets have taught and which Jesus the Jew who gladly wore the crown of thorns bequeathed to a groaning world, their case would be the world's, and I have no doubt that among the many things the Jews have given to the world, this would be the best and the brightest. It is twice blessed. It will make them happy and rich in the true sense of the word, and it will be soothing balm to the aching world. . . .

(From *Harijan*, 21 July 1946)

JAN CHRISTIAN SMUTS   *(1870–1950)*

South African prime minister, 1919–1924, 1939–1948

In a November 1934, appeal to aid immigration of German refugees to Palestine:

Today we are in for strange experiments all over the world. The suffering that was inflicted, the losses sustained, made it necessary in many ways to try new experiments, and some of them are enough to bring terror to our hearts. Gold was abandoned when it was found difficult to maintain the Gold Standard, and now the human coinage is being debased, and we are trying to find whether peace and recovery are possible at a lower level. Much of the great human progress is in danger of being destroyed and replaced by what was lower.

Harking back to the past, one of the finest contributions ever made to human advance in this respect has come from the Jews, in both the Old and the New Testaments, where you have one of the greatest insights into human hearts. Long ago they were moved from ideas of force to nobler visions of tenderness and mercy and kindness, which, to my mind, is the noblest mission ever designed for the human race.

Now we see the world of right and the gospel of love being denied to the people who preached it thousands of years ago.

We are here to testify to that great faith which must never go under again, and it is because of that great teaching that we are going all out to support this cause, to extend the hand of pity, and help those who are suffering.

To me this is a most impressive moment, this opening up of Palestine once more to the Jews. It is one of the bright spots of the world—in the new world, South Africa; in the old world, Palestine. I can see a vision of a new Palestine, see a stream of tens of thousands of Jews going back to their ancient homeland.

(Smuts, in *The African World*, p. 129)

HILAIRE BELLOC   *(1870–1953)*

British poet and novelist

The Jew must remember that not only is his domination very bitterly resented, but that his presence in any position of control whatsoever is odious to the race among which he moves. . . .

. . . There is a national antagonism to the Jewish race felt by nearly all those who are not of it and among whom it lives. . . .

. . . the average English soldier and citizen has no ties and no sympathy [with Jews]. . . .

. . . rich Europeans . . . in their habit of . . . submitting to almost any indignity for the purposes of obtaining more wealth, marry their daughters to Jews.

[Jews] stand behind those great Industrial Insurance schemes which are so detestable to the mass of the people . . . batteners upon the lapsed premiums of the poor.

[The Englishman] will not submit to be told that, in order to suit the convenience of these alien bankers, he must forgo the rights of victory. . . . Still more urgently will he deny the right of the Jewish bankers to interfere with the national reparation due to him for damage wantonly done in the course of hostilities. . . .

The Jewish Government in Moscow has taken root and is firmly established.

[Marx's *Das Kapital* is] a Jewish book written in German.

[The courage of the Jew] is of a Jewish kind, directed to Jewish ends, and stamped with a highly distinctive Jewish mark.

The conception of a national feeling must seem ridiculous to [the Jews] everywhere or, if not ridiculous, subsidiary to the more important motive of individual advantage. . . .

The Jew will serve France against the Germans, or the Germans against France, and he will do so indifferently as a resident in the country he benefits or the country he wounds; for he is indifferent to either.

("The Jewish Question" in The Eye Witness)

* * *

Belloc in his book on the Jews advocated his thesis that Jews should be treated as people separate from the nation in which they found themselves. They should be given their own ghettos in which to live live and to work. Within the ghettos they should be given complete religious freedom and full self-government under institutions of their own choosing, but they should not be treated as citizens of the country in which they found themselves. If the Napoleonic formula was accepted and they were encouraged to live as ordinary citizens, the inevitable antipathy between Jew and Christian was such, he argued, that explosions, pogroms, and massacres were inevitable. Such massacres were, as Belloc said, abhorrent. The policies which he advocated were, he argued, the only alternative to them.

It can of course be answered that at the time Belloc wrote his book, in 1922, the worst pogroms that Europe had seen had all been in Eastern Europe—a few years before in Czarist Russia, and, at the moment of writing, in Rumania and Poland—where the Jews lived under legal disabilities, lived substantially in ghettos and lived the separate life which Belloc advocated for them. Their separation had not saved them from attack by the Christians. It had on the contrary made it possible for Christians to believe absurd stories about Jewish habits and the Jewish way of life—child murders and the like. Yet most people at the time of Belloc's writing would, in spite of Eastern European pogroms or of memories of such incidents as the Dreyfus case in the West, have dismissed as absurd Belloc's suggestions of the possibility of general massacres of Jews. We were, we all thought, moving into an era of growing liberality. Such things, if they had sometimes happened in the past, could not possibly happen again in the future. Only eleven years ahead, at the time of Belloc's writing, lay Hitler. The experience of Hitler must make critics wonder, whether Belloc was indeed wholly foolish in his alleged exposure of the fragility of the Liberal formula. But at the same time it hardly gives support for Belloc's own solution. For the story of the Jews under the Nazis shows indeed that Hitler and the Nazis were alone so wicked as to wish positively to kill all Jews for being Jews, but it also shows that other governments, the American, the British and others, were not willing to put themselves even to the minor inconvenience of revising their quotas and welcoming Jews as immigrants to save their lives. . . .

The essence of Belloc's plan was that the arrangements for Jews should be made by Gentile governments. The security under them of the Jews would be dependent on Gentile good will, and experience was to prove to the Jews that they could not count on Gentile good will. . . .

(C. Hollis, The Mind of Chesterton, pp. 134–135)

* * *

There exists in the midst of European civilisation a race alien to and different from the Western blood among which it must live. This race is segregated in no artificial manner yet permanently and uniquely survives intact. So far from this segregation being due to stratification or difference of abilities between higher and lower, the Jewish nation is, and has always been, eminent in the highest intellectual employment which European civilisation could find. It has on this account been accepted sometimes as a necessity, sometimes as an advantage, but always in practice as a part of the European scheme. None the less the presence of this alien element has proved sometimes an irritant, always an element of friction, and a social arrangement in which that friction should be reduced to a minimum, and the necessary or, at any rate, normal presence of the small non-European minority in our midst shall be made as innocuous as possible, is a goal practically obtainable and eminently to be desired.

(Belloc, "The Jewish Question," in *The Eye-Witness*)

* * *

Not unless the Jewish race is to be absorbed and disappear in the mass of European blood and tradition surrounding it, that contrast and its consequent friction will increase in the near future until their worst fruit shall have ripened: a fruit of oppression, injustice, and enduring hatred.

To avoid that lamentable conclusion three policies are present. The first—and that still most generally held in Western Europe—is to regard the matter as solved; vaguely to suppose the absorption of the alien race as feasible, and its presence for the moment as something at once absurdly separate and yet not separate from the life of the community as innocuous. The second policy is that of exclusion. The third policy is to grant the Jew recognition and privilege.

Which of these three shows comprehension of our need and of the Jewish need, and which is the most likely to afford a standing answer to this gravest of modern questions?

(Belloc, "The Jewish Question," in *The Eye-Witness*)

* * *

All that is said here by way of conclusion to this series of articles, is no more than a general adumbration of that third large line of policy which the solution of the Jewish problem must take in the near future, now that the first line of absorption has certainly broken down, if we would avoid the second line of persecution.

It sounds fantastic to those who prefer words to things; it cannot be detailed because the crisis is but beginning; but it certainly marks out the road by which, and by which alone, we can avoid in the near future throughout Europe disaster to the Jewish race and shame to our own.

Every modern discussion is alive with it. You cannot speak of the South African business, of the vast religious quarrel in France, of the moral struggle in Italy, of the Young Turks, of Egypt, of India, of the influence of secret societies to-day, of any conceivable matter of real and practical import, without speaking in the same breath of the Jewish people—and alas! not in their noble aspect, the last defence of which is the inheritance of that ignoble fear of Jewish financial power, which has tarnished the whole debate.

You cannot avoid a reality so insistent, so pressing, and so enormous. You must meet it, and if you do not meet it with the intention of recognition and of privilege you will inevitably be driven to meet it in the long run with the intention of exclusion, injustice, and oppression. All history is there to teach you your lesson, and you have perhaps thirty years[3] in which to make up your minds.

(Belloc, "The Jewish Question," in *The Eye-Witness*)

JOSIAH WEDGWOOD   *(1872–1943)*

British statesman and member of Parliament

Responding to Arab riots in Palestine, then under British mandate:

For two years murder and destruction of Jewish property have gone unpunished under British rule. The administration continues to be strictly impartial between the murderers and the murdered. I have not known of such a black page of incompetence and hypocrisy in British history.

(*The Times* of London, 21 July 1938)

BERTRAND RUSSELL   *(1872–1970)*

British mathematician and philosopher

While at Broadstairs I was taken to see Sir Moses Montefiore, an old and much revered Jew who lived in the neighbourhood. (According to

---

[3]Exactly thirty years after Belloc published this series of articles—almost to the day—Hitler's *Einsatzgruppen* were pouring across Poland and Russia, slaughtering some 1.5 million Jews, in the first major actions of the Holocaust.

the Encyclopaedia, he had retired in 1824.) This was the first time I became aware of the existence of Jews outside the Bible. My people explained to me carefully, before taking me to see the old man, how much he deserved to be admired, and how abominable had been the former disabilities of Jews, which he and my grandfather had done much to remove. On this occasion the impression made by my grandmother's teaching was clear. . . .

(*The Autobiography of Bertrand Russell, 1872–1914*, p. 29)

* * *

The rejection of humility, of love of one's neighbor and of the rights of the meek, is contrary to Gospel teaching; and anti-Semitism, when it is theoretical as well as practical, is not easily reconciled with a religion of Jewish origin. For these reasons, Nazidom and Christianity have difficulty in making friends, and it is not impossible that their antagonism may bring about the downfall of the Nazis.

There is another reason why the modern cult of unreason, whether in Germany or elsewhere, is incompatible with any traditional form of Christianity. Inspired by Judaism, Christianity adopted the notion of Truth, with the correlative virtue of Faith. The notion and the virtue survived in "honest doubt," as all the Christian virtues remained among Victorian free-thinkers. But gradually the influence of skepticism and advertising made it seem hopeless to discover truth, but very profitable to assert falsehood. Intellectual probity was thus destroyed. . . .

The conception of science as a pursuit of truth has so entirely disappeared from Hitler's mind that he does not even argue against it. As we know, the theory of relativity has come to be thought bad because it was invented by a Jew. The Inquisition rejected Galileo's doctrine because it considered it untrue; but Hitler accepts or rejects doctrines on political grounds, without bringing in the notion of truth or falsehood.

(Russell, *In Praise of Idleness and Other Essays*, p. 112)

G. K. CHESTERTON   (1874–1936)

British novelist, poet, and critic

To talk of the Jews always as the oppressed and never as the oppressors
is simply absurd; it is as if men pleaded for reasonable help for exiled
French aristocrats or ruined Irish landlords, and forgot that the
French and Irish peasants had any wrongs at all!

> I am fond of Jews
> Jews are fond of money
> Never mind of whose.
> I am fond of Jews
> Oh, but when they lose
> Damn it all, it's funny.
>
> They haven't got no noses,
> They cannot even tell
> When door and darkness closes
> The park encloses,
> Where even the Law of Moses
> Will let you steal a smell.
>
> ("The Song of Quoodle")

* * *

The Syrians and Arabs, and all the agricultural and pastoral
populations of Palestine, are, rightly or wrongly, alarmed and angered
at the advent of Jews to power: for the perfectly practical and simple
reason of the reputation which the Jews have all over the world. . . .
Rightly or wrongly, certain people in Palestine fear the coming of the
Jews as they fear the coming of locusts; they regard them as parasites
that feed on the community by a thousand methods of financial
intrigue and economic exploitation.

There is not the smallest difficulty in stating in plain words what
the Arabs fear in the Jews. They fear in exact terms their knowledge,
their experience and their money. . . . Men bar themselves into their

houses, or even hide in their cellars, when such virtues are abroad in the land.

A Jewish State will be a success when the Jews in it are scaven- gers, when the Jews in it are sweeps, when they are dockers and ditchers and porters and hodsmen. . . . It is our whole complaint against the Jew that he does not till the soil with the spade. . . . It seems rather indefensible to be deaf to him if he really says "give me a land and I will love it. . . ." If he asks for the spade he must use the spade, and not merely employ the spade, in the sense of hiring half a hundred men to use spades. If he asks for the soil, he must till the soil; that is, he must belong to the soil, and not merely make the soil belong to him. . . . There can be no doubt of the patriotism and even poetic spirit in which many of them hope to make their ancient wilderness blossom like the rose. They at least would still stand among the great prophets of Israel, and none the less though they prophesied in vain. . . .

(In a newspaper article, 1920)

* * *

It was always called anti-semitism, but it was always much more true to call it Zionism. It consisted entirely in saying that Jews are Jews; and that as a logical consequence they are not Russians or Rouma- nians or Frenchmen or Englishmen. . . . For if the advantage of the ideal to the Jews is to gain the promised land, the advantage to the Gentiles is to get rid of the Jewish Problem. . . .

It is true that for anyone whose heart is set on a particular home or shrine, to be locked out is to be locked in. The narrowest possible prison for him is the whole world.

(Chesterton, The New Jerusalem, p. 283)

* * *

. . . Gilbert Chesterton . . . accepted from Belloc that there was an international money-power which was largely Jewish and which attempted to control the policies of European nations, and that Jews were men who owed their loyalty to their own Jewish nation and who were incapable of feeling patriotism to an established nation of whom they were the legal citizens. In truth there was – it was most arguable – an international money power, in the sense of a few wealthy bankers whose main interest it was to rescue the traditional monetary system, but only a few of their members were Jewish. . . .

Chesterton . . . did not abuse Jews as Jews. Few Christians wrote in more ringing admiration of the Jewish contribution to religion. In *The Everlasting Man* he was to write: "It is true in this sense humanly speaking that the world owes God to the Jews . . . Much as we may prefer that creative liberty which the Christian culture has declared and by which it has eclipsed even the arts of antiquity, we must not underrate the determining importance at the time of the Hebrew inhibition of images. . . . The God who would not have a statue remained a spirit. Nor would his statue in any case have had the disarming dignity and charm of the Greek statues then or the Christian statues afterwards. He was living in a land of monsters. We shall have the occasion to consider more fully what those monsters were, Moloch and Dagon and Tanit, the terrible goddess. If the deity of Israel had ever had an image he would have had a phallic image. By merely giving him a body they would have brought in all the worst elements of mythology; all the polygamy of polytheism; the vision of the harem in heaven. . . . It is often said with a sneer that the God of Israel was only a God of battles, a mere barbaric Lord of Hosts pitted in rivalry against other gods as their envious foe. Well it is for the world that he was a God of battles. Well it is for us that he was to the rest only a rival and a foe. In the ordinary way it would have been only too easy for them to have achieved the desolate disaster of conceiving him as a friend. It would have been only too easy for them to have seen him stretching out his hands in love and reconciliation, embracing Baal and kissing the painted face of Astarte, feasting on fellowship with the gods. . . . The more we really understand of the ancient conditions that contributed to the final culture of the Faith, the more we shall have a real and even a realistic reverence for the greatness of the prophets of Israel. As it was, the whole world melted into this mass of confused mythology; this Deity, who is called tribal and narrow, precisely because he was what is called tribal and narrow, preserved the primary religion of all mankind. He was tribal enough to be universal. He was as narrow as the universe. . . . But the world's destiny would have been distorted still more fatally if monotheism had failed in the Mosaic tradition. . . . That we do preserve something of that primary simplicity, that poets and philosophers can still indeed in some sense say a Universal Prayer, that we live in a large and serene world under a sky that stretches paternally over all the peoples of the earth, that philosophy and philanthropy are truisms of a religion of reasonable men, all that we most truly owe under heaven to a secretive and restless nomadic people, who bestowed on men the supreme and serene blessing of a jealous God."

Chesterton, then, in no way failed to understand and to honour the mystery of Judaism. He merely argued that the Jew in England was not an Englishman, the Jew in France was not a Frenchman, and so on. He was an alien and should be treated as such. It was a coherent argument but an exaggerated one. . . .

In 1911 he addressed the Jewish West End Literary Society. He praised the Jews most highly. They were, he said, the most civilised of races. One never met a Jew clod or yokel. . . .

Chesterton proclaimed without qualification that a Jew could not by his nature share the national passion of his fellow citizens. If such was the analysis . . . the question remained, "Where, then, should the Jews go?" Chesterton gave an answer to that question. He supported the solution of Zionism. The Jews should go to their natural home of Palestine, and he defended Zionism in his most lively and best of his travel books, *The New Jerusalem*. . . .

. . . In one of the chapters of *The New Jerusalem* he vigorously defended Zionism. He claimed that the accusation so commonly levelled against him of anti-semitism should rather be an accusation of Zionism. He would have liked to have seen the Jews rebuild in Palestine a Third Temple—although not of course on the site of the Dome of the Rock. The Jews, necessarily aliens everywhere else, should be allowed to return, and should return, to the one place where they could be truly at home. The test, he wrote in that book, that Palestine was the true home of the Jew would have been finally vindicated if the Jews could show that they were able to turn themselves there to agriculture. If that be the test, it seems to have been abundantly justified by the kibbutzim. . . .

. . . It is certain that, as Rabbi Wise, the famous New York rabbi, bore witness, when Hitler's persecution of the Jews began,

Chesterton was one of the first to protest against it. "When Hitlerism came," recorded Rabbi Wise, "he was one of the first to speak out with all the directness and frankness of a great and unabashed spirit. Blessing to his memory." Chesterton, we can certainly say, would never have acquiesced to a supine policy that did nothing at all to support the Jews in their agony. . . .

(Hollis, The Mind of Chesterton, pp. 135–140)

* * *

Oh, yes, I know they [the Jews] call themselves, for instance, in this country, Englishmen, and they are patriotic and loyal, and hold land and give liberally to English institutions, subsidise party funds, become peers and members of Parliament, entertain, hunt and shoot, and all the rest of it. Still the Jew is not an Englishman, because his nationality is not English. They are something different and in many ways very much better. Still, being better, they cannot be the same. They are allied, and rightly and justifiably, to their own people of their own race who are not English even in point of citizenship—Jews in Germany, Russia, France, everywhere. . . .

(The Jewish Chronicle, 28 April 1911)

* * *

Till the Jew discovers he is a separate race, with a history of its own, and a future which to be worthy he must make his own. Till thus finding himself the Jew perceives the necessity for a habitat, a centrum, wherein he can develop that which he now lacks, nationality. You see, I am not an anti-semite, I am a Zionist.

. . . I want the Jew to form a key that will fit into his own door. I believe Zionism would bring to the Jew territorial patriotism which he now lacks. It would assuredly allow him to develop his own culture in arts, in literature, in science, and it would put an end to his eternal entanglement of mutual wrong of which he is the unhappy cause between himself and the nations with whom he lives. . . .

My point is this: that the Jews being landless naturally alternate between too much power and too little, that the Jew millionaire is too safe and the Jew pedlar too harassed. It is not likely that the millionaire amongst you will be otherwise than the very few. Therefore for the many, I am afraid the future will be as the past has been—murder, outrage, persecution, insult, moral and physical torture, wandering unrest, oscillations of comfortless abasing, and uncertain toleration with grinding, evervating, cramping disabilities: in short, the Jew—at least for the most part—always burnt.

(*The Jewish Chronicle*, 28 April 1911)

* * *

. . . in one of his notebooks from the war period, where he jotted down odd thoughts as they had occurred to him from day to day, there are entries which show without any doubt that Chesterton did indeed have a bitter hatred of Jews. He wrote: "In modern Europe, Jews are not traitors, but traitors are Jews," a phrase that was mild in comparison with what was also there. "The Jews are fleas, but they are not all practically parasites. There are performing fleas." Now it is true that these phrases were written . . . when Chesterton's anger was aroused against certain individual Jews, and he obviously had not intended such jottings to be seen by anyone but himself; but they do indicate something of the way he was thinking, even if the statement about the fleas was meant to be a joke.

As I said earlier, his attitude towards the Jews was a serious blemish on Chesterton's character, for which, in as much as he was motivated by malice, he has certainly had to pay dearly. When towards the end of his life he learnt of the atrocities of Hitler towards the Jews, he wrote:

In our early days Hilaire Belloc and myself were accused of being uncompromising Anti-Semites. Today, although I still think there is a Jewish problem, I am appalled by the Hitlerite atrocities. They have absolutely no reason or logic behind them. It is quite obviously the expedient of a man who has been driven to seeking a scapegoat, and has found with relief the most famous scapegoat in European history, the Jewish people. I am quite ready to believe now that Belloc and I will die defending the last Jew in Europe.

. . . it was a little late to say it, but for the state of Chesterton's soul it was a good thing that he did.

(Ffinch, G.K. *Chesterton*, pp. 273–274)

W. SOMERSET MAUGHAM   *(1874–1965)*

British novelist, short story writer, and playwright

. . . *Lady Frederick* [1907] is interesting because it introduces a carica-tural Jewish character, the moneylender Captain Montgomerie, who is in reality the son of a Polish Jew named Aaron Levitsky. Captain Montgomerie wants to marry Lady Frederick so as to climb in society. When she turns him down he produces two bills and demands immediate payment. Conscious that Montgomerie was a burlesque figure, Maugham wrote Golding Bright to make sure that Otho Stuart did "not give the part of the rich Jew to a vulgar man since if it is exaggerated it will be grotesque."

There was in Maugham an ambivalence toward Jews. Writing to his New York literary agent Charles Hanson Towne in 1924 in response to a suggestion that Towne and Oliver Herford should dramatize his short story "The Letter," he said: "Nor have either of you that Semitic air with a dash of Czecho-Slovakia thrown in which I always thought was essential for success on Broadway." Writing to his nephew Robin in 1946 about his ocean crossing from the United States to France, he said, ". . . the passengers were for the most part children of Israel returning to Asia Minor . . . some of them seemed determined to inspire the rest of us with anti-Semitism."

In his work, Jews are usually crude and unscrupulous stereotypes in the tradition of Shylock and Fagin. In "Lady Habart" there occurs the line: "Once upon a time moneylenders were unwashed Hebrews in shabby clothes, malodorous, speaking English with an abominable accent". . . .

The theme of his letter to Robin, that Jews invite anti-Semitism by their behavior, is repeated in a passage from *The Gentleman in the Parlor*, an account of a journey to the Far East. On the steamer from Haiphong to Hong Kong the narrator meets an American Jew, Elfenbein, who is in the hosiery business. He is loud and irascible and vulgar. "He was odious," says the narrator, "but I admit that he was

often amusing; he would tell damaging stories about his fellow Jews in
a racy idiom that made them very entertaining. . . . He trod heavily
on your corns and if you kicked your feet out of the way thought you
insulted him. . . . He was the kind of Jew who made you understand
the pogrom."

In his 1909 comedy *Smith*, one of the characters is married to a
"fat old German-Jew." The critic J. T. Grien, a friend and admirer of
Maugham's, noted that "a discordant note in this comedy is the
repeated references to Jews in terms of ungraciousness . . . the impression remains that the Jews are considered, not as ordinary members of
the community, but as something exotic, akin to freakishness."

Another, much later, short story dealing with Jews, *The Alien
Corn*, was used by a Third Reich literary critic to bolster Nazi race
theories. The story is about a Jew who becomes an English gentleman.
His son, however, rebels against upper-middle-class English life and
goes to the Continent to become a pianist, reverting to his origins.
When he learns that he does not have the talent to be a first-class
concert pianist he kills himself. The story is less about being a Jew than
about the dilemma of not being able to achieve one's aims. But in a
1939 German brochure, *A Contribution on Interpreting School Literature*, Hans Kruschwitz wrote an article, "The Race Question in W. S.
Maugham's *The Alien Corn*," in which he argued that his unbiased
account proved the Nazi thesis that racial barriers are natural ones
and that the Jews will always remain the alien corn in any country
they live in.

Maugham would have been shocked to read this distorted
interpretation. The year it appeared he was living in the south of
France. At the outbreak of World War II, German exiles on the
Riviera were interned, on the theory that Nazi agents had been
planted among them. One of the interned exiles was Lion Feuchtwanger, author of *Jud Suss*, who was sufficiently anti-Nazi to have been
stripped of his German nationality. Maugham sent the French dramatist Jean Giraudoux, head of the wartime Bureau of Information in
Paris, a telegram on behalf of Feuchtwanger, who was released.

In addition, Maugham's oldest American friend was Bert Alanson, a Jewish stockbroker. His friendships with the Jewish writers S. N.
Behrman and Jerome Weidman, and with Jerome Zipkin, a Jewish real
estate heir and bon vivant, were warm and enduring. And finally, Mrs. Syrie Wellcome, whom he later married, was a woman he

believed to be Jewish. Thus one can argue both sides about Maugham and anti-Semitism. He made unpleasant cracks about Jews in his letters and depicted them in an unfavorable light in his work. He saved Feuchtwanger from internment and had many close friendships with Jews. In May 1946 Bert Alanson sent Maugham two pamphlets by a rabbi friend of his charging him with anti-Semitism. Maugham replied:

> I do not know what your rabbi means. . . . I gather that he looks upon me as anti-Semitic. God knows I have never been that; some of my best friends both in England and America are Jews and there is one, long known as the best-dressed man in San Francisco, to whom I owe more than to almost anyone in the world. I happen to think that the Zionists are mistaken in their efforts to found a Jewish state in Palestine, but that is an opinion I share with a good many Jews and I have every right to hold it.

. . . In Munich [193?] he ran into the novelist Cecil Roberts, who had been his guest at the Mauresque. Hitler had taken all the modern paintings by Jews out of the German galleries and exhibited them in Munich as Jewish art. "I must say, from what I see here," Maugham told Roberts, "that awful man seems justified. . . ."

. . . he had many friends in New York, including the playwright S. N. Behrman. They had hit it right off at their first meeting at Siegfried Sassoon's country house in 1938, for they had several things in common. Sam Behrman, the son of a rabbi in Worcester, Massachusetts, had, like Maugham, trod the uphill road to success, writing seventeen plays before the first one was produced on Broadway. Also like Maugham, he was short and believed that he was physically ugly. . . .

He and Maugham developed a kind of bantering cronyism that Maugham had with few other men. . . . But the love had a veil of teasing and humor. Maugham said that Sam was anti-Semitic, in response to which Sam sent him a set of phylacteries (small boxes containing strips of parchment inscribed with the Hebrew Scriptures), telling him that his standing with the Lord was not secure and that the phylacteries would fortify it. They carried on running jokes, such as Maugham playing the Jew to Sam's *goy* and offering to lend him money at usurious rates. . . .

(T. Morgan, *Maugham, A Biography*, pp. 139–142, 405–406, 447–448)

SIR WINSTON CHURCHILL   *(1874–1965)*

Prime Minister of England, 1940–1945, 1951–1955

Address in the House of Commons, 23 May 1939,
concerning the reduction of Jewish immigration to Palestine:

My right hon. Friend [Prime Minister Neville Chamberlain], on 13th
October, 1918, said:

> The sympathy of the British Government with Zionist aspira-
> tions does not date from yesterday. . . . My father was anxious to
> find such a territory within the limits of the British Constitu-
> tion. . . . Today the opportunity has come. I have no hesitation
> in saying that were my father alive today he would be among the
> first to welcome it and to give it his hearty support. . . .

It was in consequence and on the basis of this pledge (the Balfour
Declaration) that we received important help in the War, and after the
War we received from the Allied and Associated Powers the Mandate
for Palestine. This pledge of a home of refuge, of an asylum, was not
made to the Jews in Palestine but to the Jews scattered outside
Palestine, to that vast, unhappy mass of scattered, persecuted, wandering Jews whose intense, unchanging, unconquerable desire has
been for a National Home. . . . This is the pledge which we are now
asked to break, for how can this pledge be kept, I want to know, if in
five years' time the National Home is to be barred and no more Jews
are to be allowed in without the permission of the Arabs?
    I cannot feel that we have accorded to the Arab race unfair
treatment after the support which they gave us in the late War. The
Palestinian Arabs, of course, were for the most part fighting against us,
but elsewhere over the vast regions inhabited by the Arabs independent Arab kingdoms and principalities have come into being such as
had never been known in Arab history before. Some have been
established by Great Britain and others by France. . . .
    It is hoped to obtain five years of easement in Palestine by this
proposal; surely the consequences will be entirely the opposite. . . .
What about these five years? Who shall say where we are going to be
five years from now? Europe is more than two thirds mobilized

tonight. The ruinous race of armaments now carries whole populations into the military machine. That cannot possibly continue for five years, nor for four, nor for three years. It may be that it will not continue beyond the present year. Long before those five years are past, either there will be a Britain which knows how to keep its word on the Balfour Declaration and is not afraid to do so, or, believe me, we shall find ourselves relieved of many oversea responsibilities other than those comprised within the Palestine Mandate.

. . . Yesterday the Minister responsible descanted eloquently in glowing passages upon the magnificent work which the Jewish colonists have done. They have made the desert bloom. They have started a score of thriving industries. They have founded a great city on the barren shore. They have harnessed the Jordan and spread its electricity throughout the land. So far from being persecuted, the Arabs have crowded into the country and multiplied till their population has increased more than even all world Jewry could lift up the Jewish population. Now we are asked to decree that all this is to stop and all this is to come to an end. We are now asked to submit—and this is what rankles most with me—to an agitation which is fed with foreign money and ceaselessly inflamed by Nazi and Fascist propaganda.

It is twenty years since my right hon. Friend used these stirring words:

A great responsibility will rest upon the Zionists, who, before long, will be proceeding, with joy in their hearts, to the ancient seat of their people. Theirs will be the task to build up a new prosperity and a new civilization in old Palestine, so long neglected and mis-ruled.

Well, they have answered this call. They have fulfilled his hopes. How can he find it in his heart to strike them this mortal blow?
(Parliamentary Debate, House of Lords, vol. 113, no. 65, *House of Commons Official Report*, vol. 347, no. 107f)

* * *

Churchill to the Archbishop of Canterbury, 29 October 1942:

I cannot refrain from sending, through you, to the audience which is assembling under your Chairmanship at the Albert Hall today to protest against Nazi atrocities inflicted on the Jews, the assurance of my warm sympathy with the objects of the meeting. The systematic cruelties to which the Jewish people—men, women, and children—have been exposed under the Nazi regime are amongst the most terrible events of history, and place an indelible stain upon all those who perpetrate and instigate them. Free men and women denounce these vile crimes, and when this world struggle ends with the enthronement of human rights, racial persecution will be ended.

(Gilbert, *Road to Victory–Winston S. Churchill, 1941–1945*, p. 245)

* * *

Personal telegram to Chaim Weizmann, on the anniversary of the Balfour Declaration, 30 October, 1942:

My thoughts are with you on this anniversary. Better days will surely come for your suffering people and for the great cause for which you have fought so bravely.

(*Road to Victory*, p. 245)

* * *

At a meeting of the Chiefs of Staff Committee, 31 December 1942:

During the course of the raids, leaflets should be dropped warning the Germans that our attacks were reprisals for the persecution of the Poles and the Jews.

(*Road to Victory*, p. 287)

* * *

Told to the Spanish Ambassador, 7 April 1943, regarding the closing of the Franco-Spanish frontier to Jewish refugees and escaped POWs:

. . . if his Government (Franco's Spain) went to the length of preventing these unfortunate people seeking safety from the horrors of Nazi domination, and if they went farther and committed the offence of actually handing them back to the German authorities, that was a thing which would never be forgotten and would poison the relations between the Spanish and British peoples.

(*Road to Victory*, p. 377)

At a War Cabinet Defence Committee meeting, 19 April 1944:

. . . tell Dr. Weizmann that if such murders (in Palestine by Jewish fighters) continued and the campaign of abuse of the British in the American papers did not stop, we might well lose interest in Jewish welfare.

(Road to Victory, p. 744)

* * *

"Personal Minute" to Anthony Eden, 11 July 1944:[4]

There is no doubt that this is probably the greatest and most horrible crime ever committed in the whole history of the world, and it has been done by scientific machinery by nominally civilized men in the name of a great State and one of the leading races in Europe. It is quite clear that all concerned in this crime who may fall into our hands, including the people who only obeyed orders by carrying out the butcheries, should be put to death after their association with the murders has been proved.

(Road to Victory, pp. 846–847)

* * *

Lord Boothby's recollections of discussion with Churchill in September 1948:

I could put the case for the Jews (in Palestine) in ten minutes. We have treated them shamefully. I will never forgive the Irgun terrorists. But we should never have stopped immigration before the war.

(Gilbert, <i>"Never Despair"—Winston Churchill, 1945–1965</i>, p. 430)

* * *

In a speech of 10 December 1948, regarding the British government's refusal to recognize the new State of Israel:

The Jews have driven the Arabs out of a larger area than was contemplated in our partition schemes. They have established a Government which functions effectively. They have a victorious army at their disposal and they have the support both of Soviet Russia and of the United States.

---

[4]Written upon discovering the enormity of the mass slaughter of Jews then going on in Eastern Europe.

These may be unpleasant facts, but can they be in any way disputed? Not as I have stated them. It seems to me that the Government of Israel which has been set up in Tel Aviv cannot be ignored and treated as if it did not exist.

(*Never Despair*, p. 449)

* * *

In a speech in the House of Commons on 26 January 1949, urging British recognition of Israel:

Whether the right hon. Gentleman likes it or not, and whether we like it or not, the coming into being of a Jewish State in Palestine is an event in world history to be viewed in the perspective, not of a generation or a century, but in the perspective of a thousand, two thousand or even three thousand years. That is a standard of temporal values or time values which seems very much out of accord with the perpetual click-clack of our rapidly-changing moods and of the age in which we live.

This is an event in world history. . . .

(*Never Despair*, p. 454)

* * *

Churchill to President Weizmann, 9 February 1949, in response to his thanks for Britain's recognition of the new State of Israel:

I look back with much pleasure on our long association. The light grows.

(*Never Despair*, p. 458)

* * *

In a speech before U.S. Congress, 17 January 1952:

From the days of the Balfour Declaration I have desired that the Jews should have a national home, and I have worked for that end. I rejoice to pay my tribute here to the achievements of those who have founded the Israelite State, who have defended themselves with tenacity, and who offer asylum to great numbers of Jewish refugees.

I hope that with their aid they may convert deserts into gardens; but if they are to enjoy peace and prosperity they must strive to renew and preserve their friendly relations with the Arab world without which widespread misery might follow for all.

(*Never Despair*, p. 689)

* * *

Churchill to President Eisenhower, 16 April 1956:

I am, of course, a Zionist, and have been ever since the Balfour Declaration. I think it is a wonderful thing that this tiny colony of Jews should have become a refuge to their compatriots in all the lands where they were persecuted so cruelly, and at the same time established themselves as the most effective fighting force in the area. I am sure America would not stand by and see them overwhelmed by Russian weapons, especially if he had persuaded them to hold their hand while their chance remained.

(*Never Despair*, p. 1192)

* * *

To David Ben-Gurion on 2 June 1961, as recollected by his secretary, Yitzhak Navon:

You are a brave leader of a great nation.

(*Never Despair*, p. 1324)

THOMAS MANN   *(1875–1955)*

German novelist; author of The Magic Mountain; *Nobel Prize winner, 1929*

It is clear that the intensification of the Jewish problem is an accessory and a concomitant of the general wave of reaction against, and retrogression from, the humane and liberal ideas of the nineteenth century. . . . In times which would hardly any longer permit it to appear strange and in which the official and legal reintroduction of the rack, the wheel and of quartering would not meet with very great resistance, it cannot be an occasion for wonder if, as regards the Jewish world, too, attitudes, moods, doctrines and demands, which were perhaps excusable on the medieval level of the human mind, make their way to the forefront with saddening boldness and audacity. It is humiliating, revolting, to look upon such things, a source of deep depression not only for Jews, but also for every person who looks with reverence and sympathy upon the significant and characteristic contribution which the evolution of the human mind owes to this so highly gifted, peculiar, unusual people or race which has had so varied and fruitful a destiny.

(From a letter to the *American Hebrew*, 17 August 1932)

* * *

In March 1940:

Always when anti-Semitism breaks out, it means that the people feel ill at ease, hampered in their evil desires, that they are doing wrong, playing hookey from school, are up to bloody tricks and are eager to engage in warlike massacres instead of doing such things as are right, sensible and necessary. Then the Jews have to suffer. But they will suffer and survive. And we may all be certain that their strong sense of this world, and of social justice, will play an important part in the upbuilding of a new humanity struggling slowly out of its crisis.

(*Contemporary Jewish Record* in N. Zuckerman, ed.,
The Wine of Violence, p. 85.)

CARL JUNG   (1875–1961)

Swiss psychiatrist

One cannot, of course, accept that Freud or Adler is a generally valid representative of European mankind. . . . The Jews have this peculiarity in common with women: since they are physically weaker, they have to aim for the gaps in the armor of their adversaries, and on account of this technique, forced on them by centuries of history, the Jews themselves are best protected where others are most vulnerable. Since their culture is more than twice as ancient, they are far more conscious of human weaknesses and negative aspects than we are, and hence in this respect far less vulnerable. It is also thanks to their experience of ancient culture that it is possible for them to live in benevolent, amiable and tolerant acceptance of their own vices, while we are still too young to have no "illusions" about ourselves. Moreover, fate has destined us still to create a culture (which we are in need of), and for that purpose the so-called illusions in the form of one-sided ideals, convictions, plans, etc., are indispensable. . . .

The Aryan unconscious . . . contains powers and creative seeds that are still to be fulfilled in the future, and these must not be debased by nursery-romanticism [Jung's term for Freud's theories]. The still-young Teutonic peoples are thoroughly capable of creating new cultural forms, and this future lies in the darkness of the unconscious of every individual as an energy-laden seed, capable of becoming a mighty flame. The Jew as a relative nomad has never created, and presumably will never create, a cultural form of his own, for all his instincts and talents are dependent on a more or less civilized host people. The Jewish race possesses, in my experience, an unconscious that can bear only a very limited comparison with an Aryan one. . . .

The Aryan unconscious has a higher potential than the Jewish; that is both the advantage and disadvantage of a youthfulness not yet far removed from the barbaric. In my view it has been a grave mistake of medical psychology to apply Jewish categories, which are not even valid for all Jews, to Christian Germans and Slavs. In this way the most precious secret of Teutonic man—the deep-rooted creative awareness of his soul—has been explained away as a banal, infantile sump, while my warning voice, over the decades, was suspected of antisemitism. Freud was responsible for this insinuation. He did not know the Teutonic soul, any more than his blind followers in Germany knew it. Has the mighty phenomenon of National Socialism, at which the whole world gazes in astonishment, taught them to know better?

(*Zentralblatt fur Psychotherapie*, vol. VII, pp. 8–10)

ALBERT SCHWEITZER   *(1875–1965)*

German philosopher and medical missionary; Nobel Peace Prize, 1952

Occasionally Günsbach was visited by a Jewish peddler from a neighboring town. Since there were no Jews in Günsbach, Mäusche the peddler was both an oddity and an object lesson. The town's young boys, having heard lurid stories about the Jewish people, projected all their learned animosity upon Mäusche; to the boys, the peddler was the perfect prototype of the enemies of Christ. When Mäusche drove into town, the boys would run after his donkey cart, jeering, shouting his name and chanting invectives. Their shouting would follow the peddler all the way through town. One day young Schweitzer joined the other boys. Running close to the peddler's cart, he noticed that the man drove on, seemingly unperturbed, his freckled face wearing a patient expression except when he turned around and looked at the boys with an embarrassed but good-natured smile. It was almost as though Mäusche were sorry for them. "This smile overpowered me," Schweitzer recalled later. "From Mäusche I learned what it meant to keep silent under persecution, and this was a most valuable lesson."

(G. Marshall and D. Poling, *Schweitzer*, p. 6)

* * *

It was clear that Schweitzer was now a *persona non grata* to the government,[5] and would eventually have to leave the country. Yet many who remained in Germany found comfort in his words and position. One such person was a young minister, a former pacifist, Dietrich Bonhoeffer, who, upon the assumption of power by the Nazis, accepted an invitation to become minister of the German congregations of St. Paul and Sydenham, London. He remained there until 1935, departing only for brief visits to America, where he realized the need to make an unequivocal statement of protest against the German Christian community that had bowed silently before the totalitarian regime of Hitler. He returned to Germany to lead an emergency seminary for young ministers, and it was there that the *Philosophy of Civilization* by Dr. Schweitzer served the students as a description of the mass conformity and loss of individuality that was being witnessed in Germany on every hand. Almost alone, it seemed, Bonhoeffer tried to arouse the German religious community to withstand the restrictions and threats of Nazism. During this period, Bonhoeffer wrote *The Cost of Discipleship*, dealing with the developing crisis in Germany's cultural life and its Church. Unlike Schweitzer, he renounced his pacifism, and declared all out resistance to the course of events. The world knows the tragic cost of his discipleship, his hanging by the SS, set forth vividly in the surviving material published in English as *Letters from Prison*.

Schweitzer, however, was no longer a German national, and with a Jewish wife, could not safely re-enter Germany. His articles, lectures and books had to be his spokesmen. In addition, he had many close ties with German churchmen, whose difficult position he was

---

[5]Following his speech in Nazi Germany in 1933, referring obliquely to the "deep darkness" of the time.

forced to respect. In 1934, when both Schweitzer and Bonhoeffer were in London, they discussed common problems. Schweitzer, too, was committed to peace. He had long ago cast his lot with the free world against the Nazi menace. While in England, he decided never again to enter Nazi Germany. Hitler represented the exact kind of glorified war spirit to which Schweitzer was morally opposed. While lecturing in England, Schweitzer began to receive letters from German friends who pleaded that he not visit them if he came to Germany. They said they dared not speak out or take sides, and could not afford to risk their political neutralism or bring their thought under question by association with Schweitzer. Particularly dismaying to Schweitzer was the increasing number of religious leaders and pastors in the German State Church who wrote to him in this vein. He concluded that a state-connected Church simply could not be "the plumb line to God" (Amos 7) in an hour of national, social, political and moral failure. Accordingly Dr. Schweitzer canceled his scheduled speaking dates and concerts in Germany and, true to his word, was never to return to Germany as long as Hitler was alive. . . .

(Schweitzer, pp. 196–198)

* * *

A letter to Hamburg publisher Rowahlt Verlag (June 1963), when they sent him a copy of Rolf Hochhuth's play, *The Deputy*, which attacked Pope Pius XII for doing little to save Jews during the Holocaust:

I was an active witness of the failure which took place in those days, and I believe we must concern ourselves with this great problem of the events of history. We owe this to ourselves, for our failure made us all participants in the guilt of those days. After all, the failure was not that of the Catholic Church alone, but that of the Protestant Church as well. The Catholic Church bears the greater guilt for it was an organized, supra-national power in a position to do something, whereas the Protestant Church was an unorganized, impotent, national power. But it, too, became guilty, by simply accepting the terrible, inhuman fact of the persecution of the Jews. For in those days we lived in a time of inhumanity of culture, the beginning of which dates back to Friedrich Nietzsche at the end of the preceding century. The failure was that of philosophy, of free thought, as well.

(Schweitzer, p. 198)

The religions which decisively deny the world and life (Brahminism and Buddhism) show no interest in civilization. The Judaism of the prophetic period, the almost contemporary religion of Zarathustra, and the religious thought of the Chinese include in their ethical world—and life-affirmation—strong impulses to civilization. They want to improve social conditions, and they call men to purposeful action in the service of common aims which ought to be realized, whereas the pessimistic religions let men continue to pass their time in solitary meditation.

The Jewish prophets Amos and Isaiah (760–700 B.C.), Zarathustra (7th century B.C.), and Kungtse (560–480 B.C.) mark the great turning point in the spiritual history of mankind. Between the eighth and sixth centuries B.C., thinking men belonging to three nations, living in widely separated countries and having no relations whatever with one another, rise one and all to the perception that the ethical consists not in submission to traditional national customs, but in the active devotion of individuals to their fellow-men or to aims which should produce an improvement of social conditions. In this great revolution begins the spiritual humanizing of mankind and, with that, the civilization which is capable of the highest development. . . .

(Schweitzer, *Out of My Life and Thought, An Autobiography*, p. 215)

POPE PIUS XII   *(1876–1958)*

In a secret address to the Sacred College of Cardinals on the killing of Europe's Jews, June 1943:

Every word We address to the competent authority on this subject, and all Our public utterances have to be carefully weighed and measured by Us in the interests of the victims themselves, lest, contrary to Our intentions, We make their situation worse and harder to bear.

(Toland, *Adolf Hitler*, p. 760)

E. M. FORSTER   *(1879–1970)*

British writer; author of A Passage to India *and* A Room with a View

. . . I am asked to consider whether the people I meet and talk about are or are not Jews, and to form no opinion on them until this fundamental point has been settled. What revolting tosh! Neither science nor religion nor common sense has one word to say in its favour. All the same, Jew-consciousness is in the air, and it remains to be seen how far it will succeed in poisoning it. I don't think we shall ever reintroduce ghettoes into England; I wouldn't say for certain, since no one knows what wickedness may not develop in his country or in himself if circumstances change. I don't think we shall go savage. But I do think we shall go silly. Many people have gone so already. Today, the average man suspects the people he dislikes of being Jews, and is surprised when the people he likes are Jews. . . .

On the surface, things do not look too bad. Labour and Liberalism behave with their expected decency and denounce persecution, and respectability generally follows suit. But beneath the surface things are not so good, and anyone who keeps his ears open in railway carriages or pubs or country lanes can hear a very different story. A nasty side of our nation's character has been scratched up—the sniggering side. People who would not ill-treat Jews themselves, or even be rude to them, enjoy tittering over their misfortunes; they giggle when pogroms are instituted by someone else and synagogues defiled vicariously. 'Serve them right really, Jews.' This makes unpleasant reading, but anyone who cares to move out of his own enlightened little corner will discover that it is true. The grand Nordic argument, 'He's a bloody capitalist so he must be a Jew, and as he's a Jew he must be a Red,' has already taken root in our filling-stations and farms. Men employ it more frequently than women, and young men more frequently than old ones. The best way of confuting it is to say sneeringly 'That's propaganda.' When 'That's propaganda' has been repeated several times, the sniggering stops, for no goose likes to think that he has been got at. There is another reply which is more intellectual but which requires more courage. It is to say, 'Are you sure you're not a Jew yourself? Do you know who your eight great-grandparents were? Can you swear that all the eight are Aryan?' Cool reasonableness would be best of all, of course, but it does not work in the world of today any better than in my preparatory schools. The only effective check to silliness is silliness of a cleverer type.

Jew-mania was the one evil which no one foretold at the close of the last war. All sorts of troubles were discerned and discernable—nationalism, class-warfare, the split between the haves and the have-nots, the general lowering of cultural values. But no prophet, so far as

I know, had foreseen this anti-Jew horror, whereas today no one can see the end of it. There had been warnings, of course, but they seemed no more ominous than a poem by Hilaire Belloc. Back in India, in 1921, a colonel lent me the *Protocols of the Elders of Zion,* and it was such an obvious fake that I did not worry. . . .

To me, anti-Semitism is now the most shocking of all things. It is destroying much more than the Jews; it is assailing the human mind at its source, and inviting it to create false categories before exercising judgement. I am sure we shall win through. But it will take a long time. Perhaps a hundred years must pass before men can think back to the mentality of 1918, or can say with the Prophet Malachi, "Have we not all one father? Hath not one God created us?" For the moment, all that we can do is to dig in our heels, and prevent silliness from sliding into insanity.

(Forster, "Jew-consciousness," in *New Statesman,* 7 January 1939)

SIR (WILLIAM) MAXWELL AIKEN   *(1879–1964)*

1st Baron of Beaverbrook; Canadian financier, politician, and press lord in Great Britain

On 9 December 1938 he wrote to Frank Gannett:

> Neville Chamberlain has lost one chance after another of holding a successful election. . . . His policy of appeasement has been killed by British increased armaments, which upset the Germans, and by German persecution of the Jews which upset everybody.
>
> The Jews have got a big position in the press here. I estimate that one-third of the circulation of the *Daily Telegraph* is Jewish. The *Daily Mirror* may be owned by Jews. The *Daily Herald* is owned by Jews. And the *News-Chronicle* should really be the Jews Chronicle. Not because of ownership but because of sympathy.
>
> The *Times,* the *Daily Mail* and the *Express* are the only papers left. And I am not sure about the Mail.
>
> I have been, for years, a prophet of no war. But at last I am shaken. The Jews may drive us into war. I do not mean with any conscious purpose of doing so. They do not mean to do it. But

unconsciously they are drawing us into war. Their political influence is moving us in that direction.

This was a deplorable letter, which shows how little Beaverbrook really understood the British people. What turned the British peaple against Nazi Germany was Hitler's treatment of the Jews, not propaganda by Jews or anyone else in British newspapers. The facts made the propaganda by themselves.

In any case this letter was no more than a passing aberration. Beaverbrook had no sympathy with anti-semitism. Many years later there was criticism when a Jew was appointed to a high post on one of his papers. He reacted sharply:

> It would be intolerable if prejudice existed against Scots in England. And certainly much worse for that race if Canadians should object to them. And what is the difference between Scots and Jews.
>
> It may be claimed that the prejudice is unreasoning and nothing can be said to account for it. Certainly that is true. But it is the duty of newspaper editors to refuse to be moved by any such survival of ignorance and prejudice.
>
> (Taylor, *Beaverbrook*, p. 387)

OSWALD SPENGLER   (1880–1936)

German historian; author of The Decline of the West

The Jew could not comprehend the Gothic inwardness, the castle, the Cathedral; nor the Christian the Jew's superior, almost cynical, intelligence and his finished expertness in money-thinking. . . .

It meant a good deal for a Scottish monk to visit a Lombard monastery, and nostalgia soon took him home again; but when a rabbi of Mainz—in 1000 the seat of the most important talmudic seminary of the West—or of Salerno betook himself to Cairo or Merv or Basra, he was at home in every ghetto. . . .

This feeling of being different is more potent on both sides, the more breed the individual possesses. It is *want* of race, and nothing else, that makes intellectuals—philosophers, doctrinaires, Utopists— incapable of understanding the depth of this metaphysical hatred, which is the beat-difference of two currents of being manifested as an unbearable dissonance, a hatred that may become tragic for both. . . . During the Gothic age this difference is deep and religious, and the object of hatred is the Consensus as religion; only with the beginning of Western Civilization does it become materialist and begin to attack Jewry on its intellectual and business sides, on which the West suddenly finds itself confronted by an even challenger. . . .

The Jewish Consensus ceased to have a history at all. Its problems were solved, its inner form was complete, conclusive, and unalterable. . . . Epochs succeeded to epochs, every century witnessed fundamental human changes, but in the ghetto and in the souls of its denizens all stood still. And even when a Jew regarded himself as a member of the people amongst whom he sojourned and took part in their good and evil fortune—as happened in so many countries in 1914—he lived these experiences, not really as something *his own*, but as a partisan, a supporter; he judged them as an interested spectator, and hence it is just the deepest meanings of the struggle that must ever remain hidden from him. A Jewish cavalry-general fought in the Thirty Years' War—he lies buried in the old Jewish cemetery at Prague—but what did the ideas of Luther or Loyola mean to him?

(*Decline of the West*, vol. II, pp. 317, 319)

POPE JOHN XXIII (ANGELO GIUSEPPE RONCALLI)   *(1881–1963)*

. . . Turkish neutrality meant that Roncalli became, as he put it, the Vatican's postman for the whole of the Middle East and beyond. . . . What he does not tell his sisters, however, is that on the very day he was writing to them, September 5, 1940, he had met a party of Polish Jews who brought grim news from Nazi-occupied Poland. He helped them on their way to the Holy Land. Von Papen's assurances about the "independence" of Poland were already exposed as nonsense.

A month later—according to von Papen, the war ought to have been over—he began the most sombre retreat of his life at the villa house of the Sisters of Our Lady of Sion. It was at Terapia and overlooked the Bosphorus. But this time there were no twinkling lights of fishing boats out at sea. Following a suggestion of Pius XII, he took Psalm 51, the *Miserere*, as the basis of his meditations. So he was praying this Jewish prayer, in the midst of a community dedicated to ministering to Jews, at a time when the first inkling of the terrible fate that awaited them had begun to emerge. Some things became clearer to him.

The first was simply that no nation can claim to have God on its side. This 'murderous war that is being waged on land and sea and in the air' was certainly no crusade: 'It has been asserted, and is still being asserted, that God is bound to preserve this or that country or grant it invulnerability and final victory, because of the righteous people who live there and the good they do. We forget that although God has made the nations, he has left the constitution of states to the free decisions of men'. . . . (*Journal*, p. 257)

. . . Why should men desire what is so evidently opposed to the common good? Roncalli's answer is that war-lust is stimulated and sustained by nationalism, especially the nationalisms that are based on theories of 'racial purity'. Nationalism is the perversion of patriotism: 'Patriotism, which is right and may be holy, may also degenerate into nationalism . . . The world is poisoned by morbid nationalism, built up on the basis of race and blood, in contradiction with the Gospel. In this matter, which is of burning topical interest, 'deliver me from men of blood, O Lord. . . .' " (*Journal*, pp. 270–1)

. . . Roncalli's wartime mediation foreshadows the ecclesiology of Vatican II: he sees the Church not merely as an institution but as the living people of God, in movement, on the march, a sign and a light to the nations, *Lumen Gentium*. . . .

(Hebblewaith, *Pope John XXIII, Shepherd of the Modern World*, pp. 170–171)

* * *

. . . He needed Raymond Courvoisier and the Red Cross (known as the Red Crescent in Turkey so as not to upset Islamic sensibilities) in the other task which now engrossed him: aiding Jews. Von Papen, speaking on oath to the postulator of Pope John's beatification cause, claimed that he 'helped 24,000 Jews with clothes, money and documents' (see Zizola, in *Oggi*, April 13, 1963). It is difficult to translate charity into statistics. It would be better in this context to follow the Talmudic verse which says, 'He who saves a single life, saves the world entire.'

. . . Roncalli had been made aware of the problem at a relatively early stage of the war, through refugees from Poland. The fate of the *Struma* continued to haunt him. The *Struma* left the Rumanian port of Constanza in December 1941 carrying a human cargo of 769 Jewish refugees. It was mysteriously blown up by a mine, and there was only one survivor, Zelia Stolaric. In 1943 Mother Marie Casilda, a Sister of Our Lady of Sion, wrote to Roncalli from Bucharest about the fate of the *Struma*. She refused to believe that the Turks had simply blown the ship up. She imagined it must have been a legal cover-story to mask the rescue of the Jews who were now safe in some secret camp. Roncalli let her down gently. Her version of the story was wishful thinking. But, 'We are dealing with one of the great mysteries in the history of humanity. Poor children of Israel. Daily I hear their groans around me. They are relatives and fellow-countrymen of Jesus. May the Divine Saviour come to their aid and enlighten them' (*Actes et documents*, 9, p. 310: Letter dated April 14, 1943). To describe the holocaust as a 'mystery' is the right place to begin thinking about this ultimate in horror: it belongs to the mystery of iniquity.

Istanbul played a key-role. Turkey was still neutral, and the last escape-route out of Nazi-occupied Europe led through the Balkans and via Istanbul. It also led to Palestine, then under British mandate. But the British argument against accepting more than a limited number of refugees in Palestine was that 'there might be spies among them,' and that Jewish expansion ought to depend upon Arab consent that was unlikely to be forthcoming (see Bernard Wasserstein, *Britain and the Jews of Europe, 1939–1945*). Istanbul was at the cross-roads of information if not of immigration. Roncalli was better informed than his superiors in the Vatican. The Jewish organisation had offices in Istanbul and was desperate for help. Chaim Barlas of the Jerusalem Jewish Agency met him on January 22, 1943. It was the first of many meetings that culminated a year later in a visit from the Grand Rabbi of Jerusalem, Isaac Herzog.

Roncalli, however, did not have much freedom of action. Most of the time he was merely the link-man who forwarded requests to the Vatican. In January 1943 Chaim Barlas asked him to transmit three very modest but basic requests. Would the Vatican sound out neutrals like Portugal and Sweden to see if they would grant temporary asylum to Jews who managed to escape? This would involve no financial liability. American Jewry would look after them. Second, would the

Vatican inform the German government that the Palestine Jewish Agency had 5000 immigration certificates available? Finally Barlas wanted Vatican Radio to declare loud and clear that 'rendering help to persecuted Jews is considered by the Church to be a good deed' (*Actes et documents*, 9, pp. 87–8). That such a statement was thought necessary was a measure of how deep the roots of Christian anti-Semitism were. Though Roncalli's task here was simply to transmit, not to explain or justify, there is no reason to believe that he regarded these requests as anything other than reasonable and fulfillable.

The Vatican thought otherwise. . . . [Its] answer was disappointing, pompous and disconcerting. The Holy See had helped Jewish emigration in the past by taking soundings and providing subsidies, but 'unfortunately this help has increasingly encountered no slight difficulties which, for the time being, are insurmountable.' Since no 'subsidies' had been requested, it was impossible to understand why 'taking soundings' should run into such insurmountable difficulties. . . . [The Vatican was] distinctly cool about 'the transfer of Jews to Palestine, because one cannot prescind from the strict connection between this problem and that of the Holy Places, for whose liberty the Holy See is deeply concerned' (*Actes et documents*, 9, p. 137).

(*Pope John XXIII, Shepherd of the Modern World*, pp. 186–187)

* * *

. . . The immediate consequence of Italy switching sides was that the country including Rome became in effect German-occupied. It was urgent therefore to get the remaining Italian Jews out of the country as soon as possible. Many were put on ships heading for Palestine. Roncalli *protested* to Cardinal Maglione, not at the fact that they were helped to escape, but at their destination. Since this was the only instance of Roncalli questioning the wisdom of a Vatican decision, his feelings must have been very strong. On September 4, 1943, he wrote to the Cardinal Secretary of State:

I confess that this convoy of Jews to Palestine, aided specifically by the Holy See, looks like the reconstruction of the Hebrew Kingdom, and so arouses certain doubts in my mind. . . . That their fellow Jews and political friends should want them to go there makes perfect sense. But it does not seem to me that the

simple and elevated charity of the Holy See should lend itself to
the suspicion that by this co-operation, at least an initial and
indirect contribution is being made to the realisation of the
messianic dream.

Perhaps this is no more than a personal scruple that only
has to be admitted to be dissolved, so clear it is that the
reconstruction of the Kingdom of Judaea and Israel is no more
than a utopia. (*Actes et documents*, 9, p. 469)

After his outburst, Roncalli never referred to the matter again.
But his scruple was rather disconcerting. Before the state of Israel
existed, it was easier to make a distinction between 'helping Jews' and
'helping Zionists' and to prefer the former activity. Roncalli did so for
what at the time were valid theological reasons: since the true
Messiah had already come, it was impossible to envisage the return of
the people of Israel to their ancient homeland. Yet it was an
insensitive argument because in 1943 the problem was to find any
country at all that would take those who had escaped the
extermination camps.

Roncalli's practice was better than his theology. He continued to
help Jews on their way to Palestine. In February 1944 he had two
meetings with Isaac Herzog, grand rabbi of Jerusalem, about the fate of
the 55,000 Jews of Transnistria. . . . A bleak and inhospitable region,
it became a kind of penal colony for deported Jews. As the German
front began to crumble, the Jews were shunted westwards towards the
extermination camps. The last hope was that the Vatican would be
able to intercede with the Rumanian government. This time Roncalli
pulled out all the stops, and earned the following testimonial from
Rabbi Herzog:

Before leaving, God willing, this evening, I want to express my
deepest gratitude for the energetic steps that you have taken and
will undertake to save our unfortunate people, innocent victims
of unheard of horrors from a cruel power which totally ignores
the principles of religion that are the basis of humanity. You
follow in the tradition, so profoundly humanitarian, of the Holy
See, and you follow the noble feelings of your own heart. The
people of Israel will never forget the help brought to its unfortunate brothers and sisters by the Holy See and its highest repre-

sentatives at this the saddest moment of our history. (*Acts et documents*, p. 161: letter dated 28 February 1944).

Herzog, who had been chief rabbi in Dublin from 1925 to 1936, also sent 'the blessings of Jerusalem and Sion' to Roncalli . . . [He] was deeply touched. On March 23, 1944, he was able to report to Chaim Barlas that all the matters raised had been taken up by the Holy See, and he concluded his letter: 'May God be with you, bringing you grace and prosperity. Always at your service, and at the service of all the brothers of Israel' (*Actes et documents*, 10, p. 188).

He was to echo these words on October 17, 1960, when he met 130 U.S. Jews led by Rabbi Herbert Friedman. He told them his favourite story about Joseph recognising his brothers:

> I am your brother. Certainly there is a difference between those who admit only the Old Testament as their guide and those who add the New Testament as the supreme law and guide. But that distinction does not abolish the brotherhood that comes from a common origin. We are all sons of the same Father. We come from the Father, and must return to the Father (Righi, p. 197).

His wartime experiences in Istanbul proved that these were not empty formulas. . . .

(*Pope John XXIII, Shepherd of the Modern World*, pp. 192–193)

* * *

One particular race had special claim on his attention: the Jews. His wartime memories were still vivid. In Algiers cathedral in March, 1950 he spoke of the Jews as 'the children of promise' (Romans 9:8), 'whom I so often met in Eastern Europe, sometimes in moments of grief, but always in the mutual exchange of human and fraternal charity' (Mission, p. 120). The basis for serious theological dialogue was 'to contemplate the people of Israel in the light of Abraham, the great patriarch of all believers.' He had many Jewish friends in Paris, and rejoiced when one of them, Antonio Coen, returned to the faith of his ancestors after a bout of Freemasonry. . . .

(*Pope John XXIII, Shepherd of the Modern World*, pp. 231–232)

P. G. WODEHOUSE   (1881–1975)

British novelist and humorist

During the whole of the time Plum [Wodehouse's nickname] was interned he made notes for a book on life in camp, which he intended to write after he was released. . . . "The Camp Note Book" is not to be confused with *The Camp Book*. . . .

The suggestion has been made that certain passages about the Jews in camp may give offense on the grounds that they are anti-Semitic. Yet, if one reads Plum's comments on the Belgians and the French, on the likeness of "Mr. Big," the camp commandant, to retired British colonels who live in Cheltenham or Bexhill, or, more especially, on the English (men holding British passports) at Liège, one cannot help thinking the Jews get off fairly lightly. Plum was born one hundred years ago, and these notes were not meant to be read by anyone but himself. The quality they chiefly exhibit is the insularity so common to Englishmen at that date. Today one cannot conceive, much less explain, how it was possible for intelligent and educated people never to question these assumptions of personal superiority. Yet such attitudes were widespread right up to the Second World War, and were adopted not merely towards "foreigners," but towards people of any class lower in the social scale than one's own, and to those who held different beliefs. If the "sixteen Jews, headed by a rabbi," to whom Plum refers, had been Plymouth Brethren or even Methodists, they might well have received the same treatment, while the Frenchman, "Guts and Gaiters," and a character called 'My boy'—Young Petersen" are spoken of in terms not unlike those applied to the Jew with spectacles. All these things were for his own amusement, and Plum was not always funny when he meant to be.

I do not of course suggest that the contemporary attitude to Jews was only to be found in England, because it was widespread in the rest of Europe and in America, and in both places produced more serious results. But it could often be merely a manner of speaking, a kind of club talk, which had no bearing on actual relationships or emotions towards particular individuals. Plum was too little involved in real life to examine or reject traditional attitudes, and I very much doubt if he could be described as anti-Semitic. He had few friends, but many of the people he most liked and respected were Jews, while he was known to have real affection for several of them. Unlike contemporary writers such as Sapper, John Buchan and Dornford Yates, he never made jokes about Jews (unless they happened to be the President of Perfec-to-Zizzbaum Motion Picture Corp., when the joke was against Holly-wood). Richard Usborne tells me that when he sent Plum the original draft of his book *Wodehouse at Work*, which contained a passage making this point, he scored it heavily in the margin, and in a scribbled sentence beginning "For God's sake . . ." wrote a comment to the effect that having spent thirty years in the American theatre, he was not likely to make jokes about Jews.

(Donaldson, *P.G. Wodehouse, A Biography*, pp. 155–156)

VIRGINIA WOOLF   *(1882–1941)*

British novelist; author of Mrs. Dalloway, To the Lighthouse

In 1915, after attending a concert in the Queen's Hall, in Langham Place, then London's main concert hall, she wrote: 'I begin to loathe my kind, principally from looking at their faces in the tube. Really, raw red beef & silver herrings give me more pleasure to look upon.' And so to the next day: 'I do not like the Jewish voice; I do not like the Jewish laugh.' There was no attempt to control the irrational malice. It arose from her jealousy of her sister-in-law, who managed to publish stories while earning her living as a secretary.

(L. Gordon, *Virginia Woolf—A Writer's Life*, pp. 62–63)

* * *

[George] Steiner has argued that the Jews were persecuted not for the given reasons but in resentment of their spiritual gift, and it seems that Virginia Woolf detected this gift in her husband [Leonard Woolf, a Jew], despite his atheism. When a friend, Ethel Smyth, deplored her lack of religious sense, blaming Leonard, she retorted, 'Lord! How I detest these savers up of merit . . . ; my Jew has more religion in one toenail—more human love, in one hair.'

(*Virginia Woolf—A Writer's Life*, p. 229)

. . . While writing with enjoyment during 1940, Virginia had to concede Leonard's dread of German occupation. "The least that I could look forward to as a Jew would be to be beaten up," he told her. She knew that a Jew's wife would go to a concentration camp, but she could not work up more than mild assent to Leonard's desperate plans.

"There would be no point in waiting," he said. "We would shut the garage door and commit suicide." His first idea was that they asphyxiate themselves and he laid by a supply of petrol for that purpose. In June he acquired a supply of "protective poison" (a lethal dose of morphia) from Adrian Stephen.

"No," Virginia wrote of the first suicide pact, "I don't want the garage to see the end of me. I've a wish for 10 years more, & to write my book [*Between the Acts*] which as usual darts into my brain."

(*Virginia Woolf — A Writer's Life*, p. 271)

JAMES JOYCE   (1882–1941)

Irish novelist; author of Ulysses, Finnegans Wake

The subject of the Jews had seized upon Joyce's attention as he began to recognize his place in Europe to be as ambiguous as theirs. He was interested in a Jewish divorce case in Dublin, in the fact that Georg Brandes was a Jew, in Ferrero's theories of anti-Semitism. . . .

(R. Ellmann, *James Joyce*, p. 230)

* * *

In making his hero [of *Ulysses*] Leopold Bloom, Joyce recognized implicitly what he often spoke of directly, his affinity for the Jews as a wandering, persecuted people. "I sometimes think," he said later to Frank Budgen, "that it was a heroic sacrifice on their part when they refused to accept the Christian revelation. Look at them. They are better husbands than we are, better fathers and better sons." No doubt the incongruity of making his good Dubliner a Jew, and one so indifferent to all religious forms as to have sampled (without accepting) both Protestantism and Catholicism, attracted him with its satirical possibilities. But he must have been affected also by the Dreyfus uproar in Paris, which continued from 1892 to 1906; it had reached one of its crises in September 1902, just before Joyce's arrival in Paris, when Anatole France, a writer he respected, delivered his eloquent oration at the funeral of Zola, whose *J'accuse* was still stirring up Europe. A connection between the Jew and his artist-defender may have been fixed in Joyce's mind by the connection between Zola, France, and Dreyfus. When he returned to Dublin in 1903, he was in time for one of the rare manifestations of anti-Semitism in Ireland, a boycott of Jewish merchants in Limerick that was accompanied by some violence.

(*James Joyce*, p. 373)

* * *

He was interested too, in the way that, as he said, "A Jew is both king and priest in his own family."

(*James Joyce*, p. 373)

* * *

The question of national traits interested him very much. At the Trattoria Bonavia one day, Joyce allocated the seven deadly sins among the European nations. Gluttony, he said, was English, Pride French, Wrath Spanish, Lust German, Sloth Slavic. "What is the Italian sin? Avarice," he concluded, recalling how often he had been cheated by shopkeepers and how wickedly he had been robbed in Rome. As for his own people, the Irish, their deadly sin was Envy. . . . Schwarz asked, "Then what is the deadly sin of the Jews?" Joyce pondered, excluded one after the other, then said, "None, except of course the one mortal sin. . . ." "Which?" "To have crucified Jesus."

(*James Joyce*, p. 382)

* * *

Now that Joyce was free to devote himself to *Ulysses*, he often discussed topics related to the book. One such subject was the similarity of the Jews and the Irish, on which Joyce insisted. They were alike, he declared, in being impulsive, given to fantasy, addicted to associative thinking, wanting in rational discipline. He held, perhaps with Arnold's "Hebraism and Hellenism" in mind, that there were two basically different ways of thinking, the Greek and the Jewish, and that the Greek was logical and rational. One day he and Weiss were walking and met a Greek, with whom they talked for a long time. Afterwards Joyce remarked, "It's strange—you spoke like a Greek and he spoke like a Jew." . . . Joyce recognized his affinities to both groups. He had a little book on the Jews by a man named Fishberg, which contained pictures of Chinese Jews with pigtails, Mongolian Jews with Mongolian features, and the like. Such curiosities about the race were what especially interested Joyce. He knew little of Zionism, which was already taking hold among European Jews; but when one day Weiss commented on the possibility of a Jewish state, Joyce wryly remarked, "That's all very well, but believe me, a warship with a captain named Kanalgitter and his aide named Captain Afterduft would be the funniest thing the old Mediterranean has ever seen."

(James Joyce, pp. 395–396)

* * *

During 1921 he had time for many visitors and for some new friends, chiefly Irish and American. Most of them perceived, at least dimly, that he was a genius. Among the first of the Irishmen to see him was A. J. Leventhal, a young graduate of Trinity College and now a lecturer there. They spoke of the various Jewish families whose names were mentioned in Ulysses. . . . Joyce asked particularly about the Blooms, and was relieved to hear from Leventhal that they had all left the city. He showed Leventhal some of the Hebrew words in Ulysses, but refused to credit his suggestion that there was some confusion between the Spanish and German transliterations—an error that persists in the published text. Before his visitor left Joyce sat down at the piano and played and sang the Hebrew song, the Hatikvah. Leventhal returned to Dublin to write under the pseudonym of 'L. K. Emery' one of the first and most appreciative reviews of Ulysses.

(James Joyce, p. 513)

* * *

In general he had lost interest in his earlier book, Finnegans Wake having pre-empted its position, but he allowed himself one day to ask [Samuel, the future playwright] Beckett, 'Does anyone in Dublin read

Ulysses? 'Yes,' said Beckett. "Who?" Beckett named some names. "But they're all Jews," Joyce said. . . .

(James Joyce, p. 702)

* * *

. . . For some years he had referred to Germany derisively as "Hitlerland," and no one could have been less attracted than he to the frenzied personality of the Fuehrer. But he cultivated disengagement, and remarked one night at dinner at Paul Leon's, "Isn't this Hitler a phenomenon? Think of getting a whole people behind you." Nora picked up a knife and said, "You stop that, Jim." He spoke highly of German precision to friends whom he knew to be hostile to any favorable mention of Germany. Samuel Beckett spoke to Joyce of the Nazis' persecution of the Jews, but Joyce pointed out there had been similar persecutions before. It was not that he condoned them, but that he wished to withdraw to another perspective. . . .

On the other hand, Joyce did not blind himself to what was going on. He remarked to Maria Jolas of anti-Semitism, "It's one of the easiest and oldest prejudices to 'prove.'" When a young Harvard student wrote to him to praise *Ulysses* but complain of Joyce's attitude towards his race, Joyce remarked, "I have written with the greatest sympathy about the Jews." *Ulysses* was, in fact, if anyone cared to examine it, so anti-totalitarian a book that there was no more to be said. Joyce's views were reaffirmed by his actions; in 1938 he began to help people to escape from Nazi territory to Ireland and America. . . . Joyce had friends in the French Foreign Office and elsewhere whose help he enlisted, with his usual energy, in behalf of about sixteen refugees in various states of flight or resettlement. Joyce had Padraic Colum write to the Irish Minister of Justice, asking for a residence permit for one of these. The reply was no. Joyce would not accept the refusal. He said to Colum, "You didn't put the matter strongly enough. Write to the man again." This time the minister acceded.

(James Joyce, p. 708)

* * *

. . . Some place in Switzerland, however, became for certain the goal of the family. . . . On September 13, 1940, Joyce returned to his original idea of going to Zurich, and applied to the Swiss consulate in Lyons for visas and for permission to stay in Zurich for the duration of the war. . . . These authorities had an opportunity to display the same respect for genius that the British had shown in admitting Sigmund Freud, but they did not recognize Joyce's name and merely advised on September 30 the rejection of his application. One of Joyce's friends went to the office to ask the reason, and was told it was because Joyce was a Jew. "*C'est le bouquet, vraiment,*" Joyce exclaimed on being informed of this.

In the meantime further documents had arrived, and the Federal Aliens' Police sent the application back to Zurich on October 18 for reconsideration. An imposing group of Swiss citizens now ranged themselves on Joyce's side: in Lausanne Jacques Mercanton deposed that Joyce was not a Jew, or, in Joyce's own words to Armand Petitjean and Louis Gillet, "*que je ne suis juif de Jude mais aryen d'Erin.*"

(*James Joyce*, p. 736)

* * *

Edmund Brauchbar, a Zurich businessman who studied English with Joyce during the first World War, and subsequently moved to New York . . . was attempting to aid Jewish refugees, including some of his relations, to establish themselves in other countries. Joyce was happy to assist in this work. . . .

(R. Ellmann, *James Joyce – Letters*, vol. III, p. 430)

* * *

Translation of a postcard, written in French, to Jacques Mercanton on 29 October 1940:

We are still here, for we have not received from Berne the permit to reside in Switzerland which we applied for six weeks ago . . . Mme Giedion went to the Aliens' Police at Zurich where they seemed to believe that I am . . . a Jew! I am thunderstruck! There's a remarkable discovery! Cordially yours James Joyce

(*James Joyce – Letters*, vol. III, p. 491)

WYNDHAM LEWIS (1882–1957)

British novelist, essayist, and painter

In 1930, however, the Nazis got under his guard. On a business visit to Berlin, which he found a "Haupstadt of Vice, the excelsior Eldorado of a sexish bottom-wagging most arch old Nick, sunk within a costly and succulent rut," he was impressed by the Tarr-like professionalism of the Nazi party members. . . . The Nazi, he wrote, "is not a sex-moralist at all." He concentrates on issues of far more public moment:

> The Bank is more important than the Backside. And the young Nationalsocialist has firmly grasped this fundamental truth, in a manner that no average political Anglo-Saxon would—who always allows his pocket to be picked provided you fix his attention on something that is "wicked" or naughty.

Even the Nazi substitution of race for class seemed to him on the whole an advantage. "Race is a more *inclusive* thing than Class." Class, he had noted in *The Art of Being Ruled,* was one of the prime techniques of *divide et impera.*

> The more classes . . . that you can make him become regularly conscious of, the more you can control him, the more of an automaton he becomes. Thus, if a man can be made to feel himself acutely (a) an American, (b) a young American, (c) a middle-west young American. . . .

Hence his applause for a party that proposed one class (the "Aryan") to replace several dozen. The corollary anti-Semitism he dismissed as a mere *Agitationsmittel.* Remarking on this casualness nine years later, Lewis recalled that when he lived as a student in Munich about 1905 he "observed just as much anti-Semitism as is to be found there to-day." Hence "when I began to study Hitlerism I thought that Hitler was only going on about the Jews as Germans always had."

The apparent naivete of this must be weighed against Lewis's taste for system and his temperamental indifference to persons. The world he was observing, especially when it was characterized by political outlines on which his draughtsman's intelligence could seize, always seemed to him little more real than a Punch and Judy show. What he observed in Munich in 1905 impressed him—perhaps accurately—as a relatively harmless knockabout farce engaged in by people who on both sides had cheerfully turned themselves into racial stereotypes: no more sanguinary than Dr. Johnson's sparring with the Scots. . . .

When late in the 1930s human beings entered Lewis's world, his lack of alarm at Hitler's sanguinary grimaces required a good deal of rationalizing. *The Hitler Cult* (1939) and its outrigger *The Jews, Are They Human?* modify the original *Hitler* (1931) very considerably. "Hitler as a political corrective and Hitler as Augustus are two different things. As the latter he is neither an attractive nor an impressive spectacle. . . ."

But while events were reconciling him to the unwisdom of presenting Hitler as even "a political corrective," Lewis made use of his temporary detachment to ridicule the cant surrounding the aversion to Naziism that characterized British politics in the 1930s. In *Left Wings Over Europe* (1936) and *Count Your Dead—They Are Alive!* (1937) he described it as in part fostered, on allegedly humanitarian grounds, by "friends of the Soviet Union" whose humanitarianism was itself an *Agitationsmittel*, and who blandly ignored purges and slaughters conducted in their political homeland on a scale the Nazis hadn't then attempted to match. The Internationalists were brewing a war, and they didn't care what sentiments they exploited. In *The Jews, Are They Human?* (1939), the tone of which is a more valuable antiseptic to both anti-Semitism and its doctrinaire opposite than anything Lewis succeeds in saying, he suddenly deserts his role of dispassionate realist to cast in the teeth of indignant adversaries their indifference to the plight of the British workman:

> For it is certain that no German or Pole could be more inhuman towards a Jew, than we are towards our aged poor, or towards the Englishman or Englishman who is down and out. Our "forgotten men" are worse pariahs than any Jew is in a Central European city. We have our Ghettos too. Our Ghettos are our *slums*. That is what we call our Ghettos. But in our Ghettos we herd and starve *our own people*. That is the difference.

Though this doesn't negate Lewis's own earlier indifference, it suggests that the hands of his accusers have been far from clean. The pogroms have made it easy to misrepresent his book, composed in a time when there seemed so little reason to suppose that the Nazis would ever shed any blood that the British press treated them as a joke. In *Hitler* Lewis was certainly not advocating either anti-Semitism or a British Fuehrer. He was simply not scandalized by such possibilities, as (regarding power as inescapable) he has never been scandalized by any relatively bloodless manifestation of power. He understood the folly of not taking Hitler seriously and the folly of pretending that Germany could be indefinitely prevented from having a significant national existence. . . . Though his books in the 1920s had gotten sensationally good reviews, Lewis's reputation underwent in 1931 an occultation from which it has never recovered. His books stopped being reviewed at all, and it was arranged that his best novel should suffocate unnoticed in England and go unpublished in the United States for fifteen years.

The Hitler book, incidentally, displeased both Hitler and Goebbels. As soon as they came to power the German translation was pulped.

(H. Kenner, *Wyndham Lewis*, pp. 81–85)

JACQUES MARITAIN   *(1882–1973)*

French Catholic philosopher and theologian

First of all, there is [the people Israel's] vocation as a witness to the Scriptures. But more, while the Church is assigned the labor of supernatural and supratemporal redemption of the world, Israel, we believe, is assigned, on the plane and within the limits of secular history, a task of *earthly activization* of the mass of the world. Israel, which is not of the world, is to be found at the very heart of the world's structure, stimulating it, exasperating it, moving it. Like an alien body, like an activating ferment injected into the mass, it gives the world no peace, it bars slumber, it teaches the world to be discontented and restless as long as the world has not God — it stimulates the movement of history.

(*A Christian Looks at the Jewish Question*, p. 28)

BENITO MUSSOLINI   *(1883–1945)*

Italian fascist leader

Speech made in 1927:

We in Italy find it utterly ridiculous when we hear how the anti-Semites in Germany seek to flourish in the midst of Fascism. We protest with all our energy against Fascism being compromised in this way. Anti-Semitism is a product of barbarism.

Told to Emil Ludwig in 1932:

National pride has no need of the delirium of race. Anti-Semitism does not exist in Italy. Italians of Jewish birth have shown themselves good citizens and they fought bravely in the war.

* * *

On the report that 27 out of every 100 Jewish women in Italy married Catholic men:

These figures are proof that Italy has no anti-Semitic movement. Every Italian will welcome this increasing frequency of mixed marriages as a favourable indication of the absolute legal, juridical, political, and moral equality of the Italian people.

(A note from Mussolini to the Italo-Jewish journal *Israel*, 1932)

* * *

In an interview with Generoso Pope, publisher of several Italian newspapers in the U.S., 1937:

I authorize you to declare and to make known, immediately upon your return to New York, to the Jews of America, that their preoccupation for their brothers living in Italy is nothing but the fruit of evil informers. I authorize you to specify that the Jews in Italy have received, receive, and will receive the same treatment accorded to every other Italian citizen and that no form of racial or religious discrimination is in my thought, which is devoted and faithful to the policy of equality in law and the freedom of worship.

When [Emil] Ludwig's book came out in the early thirties, very few people in Italy and in other countries knew much about the dictator, his past, his "true" ideas, and his future intentions; they saw him only at official functions or reflected in the stories that the press office was instructed to give out. Consequently, *Talks with Mussolini*, this candid portrait of the dictator, was of considerable interest. In our day, seen against the background of all the material that has since been published on the duce, Ludwig's portrait loses its appeal. Yet many Italians still remember one of Mussolini's statements: "Anti-Semitism does not exist in Italy. Italians of Jewish birth have shown themselves good citizens, and they fought bravely in the war. Many of them occupy leading positions, in the universities, in the army, in the banks. Quite a number of them are generals. . . ." The Italian Jews, who interpreted this assertion as a pledge, were stunned when, suddenly and without warning, the anti-Semitic laws were promulgated in 1938 — and *Talks with Mussolini* was withdrawn for good from circulation.

(L. Fermi, Mussolini, pp. 290–291)

* * *

In the summer of 1938 Mussolini, pursuing the "Prussianization of Italy," doggedly pushed an anti-Semitic campaign, modeled on the Nazi pattern.

Until then there had been little anti-Semitism in Italy. There were approximately 50,000 Italian Jews, little more than one out of every thousand of the population, and in modern times they had never constituted a problem. Mussolini had often publicly recognized this fact and paid tribute to the many Italian Jews who had rendered great service to their country. . . . The launching of a policy of racial discrimination came as a surprise and antagonized not only the Jews and their friends but the Vatican and the monarchy as well: the Vatican, both because the Catholic doctrine is universal and open to all races by definition, and because the restrictions on mixed marriages and other clauses of the racial laws infringed on the holy institutions of marriage and the family; the monarchy, because anti-Semitism was against the spirit of the constitution, which assured religious freedom to all Italian citizens.

The anti-Semitic campaign was officially launched on July 14, 1938, with the publication of the *Manifesto della Razza*, a pseudoscientific document signed by five university professors and several younger "scientists." Only after World War II was it revealed that Mussolini himself had compiled the largest part of the manifesto; indeed, only Mussolini could have so shamelessly put together so many absurdities and tried to drown them in rhetoric and verbosity. The existence of human races, Mussolini asserted, is not "an abstraction of our mind, but corresponds to a material, phenomenal reality which our senses can perceive." Great and lesser races exist (according to the manifesto), and the concept of races is purely biological. Since for several centuries there has been no influx of other races in Italy, "there exists *by now* [italics added] a pure Italian race. . . . The conception of racialism in Italy must be essentially Italian and with a northern-Aryan direction. . . . This means elevating the Italians to an ideal of higher consciousness of self and greater responsibility." In a paragraph more directly concerned with the Jews, Mussolini chose to distinguish between Jews and Semites: "*Jews do not belong to the Italian race. Of the Semites who through the centuries landed on the sacred soil of our country, nothing is left. . . . The Jews represent the only population that can never be assimilated in Italy, because they are constituted of non-European racial elements, absolutely different from the elements that gave origin to the Italians." After the publication of the manifesto the campaign swiftly gathered momentum, supported by a newly founded magazine *La Difesa della Razza (The Defense of the Race)* and by the daily press, which mercilessly hammered at the faults of Italian Jews and the crimes of "international Jewry."

When the Italian Jews asked themselves the probable causes of the anti-Semitic campaign, the answer that most readily came to mind was that Mussolini had made a deal with Hitler. Perhaps he had agreed to the campaign in return for Hitler's promise that he would not annex the South Tyrol or insist on the transfer to Germany of the German-speaking minorities who lived there. . . . [But] the South Tyrol question proved to be unrelated to the artificial upsurge of Fascist anti-Semitism.

The tragedy of the Italian Jews was due to little more than a whim of the Italian dictator, to his spirit of emulation which drove him to imitate his great friend Hitler, and to his consequent desire to Prussianize Italy. There is reason to believe that Mussolini himself did not attribute any greater importance to the anti-Semitic campaign than to other measures directed at reforming "the Italian style". . . . In October, 1938, in a "very important speech," not published at the time, Mussolini told the national council of the Fascist Party that he had "given several mighty punches in the stomach to the Fascists' enemy, the *bourgeoisie*". . . . "To me the racial problem is a most important conquest, and it is most important to have introduced it in the history of Italy. . . . The racial laws of the empire will be rigorously enforced, and all those who act against them will be expelled, punished, imprisoned. . . ."

The lack of good reason, or even a good pretext, for the anti-Semitic campaign raises the question whether, in spite of his statements to the contrary, Mussolini did not nurse personal feelings against the

Jews. As far as it can be ascertained, he first encountered a definite expression of anti-Semitism in Nietzsche's works, which he read when he was twenty-five. His review articles in *Pensiero Romagnolo* indicated that he had been strongly impressed by Nietzsche's view that the Jews had brought about an inversion of spiritual values. . . . This early seed of anti-Semitism did not fall on fertile soil. In Predappio and the small towns where Mussolini had studied there had been no Jews, for they generally lived in the large cities and not in villages or towns. In the family and at school he had not met anti-Semitism, and many of the persons with whom he had later associated were Jews. . . . Nietzsche's words could not have awakened latent antipathy. But soon Mussolini evinced those vague apprehensions and misapprehensions about the Jews which are a sign of ignorance and on which anti-Semitism is often built. He said more than once that the Jews themselves created anti-Semitism by being too conspicuous and invasive, altogether too-Jewish, and he condemned those Italian Jews who participated in the Zionist movement. Of "international Jewry" he was more openly critical, and as early as 1919 he accused the great Jewish bankers of London and New York of supporting the Jews of Moscow and Budapest in their revenge on the Aryan race; in Nietzschean fashion he called bolshevism the vengeance of Judaism upon Christianity. Later he repeatedly attacked "Jewish international finance," which in his mind was the chief cause of hostility to fascism in foreign countries.

The first to suffer from this vague anti-Semitism, as wavering as many of Mussolini's opinions, was his daughter Edda, when she had fallen in love with a young Jewish suitor. Yet, until the time of the alliance with Germany, Mussolini's anti-Semitism was not dangerous and belonged rather to his cumbersome baggage of superstition than to his political beliefs. With the birth of the Rome-Berlin axis a slow, insidious change set in, of which the public could not be aware. . . .

As early as September, 1937, Ciano heard the duce talk venomously and absurdly of the Jews, saying, for instance, that America was in the hands of Negroes and Jews; that the Jews were a disintegrating element who did not want children because they feared pain; that in the future only Italians, Germans, and Japanese would play important roles in the world, while other nations would be destroyed by the acid of Judaic corruption. On November 6, 1937, the duce told Hitler's special envoy Joachim von Ribbentrop: "We are conducting a very determined and increasingly intensive anti-Semitic campaign." No racial campaign was underway at that time, and the duce's remark reveals both wishful thinking and his eagerness to show Ribbentrop he had embraced Hitler's most cherished cause.

. . . Shortly before the publication of the *Manifesto della Razza*, Mussolini told Ciano that Jewish writers and newspapermen would be banned from further activity. "The revolution," he said, "must by now impress its mark on the Italians' customs. They must learn how to be less *simpatici* and become hard, implacable, hateful: masters." In August he took the stand that since the Jews represented about one-thousandth of the Italian population they would participate only in that ratio in the over-all life of the state. In October he told Ciano: "Anti-Semitism has now been injected into the Italians' blood. It will go on circulating and developing by itself. Besides, although this evening I am conciliatory, I will be most harsh in the preparation of the laws." In November Ciano found him "more and more aroused against the Jews. He approves unconditionally the reactionary measures taken by the Nazis, and he says that under similar circumstances he would go even further." (A round of pogroms in Germany was at that time horrifying the free world.) Later the same month the duce appeared indignant because the king had indicated that he felt "infinite sympathy for the Jews."

Two sets of laws against the Jews were passed, in September and November. Mussolini was to say that the Italian racial laws were much worse on paper than in practice, that they were not strictly enforced, and that Italian Jews fared much better than the German. As far as Mussolini's own campaign is concerned, there is certainly some truth in this claim. In Germany anti-Semitism had been prevalent even before the advent of Hitler; in Italy it had not existed, and the Italian people did much to alleviate the Jews' plight. Yet Mussolini's campaign brought deep and widespread suffering, the loss of positions, the expulsion from public schools and universities of both teachers and students, many restrictions and limitations upon certain activities, the humiliation that accompanies flagrant discrimination, and, above all, the separation of families. . . . The suffering was to turn into tragedy after the fall of Mussolini, when the campaign in Italy passed to Hitler's control. Then the machinery of Fascist racial legislation facilitated the endeavor of the Nazis to persecute and exterminate the Italian Jews—more than 8,000 Italian Jews were deported to German concentration camps and gas chambers; only a little over 600 returned to Italy at the end of World War II. Because many others had left the country, the Jewish population in Italy was then about two-thirds what it had been before the anti-Semitic campaign.

Early in January, 1939, a little less than five years before the Nazi occupation of Italy in September, 1943, President Roosevelt sent a message to Mussolini proposing that the duce sponsor the settlement of European Jews in a part of Ethiopia. Mussolini replied that, while he favored a Jewish state, he felt that only three countries, the United States, Brazil, and Russia, were materially able to support such an undertaking on their own soil. A few months previously Mussolini himself had hinted at the possibility of opening some regions of Ethiopia to Jewish immigration, and his reply to Roosevelt must have been dictated by the fear, on second thought, that helping the people whom Hitler persecuted would displease the Fuehrer. Thus, out of loyalty to a friend who was the incarnation of cruelty and perversion, Mussolini missed a unique opportunity to win the sympathy of the world.

(*Mussolini*, 290–291, 363–370)

* * *

Italy became Germany's ally because of Franco-British affronts, and because Mussolini believed that nobody was going to stop Hitler. Mussolini did *not* throw in his lot with the Germans in order to participate in the systematic extermination of ethnic groups, plans for which were in 1939 and 1940 secret even from high officials of the Reich. Mussolini's alliance partner was the Hitler of Munich, not the Hitler of Auschwitz. None of what came later was foreseeable by Mussolini, any more than it was foreseeable by Stalin, Chamberlain, Roosevelt, or by the Swedes who sold Germany iron ore all during the war.

The vulgar anti-Semitism that characterized the mentality of so many Europeans of his generation, including Socialists, was alien to Mussolini. Jews had played important roles in his life from his Socialist to his Fascist days. . . . Mussolini often expressed his contempt for theories of biological determinism and backed up these expressions with real action, as when in March 1933 he instructed the Italian ambassador in Berlin to protest to Hitler about the treatment of German Jews. Shortly after the assassination of Austrian Chancellor Dollfuss, Mussolini wrote in his *Popolo d'Italia* that if German racial theories were true, the Lapps would be the highest type of humanity. . . . Biological politics directly contradicted Mussolini's beliefs in nationalism and the human will, and he explicitly condemned it in the *Enciclopedia italiana* in 1935.

But the Hitler alliance now made the introduction of anti-Semitic rhetoric and legislation into Italy inevitable. Anti-Semitism was unpopular among the cosmopolitan and tolerant Italians, especially because its official adoption was rightly seen as evidence of Mussolini's increasing subordination to Hitler. As late as February 1938, the Italian Foreign Office issued a statement that "a specific Jewish problem does not exist in Italy." Measures would be taken only against Jews who were "hostile to the regime." In the fall of 1938, nevertheless, came a spate of severe anti-Jewish legislation: any Jew who had immigrated to Italy since 1919 must leave the country within six months; Jews could no longer be state employees, teachers, or university students. Thus the sickness of official racism was introduced into a country where the Church had spoken thunderously against racialist theories, where Jews were a tiny minority of the population, and where anti-Semitism was historically of no importance.

In the style of Italian fascism, however, the bark was worse than the bite. A Jew was defined by law not simply as someone of any Jewish heritage (as in Germany) but only as a person with two Jewish parents. Specifically *exempt* from anti-Semitic laws were Jews who had joined the Fascist party in its early days or who had been members during "the last half of 1924." . . . also exempt were Jewish volunteers in World War I, wounded or decorated veterans, and those wounded in the service of the State or of fascism. These exemptions could be extended to family members as well, and also to families of Jews killed in military service or those who had "fallen in the fascist cause." Jews who were deprived of their government posts could claim retirement compensation. In all these ways the regime showed its embarrassment. The plight of the Italian Jews did not become thoroughly perilous — no executions, no concentration camps, no extermination centers — until Mussolini was overthrown in 1943.

(Joes, *Mussolini*, pp. 328–330)

CLEMENT ATTLEE   *(1883–1967)*

Prime Minister of England, 1945–1952

Reply to President Truman, 16 September 1945[6]:

One must remember that within these camps were people from almost every race in Europe and there appears to have been very little difference in the amount of torture and treatment they had to undergo. Now if our offices had placed the Jews in a special racial category at the head of the queue, my strong view is that the effect of this would have been disastrous for the Jews.

(F. Williams, ed., A Prime Minister Remembers, p. 189)

JAN MASARYK   *(1886–1948)*

Czechoslovak Foreign Minister during World War II

From a speech on the Czech program of the BBC,
9 December 1942:

. . . do everything in [your] power to make easier the life of [your] Jewish fellow-citizens. . . .

It seems that millions of Jews will be slaughtered. You know that I have always condemned anti-Semitism. But today any sign of anti-Semitism, when this small, minute, freezing, dying, ill-treated minority is handed over to the mercies of the German anti-Christs, in these times even a sign of anti-Semitism is a proof of shameful and disgusting cowardice . . . I hate cruel cowardice, and I am horrified if I think that the people which gave birth to my father helps these bestialities, even if in an insignificant fashion. . . .

(B. Wasserstein, Britain and the Jews, p. 300)

DIEGO RIVERA   *(1886–1957)*

Mexican artist and communist

For Mexico to join with the tormentors of persecuted minorities is *not only a great shame, but it is also a disgusting and loathsome act of treachery,*

---

[6]President Truman had written Attlee a memo on 26 July 1945, expressing his hope that "the British Government may find it possible without delay to take steps to lift the restrictions of the White Paper on Jewish immigration to Palestine."

a betrayal. It is a betrayal not only from the standpoint of morality and ethics, of elementary humanity and human dignity, but also from the standpoint of the truest and most genuine Mexican interests.

The Mexican who regards it as right that there should be driven out of Germany and Austria the Jews who aided in the building up of those countries' national, intellectual and spiritual wealth – that Mexican must also agree that it is right and just to drive out of the United States the Mexican workers who have there enriched the fruit-dealers, the pottery merchants, the automobile manufacturers, the railroad construction companies and all the other American industrialists who today keep more Mexican workers employed than are employed in Mexico itself. *The Mexican who will agree to this is none but a traitor.*

One can insult, persecute, torture or murder the Jews, in the name of "nationalism," with no danger and at small cost. *But on the other hand, anti-Semitism is a disgusting, fearful and criminal product.* In the case of Mexico itself, aside from being fearful and criminal, *anti-Semitism is positively idiotic.* . . . The Jew, by reason of the fact that he himself has no "fatherland," is compelled to sink his roots and his interests deep in the land of his adoption. He associates his own interests intimately and directly with the interests and advantages and with the development of the national forces of the land where he has been given shelter.

Now, when Mexico vitally needs foreign capital – what better opportunity is there than the present one to admit and welcome the Jew who has been driven out of Germany and out of Austria, and who is being persecuted by Fascist Europe, especially if this Jew possess some capital? Such an act would be profitable to Mexican economics, no matter from which angle it may be viewed.

(From an article in the Mexican newspaper *Novedades*, April 1938)

ARNOLD TOYNBEE   *(1889–1975)*

British historian

It is difficult for anyone brought up in the Christian tradition to shake himself free from the official Christian ideology. He may have discarded Christian doctrine consciously on every point; yet on this particular point he may find that he is still influenced, subconsciously,

by the traditional Christian view in his outlook on Jewish history. . . .
I am conscious that my own outlook has been affected in this way.

(Quoted in O. K. Rabinowicz and W. H. Allen, *Arnold Toynbee on*
Judaism and Zionism, preface)

* * *

Philip Toynbee: Now it has been said that you have a particular prejudice against Judaism. . . . It's said that in your treatment of
religions you always have a slight "down" on this particular one. If this
is true, is it because you feel that religious intolerance springs from
Judaism?

Arnold Toynbee: I do think it springs from Judaism, and in
that sense I suppose I do have a "down" on Judaism—I have a "down"
on the Jewish streak—it's more than a streak, it's more like the metal
rods in reinforced concrete—in Christianity and in Islam.

(Rabinowicz and Allen, *Arnold Toynbee on Judaism and Zionism*,
p. 22)

* * *

Upon the advent of Christianity or, alternatively, of Islam, the
"mandate" of Judaism and the Jews "was exhausted" (to use an apt
Chinese formula). Now, in God's own good time, the true "Chosen
people" had arrived on the scene, and the Jews' duty was clear. They
ought to have accepted Jesus or, alternatively, Muhammad at the
valuation placed on him in the official doctrine of the Judaic religion
of which he was the founder. In declining to accept him on these
terms, the Jews were failing to respond to the supreme challenge in
their history, and were thereby putting themselves permanently in the
wrong and on the shelf. Jewish history and its Israelitish antecedents
down to the beginning of Jesus's, or, alternatively Muhammad's
ministry still has validity and value as a prelude, arranged by God, to
the Christian or, alternatively, to the Muslim, dispensation. Jewish
history since one or other of those climactic dates is without significance except as a classic example of perversity on the part of the people
that, of all people, ought to have known better.

(*Arnold Toynbee on Judaism and Zionism*, p. 478)

In the unhappy relations between Jews and Gentiles, which is the classic case, the Gentile who is disgusted and ashamed at the behaviour of his anti-Semitic fellow Goyyim is also embarrassed at finding himself constrained to admit that there is some element of truth in the caricature which the Jew-baiter draws as a justification for his own bestiality.

(A. Toynbee, *Study of History*, vol. I, p. 304)

* * *

. . . [Hitler's] main idea—the fanatical worship of a jealous tribal god, at the bidding of a prophetic leader—is the original (though not ultimate) *Leitmotiv* of the Old Testament.

(A. Toynbee, *Survey for 1933*, p. 145)

* * *

On reconsideration, I do not find that I have changed my view of Zionism. I think that, in the Zionist movement, Western Jews have assimilated gentile Western civilisation in the most unfortunate possible form. The seizure of houses, lands, and property of the 900,000 Palestinian Arabs who are now refugees is on a moral level with the worst crimes and injustices committed, during the last four or five centuries, by gentile Western European conquerors and colonists overseas. This is still my judgment on the Zionists' record in Palestine since it first began to resort to violence there. At the same time, on second thought, I do think it may be true that the vehemence of my condemnation of Zionism has been out of proportion to the magnitude of Zionism's guilt. . . .

In the German Nazis, and in the English "Black-and-Tans," I see the detestable dark side of the countenance of Western Civilisation in which I myself am an involuntary participant, and in the Jewish Zionists I see disciples of the Nazis. The Jews are, of course, not the only persecuted people that has reacted to persecution by doing as it has been done by; and, of course, too, the Jews who have reacted in this tragically perverse way are only one section of Jewry. Yet the spectacle of any Jews, however few, following in the Nazis' footsteps is enough to drive a sensitive gentile or Jewish spectator almost to despair. That any Jews should inflict on a third party some of the very wrongs that Jews have suffered at Western hands is a portent that makes one wonder whether there may not be something irredeemably evil, not in Jewish human nature in particular, nor again just in Western human nature, but in the human nature common to all men.

(A. Toynbee, *Reconsiderations*, pp. 627–628)

GENERAL FRANCISCO BAHAMONDE FRANCO
(1892–1975)

Leader of fascist Spain, 1936–1975

Among the arguments used by Franco in persuading Primo de Rivera in October 1923 and July 1924 that it was Spain's duty to retain Spanish Morocco was the residence there for many centuries of "many thousands of Spaniards"—an exaggeration unless he included as Spaniards the Sephardim. In his account of the evacuation of Xauen, Franco described with unusual sensitivity the plight of the Jews as well as of the Moroccans loyal to Spain. Whether as a direct consequence of this or no (with the arbitrary and unpredictable Andalusian general little can be said for certain) Primo de Rivera decreed on 20th December 1924 that any Sephardi anywhere in the world who so wished it could opt for a fully legalized Spanish nationality. He gave them until 31st December 1930 to do so. In fact, few did. Primo de Rivera had made the fulfilment of the Spanish military service a necessary requirement. The 1931 Republic promised in its Constitution a new law to give Spanish nationality to the Sephardim, but it never came even to be drafted. A request for a Jewish cemetery in Madrid aroused the wrath of the left-wing which was then secularising all the Catholic burial grounds. . . .

The Spanish Press during the Republic was even less pre-occupied with the fate of the Jews under Hitler than that of Britain, France or the United States. To the Spanish Left, Judaism was just another religion only marginally less repugnant than Catholicism. To the Right it was irrelevant to the Spanish scene. There were hardly any Jews in Spain. A few Falangists under Nazi influence tried to arouse anti-Jewish feeling, and . . . there were churchmen who identified Jewry with Freemasonry. . . . Franco would come to have references in his speeches to Jews as synonymous with the Masons and Liberals he hated. The Spanish wartime Press had no references to Hitler's persecution of the Jews; but then it had none either to his persecution of the Catholic Church. Nevertheless behind all this, Franco was far from impassive to their fate. He protected the Jews wherever Hitler had power to the limit of his ability. He could not save them as a race, but he could and did save individuals in so far as he could extend to them the legal fiction that the Sephardim were still Spaniards although their ancestors had left Spain four-and-a-half centuries previously.

The whole story is one of constant and complicated diplomatic activity in many cities. On 17th September 1940, for example, the Spanish Consulate in Paris reported that the Sephardim were being treated like others of their race. Franco gave instructions that they were to be registered as Spaniards to make possible their defence as such against the Germans and the French. In November . . . he gave similar instructions to the Spanish Embassy in Vichy. Sephardic Jews thereafter did not have to wear the prescribed clothing nor did they have their goods confiscated. When in March 1942 cases were reported of Sephardim being molested, Franco had Serrano Suner order the Spanish Ambassador to take the matter up with the Vichy government, recalling a Protection Agreement of 1862. The Jews were released. Frontier guards on the Pyrenees were instructed to follow the spirit rather than the letter of their instructions. Refugees were allowed to enter without papers, and whereas escaped British prisoners-of-war were treated as illegal immigrants, and as such put into prisons until they were rescued by the British Embassy, Jewish refugees were usually sent to a camp, where conditions were far from ideal but the best that Spain could offer at the time.

Similar action was taken on the Sephardim's behalf by the embassies and consulates in Hungary, Bulgaria, Rumania and Greece. The Germans agreed in March 1943 to leave the Salonika community in peace. Nevertheless at the beginning of 1944 the delegate in Lisbon of the World Jewish Congress reported to Nicolas Franco, then the Spanish Ambassador in Portugal, that there were 400 Sephardim in the Haidani concentration camp in Greece awaiting deportation. Nicolas telephoned his brother. Franco had his Ambassador in Berlin take up the matter. The deportation was stopped. Some had in fact already been taken to Belsen, and the Spanish Ambassador in Berlin was instructed to importune the German Foreign Office to obtaintheir release. After many excuses—that it was impossible to find out which of the Jews were Spanish and which not, that they were scattered in various parts of the country and in different camps—259 Jews released from Belsen crossed over into Spain by Port Bou on 10th February 1944, and a further 983 on the 13th. For good measure the Spanish Government got back for them eventually the 44,000 dollars, 55,000 Swiss francs, 24 million drachmae and the gold and jewellery which the German police had taken off them in Athens.

How many Jews in all were saved by Franco's legal fiction that they were Spaniards does not appear to have been calculated; but the Sephardic communities of Greece and Bosnia survived the war; and the first ship to sail from the western Mediterranean into Haifa after the war was the Spanish ship *Plus Ultra* with 400 adults and 150 orphans who had embarked in Barcelona.

By 1949, there were in Barcelona two Jewish synagogues as against one before the Civil War, and on 2nd January of that year a new synagogue had been opened in Madrid to replace the one which had been sacked by Communists during the Civil War. By then also, the publications of the Institute of Hebraic Studies, part of Franco's Consejo Superior de Investigaciones Cientificas, . . . were beginning to attract international attention. On 20th August 1941, Franco had officially confirmed on the 14,000 Jews in Spanish Morocco their right to local self-government and allotted them a subsidy to enable the Rabbinic Courts to function.

(G. Hills, *Franco, The Man and His Nation*, pp. 408–410)

MARTIN NIEMOELLER   *(1892–1984)*

German theologian

In Germany they came first for the Communists, and I didn't speak up because I wasn't a Communist. Then they came for the Jews, and I didn't speak up because I wasn't a Jew. Then they came for the trade unionists, and I didn't speak up because I wasn't a trade unionist. Then they came for the Catholics, and I didn't speak up because I was a Protestant. Then they came for me, and by that time no one was left to speak up.

No power on earth can force me not to see in the Jew my fellow man.

You see, Germany had lost the war. We had an alarming crisis, inflation, an enormous unemployment problem. Certain Polish and Russian Jews had taken refuge in Germany; the great mass of the poor and unemployed believed them to be well-to-do. Envy developed into hatred. Instead of feeling sorry for these miserable refugees, some people begrudged them the little they had. Hitler quickly stimulated these low passions, which finally brought him to power. Today, Hitler persecutes both Jews and Christians alike.

I have seen with my own eyes and heard with my own ears how Jews have been maltreated. I had a chance to "study" this prison, which is built underground like a cave. When they whipped the Jews and I heard these poor creatures cry out like wounded animals, I knelt down and prayed to God. I never prayed so fervently before in all my life. I almost collapsed. Without my prayers, I could not have lived through the next day. But the Lord gave me new confidence and faith.
(*The National Jewish Monthly*, B'nai B'rith, May 1941)

DOROTHY L. SAYERS   (1893–1957)

British writer of detective fiction

. . . Dorothy received a rather different salute to her propagandist skills. It came in the form of a letter from General Sir Wyndham Deedes, asking for her support for, of all things, the cause of Zionism. Dorothy was a surprising choice in view of the fact that public comment had already been made about alleged anti-Semitic feeling in her writing.

The letter arrived in April 1943, and was followed a couple of months later by another, similar, approach, this time from a Miss L. M. Livingstone, who was deeply involved in the effort to combat the wave of anti-Semitism which was passing through England at the time.

Dorothy's reply to both was that she felt she was not a suitable person to take up the cudgels on behalf of the Jews, because (a) she knew comparatively little about the problem, and (b) she feared that anyone who tried to present an objective and impartial view of the situation would end up by offending Jews and Christians alike.

Typically, her main concern was not for the Jews but for her beloved English. If they were taking to anti-Semitism ("poor dears") it was because they had been driven past endurance by "bombs, blackout, restrictions, rations, coal-targets, bread-targets, clothes-coupons, call-ups, income-tax, lack of domestic help and general bedevilment"; and an influx of people with alien culture and alien standards was one imposition too many. For she believed that anti-Semitism, however horrifying its manifestations in Nazi Germany and elsewhere, was not always a matter of mindless wickedness, but was based on certain very definite incompatibilities between the Jews and their host nations; and that unless these incompatibilities were acknowledged and faced realistically, no real progress could be made.

Though the incompatibilities could be shown to have all sorts of historical sources—chiefly the inevitable division of loyalty in the majority of Jews between their host nation and the international race-religion of Jewry—the level at which they were beginning to be felt was no longer that of a generalized suspicion of foreigners, she wrote, but in what she called the "trifles of daily life experienced among the inhabitants of Hampstead and Whitechapel":

> the British Jewesses in 1939 dashing to the bank and announcing in loud tones: "Of course, we're sending all our money to America"; the children who cannot learn the common school code of honour; the Jewish evacuee offering his landlady double the rent she asked in order to secure the rooms and then informing her to the billetting authorities; the inhabitants of a London street complaining bitterly that everybody, from the high-class publishers' staff at one end to the little rookery of prostitutes at the other, eagerly did their turn of fire-watching—all except the houseful of Jews in the middle. They word it in different ways; but it all really boils down to the same thing: "bad citizens."

Since this was how Dorothy saw the situation, the solution could not in her view be found in the proposal that people should meet the Jews and get to know them, in the hope that they would then drop their prejudices; for the dislike began precisely when the Jews moved in next door.

Dorothy made it clear that she knew of many instances that totally contradicted these generalizations—individual Jews who were deeply aware of the debt they owned to the land they lived in and who would be excellent citizens of any country in the world. Nonetheless, nothing could alter the "otherness" of Jews, which indeed they themselves fostered and took pride in. Having fostered it, she maintained, they could hardly object if it was commented on and sometimes resented.

Given Dorothy's cast of mind, it was probably inevitable that she should trace back this "otherness" to the great watershed of Jewish and Christian history, the life of Christ. To a Mr. J. J. Lynx, who wrote asking for her views on the subject, she replied in June 1943: "I cannot, you see, bring myself to approach the question as though Christ had made no difference to history. I think, you see, that He was the turning-point of history, and the Jewish people, whose religion and nation are closely bound up with the course of history, missed that turning-point and got stranded: so that all the subsequent course of their history has to be looked upon in the light of that frustration."

"Naturally," she added, "I cannot expect Jewish people to sympathize with this point of view, but I do find it rather difficult to discuss a problem if I have to leave out what appears to me to be the major factor."

Dorothy's doubt whether this kind of contribution would really be welcome is more than understandable. A friend of hers, who had taught for several years at a school with a large number of Jewish pupils, had recently written an article dealing with some of the characteristics which she considered made it difficult for these pupils to be assimilated into the school community. The editor of the journal for whom she had written the article, himself Jewish, had refused to print it, claiming that it was based on lies and prejudice. In Dorothy's next letter to Mr. Lynx she quoted the experience of her friend and pointed out that "It doesn't seem worth while trying to explain the difficulties from our point of view if one isn't allowed to say plainly what those difficulties are, does it?"

(J. Brabazon, *Dorothy L. Sayers*, pp. 216–218)

LOUIS-FERDINAND CÉLINE   (1894–1961)

French writer and physician

In *Bagatelles* he exaggerates to the point of creating disbelief. Léon Blum is Jewish, he tells us correctly; Masaryk and Benes are also

Jewish, so are Gide, Maurras and the Pope; the entire English nation
is Jewish. . . .

(McCarthy, *Céline*, p. 143)

* * *

In a letter written by Céline in 1941, on Hitler's anti-Semitism:

It is the side of Hitler that most people like the least. . . . it is the side
I like the most.

(*Céline*, p. 182)

* * *

Messrs. Kikes, half-niggers, you are our gods.

(Marrus and Paxton, *Vichy France and the Jews*, p. 38)

* * *

. . . if you really want to get rid of the Jews, then, not thirty-six
thousand remedies, thirty-six thousand grimaces: racism! That's the
only thing Jews are afraid of: racism! And not a little bit, with the
fingertips, but all the way! Totally! Inexorably! Like complete Pasteur
sterilization.

(*Vichy France and the Jews*, p. 42)

JUAN PERÓN   *(1895–1974)*

Argentine dictator

A point at which Perón openly parted company with Nazism was the
latter's emphasis on racial purity. Despite charges that he was anti-Semitic, he criticized anti-Semitism and took steps to discourage his
ultra-nationalist supporters from persecuting the large Jewish community in Buenos Aires. He did so, however, on practical rather than
moral grounds. In taped memoirs, he recorded his response to a
German who, having escaped to Argentina after the war, urged Perón
to do something about the Jewish problem: if Hitler couldn't solve it

with 100 million Germans, how could he, Perón, accomplish anything with only 20 million Argentines, the colonel asked. Moreover, he pointed out that it was impossible to kill them or deport them. Therefore, the best way to deal with them was to incorporate them into Argentine society as much as possible.

Another marked difference between Perón and those who would have reproduced a true Nazi or Fascist regime in Argentina was the colonel's visceral distaste for violence. It is true that he would often close his eyes to brutalities committed by others in his name, and that from time to time he would indulge in inflammatory rhetoric. But he never had the slightest inclination to make violent action a center-piece of his political philosophy in the manner of Mussolini or Hitler.

(J. A. Page, *Perón, a Biography*, p. 90)

* * *

. . . The ALN, whose young militants had functioned as civilian shock troops for the regime since August, enrolled in the crusade with great zeal, despite their disdain for elections. In a ceremony befitting the seriousness with which the group held itself, the ALN solemnly installed Peron its leader. One of the organization's officials then tried to lecture him in the art of running a campaign. "I'm your leader now," Peron reminded him. "I give the orders and you follow them." But despite his admonition, ALN members continued to set off outbursts of violence and engage in occasional acts of anti-Semitism. Peron deplored these excesses, but would not disassociate himself from the ALN.

(*Perón, a Biography*, p. 139)

* * *

In 1967 he published a book that sought to substantiate his pretension to hemispheric statesmanship. . . . Peron's references to the "international synarchy" permit a glimpse at the dark side of his intellect. He professed a belief in the existence of a conspiracy among capitalists, Communists, Masons, Zionists and the Catholic Church to impose a world order upon all nations. Thus there was only one kind of imperialism, which operated through the media of "dark forces," "sepoys," political and economic pressures, and, if necessary, armed conflict. . . .

This fantastic confection belongs to a tradition of conspiracy theories dating back at least to the nineteenth-century view that the French Revolution was a Jewish-Masonic plot. Intelligent Peronists were (and still are) embarrassed by their leader's references to the synarchy and dismissed them as tactical pronouncements. However, Peronism's lunatic fringe harbored a number of individuals with paranoid tendencies which fed upon talk of a shadowy worldwide conspiratorial movement. . . .

(Perón, a Biography, pp. 404–405)

JOSEF GOEBBELS   (1897–1945)

Reich minister of propaganda during World War II

From his diary in February 1942:

The Führer once more expressed his determination to clean up the Jews in Europe pitilessly. There must be no squeamish sentimentality about it. The Jews have deserved the catastrophe that has now overtaken them. Their destruction will go hand in hand with the destruction of our enemies. We must hasten this process with cold ruthlessness. We shall thereby render an estimable service to a humanity tormented for thousands of years by the Jews.

(Wasserstein, *Britain and the Jews of Europe*, p. 137)

* * *

Written in March 1942, after Goebbels learned the exact meaning of the term "Final Solution":

. . . A judgment is being visited upon the Jews that, while barbaric, is fully deserved. . . . One must not be sentimental in these matters. If we did not fight the Jew, they would destroy us. It's a life-and-death struggle between the Aryan race and the Jewish bacillus. No other government and no other regime would have the strength for such a global solution of this question.

(L. P. Lochner, ed., *The Goebbels Diaries*, p. 138)

HELMUT HESSE   (?–1943)

A German parson during the Nazi era

As Christians we can no longer tolerate the silence of the church on the persecution of Jews. What leads us to this conclusion is the simple commandment to love one's neighbor. The Jewish Question is an Evangelical, not a political, question. The church has to resist anti-Semitism in its territories. The church must stand up against the state to testify to the holy historical meaning of Israel and make every attempt to oppose the destruction of Jewry. Every non-Aryan, whether Jew or Christian, has presently fallen victim to murderers in Germany.[7]

(S. Gordon, *Hitler, Germans and the "Jewish Question,"* p. 258)

HAJ AMIN AL-HUSSEINI   (1897–1974)

Grand Mufti of Jerusalem during World War II

June 28, 1943
His Excellency
The Minister of Foreign Affairs for Hungary

Your Excellency:

You no doubt know of the struggle between the Arabs and Jews of Palestine, what it has been and what it is, a long and bloody fight, brought about by the desire of the Jews to create a national home, a Jewish State in the Near East, with the help and protection of England and the United States. In fact, behind it lies the hope which the Jews have never relinquished, namely, the domination of the whole world through this important strategic center, Palestine. In effect, their program has, among other purposes, always aimed at the encouragement of Jewish emigration to Palestine and the other countries of the Near East. However, the war, as well as the understanding which the members of the Three-Power Pact have of the responsibility of the Jews

---

[7]After preaching vehemently against the persecution of Jews in 1943, Hesse was arrested and sent to Dachau, where he died a few days later.

for its outbreak and finally their evil intentions towards these countries which protected them until now—all these are reasons for placing
them under such vigilant control as will definitely stop their emigration to Palestine or elsewhere.

Lately I have been informed of the uninterrupted efforts made by
the English and the Jews to obtain permission for the Jews living in
your country to leave for Palestine via Bulgaria and Turkey.

I have also learned that these negotiations were successful, since
some of the Jews of Hungary have had the satisfaction of emigrating to
Palestine via Bulgaria and Turkey and that a group of these Jews
arrived in Palestine towards the end of last March. . . . The Jewish
Agency quotes, among other things, its receipt of a sufficient number
of immigration certificates for 900 Jewish children to be transported
from Hungary, accompanied by 100 adults.

To authorize these Jews to leave your country under the above
circumstances and in this way, would by no means solve the Jewish
problem and would certainly not protect your country against their
evil influence—far from it!—for this escape would make it possible for
them to communicate and combine freely with their racial brethren in
enemy countries in order to strengthen their position and to exert a
more dangerous influence on the outcome of the war, especially since,
as a consequence of their long stay in your country, they are necessarily in a position to know many of your secrets and also about your
war effort. All this comes on top of the terrible damage done to the
friendly Arab nation which has taken its place at your side in this war
and which cherishes for your country the most sincere feelings and the
very best wishes.

This is the reason why I ask your Excellency to permit me to
draw your attention to the necessity of preventing the Jews from
leaving your country for Palestine; and if there are reasons which
make their removal necessary, it would be indispensable and
infinitely preferable to send them to other countries where they find
themselves under active control, for example, in Poland, in order
thereby to protect oneself from their menace and avoid the
consequent damage.[8]

(J. Peters, *From Time Immemorial*, p. 372)

---

[8]As a consequence of this request, 400,000 Jews were subsequently killed during the Holocaust, shipped to Auschwitz from Hungary.

ANTHONY EDEN   (1897–1977)

1st Earl of Avon; British Foreign Secretary; Prime Minister,
1955–1957

. . . The meeting with Eden was most discouraging [in 1943] and presaged the outcome of the Bermuda Conference. Opening the discussion, Proskauer stressed the request that Britain and the United States call on Germany to permit the Jews to leave occupied Europe. Eden rejected that plan outright, declaring it "fantastically impossible." Nor was he taken by the proposal to send food to European Jews. To a suggestion that Britain help in removing Jews from Bulgaria, Eden responded icily, "Turkey does not want any more of your people." Any such effort, furthermore, would require Allies to ship additional goods to Turkey, and that would be difficult. All in all, Eden offered no reasonable hope of action. . . .

The meeting with Eden dealt a crushing blow to the American Jewish leadership, as is reflected in the following description of the reaction of the Joint Emergency Committee. . . .

> Over the entire meeting hung the pall of Mr. Eden's attitude toward helping to save the Jews in occupied Europe. Without expressing it, the people at the meeting felt that there was little use in continuing to agitate for a demand [for action] on the part of the United Nations by the Jews of America.

Incredible though it may sound, what lay behind Eden's adamant opposition to the plea that the Allies call on Germany to release the Jews was the fear that such an effort might in fact succeed. Later during the same day on which Eden spoke with Proskauer and Wise, he met with Roosevelt, Hull, Welles, and the British ambassador to the United States, Lord Halifax. Also present were a British Foreign Office official and Harry Hopkins, Roosevelt's special assistant. Hull raised the issue of the 60,000 to 70,000 Jews in Bulgaria who were threatened with extermination unless the British and Americans could get them out. He pressed Eden for a solution. According to Hopkins's notes, Eden replied

> that the whole problem of the Jews in Europe is very difficult and that we should move very cautiously about offering to take all

Jews out of a country like Bulgaria. If we do that, then the Jews of the world will be wanting us to make similar offers to Poland and Germany. Hitler might well take us up on any such offer and there are simply not enough ships and means of transportation in the world to handle them.

Nothing in Hopkins's notes indicates that anything was said questioning, let alone objecting to, this brutal statement. In a group that included all of the foremost statesmen of the democratic world except Winston Churchill—a group that was well aware of what was happening to the Jews of Poland and Germany—no one expressed any qualms about Eden's callousness. Nor did anyone challenge the contrived reason Eden gave for advising care lest Hitler be encouraged to release the Jews.

Even if one accepts Eden's contention that transportation was not available, can anyone doubt that Jews would have *walked*, if necessary, across the Balkans and out through Turkey? The hard fact of the matter is that, despite the excuse used constantly throughout World War II that the rescue of Jews was impossible because of the shortage of transportation, shipping and other resources were somehow found for non-military purposes when the Allied leadership so desired. . . . [L]et it be noted that ten days after Eden's discussion with Roosevelt and the other statesmen, the British government announced plans to take 21,000 non-Jewish Polish refugees to East Africa. They were some of the 100,000 non-Jewish Polish, Yugoslav, and Greek refugees whom the Allies moved to sanctuaries in the Middle East and Africa during World War II.

The real problem as far as Eden and the British were concerned was not ships. It was the immense pressure that the release of thousands of Jews from Europe would place on the British policy of placating the Arabs by strictly limiting Jewish immigration into Palestine. Placed in its broader context, this was part of the fundamental problem of where Jews could be put if they *were* rescued. No country wanted to take them in, as had been proved between 1933 and 1941 when persecuted Jews had been free to leave Nazi Europe. American Jewish groups had been correct in devising several proposals for havens of refuge for those who could get out. Unwillingness to offer refuge was a central cause for the Western world's inadequate response to the Holocaust.

Eden's fear that the Axis powers might agree to send the Jews to the Allies instead of to the killing centers was by no means unique. For instance, in December 1943 the British government opposed a plan for evacuating Jews from France and Rumania because "the Foreign Office are concerned with the difficulties of disposing any considerable number of Jews should they be rescued from enemy occupied territory. . . . They foresee that it is likely to prove almost if not quite impossible to deal with anything like the number of 70,000 refugees whose rescue is envisaged." Six months later, the British War Cabinet's Committee on Refugees declined to pursue a possible arrangement for the exodus of large numbers of Jews from Nazi Europe, partly because it could "lead to an offer to unload an even greater number of Jews on our hands."

The same callousness prevailed on the American side. . . .

(D. Wyman, *The Abandonment of the Jews: America and the Holocaust, 1941–1945*, pp. 96–99)

ADRIAN ARCAND   (1899–1967)

Canadian fascist leader

We don't attack Jews, we simply defend our country against their conspiracy.

(Quoted in *Maclean's* magazine, 15 April 1938)

HEINRICH HIMMLER   (1900–1945)

Leader of the Nazi SS

From a speech to SS leaders in Poznan, 4 October 1943:

I want to tell you about a very grave matter in all frankness. We can talk about it quite openly here, but we must never talk about it publicly. . . . I mean the evacuation of the Jews, the extermination of the Jewish people. It is one of the things one says lightly – "The Jewish people are being liquidated," party comrades exclaim; "naturally, it's in our program, the isolation of the Jews, extermination, okay, we'll do it." And then they come, all 80 million Germans, and every one of them has his decent Jew. Of course, the others may all be swines, but this particular one is an A-1 Jew. All those who talk like this have not seen it, have not gone through it. Most of you will know what it means to see 100 corpses piled up, or 500, or 1,000. To have gone through this and—except for instances of human weakness—to have remained decent, that has made us tough. This is an unwritten, never to be written, glorious page of our history.

(Gordon, *Hitler, Germans and the "Jewish Question,"* p. 196)

* * *

At a meeting of the heads of Nazi administrative units,
6 October 1943:

. . . Remember how many people, Party members included, send their precious plea for clemency to me or some other authority; they invariably say that all Jews are, of course, swine but that Mr. So-and-so is the exception, a decent Jew who should not be touched. I have no hesitation in saying that the number of these requests and the number of differing opinions in Germany leads one to conclude that there are more decent Jews than all the rest put together.

(*Hitler, Germans and the "Jewish Question,"* pp. 195–196)

* * *

In a speech to a group of Gauleiters and Reichsleiters,
6 October 1943:

The sentence "The Jews must be exterminated," with its few words, gentlemen, can be uttered easily. But what that sentence demands of the man who must execute it is the hardest and toughest thing in existence. I ask you really only to hear and never to talk about what I tell you in this circle. When the question arose, "What should be done with the women and children?" I decided here also to adopt a clear solution. I did not deem myself justified in exterminating the men, that is to say, to kill them or let them be killed, while allowing their children to grow up to avenge themselves on our sons and grandchildren. The hard decision had to be taken—*this people must disappear from the face of the earth.*

It [this assignment] was carried out—I think I can say—without our men and our leaders suffering the slightest damage to spirit or soul. . . . You now know what is what and you must keep it to yourself. Perhaps at a much later time we shall consider whether something about it can be told to the German people. But it is probably better to bear the responsibility on behalf of our people and take the secret with us into our graves. . . .

(B. Smith and A. Peterson, *Heinrich Himmler Geheimreden*, p. 162)

GEORGE ORWELL   *(1903–1950)*

British novelist and journalist

From a review in *New English Weekly*, 12 November 1936:

Nevertheless, as I have said, *The Calf of Paper* [a novel by Scholem Asch] deserves to be read by everybody, if only because it makes clear why the Nazis triumphed and were probably bound to triumph. The only point upon which the author, who is presumably a Jew himself, seems to be in doubt, is the real reason for antisemitism. But curiously enough, he supplies a clue, unconsciously, in one of the very few scenes in which a Jew (a young Bolshevik military officer) is held up for our admiration. This scene is a reminder that if you want antisemitism explained, the best book to read is the Old Testament.

(S. Orwell and I. Angus, eds., *An Age Like This*, p. 248)

* * *

Orwell in *The Tribune*, 4 February 1944:

. . . Whether a poet, as such, is to be forgiven his political opinions is a different question. Obviously one mustn't say "X agrees with me: therefore he is a good writer," and for the last ten years honest literary criticism has largely consisted in combating this outlook. Personally I admire several writers (Céline, for instance) who have gone over to the Fascists, and many others whose political outlook I strongly object to. But one has the right to expect ordinary decency even of a poet. I never listened to [Ezra] Pound's broadcasts, but I often read them in the BBC Monitoring Reports, and they were intellectually and morally disgusting. Antisemitism, for instance, is simply not the doctrine of a grown-up person. People who go in for that kind of thing must take the consequences. But I do agree with our correspondent in hoping that the American authorities do not catch Pound and shoot him, as they have threatened to do. It would establish his reputation so thoroughly that it might be a good hundred years before anyone could determine dispassionately whether Pound's much-debated poems are any good or not. . . .

(Orwell and Angus, eds., *As I Please*, pp. 84–85)

* * *

Orwell in *The Tribune*, 11 February 1944:

There are two journalistic activities that will always bring you a come-back. One is to attack the Catholics and the other is to defend the Jews. Recently I happened to review some books dealing with the persecution of the Jews in medieval and modern Europe. The review brought me the usual wad of antisemitic letters, which left me thinking for the thousandth time that this problem is being evaded even by the people whom it concerns most directly.

The disquieting thing about these letters is that they do not all come from lunatics. I don't greatly mind the person who believes in the Protocols of the Elders of Zion, nor even the discharged army officer who has been shabbily treated by the Government and is infuriated by seeing "aliens" given all the best jobs. But in addition to these types there is the small business or professional man who is firmly convinced that the Jews bring all their troubles upon themselves by underhand business methods and complete lack of public spirit. These people write reasonable, well-balanced letters, disclaim any belief in racialism, and back up everything they say with copious instances. They admit the existence of "good Jews," and usually declare (Hitler says just the same in *Mein Kampf*) that they did not start out with any anti-Jewish feeling but have been forced into it simply by observing how Jews behave.

The weakness of the left-wing attitude toward antisemitism is to approach it from a rationalistic angle. Obviously the charges against the Jews are not true. They cannot be true, partly because they cancel out, partly because no one people could have such a monopoly of wickedness. But simply by pointing this out one gets no further. The official left-wing view of antisemitism is that it is something "got up" by the ruling classes in order to divert attention away from the real evils of society. The Jews, in fact, are scapegoats. This is no doubt correct, but it is quite useless as an argument. One does not dispose of a belief by showing that it is irrational. Nor is it any use, in my experience, to talk about the persecution of the Jews in Germany. If a man has the slightest disposition towards antisemitism, such things bounce off his consciousness like peas off a steel helmet. The best argument of all, if rational arguments were ever of any use, would be to point out that the alleged crimes of the Jews are only possible because we live in a society which rewards crime. If all Jews are crooks, let us deal with them by so arranging our economic system that crooks cannot prosper. But what good is it to say that kind of thing to the man who believes as an article of faith that Jews dominate the Black Market, push their way to the front of the queues and dodge military service?

We could do with a detailed enquiry into the causes of antisemitism, and it ought not to be vitiated in advance by the assumption that those causes are wholly economic. However true the "scapegoat" theory may be in general terms, it does not explain why the Jews rather than some other minority group are picked on, nor does it make clear what they are a scapegoat *for*. A thing like the Dreyfus Case, for instance, is not easily translated into economic terms. So far as Britain is concerned, the important things to find out are just what charges are made against the Jews, whether antisemitism is really on the increase (it may actually have decreased over the past thirty years), and to what extent it is aggravated by the influx of refugees since about 1938.

One not only ought not to assume that the causes of antisemitism are economic in a crude, direct way (unemployment, business jealousy, etc.), one also ought not assume that "sensible" people are immune to it. It flourishes especially among literary men, for instance. Without even getting up from this table to consult a book I can think of passages in Villon, Shakespeare, Smollett, Thackeray, H.G. Wells, Aldous Huxley, T.S. Eliot and many another which would be called antisemitic if they had been written since Hitler came to power. Both Belloc and Chesterton flirted, or something more than flirted, with antisemitism, and other writers whom it is possible to respect have swallowed it more or less in its Nazi form. Clearly the neurosis lies very deep, and just what it is that people hate when they say that they hate a non-existent entity called "the Jews" is still uncertain. And it is partly the fear of finding out how widespread antisemitism is that prevents it from being seriously investigated.

(Reprinted in *As I Please*, pp. 89–91)

REINHARD HEYDRICH *(1904–1942)*

Chief lieutenant in the Nazi SS

In a speech prepared for him by Adolf Eichmann, at the Wannsee Conference, 20 January 1942:

Instead of emigration, there is now a further possible solution to which the Fuhrer has already signified his consent—namely deportation to the east. Although this should be regarded merely as an interim measure, it will provide us with practical experience which will be especially valuable in connection with the future final solution. . . .

    In pursuance of the final solution, special administrative and executive measures will apply to the conscription of Jews for labour in the eastern territories. Large labour gangs of those fit to work will be formed, with the sexes separated, which will be directed to these areas for road construction, and undoubtedly a large part of them will fall out through natural elimination. Those who remain alive—and they will certainly be those with the greatest powers of endurance—will be treated accordingly. If released, they would, being a natural selection of the fittest, form a new cell from which the Jewish race could again develop. (History teaches us that.) In the course of the practical implementation of the final solution, Europe will be combed from west to east.

    (Wasserstein, *Britain and the Jews of Europe, 1939–1945*, p. 136)

NANCY MITFORD *(1904–1973)*

British novelist and biographer

Nancy returned to England at the end of August to find herself on the brink of what was to turn into a row of truly Mitford proportions. In the spring of 1934, before her holiday in Italy, she had started work on a new novel, the idea being a tease on Unity and Diana, whose recent conversion to Fascism had provided Nancy with her inspiration. The heroine was modelled on Unity, and there was a lot of comic business about the Fuhrer, and about the English Leader, Captain Jack (Mosley), and his uniformed band of Union Jackshirts (the British Union of

Fascists). Unfortunately this was a tease that neither Unity nor Diana found in the least amusing. . . .

. . . To the liberal-aesthete circle, Mosley's brand of Fascism, distinct from but sympathetic towards the German version, was abhorrent. When in the summer of 1933 Diana returned from her first visit to Germany, full of enthusiasm for what she had seen of the Nazi Party on show at the Nuremberg Parteitag, several of them tried to argue her out of her, as they saw it, disastrous illusion. It seemed inconceivable that a woman as charming and sophisticated as Diana, a lover of the arts, a passionate subscriber to all that was most civilised in their world, should be in thrall to such a dark and ugly creed. But in thrall she was, and argument was a waste of breath.

Fanatical as Diana's committal to her Leader and his cause appeared to most of her friends, Unity's seemed little short of lunatic. Having met Mosley with Diana at Eaton Square, she had succumbed at once to his mesmerising charm and the appealing simplicity of his argument. Eagerly she joined the Movement, and accompanied her sister on that decisive first visit to Germany in 1933. She and Diana drew close over their common interest. . . . Transported by the martial music and the sight of thousands of marching men, ecstatic under the spell of the Fuhrer's hypnotic oratory, she took to Hitler and Fascism as a born-again Christian takes to God. . . .

. . . to Nancy [Unity's] obsession with Nazism, uncomprehending though it may have been, was anything but endearing. By her taunts she tried to emphasise the ridiculous aspects of Unity's behaviour, while at the same time maintaining a facade of good-natured sisterly affection. She loved her sisters, but she loathed their politics, and this love and loathing were difficult to reconcile. . . .

She responded with mockery to every aspect of Unity's obsession: to Horst Wessel ("Hoarse Vessel") to Hitler and the whole of the Nazi regime: "By the way aren't you going abroad, to England, quite soon. Well then I shan't bother to send this to the nasty land of blood baths & that will save me ld. We were asked to stay with somebody called Himmler or something, tickets & everything paid for, but we can't go as we are going to Venice & the Adriatic for our hols . . . Actually he wanted to show us over a concentration camp, now why? So that I could write a funny book about them."

Nancy remained all her life politically immature, her opinions too frivolous and too subjective to be taken seriously—a limitation which restrained her not at all in the airing of these opinions. Her loathing of the Fascist Right coupled with a feeling for moderation and a dislike of extremes of behaviour in any direction led her towards a middle-of-the-road Socialism. She considered herself a Socialist, and as such could hardly be expected to show sympathy to the family Fascists, but, as always, her feelings were ambivalent, particularly where they concerned Diana. . . .

As Blomfield Road was such a favourite target of the Luftwaffe . . . Nancy moved to Rutland Gate, to the mews flat at the back, as the main house had been requisitioned to provide provisional living-quarters for families of Polish Jews evacuated from the East End. Nancy was fascinated by these East End families and took on the job of looking after them with enthusiasm. They were 'so hard working clean & grateful,' and there was always some interesting drama going on to take her mind off the bombs. 'Oh dear a little creature here aged 16 is in the family way. I advised her, in the words of Lady Stanley, a tremendous walk a hot bath & a great dose but will this have any effect on a tough little Jewess? Or shall I be obliged to wield a knitting needle & go down to fame as Mrs Rodd the abortionist? (I might join Diana which would be rather nice) Really, talk about big families I feel like the mother of 10 here or old Mummy Hubbard.'

(Hastings, *Nancy Mitford*, pp. 92–95, 135)

ALBERT SPEER   *(1905–1981)*

Hitler's chief architect and minister of war production

For had I only wanted to, I could have found out even then [1931] that Hitler was proclaiming expansion of the Reich to the east; that he was a rank anti-Semite; that he was committed to a system of authoritarian rule; that after attaining power he intended to eliminate democratic procedures and would thereafter yield only to force. Not to have worked that out for myself; not, given my education, to have read books, magazines, and newspapers of various viewpoints; not to have tried to see through the whole apparatus of mystification — was already criminal. At this initial stage my guilt was as grave as, at the end, my work for Hitler. For being in a position to know and nevertheless shunning knowledge creates direct responsibility for the consequences—from the very beginning. . . .

Even after joining the party I continued to associate with Jewish acquaintances, who for their part did not break relations with me although they knew or suspected that I belonged to this anti-Semitic organization. At that time I was no more an anti-Semite than I became in the following years. In none of my speeches, letters, or actions is there any trace of anti-Semitic feelings or phraseology.

Had Hitler announced, before 1933, that a few years later he would burn down Jewish synagogues, involve Germany in a war, and kill Jews and his political opponents, he would at one blow have lost me and probably most of the adherents he won after 1930. . . .

In 1931 I had no idea that fourteen years later I would have to answer for a host of crimes to which I subscribed beforehand by entering the party. I did not yet know that I would atone with twenty-one years of my life for frivolity and thoughtlessness and breaking with tradition.[9] Still, I will never be rid of that sin.

(Speer, *Inside the Third Reich*, pp. 19–20)

* * *

On November 10 [1938], driving to the office, I passed by the still smoldering ruins of the Berlin synagogues. That was the fourth momentous event that established the character of this last of the prewar years. Today, this memory is one of the most doleful of my life, chiefly because what really disturbed me at the time was the aspect of disorder that I saw on Fasanenstrasse: charred beams, collapsed facades, burned-out walls—anticipations of a scene that during the war would dominate much of Europe. Most of all I was troubled by the political revival of the "gutter." The smashed panes of shop windows offended my sense of middle-class order. . . .

I accepted what had happened rather indifferently. . . . It has repeatedly surprised me, in later years, that scarcely any anti-Semitic remarks of Hitler's have remained in my memory . . . but Hitler's hatred for the Jews seemed to me so much a matter of course that I gave it no serious thought.

---

[9]Speer confessed his guilt at the Nürnberg trials in 1945–46 and served a twenty-year sentence at Spandau prison in West Berlin.

. . . Today it seems to me that I was trying to compartmentalize my mind. On the one hand there was the vulgar business of carrying out a policy proclaimed in the anti-Semitic slogans printed on streamers over the entrances to towns. On the other hand there was my idealized picture of Hitler. I wanted to keep these two apart. Actually, it did not matter, of course, who mobilized the rabble of the gutter to attack synagogues and Jewish businesses, it did not matter whether this happened at Hitler's direct instigation or merely with his approval.

During the years after my release from Spandau I have been repeatedly asked what thoughts I had on this subject during my two decades alone in the cell with myself; what I actually knew of the persecution, the deportation, and the annihilation of the Jews; what I should have known and what consequences I ought to have drawn.

I no longer give the answer with which I tried for so long to soothe the questioners, but chiefly myself: that in Hitler's system, as in every totalitarian regime, when a man's position rises, his isolation increases and he is therefore more sheltered from harsh reality; that with the application of technology to the process of murder the number of murderers is reduced and therefore the possibility of ignorance grows; that the craze for secrecy built into the system creates degrees of awareness, so it is easy to escape observing cruelties.

I no longer give any of these answers. For they are efforts at legalistic exculpation. It is true that as a favorite and later as one of Hitler's most influential ministers I was isolated. It is also true that the habit of thinking within the limits of my own field provided me, both as architect and as Armaments Minister, with many opportunities for evasion. It is true that I did not know what was really beginning on November 9, 1938, and what ended in Auschwitz and Maidanek. But in the final analysis I myself determined the degree of my isolation, the extremity of my evasions, and the extent of my ignorance.

I therefore know today that my agonized self-examinations posed the question as wrongly as did the questioners whom I have met since my release. Whether I knew or did not know, or how much or how little I knew, is totally unimportant when I consider what horrors I ought to have known about and what conclusions would have been the natural ones to draw from the little I did know. Those who ask me are fundamentally expecting me to offer justifications. But I have none. No apologies are possible.

(*Inside The Third Reich*, pp. 111–113)

. . . I dismissed my escort, sat down on the stump of a tree, and drafted a rebel's speech which I wrote out at one sweep. Only five days ago [April 11, 1945] Hitler had censored my official speech to such an extent that it was no longer worth giving. This time I wanted to issue a call for resistance, to bluntly forbid any damage to factories, bridges, waterways, railroads, and communications, and to instruct the soldiers of the Wehrmacht and the militia to prevent demolitions "with all possible means, if necessary by the use of firearms." The speech also called for surrendering political prisoners, which included Jews, unharmed to the occupying troops, and stipulated that prisoners of war and foreign workers not be prevented from making their way back to their native lands. . . .

(Inside the Third Reich, p. 469)

* * *

. . . by my abilities and my energies I had prolonged that war by many months. I had assented to having the globe of the world crown that domed hall which was to be the symbol of new Berlin. Nor was it only symbolically that Hitler dreamed of possessing the globe. It was part of his dream to subjugate the other nations. France, I had heard him say many times, was to be reduced to the status of a small nation. Belgium, Holland, even Burgundy, were to be incorporated into his Reich. The national life of the Poles and Soviet Russians was to be extinguished; they were to be made into helot peoples. Nor, for one who wanted to listen, had Hitler ever concealed his intention to exterminate the Jewish people. In his speech of January 30, 1939, he openly stated as much. Although I never actually agreed with Hitler on these questions, I had nevertheless designed the buildings and produced the weapons which served his ends.

(Inside the Third Reich, p. 523)

* * *

In the description of Hitler as he showed himself to me and to others, a good many likable traits will appear. He may seem to be a man capable and devoted in many respects. But the more I wrote, the more I felt that these were only superficial traits.

For such impressions are countered by one unforgettable experience: the Nuremberg Trial. I shall never forget the account of a Jewish family going to their deaths: the husband with his wife and children on the way to die are before my eyes to this day.

> (Foreword to *Inside the Third Reich*, 11 January 1969)

W. H. AUDEN   *(1907–1973)*

British poet and playwright

—As told to editor Allan Gould, when Auden visited Canada in 1972:

I know that all the verse I wrote, all the positions I took in the thirties, didn't save a single Jew from Auschwitz.

FATHER RUFFINO NICCACCI OF ASSISI   *(1911–?)*

Italian Franciscan friar and head of a Catholic seminary during World War II

The story of Father Ruffino Niccacci of Assisi is remarkable enough: 32 years old in 1943, when the Italian fascist regime collapsed in ruins and the Nazis occupied their former ally, the young Franciscan friar found himself entrusted with a task for which his theological training left him totally unprepared—he was to organize the rescue of hundreds of imperiled Jews from deportation and certain death.

Father Niccacci, head of the local Catholic seminary, fashioned a brilliant escape network. The monasteries and convents of Assisi, patriots and ex-fascists, ordinary parishioners, and even the town atheist were painstakingly enlisted in the cause. Everyone gained heart from Father Niccacci. . . .

[He] encouraged, cajoled, pleaded and, by his own example, inspired the concealment and the smuggling to safety of several thousand Jews destined for the Nazis' Final Solution.

A town of 5,000 in 1943, Assisi soon grew to twice that number, as refugees found refuge within its walls. Not one was betrayed. And not one was captured. The local bishop, Giuseppe Niccolini, and

Cardinal Elia della Costa, the archbishop of Florence, provided encouragement. Reportedly, Pope Pius XII himself gave his blessing.

But it was Father Niccacci who took the immediate risks and honed the skills more associated with his peasant background than his priestly calling: he showed constant ingenuity in outwitting the Nazi authorities; he managed bare-faced lies when facing the dreaded SS, and he showed boundless courage while under brutal interrogation. Why did he do it? Father Niccacci's response matches that of so many rescuers whom historians are now beginning to study systematically: What else could we do? they all seem to say, as if the question itself were impertinent or at least out of place.

Father Niccacci followed the example of Saint Francis, the patron saint of his own monastic order. "God commanded him to find a leper and embrace and kiss him," Father Niccacci told the astonished sisters of a convent in which Jews hid behind the cloisters. "Once more we live in the Dark Ages," he said. "The men and women who have come to you today to seek your refuge and protection—they are the lepers of the modern world. They are Jews, who are being persecuted by the Germans and fascists, sent to concentration camps, then tortured and put to death."

. . . of the 47,000 Jews in Italy at the beginning of the war, about eighty-five per cent were saved.

Up and down the Italian peninsula, Italians befriended Jews. In some sense, in honoring Father Ruffino Niccacci we honor all those who extended a helping hand. Even more, we draw attention to the fact that along with the perpetrators and those who stood by and did nothing, the history of the Holocaust is also an account of men and women who helped, at great risk to themselves. . . .

(Michael R. Marrus, "Analysis—A Light in an Age of Darkness,"
Toronto Globe and Mail, 30 March 1990, p. A8)

LORD MOYNE

British minister of state for the Middle East

What would I do with one million Jews?
(He was later assassinated by the Stern Group in 1944 in Palestine.)

14

Reflections on the Holocaust
and the State of Israel

CARL SANDBURG   (1878–1967)

Author and poet; Pulitzer Prize 1953

I have often thought that Carl is one of the kindest men I've ever known. The only sign of hatred I have seen or heard him express is directed at anti-Semites and racial segregationists.

When the Associated Press carried his statement on December 29, 1958, after the arrest of several swastika painters in Cologne, Germany, "I believe that every swastika painter deserves the death penalty," liberals accused Sandburg of compromising his stand against capital punishment. The statement annoyed some of his closest friends, others saying, "Shoot to kill."

Most of the Gentile liberals I have met stand on their detestation of all prejudice and let it go at that. For Carl Sandburg the fight against anti-Semitism and Negrophobia has been a special project. He admits to me anti-Semitism has puzzled him as much as it angers him. "I came across anti-Semitism in the union halls among my fellow Socialists, and I've heard it among the I.W.W.'s, and I've had it expressed to me by some of my dearest friends, and I find it sad beyond words, beyond words."

In answer to the rash of criticism his public statement provoked Sandburg answered the question was he serious about the swastika painters with:

"Yes. The swastika stands not for the murder of an individual or for a few individuals but for the death of a race. It is the symbol of race murder; it is the ghastliest graphic symbol in the story of mankind."

(H. Golden, *Carl Sandburg*, p. 109)

KARL JASPERS   (1883–1969)

German existentialist philosopher

There is no other way to realize truth for the German than purification out of the depth of consciousness of guilt.

Purification in action means, first of all, making amends.

Politically this means delivery, from inner affirmation, of the legally defined reparations. It means tightening our belts, so part of their destruction can be made up to the nations attacked by Hitler Germany. . . .

There is more to reparation, however. Everyone really affected by the guilt he shares will wish to help anyone wronged by the arbitrary despotism of the lawless regime.

There are two different motivations which must not be confused. The first calls on us to help wherever there is distress, no matter what the cause—simply because it is near and calls for help. The second requires us to grant a special right to those deported, robbed, pillaged, tortured and exiled by the Hitler regime.

Both demands are fully justified, but there is a difference in motivation. Where guilt is not felt, all distress is immediately leveled on the same plane. If I want to make up for what I, too, was guilty of, I must differentiate between the victims of distress. . . .

Clarification of guilt is at the same time clarification of our new life and its possibilities. From it spring seriousness and resolution.

Once that happens, life is no longer simply there to be naively, gaily enjoyed. We may seize the happiness of life if it is granted to us for intermediate moments, for breathing spells—but it does not fill our existence; it appears as amiable magic before a melancholy background. Essentially, our life remains permitted only to be consumed by a task. . . .

Our progress with inner purification on the basis of guilt consciousness can be checked by our reaction to attacks.

Without guilt consciousness we keep reacting to every attack with a counterattack. . . .

Such purification makes us free. The course of events lies not in man's hand, though man may go incalculably far in guiding his existence. There remains uncertainty and the possibility of new and greater disasters, while no new happiness is guaranteed by the awareness of guilt and the resulting transformation of our being. There are the reasons why purification alone can free us so as to be ready for whatever comes. For only the pure soul can truthfully live in this tension: to know about the possible ruin and still remain tirelessly active for all that is possible in the world.

In regarding world events we do well to think of Jeremiah. When Jerusalem had been destroyed, state and country lost, the prophet forcibly taken along by the last few Jews who were fleeing to Egypt—

when he had to see those sacrificing to Isis in the hope that she would do more for them than Jehovah, his disciple Baruch despaired. And Jeremiah answered, "The Lord saith thus: Behold; that which I have built will I break down, and that which I have planted I will pluck up, and seekest thou great things for thyself? Seek them not." What does that mean? That God is, is enough. When all things fade away, God is—that is the only fixed point.

But what is true in the face of death, in extremity, turns into a dangerous temptation if fatigue, impatience, despair drive man to plunge into it prematurely. For this stand on the verge is true only if borne by the unswerving deliberation always to seize what remains possible while life endures. Our share is humility and moderation.

(Jaspers, *The Question of German Guilt*, trans. E.B. Ashton, pp. 118–123)

NIKOS KAZANTZAKIS *(1883–1957)*

Greek novelist; author of Zorba the Greek, The Last Temptation of Christ

At a later point, he would talk about his "Jewesses," and he succeeded in making me love them all: Rahel, Elsa, Leah, Itka, Dina. However, it was mainly with the first two—one the daughter of a rabbi from Warsaw and the other a pure Aryan from Jena—that he played. . . . Rahel, Elsa, Leah, Itka . . . Once upon a time . . . A new tale is beginning.

(H. Kazantzakis, *Nikos Kazantzakis, A Biography Based on his Letters*, p. 83)

* * *

October 16, 17, 18, 1922:[1] I told her about my Buddha. We ate chocolate, then talked about our relationship. I said to her: "You are Jewish, a predatory spirit, Spinoza and Shylock. You want to benefit as much as possible from knowing me. When I have nothing left to give you, you'll abandon me." . . .

November 19: If her mother were to learn that she was living with me, she would die of it.

---

[1]The entries are from Kazantzakis's diaries.

His wife and biographer continues: And so by this most delicious ruse, disguising Himself as a slender young girl, exquisite, vibrant, a visionary poet as well, Jehovah had taken the Cretan in hand, allowing him to apprehend certain mysteries of the Bible — of the Bible in which he was already thoroughly versed, this man enamored of Judaism. "The Jews are the salt of the earth," he proclaimed as a mature man; and as a child, he had gotten his father to let him penetrate the ghetto, so that a rabbi could give him Hebrew lessons.

While the young Jewish girl was initiating the Cretan into the rich traditions of her race, the Cretan for his part was gradually revealing to her his conception of the world. He talked to her of Homer, Dante, Buddha, and "his" Crete. . . .

The years passed. The young girl returned home and was imprisoned. Our efforts to have her come to Greece were unsuccessful. She married and had a son. When the war broke out, she was in Paris. She stayed there to help in the work of rescuing the children of her race. She had given up Communism and the gospel of hatred. But the poet wanted to immortalize her in her original flamelike guise. And so, both in *The Odyssey* and in *Toda Raba*, we encounter Rala in her orange blouse, sacrificing herself to her revolutionary ideal and choosing to die rather than compromise with Socialism, whose weakness had allowed the present state of things to come about.

(*Nikos Kazantzakis, A Biography*, pp. 87–89)

* * *

Kazantzakis to Leah, 10 March 1925:

Leah, Leah, dear herring-comrade; beautiful, marvelous Jewess. . . . How often and how deeply I think of you. I hope to see you this year. I'm going to Palestine this summer — I've become a Zionist. Ah, why am I not a Jew? I feel no affinity at all with my own people. I find myself at home, in my own climate, when I talk with Jews, when I laugh and am silent with them. . . .

(*Nikos Kazantzakis, A Biography*, p. 120)

* * *

To "Lenotschka," 13 September 1926:

I've reached the towering, ascetic stronghold of El Greco. My heart was pounding violently all the way from Madrid. . . . I crossed the threshold and made my way into El Greco's garden and went up to his house in the ghetto—El Greco loved the Jews so much that all his life he lived in the Jewish quarter. . . .

(*Nikos Kazantzakis, A Biography*, pp. 145–146)

* * *

To Leah, 23 March 1951:

. . . Thank you for not having forgotten us. I too think of you very often, dear Leah, and I still hope to see you again one day—not in Paris, that accursed, seductive Babylon, but in Jerusalem, Tel Aviv, in the Promised Land, which I love so much! There's a very large drop of Hebrew blood (in my veins)[2] and this drop produces an effervescence and commotion in all my Hellenic and Cretan blood. I am obsessed and possessed by the Hebraic destiny. When I was ten years old, I begged my father to let me go to the home of the Rabbi of Canea to learn Hebrew. I went three times, and took three lessons. But my uncles, and more especially my aunts, were afraid and revolted against it. They were fearful that the Jews might drink my blood, and my father withdrew me from the rabbinical school.

Here in solitude, I am working hard and well. I am writing a book on a Hebrew subject now (The Last Temptation). It takes place in Palestine, and you can understand how interesting it would be for me to see the Holy Land again. But that seems impossible. . . .

(*Kazantzakis, A Biography*, pp. 495–496)

HARRY S TRUMAN   *(1884–1972)*

33rd president of the United States, 1945–1953

Mr. Truman was speaking [to the author] of April 20, 1945, the eighth day of his Presidency. . . .

"I had a long list of appointments that day, and one of them, you were asking earlier about Palestine, one of them was with Rabbi Wise [Dr. Stephen S. Wise, chairman of the American Zionist Emergency Council]. I saw him late that morning, and I was looking forward to it

---

[2]Here the biographer adds: "Nikos is playing with words. Actually he had no Hebrew blood in his veins."

because I knew he wanted to talk about Palestine, and that is one part of the world that has always interested me, partly because of its Biblical background, of course. . . .

It wasn't just the Biblical part about Palestine that interested me. The whole history of that area of the world is just about the most complicated and most interesting of any area anywhere, and I have always made a very careful study of it. There has always been trouble there, always been wars from the time of Darius the Great and Rameses on, and the pity of it is that the whole area is just waiting to be developed. And the Arabs have just never seemed to take any interest in developing it. I have always thought that the Jews would, and of course, they have. But what has happened is only the beginning of what could happen, because potentially that is the richest area in the world. . . .

But getting back to what you were asking about, that morning I saw Rabbi Wise. It was late in the morning, and I remember he said, 'Mr. President, I'm not sure if you're aware of the reasons underlying the wish of the Jewish people for a homeland.'

He was just as polite as he possibly could be, but I've told you in those days nobody seemed to think I was *aware* of anything. I said I knew all about the history of the Jews, and I told the rabbi I'd read all Roosevelt's statements on Palestine, and I'd read the Balfour Declaration, and of course, I knew the Arab point of view.

I also said that I knew the things that had happened to the Jews in Germany, not that I . . . at that time I didn't really know what had happened. At that time I couldn't even have *imagined* the kind of things they found out later.

But I said as far as I was concerned, the United States would do all that it could to help the Jews set up a homeland. I *didn't* tell him that I'd already had a communication from some of the "striped pants" boys warning me . . . in effect telling me to watch my step, that I didn't really understand what was going on over there and that I ought to leave it to the *experts*.

The rabbi—he was just about the most courteous man I've ever seen—said he believed me, but he said he was sure a great many people, including some State Department people, wouldn't go along with me. The *experts* on the Middle East, he said.

I told him I knew all about *experts*. I said that an *expert* was a fella who was afraid to learn anything new because then he wouldn't be an *expert* anymore. . . ."

But pressure on the White House from American Zionists was, as Mr. Truman told me, so great that: "Well, there'd never been anything like it before, and there wasn't after. Not even when I fired MacArthur, there wasn't. And I said, I issued orders that I wasn't going to see anyone who was an extremist for the Zionist cause, and I didn't care who it was. There were . . . I had to keep in mind that much as I favored a homeland for the Jews, there were simply other matters awaiting . . . that I had to worry about."

And then late on the morning of March 13 [1948] Truman got a telephone call from the Statler, where his old friend and business partner Eddie Jacobson was staying. Eddie wanted to come to the White House to see the President.

"I said to him, 'Eddie, I'm always glad to see old friends, but there's one thing you've got to promise me. I don't want you to say a *word* about what's going on over there in the Middle East. Do you promise?' And he did."

A little later Eddie was ushered into the Oval Room, and this is the way Harry Truman described what followed:

"Great tears were running down his cheeks, and I took one look at him, and I said, 'Eddie, you son of a bitch, you promised me you wouldn't say a word about what's going on over there.' And he said, 'Mr. President, I haven't said a word, but every time I think of the homeless Jews, homeless for thousands of years, and I think about Dr. Weizmann, I start crying. I can't help it. He's an old man, and he's spent his whole life working for a homeland for the Jews, and now he's sick, and he's in New York and wants to see you. And every time I think about it I can't help crying.'

"I said, 'Eddie, that's enough. That's the last word.'

"And so we talked about this and that, but every once in a while a big tear would roll down his cheek. At one point he said something about how I felt about old Andy Jackson, and he was crying again. He said he knew he wasn't supposed to, but that's how he felt about Weizmann.

"I said, 'Eddie, you son of a bitch, I ought to have you thrown right out of here for breaking your promise; you knew damn good and well I couldn't stand seeing you cry.'

"And he kind of smiled at me, still crying, though, and he said, 'Thank you, Mr. President,' and he left.

"After he was gone, I picked up the phone and called the State Department, and I told them I was going to see Weizmann. Well, you should have heard the carrying-on. The first thing they said—they said Israel wasn't even a country yet and didn't have a flag or anything. They said if Weizmann comes to the White House, what are we going to use for a flag?

"And I said, 'Look here; he's staying at the Waldorf-Astoria hotel in New York, and every time some foreign dignitary is staying there, they put something out. You find out what it is, and we'll use it. And I want you to call me right back.' "

On March 18 Chaim Weizmann came to the White House, but no flag was necessary. He came in through the east gate, and the fact of his visit was not known until later.

In any case, only eleven minutes after Israel became a state in May, its existence was officially recognized by the United States.

A year later the Chief Rabbi of Israel came to see the President, and he told him, "God put you in your mother's womb so that you could be the instrument to bring about the rebirth of Israel after two thousand years."

At that, great tears started rolling down Harry Truman's cheeks.

(Miller, *Plain Speaking*, pp. 230–236)

PAUL TILLICH   (1886–1965)

German-born American philosopher and theologian

. . . a story told of himself by Dr. Paul Tillich of Union Theological Seminary in a discussion after one of his seminars. Dr. Tillich explained that he had never at first approved of the Zionist movement. He had thought it a good thing that a group—the Jews—should survive in the modern world to represent a religious faith independent of patriotism, whose kingdom—since they had no country—could not be of this world. But it was then pointed out to him by a Jewish friend that he was being quite unfair to "the petty bourgeois Cohens and Levis," who could hardly be expected to be Moseses and Isaiahs, and who ought not to be restricted to the status of aliens in countries in which they were still not accepted on quite the same basis as other natives and which were liable to anti-Semitic panics. Dr. Tillich was so struck by the justice of this that he at once joined a Zionist organization.

(E. Wilson, *A Piece of My Mind: Reflections at Sixty*, pp. 106–107)

ELIZABETH ARDEN   *(1887–1966)*

U.S. cosmetics executive

To be a Catholic or Jewish isn't chic. Chic is Episcopalian.
(Lewis and Woodworth, *Miss Elizabeth Arden*, p. 2)

RAYMOND CHANDLER   *(1888–1959)*

U.S. detective story writer

Chandler to Miss Aron, 11 January 1946:

. . . I might say that I have received about a dozen letters on this subject, ranging from the pathological-vituperative to the courteous (of which yours is the only true example).

This book [*The High Window*] was published in 1942. It has been for sale and in rental libraries for quite a long time. Apparently the outburst is due to the 25¢ edition. I had heard no previous whisper of complaint. I have many Jewish friends. I even have Jewish relatives. My publisher is a Jew. Are you one of those who object to that word? If so, what would you like me to substitute? I am *not* being sarcastic. Also *all* the letters have come from the east. Out here [Los Angeles] the Jews seem to be in a fair way to lose their inferiority complex. At least my doctor thinks so. He is a Jew also.

You say why don't I introduce a character as a "thin-blooded Roman Catholic or a rugged Episcopalian"? Simply, my dear, because religion has nothing to do with it. You may happen to be an orthodox Hebrew, but there are Roman Catholic Jews and Christian Scientist Jews and Jews with no religion at all, and Jews — very, very many — who are Hebrews just once a year, on the Day of Atonement. I call a character a Jew for purely intellectual reasons occasionally, since there is, except on the most exalted levels of personality, a Jewish way of thought too.

The Jew is a type and I like types, that being as far as I have gone. He is of course many types, some recognizable a block away, some only on more intimate study, some hardly at all. I know there are Jewish people whom even Jews cannot pick out. I have had two secretaries who told me that, both being Jewish girls. There is a tone of voice, there is a certain eye, there is a coloring. It is not, dear lady, a matter of noses.

You are kind enough not to accuse me of anti-semitism. I am grateful for that since I am horribly tired of the whole subject. And at the same time I am terribly sorry for these tormented minds which cannot leave it alone, which worry it and keep it sore. A writer in the Saturday Review of Literature lately said that what the Jews demand is not the right to have geniuses, but the right to have scoundrels. I agree. And I demand the right to call a character named Weinstein a thief without being accused of calling all Jews thieves. That right, with certain people, I do not have.

Incidentally Dr. Carl Moss is a portrait of my publisher, Alfred Knopf. Not exact, but with the offhand respect which is all Philip Marlowe would have for anyone. And I am *not* Philip Marlowe.

Let me in all kindness say one final word. You are yourself not the type, but if among your friends there is an impulse to go on an anti-semitic witch hunt, let them look for their enemies not among those who call a Jew a Jew, who put Jewish characters in their books because there are many Jews in their lives and all interesting and all different and some noble and some rather nasty—like other people—but let them look for their enemies among the brutes (whom they can easily recognize) and among the snobs who do not speak of Jews at all.

You are safe and more than safe with outspoken people like me.
(MacShane, *Selected Letters of Raymond Chandler*, pp. 65–67)

* * *

Chandler to publisher Hamish Hamilton, 11 January 1950:

. . . I don't think there is much chance of any motion picture outfit buying the screen rights to LS.[3] They're tired of the private dick stories (having run them to death with a series of imitations) and the book is not too admiring of Hollywood. Fundamentally it is probably a

---

[3]*The Little Sister*, written in 1949.

question of money. Lots of stories are now sold for five or ten thousand dollars. I'm asking fifty. There was one producer at Warner's named Harry Kurnitz wanted to do it, but Jack Warner evidently said no. Nor do I think there is any feeling against me as an anti-Semitic. After all I dealt with dozens and dozens of Jews in Hollywood and was never accused by any of them of any such feeling. The people who do raise the point belong to that extreme fringe who resent anyone's using the word Jew at all. Some of my most stalwart supporters are Jewish. My favorite doctor is Jewish. He once said, "There's a bit of the anti-Semitic in all of us, Jews and Gentiles alike." What they seem to resent is the feeling that the Jew is a distinct racial type, that you can pick him out by his face, by the tone-quality of his voice, and far too often by his manners. In short, to some extent the Jews are still foreigners, especially the middle-Europeans. It was not so in England when I was a schoolboy. I must have known Jewish boys at school, but I can't remember which were which. One just didn't think about it. The only time I ever heard a man called a Jew in England was by one of his closest friends, and all he meant was that he was an orthodox Hebrew. Over here it is different. They are of all religions or no religion. When you call a man a Jew you are not thinking of his religion, but of certain personal characteristics of appearance and behaviour, and the Jews don't like that, because they know that is what you mean. They want to be like everyone else, indistinguishable from everyone else, except that they want to be Jews to themselves, and they want to be able to call non-Jews by the name of Gentiles. But even then they are not happy, because they know very well you can't insult a man by calling him a Gentile, whereas you *can* insult him by calling him a Jew. As long as that is so I don't see how you can expect the Jews not to be oversensitive, but at the same time I don't see why I should be so unnaturally considerate of this oversensitiveness as never to use the word Jew. It's not so one-sided. I've lived in a Jewish neighbourhood, and I've watched one become Jewish, and it was pretty awful. I don't know the answer, and I'm pretty sure it will take a long time to find it. It really seems at times that the Jews ask too much of us. They are like a man who insists upon being nameless and without an address and yet insists on being invited to all the best parties.

(*Selected Letters*, pp. 206–208)

CHARLES DE GAULLE   (1890–1970)

French World War II Resistance leader; president of the Republic, 1958–1969

On the 27th, de Gaulle called another press conference. What sensations did he still hold in reserve? . . . In the following day's newspapers, the second No to Britain competed for space and headlines with a passage in which de Gaulle, referring to the Six-Day War, described the Jews as "an *elite* people, sure of itself and dominating." Had de Gaulle turned anti-semitic? Certainly there had never been any sign of it, and there had always been Jews among his close associates. But his remarks aroused much unfavourable comment, and provoked the sociologist of Jewish origin, Raymond Aron, to publish a book, *De Gaulle, Israel et les Juifs*, expressing his indignation at the implication that Jewish Frenchmen were not to be regarded as French in the full sense.

(Crozier, *De Gaulle*, p. 581)

* * *

This chapter cannot be concluded without a reference to de Gaulle's famous description of the Jews at his press conference of 27 November 1967 as "an elite people, self-confident and dominating." The word "dominating" caused an outcry in the Western world, and was regarded as an injustice even by some members of the General's family. De Gaulle did not withdraw it but invited the Chief Rabbi to the Elysée and assured him he had meant no slight on the Jewish people. This was a gesture of appeasement without precedent or sequel during the General's decade as President, but it did not assuage the critics. In his family circle de Gaulle insisted that he had done no more than repeat what his father Henri had told his children long ago. In fact he was echoing Charles Maurras's description of the Jews long before the Nazi era. "Dominating" was his favourite adjective for them, and it must have lodged in the tenacious memory of de Gaulle, so long a reader of *L'Action Française.*

In terms of public relations there was a price which de Gaulle had to pay for his abandonment of the Israeli cause. An influential section of the French and American press turned against him permanently after the Six-Day War, and he forfeited the long-standing sympathy of French Jewry. Arab goodwill, however, increased. He had achieved that aim at least, and it was not without material importance for France.

(B. Ledwidge, De Gaulle, pp. 332–333)

HENRY MILLER   (1891–1980)

U.S. novelist; author of Tropic of Cancer, Tropic of Capricorn

Miller to Elmer Gertz, 16 March 1962:[4]

... When you take a vacation cut your bridges behind you—never leave addresses and phone numbers. Die to the world—utterly—even if only for 36 hours. Otherwise, the "world" will kill you. I haven't a single Jewish friend (always a professional, of course) who knows how to take a real vacation. I think sometimes the Jews are farther from the Orient than any Westerner. The Orient for us (I include myself, notice) is what sleep is to the body cells. To forget, to just not give a damn, to laze away the days—what a gift!

Take it still easier, please.

Henry Miller

P.S. one exception—my friend and beau-frère, Bezalel Schatz—but then he was raised different—in his father's wonderful school in Jerusalem, where creative activity, music and play were the paramount things. Man, he sure can relax!

(Gertz and Flanery, Henry Miller—Years of Trial and Triumph,
1962-1964, pp. 68–69)

KARL MENNINGER   (1893–1990)

*U.S. psychiatrist; founder, with his father and brother, of the
Menninger Diagnostic Clinic in Kansas*

If we had no further illustration than the character of Sigmund Freud, we should have a basis for suspecting some connection between the Jew and psychological genius. It would take us too far to list all the outstanding Jewish psychologists and psychiatrists, nor would it, in my own mind, be fitting to associate lesser names with that of such a

---

[4] A Jewish lawyer who fought and won many of Miller's censorship battles.

master as he. It is one thing to show that proportionately many Jews have an interest in psychiatry and another to show that they have some special abilities in that direction. The fact is well known that Jewish physicians are distinguished for their scientific accomplishments in all fields of medicine, and, in writing such an article as this, one is dangerously close to the dilemma that if one holds that Jews are brilliant in all fields of science, it is the more difficult to show that they have some outstanding genius in psychiatry. Furthermore, as a Gentile, I am apt—like all Gentiles—to overestimate the superiorities and attainments of the Jews (a psychological fact which no doubt contributes in part to anti-Semitic reactions).

Nevertheless, I shall proceed on the basis of my empirical impressions, an unscientific but not necessarily invalid method. Some physicians accuse psychiatry of being more of an art than a science and say that psychiatrists are, therefore, born rather than made (not in the sense of inheriting something, but of coming by their special gifts by very early childhood influences, rather than from later training). This perhaps substantiates me in my belief that some Jews seem to have a special gift which makes them more likely than the average person in those requirements that make for skill, if not genius, in psychiatry, gifts which are peculiarly related to their Jewish origin. Since the recognition of the psychological elements of disease and behavior are so rapidly increasing in scientific circles as well as among laymen, and since the demands for psychiatrists so far exceed the supply, the recognition of such gifts might therefore be of considerable practical value, and it behooves us to inquire into the reasons for it and the possibilities of its being cultivated. . . .

. . . Does the Jewish child suffer more than the Gentile child, and, if so, does he suffer in a way which is likely to increase this propensity for interest in the sufferings of other people?

My impression is that perhaps, if we may generalize, the Jewish child does suffer somewhat more or somewhat more frequently than the Gentile child. However, I do not think that this is due to the immediate effects of Gentile prejudice. My impression is that it is due to the child's reaction to the parents' reaction to the entire social situation in which the Jews live. This includes, of course, their religious and historical traditions. . . .

. . . many Jewish children grow up with an extraordinary interest in and curiosity about people, reinforced no doubt by the background of religion and philosophy which is their heritage. Their own detachment when successfully achieved enables them to be more objective, more analytical and at the same time more discerning in their judgment of others, partly because they understand, and partly because they have been able to rise above suffering and even feel able to relieve it in others.

There is another point to be made in tracing childhood experiences to the adult vocation of psychiatry. Everyone learns sooner or later that one must expect disappointments in love—that his loved ones hurt him oftentimes as grievously as his enemies—but it has seemed to me that the individual Jew learns this at an earlier and more vulnerable age than do others. He learns it first because of his initial disappointment in his parents; their overtenderness and overestimation of him leads to inevitable disappointment because the least indifference on their part or perhaps the enthusiastic reception of another infant is interpreted by the child as a tragic rejection. Thus the individual Jew learns again what the Jews as a group (from their social experiences) long ago learned, namely, that no one can be implicitly and completely trusted. This saves them the painful disillusionment which the Gentile is continually experiencing because of his more gullible naiveté. The Jew knows from bitter experience that those who appear to love one another most, have a hostile component in their interpersonal bond which may under certain circumstances show itself directly or indirectly, overtly or covertly. They know that in one sense there is no such thing as disinterested friendship.

Theoretically—on the basis of their social experience—this attitude might be thought to apply only to Gentiles and not to fellow Jews. Practically, however, the early disillusionment extends to all relationships. Because of his experience within a closely allied group, the Jewish child has an opportunity to learn what every idealistic person who joins a social group or cause in search of understanding and inspiration discovers—that close association breeds hostilities and jealousies as well as love and sympathy.

This knowledge that even one's brothers, those whom one has been taught to turn to for comfort, are not exempt from envy, jealousy, craftiness, and hate, and, above all, actions of self-interest to the hurt of the others, leaves the Jew peculiarly exposed to *feelings of insecurity*. He has too keen an insight into human nature for his own comfort. He is so aware of the possibility of an attack or a desertion or a "double-cross" from his friends that he often anticipates it, even provokes it. But if he learns to understand and control this sensitiveness, he can turn to account his perception of unseen motives with telling effect, as he often does in psychiatry.

Still another reason that those raised in the Jewish tradition may have some special gift for psychiatry is that of the high value placed by them throughout history on verbal expression of feelings as exemplified by the incomparable poetry of the Psalms and the extraordinary quality of their religious literature, and also upon studious scholarly organization of their thinking. The Irish are gifted verbally but do not have the scientific essential of orderliness; the Swedes are orderly but not so gifted verbally. Now, in psychiatry the reduction of relatively intangible things such as feelings and attitudes to verbal expression is highly important. It is necessary to the scientific evaluation of mental processes and it has been shown by the work of Freud to have a therapeutic value for the patient. It is a very old observation that quarreling Irish may throw bricks at one another, and Italians knives, but Jews throw sharp words. This is a destructive use of the same gift. To convert this talent for verbalization into scientific purposes is in no branch of science more useful than in psychiatry. . . .

(K. Menninger, "The Genius of the Jew in Psychiatry," in
A Psychiatrist's World, pp. 415–424)

ROBERT GRAVES   *(1895–1985)*

British poet and author

From a talk delivered to the Israel and Commonwealth
Association in Tel Aviv, 19 January 1959:

What does it feel like to be a *goy?* Most modern Jewish fiction, or autobiography disguised as fiction, answers the complementary question "What does it feel like to be a Jew?" The *goyim* who surround each protagonist in these very similar dramas are described objectively; but the Jewish reader and the author himself can only guess what goes on behind their masks. Are they cruel, insensitive, or merely ignorant?

I am a *goy*, and the son of *goyim*: several generations at least on both sides of the family. It has recently become the fashion in the United States for young non-Jewish intellectuals to ransack their yellowing archives in search of a Jewish great-great-grandmother. The other day one of the Lowells of Boston told me with sparkling eyes that he actually *has* a Jewish great-grandmother. I cannot make any such claim. My father's pedigree contains several mediaeval Kings of England, albeit through an illegitimate line, several Spanish Kings maternally descended from the Prophet Mahomet and—since we Graveses married into several Irish families—any amount of legendary Irish kings and heroes. No Cohens or Levis, not one! I did have a German great-grandmother named Schubert, but unfortunately she came of solid Lutheran stock. . . .

. . . At all events, write me down as a *goy* and as a Protestant *goy*: than which nothing in the world could be more *goyesque*. . . .

It was an old Christian dogma that the Mosaic Law, entrusted by God to the Jews, remained valid only until the Messiah came—that the Messiah had come in the person of Jesus the Nazarene—that though the New Testament was inspired by him to replace it, the prophecies contained in the Old were authoritative proof of his destined Messiahship—that Christians were a New Israel, successors of the Old Israel which had denied Christ and been therefore rejected by God. So my Protestant ancestors, in order fully to understand their New Testament, pored over the Old, and came to remarkable and unsettling conclusions. Some, finding Jesus to have declared that the Law of Moses would never pass away until the end of the world, now regarded Jewish ritual obligations (so far as they could be observed without a Temple or priesthood) as still binding on Christians. For instance they wanted to keep the Jewish Sabbath instead of the Christian Sunday which the Christians had borrowed from Mithraism, along with Mithras's Nativity Feast on December 25th, adoring shepherds and all. They also thought it wicked to eat blood-sausage, and would not remove their hats in church. . . .

What does it feel like to be a *goy?* Embarrassing, for careful students of religious history. The trouble began with Saul of Tarsus—later Paul—who once, when in danger of his life from an angry pilgrim crowd, claimed Jewish birth. He certainly became a Jew by adoption early in his career, but according to the Ebionites (the austere apocalyptic section of Nazarenes) was the son of Greek parents; and the Ebionites can hardly be suspected of deliberate falsehood. . . .

. . . Paul presently claimed that Jesus' crucifixion totally annulled the Mosaic Law, and that an act of repentance and a confession of belief in his Messiahship was the needful passport to Heaven. Mystical accretions—some of them, like the Trinity doctrine, now given a

Gnostic origin, others borrowed from paganism—expanded the Pauline faith. Yet Paul's adoption of the Jewish ethic, as whittled down and reconciled by the God-fearers with obedience to their Roman overlords, stuck; and is still Christian dogma for Catholics and Protestants alike.

When Judaism had been proscribed and nearly battered out of existence, the Christians escaped by joining the hue and cry against their parent faith, accusing the Jews of Jesus' murder, and rewriting the Gospels to present him as an original thinker who detested the Pharisees, knew better than Moses, and was honourably treated by Pontius Pilate, the Roman Procurator. To substantiate the Trinity doctrine, they even went so far as to make Jesus identify blasphemously with God. . . .

To us English, all Jews were a mystery for over four hundred years before Cromwell invited them back. They had been expelled in an access of religious hysteria: being accused of numerous unexplained crimes—especially the ritual murders of children, laid at their door, it seems, by members of a primitive pagan cult surviving in East Anglia, who actually committed them. Thus Shakespeare, who pilloried Shylock, the villainous Jew, in his *Merchant of Venice*, is unlikely ever to have met a Jew—unless perhaps a Sephardic physician attached to the Spanish Embassy in London. The tradition of wicked Jews who spat at Christ being endorsed by the Gospels, a Jew was a safe target; and Shakespeare borrowed his story from the Venetians, who had cause to be jealous of their Jewish trade rivals. An unusual feature in the case is Shakespeare's sympathetic understanding of Shylock's troubles.

Cromwell invited the Jews back for political, not religious reasons. They brought modern banking methods to London from Holland, and the City's present financial strength rests squarely on the foundations they laid. Their descendants have met with little trouble since those days, always showing gratitude and loyalty to England. Yet although, a century ago, religious toleration reached a point where Jews could be enrolled in the British nobility, and one even became Prime Minister [Disraeli] and founded the Primrose League (the most true-blue Conservative institution of all) it would be foolish to pretend that they have been fully assimilated into British social life. Jewish dietary laws, and the yearly reminder at Pesach that their true home lay far away, made this impossible. They remained guests, albeit honoured guests.

. . . So at last you Jews won what you had always prayed for: a return to your own land! I foresaw that "What it feels like to be a *goy*" would soon acquire a new sense. A *goy*, in relation to Jews dispersed all over the world, who are living on sufferance as guests in a generally hostile environment, is one thing; a *goy* in relation to a small though dynamic *nation* of Jews, based on their original homeland, is another thing altogether.

Until that miraculous day, most European Jews were taught from earliest infancy: "Be careful! Never listen to the *goyim*! Swallow insults, keep the Law! Be patient; you are one of God's Chosen, and precious in His sight. One day He will make us a nation again!" It was a superiority complex, and difficult for a sensitive *goy* to understand. Though he might be welcomed in a Jewish home and treated like a king, with all the extravagant hospitality of which perhaps the Irish alone are equally capable, he felt inferior and guilty; because he had not suffered a million slights and snubs and insults; and because he had been faithful to his national identity. Often twenty generations of his ancestors had been around in those parts; but the Jews had been denied an ancestral home three times as long. Pity was not what he felt towards them, nor envy—it was a certain awe. And the Protestant in him said: "Not surprising; the Bible says that they are God's Chosen People." Even St. Paul in his Epistle to the Corinthians had blurted out: "What advantage then hath the Jew? Much, chiefly that to the Jews were committed the holy oracles of God."

Of course, a "but" followed; nevertheless. . . .

Ten years after the Lord turned again the captivity of Zion, your Government invited me to visit Israel. I answered in hot sincerity that it was the greatest honour ever paid me. Whatever vicarious guilt I felt for the persecution of your ancestors by mine, was at last officially purged. Here in Israel I am a *goy* in the new, different sense. The *awe* remains: that Israel is a nation once more, and not a sentimental show-piece either, a mock-antique, but a strong, proud, energetic, well-disciplined nation—one that continues to welcome homeless Jewish immigrants into an already crowded country, and establish them as useful citizens. . . .

My sense of awe has been heightened by the realization that Hebrew is again a living spoken language—the same Hebrew from which our vernacular Old Testament was translated at third hand, through Latin and Greek. And the blood-curdling life-histories of those who came here as ragged refugees, and can now hold their heads high again, seem to me a sufficient guarantee that the New Israel will endure. . . .

Colonel T. E. Lawrence, whose official biographer I was, thoroughly approved of the Balfour Declaration, and wrote to me before he died in 1935: "It is a problem of the third generation." If he meant "the third generation from now" (for your Rothschild settlements had already attained a fifth or sixth generation of "Sabras"), he was wrong. Unlike Moses, who kept Israel forty years in the Wilderness, you have not needed to await that third generation. The first generation has speeded up history. . . .

Our British Welfare State rests on a theory of social justice and fair shares for all. But "Fair Shares for All" does not encourage overtime, or doing without luxuries so that as many poor fellows as possible can benefit from one's own industry. "Love thy neighbour!" is a positive injunction—like "Six days *shalt* thou labour!" "Fair Shares for All!" is negative.

What advantage therefore hath a Jew? Much: chiefly that unto the Jews were committed the holy oracles of God! And, though there have been saints in every land, and under every religion, Israel was the first nation to make brotherly love and mercy head the list of moral virtues. So, if asked to pronounce on the knotty question: "What is a Jew?" I should answer: "Anyone who feels himself a Jew and will faithfully obey that Levitical text." All other considerations seem to me legalistic and unworthy of Israel's historical role.

(Graves, *The Crane Bag and Other Disputed Subjects*, pp. 103–114)

THORNTON WILDER   *(1897–1975)*

U.S. novelist and playwright; wrote Our Town,
The Skin of Our Teeth; *Pulitzer Prize, 1938*

The next religions that arise in the world will also undoubtedly draw their strength in large part from a slain-god myth and/or from a denunciation of the senses; but it may be assumed that in each successive "relevation" these emphases will play less dominant a part. The Crucifixion is still the most magnificent metaphor ever found for mankind's falling short of the perfection to which it might attain; but the Crucifixion's involvement in blood and murder reawakens the latent anguish of the infantile life and fills the inner mind with such vibrating nerves and such despairing self-abasement that the spiritual values can barely make themselves heard. The business of a preacher should be to divorce the specific dramatic elements of the story of Christ from the "educative" elements, and, like an analyst, ceaselessly turn the light of explanation into the dark pockets of over-emotional identification with the blood-guilt aspects of the story.

Obiter dicta: No wonder the Jews rejected the [Crucifixion] metaphor; their sense of guilt carries only one of those burdens: they loathe the flesh, but they are not killers. If it weren't for that element they'd have been the best of all Christians—as would the Chinese, too.

Like that other testimony to order and meaning in the universe, art, religion was communicated to the world by neurotics, and betrays its origin at every turn (look at St. Paul and Pascal and the Old Testament). . . .

(Wilder, "On Religion and Psychoanalysis," 17 February 1940, in *The Journals of Thornton Wilder, 1939–1961*, p. 10)

* * *

. . . Communism was designed by a Jew. Jews are not impatient. (Jews can pump themselves up into an impatience, but it is not a true impatience. It is doubtful whether Jews believe in the perfectibility of man, even on a millenary basis.)* Communism fell, however, into the hands of non-Jews, and look what has happened.

It is very Jewish that Communism describes a society in which every man is (1) patient, (2) a good citizen, and (3) willing to sacrifice a great deal of initiative for a security provided by an overruling force—the Government. That dream is very intoxicating—by antithesis—to the impatient, the unsocial, and the individualist. How fascinating, doubly fascinating, to those who feel themselves to be rulers is a state-plan in which there are no rulers. . . .

*(N.B. To consider: did the—do the—Jews await a Messiah?)
(Wilder, "Of Utopias and Panaceas," 17 February 1940, in *The Journals of Thornton Wilder*, pp. 11–12)

From a letter written at Harvard University, 30 November
1950:

A Miss [X] had written me asking if she might send a "rare blue-cloth
binding" first edition of *The Cabala* for my signature—in fact for a
"signed presentation inscription with a few lines regarding its incep-
tion." I wrote that I had a terrible time finding paper, cord, and post
office, and wouldn't she like to bring it to my lecture on Emily Dickinson, January 13, at the Poetry Center, YMHA/YWHA, New York.
   She wrote back on November 24:

> I am duly in receipt of your postal of the 21st instant, and, in
> reply thereto, beg to advise you that I have no interest whatever
> in the Young Men's Hebrew Association, or anything connected
> with the race in other than a fictional or historical relation.

Then a great deal of directions about the book, her sincere
appreciation, and her "Cordially yours," and a postscript asking also
for a photograph.
   I reply:

Dear Miss [X],
The first sentence of your letter made me shudder so that I keep it by
me all the time to remind me of how slowly the world is learning the
lessons by which it must live and pursue happiness and attain peace. I
need to be reminded of this constantly—for the background of my
teaching these young people at Harvard and Radcliffe. Although you
would not wish me to, I thank you for this bitter reminder.

Sincerely yours.

                      (*The Journals of Thornton Wilder*, pp. 81–82)

FRANK CAPRA   *(1897–)*

U.S. film director; directed It's a Wonderful Life,
It Happened One Night

That's why only the Jews could make good films: They could lose and
smile; they could *win* and smile. They were gamblers, first of all—they
were gamblers.

The fact is that the Jews—every one of them had an education. Education is the prime thing about a Jew. If you're not educated, you're not a Jew: They won't accept you. So—*accomplishment!!*

[The famed movie producer] Harry Cohn was very, very proud of his films; goddam proud of them—that they could make people laugh. He was *not* just a money-making guy! He was a very proud man, and proud that his material was going out and entertaining people. He was a showman.

Now, the showmen are all gone. I think that Mr. Warner—Jack Warner—was the last one. Now we have those who are not show-biz people. They don't have this feeling that they want to make people laugh. Now [in Hollywood] it's money, pure money. I hope this doesn't last very long.

(As told by Capra to editor Allan Gould in 1982)

VLADIMIR NABOKOV   *(1899–1977)*

Russian-American novelist and poet; author of Pnin, Lolita

. . . He met the aphoristic poet Baron Anatoly Shteiger and came to know him. . . . There were obstacles to Nabokov's appreciation of Shteiger, chief among them that he was a close friend of Georgy Adamovich and one of the most important figures in Adamovich's "Paris School." There were other things they disagreed strongly about as well: Shteiger was a homosexual, and he had the easy anti-Semitism of the Russian aristocracy that Nabokov had fought against so bitterly for so many years. . . .

. . . If, given his views, Nabokov showed considerable restraint in regard to his political convictions with [critic Edmund] Wilson, Wilson for his part must have been extremely careful in regard to the expression of his anti-Semitic views (known to those who have worked with Wilson correspondence in archives), and he told a friend that he lived in terror of forgetting to include a warm greeting to Vera [Nabokov's Jewish wife] every time that he wrote to Nabokov. . . .

Real or imagined anti-Semitism became the focus for sporadic irritability in Nabokov in the mid-fifties. He claimed to see it in both the faculty and the student body at Cornell. He was friendly with

Cornell's best-known writer, Arthur Mizener, with whom he nearly fought seriously over alleged anti-Semitism. (Mizener liked Nabokov enough that he had invited him to his daughter's wedding. Nabokov spent the ceremony studying the details of the church.) In 1954 Mizener was one of a group of faculty friends invited to a cocktail party by Nabokov, and at that party Mizener told the story of an argument he had witnessed between Delmore Schwartz and Robert Lowell over the award of the Bollingen prize to Ezra Pound. Schwartz accused Lowell to his face of being an anti-Semite like Pound. In telling the story Mizener expressed confidence that Lowell, who had been one of the three judges who had made the award, had made his decision on the basis of the quality of the poetry alone, and he expressed sympathy for the very difficult position that Lowell found himself in. Nabokov, who had been listening to the story at a slight distance, paled and took another guest, Professor M.H. Abrams, with him into a nearby room. Nabokov expressed consternation at the dilemma that faced him: Mizener was his friend, but he was going to have to throw him out of his house for talking in an anti-Semitic way. Abrams was astonished at Nabokov's interpretation of what Mizener had said and only just managed to calm Nabokov down. Nor did Nabokov let the matter pass. He consulted Philip Rahv of *Partisan Review* to discover if there was anything anti-Semitic known in Mizener's past. The matter concerns only Nabokov's extreme hypersensitivity in regard to the question. Nabokov's allegation was wholly unfounded.

(Field, *VN, The Life and Art of Vladimir Nabokov*, pp. 183, 262, 302–303)

AYATOLLAH KHOMEINI   (1900–1989)

Leader of the Revolutionary Islamic government of Iran, 1979–1989

. . . His views were always stern. He believed that there was either good or evil, with no gray area in between. Thus corruption cannot be reformed but must be destroyed. He used to recount a parable of a clean spring and a stagnant pond. The spring can pour into the pond, but the pond will remain stagnant unless it is drained.

It was inevitable that Khomeini would loath the attacks that Reza Shah made on the power of the mullahs. After Reza Shah's abdication, Khomeini wrote a book in which he described the King as a usurper who had ignored Islamic precepts and had run a corrupt, cruel, and illegitimate state. His later declarations were filled with similar anger at the way in which Mohammed Reza was substituting Western values for the Islamic tradition in Iran. . . .

In the fifties Khomeini attempted, vainly, to obtain clemency for members of the Islamic fedayeen (the precursors of Islamic Jehad and Hezbollah which came to prominence in Lebanon in the 1980s), who had been sentenced to death for assassinating prominent members of the Shah's regime. He abhorred the Shah's relationship with Israel. . . .

Khomeini described the Shah's attempt to enfranchise women as an effort "to corrupt our chaste women." . . . Land reform endangered their financial independence. Khomeini asserted that many of the reforms were "perhaps drawn up by the spies of the Jews and the Zionists. . . . The Koran and Islam are in danger." On some issues he managed to force changes in government policy. It gave him a sense of his power.

When the land reform began to take effect in 1963, the Shah himself denounced the religious opposition as "black reaction" and dismissed the clerics as "lice-ridden mullahs." Land reform was popular and the National Front politicians, what remained of them, could hardly oppose it. But Khomeini again insisted that it was all being done for foreign enemies. "In the interest of the Jews, America, and Israel, we must be jailed and killed; we must be sacrificed to the evil intentions of foreigners."

In June 1963, Khomeini denounced the Shah particularly harshly as a Zionist agent, and was arrested. This caused wide-spread riots that the government suppressed with brutality. Estimates of the number of people who were killed by the military varied from several hundred to several thousand. . . .

(Shawcross, *The Shah's Last Ride*, pp. 112–114)

JEAN-PAUL SARTRE   *(1905–1980)*

French philosopher, novelist, and playwright

The anti-Semite readily admits that the Jew is intelligent and hard-working; he will even confess himself inferior in these respects. This concession costs him nothing, for he has, as it were, put those qualities in parentheses. Or rather they derive their value from the one who possesses them: the more virtues the Jew has the more dangerous he will be. The anti-Semite has no illusions about what he is. He considers himself an average man, modestly average, basically mediocre. There is no example of an anti-Semite's claiming individual superiority over the Jews. But you must not think that he is ashamed of his mediocrity; he takes pleasure in it; I will even assert that he has chosen it. This man fears every kind of solitariness, that of the genius as much as that of the murderer; he is the man of the crowd. However small his stature, he takes every precaution to make it smaller, lest he stand out from the herd and find himself face to face with himself. He has made himself an anti-Semite because that is something one cannot be alone. The phrase, "I hate the Jews," is one that is uttered in chorus; in pronouncing it, one attaches himself to a tradition and to a community — the tradition and community of the mediocre.

(Sartre, *Anti-Semite and Jew*, p. 22)

* * *

. . . Don't the Jews have all the scholarships? All that intelligence, all that money can acquire one leaves to them, but it is as empty as the wind. The only things that count are irrational values, and it is just these things which are denied the Jews forever. Thus the anti-Semite takes his stand from the start on the ground of irrationalism. He is opposed to the Jew, just as sentiment is to intelligence, the particular to the universal, the past to the present, the concrete to the abstract, the owner of real property to the possessor of negotiable securities. . . .

(*Anti-Semite and Jew*, p. 25)

* * *

Since the Jew is dependent upon opinion for his profession, his rights, and his life, his situation is completely unstable. Legally not open to attack, he is at the mercy of the whims and passions of the "real" society. He carefully watches the progress of anti-Semitism; he tries to foresee crises and gauge trends in the same way that the peasant keeps watch on the weather and predicts storms. He ceaselessly calculates the effects that external events will have on his own position. He may accumulate legal guarantees, riches, honors; he is only the more vulnerable on that account, and he knows it. Thus it seems to him at one and the same time that his efforts are always crowned with success—for he knows the astonishing successes of his race—and that a curse has made them empty, for he will never acquire the security enjoyed by the most humble Christian.

This is perhaps one of the meanings of *The Trial* by the Jew, Kafka. Like the hero of that novel, the Jew is engaged in a long trial. He does not know his judges, scarcely even his lawyers; he does not know what he is charged with, yet he knows that he is considered guilty; judgment is continually put off—for a week, two weeks—he takes advantage of these delays to improve his position in a thousand ways, but every precaution taken at random pushes him a little deeper into guilt. His external situation may appear brilliant, but the interminable trial invisibly wastes him away, and it happens sometimes, as in the novel, that men seize him, carry him off on the pretense that he has lost his case, and murder him in some vague area of the suburbs.

The anti-Semites are right in saying that the Jew eats, drinks, reads, sleeps, and dies like a Jew. What else could he do? They have subtly poisoned his food, his sleep, and even his death. How else could it be for him, subjected every moment to this poisoning? As soon as he steps outside, as soon as he encounters others, in the street or in public places, as soon as he feels upon him the look of those whom a Jewish newspaper calls "Them"—a look that is a mixture of fear, disdain, reproach, and brotherly love—he must decide: does he or does he not consent to be the person whose role they make him play? And if he consents, to what extent? If he refuses, will he refuse all kinship with other Israelites, or only an ethnic relationship?

(*Anti-Semite and Jew*, pp. 87–89)

* * *

. . . the rationalism to which the Jew adheres so passionately is first of all an exercise of asceticism and of purification, an escape into the universal. The young Jew who feels a taste for brilliant and abstract argument is like the infant who touches his body in order to become acquainted with it: he experiments with and inspects his intoxicating condition as universal man; on a superior level he realizes that accord and assimilation which is denied him on the social level.

The choice of rationalism is for him the choice of a human destiny and a human nature. That is why it is at once both true and false that the Jew is "more intelligent than the Christian." We should say rather that he has a taste for pure intelligence, that he loves to exercise it with reference to anything and everything, that the use he makes of it is not thwarted by the innumerable taboos which still affect the Christian, or by a certain type of particularist sensibility which the non-Jew cultivates willingly. And we should add that there is in the Jew a sort of impassioned imperialism of reason: for he wishes not only to convince others that he is right; his goal is to persuade them that there is an absolute and unconditioned value to rationalism. He feels himself to be a missionary of the universal; against the universalism of the Catholic religion, from which he is excluded, he asserts the "catholicity" of the rational, an instrument by which to attain to the truth and establish a spiritual bond among men. . . .

The anti-Semite reproaches the Jew with "not being creative," with having "a destructive intelligence." This absurd accusation (Spinoza, Proust, Kafka, Milhaud, Chagall, Einstein, Bergson—are they not Jews?) has been given a semblance of truth by the fact that the Jewish intelligence willingly takes a critical turn. But here again it is not a question of the disposition of cerebral cells but of a choice of weapons. In effect, the Jew finds arrayed against him the irrational powers of tradition, of race, of national destiny, of instinct: it is pretended that these powers have built monuments, a culture, a history—practical values that retain much of the irrationality of their origins and are accessible only to intuition. The defense of the Israelite is to deny intuition as well as the irrational, to make the obscure powers vanish—magic, unreason, everything that cannot be explained on the basis of universal principles, everything that betrays a tendency to the singular and the exceptional. He is distrustful on principle of those totalities which the Christian mind from time to time produces: he *challenges*.

(*Anti-Semite and Jew*, pp. 112–114)

* * *

This universalism, this critical rationalism, is what one normally finds in the democrat. In his abstract liberalism, he affirms that Jews, Chinese, Negroes ought to have the same rights as other members of society, but he demands these rights for them as men, not as concrete and individual products of history. Thus certain Jews look at their own personalities with the eyes of the democrat. Haunted by the specter of violence, by the unassimilated residues of particularist and warrior societies, they dream of a contractual community in which thought itself would be established under form of contract—since it would be a dialogue in which the disputants would agree on principles at the start—and in which the "social contract" would be the sole collective bond. The Jews are the mildest of men, passionately hostile to violence. That obstinate sweetness which they conserve in the midst of the most atrocious persecution, that sense of justice and of reason which they put up as their sole defense against a hostile, brutal, and unjust society, is perhaps the best part of the message they bring to us and the true mark of their greatness.

(*Anti-Semite and Jew*, pp. 117–118)

* * *

Anti-Semitism is a problem that affects us all directly; we are all bound to the Jew, because anti-Semitism leads straight to National Socialism. And if we do not respect the person of the Israelite, who will respect us? If we are conscious of these dangers, if we have lived in shame because of our involuntary complicity with the anti-Semites, who have made hangmen of us all, perhaps we shall begin to understand that we must fight for the Jew, no more and no less than for ourselves.

(*Anti-Semite and Jew*, p. 151)

* * *

. . . Richard Wright, the Negro writer, said recently: "There is no Negro problem in the United States, there is only a White problem." In the same way, we must say that anti-Semitism is not a Jewish problem; it is *our* problem. Since we are not guilty and yet run the risk of being its victims—yes, we too—we must be very blind indeed not to see that it is our concern in the highest degree. It is not up to the Jews first of all to form a militant league against anti-Semitism; it is up to us.

. . . The cause of the Jews would be half won if only their friends brought to their defense a little of the passion and the perseverance their enemies use to bring them down.

In order to awaken this passion, what is needed is not to appeal to the generosity of the Aryans—with even the best of them, that virtue is in eclipse. What must be done is to point out to each one that the fate of the Jews is *his* fate. Not one Frenchman will be free so long as the Jews do not enjoy the fullness of their rights. Not one Frenchman will be secure so long as a single Jew—in France or *in the world at large*—can fear for his life.

(*Anti-Semite and Jew*, pp. 152–153)

C. P. SNOW   *(1905–1980)*

British novelist and scientist

When I was very poor and very young, I was taken up by one of the rich patrician Anglo-Jewish families. It was a startling experience. I was a Gentile, and I had never seen the inside of a Jewish family before. What impressed me more at the time, I had never been inside an influential family before. This was my first contact with the easy, interconnected, confident world of the English ruling classes. Up to that time, cabinet ministers, high court judges, bosses of the civil service were, for me, people one read about in newspapers. At my friends' houses I met these people; in fact, my friends' relatives occupied just such jobs. It was a slightly off-beat introduction to a layer of English society which later on I happened to get to know quite well. The introduction was off-beat, of course, because my friends' family, in ninety-nine ways out of one hundred indistinguishable from an upper-class English family, in one way was not. They were, after all, Jewish: and the younger ones, my own generation, were conscious of it. When I got fascinated by the argumentativeness, the brilliance, the vivacity of the great family parties, my friends were anxious, pressingly anxious, that I should not take them at a false valuation. "You seem to think," they used to say, "that Jews are more intelligent than anyone else. You must get it into perspective. We can produce Jews for you who are much stupider and much duller than anyone you can possibly believe. You just have a look at Cousin X and Aunt Y."

My friends' desire was to prove that everyone is much the same, which is a very praiseworthy thing to do. Also they didn't want me to be beglamoured. I suppose I was a bit beglamoured then. To an extent I have remained so ever since. It is very difficult, and pretty disreputable intellectually, to make generalizations about large groups of people whose main connection is that they are called by the same label. But I should have thought that, if one were going to play that game at all, Jews have—to a slight but significant extent—thrown out more ability in relation to their numbers than any other group on earth.

It is worth remembering that, when one estimates how many Jews have ever lived, the number is quite small. Yet the amount of Jewish genius and talent in almost every high level of activity can bear comparison, not in relative but in absolute terms, with that of far larger groups such as the Russians or the English or the French, who themselves have a creditable record.

It is a bit of a mystery why this should be so. Part of it must be owing to the genes, and the Jews, who have not been lucky in much, have obviously been lucky in the genes. Where has this wonderful gene pool come from? No one has given me an answer which seems remotely satisfactory. If the marriage laws had been kept, all the genes would date back to before the Babylonian captivity. But with all respect to tradition, I just do not believe that is true. You have only got to look at Jews from different parts of the world to see that the structure of the gene pool is more complicated than that. It would be of the deepest interest to see a genetic reconstruction of the Jewish "race" from the diaspora onward.

Then, as well as the genetic inheritance, there is environment. You can't persecute a group of people for nearly two thousand years, keep them out of various sorts of jobs, set them apart and cause them to set themselves apart, without producing certain minimum effects. Some of these effects, of course, inhibited the emergence of Jewish talents. For instance, it must have been difficult for a Jew to show his athletic prowess in Western Europe in the Middle Ages, or almost up to the time of the emergence of the great Jewish boxers in the eighteenth century. But some talents, particularly the intellectual talents, based on the belief that the mind is a good and private thing, the centuries of persecution probably reinforced.

In any case, the result is on the table. As I said before, in almost every sphere of human activity, the Jews have made a contribution utterly out of proportion to their numbers. I have often heard this contribution undervalued, even in England, which, of the countries I know well, is probably the least anti-Semitic. The technique is always the same. It consists of praising the Jewish talent for one kind of activity, in order to dispraise it for another, which for the purposes of argument is regarded as more significant. Thus: Jews have done pretty well in mathematics, or theoretical physics, or idea-spinning, but have never really been any good at experimental science, at really plucking out the secrets of nature. I used to hear that thirty years ago. It sounds very silly now. Of the last dozen Nobel Prize winners for experimental physics, three have been Jewish. Only the other day I heard one of these ranked by his peers as the greatest experimental physicist alive. In exactly the same way, it used to be said that in literature Jews produced some of the best critics, but not the first-class creative artists. This was still being said in England in the thirties after Proust's great book, after Svevo, after heaven knows how many others. Now I think it would take some nerve to say it. Try writing down the ten most interesting creative artists in prose fiction in the United States at the present day [1961] under the age of fifty. Most of us will include five or six Jewish names. In productive industry one hears the same dismal trick. Jews are all right in the City, or Wall Street, as the case may be, but are no use at making the hardware. Yet, from H. R. Ricardo down increasingly to the present day, American and British industry employs in the highest ranks of engineers about five times as many Jews as is statistically reasonable.

I am sick and tired of all this special pleading, of all these attempts to prove that one group of people, for the moment disapproved of, Jews or Russians or Japanese, are in some subtle way less creative than our own. These attempts are nonsense and, consciously or unconsciously, dishonest nonsense. This is specially true when applied to the Jewish talent. The only point about the Jewish talent that ought to matter deeply to the world is that there is a lot of it.

My first Jewish friends were, of course, right when they didn't want me to see or think of Jews as a collective entity. It is an outrage to human dignity to think of someone first as a label and then as a man. That is why all class structures and all "race" structures degrade, in an unnecessary and trivial fashion, the human condition. Yet we are still living, let us hope temporarily, in just such structures. Ilya Ehrenburg [a Soviet Russian writer], in a speech on his seventieth birthday, recently said that he liked to think of himself first and

foremost as a man, but that while there is a single anti-Semite alive, he is proud to be a Jew. Perhaps our Jewish friends will forgive us if we, who are not Jews, say much the same thing. While there is a single anti-Semite alive, we are proud to be on the other side.
(From C. P. Snow's Introduction to Arnold A. Rogow's *The Jew in a Gentile World*, pp. xv–xvii)

ROBERT PENN WARREN   *(1905–1989)*

U.S. poet and novelist; author of At Heaven's Gate, All the King's Men; *Pulitzer Prize 1947*

. . . In one of Faulkner's novels, a returning black soldier (one of the early novels)—a returning black soldier was a shock. He was wearing a uniform. It was a different world. From that time on, it was a different world. This whole encounter with the outside world . . . is very important to the South . . . as a rebellious minority . . . the explosion suddenly in all different directions. And I think you can make a case for this. You have the same thing in different ways happening with the sudden great burst of Jewish literary genius in this country; and black, the same way. The same kind of shock—the breaking up of a fixed situation, where some people have been more or less enclosed, brought into a fruitful relation and a shocking relation to the world outside . . .

[Interviewer: I suppose you see it in another way with Willa Cather—in the West?]

Yes. But that society was firmly fixed. It was rigid, you see, and it wasn't in the sense of minority society, as Southern society was, or Jewish society, or black society, you see. These are fairly firmly fixed, enclosed groups, with their own order of life, and their own special kind of limitations and deprivations, and their own inner problems and tensions.
(F. C. Watkins and J. T. Hiers, *Robert Penn Warren Talking, Interviews 1950–1978*, pp. 162–163)

* * *

[Interviewer]: When you look at the current American novel—Bellow, Malamud, Barth, Pynchon—do you feel very much that these writers are of a different generation? Do you feel that they're talking about a different world, concerned with different things, interested in different techniques? Do you feel apart from them?

Warren: Well, one *has* to feel apart—I'm older—apart from them in that sense. But I feel very close to my *interests.* I feel very close imaginatively to Saul Bellow's work. He's a wonderful writer, a powerful imagination. And of course, in one sense he's writing about a strange Jewish world which I know only by report and through friends like Saul Bellow or through the work of people like him. But I think there's a strange kind of possibility of rapport: Jewish writing in America has a minority psychology to it, so does Southern writing. As my wife once said, "You're just like Jews, you Southerners," and I think there's some truth in that. This is reflected, I think, in the literature. There's a certain *insideness* of the *outsider,* and intensities of inside effects sometimes look queer to those who are not inside. Malamud, I admire greatly. . . .

(*Robert Penn Warren Talking, Interviews 1950–1978,* p. 190)

JOHN KENNETH GALBRAITH   *(1908–)*

Canadian-born U.S. economist; author of The Affluent Society, The New Industrial State, The Age of Uncertainty

. . . Each club [at Princeton in the late 1930s] had its exact position in the general order, beginning at the top with the one called Ivy. I was never quite sure which came last. Jews and other outcasts were firmly excluded from all clubs. At first I was rather indifferent to these awful proceedings. Then two or three students sought me out to confide their terrible fear that they would not be selected. For all of their bright college careers they would be formally designated as undesirables. There was nothing one could do. I learned that Woodrow Wilson, when president of the university, had also been appalled but was equally helpless to change the system. . . .

(*Galbraith, A Life in Our Times, Memoirs,* pp. 19–20)

* * *

Early in my service [at Harvard] I admitted my best student, Theodore H. White. Later that day Dr. Ferry looked over the list, and his face became grim. Pointing to White, he told me that we were already up to our Jewish quota. I protested that White was not a Jewish name. He looked at me with a hopeless gesture and said that names meant nothing. Teddy was disaccepted over my objection. I was greatly distressed, and my relations with Ferry were strained for some time. As for White, he went to a more distinguished house and in more civilized times became a member of the Harvard Board of Overseers.

In my second year I was assigned to teach in the elementary course in economics, then called Economics A, and here I found anti-Semitism a blessing. A committee of instructors of which I became a member made up the small sections in which all the beginning teaching was then done. We were not allowed to see the grades or academic rank of the students, for then we would be tempted to assign the best students to ourselves. I accomplished the same result by putting in my sections the largest plausible number of truly Jewish names, judging that their owners had to be a lot better to get in. I had always, in consequence, an especially apt and articulate group of overachievers. My high grades came eventually to the attention of Burbie, who supervised the course. He advised me that he was taking my blue books with him to Maine to make sure that my marks were not inflated. He often said he was doing this; we knew, in fact, that the books, which were stored in a closet near his office in Holyoke House, were never disturbed.

(*A Life in Our Times, A Memoir*, pp. 51–52)

* * *

In Deya [on Majorca], on the olive-tree-covered slopes down to the Mediterranean . . . Robert Graves . . . lived just across the way. One afternoon as I finished work, Graves came into our living room and glanced at the *International Herald Tribune* beside my typewriter. The headline was large and black: Gamal Abdel Nasser had just closed the Gulf of Aqaba. War between Israel and Egypt now seemed inevitable.

Turning from the newspaper to me, Graves said, "You aren't worried about those Israels [sic], are you?"

I said that I was. A small country surrounded by so many hostile neighbors.

"Your generation, my dear Ken, had no preclassical history, did it?" It was not, in fact, a major subject at the Ontario Agricultural College.

Graves continued, "Do you realize that the Egyptian Army had its last military success at Kadesh against the Hittites in 1299 B.C.?"

(*A Life in Our Times, A Memoir,* pp. 522–523)

HARRISON SALISBURY   *(1908–   )*

U.S. reporter and author; Pulitzer Prize 1955

If anyone had told me that I was growing up in a ghetto, I would not have known what they meant. When I came home from my first day at Sumner School, my mother asked me about the children in my class. I said there were "five Sullivans." She was skeptical. So was my father. There were, in fact, five Solomons in my class. I knew no more of Jews than did my aunt Mary, growing up thirty years before in the Welsh community of the Western Avenue M.E. Church. She had a handsome young suitor, of whom she was very fond. One day a friend asked her, a bit hesitantly, if she knew that the young man was Jewish. "What do you mean?" my aunt asked. "Is that some kind of disease?"

In Miss MacPherson's first-grade classroom there were probably twenty-four children, of whom I suppose twenty were Jewish, one was black—a handsome boy named Booker T. Washington, who later became a professional singer—two were blond Scandinavian girls and one was myself. I do not believe any of us felt differences of creed, color or national origin. We wouldn't have understood that. Sumner School was about 95 percent Jewish, but years later, former classmates told me that neither they nor their parents had thought of it as a "Jewish" school. Nor did I. No one noticed that there were no Jewish teachers until, in 1918, Miss Levy appeared and took over grade three.

We all enjoyed the usual holidays—Christmas vacation, Lincoln's and Washington's birthdays, Easter vacation and, later on, Armistice Day, November 11. But the Jewish children got extra holidays—Rosh Hashanah, Yom Kippur and Passover. On those days, our little band of four or five goyim huddled in the deserted classroom while our teacher tried to find a way to occupy us. Outside on Sixth Avenue, my friends walked with their parents in their best clothes, or played shinny and marbles. It wasn't fair. When I grew a bit older, three of us would be selected as "writers" and go to the big Keneseth Israel Temple, very Orthodox, escorted by serious men in black suits. There we would record the financial pledges, the names, addresses and amounts. Writing was forbidden on the high holy days. For this we got a dollar. Almost every holiday, a worried old grandmother—a babushka, as I would come to say in Russia—would encounter me as I was walking home from school, grasp my wrist and ask me to light the stove in her kitchen. It was forbidden to light a fire until sundown, but if the little goy would do it she could get supper going. For this I got a nickel.

The nickels and dollars did not wash away the discrimination. I was a member of a small minority amid a large and powerful majority. We were friends, but there were lines I could not cross. School ended at three o'clock. I came home, had a glass of milk and a butter-and-sugar sandwich, and was ready to play. But my friends who went to *heder*, the Hebrew school, weren't free until five. I could see no reason, nor did they, why I shouldn't go to *heder* too. Finally, my mother went to the school and asked if I could be admitted. The rabbi was outraged. Positively not. This was not a school for the goyim.

In time I came to know a great deal about discrimination, about anti-Semitism in American country clubs and in the higher ranks of the Soviet government, about *numerus clausus* at Harvard and in the Academy of Science in Moscow. One of my childhood friends adopted a new, "non-Jewish" name and several of my Russian friends conveniently "lost" their internal passports and got new ones which specified their nationality as Russian, not Jewish. I had walked across the neatly kept ghetto in Warsaw, its carefully piled bricks and fresh-swept rubble marking where the streets and houses had been. I had met survivors of Auschwitz. I knew the results of the dirty little game that starts with "some of my best friends are Jews" and ends with extermination ovens. I went south in 1960 for the opening of the great struggle to bring America to live under the reality of our Constitution. I knew Malcolm X before he was murdered. I learned a good bit about the rawest edges of racism.

(Salisbury, *A Journey for Our Times, A Memoir*, pp. 28–29)

JEAN-LOUIS BARRAULT   (1910-   )

French actor and director, starred in Children of Paradise

Israel would be worth at least a month: we could stay there only two weeks. And so we went at it greedily . . . we soon got into the rhythm of the country. At Tel Aviv we performed in the Habimah theatre [in 1960]. In Haifa we camped in a cinema. At Jerusalem again a cinema— this one more comfortable. From that stay I now retain three sources of enrichment:

     –the exemplary courage of the Israeli people;
     –my encounter with fundamental Christianity;
     –the geographical position of the country, where Hope and Tragedy ferment simultaneously, under the sign of the Eternal.
     There is a saying, I think, somewhere in the Scriptures: "This land shall be his who shall restore its greenness."
     That is what the Israeli nation has succeeded in doing. Nothing but orchards everywhere: orange trees, lemon trees, grapefruit trees, vines, cereals; irrigation canals; reafforestation. The Caesarea of antiquity is today reappearing from under the dunes. . . .
     Israel is a people in arms, as the French nation was at the time of Valmy. Can one be anything else when one is threatened from all sides? And how not be on edge because of it.
     It is also a people with ploughs and trowels. By an irony of fate the winds bring the sands of Egypt and are constantly trying to make this land a desert.
     It is a continual struggle against men and against nature. The Israeli people have an acute sense of this. Anyone would, after what they have had to suffer over the centuries and—in the course of that terrible war—from cruel genocide. Their courage exacts admiration and respect. In spite of their ready aggressiveness, one loves them; one takes their side.
     Unfortunately, that does not resolve the cruel ordeal of the Palestinian population: this too we share. It is more than a matter of conscience: the problem seems almost insoluble. . . .
     On the top of the cliff a desert plateau begins. If you raise your head you can make out, as though on a balcony, Arab sentinels squatting, with a rifle across their knees, waiting for the order to fire.
     Down below, in the orchards, the Jews are working. They have

shown that they are peasants, craftsmen, creators. They have restored to this land its greenness, they deserve it.

If for centuries money became their speciality, this is because it was the only material that "those dogs of Christians" and the others allowed them to manipulate. I have acted Shylock. I have felt that rage, and Shakespeare is a just man.

In Jerusalem we were received by Ben Gurion. The man was impressive: a mixture of sage and saint.

From the roof of the Convent of Notre Dame de France, which is on Israeli territory, you have a view of Jordanian Jerusalem. We could not go there. Three years back, when we were in Lebanon, at Baalbek, members of our company could go there. Politics, politics!

The place is all the more overwhelming because it is very small. Scarcely a ventricle of the world, yet one feels its pulsation there. . . .

(*Memories for Tomorrow — The Memoirs of Jean-Louis Barrault*, trans. Jonathan Griffin, pp. 252–255)

MARSHALL McLUHAN   *(1911–1980)*

Canadian media expert; author of The Gutenberg Galaxy, Understanding Media

McLuhan to Wyndham Lewis, 13 December 1944:

. . . Oh the mental vacuum that is Canada. Bruce Hutchison has out a novel "The Hollow Men." Not very good. But he does resist and protest. He struggles against this tepid bathos. There is terrible social cowardice, and all action here seems so furtive that one can only conclude that some unacknowledged guilt is behind it all. Canada needs about 2 million Jews to bring life to it. . . .

(*Letters of Marshall McLuhan*, p. 165)

* * *

McLuhan to United Church Minister William Glenesk,
5 January 1970:

. . . Have a look at Luke 8:18: "Heed *how* you hear." Note the importance of the *how* figure-ground relationship of the seed and ground in the verses above it. Those who conceptualize the seed without perceptualizing are those who are not with it and therefore cannot keep it. After all, the church is a thing, and not a theory. That is why the poor and the children of the world can grasp it, whereas the wise and the learned have serious conceptual problems blocking their perceptual lives. The Jews had many concepts about the Messiah which defeated their confrontation with Him. . . .

(*Letters of Marshall McLuhan*, p. 394)

* * *

McLuhan to Dr. Sidney Halpern, 9 January 1974:

Your request for some statement from me concerning the role of Israel, presents many aspects. As a Roman Catholic I have long employed the aid of a Hebrew maiden, the Blessed Virgin Mary. She has been a constant help to me in my studies and has been called "Our Lady of Good Studies" by Roman Catholics because of her own studies of the Scriptures in the temple as a child. To myself, as to most Catholics, a conscious debt to Israel is enormous, since we regard ourselves as being in the continuous line of Judaic development. On the other hand, the role of non-Christian Israel in the world has always been opaque and a divine mystery to the Roman Catholic. About anything so profound, it is merely irrelevant to have a personal point of view. What would appear more relevant to me is that we discuss these matters by kneeling in prayer together. The apocalyptic role of Israel has become more intensely manifest during the past few years. Many people are meditating and praying about this by way of *action*.

My own writing has been concerned with the development, in the simultaneous electric world, of the physical unity of the human family. I would be happy if you could suggest to me an effective approach to these matters that would enable me to make a forceful and convincing statement. As a Catholic who thinks of himself as a Jew spiritually, and as a student of the media, who thinks of us all politically, as members of the same family, what do you suggest I might say?

(*Letters of Marshall McLuhan*, p. 488)

RICHARD M. NIXON   *(1913–   )*

37th president of the United States, 1969–1974

The transcripts would be Nixon's undoing. Even if he clung to office, how would he govern after this? All moral authority was gone, Kissinger said. The deletions and denigrating characterizations suggested something else, long concealed, about the Nixon character. Rumors and some reliable reports circulated that Nixon regularly employed ethnic slurs, particularly anti-Semitic ones, and that some had been deleted from the transcripts. Was Nixon a racist? An anti-Semite?

For his part, Kissinger was convinced that the President was anti-Semitic. He had believed it for years. As the son of German Jews who had fled the Nazis, he was particularly sensitive to what he regarded in Nixon as a dangerous brand of anti-Jewish prejudice born of ignorance. He saw in the President an antagonistic, gut reaction which stereotyped Jews and convinced Nixon that they were his enemies. Many times Kissinger returned from a meeting with Nixon and told his deputy, Lawrence Eagleburger: "That man is an anti-Semite." The remark by Nixon which most often unsettled Kissinger was well known to the President's close associates: "The Jewish cabal is out to get me." The meaning of the often-repeated comment was a source of debate within the Administration. Many believed that it reflected hostility more to intellectuals than to Jews.

Late in 1971, Nixon had summoned the White House personnel chief, Fred Malek, to his office to discuss a "Jewish cabal" in the Bureau of Labor Statistics. The "cabal," Nixon said, was tilting economic figures to make his Administration look bad. How many Jews were there in the bureau? he wanted to know. Malek reported back on the number, and told the President that the bureau's methods of weighing statistics were normal procedure that had been in use for years. Later, there was another suspected "Jewish cabal" in another department.

Malek, a young West Point and Harvard Business School graduate who had been brought into the Administration by Haldeman, knew that these tirades were not reserved for Jews. The President had once told him that he did not want any more "fucking academics" or "goddam Ivy Leaguers" appointed to high positions. They were wrecking his programs; most if not all of the problems in government could be traced to them. Haldeman had directed Malek to ignore presidential orders which suggested departmental purges or quotas, and Nixon did, in fact, continue to approve appointments of academics, even Ivy League ones and Jews.

Arthur Burns, himself a Jew, was convinced that Nixon was not truly anti-Semitic. There were, however, ugly strands of prejudice in the man. Burns had concluded, and he was not surprised that there were, apparently, anti-Semitic remarks on the tapes. The President really didn't have much love for humanity, Burns believed. Why should Nixon love Jews any more than Japanese or Italians or Catholics? Nixon regularly employed epithets for whole sections of mankind, he knew.

Burns and Kissinger had often discussed the question. Burns used to point out that the President greatly admired Israel, and that a large number of Jews served in his Administration. What disturbed Burns was something he considered apart from anti-Semitism: if the President perceived that Jews or Israel, or anyone else, for that matter, got in his way, he was prepared to stomp them. Burns vividly recalled a 1973 White House meeting during which the President had a tantrum about an amendment to his trade bill; the amendment would have restricted business with the Soviet Union if Russia did not ease its persecution of Jews. "Members of the Jewish community" were causing him difficulties, Nixon had said, because of their support for the amendment. A wave of anti-Semitism might descend on American Jews if they persisted, he predicted. Burns watched Nixon very closely on that occasion, and he was impressed by the President's fury. Burns felt that Nixon was saying that Jews might suffer for thwarting his will. . . .

There *were* ethnic references on the same tapes—including some that might be regarded as anti-Semitic. . . . The President had, in fact, said on one tape that it was not going to be his policy to have a Jewish seat on the Supreme Court, as it had been for some other Presidents. Jews, he said, were intelligent and aggressive and were everywhere in the government. If any minority group needed a leg up, it clearly was not the Jews. . . .

There were protests. The President talking about Herb Klein: "[he] doesn't have his head screwed on right." The President not giving a shit about the lira. The arts: "The arts, you know, they're Jews, they're left wing—in other words, stay away. . . ."

(Woodward and Bernstein, *The Final Days*, pp. 169–171, 377)

JOHN BERRYMAN   *(1914–1972)*

U.S. poet; wrote Homage to Mistress Broadstreet, 77 Dream Songs

[Certain poems] were written in the period ending on about 1 April 1949 (a day when Berryman wept on reading about the murder of the

Polish professors in *The Black Book of Poland,* a work which informs his own). The finished passages manage a dense, dissonant rendering of the Jewish holocaust . . . [and an] extract "from the Black Book" . . . about the gas chambers. . . .

. . . In an interview with Jonathan Sisson in 1966, Berryman recalled his problems with writing the sequence:

> It was in the form of a Mass for the Dead. It was designed to have 42 sections, and was about the Nazi murderers of the Jews. But I just found I couldn't take it. The sections published . . . are unrelievedly horrible. I wasn't able at this time . . . to find any way of making palatable the monstrosity of the thing which obsessed me.
>
> (Haffenden, *The Life of John Berryman,* pp. 205–206)

* * *

. . . He and Bellow shared a passion for literature and would match each other with ideas and repartee. Anita felt that he wanted to exercise a talent for friendship, and (in relation to that circle of friends) fiercely to borrow the passion of the Jews and to make a real connection with them. . . .

Early in his days at Iowa he took up Hebrew under Frederick Peretz Bargebuhr, a man he considered a "brilliant scholar" who had been an architect and had come late to teaching from Germany via Palestine. . . . In his first enthusiasm for Hebrew, Berryman studied hard and outstripped the other student in the class who shared Bargebuhr's regularity of approach. . . . As an offshoot of his studies, Berryman even drafted a hundred lines of a poem. ("Part is in Hebrew," he announced grandly). . . .

(*The Life of John Berryman,* pp. 236–237)

* * *

While in hospital he took the notion of becoming a Jew, partly, it would seem, from impatience with the mediation of the Christian church (he had scarcely ever doubted the existence of God, but now felt the fervent wish to appeal directly to Him, and not by virtue of clerical intercession), and partly from a desire to identify more closely with his son, Paul, and with his dead friend, Delmore Schwartz. On 13 November, he jotted the following notes:

> To become a Jew—the wonder of my life—it's possible! Rabbi Milgrom is coming at 2:30.
>
> My uneasiness with Xt'y [Christianity] came to a head in Mass . . . this morning. Worship God but where? . . . Left and came to my room and incredibly thought of *becoming a Jew.* Always held it impossible because of inadequate concept of God. . . . hostile to Trinity, dubious of X [Christ], hostile to the Blessed Virgin, anti-Pope, deep sympathy with the Church, but *not* for *me.*

As a Jew, he considered, he might be "alone with God, yet *not* alone, one of many worshippers, like them except in blood (who cares?)." He felt a great affinity with Jewish writings and thought, and for years had respected Jewish friends, writers, metaphysicians, musicians. He had already worked to learn Hebrew, begun a translation of Job, borne in mind a project to compile an anthology of Yiddish poetry, and finally, as he put it, "resented/liked name 'Berryman' *being thought Jewish.*" His inclination did not last long, however, and he professed a regular Catholicism throughout 1971. When he completed *Opus Dei,* a section of his next book *Delusions, Etc.,* based on the Offices of the Church, by the next summer, he decided (as he told Eileen): "I'm giving Silvers [editor of the *New York Review of Books*] first look at, though I doubt if those lucky Jews (I worked hard to become a Jew myself last Fall in hospital, the write-up in my novel [never completed] will kill you laughing) can bear the open Xtianity."

(The Life of John Berryman, pp. 382–383)

ANTHONY BURGESS   *(1917–   )*

British novelist; author of A Clockwork Orange *and* Earthly Powers

Cats will leap on the knees of cat-haters. It was through going with a Jewish girl that I learned the extent of British antisemitism. It was not of the ideological Nazi kind but the public bar stupidity of "them with long noses" and "blame it all on the bleedin' Jews.' Wherever we went her presence, though unnoticed, called it forth. I could hit out, but I could not become a Jew. I longed for diatribes against the Catholics and occasionally got them, which made me feel better. The sense of being cut off from the main stream of British life, inhibited during the war, was returning. Catholic or Jew made little difference so long as one was not Protestant. The real religion, hence the real culture, lay somewhere east.

I should have married this girl, but, though I had good enough grounds, I could not now seek divorce. Moreover, her Judaism was reinforcing my Catholicism and making the notion untenable. And my wife was turning herself into my poor wife, sick, lonely, neglected. Guilt, guilt, and then the leap of the hungry dark forces in a hotel bedroom smelling of bedcrumbs. There is no poetry for such transports, except perhaps in the Song of Solomon. . . .

(Burgess, Little Wilson and Big God, p. 344)

* * *

Mr. Rosten's subtitle [of his book *Hooray for Yiddish!*] is "A Book about English." Take title and subtitle together and you get the truth—the manner in which, chiefly in New York, Yiddish has impregnated English and produced a wonderful hybrid which Mr. Rosten calls Yinglish and I prefer to call Yidglish. After all, Yinglish could be Yankee English or English expressive of the Yin as opposed to the Yang. . . .

How far a Gentile or *goy* is permitted to use Yidglish is not a point argued by Mr. Rosten. As American showbiz is a Jewish province, it is inevitable that showbiz language, even in Britain, should partake of Yidglish idioms, which include modes of emphasis and inversion as well as calques and straight borrowings from Yiddish. I have heard a distinguished British stage producer say "We need that like a *loch in kop*' and "Hamlet he wants to play" and "Mummerset yet." The production of plays and films places its participants in situations of stress and despair analogous to those of a whole long-suffering people, and Yidglish provides ironic tropes which contrast dramatically with the agonized cries and lavish curses of the Old Testament. You can rant prophetically in the desert or wail by the waters of Babylon; in the exile of the cities, where nobody listens anyway, you use Yidglish.

Mr. Rosten's last book sold well because it was funny, and this is funny too. New York Jewish jokes are the best in the world; here they are in the service of subtle differentiations of usage. . . .

But Yidglish is brilliant always in doing so much with so little — an inversion, an intonation — and is remarkable in seeming to carry in every form the whole experience of a race that has learned to respond to tribulation with grim humour. . . .

Englishmen, naturally *goyim*, since there is an assumption that an Englishman cannot be a Jew, despite Disraeli and Siegfried Sassoon, come occasionally into Rosten's stories. . . .

A male *goy*, like that Englishman, is a *sheygets* and his mother a *shikse*. The plural of *goy* comes aptly in a reply to the quatrain written surely, by Sir Walter Raleigh the professor, not — as Rosten thinks — Hilaire Belloc: "How odd/of God/ To choose/The Jews." It deserves to be set out in lineate glory:

> Not odd
> Of God:
> Goyim
> Annoy 'im.
> (Burgess, *But Do Blondes Prefer Gentlemen?* pp. 181–183)

CONOR CRUISE O'BRIEN   *(1917–   )*

Irish literary critic and historian

The greatest concentration of murderous hatred ever attained on earth came about in our own century in the shape of Hitler's Third Reich. And that concentration could not have been possible without the bonding of collective passion brought about by German nationalism. . . .

Followers of Jesus Christ might perhaps have been expected to manifest some disapproval of the greatest preacher and practitioner of hatred and revenge who ever walked on earth. . . .

The failure of the churches even to try to stop the persecution of the Jews—was one of the greatest and most tragic missed opportunities in history. . . .

(*The New York Review of Books*, April 1989)

BILLY GRAHAM *(1918–   )*

American evangelist

. . . Inexhaustibly ingratiating, he will hastily assure a Jewish interviewer, "I am very pro-Jewish. We Christian gentiles have committed our lives to a Jew, you know." During his 1957 New York crusade, he was even inspired to confide to one Jewish journalist that Israel was destined to expand until the nation included the entire territory promised to the descendants of Abraham in the Bible—that is, from the Nile to the Euphrates—and after the Six-Day War in 1967, he heartily encouraged Israel to hold steadfast against demands she return seized territory, declaring that Jerusalem must be reunited as a Jewish city. But when he was once denied a visa by Jordan for "propaganda activities for Israel," he seemed genuinely bewildered and aghast, insisting, "I'm sure if they had done this, they would have notified our Minneapolis office". . . .

(Frady, *Billy Graham*, p. 247)

* * *

It was in 1960 that he finally paid his first visit to the Holy Land. . . . Graham happened to make his entry into the Holy Land in a blazing of flashbulbs, and he immediately announced, "Man, I feel as if I belong here!" At a press conference at the Mandelbaum Gate, he explained, "I became a Christian back in North Carolina at the age of sixteen, and ever since then, I've always wanted to come see where Jesus lived, where he died." Over the following days, he loped buoyantly about those gaunt hills and ruins in a mesh golf cap and sunglasses, with reporters and photographers clambering over the stones after him in a constant whir and snick of cameras. There occurred a brief row over what facilities ought to be made available to him for any public addresses, Ben-Gurion finally wiring from the

United States that he would be agreeable to most any arrangements so long as Graham "refrained from mentioning Jesus Christ before a Jewish audience." But Graham himself quickly charmed away this small awkwardness by appearing at a press conference at the King David Hotel to peal in his golden tones, "Shalom," and then proclaim, "I am going to address only Christian audiences. I have no intention of proselyting. In fact, I must be grateful to you for proselytizing *me*. For Jesus Christ was a Jew, all his apostles were Jews, and the whole early church was Jewish."

(*Billy Graham*, pp. 342–343)

ROBERT F. KENNEDY   *(1925–1968)*

U.S. senator, brother of President John F. Kennedy

He was considerably impressed by the Jews [during a stay in Palestine in 1948]. "They are different from any Jews I have ever know[n] or seen." As for the Arabs, "I just wish they didn't have that oil."

On May 14 the British mandate came to an end. . . . The *Boston Post* ran four articles from its "Special Writer" in the Middle East on June 3–6. . . .

His second piece revealed his own commitment. The Jews in Palestine, he wrote, "have become an immensely proud and determined people. It is already a truly great modern example of the birth of a nation with the primary ingredients of dignity and self-respect." His original draft added at this point: "Many of the leading Jewish spokesmen for the Zionist cause in the United States are doing immeasurable harm for that cause because they have not spent any or sufficient time with their people to absorb the spirit." On reflection he deleted this thought and simply praised the Jews in Palestine as "hardy and tough," their "spirit and determination" created not only by their desire for a homeland but by "the remembrance of the brutal inhuman treatment received by the Jews in the countries of Europe." He gave a lyrical account of his kibbutz visit, omitting the reservations expressed in his diary. The Jews, he said, had "an undying spirit" the Arabs could never have. "They will fight and they will fight with unparalleled courage."

The third piece was sharply critical of British policy for its "bitterness toward the Jews." . . . In any case, peace-loving nations could not stand by and watch people kill each other. "The United States through the United Nations must take the lead in bringing about peace in the Holy Land."

His father, with his dread of American meddling, conceivably winced a little at this last proposition. Not too much, probably: he cared less what his sons said than whether they said it persuasively. On these grounds he must have admired Robert's series. The pieces showed a maturity, cogency and, from time to time, literary finish creditable for a football player of twenty-two hardly out of college.

(A. M. Schlesinger, Jr., *Robert Kennedy and His Times*, pp. 76–77)

* * *

[In 1968] . . . labor, the party regulars and the south brought Humphrey great strength. He also had a long record of service to Jewish causes, and 60 percent of American Jews lived in the climactic primary states, California and New York. McCarthy too had strong Jewish support. The Jewish community saw him, said Adam Yarmolinsky, as "the professor who gave your bright son an A, and Bobby Kennedy was the tough kid on the block who beat up your son on his way to school." When Kennedy came to New York the day after Indiana, a group of rabbis waited on him. "Why do I have so much trouble with the Jews?" he asked. "I don't understand it. Nobody has been more outspoken than I have. . . . Is it because of my father when he was in England? *That was thirty years ago.*" One of his visitors said that, after the Six-Day War, American Jews needed "continual reassurance" about Israel. Kennedy wearily said he would make his position clear again on the west coast.

(*Robert Kennedy and His Times*, p. 884)

* * *

There was one important group of white middle-class voters, however, which Kennedy believed he could attract to his side and that was the Jews. . . . The equation was simple. To win the nomination he had to win New York and California. To win New York and California he had to win the Jewish vote. To win the Jewish vote he had to take a strong pro-Israel stand.

Robert Kennedy had a long record of sympathy for Israel and the Jews. . . . Being a Kennedy, and therefore an advocate of the virtues of toughness, hard work, competitiveness, and ambition, Kennedy soon took the side of the Jews against that of the Palestinian Arabs. The Jews seemed to possess the qualities he admired most. . . .

Robert Kennedy, as we know, was a black and white thinker, with a pronounced strain of the moralist in his makeup. After his 1948 experience in Palestine he became a black and white thinker on the Jewish-Arab question. The Jews were good; the Arabs were bad. It was an attitude characteristic of most Americans' thinking on the subject at the time. Thus Kennedy proved incapable of seeing any justification to the Palestinian Arabs' cause. . . .

Two and a half million Jews lived in New York state at the time Robert Kennedy ran for senator from New York in 1964. Assiduously he cultivated the Jewish vote in that whirlwind "hit and run" campaign, doing things few non-Jewish candidates had ever done before. Having himself photographed eating a knish was pretty innocent. But donning a yarmulke, the traditional Jewish skullcap, for speeches in synagogues and having himself photographed wearing it was a bit much. No non-Jewish politician running for the Senate had ever done that before.

Naturally in all his speeches before Jewish audiences Kennedy reminded his listeners of John F. Kennedy's support for Israel, recalling that during his late brother's administration JFK had advocated sending Hawk missiles to the Jewish state.

Joseph Kennedy had had a reputation for being an anti-Semite, and, of course, as ambassador to Great Britain, he had advised Roosevelt not to go to war against Hitler. But Robert Kennedy, with his pro-Israel sympathies, succeeded in overcoming that reputation. He won the New York state Jewish vote and that probably won him his election to the Senate. As a token of thanks to the Jews of New York, the Kennedy family gave $1,450,000 to Yeshiva University after the election.

But Robert Kennedy, in his courting of the Jewish vote, went several steps further. He also openly criticized the Arabs.

In June 1967, speaking at a meeting of Jewish labor union leaders, he made a remark that reverberated throughout the Arab world like a cannon volley. Clearing his throat in a mock cough, he made a sour face and said, "I've just drunk a cup of bitter Arab coffee and have not had time to wash my mouth."

The remark elicited a big laugh from his audience, and feelings of shock and outrage throughout the entire Arab world, where it was interpreted as an insult to the Arab people and to Arab hospitality.

As it turned out, Kennedy's "bitter Arab coffee" remark was to dog him throughout the remaining days of his life—he would eat knishes, the Arabs would say, and attend bar mitzvahs, and wear the yarmulke, but he would not drink Arab coffee—and the line was even quoted in his obituaries in Arab newspapers after his death at the hands of a young Palestinian Arab. . . .

(J. H. Davis, *The Kennedys—Dynasty and Disaster 1848–1983,*
pp. 540–542)

RICHARD BURTON   *(1925–1984)*

Welsh-born actor; starred in Who's Afraid of Virginia Woolf,
The Spy Who Came in from the Cold

The 1972 Notebooks begin in Arizona, where he has gone with Elizabeth to look after her mother, Sarah. Sarah is ill again and the family gathers around to set her on her feet and put her into society. Burton had expected a true democratic American town. He admired the openness and republicanism of the USA. He was very quickly disillusioned.

(Jan. 28) Last night I had an unique experience—for me that is. I went to have dinner with the Ws in the swankest country club in the area, or the richest, or both. However, the uniqueness was that I discovered towards the end of the dinner that the club was restricted to Gentiles only. NO JEWS ALLOWED. Mary Frances told me so. She said that they, the club, had told them, the Jews, that there are just too many of you and before long you'll be running the place so why don't you form a club of your own. I was flabbergasted. I shld[5] have immediately announced

---

[5]The abbreviations "shld," "wld," and "cld" are Burton's. —ED.

this to the rest of the family and we wld have undoubtedly swept out en masse. However I thought of Sarah and that the only reason why we were dining with the Ws was to get her out as easily and unrancorously as possible, but I simply couldn't sit there and say nothing. She promptly gave me an opportunity to salvage my conscience as she said with twinkling glee, "And do you know, Richard, they ran into financial difficulties and had to appeal to us Gentiles for help. What about that!" I swooped. "How strange to hear that," I said. "Our lot doesn't usually get into that kind of difficulty." She took the blow with an air of not knowing quite whether I was making a little British joke or not. I now laid it on. "Elizabeth, as you obviously don't know, is a convert to Judaism and our daughter Liza is of course a Jewess and my grandfather was a Jew." She was helpless. She said "Yes" but it had several additional vowels in it, impossible to write down but it was something like "Yeaaeahowes."

To re-iterate here the platitudinous idiocies of their conversation would be tedious. . . . We all agreed afterwards that they were so brain-washed that nothing, no argument, no appeal to intelligence, cld possibly change them. For instance, and only one example will I give, W. said that the thing that had made this country great was that it was a melting pot for all the peoples of the world. Yawn. Yawn. But they had just said that Jews were not allowed in their club! There was therefore absolutely no point in asking about the blacks.

We reduced ourselves to hysteria in the course of the post mortem in our suite but under it all we were sick at heart.

(Bragg, RICH: The Life of Richard Burton, pp. 399–400)

* * *

(Feb. 20) [The Jewish writer Wolf Mankowitz] was at his most engagingly Cockney and obviously adored Elizabeth who reciprocated and said, "Now that's the kind of man I could love if you weren't around, I adore him." Bloody daft thing to say, I said, hurting. But good taste all the same, I thought. There is always an oddity about people's preferences in types. I've always lusted for medium-height dark-haired Jewesses, or those who could be first racial cousins. Elizabeth has always fancied Jews, period. She seems to have a rapport with them which she doesn't have with the ordinary Anglo-Saxon. She and Wolf could obviously have talked all night. . . .

(RICH: *The Life of Richard Burton*, p. 406)

WILLIAM STYRON   (1925–   )

U.S. novelist; author of The Confessions Nat Turner, Sophie's Choice; *Pulitzer Prize, 1968*

Springtime at Auschwitz. The phrase itself has the echo of a bad and tasteless joke, but spring still arrives in the depths of southern Poland, even at Auschwitz. Just beyond the once electrified fences, still standing, the forsythia puts forth its yellow buds in gently rolling pastures where sheep now graze. The early songbirds chatter even here, on the nearly unending grounds of this Godforsaken place in the remote hinterland of the country. At Birkenau, that sector of the Auschwitz complex that was the extermination camp for millions, one is staggered by the sheer vastness of the enterprise stretching out acre upon acre in all directions. The wooden barracks were long ago destroyed, but dozens of the hideous brick stablelike buildings that accommodated the numberless damned are still here, sturdily impervious, made to endure a thousand years.

Last April, as this visitor stood near Crematorium II, now flattened yet preserved in broken-backed rubble, his gaze turned and lingered upon the huge pits where the overflow of the bodies from the ovens were burned; the pits were choked with weeds but among the muck and the brambles there were wildflowers beginning to bloom. He reflected that "forsythia" was one of two loan words from Western languages that he recognized amid his meager command of Polish. The other word, from the French, was *cauchemar*–"nightmare." At the beginning of spring, the two images mingle almost unbearably in this place. . . .

Hulking and Teutonic in their dun-colored brick, the rows of barracks where hundreds of thousands perished of disease and starvation, or were tortured and hanged or shot to death, now shelter the principal museum exhibits: the mountains of human hair, the piles of clothes, the wretched suitcases with crudely or neatly painted names like Stein and Mendelson, the braces and crutches, the heaps of toys and dolls and teddy bears — all of the heart-destroying detritus of the Holocaust from which one stumbles out into the blinding afternoon as if from the clutch of death itself. Even thus in repose — arrested in time, rendered a frozen memorial, purified of its seething mass murder — Auschwitz must remain the one place on earth most unyielding to meaning or definition.

I was unable to attend the recent symposium on Auschwitz at the Cathedral Church of St. John the Divine in New York City, but many of the aspects of the proceedings there, at least as reported, troubled and puzzled me, especially because of the overwhelming emphasis on anti-Semitism and Christian guilt. My interest in the meeting was deep, since although I am not nominally a Christian, my four children are half-Jewish and I claim perhaps a more personal concern with the idea of genocide than do most gentiles.

There can be no doubt that Jewish genocide became the main business of Auschwitz; the wrecked crematoria at Birkenau are graphic testimony to the horrible and efficient way in which the Nazis exterminated two and a half million Jews — mass homicide on such a stupefying scale that one understands how the event might justify speculation among theologians that it signaled the death of God.

The Holocaust is so incomprehensible and so awesomely central to our present-day consciousness — Jewish and gentile — that one almost physically shrinks with reticence from attempting to point out again what was barely touched on in certain reports on the symposium: that at Auschwitz perished not only the Jews but at least one million souls who were not Jews. Of many origins but mainly Slavs — Poles, Russians, Slovaks, other — they came from a despised people who almost certainly were fated to be butchered with the same genocidal ruthlessness as were the Jews had Hitler won the war, and they contained among them hundreds of thousands of Christians who went to their despairing deaths in the belief that *their* God, the Prince of Peace, was as dead as the God of Abraham and Moses. . . .

Because of this I cannot accept anti-Semitism as the sole touchstone by which we examine the monstrous paradigm that Auschwitz has become. Nor can I regard with anything but puzzled mistrust the chorus of *mea culpas* from the Christian theologians at the symposium, rising along with the oddly self-lacerating assertion of some of them that the Holocaust came about as the result of the anti-Semitism embedded in Christian doctrine.

I am speaking as a writer whose work has often been harshly

critical of Christian pretensions, hypocrisies and delusions. Certainly one would not quarrel with the premise that Christian thought has often contained much that was anti-Semitic, but to place all the blame on Christian theology is to ignore the complex secular roots of anti-Semitism as well. The outrages currently being perpetrated against the Jews by the secular, "enlightened," and anti-Christian Soviet Union should be evidence of the dark and mysterious discord that still hinders our full understanding of the reasons for this ancient animosity.

To take such a narrow view of the evil of Nazi totalitarianism is also to ignore the ecumenical nature of that evil. For although the unparalleled tragedy of the Jews may have been its most terrible single handiwork, its threat to humanity transcended even this. If it was anti-Semitic, it was also anti-Christian. And it attempted to be more final than that, for its ultimate depravity lay in the fact that it was anti-human. Anti-life.

This message was plainly written in the spring dusk at Auschwitz only short weeks ago for one observer, who fled before the setting of the sun. To linger in Auschwitz after nightfall would be unthinkable.

(Styron, *This Quiet Dust and Other Writings*, pp. 302–305)

GORE VIDAL   (1925–   )

U.S. novelist and essayist

In a letter to a friend, George Orwell wrote, "It is impossible to mention Jews in print, either favorably or unfavorably, without getting into trouble." But there are times when trouble had better be got into before mere trouble turns into catastrophe. Jews, blacks and homosexualists are despised by the Christian and Communist majorities of East and West. Also, as a result of the invention of Israel, Jews can now count on the hatred of the Islamic world. Since our own Christian majority looks to be getting ready for great adventures at home and abroad, I would suggest that the three despised minorities join forces in order not to be destroyed. This seems an obvious thing to do. Unfortunately, most Jews refuse to see any similarity between their special situation and that of the same-sexers. At one level, the Jews are perfectly correct. A racial or religious or tribal identity is a kind of fact. Although sexual preference is an even more powerful fact, it is not one that creates any particular social or cultural or religious bond between those so-minded. Although Jews would doubtless be Jews if there was no anti-Semitism, same-sexers would think little or nothing at all about their preference if society ignored it. So there *is* a difference between the two estates. But there is no difference in the degree of hatred felt by the Christian majority for Christ-killers and Sodomites. In the German concentration camps, Jews wore yellow stars while homosexualists wore pink triangles. I was present when Christopher Isherwood tried to make this point to a young Jewish movie producer. "After all," said Isherwood, "Hitler killed six hundred thousand homosexuals." The young man was not impressed. "But Hitler killed six *million* Jews," he said sternly. "What are you?" asked Isherwood. "In real estate?"

Like it or not, Jews and homosexuals are in the same fragile boat, and one would have to be pretty obtuse not to see the common danger. But obtuseness is the name of the game among New York's new class. Elsewhere, I have described the shrill fag-baiting of Joseph Epstein, Norman Podhoretz, Alfred Kazin, and the Hilton Kramer Hotel. *Harper's* magazine and *Commentary* usually publish these pieces. . . .

. . . Meanwhile, like so many Max Naumanns (Naumann was a German Jew who embraced Nazism), the new class passionately supports our ruling class—from the Chase Manhattan Bank to the Pentagon to the Op-Ed page of *The Wall Street Journal*—while holding in fierce contempt faggots, blacks (see Norman Podhoretz's "My Negro Problem and Ours," *Commentary*, February 1963), and the poor (see Midge Decter's "Looting and Liberal Racism," *Commentary*, September 1977). Since these neo-Naumannites are going to be in the same gas chambers as the blacks and the faggots, I would suggest a cease-fire and a common front against the common enemy, whose kindly voice is that of Ronald Reagan and whose less than kindly mind is elsewhere in the boardrooms of the Republic.

(Vidal, "Pink Triangle and Yellow Star," in *The Nation*,
14 November 1981)

A. ROY ECKARDT   (1918–   )

U.S. Protestant theologian

The guilt of the Christian community for its dominant silence amid the Nazi slaughters of the Jewish people has in recent years been increasingly confessed within both Catholic and Protestant circles.

Yet when within past weeks the extermination of the entire nation of Israel almost occurred, once again there was silence in the churches.

The few voices that were raised merely helped to make the general stillness louder. When at the beginning of the crisis Protestant and Catholic organizations were asked by the American Jewish community to call upon our government to stand by Israel, there was no institutional response. The U.S. Conference of Catholic Bishops gave no word and the [Protestant] National Council of Churches was content to urge "compassion and concern for all the people of the Middle East" and the formulating of a solution by the United Nations. Some Christians found an element of presumptuousness in the Jewish request; they claimed it did not allow them to reach a moral judgment of their own. But the fact is that church groups either ignored the entire problem or announced a policy of neutralism. . . .

. . . The moral tragedy is that the only tangible way open to us to atone for our historic crimes against original Israel is by assuming a special responsibility for the rights and welfare of Jews. The present refusal to bear this obligation may well reflect the Christian community's wish to exonerate itself from the culpability for the long years of antisemitism.

Karl Barth once said: "In order to be chosen we must, for good or ill, either be Jews or else be heart and soul on the side of the Jews." It almost seems that the entire history of Christianity, including the churches' current response to the Middle Eastern crisis, has been an attempt to make Barth's words as irrelevant as is humanly possible. Writing as Christians who oppose that attempt, we say to our Jewish brothers: we too have been shocked by the new silence. And we are greatly saddened. But we have not been surprised. The causes of the silence lie deep in the Christian soul. Therefore we can only mourn and pray and hope.

(A. Roy and Alice Eckhardt, "Again, Silence in the Churches," in
The Christian Century, 26 July and 2 August 1967)

RICHARD VON WEIZSAECKER   *(1920–   )*

President of West Germany

Speech to the full parliament, on the 40th anniversary of the surrender of Nazi Germany in World War II:

The genocide of the Jews is . . . unparalleled in history . . . every German was able to experience what his Jewish compatriots had to suffer . . . whoever opened his eyes and his ears and sought information could not fail to notice that Jews were being deported. The nature and scope of the destruction may have exceeded human imagination, but apart from the crime itself, there was, in reality, the attempt by too many people, including those of my generation . . . not to take notice of what was happening. . . . When the unspeakable truth of the Holocaust then became known at the end of the war, all too many of us claimed that they had not known anything about it or even suspected anything. . . .

The Jewish nation remembers and will always remember. We seek reconciliation. Precisely for this reason we must understand that there can be no reconciliation without remembrance. The experience of millionfold death is part of the very being of every Jew in the world, not only because people cannot forget such atrocities, but also because remembrance is part of the Jewish faith. . . .

. . . Remembrance is experience of the work of God in history. It is the source of faith in redemption. . . . If we for our part sought to forget what has occurred, instead of remembering it, this would not only be inhuman. We would also impinge upon the faith of the Jews who survived and destroy the basis of reconciliation. We must erect a memorial to thoughts and feelings in our own hearts. . . .

(Reprinted in the *New York Times*, 9 May 1985, p. 10)

PHILIP WYLIE *(1902–1971)*

U.S. author of Opus 21, Tomorrow! The Innocent Ambassadors

Hitler *rescued the German ego*—which was . . . bound up in the idea of arms, destruction, and invincibility, and which had been frustrated. He told them that, because of their *purity* and *integrity* of motive, they had been the innocent victims of—*the Jews!* The mechanism is that which I have described, whereby a man behaves like a woman. Because he used it, Hitler is really more of a Delilah than an Antichrist.

While the Germans were furiously (and victoriously) storming every fort in the west and the east, Hitler said, the Jews had gnawed down their house from within. This is the oldest dirty trick man knows—the trick of begging the question via the whipping boy—illogical, feline, dissembling, and vile. Hitler found a fall guy for the Germans and then persuaded them that their original premise of might making right had been sound, after all. . . . many democratic men accepted the debased German invention of a fall guy—the Jew—and therein found another quantum of "rightness" which set them spiritually, if not alongside the Nazis, at least not against them.

The use of anti-Semitism by Hitler at this time is an astonishing evidence of the principle of opposites in the workings of man's soul.

There is a reason behind it which even the Jews do not understand. And yet, by every social and economic measurement to which man is accustomed, there is no sense whatever in anti-Semitism. The statements and figures upon which Hitler bases his monstrous accusation are simply crap. The Jews did not betray Germany before or during or after the war, any more than the Gentiles. Germany was whipped and it had to surrender when its one hundred per cent Aryan navy turned red and refused to sail. Such was the immediate occasion. The Jews in Germany gave just as many lives in the war, per capita, as the Protestants or Catholics. They gave as much money. They were neither richer nor poorer than the others. They maintained the fatherland, along with every common man, right up until it collapsed. Afterward, within the fatherland, so many of them persevered in civilized activities that even Hitler had to "create" thousands of them "Aryans" to maintain his state—and of those he lost, many brilliant ones are making a deficit for Nazism in their laboratories which will tell sorely against the cause of the Herrenvolk in the end. If they had been allowed to stay decently in Germany, as Germans, they would be experimenting and planning for the Reich, even today.

There is this same anti-Semitism in America. I hear the swirl and mutter of it around me in restaurants, at clubs, on the beach, in Washington, in New York, and here at home. No basis exists for the statements that accompany it in *any measurable fact.* "The Jews," people say, "own the radio, the movies, the theaters, the publishing companies, the newspapers, the clothing business and the banks. They are just one big family, banded together against the rest of humanity, and they are getting control of the media of articulation so that they can control us. They have depraved every art form. They are doing it simply to break down our moral character and make us easy to enslave. Either we will have to destroy them, or they will ruin us."

The garbage goes in somewhat that vein. It has been shown, time and again, that the widespread impression of what Jews own in America is idiotic. They own two or three large banks, among hundreds—a number out of proportion to their ratio in the whole population. Banks—Gentile banks—own the movies. There are more Gentiles than Jews in the movie business. Their race bears no relation to the quality or the moral viewpoint of the pictures which they produce. America was a whoring, rum-swilling, vulgar nation from the start. Protestantism, Catholicism, and Victorianism combined to give it a veneered notion that it was a land of purity, sweetness, and light—but it never was; and the Jews who profit by the venality and prurience of our folk are no more numerous in proper ratio than the micks, wops, and so on, who do the same. There were some Jewish gangsters in the Volstead era—but there were shanty Irish rum barons, and Sicilians and Italians, out of all proportion to their incidence here. Jews own a good many theaters because what we call "the theaters" occur in New York, and New York is where the majority of America's Jews live. Jews own half a dozen conspicuous newspapers, including the New York *Times*, which is regarded by Gentiles as the best newspaper in the world, and Gentiles *own all the rest*. The Hearst papers, the Scripps-Howard papers, the McCormick-Patterson papers, the papers owned by John Knight, alone, represent chains that fantastically outweigh all the papers owned by Jews—and in those chains are many papers which are a blight on decency and sanity: strictly Gentile dirty work, prejudice, and corruption. The Jews own a big piece of the radio, which also centers in New York. They own some of the clothing business—but only a fraction of the whole.

There isn't *any* sense in the accusation that Jews belong to some sort of international cabal which plans to control the world. A person might as reasonably believe that a lama in Tibet decides everything for everybody. "Zion" is an idea of the same silly order of magnitude. The Jews do "stick together," locally, to some small extent—and so do the Catholics and so do the Methodists—and so would you if you belonged to a group that had been persecuted for two thousand years by everybody. But there are Jews in every nation, and they are loyal to that nation as are the rest of the people in it, and Jews within a nation struggle one against the other as hard as the other people and in the same way. There are myriads of poor, vulgar Jews in a few big cities; their collective behavior is not nice to look at—but there are the same steaming slews of wops and micks, and they behave in the same way or even worse. In Oklahoma, or in Georgia, are wildernesses of people who, for sheer miserliness of soul and hog-trough behavior, have never been approached by any Jews there is a record of. Life is measurelessly finer in the Bronx than on Tobacco Road.

The "factual case against the Jews," upon investigation, crumbles away so completely that a man who was anti-Semitic (if he had intelligence—an impossibility, however, since being anti-Semitic precludes the attribute) would have to change his opinion *at once*, when confronted with the data. Anti-Semites have been shown the facts, of course, but they persist in their attitude. Indeed, after thoroughly investigating the facts and the sources of the facts, they go on repeating the then proven lies of their original false position. This is, of course, a suicide of all reason by the deliberate self-deceiver and represents the birth of a treacherous man—a man who, having seen the truth and recognized it, adheres nevertheless to a dishonesty.

Why?

. . . One reason is simple. The so-called "case against the Jew" is the case against humanity. The fault of the Jew is the fault of mankind. But it happens that, in every large nation, there exists a minority of Jews who have carefully maintained their separate identity. To ascribe to them the faults of common man—and to them solely—furnishes a convenient alibi for common man, whose doting vanity has now got him in such shape that he can bear neither to continue as he is nor to look at *himself* for the reasons of his course. The psychology is primitive and therefore, in modern man, infantile. It is the psychology of the school child who says, "Jimmy put me up to it" or "Tony dared me." Even the teacher is sometimes taken in by that specious formula. And it is easier for everybody, Americans included, to say, "The Jews corrupted us" or "The Jews wouldn't play according to the rules so we had to cheat, also," than it is to say what is true: we Americans have always been the slickest bunch of cheaters in the history of time, and furthermore, proud of it! . . .

However, that is only part of the ferocious rot. Anti-Semitism has stained the centuries. There must have been, once, a reason for it, a point of origin. And there was—long ago. The Jews, sadly enough, have their religion to blame for their now senseless predicament. The

Old Testament described punishments that will be passed on to the "fathers and sons, unto the third and the fourth generation." They are suffering such punishment, now. . . .

It was effective, if obvious, of Hitler to select the Jews as his whipping people: there they were still partially identifiable and somewhat clannish—with a history of having been scourged for centuries without retaliation. But it was also ironic. For, by the choice, the Nazis began making themselves into the Jews of the future, and in exactly the same way the Jews begot their spitefully preserved tragedy. To the extent that the Nazis are successful in perpetrating and maintaining their arrogant pride of "race" they, too, will pay off through the centuries; for *that* was the crime-against-man of ancient Israel. . . .

The Jews, beyond all men until the Nazis, carried that particular vanity to its outermost excess—the segregation of themselves from the rest of humanity, into a "superrace." Their vainglorious beginnings are traceable in the Old Testament. Under Joshua, and others, they rolled over the Near East, burning cities, leveling them, sowing salt in the ruins, carrying away the women for concubines, and putting the males to death. If you take the trouble to read the Talmud, you will find that the orthodox Jews had a code (which *they* practice no more than we do the villainous codes of *our* Old Testament) whereby there was a separate morality for Jews. It was necessary for them to be honest and decent only with each other. All the rest of mankind was cold turkey, to be preyed upon, cheated, lied to, swindled, and knocked on the head. No punishment for gutting a goy. Ten points and a gold star, rather—as in Mohammedanism.[6]

These wiper-outers of three millennia or more were, in their turn, conquered and dissipated. But they clung to their orthodoxy, or parts of it, wherever they went for a long time. They remained "The Chosen People" and their orthodox religion insisted that the day of judgment

---

[6]Note to the 20th edition of this book, published in 1955: This, in its literal sense, is an error. I have since read the Talmud and realize my impression came from a published *discussion* of it—the work, beyond any doubt, of an anti-Semite. However, in the psychological sense, the sense that Jews considered themselves the master race, the "chosen people"—and in the historical sense that the Twelve Tribes dealt ferociously with their Gentile neighbors—the assertion holds valid.

One needs not to read the Talmud, a just and wonderful book, but only the Old Testament, to learn these things. Indeed, the Bible itself is a long, seldom-broken account of sado-masochistic reflexes in various tormented, arrogant people. Barbaric people, to be sure; yet its uncounted murders, massacres, tortures, crucifixions and the like form the acknowledged *basis* of our Western society! . . .

would eventually arrive when Jehovah would appear and hang up all their enemies so that Jews could spit upon them while they squirmed in torment. Such religious patterns are more or less universal—the product of man's instinctual investiture of his creeds with his own inner nature, whether it is good and altruistic or frustrated and vengeful. Read the Bible. Moreover, because they felt themselves to be superior and select, the Jews refused to *breed* with other men.

That was the insult supreme. . . .

. . . This excessive and ostentatious practice of superiority was unbearable to the neighbors. They threw the Jews into ghettos, took their money, tormented them, raped their good-looking women, and generally raised hell with them. The Jews, in millions of cases reduced to nothing except their belief in their essential superiority, clung to that all the harder—and were kicked the more—and thus became professionally a martyred class for a thousand and more years. In the period, having to work harder to live than their fellows, they naturally survived to some extent through the genes of the most crafty, the fastest thinking, and the slyest. Thus there may have developed in them, a little more than in other men, a strain of intelligence and guile which made effective traders of them. At any rate, they became effective, also, as scientists and doctors and musicians and teachers. Possibly their average I.Q. was never any higher than the human norm; but certainly they managed to produce a somewhat higher ratio of effective brains on the level near the top. . . .

The smartness of Jews, to the extent that it was real, or the mere reputation for it, if it was not, annoyed the never-bright multitudes. It gave no discernible trouble to smart Gentiles, that I have found a record of. But the subjective quantum became extraordinarily conspicuous because of the self-pronounced superiority of the Jews and their actual unwillingness to mix themselves biologically with the rest of the species. For those two crimes, above all others, they were condemned and officially held down. Out of those acts came a great and terrible prejudice. A thoroughly reasonable, self-protective prejudice, in a sense, and in its long-vanished time. For if ever there does appear upon this planet a tightly knit minority of really superior people, it will be the end of all the rest of mankind—and mankind knows it, not having come through a billion-odd years of evolutionary struggle for nothing.

Had the Jews been humble, they would have avoided their

suffering. But they were bound to suffer, century after century, so long as they refused to marry other people, as indeed even the humblest Catholics have. And a people that calls itself "chosen" can scarcely be credited with humility. The original device of self-styling themselves the top people on earth was to compensate, doubtless, for those feelings of guilt-born inferiority which are inevitable among all conquering men. It is a futile, dangerous device. Christ railed at the Jews for it, until he lost all popularity with them, and he has enjoyed none among them since. He was the enemy of business, of banking, of interest—and mortgage-brokers, of the ladies' guild and the self-important tax assessor, and the people didn't like it then any better than they do now. The Jews crucified Christ, their greatest hero, and are almost the only people to have done such a thing. (We Americans have skimmed close to it on occasion; we shot Lincoln; and, of course, the Nazis have crucified all heroes.) That single act was an expression of the wrongness of the behavior of Jews two thousand years ago.

It has nothing to do with the behavior of most Jews today.

Indeed, very little of the substance in this explanation pertains to *any* Jew alive today. Orthodoxy, even in its mild and later forms, is perishing. Jews marry Gentiles by thousands. It is no longer possible to tell them from other men by the way they look or talk—and it probably has not been possible for centuries. Jews shudder when they hear the word "chosen people" because it gives them, now, no sense of vanity but only a frightful awareness of the retribution man has charged against their assumption, long ago, of that title. If overnight, all the people on earth could forget that there had been "Jews" in their various nations, it would be impossible to pick out, by any criteria, who had once been one sort (Jewish) and who had been another (Gentiles). There is no longer any way to determine the matter, if there ever was one, and if there are hooked noses on more Jews, there are still hooked noses on plenty of bishops.

Unfortunately, the consciousness of Jewishness cannot be eliminated overnight, either from Gentiles or from Jews. It represents a memory—a memory of a race of people, once conquerors, once authors of the idea of superiority, once the terror of the Near East, and afterward for two thousand years and more so recklessly determined to stick to the notion of superiority that they reviled the rest of man—no matter what penalty they had to pay for doing it. Such is the cost of every "Herrenvolk" idea. Contemporary Jews—innocent of any blame whatever, but still attacked at every turn by the long, harsh, reasonless, race memories of man—are born and live and die in the fantastic and irrelevant predicament of merely being Jewish.

It is little wonder that, no matter how they try to escape the fabulous rage of the memory, no matter how often and how meritoriously they protest the utter injustice of it, no matter what they change their name to or whom they marry, a difference often clings to them. The Anti-Semite—dull, unperceptive, and uncomprehending— *compels* that difference by his savage tradition of revenge. He makes believe that the old, instinctually valid accusations of the Jews are still real and current. He supports his lickspittle racial document with popeyed fabrications. He persecutes with words and innuendo and blackball where he no longer has gall enough to do it with blows— substituting mental barbarism for physical attack because he resents the colossal indignity that the whole business is now bringing upon his own head. Indignity—since it is unworthy of him, having lost all relation even to the basest of his instincts.

The Jew gravely seeks some means to endure this. As long as it continues, he will not be quite the same as the others. Either he will have to defend himself by direct counterattack of it, or by exemplary and sadly proud conduct—or else he will have to hide away from it, or try to forget it by living as much as he can only with other Jews. That is his last ordeal for the old sins of his forebears; a neurosis—both personal and collective—imposed upon himself and the rest of his kind by the dastardliness of common men who go on for stupid generations practicing revenge when the cause of it has vanished, practicing it because it gives them pleasure, because it diverts their sensibilities from their own vast nastiness—and so appears, for little instants, to lighten the crushing burden of *their* inferiorities.

Out of such scant traces of pre-Christian Judaism as he could uncover, and out of this pitiful neurosis, Hitler made his case against the Jews. Onto it, when he had got the fire going again, he heaped all the wickedness of man.

Then he swallowed the fire. Or, perhaps, it swallowed him.

He led the German people, the good with the bad, the bright with the ignorant, the Protestants and Catholics and the tree worshipers, on toward a new Jericho.

Here is the marvel and the joke! Here is the cosmic laugh—the cruel fun for the ages! Hitler made the Germans over into the living image of the long-dead Jews. As Joshua, the man who could plaster the sun and the moon against the sky, created he the superman, the Herrenvolk. . . .

The Germans, it seems, were the chosen people, and not the Jews. The Jews, indeed, were the scum of the earth and first on the extirpation list. The jubilant and resurrected Herrenvolk extirpated them. All other men, according to Hitler, were muck and could be cheated and rooked at will—a page out of the Talmud. Cheating a non-Nazi stepped you up in party favoritism—a little something from the Koran. Conquer Europe, Hitler said, with the sword, and the rest of the world with shekels—another precept of the Jew of antiquity. . . .

(Wylie, *Generation of Vipers*, ch. IX, pp. 135–149)

ROALD DAHL   *(1916–   )*

British author of Kiss Kiss *and* Chitty Chitty Bang Bang

. . . there aren't any non-Jewish publishers anywhere.

. . . I'm certainly anti-Israel and I've become anti-Semitic, inasmuch as you get a Jewish person in another country like England strongly supporting Zionism. . . .

[Israel] killed 22,000 civilians when they bombed Beirut. It was very hushed up in the newspapers, because they are primarily Jewish-owned. . . .

(From a 1990 interview with the *Jewish Chronicle* of London)

LECH WALESA   *(1943–   )*

Leader of Poland's Solidarity Movement

Monday, 18 April 1983

8:00 A.M.: Lech leaves for Warsaw with Father Jankowski and Jozef Duryasz to take flowers to the Warsaw Ghetto monument and the cemetery. Informs journalists after they're gone:

This trip we took to commemorate the anniversary of the

Warsaw Ghetto uprising is a perfect example of how Solidarity not only looked to the future, but also felt bound by its obligations with regard to the past. In Poland today, anti-Semitism is no longer the issue it once was, but that doesn't mean we can overlook the major part it played in our past. Even if it seems to have little bearing on current events, we are duty-bound to bear witness to the fate of those who, especially under the Nazis, were no longer even fighting for their lives, but merely for a dignified death. This is why I took with me to Warsaw a short note to Dr. Marek Edelman, delegate to the Solidarity Congress and sole surviving leader from the Warsaw Ghetto uprising of 1943.

To Dr. Marek Edelman

Dear friend,

Although our paths in life have been so very different, we have already met as representatives of the same cause, the human cause: in the one life we have been given to live, we have committed ourselves to express a common truth and a common belief, and to act according to the dictates of our conscience — with our heads held high, in the manner befitting true men.

I have tried to imagine the tragic days of the Warsaw Ghetto uprising when you yourself faced your most difficult ordeal. I respect you deeply for the part you played as leader of that life-and-death struggle. I am also deeply respectful of your last public declaration, in which you stated so very clearly that you weren't fighting just for lives, but for the right to live in peace and dignity.

Despite the differences in our backgrounds, we find ourselves together once again, as men and citizens guided by a solid and unshakable determination to act within the framework of this organization: an organization that was created by the workers of Poland so that they could live decent and honest lives. So that they could live their lives according to religious beliefs and the natural rights of man.

It is these aspirations that have brought Solidarity into being. We are still traveling together toward those same goals, fighting to win for man his rightful place on this earth and thereby in Poland itself.

(L. Walesa, *A Way of Hope*, pp. 261–262)

THE PALESTINE NATIONAL CHARTER OF THE PALESTINE LIBERATION ORGANIZATION

National Congress of the PLO, held in Cairo (1–17 July 1968)

1. Palestine is the homeland of the Palestinian Arab people; it is an individible part of the Arab homeland, and the Palestinian people are an integral part of the Arab nation.

6. The Jews who had normally resided in Palestine until the beginning of the Zionist invasion will be considered Palestinians. . . .

9. Armed struggle is the only way to liberate Palestine. Thus it is the overall strategy, not merely a tactical phase. . . .

15. The liberation of Palestine, from an Arab viewpoint, is a national duty and it attempts to repel the Zionist and imperialist aggression against the Arab homeland, and aims at the elimination of Zionism in Palestine. . . .

16. The liberation of Palestine, from a spiritual point of view, will provide the Holy Land with an atmosphere of safety and tranquillity, which in turn will safeguard the country's religious sanctuaries and guarantee freedom of worship and of visit to all, without discrimination of race, color, language, or religion. . . .

19. The partition of Palestine in 1947 and the establishment of the state of Israel are entirely illegal, regardless of the passage of time, because they were contrary to the will of the Palestinian people and to their natural right in their homeland, and inconsistent with the principles embodied in the Charter of the United Nations, particularly the right to self-determination.

20. The Balfour Declaration, the mandate for Palestine and everything that has been based upon them, are deemed null and void. Claims of historical or religious ties of Jews with Palestine are incompatible with the facts of history and the true conception of what constitutes statehood. Judaism, being a religion, is not an independent nationality. Nor do Jews constitute a single nation with an identity of its own; they are citizens of the states to which they belong.

21. The Palestinian Arab people, expressing themselves by the armed Palestinian revolution, reject all solutions which are substitutes for the total liberation of Palestine and reject all proposals aiming at the liquidation of the Palestinian problem, or its internationalization.

22. Zionism is a political movement organically associated with

international imperialism and antagonistic to all action for liberation and to progressive movements in the world. It is racist and fanatic in its nature, aggressive, expansionist and colonial in its aims, and fascist in its methods. Israel is the instrument of the Zionist movement, and a geographical base for world imperialism placed strategically in the midst of the Arab homeland to combat the hopes of the Arab nation for liberation, unity and progress. Israel is a constant source of threat *vis-à-vis* peace in the Middle East and the whole world. Since the liberation of Palestine will destroy the Zionist and imperialist presence and will contribute to the establishment of peace in the Middle East, the Palestinian people look for the support of all progressive and peaceful forces and urge them all, irrespective of their affiliations and beliefs, to offer the Palestinian people all aid and support in their just struggle for the liberation of their homeland.

23. The demands of security and peace, as well as the demands of right and justice, require all states to consider Zionism an illegitimate movement, to outlaw its existence, and to ban its operations, in order that friendly relations among peoples may be preserved, and the loyalty of citizens to their respective homelands safeguarded.

24. The Palestinian people believe in the principles of justice, freedom, sovereignty, self-determination, human dignity, and in the right of all peoples to exercise them.

29. The Palestinian people possess the fundamental and genuine legal right to liberate and retrieve their homeland. . . .

(In J. Peters, *From Time Immemorial*, pp. 417–420)

15

Afro-American Reflections
on the Jews

JAMES WELDON JOHNSON   *(1871–1938)*

Afro-American novelist and poet; author of God's Trombones

It is most likely that all of us have at some time toyed with the Arabian Nights-like thought of the magical change of race. As for myself, I find that I do not wish to be anyone but myself. To conceive of myself as some one else is impossible, and the effort is repugnant. If the jinnee should suddenly appear before me and by way of introduction, say, . . . "Name some boon you desire, and it shall be granted," I think I should reply, "Grant me equal opportunity with other men, and the assurance of corresponding rewards for my efforts and what I may accomplish." If, coming to the principal matter, he should say, "Name any person into whom you would like to be changed, and it shall be done," I should be absolutely at a loss. If, continuing, he should say, "Name any race of which you would like to be made a member, it shall be done," I should likewise be at a loss. If the jinnee should say, "I have come to carry out an inexorable command to change you into a member of another race; make your choice!" I should answer, probably, "Make me a Jew."

(Johnson, *Along This Way*, an autobiography, 1933)

PAUL ROBESON   *(1898–1976)*

Afro-American singer, actor, and political activist

Sometimes I think I am the only Negro living who would not prefer to be white.

It has been said that I am to leave Europe and go back among my own people. . . . Where I live is not important. But I am going back to my people in the sense that for the rest of my life I am going to think and feel as an African—not as a white man.

Perhaps that does not sound a very important decision. To me, it seems the most momentous thing in my life.

555

Only those who have lived in a state of inequality will understand what I mean—workers, European Jews, women . . . those who
have felt their status, their race, or their sex a bar to a complete share
in all that the world has to offer.

All these people will understand what it is that makes most
Negroes desire nothing so much as to prove their equality with the
white man—*on the white man's own ground.*

(Foner, *Paul Robeson Speaks*, p. 91)

* * *

From a speech over the Mutual Broadcasting System, 23
September 1946:

. . . lynching is undermining the fundamental democracy of all. It is
not the special or exclusive concern of Negro Americans. The good
Aryan who stood idly by when the German Jew was persecuted lived
to learn that that was the beginning of the end of his own freedom. Let
us not some day live to learn that the persecution of the Negro was the
beginning of the end of all American freedom.

(*Paul Robeson Speaks*, p. 177)

* * *

From a speech to a protest meeting, London, 25 March 1949:

The picture South Africa presents today recalls the Germany of the
years before the war. The pogroms against the Jews in those years led
inevitably and inexorably to the horrors of Auschwitz and Belsen.
Can that be the intention of the present rulers of South Africa? Are
they preparing by their present acts to commit finally the act of
genocide?

(*Paul Robeson Speaks*, p. 195)

* * *

From an interview in the *Daily Worker* of London, 14 January
1960:

When I hear of these anti-semitic acts [taking place in West Germany
in 1959] I feel "This is where I came in." Some of my first work here in
Britain, in 1933, was singing in aid of Jewish refugee children.

I was shaped, myself, in the struggle against fascism. I was at Dachau after the war. . . .

This persecution is not just a Jewish problem, for it could lead to the destruction of the world.

My grandchildren are half-Jewish, so I feel it particularly. Whoever attacks a Negro may attack a Jewish boy, and vice-versa. . . .

(*Paul Robeson Speaks*, p. 462)

LANGSTON HUGHES   *(1902–1967)*

Afro-American poet and writer

Central was the high school of students of foreign-born parents—until the Negroes came. It is an old high school with many famous graduates. It used to be long ago the high school of the aristocrats, until the aristocrats moved farther out. Then poor whites and foreign-born took over the district. Then during the war, the Negroes came. Now Central is almost entirely a Negro school in the heart of Cleveland's vast Negro quarter. . . .

Although we got on very well, whenever class elections would come up, there was a distinct Jewish-Gentile division among my classmates. That was perhaps why I held many class and club offices in high school, because often when there was a religious deadlock, a Negro student would win the election. They would compromise on a Negro, feeling, I suppose, that a Negro was neither Jew nor Gentile!

. . . I had lots of Jewish friends, too, boys named Nathan and Sidney and Herman, and girls named Sonya and Bess and Leah. I went to my first symphony concert with a Jewish girl—for these children of foreign-born parents were more democratic than native white Americans, and less anti-Negro. They lent me *The Gadfly* and *Jean-Christophe* to read, and copies of the *Liberator* and the *Socialist Call*. They were almost all interested in more than basketball and the glee club. They took me to hear Eugene Debs. And when the Russian Revolution broke out, our school almost held a celebration. . . .

(Hughes, *The Big Sea*, an autobiography, pp. 29–31)

RICHARD WRIGHT   *(1908–1960)*

Afro-American critic and novelist; author of Native Son

. . . The two women [Wright's mother and his sister] were soon at work in the homes of whites, and the two boys joined the bands of roaming neighborhood children. From them, the elder Wright learned a great deal. A girl not much older than himself pointed out that the other half of the double apartment in which he lived was one of the centers of prostitution in the area. From others, he learned anti-Semitic slogans, folk ditties, cruel bits of doggerel, all part of the defensive armory of the poverty-stricken, the powerless. And again, events added to his growing knowledge of whites.

[Wright, newly migrated to Chicago] rode in search of a job, and he found one in a family delicatessen owned by a Jewish couple. He learned later that the Hoffmans were foreigners, migrants like himself. Their English was heavily dialectical, almost incomprehensible. Yet, he noted, they were able to own a store in a neighborhood across the boundary line of the black belt, away from the dirt and grime, in this neighborhood from which he was barred from living. He became envious and contemptuous of them and attributed their good fortune to the whiteness of their skin. Automatically, intuitively, he was beginning to interpret his new environment by signals derived from the old. . . .

At work, the Hoffmans were kind, friendly, and they treated him well. He appeared shy and reserved to them, but they knew something of the South and attributed his attitude to his having lived there. He was a good worker. He kept the store clean, ran errands, made deliveries, and stocked the shelves. He did not complain. He appreciated their kindnesses and regretted that he had once sung folk ditties and told the obscene jokes about Jews. Still, he could not trust the Hoffmans. Jews or no, they were still white people and they had a measure of control over his life. To believe that they were different from the whites of his past would have been emotionally rewarding, but he could not do that. Until he wanted time off to apply for a better job, however, he was unaware of how prevalent, how corrosive, his fear of them was. . . .

(Gayle, *Richard Wright: Ordeal of a Native Son*,
pp. 18, 50, 51)

LOUIS FARRAKHAN *(1934–   )*

American Black Muslim minister and political leader

In a March 1984 radio broadcast:

. . . the Jews don't like Farrakhan, so they call me Hitler. Well, that's a good name. Hitler was a very great man.

* * *

At the National Press Club, June 1984:

Judaism is a dirty religion.

* * *

In a Washington, D.C. speech, July 1985:

Jews know their wickedness, not just Zionism, which is an outgrowth of Jewish transgression.

* * *

In a Los Angeles speech, September 1985

Don't push your six million [Holocaust victims] when we lost 100 million [in slavery].

* * *

At New York City's Madison Square Garden, October 1985

—Jesus had a controversy with the Jews. Farrakhan has a controversy with the Jews. Jesus was hated by the Jews. Farrakhan is hated by the Jews. Jesus was scourged by Jews in their temple. Farrakhan is scourged by Jews in their synagogues. . . .

And I respectively say to my Jewish friends, please don't call me anti-Semitic. Go and study the state of Israel. The Ashkenazi Jews are European Jews who converted to Judaism. They never had any roots in Palestine. They never came from Palestine. These are Europeans who have come into Palestine and now the Falasha Jews and the Black Hebrew Israelites, they are suffering under the rule of the real anti-Semite, who is Yitzhak Shamir.

Where are the Asiatic Jews? Where are the African Jews? Why don't they have an equal share of power in Israel? It is because the real anti-Semite is in power and he clutches the Semitic people who are of Afro, Asian, and Semitic origin, not these Yiddish and Polish speaking people. . . .

(From his speech, "Empowerment in the Black Community Through Politics and Economics," given at the University of the District of Columbia, March 1988)

* * *

You can't be controlled by religion anymore. Politicians can't control you. Preachers can't control you. Mom and Dad can't control you, but drugs, and drugs can keep you in a stupor. And they're drugging you because they don't know what to do with you and they're afraid. They are afraid that the right voice with the right message will come along at the right time. And when the right voice with the right message at the right time reaches the right heart and the right mind, it will produce the rise of the people and this is what they fear. And this is why they must put a shroud over Farrakhan and call him an anti-Semite, a hater, a bigot, so that you will not listen to what your brother has to say. . . .

Can you imagine any white writer, any of you to have the unmitigated gall, the un-mit-i-gat-ed gall, to call me, a victim of white racism, a racist. I'm a victim of your bigotry, and now you call me a bigot. . . . Can you imagine Mr. Cohen [Richard Cohen, a columnist with the *Washington Post*] today saying that anti-Semitism is retreating all over the world except, except in the black community. Can you imagine Mr. Cohen with the audacity to say that you are anti-Semitic. You have never harmed a Jew. I'm speaking about collectively; we know there are some blacks and Jews that have problems. But I'm talking about as a collective people. Now, we have not done anything to deserve this. And we know it's right.

We've been loyal to you. We've cleaned your floors and when you asked us, "And you do do windows, don't you?" we said, "Yes." We left our homes uncleaned to clean yours. We left our children unkempt to clean yours. We give you our talent. You manage us. You get the money. We get the fame and then end up on drugs with no money. You are our manager, you are our agents. How have we been against you? You run the institutions quietly behind the scenes. You pull the strings where education is concerned. You're the scriptwriters. You're the Hollywood promoters that promoted us as Little Black Sambo and . . . Stepin Fetchit.

What have we done to Jews in America? Talk back to me! We are not your enemy. We didn't burn you in no oven. . . . A black man wouldn't come to your synagogue and mark no swastika. . . . We are not haters of Jews. But I ask you, who taught us to hate ourselves? Who writes the textbooks that write us out of history? Who makes the movies that show us as nothing but Toms and bug-eyed dancers? We don't do this to you. It has been done to us. But why do you call my brothers and sisters anti-Semitic? It is because you view me as that and my people will not rise up to kill me as they have done other black leaders in the past at your insistence and this is why you say he is anti-Semitic. It's a damned lie. . . . You want my people to kill me. . . .

("Empowerment in the Black Community Through Politics and Economics")

RALPH ELLISON   *(1914–   )*

Afro-American novelist; author of Invisible Man

. . . many Negroes, like myself, make a positive distinction between "whites" and "Jews." Not to do so could be either offensive, embarrassing, unjust or even dangerous. If I would know who I am and preserve who I am, then I must see others distinctly whether they see me or no. Thus I feel uncomfortable whenever I discover Jewish intellectuals writing as though *they* were guilty of enslaving my grandparents, or as though the *Jews* were responsible for the system of segregation. Not only do they have enough troubles of their own, as the saying goes, but Negroes know this only too well.

The real guilt of such Jewish intellectuals lies in their facile, perhaps unconscious, but certainly unrealistic, identification with what is called the "power structure." Negroes call that "passing for white." Speaking personally, both as writer and as Negro American, I would like to see the more positive distinctions between whites and Jewish Americans maintained. Not only does it make for a necessary bit of historical and social clarity, at least where Negroes are concerned, but I consider the United States freer politically and richer culturally because there are Jewish Americans to bring it the benefit of their special forms of dissent, their humor and their gift for ideas which are based upon the uniqueness of their experience. The diversity of American life is often painful, frequently burdensome and always a source of conflict, but in it lies our fate and our hope.

(from *The New Leader*, 9 December 1963)

* * *

Among his peers Ellison's presence or even the mention of his name causes the immediate arming of intellectual equipment. There can be no soft-pedaling, no relaxation of intellect where he is involved. At Brown University in November of 1969, novelists and critics gathered at the annual Wetmore Lecture to discuss form, the future of the novel, and each other. Critic Robert Scholes opened one discussion on form by reading from Ellison's acceptance speech before the National Book Award Committee. "Ah, Ellison," Leslie Fiedler said, throwing his arm out in a gesture of dismissal. "He's a black Jew."

Ellison chuckles. "Leslie's been trying to make me a Jew for years," he says. "I have to look at these things with a Cold Oklahoma Negro Eye. But someone should have said that *all* us old-fashioned Negroes are Jews."

(McPherson, "Indivisible Man," in *Atlantic Monthly*, December 1979)

MALCOLM X (LITTLE)   *(1925–1965)*

U.S. militant Afro-American leader and Black Muslim

After a while, I worked downtown for a Jew. He liked me because of something I had managed to do for him. He bought run-down restaurants and bars. Hymie was his name. He would remodel these places, then stage a big, gala re-opening, with banners and a spotlight outside. The jampacked, busy place with the big "Under New Management" sign in the window would attract speculators, usually other Jews who were around looking for something to invest money in. Sometimes even in the week of the new opening, Hymie would re-sell, at a good profit.

Hymie really liked me, and I liked him. He loved to talk. I loved to listen. Half his talk was about Jews and Negroes. Jews who had anglicized their names were Hymie's favorite hate. Spitting and curling his mouth in scorn, he would reel off names of people he said had done this. Some of them were famous names whom most people never thought of as Jews.

"Red, I'm a Jew and you're black," he would say. "These Gentiles don't like either one of us. If the Jew wasn't smarter than the Gentile, he'd get treated worse than your own people."

Hymie paid me good money while I was with him, sometimes two hundred and three hundred dollars a week. I would have done anything for Hymie. I did do all kinds of things. But my main job was transporting bootleg liquor that Hymie supplied, usually to those spruced-up bars which he had sold to someone. . . .

But one weekend on Long Island, something happened involving the State Liquor Authority. One of New York State's biggest recent scandals has been the exposure of wholesale S.L.A. graft and corruption. In the bootleg racket I was involved in, someone high up must have been taken for a real pile. A rumor about some "inside" tipster spread among Hymie and the others. One day Hymie didn't show up where he had told me to meet him. I never heard from him again . . . but I did hear that he was put in the ocean, and I knew he couldn't swim.

(*The Autobiography of Malcolm X*, pp. 124–125)

* * *

Spinoza impressed me for a while when I found out that he was black. A black Spanish Jew. The Jews excommunicated him because he advocated a pantheistic doctrine, something like the "allness of God," or "God in everything." The Jews read their burial services for Spinoza, meaning that he was dead as far as they were concerned; his family was run out of Spain, they ended up in Holland, I think.

(*The Autobiography of Malcolm X*, p. 181)

* * *

In fact, history's most tragic result of a mixed, therefore diluted and weakened, ethnic identity has been experienced by a white ethnic group—the Jew in Germany.

He had made greater contributions to Germany than Germans themselves had. Jews had won over half of Germany's Nobel Prizes. Every culture in Germany was led by the Jew; he published the greatest newspaper. Jews were the greatest artists, the greatest poets, composers, stage directors. But those Jews made a fatal mistake—assimilating.

From World War I to Hitler's rise, the Jews in Germany had been increasingly intermarrying. Many changed their names and many took other religions. Their own Jewish religion, their own rich Jewish ethnic and cultural roots, they anesthetized, and cut off . . . until they began thinking of themselves as "Germans."

And the next thing they knew, there was Hitler, rising to power from the beer halls—with his emotional "Aryan master race" theory. And right at hand for a scapegoat was the self-weakened, self-deluded "German" Jew.

Most mysterious is how did those Jews—with all their brilliant minds, with all of their power in every aspect of Germany's affairs—how did those Jews stand almost as if mesmerized, watching something which did not spring upon them overnight, but which was gradually developed—a monstrous plan for their own *murder*.

Their self-brainwashing had been so complete that not long after, in the gas chambers, a lot of them were still gasping, "It *can't* be true!"

If Hitler *had* conquered the world, as he meant to—that is a shuddery thought for every Jew alive today.

The Jew never will forget that lesson. Jewish intelligence eyes watch every neo-Nazi organization. Right after the war, the Jews' Haganah mediating body stepped up the longtime negotiations with the British. And this time the British acquiesced and helped them to wrest Palestine away from the Arabs, the rightful owners, and then the Jews set up Israel, their own country—the one thing that every race of man in the world respects, and understands.

(*The Autobiography of Malcolm X*, pp. 280–281)

* * *

Question-and-answer periods are another area where, by now, again blindfolded, I can often tell you the ethnic source of a question. The most easily recognizable of these to me are a Jew in any audience situation, and a bourgeois Negro in "integrated" audiences.

My clue to the Jew's question and challenges is that among all other ethnic groups, his expressed thinking, his expressed concerns, are the most subjective. And the Jew is usually hypersensitive. I mean, you can't even say "Jew" without him accusing you of anti-Semitism. I don't care what a Jew is professionally, doctor, merchant, housewife, student, or whatever—first he, or she, thinks Jew.

Now, of course I can understand the Jew's hypersensitivity. For two thousand years, religious and personal prejudices against Jews have been vented and exercised, as strong as white prejudices against the non-white. But I know that America's five and a half million Jews (two million of them are concentrated in New York) look at it very practically, whether they know it or not: that all the bigotry and hatred focused upon the black man keeps off the Jew a lot of heat that would be on him otherwise.

For an example of what I am talking about—in every black ghetto, Jews own the major businesses. Every night the owners of the businesses go home with that black community's money, which helps the ghetto to stay poor. But I doubt that I have ever uttered this absolute truth before an audience without being hotly challenged, and accused by a Jew of anti-Semitism. Why? I will bet that I have told five hundred such challengers that Jews as a group would never watch some other minority systematically siphoning out their community's resources without doing something about it. I have told them that if I tell the simple truth, it doesn't mean that I am anti-Semitic; it means merely that I am anti-exploitation.

(The Autobiography of Malcolm X, pp. 286–287)

* * *

. . . From the consistent subjectivity in just about everything he asked and said, I had deduced something, and I told him, "You know, I think you're a Jew with an Anglicized name." His involuntary expression told me I'd hit the button. He asked me how I knew. I told him I'd had so much experience with how Jews would attack me that I usually could identify them. I told him all I held against the Jew was that so many Jews actually were hypocrites in their claim to be friends of the American black man, and it burned me up to be so often called "anti-Semitic" when I spoke things I knew to be the absolute truth about Jews. I told him that, yes, I gave the Jew credit for being among all other whites the most active, and the most vocal, financier, "leader" and "liberal" in the Negro civil rights movement. But I said at the same time I knew that the Jew played these roles for a very careful strategic reason: the more prejudice in America could be focussed upon the Negro, then the more the white Gentiles' prejudice would keep diverted off the Jew. I said that to me, one proof that all the civil rights posturing of so many Jews wasn't sincere was that so often in the North the quickest segregationists were Jews themselves. Look at practically everything the black man is trying to "integrate" into, for instance; if Jews are not the actual owners, or are not in controlling positions, then they have major stockholdings or they are otherwise in powerful leverage positions—and do they really sincerely exert these influences? No!

And an even clearer proof for me of how Jews truly regard Negroes, I said, was what invariably happened wherever a Negro moved into any white residential neighborhood that was thickly Jewish. Who would always lead the whites' exodus? The Jews! Generally in these situations, some whites stay put—you just notice who they are: they're Irish Catholics, they're Italians; they're rarely ever any Jews. And, ironically, the Jews themselves often still have trouble being "accepted."

Saying this, I know I'll hear "anti-Semitic" from every direction again. Oh, yes! But truth is truth.

(*The Autobiography of Malcolm X*, pp. 378–379)

MARTIN LUTHER KING, JR.　　*(1929–1968)*

U.S. minister, civil rights leader; Nobel Peace Prize 1964

King meanwhile had gone to New York City, where Mayor Robert Wagner conferred with him about cooling Harlem down. The trip was a disaster. While King toured the riot sites, embittered Harlemites booed him and spouted anti-Semitic vitriol that made him grimace. At the same time, local Negro leaders fumed that no "outsider" imported by the mayor had the right to invade their territory and tell them what to do.

King was greatly troubled. He warned Harlem Negroes that violence would only exacerbate their problems and beseeched them to follow his course of nonviolent resistance. . . . As for black anti-Semitism, "I solemnly pledge to do my utmost to uphold the fair name of Jews. Not only because we need their friendship, and surely we do, but mainly because bigotry in any form is an affront to us all."

(Oates, Let the Trumpet Sound, The Life of Martin Luther King, Jr., p. 306)

* * *

Not that he was going to give up on white America and stoop to some black nationalist or Black Power argument that all whites were devils. He had to remind himself that when the brick struck him in Marquette Park a white man was marching at his side. He had to remind himself that "We've got some black devils too." He had met some in the slums of Chicago—"street corner preachers" who exhorted Negroes to burn America down, and other blacks so caught up in frustration and irrational rage that they mouthed racist epithets against Jews, blaming them for all their woes. For King, black anti-Semitism in the ghettoes was "a freakish phenomenon" and deeply troubling. He understood that many slumlords and ghetto shop owners were Jews, and that ghetto Negroes, surrendering to racial stereotypes, generalized about a group of people on the basis of a few. They seemed impervious to the fact that Jews had been heavily involved in the civil-rights movement from the outset. In Chicago, King had taken a strong stand against black anti-Semitism "because it's wrong, it's unjust, and it's evil." It still left him depressed. The whole Chicago experience left him depressed. He didn't know where he was going from here.

(Let the Trumpet Sound, pp. 418–419)

* * *

Then came the question he had been expecting—one that Wachtel had warned him was on all the rabbis' minds. Would King comment on "the vicious anti-Semitism" and anti-Israel sentiments of the H. Rap Browns and Stokely Carmichaels?

King knew what they were referring to. After the Six-Day War in the Middle East the year before, SNCC had blamed "the Palestine problem" on "Zionist imperialists," denounced U.S. aid to Israel, and ranted against Zionism itself. King explained what he had said before—that black anti-Semitism, "virtually nonexistent in the South," was an ugly product of the northern ghetto. "We have made it clear that we cannot be the victims of the notion that you deal with one evil in society by substituting another evil," King said. "You cannot substitute one tyranny for another, and for the black man to be struggling for justice and then turn around and be anti-Semitic is not only a very irrational course but it is a very immoral course, and wherever we have seen anti-Semitism we have condemned it with all our might."

Thus far, King's answers reflected his maturest ideas to date on some of the critical racial problems besetting the country. Then he attempted to answer a difficult and wordy question about what he would say to those Negroes who supported the Arabs against Israel solely because of color. King ascribed that view to some "so-called young militants" who did not represent the vast majority of American Negroes. "There are some who are color-consumed and they see a kind of mystique in being colored," King said, "and anything non-colored is condemned. We do not follow that course in the Southern Christian Leadership Conference." He went on to offer an opinion about the Middle East crisis itself. What the Middle East needed, obviously, was peace. But that meant one thing for Israel, another for the Arab states. "Peace for Israel means security, and we must stand with our might to protect its right to exist, its territorial integrity. I see Israel, and never mind saying it, as one of the great outposts of democracy in the world and a marvelous example of what can be done, how desert land almost can be transformed into an oasis of brotherhood and democracy."

On the other hand, peace for the Arabs meant security on another level. It meant economic security. This was how those in the Southern Christian Leadership Conference tried to see the problem. "These nations, as you know, are part of that third world of hunger, of disease, of illiteracy," and these conditions caused tensions and led to "an endless quest to find scapegoats. So there is a need for a Marshall Plan for the Middle East, where we lift those who are at the bottom of the economic ladder and bring them into the mainstream of economic security."

Of course, economic problems alone scarcely accounted for the Arab view of Israel or for the manifold troubles of many Arab states. Though King was speaking extemporaneously and was probably getting tired, his remarks about the Arabs did betray a shallowness of thought, indicating that he had yet to refine his ideas about the complex and troublesome Middle East.

(*Let the Trumpet Sound*, pp. 474–475)

* * *

To a black student who attacked "Zionists":

When people critize Zionists they mean Jews. You're talking anti-Semitism.

WHITNEY YOUNG, JR.   *(1921–1971)*

Afro-American leader, executive director of the
National Urban League

Replying to a critic objecting to his signature on a
New York Times advertisement in support of Israel,
7 October 1970:

. . . I know of no real aid oil-rich Arab countries have given the struggling new nations of black Africa, although the Israelis have a very impressive program of technical assistance of the no-strings-attached variety, even in nations that take the Arab line in the UN. . . .

[Until peace comes to the Middle East] I would continue to favor providing Israel with the weapons she needs to defend herself against those who have sworn to destroy her. . . .

Arab history and culture is replete with instances of racial prejudice. Today, the Arab leaders of the Sudan are waging a merciless war against the black people of the southern region of that country, and Arabs in Chad are at war with the black government of that country. . . .

If the Arab nations had really been concerned with improving "the social, economic, and political existences" of their people, they would long ago have ceased threatening to push Israel into the sea and concentrated their energies on improving the lives of their people. . . .

(Chertoff, *The New Left and the Jews*, p. 183)

STOKELY CARMICHAEL   *(1941–   )*

U.S. Black Power leader

From a speech before a convention of the Organization of
Arab Students, 31 August 1968:

We have begun to see the evil of Zionism, and we will fight to wipe it
out wherever it exists, be it in the Ghetto of the United States or in the
Middle East.

(Chertoff, *The New Left and the Jews*, p. 179)

* * *

At a rally for Louis Farrakhan, at Madison Square Garden in
New York City, 7 October 1985:

As Kwame Toure, now head of the All African People's Revolutionary
Party said:
   Africa gave Judaism to the world. Moses was an Egyptian! Moses
was an African!

AMIRI BARAKA/LEROI JONES   *(1934–   )*

Afro-American playwright and poet

The alliance [of Jewish Hettie Cohen and the black poet in marriage]
was to cause wonder and outright negative criticism in the years to
follow, mainly because of Jones's anti-Jewish sentiment and strong
separatist stance. Baraka-who-was-once-Jones is not eager to discuss
this marriage. He explains, "I came to the Village looking to be a
writer, an artist, and that was one of the first people I met down there."

(Hudson, *From LeRoi Jones to Amiri Baraka*, p. 13)

* * *

   Significant in view of his later anti-Jew statements, a disproportionate number of Jones's friends and associates at the time were
Jews. . . .

(*From Leroi Jones to Amiri Baraka*, p. 14)

In "Letter to Jules Feiffer," a rebuttal to a letter Feiffer had published in
The Village Voice, Jones . . . [reminds] Feiffer, "I can think of 5,000,000
people who used to live in Europe, who should've fought back when
they were assaulted by racists. Can't you?" By the time of the writing
of this essay, Jones had stopped calling himself a Negro, and he asks
Feiffer, "Why so much fuss about Negroes wanting to call themselves
Afro-Americans? And if you want to call yourself a Judeo (Judaeo?)
American, it's perfectly all right with me. In fact, I think if perhaps
there were more Judeo-Americans and a few less bland, cultureless,
middle-headed [sic] AMERICANS, this country might still be a great
one."

(*From Leroi Jones to Amiri Baraka*, p. 83)

* * *

. . . Jones draws an analogy between the nonviolent American
Negro and "the European Jews and more specifically the fate of the
German Jews at the hands of Adolph Hitler. The German Jews, at the
time of Hitler's rise to power, were the most assimilated Jews in
Europe. They believed, and with a great deal of emotional investment,
that they were Germans. . . . Even when the anti-Jewish climate
began to thicken and take on the heaviness of permanence, many
middle-class Jews believed that it was only the poor Jews, who, perhaps
rightly so, would suffer in such a climate."

(*From Leroi Jones to Amiri Baraka*, p. 84)

* * *

. . . in "Negro Theater Pimps Get Big Off Nationalism," the eye
focuses on those he considers the idolators and the misled ("Eldridge
Cleaver and his misguided jeworiented revolutionaries"). . . .

(*From Leroi Jones to Amiri Baraka*, p. 107)

* * *

Looking back over the corpus of Jones's poetry, we notice a
gradual change from a subjective, tentative lyricist to an activist
priest-poet. As to subject matter, the Jonesian and Barakan themes
are there: the negative themes—anti-middle-class Negro, anti-Jew,

anti-white liberal, anti-Christianity, anti-Western culture, and the positive themes—blacks as the saviors-survivors in the coming world, the need for new gods, black aestheticism, theories of art and culture, revolution as necessary and justifiable on spiritual grounds, the physical and spiritual beauty of black people.

(*From Leroi Jones to Amiri Baraka*, p. 145)

HARRY BELAFONTE (1927–   )

Black-American singer, entertainer, and civil rights activist

There is no absence of participation on the part of Jews when it comes to assisting on things that are of substance to black Americans and vice versa. When we began organizing the Mandela trip [to the United States in mid-1990], we turned to some of our traditional allies who are not black—whites of various persuasions and Jews—for assistance and expertise. When we looked around for money, there were a number of people of the Jewish faith who were quite responsive to us. A lot of what went on was very low profile. . . .

There are some of us who believe that, given the Jewish religious ethic and historical experience, there should be greater sensitivity expressed on the part of Jews to the experience and struggles that blacks have had, so we hold them more responsible. . . .

Still, Jews played a large part in opening doors that had been closed to blacks. Had they not, we would not have been able to achieve a lot that we have. We need to talk very seriously and completely about this thing that is suffocating us: This anti-black perception in Jews and this anti-Semitic perception in blacks. We'll all be better for it.

(From an interview in *The New York Times*, July 29, 1990,
Section E, p. 5)

Epilogue

PAUL JOHNSON

U. S. author of A History of the Jews

In his *Antiquities of the Jews*, Josephus describes Abraham as "a man of great sagacity" who had "higher notions of virtue than others of his time." He therefore "determined to change completely the views which all then had about God." One way of summing up 4,000 years of Jewish history is to ask ourselves what would have happened to the human race if Abraham had not been a man of great sagacity, or if he had stayed in Ur and kept his higher notions to himself, and no specific Jewish people had come into being. Certainly the world without the Jews would have been a radically different place. Humanity might eventually have stumbled upon all the Jewish insights. But we cannot be sure. All the great conceptual discoveries of the intellect seem obvious and inescapable once they have been revealed, but it requires a special genius to formulate them for the first time. The Jews had this gift. To them we owe the idea of equality before the law, both divine and human; of the sanctity of life and the dignity of the human person; of the individual conscience and so of personal redemption; of the collective conscience and so of social responsibility; of peace as an abstract ideal and love as the foundation of justice, and many other items which constitute the basic moral furniture of the human mind. Without the Jews it might have been a much emptier place.

Above all, the Jews taught us how to rationalize the unknown. The result was monotheism and the three great religions which profess it. It is almost beyond our capacity to imagine how the world would have fared if they had never emerged. Nor did the intellectual

573

penetration of the unknown stop at the idea of one God. Indeed monotheism itself can be seen as a milestone on the road which leads people to dispense with God altogether. The Jews first rationalized the pantheon of idols into one Supreme Being; then began the process of rationalizing Him out of existence. In the ultimate perspective of history, Abraham and Moses may come to seem less important than Spinoza. For the Jewish impact on humanity has been protean. In antiquity they were the great innovators in religion and morals. In the Dark Ages and early medieval Europe they were still an advanced people transmitting scarce knowledge and technology. Gradually they were pushed from the van and fell behind until, by the end of the eighteenth century, they were seen as a bedraggled and obscurantist rearguard in the march of civilized humanity. But then came an astonishing second burst of creativity. Breaking out of their ghettos, they once more transformed human thinking, this time in the secular sphere. Much of the mental furniture of the modern world too is of Jewish fabrication.

The Jews were not just innovators. They were also exemplars and epitomizers of the human condition. They seemed to present all the inescapable dilemmas of man in a heightened and clarified form. They were the quintessential "strangers and sojourners." But are we not all such on this planet, of which we each possess a mere leasehold of threescore and ten? The Jews were the emblem of homeless and vulnerable humanity. But is not the whole earth no more than a temporary transit-camp? The Jews were fierce idealists striving for perfection, and at the same time fragile men and women yearning for flesh-pots and safety. They wanted to obey God's impossible law, and they wanted to stay alive too. Therein lay the dilemma of the Jewish commonwealths in antiquity, trying to combine the moral excellence of a theocracy with the practical demands of a state capable of defending itself. The dilemma has been recreated in our own time in the shape of Israel, founded to realize a humanitarian ideal, discovering in practice that it must be ruthless simply to survive in a hostile world. But is not this a recurrent problem which affects all human societies? We all want to build Jerusalem. We all drift back towards the Cities of the Plain. It seems to be the role of the Jews to focus and dramatize these common experiences of mankind, and to turn their particular fate into a universal moral. But if the Jews have this role, who wrote it for them?

Historians should beware of seeking providential patterns in events. They are all too easily found, for we are credulous creatures, born to believe, and equipped with powerful imaginations which readily produce and rearrange data to suit any transcendental scheme. Yet, excessive scepticism can produce as serious a distortion as credulity. The historian should take into account all forms of evidence, including those which are or appear to be metaphysical. If the earliest Jews were able to survey, with us, the history of their progeny, they would find nothing surprising in it. They always knew that Jewish society was appointed to be a pilot-project for the entire human race. That Jewish dilemmas, dramas, and catastrophes should be exemplary, larger than life, would seem only natural to them. That Jews should over the millennia attract such unparalleled, indeed inexplicable, hatred would be regrettable, but only to be expected. Above all, that the Jews should still survive, when all those other ancient people were transmuted or vanished into the oubliettes of history, was wholly predictable. How could it be otherwise? Providence decreed it and the Jews obeyed. The historian may say: there is no such thing as providence. Possibly not. But human confidence in such an historical dynamic, if it is strong and tenacious enough, is a force in itself, which pushes on the hinge of events and moves them. The Jews believed they were a special people with such unanimity and passion, and over so long a span, that they became one. They did indeed have a role because they wrote it for themselves. Therein, perhaps, lies the key to their story.

(Johnson, A *History of the Jews*, pp. 585–587)

Bibliography

Abélard, Peter. *Dialogus inter Philosophum, Judaeum et Christianiaum.* ed. F. H. Rheinwald. Berlin, 1831.

Ackroyd, Peter. *T. S. Eliot, A Life.* New York: Simon & Schuster, 1984.

Adams, Henry. *Lectures and Biographical Sketches.* Boston: Houghton Mifflin, 1884.

Andersen, Hans Christian. *The Story of My Life.* Boston: Houghton, Osgood, 1880.

Ambrose, Stephen E. *Eisenhower.* New York: Simon & Schuster, 1983.

Angoff, Charles. *H. L. Mencken, A Portrait from Memory.* New York: A. S. Barnes, 1956.

Arnold, Matthew. *Literature and Dogma.* London: Smith Elder, 1873.

Arnold, Thomas, ed. *Addison: Selections from Addison's Papers Contributed to "The Spectator."* Oxford, England: Clarendon Press, 1984.

Attlee, Clement. *A Prime Minister Remembers.* London: William Heinemann, 1961.

Augustine. "Treatise against the Jews." In *Patrologia Latina.* Paris: Garnier, 1878–1890.

_____ "Creed." In *The Fathers of the Church,* vol. 27. New York: Christian Heritage, 1946.

_____ *The City of God.* Trans. Marcus Dods. New York: Random House, Modern Library, 1950.

Bald, R. C. *John Donne: A Life.* Oxford, England: Clarendon Press, 1970.

Balzac, Honore de. "The Influence of the Jews on the Progress of the World." In *Selected Addresses and Papers of Simon Wolf.* Cincinnati, 1926.

Bander, Edward J. *Mr. Dooley and Mr. Dunne.* Charlottesville, VA: Michie Company Law Publishers, 1981.

Barrault, Jean-Louis. *Memories for Tomorrow*. Trans. Jonathan Griffin. New York: Dutton, 1974.

Belloc, Hilaire. "The Jewish Question." In *The Eye-Witness*, Autumn 1911.

Beñes, Eduard. *Democracy Today and Tomorrow*. New York: Macmillan, 1939.

Benston, Kimberly, ed. *Speaking for You, The Vision of Ralph Ellison*. Washington, DC: Howard University Press, 1987.

Berenson, Bernard. *Humor and Reflection*. New York: Simon & Schuster, 1952.

Besterman, Theodore. *Voltaire*. London: Longmans Green, 1969.

Bierce, Ambrose. *Devil's Dictionary*. Mineola, NY: Dover, 1911.

Blake, William. *Selections from Jerusalem*. Vol. 27. London, 1804–1820.

Blotner, Joseph. *Faulkner: A Biography*. New York: Random House, 1974.

Booth, Bradford A. *Anthony Trollope: Aspects of His Life and Art*. Bloomington, IN: Indiana University Press, 1958.

Brabazon, James. *Dorothy L. Sayers*. Toronto: General Publishing, 1981.

Bradshaw, John, ed. *Letters of the Earl of Chesterfield*. New York: Charles Scribner's Sons, 1892.

Bragg, Melvyn. *RICH: The Life of Richard Burton*. London: Hodder & Stoughton, 1988.

Browne, Thomas. *Religio Medici*, 1635.

Bryant, William Cullen. *New York Post*. January, 1867.

Burgess, Anthony. *But Do Blondes Prefer Gentlemen?* New York: McGraw-Hill, 1986.

———— *Little Wilson and Big God*. Toronto: Stoddart, 1987.

Byrnes, R. F. *Pobedonostsev*. Bloomington, IN: Indiana University Press, 1968.

Byron, William. *Cervantes, A Biography*. Garden City, NY: Doubleday, 1978.

Capek, Karel. *President Masaryk Tells His Story*. London: Ayer, 1934.

Carr, Virginia Spencer. *The Lonely Hunter*. Garden City, NY: Doubleday, 1975.

Chertoff, Mordecai S. *The New Left and the Jews*. New York and Toronto: Pitman, 1971.

Chrysostom, St. John. Homilies Against the Jews. In *Patrologia Graeca*, vol. 8, pp. 843–892. Paris: Garnier, 1857–1866.

Churchill, Winston. Parliamentary Debate, House of Lords, vol. 113, *House of Commons Official Report*, vol. 347.

Chute, Marchette. *Geoffrey Chaucer of England*. New York: Dutton, 1946.

Cohen, Mary M. "Browning's Hebraic Sympathies." *Poet-Lore* 3 (1891): 250–254.

Cohen, Morton. *Rider Haggard, His Life and Work*. London and Toronto: Macmillan, 1968.

Collier, Peter, and David Horowitz. *The Fords—An American Epic*. New York: Simon & Schuster, 1987.

Colvin, Sidney, ed. *The Letters of Robert Louis Stevenson.* Charles Scribner's Sons, 1899.

The Complete Works of Samuel Taylor Coleridge. Ed. W. G. Shedd. New York: 1884.

Crozier, Brian. *De Gaulle.* New York: Charles Scribner's Sons, 1973.

Cushman, Harvey. *The Life of Sir William Osler.* Oxford, England: Clarendon Press, 1925.

Davis, John H. *The Kennedys—Dynasty and Disaster, 1848-1983.* Toronto and New York: McGraw-Hill, 1984.

De Quincey, Thomas. "Language." London, 1858.

Dickens, Charles. *Child's History of England,* 1907.

Djilas, Milovan. *Party of a Lifetime,* New York: Harcourt Brace Jovanovich, 1975.

Donald, David Herbert. *Look Homeward—A Life of Thomas Wolfe.* New York: Ballantine, 1987.

Donaldson, Frances. *P. G. Wodehouse, A Biography.* New York: Knopf, 1982.

Doob, Leonard, ed. "Ezra Pound Speaking." Broadcast 32, 30 April 1942. Westport, CT: Greenwood Press, 1978.

Dostoyevsky, Fyodor. "The Jewish Question." In *The Diary of a Writer.* Trans. Boris Brasol. New York: Charles Scribner's Sons, 1949.

Douglas, D., ed. *Familiar Letters of Sir Walter Scott,* 1894.

Dreiser, Theodore. *Letters of Theodore Dreiser,* vol. 2, p. 405.

Duberman, Martin. *James Russell Lowell, Poet, Critic, Editor.* Boston: Houghton Mifflin, 1966.

Edel, Leon, ed. *The Thirties: From Notebooks and Diaries of the Period.* New York: Farrar, Straus & Giroux, 1980.

Eliot, George. "The Modern Hep! Hep! Hep!" In *Impressions of Theophrastus Such,* 1879.

Eliot, T. S. *After Strange Gods.* New York: Harcourt, Brace, 1934.

Ellis, Havelock. "The Jewish Question." In *Questions of Our Day.* New York: Vanguard Press, 1936.

Ellmann, Richard. *James Joyce.* New York: Oxford University Press, 1982.

Ellmann, Richard, ed. *James Joyce—Letters.* New York: Viking Press, 1966.

Farwell, Byron. *Burton.* New York: Holt, Rinehart & Winston, 1963.

Fermi, Laura. *Mussolini.* Chicago: University of Chicago Press, 1961.

Ffinch, Michael. *G. K. Chesterton.* London: Weidenfeld and Nicolson, 1986.

Field, Andrew. *The Life and Art of Vladimir Nabokov.* New York: Crown, 1986.

Fischer, Louis, ed. *The Essential Gandhi, An Anthology.* New York: Random House, 1962.

Fitzgerald, Sally, ed. *Letters of Flannery O'Connor—The Habit of Being.* New York: Farrar, Straus & Giroux, 1979.

Foner, Philip S., ed. *Paul Robeson Speaks*. Secaucus, NJ: Citadel Press, 1978.

Foreign Relations, pp. xii–xiii. Washington, DC, 1892.

Forster, Edward M. *Two Cheers for Democracy*. London: Penguin Books, 1965.

Frady, Marshall. *Billy Graham*. Boston and Toronto: Little, Brown, 1979.

Franklin, Benjamin. *The Autobiography of Benjamin Franklin*, ed. Leonard W. Larabee. New Haven, CT: Yale University Press, 1964.

Friedman, Lee M. "Cotton Mather and the Jews." In vol. 26 of *American Jewish Historical Publications*. Baltimore: Lord Baltimore Press, 1918.

_____ *Pilgrims in a New Land*. New York: Farrar, Straus & Giroux, 1948.

Galante, Abraham. *Turcs et Juifs*.

Galbraith, John Kenneth. *A Life in Our Times, Memoirs*. Boston: Houghton Mifflin, 1981.

Gallup, Donald, ed. *The Journals of Thornton Wilder, 1939–1961*. New Haven, CT: Yale University Press, 1985.

Gayle, Addison. *Richard Wright: Ordeal of a Native Son*. Garden City, NY: Doubleday, 1980.

George, Henry. *The Writings of Henry George*. New York: Doubleday & McLure, 1898.

Gertz, Elmer, and Lewis, Felice Flanery, eds. *Henry Miller – Years of Trial and Triumph, 1962–1964*. Carbondale, IL: Southern Illinois University Press, 1978.

Gifford, R., and Lee, L. *Saroyan: A Biography*. New York: Harper & Row. 1984.

Gilbert, Martin. *Road to Victory – Winston Churchill, 1941–1945*. Toronto: Stoddart, 1986.

_____ *Never Despair – Winston Churchill, 1945–1965*. Toronto: Stoddart, 1988.

Givner, Joan. *Katherine Anne Porter, A Life*. New York: Simon & Schuster, 1982.

Gladstone, William Ewart. "The Place of Ancient Greece in the Providential Order." In *Gleanings of Past Years*, vol. 7, pp. 79f. New York: Charles Scribner's Sons, 1879.

Goethe, Johann Wolfgang von. *Maximen und Reflexionen*.

_____ *Wilhelm Meister's Travels*. Trans. T. Carlyle and R. D. Boylan, 1821.

_____ *Gespräche*, ed. F. Biedermann. Leipzig, 1909.

Golden, Harry. *Carl Sandburg*. New York: World Publishing Co., 1961.

Gordon, Lyndall. *Virginia Woolf – A Writer's Life*. New York: Oxford University Press, 1984.

Gordon, Sara. *Hitler, Germans and the "Jewish Question."* Princeton, NJ: Princeton University Press, 1984.

Graetz, Hermann. *Geschichte der Juden*, vol. 4. Leipzig: Leiner, 1873.

Graves, Robert. *The Crane Bag and Other Disputed Subjects*. London: Cassel & Company, 1969.

Gregory. Homilies of the Resurrection, 5. In *Patrologia Graeca*. Paris: Garnier, 1857–1866.

Grotius, Hugo. *The Truth of the Christian Religion*. 11th ed. Trans. John Clarke. London, 1800.

Grunfeld, Frederic V. *Prophets Without Honor*. New York: Holt, Rinehart & Winston, 1979.

Haffenden, John. *The Life of John Berryman*. Boston: Routledge & Kegan Paul, 1982.

Harap, Louis. *The Image of the Jew in American Literature*. Philadelphia: The Jewish Publication Society, 1974.

Harris, Leon. *Upton Sinclair: American Rebel*. New York: Thomas Y. Crowell, 1975.

Harvard Anniversary Literary and Political Addresses. Boston, 1892.

Hassall, Christopher. *Rupert Brooke, A Biography*. London: Faber and Faber, 1964.

Hastings, Selina. *Nancy Mitford*. London: Hamish Hamilton, 1985.

Hazlitt, William. *Notes of a Journey through France and Italy*. 1826.

———— "On Jewish Emancipation." *The Tatler* (28 March 1831).

Headlam, James Wycliffe. *Bismarck and the Foundations of the German Empire*. New York: AMS Press, 1899.

Hebblewaith, Peter. *Pope John XXIII, Shepherd of the Modern World*. Garden City, NY: Doubleday, 1985.

Hertzberg, Arthur. *The French Enlightenment and the Jews*. New York and Philadelphia: Columbia University Press and the Jewish Publication Society, 1968.

Higham, Charles. *Orson Welles*. New York: St. Martin's Press, 1985.

Hilberg, Raul. *The Destruction of the European Jews*. New York: Holmes & Meier, 1985.

Hills, George. *Franco, the Man and His Nation*. New York: Macmillan, 1967.

Hitler, Adolf. *Mein Kampf*. Trans. Ralph Manheim. Boston: Houghton Mifflin, 1943.

———— *Hitler's Secret Conversations*. New York: Signet, 1961.

Hobbes, Thomas. "The Question Concerning Liberty, Necessity, and Chance." In *The English Works of Thomas Hobbes of Malmesbury*, ed. Sir William Molesworth, 2:232. London: Bohm, 1839–1845.

Hollis, Christopher. *The Mind of Chesterton*. London: Hollis & Carter, 1970.

Holmes, Oliver Wendell. *Over the Teacups*. Boston: Houghton Mifflin, 1891.

Hudson, Theodore R. *From Leroi Jones to Amiri Baraka*. Durham, NC: Duke University Press, 1973.

Hughes, Langston. *The Big Sea*. New York: Knopf, 1940.

Hugo, Victor. *Stars and Sand*, Philadelphia: Jewish Publication Society, 1942.

Hume, David. *History of England*, vol. 1. New York: Harper & Bros., 1761.

Huxley, Thomas. *Science and Hebrew Tradition*. New York: D. Appleton and Company, 1920.

Ingersoll, Robert G. *Some Mistakes of Moses*. Buffalo, NY: Prometheus Books, 1986.

James, Anthony. *Mussolini*. New York: Franklin Watts/Grolier, 1982.

James, William. *The Will to Believe*. Cambridge, MA: Harvard University Press, 1979.

Jaspers, Karl. *The Question of German Guilt*. Trans. E. B. Ashton. New York: Capricorn Books, 1961.

Jerome. *Les Juifs dans l'Empire Romain*, vol. 2 Paris: Guenthner, 1914.

Joes, Anthony James. *Mussolini*. New York: Franklin Watts, 1982.

Johlinger, Otto. *Bismarck und die Juden*. Berlin, 1921.

Johnson, Diane. *Dashiel Hammett, A Life*. New York: Random House, 1983.

Johnson, Edgar. *Charles Dickens—His Tragedy and Triumph*. New York: Simon & Schuster, 1952.

Johnson, James Weldon. *Along This Way*. New York: Viking Press, 1933.

Johnson, Paul. *A History of the Jews*. New York: Harper & Row, 1987.

Jones, Ernest. *Free Associations: Memories of a Psycho-Analyst*. New York: Basic Books, 1959.

Karl, Frederick R. *Joseph Conrad: The Three Lives*. New York: Farrar, Straus & Giroux, 1979.

Karl Marx: Early Writings. Ed. and trans. Bottomore. New York: McGraw–Hill, 1964.

Kazantzakis, Helen. *Nikos Kazantzakis, A Biography Based on His Letters*. New York: Simon & Schuster, 1968.

Kenner, Hugh. *Wyndham Lewis*. Norfolk, VA: New Directions, 1954.

Kierkegaard, Søren. *Fear and Trembling*. Trans. Robert Payne. London: Oxford University Press, 1939.

Kiernan, Thomas. *The Intricate Music, A Biography of John Steinbeck*. Boston and Toronto: Little, Brown, 1979.

The Koran. Trans. J. M. Rodwell. London: Everyman's Library, 1909.

Korn, Bertram Wallace. *American Jewry and the Civil War*. Philadelphia: The Jewish Publication Society, 1951.

Krausnick, Helmut. *Anatomy of the SS State*. New York: Walker, 1968.

Kropotkin, Peter. *Memoirs of a Revolutionist*. New York: Horizon Press, 1968.

Lamb, Charles. "Jews, Quakers, Scotchmen, and Other Imperfect Sympathies." *London Magazine* (1808):152.

Lamm, R. *Joseph Campbell. Unpublished Study*. New York.

Languth, A. J. *Saki: A Life of H. H. Munro*. New York: Simon & Schuster, 1981.

Ledwidge, Bernard. *De Gaulle*. New York: St. Martin's, 1982.

Lee, A. *Henry Ford and the Jews*. New York: Stein & Day, 1980.

Lawrence, Lee, and Gifford, Barry. *Saroyan, A Biography*. New York: Harper & Row, 1984.

Leibnitz, Gottfried Wilhelm von. *Essais de Théodicée sur la bonté de Dieu, la liberté de l'homme et l'origine du mal*, 1:316. Amsterdam, 1710.

Lenin, Vladimir. *Lenin on the Jewish Question*. New York: International Universities Press, 1934.

Lessing, Gotthold Ephraim. *Rettung des Hieronimus Cardnus*, vol. 3 of *Schriften*, 1754.

Letters of Sidney and Beatrice Webb, vol. 1, ed. by Norman Mackenzie. Cambridge, England: Cambridge University Press.

Letters from Africa, 1914–1931. Trans. Anne Born. Chicago: Chicago University Press, 1981.

Letters of Anton Chekhov. Ed. Avraham Yarmolinsky. New York: Viking Press, 1973.

Letters of Evelyn Waugh. Ed. Mark Amory. London: Weidenfeld and Nicholson, 1980.

Letters of Henrik Ibsen. Trans. John Wilsen Laurvik and Mary Morrison. New York: Fox, Duffield, 1905.

Letters of Henry Adams, 1892–1918. Boston, 1930.

The Letters of Jack London. Ed. Earle Labor, Robert E. Leitz III, and I. Milo Shepard. Stanford, CA: Stanford University Press, 1988.

Letters of Marshall McLuhan, selected and edited by Matie Molinaro, Corinne McLuhan, William Toye. Toronto: Oxford University Press, 1987.

Letters of Wallace Stevens. Sel. and ed. Holly Stevens. New York: Knopf, 1966.

Levin, Nora. *The Jews in the Soviet Union Since 1917*. New York: New York University Press, 1988.

Lewis, Alfred Allen, and Woodworth, Constance. *Miss Elizabeth Arden*. New York: Coward, McCann & Geoghegan, 1972.

Lindbergh, Anne Morrow. *The Flower and the Nettle, Diaries and Letters, 1936–1939*. New York: Harcourt Brace Jovanovich, 1938.

Littell, Franklin H. *The Crucifixion of the Jews*. New York: Harper & Row, 1975.

Lochner, Louis P., ed. *The Goebbels Diaries*. Garden City, NY: Doubleday, 1948.

Locke, John. "A Letter Concerning Toleration." In vol. 6 of *Works*, 11th ed., pp. 17f, 40, 51f. London: Adler's Foreign Books, 1812.

Lockhart, J. G. *Memoirs of Sir Walter Scott*, vol. 4. London, 1914.

Lonsbach, R. M. *Nietzsche und die Juden*. Stockholm: Berman-Fischer, 1939.

Lopez, H. "A Country and Some People I Love." *Harpers*, September 1965.

Lowell, J. R. *Literacy and Public Addresses*, vol. 6. In *Writings*. Boston: Houghton, Mifflin, 1899.

Ludington, Townsend. *John Dos Passos, A Twentieth-Century Odyssey*. New York: Dutton, 1980.

Luther, Martin. *The Table Talk of Martin Luther*. Bohn's Library.

Lynn, Kenneth S. *Hemingway*. New York: Simon & Schuster, 1987.

Macaulay, Thomas Babington. "Civil Disabilities of the Jews." *The Edinburgh Review* (January 1831).

Mack, John E. *A Prince of Our Disorder: The Life of T. E. Lawrence*. Boston: Little, Brown, 1976.

MacShane, Frank, ed. *Selected Letters of Raymond Chandler*. New York: Columbia University Press, 1981.

Maistre, Joseph Marie Comte, de. *Les Soirées de Saint-Petersbourg, ou, Entretiens sur le Gouvernement Temporal de la Providence*. 12th ed., vol. 2. Lyon, France: L. B. Pelegaud, 1874.

Malcolm X. *The Autobiography of Malcolm X*. With Alex Haley. New York: Grove Press, 1965.

Marchand, Leslie A. *Byron—A Portrait*. New York: Knopf, 1970.

Marcus, Jacob R. *The Jew in the Medieval World*. New York: Atheneum, 1973.

Maritain, Jacques, *A Christian Looks at the Jewish Question*.

Marrus, Michael R. "Analysis—A Light in an Age of Darkness" in *Toronto Globe and Mail*, March 30, 1990, p. 8.

Marrus, Michael R., and Paxton, Robert O. *Vichy France and the Jews*. New York: Basic Books, 1981.

Marshall, George, and Pauling, David. *Schweitzer*. Garden City, NY: Doubleday, 1971.

Maude, Aylmer. *The Life of Tolstoy: Later Years*. New York: Oxford University Press, 1987.

McCall, S. M. *Patriotism of the American Jew*. New York: Plymouth Press, 1924.

McCarthy, Patrick. *Céline*. New York: Viking Press, 1975.

McPherson, James Alan. "Indivisible Man. *The Atlantic Monthly*, 1970.

Mead, Margaret. *An Anthropologist at Work: Writings of Ruth Benedict*. Boston: Houghton Mifflin, 1959.

Menninger, Karl. "The Genius of Psychiatry." In *A Psychiatrist's World*, New York: Viking Press, 1959.

Menorah Monthly (official organ of B'nai B'rith 1860–1901).

Meyers, Jeffrey. *Hemingway, A Biography*. New York: Harper & Row, 1985.

Mickiewicz, Adam. *Kurs Literatury Slowianskiej*, vol. 3. Paris, 1841–1844.

Mill, John Stuart. *Considerations on Representative Government*. New York: Holt, 1861.

Miller, Merle. *Plain Speaking* (an oral biography of Harry S Truman). New York: Berkley, 1985.

Miller, Nathan. *FDR—An Intimate History*. Garden City, NY: Doubleday, 1983.

Moore, H. T., ed. *The Collected Letters of D. H. Lawrence.* New York: Viking Press, 1962.

Morgan, Ted. *Literary Outlaw: The Life and Times of William S. Burroughs.* New York: Henry Holt, 1988.

—————— *Maugham, A Biography.* New York: Simon & Schuster, 1980.

Morris, M. H. "Roger Williams and the Jews." In vol. 3 of *American Jewish Archives,* January 1951.

Newton, Thomas. *Dissertations of the Prophecies.* London, 1754.

Niebuhr, Reinhold. *The Children of Light and the Children of Darkness.* New York: Charles Scribner's Sons, 1944.

Nietzsche, Friedrich. *The Antichrist.* Trans. H. L. Mencken. New York: Knopf, 1920.

—————— *Beyond Good and Evil.* Trans. Walter Kaufman. New York: Random House, 1989.

—————— *The Dawn of Day.* New York: Gordon, 1974.

Oates, Stephen B. *Let the Trumpet Sound, the Life of Martin Luther King, Jr.* New York: New American Library, 1985.

O'Brien, Conor Cruise. *The Siege, the Saga of Israel and Zionism.* New York: Simon & Schuster, 1986.

O'Connor, Flannery. *The Habit of Being.* New York: Farrar, Straus and Giroux, 1979.

Ohmann, F., ed. *Kants Briefe.* Leipzig: Insel Verlag, 1911.

Orwell, George. *As I Please, 1943–1945.* New York: Harcourt, Brace and World, 1968.

Orwell, Sonia, and Angus, Ian, eds. *An Age Like This.* Vol. 1 of *The Collected Essays, Journalism and Letters of George Orwell.* London: Secker & Warburg, 1968.

Padover, Saul K. *Democracy by Thomas Jefferson.* New York: Appleton, 1939.

Page, Joseph A. *Perón, A Biography.* New York: Random House, 1983.

Paine, Thomas. *The Age of Reason.* New York: Citadel, 1976.

Parliamentary History of England from the Earliest Period to the Year 1803.

Pascal, Blaise. "Advantages of the Jewish People." In *Thoughts,* trans. W. F. Trotter. New York: P. F. Collier & Son, 1910.

Patai, Raphael, and Patai, Jennifer. *The Myth of the Jewish Race.* New York: Charles Scribner's Sons, 1975.

Payne, Robert. *The Rise and Fall of Stalin.* New York: Avon Books, 1965.

Penn, William. "The Great Case of Liberty of Conscience." In *Works,* vol. 1, p. 459. London: 1687.

Peters, Joan. *From Time Immemorial.* New York: Harper & Row, 1984.

Porges, Irwin. *Edgar Rice Burroughs — The Man Who Created Tarzan.* New York: Ballantine, 1975.

Poschinger, Heinrich von. *Conversations with Bismarck,* 1900.

Priestley, Joseph. *A Comparison of the Institutions of Moses with Those of the Hindoos and Other Ancient Nations,* 1799.

Public Papers of Woodrow Wilson. New York, 1925.

Rabinowicz, Oskar M., and Allen, W. H. *Arnold Toynbee on Judaism and Zionism.* London: Howard & Wyndham Ltd., 1974.

Renoir, Jean. *Renoir, My Father.* London: William Collins & Sons, 1962.

Reuchlin, John. "Advice Whether to Take, Carry Off and Burn All the Books of the Jews. In *Augenspiegel,* pp. 227–240. In *Johann Reuchlin, sein Leben und seine Werke,* L. Geiger, compiler. Leipzig, 1871.

Robinson, Phyllis C. *Willa—The Life of Willa Cather.* Garden City, NY: Doubleday, 1983.

Roger William and the Jews, American Jewish Archives.

Roosevelt, Theodore. *Theodore Roosevelt, An Autobiography.* New York: Charles Scribner's Sons, 1922.

Ross, Walter S. *The Last Hero.* New York: Harper & Row, 1968.

Roth, Cecil. *The Spanish Inquisition.* New York: Norton, 1964.

Rousseau, Jean Jacques. *Emile ou de l'éducation.* Trans. Barbara Foxley, pp. 267f. New York: Dutton, 1911.

Ruskin, John. "Morals and Religion." In *The True and the Beautiful.* London: Allen & Unwin.

Russell, Bertrand. *The Autobiography of Bertrand Russell.* Toronto: McClelland & Stewart, 1967.

———— *In Praise of Idleness and Other Essays.* New York: Norton, 1935.

Salisbury, Harrison E. *A Journey for Our Times, A Memoir.* New York: Harper & Row, 1983.

Samuels, E. *Bernard Berenson: The Making of a Connoisseur.* Cambridge, MA: Harvard University Press, 1979.

Sanders, Marion K. *Dorothy Thompson—A Legend in Her Time.* Boston: Houghton Mifflin, 1973.

Sartre, Jean Paul. *Anti-Semite and Jew.* New York: Schocken Books, 1948.

Schaff, P. *Select Library of the Nicene and Post-Nicene Fathers,* vol. 8. New York, 1888.

Schiller, Friedrich von. "Die Sendung Moses." *Thalia,* 1790.

Schlegel, Friedrich. *Lectures on the History of Literature, Ancient and Modern.* Philadelphia, 1818.

Schlesinger, Arthur M., Jr. *Robert Kennedy and His Times.* Boston: Houghton Mifflin, 1978.

Schorer, Mark. *Sinclair Lewis, An American Life.* New York: McGraw-Hill, 1961.

Schuh, Willi. *Richard Strauss.* Trans. Mary Whittall. New York: Cambridge University Press, 1976.

Schweitzer, Albert. *Out of My Life and Thought, An Autobiography.* Trans. C.

T. Campion. New York: Henry Holt, 1933.

Science and the Hebrew Tradition. New York and London: D. Appleton, 1920.

Selected Letters of e.e. cummings. Ed. F. W. Dupee and George Stade. New York: Harcourt Brace Jovanovich, 1969.

Selected Letters of Richard Wagner. Ed. Stewart Spencer and Barry Millington. New York: Norton, 1987.

Shaw, George Bernard. "Preface on Bosses." In *The Millionairess.* London: Penguin Books, 1936.

_____ Interview in the *London Daily Express.* Reprinted in *The Churchman,* November 15, 1938.

Shawcross, William. *The Shah's Last Ride.* London: Chatto & Windus, 1989.

Shelley, Percy Bysshe. *A Philosophical View of Reform,* 1819.

Sheppard, R. Z. "Notes from the Underground." *Time* Dec. 25, 1989.

Singer, S. W., ed. *Reverend Joseph Spence, Anecdotes, Observations, and Characters of Books and Men, 1728–1744.* London, 1820.

Smith, Bradley, and Peterson, Agnes. *Heinrich Himmler Geheimreden.*

Smith, David C. *H. G. Wells, Desperately Mortal.* New Haven, CT: Yale University Press, 1986.

Smuts, Jan. *The African World.* November 10, 1934, Johannesburg.

Snow, C. P. Introduction to A. Rogow's *The Jew in a Gentile World.* New York: Macmillan, 1961.

Speer, Albert. *Inside the Third Reich.* New York: Macmillan, 1970.

Spencer, S., and Millington, B. Selected Letters of Richard Wagner. New York: Norton, 1988.

Spengler, Oswald. *The Decline of the West.* New York: Knopf, 1928.

Stalin, Joseph. "Report on the London Congress." In *Stalin: Collected Works,* vol. 2.

Stannard, Martin. *Evelyn Waugh, The Early Years, 1903–1939.* Toronto: Fitzhenry & Whiteside, 1986.

Stanton, Elizabeth Cady. *Eighty Years and More.* New York: European, 1898.

Stars and Sand, ed. Joseph L. Baron. Philadelphia: The Jewish Publication Society, 1943.

Steffens, Lincoln. *The Autobiography of Lincoln Steffens.* New York: Harcourt, Brace, 1931.

Stern, Menachem. *Greek and Latin Authors on Jews and Judaism,* vol. 1. Jerusalem: The Israel Academy of Sciences and Humanities, 1974.

Stubbs, Charles William. *God and the People.* London: T. Fisher Unwin, 1896.

Styron, William. *This Quiet Dust and Other Writings.* New York: Random House, 1982.

Swanberg, W. A. *Dreiser.* New York: Charles Scribner's Sons, 1965.

_____ *Luce and His Empire.* New York: Charles Scribner's Sons, 1972.

Synan, Edward A. *The Popes and the Jews in the Middle Ages.* New York: Macmillan, 1965.

Taylor, A. J. P. *Beaverbrook.* London: Hamish Hamilton, 1972.

Tebbel, John. *The Life and Good Times of William Randolph Hearst.* New York: Dutton, 1952.

Thackeray, H. St. J. *Josephus against Apion,* vol. I. Cambridge, MA: Harvard University, 1926.

Tilton, Eleanor M. *Amiable Autocrat—The Biography of Dr. Oliver Wendell Holmes.* New York: Henry Schumann, 1947.

Toland, John. *Adolf Hitler.* Garden City, NY: Doubleday, 1976.

Toynbee, Arnold. *Study of History.* New York: Oxford University Press, 1987.

Twain, Mark. "Concerning the Jews." *Harper's Magazine* 99 (June 1889): 527–535.

Van Doren, Carl. *Benjamin Franklin.* New York: Viking Press, 1938.

Veblen, Thorstein. "The Intellectual Pre-eminence of Jews in Modern Europe." *Political Science Quarterly* (March 1919). In *The Portable Veblen,* ed. Max Lerner, pp. 467–479. New York: Viking Press, 1934.

"Victory and Peace." 1942. In *Our Bishops Speak,* p. 113. Milwaukee: Bruce, 1952.

Vidal, Gore. "Pink Triangle and Yellow Star." In *The Second American Revolution and Other Essays (1976–1982),* pp. 169–184. New York: Random House, 1982.

Volkov, Solomon, ed. *Testimony, the Memoirs of Dmitri Shostakovich.* New York: Harper & Row, 1979.

Wagenknecht, Edward. *Harriet Beecher Stowe, the Known and the Unknown.* New York: Oxford University Press, 1965.

Walesa, Lech. *A Way of Hope.* New York: Henry Holt, 1987.

Wasserstein, Bernard. *Britain and the Jews.* London: Oxford University Press, 1979.

Watkins, Floyd C., and Hiers, John T., eds. *Robert Penn Talking, Interviews 1950–1978.* New York: Random House, 1980.

Weizmann, Chaim. *Trial and Error.* London: Hamish Hamilton, 1949.

Wells, H. G. *Short History of the World.* New York: The Review of Reviews Corp., 1923.

Wheatly, Henry B., ed. *Diary of Samuel Pepys,* vol. 3. London: AMS Press, 1929.

Whitehead, Alfred N. "An Appeal to Sanity" in *The Atlantic Monthly,* 1970.

Williams, Francis, ed. *A Prime Minister Remembers.* London: Heinemann, 1961.

Wilson, Angus. *The Strange Ride of Rudyard Kipling.* London: Secker & Warburg, 1977.

Wilson, Edmund. "The Jews." In *A Piece of My Mind: Reflections at Sixty.* New York: Farrar, Straus & Giroux, 1956.

_____ *The Thirties: From Notebooks and Diaries of the Period.* New York: Farrar, Straus and Giroux, 1980.

Wilson, Woodrow. *The State.* Boston: Heath & Co., 1890.

Wolf, Simon. Letter to Portalis. In *Selected Addresses and Papers of Simon Wolf.* Cincinnati, 1926.

Wolfe, Bertram D. *Three Who Made a Revolution.* New York: Dell Publishing, 1964.

Wolfe, Lucien, ed. *Menasseh ben Israel's Mission to Oliver Cromwell.* London, 1901.

Woodress, James. *Willa Cather, A Literary Life.* Lincoln: University of Nebraska Press, 1987.

Woodward, Bob, and Bernstein, Carl. *The Final Days.* New York: Simon & Schuster, 1976.

Wylie, Philip. "The New Order for Common Man." In *Generation of Vipers,* pp. 135–149. New York: Holt, Rinehart & Winston, 1955.

Wyman, David. *The Abandonment of the Jews: America and the Holocaust, 1941–1945.* New York: Pantheon Books, 1984.

Zionism and Anti-Semitism: The Absurd Folly of Jew Baiting. New York: American Jewish Congress, 1923.

Zuckerman, Nathan. *The Wine of Violence.* New York: Association Press, 1947.

Acknowledgments

The editor gratefully acknowledges permission to reprint excerpts from the following:

Byron: A Portrait by Leslie A. Marchand. Copyright © 1970 by Leslie A. Marchand. Reprinted by permission of Alfred A. Knopf Inc.

Letters of Wallace Stevens edited by Holly Stevens. Copyright © 1966 by Holly Stevens. Reprinted by permission of Alfred A. Knopf Inc.

"Roger Williams and the Jews." *American Jewish Archives.*

The Crane Bag and Other Disputed Subjects by Robert Graves. Reprinted by permission of AP Watt Limited.

"An Appeal to Sanity" by Alfred North Whitehead. Copyright © 1939 by *The Atlantic Monthly.*

"Indivisible Man" by James Alan McPherson. Copyright © 1970 by *The Atlantic Monthly.*

Free Association: Memoirs of a Psycho-Analyst, by Ernest Jones. Copyright © 1987 by Katherine Jones. Reprinted by permission of Basic Books, Inc., Publishers, New York.

Edgar Rice Burroughs, Vol. II, by Irwin Porges. Copyright © 1975 by Irwin Porges. Reprinted by permission of Brigham Young University Press.

Letters of Sidney and Beatrice Webb, Vol. 1 edited by Norman Mackenzie. Reprinted by permission of Cambridge University Press.

Richard Strauss by Willi Schuh, translated by Mary Whittall. Copyright © 1976. Reprinted by permission of Cambridge University Press.

De Gaulle. Copyright © 1973 Brian Crozier. Published by Charles Scribner's Sons, New York. Reprinted by permission of the author.

The Diary of a Writer, Volume II by F. M. Dostoievsky, translated by Boris Brasol. Reprinted with permission of Charles Scribner's Sons, an imprint of Macmillan Publishing Company. Copyright © 1949 Charles Scribner's Sons; copyright renewed 1976 Maxwell Fassett.

Dreiser by W. A. Swanberg. Reprinted with permission of Charles Scribner's Sons, an imprint of Macmillan Publishing Company. Copyright © 1965 W. A. Swanberg.

Luce and His Empire by W. A. Swanberg. Reprinted with permission of Charles Scribner's Sons, an imprint of Macmillan Publishing Company. Copyright © 1972 W. A. Swanberg.

The Shah's Last Ride by William Shawcross. Copyright © 1989. Reprinted by permission of Chatto & Windus.

"Again Silence in the Churches." Copyright © 1967 Christian Century Foundation. Reprinted by permission from the August 2, 1967 issue of *The Christian Century.*

An interview in the *London Daily Express* by George Bernard Shaw. Reprinted by permission from the November 15, 1938 issue of *The Churchman.*

From LeRoi Jones to Amiri Baraka, by Theodore R. Hudson. Copyright © 1973 by Theodore R. Hudson. Reprinted by permission of Duke University Press.

Henry Miller, Years of Trial and Triumph 1962–1964 by Elmer Gertz. Copyright © 1978. Reprinted by permission of Elmer Gertz.

Evelyn Waugh, The Early Years by Martin Stannard. Copyright © 1986 by Martin Stannard. Reprinted by permission of Fitzhenry & Whiteside.

Mussolini by Anthony James. Copyright © 1982. Reprinted by permission of Franklin Watts/Grolier.

Ezra Pound Speaking, Leonard Doob, ed. (Greenwood Press, an imprint of Greenwood Publishing Group, 1978). Copyright © 1978 by Ezra Pound Literary Property Trust. Reprinted with permission.

Beaverbrook by A. J. P. Taylor. Copyright © 1972. Reprinted by permission of Hamish Hamilton Ltd.

Nancy Mitford by Selina Hastings. Copyright © 1985. Reprinted by permission of Hamish Hamilton Ltd.

A Journey for Our Times, A Memoir, by Harrison Salisbury. Copyright © 1983 by Harrison Salisbury. Reprinted by permission of Harper & Row, Publishers, Inc.

From Time Immemorial by Joan Peters. Copyright © 1984 by Joan Peters. Reprinted by permission of Harper & Row, Publishers, Inc.

Hemingway: A Biography by Jeffrey Meyers. Copyright © 1985 by Jeffrey Meyers. Reprinted by permission of Harper & Row, Publishers, Inc.

Testimony, the Memoirs of Dmitri Shostakovich, edited by Solomon Volkov. Copyright © 1979 by Solomon Volkov. Reprinted by permission of Harper & Row, Publishers, Inc.

Upton Sinclair: American Rebel by Leon Harris. Copyright © 1975 by Leon Harris. Reprinted by permission of Harper & Row, Publishers, Inc.

Bernard Berenson: The Making of a Connoisseur by Ernest Samuels. Reprinted by permission of Harvard University Press, Cambridge, Mass. Copyright © 1979 by the President and Fellows of Harvard College.

Josephus Against Apion, Volume I, translated by H. St. J. Thackeray. Reprinted by permission of the publishers and the Loeb Classical Library, Harvard University Press, Cambridge, Mass. 1926.

James Russell Lowell by Martin Duberman. Copyright © 1966 by Martin Duberman. Reprinted by permission of Houghton Mifflin Co.

Robert Kennedy and His Times by Arthur M. Schlesinger, Jr. Copyright © 1978 by Arthur M. Schlesinger, Jr. Reprinted by permission of Houghton Mifflin Company.

Anthony Trollope, by Bradford A. Booth. Reprinted by permission of Indiana University Press.

Pobedonostsev, by R. F. Byrnes. Copyright © 1968. Reprinted by permission of Indiana University Press.

Greek and Latin Authors on Jews and Judaism, Vol. I, II by Menahem Stern. Copyright © 1974, 1980. Reprinted by permission of the Israel Academy of Sciences and Humanities.

A Prince of our Disorder: The Life of T. E. Lawrence, by John E. Mack, M.D. Copyright © 1976 by Thomas Kiernan. Reprinted by permission of Little, Brown and Company.

But Do Blondes Prefer Gentlemen, by Anthony Burgess. Copyright © 1986 by Anthony Burgess. Reprinted by permission of McGraw-Hill Publishing Company.

Karl Marx: Early Writings, edited and translated by Bottomore. Copyright © 1964 by Bottomore. Reprinted by permission of McGraw-Hill Publishing Company.

Sinclair Lewis: An American Life by Mark Schorer. Copyright © 1961. Reprinted by permission of McGraw-Hill, Inc.

The Kennedys: Dynasty and Disaster, by Burgess and Davis. Copyright © 1984 by Burgess and Davis. Reprinted by permission of McGraw-Hill Publishing Company.

"Is Dreiser Anti-Semitic?" Reprinted from the April 17, 1935 issue of *The Nation* with permission.

An article by Reinhold Niebuhr. Reprinted from the February 28, 1942 issue of *The Nation* with permission.

"Harijan" by Mahatma Gandhi. Reprinted by permission of the Navajivan Trust.

The Jews in the Soviet Union since 1917, vol. 1, by Nora Levin. Reprinted by permission of New York University Press. Copyright © 1988 by Nora Levin.

H.L. Mencken, A Portrait from Memory by Charles Angoff. Copyright © 1956 by Charles Angoff. Reprinted by permission of Oak Tree Publishing.

Hitler, Germans and the "Jewish Questions" by Sarah Gordon. Copyright © 1984 by Princeton University Press.

Anti-Semite and Jews by Jean-Paul Sartre, translated by George Becker. Copyright © 1948 and renewed 1976 by Schocken Books, Inc. Reprinted by permission of Schocken Books, published by Pantheon Books, a Division of Random House Inc.

Dashiell Hammet: A Life by Diane Johnson. Copyright © 1983 by Diane Johnson. Reprinted by permission of Random House Inc.

Faulkner—A Biography, Vol. II by Joseph Blotner. Copyright © 1974 by Joseph Blotner. Reprinted by permission of Random House Inc.

The Abandonment of the Jews: America and the Holocaust 1941-1945 by David S. Wyman. Copyright © 1984 by David S. Wyman. Reprinted by permission of Pantheon Books, a division of Random House Inc.

This Quiet Dust and Other Writings by William Styron. Copyright © 1982 by William Styron. Reprinted by permission of Random House Inc.

copyright © 1968 by Arna Boutemps and George Houston Bass. Reprinted by permission of Hill and Wang, a division of Farrar, Straus and Giroux.

Lenin on the Jewish Question by Vladimir Lenin. Copyright © 1934. Reprinted with permission of International Publishers.

Road to Victory, Never Despair by Dorothy L. Sayers. Reprinted with permission of Stoddart Publishing Co.

Little Wilson and Big God by Dorothy L. Sayers. Reprinted with permission of Stoddart Publishing Co.

A History of the Jews by Paul Johnson. Copyright © Harper & Row, 1987.

Introduction by C. P. Snow in *The Jew in The Gentile World* by Arnold A. Rogow. Reprinted with permission of Macmillan Publishing Co. Copyright © 1961 by Arnold A. Rogow.

The Popes and the Jews in the Middle Ages, by Edward A. Synan. Reprinted with permission of Macmillan Publishing Co. Copyright © 1965 by Edward A. Synan.

Inside the Third Reich by Albert Speer. Translated by Richard and Clara Winston. Reprinted with permission of Macmillan Publishing Co. Copyright © 1970 by Macmillan Publishing Co.

Franco, The Man and His Nation, by George Hills. Reprinted with permission of Macmillan Publishing Co. Copyright © 1968 by George Hills.

The Jew in the Medieval World by Jacob R. Marcus. Reprinted with permission of the Jewish Publication Society. Copyright © by McClelland and Stewart.

American Jewry and the Civil War by Bertram Wallace Korn. Reprinted with permission of the Jewish Publication Society. Copyright © 1951 by the Jewish Publication Society.

Major Noah by Isaac Goldberg. Reprinted with permission of the Jewish Publication Society. Copyright © 1936 by the Jewish Publication Society.

The Image of the Jew in American Literature by Louis Harap. Reprinted with permission of the Jewish Publication Society. Copyright © 1974 by the Jewish Publication Society.

The Crucifixion of the Jews by Franklin H. Littell. Reprinted with permission of Harper and Row. Copyright © 1975 by Franklin H. Littell.

Index

Allan Gould is the author of sixteen books, including *The Unorthodox Book of Jewish Records and Lists* (co-authored with Danny Siegel); he also wrote the introduction to *The Holocaust: The Nazi Destruction of Europe's Jews*, a classic anthology of documents and photographs. He lectures frequently on Jewish humor, literature, Midrash, ethics, and the Holocaust, and has had over 500 articles published in many national magazines. Mr. Gould lives in Toronto.